THEORIES OF LEARNING

THE CENTURY PSYCHOLOGY SERIES

Richard M. Elliott, Gardner Lindzey & Kenneth MacCorquodale

Editors

THEORIES OF LEARNING

third edition

Ernest R. Hilgard

Gordon H. Bower

Both of Stanford University

New York

APPLETON-CENTURY-CROFTS
EDUCATIONAL DIVISION
MEREDITH CORPORATION

ACKNOWLEDGMENTS

Figures and Tables

Table 3-2 is from HILGARD AND MARQUIS' CONDITIONING AND LEARNING, Second edition, by Gregory A. Kimble. Copyright © 1961 by Appleton-Century-Crofts, Inc. Reprinted by permission of Appleton-Century-Crofts, Division of Meredith Publishing Company.

Figure 3-3 and Table 3-1 are from Pavlov, *Conditioned Reflexes* (Clarendon Press, 1927).

Figure 5-6 is redrawn from SCHEDULES OF REINFORCEMENT by C. B. Ferster and B. F. Skinner. Copyright © 1957 by Appleton-Century-Crofts, Inc. Reprinted by permission of Appleton-Century-Crofts, Division of Meredith Publishing Company.

Figure 6-7 is redrawn from PERSONALITY AND THE BEHAVIOR DISORDERS, Volume I— Edited by J. McV. Hunt. Copyright 1944 by the Ronald Press Company.

Figure 13-1 is redrawn from NEW DIRECTIONS IN PSYCHOLOGY II, Frank Barron, *et al.* Copyright © 1965 by Holt, Rinehart and Winston, Inc. Reprinted by permission of the publisher. All rights reserved.

Figure 13-4 is redrawn from J. W. Fuster, *Science 127,* page 150, 17 January 1958.

Figure 13-10 is redrawn from R. W. Sperry, *Science 133,* pages 1749–1757, 2 June 1961.

Figure 15-1 is redrawn from H. S. Terrace, *Science 144,* pages 78–80, 3 April 1964.

Figures 16-4 and 16-5 are redrawn from *The Conditions of Learning,* by Robert M. Gagné, copyright © 1965 by Holt, Rinehart and Winston, Inc. All rights reserved.

Quotations

The quotation appearing on pages 54–55 is from CONDITIONING AND LEARNING by Ernest R. Hilgard and Donald G. Marquis. Copyright © 1940 by D. Appleton-Century Company, Inc. Reprinted by permission of Appleton-Century-Crofts, Division of Meredith Publishing Company.

The quotations appearing on pages 128 and 134 are from B. F. Skinner, *Science and Human Behavior,* copyright 1953, The Macmillan Company, and are used with the permission of the publisher.

The quotation appearing on pages 245–246 is from GESTALT PSYCHOLOGY by Wolfgang Köhler by permission of LIVERIGHT Publishers, New York. Copyright 1929, Horace Liveright Inc.; copyright 1947, LIVERIGHT Publishing Corp.

The quotations appearing on pages 265 and 268–269 are from BEYOND THE PLEASURE PRINCIPLE by Sigmund Freud, by permission of LIVERIGHT Publishers, New York.

The quotation appearing on page 277 is from GROUP PSYCHOLOGY AND THE ANALYSIS OF THE EGO by Sigmund Freud by permission of LIVERIGHT Publishers, New York.

The quotations appearing on pages 305 and 306 are from W. S. Monroe, editor, *Encyclopedia of Educational Research,* copyright 1941, The Macmillan Company, and are used with the permission of the publisher.

PREFACE

Interest in the psychology of learning, already high when the previous editions of this book appeared, has accelerated during the ten years since the second edition. This is due, in part, to an increasing concern with education generally, coming about through the social pressures of increasing population, the rise of developing nations, and competition among nations for technological supremacy requiring highly educated manpower. If education is to be more efficient it must be based upon sound knowledge about how learning goes on.

Investigation of learning in its basic science aspects gains social and economic support as a kind of "fall-out" from the realization that the sounder our basic knowledge about learning processes, the sounder will be our technological applications in training and education as broadly conceived. The basic advances in learning theory have profited in the very recent past from adjacent developments in brain physiology and brain chemistry, and the development of information-processing by way of electronic computers.

It is the purpose of this revision to continue the orientation to the main influences on learning theory prominent in the first half of this century, and to note how they are represented in contemporary experimentation and theorizing. But in this revision we make note also of the newer developments not well coordinated with these by now "classical" theories. Finally, in view of the importance of new technologies of instruction, a chapter is devoted to them.

Comparison with the second edition will reveal the following major changes in addition to minor revisions throughout. First, there is a new chapter on Pavlov, in view of a resurgence of interest in his views, particularly as represented in current developments from the USSR, with recognition given to the significance in human learning of the "second signal system" (language). Second, and somewhat regretfully, the chapter on Kurt Lewin has been dropped because his views on learning have not been sufficiently influential in recent years to justify this attention to them in the context of learning theory.[1] Third, the chapters on mathematical models and current developments are so new that they may be considered as replacements for rather than revisions of the corresponding chapters in the second edition. The chapter on information processing models and that on the neurophysiology and neurochemistry of learning are entirely new. Finally, the chapter on the technology of instruction is also new. The primary authorship of each chapter is indicated in the table of contents.

It is hoped that with these changes this edition may serve as an introduction to contemporary learning theory and as a background for the exciting developments that will surely occur in the years ahead.

We wish to acknowledge the wise suggestions given by Richard M. Elliott and Kenneth MacCorquodale as editors. Much of the work in seeing the manuscript through to the printer, in checking bibliographies, and in other ways bringing the task to completion we owe to the care and patience of Arlene H. Morgan and Janis Christiansen, for whose help we are most grateful.

Permissions for the reproduction of copyrighted material have been generously granted. The sources are acknowledged wherever such material has been used.

E.R.H.
G.H.B.

---

[1] It may be recalled that the views of Raymond H. Wheeler which were represented in the first edition were omitted from the second. Lewin's views are currently very much alive in social psychology and in relation to some aspects of human motivation. Lewin's views, as represented in the second edition, have not been specifically challenged or refuted; the earlier chapter is still an acceptable introduction to them.

CONTENTS

The Nature
of Learning Theories

The study of learning is shared by many disciplines. Physiologists, biochemists, and biophysicists have a legitimate interest in it; parents, teachers, industrial managers, rehabilitation workers, and others faced by the practical problems of the control of learning have their own needs which require that they understand the basic processes and how to manage them. Yet the scientific study of learning is carried on primarily by psychologists. Psychology's claim to the field was staked out in part by masterly pioneers such as Ebbinghaus (1885),[1] Bryan and Harter (1897, 1899), and Thorndike (1898). Those who have followed in their footsteps have been primarily psychologists. Professional educators have welcomed educational psychology as a foundation science upon which to build their practices, and studies of learning have gone on concurrently in laboratories of general psychology and laboratories of educational psychology, with interplay between the pure and applied fields. Under the circumstances, it is very natural for psychologists to feel that the study of learning belongs to them.

In addition to historical reasons, there is another basis on which to account for the psychologist's interest in learning. This is the centrality of learning in the more general systems of psychological theory. A scientist, along with the desire to satisfy his curiosity about the facts of nature, has a predilection for ordering his facts into systems of laws and theories. He

[1] References cited can be found by author and date in the list at the end of the book.

is interested not only in verified facts and relationships, but in neat and parsimonious ways of summarizing these facts. Psychologists with a penchant for systems find a theory of learning essential because so much of man's diverse behavior is the result of learning. If the rich diversity of behavior is to be understood in accordance with a few principles, it is evident that some of these principles will have to do with the way in which learning comes about.

THE DEFINITION OF LEARNING

What Learning Includes

There are many activities which everyone will agree count as illustrations of learning: acquiring a vocabulary, memorizing a poem, learning to operate a typewriter. There are other activities, not quite as obviously learned, which are easily classified as learned once you have reflected upon them. Among these are the acquiring of prejudices and preferences and other social attitudes and ideals, including the many skills involved in the social interplay with other people. Finally there are a number of activities whose acquisition is not usually classifiable as a gain or improvement because their utility, if such there be, is not readily demonstrable. Among these are tics, mannerisms, and autistic gestures.

Such a pointing to illustrations of learning serves very well as a first approximation to a definition. It is, in fact, extremely difficult to write an entirely satisfactory definition. Although we are tempted to define learning as improvement with practice, or as profiting by experience, we know very well that some learning is not improvement, and other learning is not desirable in its consequences. To describe it alternatively as any change with repetition confuses it with growth, fatigue, and other changes which may take place with repetition. The following definition may be offered provisionally:

Learning is the process by which an activity originates or is changed through reacting to an encountered situation, provided that the characteristics of the change in activity cannot be explained on the basis of native response tendencies, maturation, or temporary states of the organism (e.g., fatigue, drugs, etc.).

The definition is not formally satisfactory because of the many undefined terms in it, but it will do to call attention to the problems involved in any definition of learning. The definition must distinguish between (1) the kinds of changes, and their correlated antecedents, which are included as learning, and (2) the related kinds of changes, and their antecedents, which are not classified as learning. We can now go on to consider some of the changes that are excluded by our provisional definition.

Native Response Tendencies versus Learning

The older catalogs of innate behavior usually included among unlearned activities the reflexes (such as pupillary constriction to light), the tropisms (such as a moth's dashing into a flame), and the instincts (such as a bird's nest-building). We may continue to acknowledge such activities as characteristic of various species, and those more nearly idiosyncratic to one species as *species-specific*.

The concept of instinct has been the most controversial of these terms, partly because of a vagueness of connotation, partly because of a tendency to use the word as explanatory, hence as a cloak for ignorance. After a period of some years in which it was virtually taboo, the respectability of instinct was briefly revived by a group of European naturalists known as ethologists (e.g., Tinbergen, 1951; Thorpe, 1956) only to lead to so much controversy that its advocates have again abandoned it in favor of *species-specific behavior* (Hinde and Tinbergen, 1958).

The problem of what is naturally characteristic of a given species is not solved by attempting to classify some behavior as altogether innate, other behavior as altogether learned. The objections to the concept of instinct that come from finding much learning in so-called instinctive behavior (Beach, 1955), though useful in providing warning signs against overstating the case for instinct, do not meet the problem that some things are much easier for one organism to acquire than for another. Thus if learning is used exclusively in describing behavior, it ought to be possible to teach all birds to home as some pigeons do, or to teach an oriole to build a robin's nest. The in-between nature of behavior with large instinctive components is well illustrated by the experiments on imprinting (e.g., Lorenz, 1952; Hess, 1958). A young duckling, for example, is prepared instinctively to accept a certain range of mother-figures, characterized by size, movement, and vocalization. Once such a mother-figure has been accepted and followed about, only this *particular* mother can satisfy the instinctive demand. The selected mother (who may be Professor Lorenz crawling on hands and knees) has become imprinted, and is the only "mother" the duckling will follow. Imprinting is then a form of learning, but a form very closely allied to the instinctive propensities of a particular kind of organism of a particular age. (We lack at present clear evidence for imprinting except in fowls and other birds.) The problem of distinguishing between the instinctive and learned components of the behavior illustrated by imprinting is an experimental problem, depending for its clarification upon the ingenuity of the experimenter in designing appropriate control experiments.

Maturation versus Learning

Growth is learning's chief competitor as a modifier of behavior. If a behavior sequence matures through regular stages irrespective of intervening practice, the behavior is said to develop through maturation and not through learning. If training procedures do not speed up or modify the behavior, such procedures are not causally important and the changes do not classify as learning. Relatively pure cases such as the swimming of tadpoles and the flying of birds can be attributed primarily to maturation. Many activities are not as clear-cut, but develop through a complex interplay of maturation and learning. A convenient illustration is the development of language in the child. The child does not learn to talk until old enough, but the language which he learns is that which he hears. In such cases it is an experimental problem to isolate the effects of maturation and of learning. The ambiguity in such cases is one of fact, not of definition.

Fatigue and Habituation versus Learning

When activities are repeated in rapid succession, there is often a loss in efficiency commonly attributed to fatigue. Such changes in performance are called *work decrements* in the experimental laboratory. The units of a work curve are like those of a practice curve: performance plotted against trials or repetitions. Hence the experimental arrangements in obtaining a work curve are essentially those of a learning procedure and, at first sight, it appears to be a form of question-begging to define the processes involved by the results obtained. It would be question-begging, however, only if we were to equate learning or fatigue with the change in performances, and it is permissible to make such inferences as the obtained performances require or suggest. Fatigue curves tend to show decreasing proficiency with repetition and recovery with rests. Learning curves ordinarily show gains with repetitions and forgetting over rests. These typical differences between learning effects and fatigue effects are evident enough, but the inferences from performance are made on somewhat more complex evidence. It is because of the complexity of these inferences that it is difficult to state a concise definition of learning which will conserve the learning inferences from performance while eliminating the fatigue inferences. The problem is logically the same as distinguishing changes due to maturation and to learning. But again the ambiguity is one of fact, not of definition.

Another kind of repeated situation that produces progressive changes in the direction of reduced responsiveness is known as *habituation*. This differs from fatigue in that little work is involved: what is reduced is responsiveness to a repeated stimulus. If you try to study (or to go to sleep) in a room with a loudly ticking clock this is at first very disrupting, but you soon "get used" to it, and it no longer bothers. This becoming accustomed is called habituation. While habituation has long been recognized as having some affiliations with learning (e.g., Humphrey, 1933; Thorpe, 1956), attention has again been called to it through the prominence given recently by Russian workers to the *orientation reflex* and its diminution with repetition (Sokolov, 1963). Some habituation may be due to sensory adaptation, as when the odor of a fish market or a laboratory is not detected by those who work there, but other effects are probably central, and more nearly related to learning and to that aspect of learning known as extinction. The effects of repeated habituation may be relatively enduring, so that later habituations are more rapid than earlier ones. Hence some learning is involved in habituation, but it is again a marginal case.

Learning must always remain an inference from performance, and only confusion results if performance and learning are identified. A clear illustration is provided by performance under the influence of drugs or intoxicants. The fact that learned behavior fails when the organism is in such a state does not mean that forgetting has occurred. When the normal state has been restored, the performance may return to normal levels although there has been no intervening training.

Learning and the Nervous System

Some definitions of learning avoid the problem of performance by defining learning as a change in the central nervous system. So long as this change in the nervous system persists, temporary changes in state, such as those in fatigue and intoxication, affect performance but not learning. This definition asserts that learning is an inference, but it goes on to make a particular sort of inference about the role of the nervous system in learning. In view of the lack of knowledge of what actually does take place inside the organism when learning occurs, it is preferable not to include hypothetical neural processes in the definition of learning. We know that learning takes place. We should therefore be able to define what we are talking about without reference to any speculation whatever. This position does not deny that what we are calling learning may be a function of nervous tissue. It asserts only that it is not necessary to know anything about the neural correlates of learning in order to know that learning occurs.

Learning, Problem-Solving, and Reasoning

After you have learned, there are many things which you are able to do. If you can add and subtract, you can solve many novel problems without learning anything new. Where the solution of problems is relatively mechanical (as in addition and subtraction), the problem may be thought of as merely the exercise or utilization of a learned bit of behavior. When, however, there is greater novelty, more putting of things into relationship, as in reasoning or inventiveness, the process is interesting in its own light, and is not to be described simply as the running off of old habits.

The question has been raised, especially by Maier (1931), as to the appropriateness of including processes like reasoning within the same classification as other kinds of learning. Our preference is for including them. Leaving them in does not prejudge their explanation. There may be several kinds of learning from the simpler to the more complex, not all following the same principles. If so, we have no assurance that the only sharp break comes when "reasoning" appears. Leaving the doubtful processes in simply asserts that a complete theory of learning must have something to say about reasoning, creative imagination, and inventiveness, in addition to what may be said about memorizing and retaining or about the acquisition of skill.

Definition Not a Major Source of Disagreement Between Theories

While it is extremely difficult to formulate a satisfactory definition of learning so as to include all the activities and processes which we wish to include and eliminate all those which we wish to exclude, the difficulty does not prove to be embarrassing because it is not a source of controversy as between theories. The controversy is over fact and interpretation, not over definition. There are occasional confusions over definition, but such confusions may usually be resolved by resort to pointing, to denotation. For the most part it is satisfactory to continue to mean by learning that which conforms to the usual socially accepted meaning that is part of our common heritage. Where distinctions have to be made with greater precision, they can be made through carefully specified types of inference from experiments.

SOME TYPICAL PROBLEMS CONFRONTING LEARNING THEORIES

The preferences of the theorist often lead him to concentrate upon one kind of learning situation to the neglect of the others. His theory is then appropriate to this situation, but becomes somewhat strained in relation to other problems of learning. A comprehensive learning theory ought to answer the questions which an intelligent nonpsychologist might ask about the sorts of learning which are met in everyday life. A few such questions will be listed here, and then used later in appraising the theories which different writers present.

1. What are the limits of learning?   Here is raised the question of the capacity to learn, of individual differences among learners of the same species and of unlike species. There are questions not only of persistent differences in capacity, but of change in capacity with age. Who can learn what? Are the limits set at birth? Do people get more or less alike with practice? These are the sorts of questions which it is natural to raise.

2. What is the role of practice in learning?   The old adage that practice makes perfect has considerable historical wisdom behind it. Surely one learns to roller skate or to play the piano only by engaging in the activity. But what do we know about practice in detail? Does improvement depend directly on the amount of repetition? If not, what are its conditions? What are the most favorable circumstances of practice? Can repetitive drill be harmful as well as helpful to the learner?

3. How important are drives and incentives, rewards and punishments?   Everybody knows in a general way that learning can be controlled by rewards and punishments, and that it is easier to learn something which is interesting than something which is dull. But are the consequences of rewards and punishments equal and opposite? Is there a difference between intrinsic and extrinsic motives in their effect upon learning? How do goals and purposes affect the process?

4. What is the place of understanding and insight?   Some things are learned more readily if we know what we are about. We are better off as travelers if we can understand a timetable or a road map. We are helpless with differential equations unless we understand the symbols and the rules for their manipulation. But we can form vowels satisfactorily without knowing how we place our tongues, and we can read without being aware of our eye movements. Some things we appear to acquire blindly and automatically; some things we struggle hard to understand and can finally master only as we understand them. Is learning in one case different from what it is in the other?

5. Does learning one thing help you learn something else?   This is the problem of formal discipline, as it used to be called, or of transfer of training, to use a more familiar contemporary designation. Some transfer of training must occur or there would be no use in developing a foundation for later learning. Nobody denies that it is easier to build a vocabulary in a language after you have a start in it, or that higher mathematics profits from mastery of basic concepts. The question is really one of how much transfer takes place, under what conditions, and what its nature is.

6. What happens when we remember and when we forget? The ordinary facts of memory are mysterious enough, but in addition to familiar remembering and forgetting, our memories may play peculiar tricks on us. Some things we wish to remember are forgotten; some things we would be willing to forget continue to plague us. In cases of amnesia there are often gaps in memory, with earlier and later events remembered. Then there are distortions of memory, in which we remember what did not happen, as is so strikingly demonstrated in testimony experiments. What is taking place? What control have we over processes involved?

These six questions will serve as useful ones to ask of each of the major theories. They suffice to illustrate the kinds of questions which give rise to theories of learning.

ISSUES ON WHICH LEARNING THEORIES DIVIDE

In the preceding section we asked certain common-sense questions about learning on the assumption that a good learning theory should have something to say about each of them. Such questions can be raised before we know anything about actual learning theories. Now we wish to turn, however, to certain issues that have arisen in the formulation of actual theories. By alerting us in this way to what is to follow, we are better prepared for some of the differences in flavor that we shall meet as we review one theory after another.

Learning theories fall into two major families: *stimulus–response* theories and *cognitive* theories, but not all theories belong to these two families. The stimulus–response theories include such diverse members as the theories of Thorndike, Pavlov, Guthrie, Skinner, and Hull. The cognitive theories include at least those of Tolman and the classical gestalt psychologists. Not completely and clearly classifiable in these terms are the theories of functionalism, psychodynamics, and the probabilistic theories of the model builders. The lines of cleavage between the two families of theories are not the only cleavages within learning theories; there are other specific issues upon which theories within one family may differ.

General Issues Producing a Cleavage Between Stimulus–Response and Cognitive Theories

The cleavages between the theorists of opposing camps are difficult to understand because many of the distinctions which at first seem to contrast sharply later are found to be blurred. All reputable theorists accept a common logic of experimentation, so that disagreements over experimentally obtained facts are readily arbitrated. In the end, all the theorists accept a common body of demonstrated relationships at the factual or descriptive level; any theorist who denied an established fact, a reproducible experimental finding, would lose status among his scientific colleagues, and his theories would no longer command respect. The first rule that we must be prepared to accept as we judge the relative merits of different theories is this: *All the theorists accept all of the facts.* Some experimental findings are doubted when they are first announced and the status of findings *as fact* may for a long time be doubted; but once the status as fact is established, all accept the fact as true. Hence the differences between two theorists are primarily differences in interpretation. Both theories may fit the facts reasonably well, but the proponent of each theory believes his view to be the more fruitful. We shall be better prepared later on to discuss the ways in which theories are validated or modified after we are acquainted with them in more detail. For the present, we must be prepared to accept the historical truth that opposing theories have great survival value, and that an appeal to the facts as a way of choosing between theories is a very complex process, not nearly as decisive in practice as we might expect it to be.

We may begin by examining three kinds of preferences on which stimulus–response theorists tend to differ from cognitive theorists.

1. *"Peripheral" versus "Central" Intermediaries.* Ever since Watson promulgated the theory that thinking was merely the carrying out of subvocal speech movements, stimulus–response theorists have preferred to find response or movement intermediaries to serve as integrators of behavior sequences. Such movement-produced intermediaries can be classified as "peripheral" mechanisms, as contrasted with "central" (ideational) intermediaries. The stimulus–response theorist tends to believe that some sort of chained muscular responses, linked perhaps by fractional anticipatory goal responses, serve to keep a rat running to a distant food box. The cognitive theorist, on the other hand, more freely infers central brain processes, such as memories or expectations, as integrators of goal-seeking behavior. The differences in preference survive in this case because both kinds of theorists depend upon *inferences* from observed behavior, and the inferences are not directly verified in either case. It is potentially easier to verify tongue movements in thinking than it is to discover a revived memory trace in the brain, but in fact such verification is not offered with the precision necessary to compel belief in the theory. Under the circumstances, the choice between the peripheral and the central explanation is not forced, and favoring one or the other position depends upon more general systematic preferences.

2. *Acquisition of Habits versus Acquisition of Cognitive Structures.* The stimulus–response theorist and the cognitive theorist come up with different answers to the question, What is learned? The answer of the

former is "habits"; the answer of the latter is "cognitive structures." The first answer appeals to common sense: we all know that we develop smooth-running skills by practicing them; what we learn is *responses*. But the second answer also appeals to common sense: if we locate a candy store from one starting point, we can find it from another because we "know where it is"; what we learn is *facts*. A smooth-running skill illustrates a learned habit; knowing alternate routes illustrates cognitive structure. If all habits were highly mechanical and stereotyped, variable nonhabitual behavior would force us to admit cognitive structures as part, at least, of what is learned. But the stimulus–response psychologist is satisfied that he can deduce from the laws of habit formation the behavior that the cognitive theorist believes supports his interpretation. Hence we cannot choose between the theories by coming up with "decisive" illustrations of what we learn, for both groups of theorists will offer explanations of all our examples. The competing theories would not have survived thus far had they been unable to offer such explanations.

3. Trial and Error versus Insight in Problem-Solving. When confronted with a novel problem, how does the learner reach solution? The stimulus–response psychologist finds the learner assembling his habits from the past appropriate to the new problem, responding either according to the elements that the new problem has in common with familiar ones, or according to aspects of the new situation which are similar to situations met before. If these do not lead to solution, the learner resorts to trial and error, bringing out of his behavior repertory one response after another until the problem is solved. The cognitive psychologist agrees with much of this description of what the learner does, but he adds interpretations not offered by the stimulus–response psychologist. He points out, for example, that granting all the requisite experience with the parts of a problem, there is no guarantee that the learner will be able to bring these past experiences to bear upon the solution. He may be able to solve the problem if it is presented in one form and not solve it if it is presented in another form, even though both forms require the same past experiences for their solution. According to the cognitive theorist, the preferred method of presentation permits a perceptual structuring leading to "insight," that is, to the understanding of the essential relationships involved. The stimulus–response psychologist tends, by preference, to look to the past history of the learner for the sources of solution, while the cognitive psychologist, by preference, looks to the contemporary structuring of the problem. His preference for the past does not require the stimulus-response psychologist to ignore the present structuring of the problem, nor does this preference for the present require the cognitive psychologist to ignore the past. One must not assume because there is a difference in preference that either theorist is blind to the totality of the learning situation. The facts of the insight experiment are accepted by both theo-rists, as are the facts of skill learning. We may remind ourselves again that no single experiment will demolish either the interpretation according to trial and error or the interpretation according to insight.

These three issues—peripheral versus central intermediaries, acquisition of habits versus acquisition of cognitive structures, and trial and error versus insight in problem-solving—give something of the flavor of the dif-ferences between these two major families of theories.

Specific Issues Not Confined to the Major Families

Some issues lie outside the conflict between the stimulus–response and the cognitive theories. Thus two stimulus–response psychologists may differ as to the role of reinforcement in learning, and two cognitive theo-rists may differ as to the necessity for a physiological explanation of learn-ing. Four of these issues will suffice to alert us to the many problems that learning theorists face.

1. *Contiguity versus Reinforcement.* The oldest law of association is that ideas experienced together tend to become associated. This has come down in one form or another to the present day as the principle of association by contiguity, although it is now more fashionable to de-scribe the association as between stimuli and responses rather than as be-tween ideas. Some theorists have accepted the principle of contiguous association, for example, Guthrie (a stimulus–response psychologist) and Tolman (a cognitive psychologist). Other theorists insist that learning does not take place through contiguity alone, unless there is some sort of reinforcement, some equivalent of reward or punishment.

2. *Learning as Jumpwise or by Small Increments.* The possibility that learning takes place at base in all-or-none fashion was early pro-posed by Guthrie, and it now has received support from a number of sources. The alternative is, of course, that learning takes place gradually, modifications taking place even below threshold, so that several trials may be necessary before the results of learning reach threshold and begin to be revealed in performance. This was Hull's position. This issue, then, is not one between S–R and cognitive psychologists, but is being fought out among S–R psychologists. The conclusion may very well be that there are a few stages in learning, not just one, and not a very large number. As we shall see, the issue is not one calling for cantankerous opposite views, be-cause a single theorist, such as Estes, may try out models based on either assumption, without an *a priori* preference favoring one or the other.[2]

---

[2] The issue is treated in Chapter 11, where the pertinent literature is cited.

3. One or More Kinds of Learning? The contiguity–reinforcement dilemma may be resolved by accepting both, thus defining two varieties of learning. This solution has appealed to theorists such as Thorndike and Skinner and Mowrer. But these two varieties are not the only possibilities. Perhaps by using the common name "learning" to cover the acquisition of motor skills, the memorization of a poem, the solving of a geometrical puzzle, and the understanding of a period in history, we are deceiving ourselves by looking for common laws that explain processes that have little in common. It may be that the jumpwise–incremental issue will also be resolved by recognizing more than one kind of learning.

Hence the theorist has to choose between a single-factor theory and a multi-factor one. Tolman at one time pointed to the possibility of seven kinds of learning. More recently a symposium volume has appeared dealing very largely with this problem of appropriate categories of learning (Melton, 1964), without actually settling the issue.

4. Intervening Variables versus Hypothetical Constructs. We have already considered a contrast between two types of intermediary, the peripheral and the central types. But as theories become more refined, additional problems arise concerning the way in which inferred intermediaries should be specified. One kind of intermediary found in theories is a mathematical constant that reappears in various contexts, such as the acceleration of a free-falling body (*g*) that appears in equations describing the movement of a pendulum, the path of a projectile, or the way in which balls roll down inclined planes. Such an integrating intervening variable need have no properties other than those expressed in its units of measurement, that is, it need have no independent existence, apart from the functional relationships it has in its systematic context. This kind of integrating intermediary, without surplus meanings, is called an *intervening variable* (MacCorquodale and Meehl, 1948; Hilgard, 1958). By contrast, some kinds of intermediaries are concrete, tangible, palpable, with properties of their own. Suppose, for example, we describe the behavior that results when a cat is confronted with a barking dog. The cat arches its back, hisses, its hair stands on end, and numerous changes take place within its digestive and circulatory system. Many of the internal changes can be *explained* by the use of a demonstrable intermediary, adrenalin, the hormone of the adrenal glands. Suppose that before adrenalin was isolated a theorist had inferred that some substance in the blood stream was causing the internal changes. This would have been a *hypothetical construct* at this stage, an inferred intermediary with palpable qualities. The discovery of adrenalin would have then confirmed the hypothesis that such a substance in the blood stream was, in fact, causing many of the changes. Adrenalin, as a substance, has other properties than those inferred from bodily changes in emotion. In this it differs from a mere intervening variable, which has no further properties beyond its systematic ones.

Those who hold with intervening variables in their learning theories are free to choose such variables as they wish, provided they serve their systematic purposes of producing a more coherent and parsimonious theory than can be produced without them. Those who prefer hypothetical constructs must seek either demonstrable movements or secretions (if they are peripheralists), or some physiological brain processes (if they are centralists). Again, the issue over intervening variables or hypothetical constructs is not confined to one or the other of the major theoretical families.

One extreme position is that we can do away with intermediaries entirely (Skinner). Thus, on this issue as on the others, we have nearly all possible views represented.

This brief introduction to three contrasts between stimulus–response theories and cognitive theories, and four issues that are not confined to the two major families, should make it clear that what seem to be diametrically opposed points of view may turn out to be based on differences in preference, each being possible of persuasive statement, and to a point justifiable. The opposed cases are each made by intelligent men of good will. We shall have to wait until later to consider how a more unified outlook may eventually be achieved.

THE PLAN OF THIS BOOK

The student of learning, conscientiously trying to understand learning phenomena and the laws regulating them, is likely to despair of finding a secure position if opposing points of view are presented as equally plausible, so that the choice between them is made arbitrary. He may fall into a vapid eclecticism, with the general formula, "There's much to be said on all sides."

This is not a necessary outcome of a serious attempt to understand opposing points of view. Science ought to be systematic, not eclectic, but a premature systematic position is likely to be dogmatic and bigoted just as an enduring eclecticism is likely to be superficial and opportunistic. It is possible to have systematization of knowledge as the goal without permitting the desire for system to blind the seeker after it to the truths unearthed by those with views unlike his own.

Throughout the chapters that follow, in presenting one after the other a variety of systematic positions with illustrative experiments testing their assertions, the effort is made to show that there is something to be learned from each of them. Each has discovered phenomena which move us forward in our knowledge about learning. At the same time, no one has succeeded in providing a system invulnerable to criticism. The construction of a fully satisfactory theory of learning is likely to remain for a long time an uncompleted task.

SUPPLEMENTARY READINGS

General Sources on the Psychology of Learning:

BUGELSKI, B. R. (1956) *The psychology of learning.*

DEESE, J. (1958) *The psychology of learning* (revised).

KIMBLE, G. A. (1961) *Hilgard and Marquis' Conditioning and learning* (2nd edition).

McGEOCH, J. A., and IRION, A. L. (1952) *The psychology of human learning* (revised).

OSGOOD, C. E. (1953) *Method and theory in experimental psychology.* Chapters 8-16.

STEVENS, S. S. (Editor) (1951) *Handbook of experimental psychology.* Chapters 13, 15-21, 34.

WOODWORTH, R. S., and SCHLOSBERG, H. (1954) *Experimental psychology* (revised). Chapters 18-26.

Contrasting Points of View Toward Learning:

ESTES, W. K., KOCH, S., MacCORQUODALE, K., MEEHL, P. E., MUELLER, C. G., JR., SCHOENFELD, W. N., and VERPLANCK, W. S. (1954) *Modern learning theory.*

GOLDSTEIN, H., KRANTZ, D. L., and RAINS, J. D. (1965) *Controversial issues in learning.*

HILGARD, E. R. (Editor) (1964a) *Theories of learning and instruction.* Nat'l. Soc. Stud. Educ., 63rd Yearbook, Part II.

HILL, W. F. (1963) *Learning: A survey of psychological interpretations.*

MARX, M. H. (Editor) (1963) *Theories in contemporary psychology.*

MELTON, A. W. (Editor) (1964) *Categories of human learning.*

The *Annual Review of Psychology,* appearing first in 1950, each year reviews critically the current experimental and theoretical literature on learning. The reviews are valuable not only as indexes to the literature but for the trends in experiment and theory detected by the reviewers.

Thorndike's Connectionism

For nearly half a century one learning theory dominated all others in America, despite numerous attacks upon it and the rise of its many rivals. It is the theory of Edward L. Thorndike (1874–1949), first announced in his *Animal intelligence* (1898). Its pre-eminence was aptly assessed by Tolman:

The psychology of animal learning—not to mention that of child learning—has been and still is primarily a matter of agreeing or disagreeing with Thorndike, or trying in minor ways to improve upon him. Gestalt psychologists, conditioned–reflex psychologists, sign–gestalt psychologists—all of us here in America seem to have taken Thorndike, overtly or covertly, as our starting point (Tolman, 1938, page 11).

The basis of learning accepted by Thorndike in his earliest writings was association between sense impressions and impulses to action. Such an association came to be known as a "bond" or a "connection." Because it is these bonds or connections which become strengthened or weakened in the making and breaking of habits, Thorndike's system has sometimes been called a "bond" psychology or simply "connectionism." As such it is the original stimulus–response or S–R psychology of learning.

While many more recent versions of S–R psychology have reduced the prominence now given to Thorndike's interpretations of learning, it must not be supposed that his views are of historical interest only, for they continue to influence much recent experimentation. Nearly a quarter of a century after Tolman made the statement just quoted, Postman, another active worker in the field of learning, had this to say:

The picture of the learning process which Thorndike sketched more than fifty years ago is still very much on the books. No comprehensive theory of human learning can afford to ignore the heritage left to us by Thorndike (Postman, 1962, page 397).

CONNECTIONISM BEFORE 1930

There were few changes in Thorndike's theory between 1898 and 1930. During these years Thorndike devoted himself largely to applications of his established theory to problems of educational and social importance. Because of the stability of the concepts during these years, it is possible to select any one of Thorndike's many publications to serve as a guide to his theory. The major work, from which most of the quotations in what follows have been taken, is the three-volume *Educational psychology* (1913–1914), which represents the system at the height of its popularity.

The most characteristic form of learning of both lower animals and man was identified by Thorndike as trial-and-error learning, or, as he preferred to call it later, learning by selecting and connecting. The learner is confronted by a problem situation in which he has to reach a goal such as escape from a problem-box or attainment of food. He does this by selecting the appropriate response from a number of possible responses. A trial is defined by the length of time (or number of errors) involved in a single reaching of the goal. Thorndike's earliest experiments were of this kind, done chiefly with cats, although some experiments with dogs, fish, and monkeys were included (1898, 1911).[1] The typical experiment is that of a hungry cat confined in a box with a concealed mechanism operated by a latch. If the cat correctly manipulates the latch, the door opens, and the cat gains access to the food outside. The first trials are characterized by a great amount of clawing, biting, and dashing about before the latch is moved. The score, as measured in elapsed time, is high. On succeeding trials the time scores get lower, but slowly and irregularly. It is this gradualness which suggests that the cat does not really "catch on" to the manner of escape, but learns it instead by the stamping in of correct responses and the stamping out of incorrect ones.

Experiments like this have become so commonplace that the importance of their introduction by Thorndike is easily overlooked. By contrast with the other laboratory arrangements within which learning was studied, the problem-box brought to the fore the problems of motivation, of rewards and of punishments. The typical laboratory experiments on learning be-

[1] When years only are given, the name of the author can be understood from the context.

fore Thorndike were either the experiments introduced by Ebbinghaus on the memorization and recall of verbal materials or the experiments on acquisition of skill exemplified by the Bryan and Harter studies of learning telegraphy. In both of these, motivation remains in the background as one of the contextual features, along with learning capacity and other factors not entering as manipulated variables. In his "law of effect" Thorndike brought motivation into the foreground. Trials were defined not by a repetition of a list (Ebbinghaus) or by so many minutes of practice (Bryan and Harter) but by the performance prior to successful (or unsuccessful) goal attainment.

Thorndike saw that in his law of effect he had added an important supplement to the familiar law of habit formation through repetition:

> But practice without zeal—with equal comfort at success and failure—does *not* make perfect, and the nervous system grows *away* from the modes in which it is *exercised with resulting discomfort.* When the law of effect is omitted—when habit-formation is reduced to the supposed effect of mere repetition—two results are almost certain. By the resulting theory, little in human behavior can be explained by the law of habit; and by the resulting practice, unproductive or extremely wasteful forms of drill are encouraged (1913b, page 22).

The interest in rewards and punishments which grew out of his experiments with animals continued naturally enough as he turned his attention to learning as it occurs in schools. There the arguments over punishment, promotion, school marks, and other incentive devices were rife, even though academic psychologists had not yet awakened to the centrality of motivational concepts.

Thorndike's experiments on animals had a very profound influence upon his thinking about human learning. He became convinced, contrary to the then popular beliefs, that animal behavior was little mediated by ideas. Responses were said to be made directly to the situation as sensed. While he did not go so far as to deny ideation among animals, he was convinced that the great bulk of their learning could be explained by the direct binding of acts to situations, unmediated by ideas. A comparison of the learning curves of human subjects with those of animals led him to believe that the same essentially mechanical phenomena disclosed by animal learning are the fundamentals of human learning also. Although always aware of the greater subtlety and range of human learning, he showed a strong preference for understanding more complex learning in terms of the simpler, and for identifying the simpler forms of human learning with that of animals.

> Both theory and practice need emphatic and frequent reminders that man's learning is fundamentally the action of the laws of readiness, exercise, and effect. He is first of all an associative mechanism working to avoid what disturbs the life-processes of the neurones. If we begin by fabricating imaginary powers

and faculties, or if we avoid thought by loose and empty terms, or if we stay lost in wonder at the extraordinary versatility and inventiveness of the higher forms of learning, we shall never understand man's progress or control his education (1913b, page 23).

The systematic position is best understood through the three laws to which he refers: readiness, exercise, and effect. It is in accordance with these laws that animal and human learning takes place.

The Law of Readiness

The law of readiness is an accessory principle which describes a physiological substratum for the law of effect. It states the circumstances under which a learner tends to be satisfied or annoyed, to welcome or to reject. There are three such circumstances (1913a, page 128):

1. When a conduction unit is ready to conduct, conduction by it is satisfying, nothing being done to alter its action.
2. For a conduction unit ready to conduct not to conduct is annoying, and provokes whatever response nature provides in connection with that particular annoying lack.
3. When a conduction unit unready for conduction is forced to conduct, conduction by it is annoying.

Although "conduction units" were referred to in his earlier writings as though he were talking about actual neurones, Thorndike did not, in fact, pay much attention to neuroanatomical details. He talked about neurones to be clear that he was talking about direct impulses to action, and not about "consciousness" or "ideas." It must be remembered that his system antedated behaviorism, even though its emphasis was definitely toward an objective account of behavior. The physiological language was the most available vocabulary for the objectivist prior to the rise of behaviorism. Actually Thorndike's "conduction units" have no precise physiological meaning. It would be difficult, for example, to understand how a physiological unit unready to conduct could be made to conduct.

If for "conduction unit" a term such as "action tendency" is substituted, the psychological meaning of Thorndike's law of readiness becomes clearer. When an action tendency is aroused through preparatory adjustments, sets, attitudes, and the like, fulfillment of the tendency in action is satisfying, nonfulfillment is annoying. Readiness thus means a preparation for action. Thorndike uses the illustration of an animal running after its prey, getting ready all the while for jumping upon it and seizing it. He describes a child seeing an attractive object at a distance, getting ready to approach it, seize it, and manipulate it. He says that it is the neurones which prepare prophetically for later actions in the sequence. This somewhat objectionable manner of describing what goes on need not detract from the reality of the psychological observation that satisfaction and frustration depend upon what the organism is prepared to do.

There is another kind of readiness familiar to educators. This is illustrated by the use of "reading readiness" to refer to the child's reaching a maturity level appropriate to the beginning of reading. Thorndike did not use his law of readiness in this way, and it would be historically inaccurate to construe his law of readiness as an anticipation of maturational readiness. There is, of course, a logical relationship between the two kinds of readiness, because interests and motives mature along with capacities. But Thorndike's readiness was a law of preparatory adjustment, not a law about growth.

The Earlier Law of Exercise

The law of exercise refers to the strengthening of connections with practice (Law of Use) and to the weakening of connections or forgetting when practice is discontinued (Law of Disuse). Strengthening is defined by the increase in probability that the response will be made when the situation recurs. This probability may be either a *greater* probability of occurrence if the situation is repeated immediately, or an *equal* probability persisting longer in time. That is, a stronger connection is in a favored competitive position relative to other habits, either at the time of its strengthening or if tested after there has been opportunity for forgetting.

The definition of strength by probability of occurrence (1913b, page 2) has a very contemporary ring. It is acceptable in itself to those who might go on to reject the structural basis assigned by Thorndike to changes in strength of connections. Although changes were said to occur in neurones and synapses, even in his earlier writings the precise properties attributed to neurones were cautiously stated and not actually essential to the theory.

The kinds of phenomena falling under the law of exercise are chiefly those of repetitive habits, as in rote memorizing or the acquiring of muscular skills. Learning curves in which performance is plotted against trials represent the quantification of the law of use; forgetting curves give quantitative details for the law of disuse. During the period under discussion, Thorndike accepted uncritically the prevailing principle of learning by doing, even though he had criticized the use of the principle independent of the law of effect. He later altered his position and greatly reduced the emphasis upon the law of exercise.

The Earlier Law of Effect

The law of effect refers to the strengthening or weakening of a connection as a result of its consequences. When a modifiable connection is made and is accompanied by or followed by a satisfying state of affairs, the strength of the connection is increased; if the connection is made and followed by an annoying state of affairs, its strength is decreased.

Two chief objections have been made to the law of effect by its critics. At the height of behaviorism it was objected that satisfaction and annoyance were subjective terms, inappropriate for use in describing animal behavior. But Thorndike was in reality ahead of his critics, for he had early stated what he meant by such states of affairs in what would today be called operational terms:

> By a satisfying state of affairs is meant one which the animal does nothing to avoid, often doing things which maintain or renew it. By an annoying state of affairs is meant one which the animal does nothing to preserve, often doing things which put an end to it (1913b, page 2).

These definitions are not circular, so far as the law of effect is concerned. That is, the states of affairs characterized as satisfying and as annoying are specified independently of their influence upon modifiable connections. The law of effect then states what may be expected to happen to preceding modifiable connections which are followed by such specified states. The objection that Thorndike was lacking in objectivity in the statement of the law of effect is not a valid one.

The second objection was that the backward effect of a state of affairs on something now past in time is not conceivable. The past is gone, effects can be felt only in the present, or perhaps revealed in the future. The criticism, like the first, is a faulty one. The effect is revealed in the probability of occurrence of the response when the situation next occurs; whether or not such an effect occurs is a matter of observation and experiment, not something to be denied on *a priori* grounds. In fairness to his critics, it must be said that Thorndike's insistence on a backward influence upon neurones encouraged such objections to the law of effect. Some of his statements were indeed objectionable, but the objectionable statements never did express the essence of the law of effect, which is essentially an empirical matter.

Translated into more familiar words, Thorndike is saying in this law that rewards or successes further the learning of the rewarded behavior, whereas punishments or failures reduce the tendency to repeat the behavior leading to punishment, failure, or annoyance. So much would merely be a reassertion of common observations. But he went further and insisted that the action of consequences is direct and need not be mediated by ideas. In this insistence his law of effect anticipates the reinforcement principle adopted in many conditioned-response theories. The later changes in theory reduced the importance of annoyers relative to satisfiers and added some new phenomena, but the central importance of a modified law of effect persisted in Thorndike's final statements of his position.

Subordinate Laws

The major laws of readiness, exercise, and effect were said to have five subsidiary laws applicable to both animal and human learning (1913b, pages 23-31). Among these occurs one, associative shifting, which is so similar to one variety of conditioned-response theory that it deserves special mention, even though it was listed as the fifth of the subordinate principles.

In a short account of Thorndike's views, the impression may be given that Thorndike was a very systematic writer. His "system," apart from a few persistent preferences, is in fact a rather loose collection of rules and suggestions. What was called a "law" at any one time was a statement which at the time appeared to Thorndike to have some generality of application. No effort was made to retain internal coherence among the concepts used, or to establish any genuine relationship of coordination or subordination among the laws. The five "subordinate laws" to be discussed are principles which seemed to Thorndike somewhat less important than the major laws of readiness, exercise, and effect. They are not related to the major laws in any clear manner, and in later writings they were occasionally omitted, occasionally revived.

1. Multiple response. The first of the five principles is that of multiple response or varied reaction. In order for a response to be rewarded, it must occur. When the learner faces a problem he tries one thing after another. When the appropriate behavior is stumbled upon, success follows and learning is possible. Were the organism unable to vary its responses, the correct solution might never be elicited.

2. Set or attitude. The second principle is that learning is guided by a total attitude or "set" of the organism. Responses are determined in part by enduring adjustments characteristic of individuals raised in a given culture. But they are also influenced by more momentary tendencies. The attitude or set determines not only what the person will do, but what will satisfy or annoy him. Thorndike says that a more ambitious golfer will be annoyed by shots which the more modest would cherish. This principle is related to a series of conceptions coming to prominence later in discussions of level of aspiration.

3. Prepotency of elements. The third principle states that the learner is able to react selectively to prepotent elements in the problem. That is, a man can pick out the essential item and base his responses upon it, neglecting other adventitious features which might confuse a lower animal. This ability to deal with the relevant parts of situations makes analytical and insightful learning possible.

4. Response by analogy. The fourth principle is that of assimilation, or response by analogy. How does man react to novel situations? He responds to a new situation as he would to some situation like it, or he responds to some element in the new situation to which he has a response in his repertory. Responses can always be explained by old acquisitions, together with inborn tendencies to respond; there is nothing mysterious about responses to novelty.

5. Associative shifting. The fifth of these subsidiary laws is called associative shifting. The fundamental notion is that if a response can be kept intact through a series of changes in the stimulating situation, it may finally be given to a totally new stimulus. The stimulating situation is changed first by addition, then by subtraction, until nothing from the original situation remains. Thorndike illustrates by the act of teaching a cat to stand up at command. First a bit of fish is dangled before the cat while you say, "Stand up." After enough trials, by proper arrangement, the fish may be omitted, and the oral signal will alone evoke the response. The most general statement of the principle of associative shifting is that we may "get any response of which a learner is capable associated with any situation to which he is sensitive" (1913b, page 15). This is obviously related to that type of conditioning in which the process is described as substituting a conditioned stimulus for an unconditioned one. Thorndike noted the similarity, but he believed the conditioned response to be a more specialized case under the broader principle of associative shifting. While in his earlier writings associative shifting was but the fifth of the subordinate laws, in later books it was "promoted," becoming a kind of learning second to that by selecting and connecting (1935, pages 191-197).

Controlling Learning

There is always some danger of misunderstanding a systematic writer's influence if attention is confined to the more abstract and generalized laws which he proposes, to the neglect of some of the accessory details which give both flavor and body to his teaching. Thorndike as early as 1913 was giving much more attention to the dynamics of learning than a formal consideration of his laws suggests.

Within the framework of his primary laws, he saw three considerations which affected the teacher's problem in using them in the classroom.

These were: (1) ease of identification of the bonds to be formed or broken; (2) ease of identification of the states of affairs which should satisfy or annoy; and (3) ease of application of satisfaction and annoyance to the identified states of affairs (1913b, pages 213-217). The teacher and the learner must know the characteristics of a good performance in order that practice may be appropriately arranged. Errors must be diagnosed so that they will not be repeated. When there is lack of clarity about what is being taught or learned, practice may be strengthening the wrong connections as well as the right ones. At the same time, needed connections may be weakened by disuse. It is especially hard to teach imagination, force, and beauty in literary expression because it is difficult to be specific about the conduct which should be made satisfying at the time it occurs. The importance of specificity runs throughout Thorndike's writings. As we shall see later, this is at once a source of strength in his system and one of its points of vulnerability.

But Thorndike's advice is not limited to the application of his major laws. He refers also to a number of motivational features not readily deducible from the laws of readiness and effect. Five aids to improvement he lists as the interest series (1913b, pages 217-226). These he believes to be commonly accepted by educators:

1. Interest in the work
2. Interest in improvement
3. Significance
4. Problem-attitude
5. Attentiveness

To these five he added two more which he felt were open to some dispute. They were the absence of irrelevant emotion and the absence of worry. In his emphasis upon satisfiers and annoyers he is not talking about "crude emotional states," which he believes are to be avoided.

In the case of improvement in skill, the balance turns again toward freedom from all the crude emotional states and even from all the finer excitements, save the intrinsic satisfyingness of success and a firm repudiation of errors which can hardly be called exciting (1913b, pages 226-227).

Thus to his rather harsh and brittle doctrine of specificity of connections he added informal considerations which did much to temper it. The active role of the learner, who comes to the learning situation with needs and problems which determine what will be satisfying to him, is recognized implicitly in the commentary on the laws, although it lacks explicit statement in the laws themselves. It is probably these accessory features which have commanded ardent support by Thorndike's followers, while it is the most abstract features which have been the focus of attack by those who have disagreed with him.

The Identical-Elements Theory of Transfer

Schools are publicly supported in the hope that more general uses will be made of what is learned in school. To some extent all schooling is aimed at a kind of transfer beyond the school. Whether the proper way to achieve this end may turn out to be to teach more formal subject matter, like mathematics and the classics, or to give more attention to practical subject matter like manual training and social studies, the problem is a central one for educators.

Thorndike early interested himself in the problem. His theory began to take form in an experimental study done in collaboration with Woodworth (Thorndike and Woodworth, 1901), and was formally stated in his early *Educational psychology* (1903). The theory proposes that transfer depends upon the presence of identical elements in the original learning and in the new learning which it facilitates. These may be identities of either substance or procedure. Thus the ability to speak and write well are important in all schoolroom classes and many tasks of ordinary life. Hence mastery of these skills will serve in different pursuits, and transfer will be effected through what the different situations require in common. The substance of what is required in different situations may be unlike, but there may be procedures in common. The procedures of looking things up in such diverse sources as a dictionary, a cookbook, and a chemist's handbook have much in common, despite the unlike contents of the three kinds of book. If an activity is learned more easily because another activity was learned first, it is only because the two activities overlap. Learning is always specific, never general; when it appears to be general, it is only because new situations have much of old situations in them.

Intelligence as measured by tests may be thought of as to some extent a measure of the transfer-capacity of an individual. That is, the test measures the ability to give right answers in relatively novel situations. It is logically sound that Thorndike's theory of intelligence was, like his theory of transfer, a matter of specific connections. The more bonds the individual has which can be used, the more intelligent he is.

Thorndike's specificity doctrines of transfer and of intelligence have been highly influential and have led to a great deal of experimental work. Although the problems of the nature of and measurement of intelligence lie outside the scope of this volume, there will be occasion later to consider some of the alternative explanations of transfer.

During the stable period of Thorndike's system there were many changes in psychological climate, but these left him unruffled. The rise of behaviorism and the new importance attributed to the conditioned response affected him but little, because the new enthusiasts were talking a congenial language, even when they included him in their sweeping attacks on everything which preceded them. The attacks by the gestalt psychologists in the '20's were more telling, and he began later to meet some of their criticisms. But it was his own experiments which led him to come before the International Congress of Psychology in New Haven in September, 1929, with the statement, "I was wrong." He there announced two fundamental revisions in his laws of exercise and effect which became the basis for a number of publications dating from 1930.

CONNECTIONISM AFTER 1930

The revisions of his fundamental laws were reported by Thorndike in a number of journal articles and monographs with various collaborators, the main results being gathered in two large volumes under the titles *The fundamentals of learning* (1932a) and *The psychology of wants, interests, and attitudes* (1935). The law of exercise was practically renounced as a law of learning, only a trivial amount of strengthening of connections being left as a function of mere repetition. The law of effect remained only half true, the weakening effects of annoying consequences being renounced. For the two central laws there was substituted half the original law of effect.

Disproof of the Law of Exercise

The type of experiment used to disprove the law of exercise was that in which repetition went on under circumstances in which the law of effect could not be applicable. For example, repeated attempts to draw a line exactly 3 inches long while blindfolded did not lead to improvement, no matter how frequent the repetitions. Practice brings improvement only because it permits other factors to be effective; practice itself does nothing. Thorndike intended that his "repeal" of the law of exercise should be a safeguard against its misuse, not a denial of the importance of controlled practice. The laws of habit strengthening must be those of the conditions under which practice takes place; mere repetition of situations is not enough. If the person is informed each time after his attempt to draw a 3-inch line that his product is too long or too short, he will improve with repetition (Trowbridge and Cason, 1932).[2]

The law of exercise was not, in fact, fully repealed. It was said that repetition of *situations* produces no change in strength of connections, but repetitions of *connections* may produce a small advantage for that connection as against competing connections attached to the same situation.

---

[2] There was indeed more regularizing of performance in his own experiments than Thorndike believed, according to recomputation of his data by Seashore and Bavelas (1941).

The strengthening is almost negligible; for all practical purposes, connections get strengthened by being rewarded, not by just occurring. In one of those curious and optimistically quantitative summaries which Thorndike occasionally made, he concluded that a single occurrence followed by reward strengthens a connection about six times as much as it would be strengthened by merely occurring (1940, page 14).

The Truncated Law of Effect

A number of experiments yielded data showing that the effects of reward and punishment were not equal and opposite, as had been implied in earlier statements of the effects of satisfiers and of annoyers. Instead, under conditions in which symmetrical action was possible, reward appeared to be much more powerful than punishment. This conclusion, if confirmed, is of immense social importance in such fields of application as education and criminology.

One of these experiments was done with chicks (1932b). A simple maze gave the chick the choice of three pathways, one of which led to "freedom, food, and company"—that is, to an open compartment where there were other chicks eating. The wrong choices led to confinement for 30 seconds. Statistics were kept on the tendencies to return to the preceding choice if it had led to reward, and to avoid the preceding choice if it led to punishment. Thorndike interpreted his findings as follows: "The results of all comparisons by all methods tell the same story. Rewarding a connection always strengthened it substantially; punishing it weakened it little or not at all" (1932b, page 58).

The corresponding experiment with human subjects consists of a multiple-choice vocabulary test. For example, a Spanish word is given with five English words, one of which is its correct translation. A second and a third word follow, and so on through a list, each word with alternative translations arranged in the same manner. The subject guesses the word which is correct, underlines it, and then hears the experimenter say *Right* ("rewarded" response) or *Wrong* ("punished" response). How will he change his responses the next time through the list? As with the chicks, reward leads to repetition of the rewarded connection, but punishment does not lead to a weakening of the punished connection. In six experiments of this general sort, Thorndike concluded that the announcement of *Wrong* did not weaken connections enough to counterbalance the slight increase in strength gained from just occurring (1932a, page 288).

Thorndike and his staff went on to collect a series of testimonials about the relative efficacy of rewards and punishments from published biographies and other sources, going back many years. The almost universal evidence of the greater beneficial effect of reward than of punishment gave practical support to the findings of the experiments, which otherwise could be criticized as too far removed from ordinary life (1935, pages 135-144; 248-255).

There were some statistical difficulties in Thorndike's interpretations of his data which caused him to underestimate the significance of punishment. On the whole, however, he probably did a service through calling attention to the asymmetry of the effects of reward and of punishment.

As in the disproof of the law of exercise, the repeal of the principle of weakening by annoying aftereffects is not absolute. It is only direct weakening which is denied. Punishments do, according to Thorndike, affect learning indirectly. Thorndike says that their indirect effect comes chiefly from leading the animal to do something in the presence of the annoyer which makes him less likely to repeat the original connection. But this is not necessarily the case.

An annoyer which is attached to a modifiable connection may cause the animal to feel fear or chagrin, jump back, run away, wince, cry, perform the same act as before but more vigorously, or whatever else is in his repertory as a response to that annoyer in that situation. But there is no evidence that it takes away strength from the physiological basis of the connection in any way comparable to the way in which a satisfying after-effect adds strength to it (1932a, pages 311-313).

Thorndike was less successful in his attempts to explain the action of effect than in demonstrating that there are phenomena to which his principles apply. He distinguished between a direct *confirming influence* and the *informative influence* of rewards. Control of behavior according to the information supplied by its consequences implies mediation by ideas of the sort, "If I do this, I get fed; if I do that, I get slapped." Thorndike believed that he kept this kind of deliberation at a minimum in his experiments, so that what he had to explain was the direct confirmatory reaction which he said was responsible for the strengthening of responses through reward. This confirming reaction is vaguely described as an "unknown reaction of the neurones" which is aroused by the satisfier and strengthens the connection upon which it impinges (1933c). The confirming reaction is said to be independent of sensory pleasures, and independent of the intensity of the satisfier. It is highly selective, depending upon aroused drives or "overhead control in the brain." While such an account is far from satisfactory, it at least helps to show where Thorndike stood. He was against mediation by ideas, as an interpretation of effect according to information would imply. At the same time, he recognized the complexity of the reinforcement process and was not committed to a simple hedonism. The law of effect was for him no longer a law of affect, as Hollingworth (1931) once named it.

Belongingness

In addition to the revisions of the laws of exercise and effect, several new terms entered as Thorndike's system was revised. One of these, *belongingness,* by its recognition of an organizational principle foreign to the structure of Thorndike's theory of specificity and mechanical action, made slight concessions to the gestalt psychologists.[3] According to this principle, a connection is more easily learned if the response belongs to the situation, and an aftereffect does better if it belongs to the connection it strengthens. For example, a series of sentences may be each of the form "John is a butcher. Henry is a carpenter." The association John–butcher is a stronger one following such a reading than the association butcher–Henry, even though the latter connection is based on more nearly contiguous items. The reason is that a subject and predicate belong together in a way in which the end of one sentence and the beginning of another do not. The belongingness of a reward or punishment depends upon its appropriateness in satisfying an aroused motive or want in the learner, and in its logical or informative relationship to the activities rewarded or punished. Thus to be rewarded by having your thirst quenched when you lift a glass of cool water to your lips is reward with belonging. If the same series of movements led sporadically to an electric shock on your ankle, that would be punishment without belonging. Although Thorndike states that aftereffects are influential without either belongingness or relevance, he points out at the same time that they are more effective when they do belong and when they are relevant (1935, pages 52-61).

While the principle of belongingness may be interpreted as something of a concession, the principle of *polarity* is emphasized as defying gestalt principles (1932a, page 158). The principle of polarity is that connections act more easily in the direction in which they were formed than in the opposite direction. If you have learned the items of a German–English vocabulary, it is easier to respond to the German word by its English equivalent than to the English word by its German equivalent. If a connection is thought of as a new whole, Thorndike contends, the polarity principle ought not be important. It ought then to be as easy to dissociate parts from the whole in one direction as in another.

Other new terms introduced, such as "impressiveness," "identifiability," "availability," and "mental systems," represent informal extensions of notions already latent in the earlier writings.

Discovery of the Spread of Effect

In 1933 a new kind of experimental evidence was offered in support of the law of effect, evidence described as the *spread of effect* (1933a,

---

[3] The point was made early by Brown and Feder (1934). See also Guthrie (1936b).

1933b). The experiments purported to show that the influence of a rewarding state of affairs acts not only on the connection to which it belongs but on adjacent connections both before and after the rewarded connection, the effect diminishing with each step that the connection is removed from the rewarded one. The effect acts to strengthen even punished connections in the neighborhood of the rewarded one. The experiments lent support to the automatic and mechanical action of effect. A characteristic experiment was that in which the subject was asked to state a number from 1 to 10 following the announcement of a stimulus word by the experimenter. The experimenter then called his response *Right* or *Wrong,* these "rewards" and "punishments" conforming either to a prearranged assignment of correct numbers to each word, or to some systematic pattern of "rights" or "wrongs." In either case, the assignment of numbers from the point of view of the subject is arbitrary, and the cue to repeat the number first assigned or to change it comes from what the experimenter says following each word. The lists are so long that the subject cannot recall on the second trial just what was done on the first one.

After the list has been read a number of times in this manner, the responses of the subject are classified to find the number of times the responses were repeated. Not only are the rewarded responses repeated more often than the others, but responses called *Wrong* are repeated beyond chance expectancy if they occur near in time to a response called *Right.* To some extent the phenomena included in the spread of effect come nearest to a "discovery" in the whole of Thorndike's work. Because of the novelty of the phenomena and their systematic relevance, typical experiments in support of and critical of the spread of effect are reviewed below as illustrative of Thorndike's influence upon experimentation in the field of learning.

EXPERIMENTS ON THE SPREAD OF EFFECT

The experimental study of the spread of effect is the most characteristic contemporary laboratory residue of connectionism.[4] It illustrates at once both the relative potency of rewards and punishments and the semiautomatic manner in which effects act upon connections, whether or not they "belong." To the extent that the phenomena of the spread of effect stand upon firm ground, Thorndike's basic conceptions are buttressed against attacks by his critics.

[4] Another laboratory topic owing to Thorndike has to do with learning with and without awareness, but these experiments have many other roots as well. For a discussion of them in relation to Thorndike, see Postman (1962, pages 386-392).

Punishment May Be More Effective Than Thorndike Believed

Thorndike had already changed his mind about the effectiveness of annoyers in weakening connections before the spread-of-effect experiments were announced. He interpreted his results on the spread of effect as confirming his recently acquired belief in the relative ineffectiveness of punishments in weakening connections. The spread of effect is then, to him, a spread of positive effects, a gradient of reward. Reward is said to strengthen even neighboring punished connections.

In several of his experiments, Thorndike made a faulty assumption about the baseline of chance expectation. He assumed that one alternative in a series of multiple possibilities was as likely to occur as another. That is, if there were four choices, by chance each should occur 25% of the time. When the opportunity is given to repeat the responses, the same one chosen last time should be chosen again in 25% of the cases, if the tendency to respond has been neither strengthened nor weakened during the first occurrence. In practice this chance repetition seldom occurs, for whatever predisposition leads to a preference for one of the choices the first time tends to favor that same choice the next time. Suppose there are four alternatives, and the series is presented twice. If there is a 35% agreement on choices between the first and the second time, this does not mean that the gain over chance resulted from repetition. The above-chance preference may have been there on the first trial. This criticism was made by Stephens (1934) and Hull (1935b), among others, and empirical results show that punishment may in fact lead to fewer repetitions. The result of Thorndike's use of too low a base for chance repetition was automatically to assign too much strengthening to rewards and too little weakening to punishments. The asymmetry could be entirely a statistical artifact.

Tilton, earlier an associate of Thorndike, repeated the spread-of-effect experiment with careful controls to determine what the empirical level of repetition would be without the saying of *Right* and *Wrong,* and then proceeded to plot the spread of effect on either side of a rewarded and a punished response (Tilton, 1939, 1945). He made a correction also for a serial position effect, that is, for a tendency to repeat the same response to items near the beginning and the end of the list. When correction is made, it is found that the effects of *Right* and *Wrong* are about alike, the announcement of *Wrong* decreasing repetitions about as much as *Right* increases them. A replotting of Tilton's results is shown in Figures 2-1 and 2-2.

Tilton's study shows that there is a tendency for punished responses in the neighborhood of reward to be repeated more frequently than such responses remote from reward. Their punishment (being called *Wrong*) suffices however, even one step from reward, to lead to *less* repetition than would occur if the response were neither rewarded nor punished (Figure 2-1). Similarly, when a response called *Wrong* (punished) occurs in the midst of a series of rewarded responses, the neighboring rewarded responses are repeated less frequently than they would have been had they not been in the neighborhood of the punished response. Again, however, their reward (being called *Right*) is enough to lead to their repetition at a *greater* frequency than that represented by the neutral baseline (Figure 2-2).

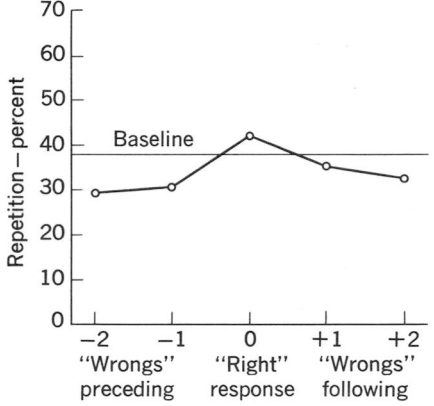 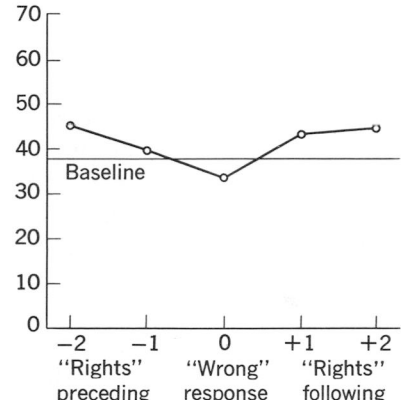

Figure 2-1   Gradient of effect around a *Right* response. Calling a response *Right* increases its repetition, calling a response *Wrong* decreases its repetition. The decrease from being called *Wrong* is less, however, when the response called *Wrong* is near an isolated *Right*. Redrawn from Tilton (1945).

Figure 2-2   Gradient of effect around a *Wrong* response. Calling a response *Wrong* decreases its repetition, calling a response *Right* increases its repetition. The increase from being called *Right* is less, however, when the response called *Right* is near an isolated *Wrong*. Redrawn from Tilton (1945).

Because Tilton used the conventional method of obtaining spread of effect, repeating lists over and over again, and allowing right responses and wrong responses to appear with any degree of separation, he had to make a rather elaborate analysis in order to exhibit just what was in fact happening within his experiment. Martens (1946) introduced a corrective by arranging the experimental situation so that each position before and after reward has an equal opportunity to be represented in the final spread-of-effect pattern. This she did by limiting the training and testing to one trial each on each list. That is, on one trial through a list of words the subject arbitrarily assigned numbers and was informed each time whether the number was right or wrong. The experimenter was able to assign the word *Right* to prearranged positions, all other positions being assigned the word *Wrong*. Then a single additional trial was used to determine the extent to which the subject would repeat the numbers called *Right* and repeat or change the numbers called *Wrong*. The statistical handling and interpretation of the effects of *Right* and *Wrong* are greatly simplified, for according to the prearranged pattern there are an equal number of opportunities to give the same response or a different response to each of several positions before and after the rewarded connection. The control situation consisted in the subject's assigning numbers as in a free association experiment, with the list repeated twice, no announcements of *Right* or *Wrong* being used. Her results in this modified situation supported Tilton's, so far as the effect of a rewarded response imbedded in the midst of punished responses is concerned. That is, the effect of *Wrong*, even adjacent to the rewarded connection is greater than whatever influence can be attributed to the spread of the effect of *Right*. The direct effects of both *Right* and of *Wrong* are greater than any spread from one to the other.

Stephens (1941), like Tilton, a former student of Thorndike, made an interesting mediating suggestion that "symbolic" reward strengthens weak connections more than "symbolic" punishment weakens them, but symbolic punishment weakens strong connections more than symbolic reward strengthens them. According to this view, it was because Thorndike tended to work mostly with weak connections that he got the results he did. Stephens' experiment was done by using statements such as appear on attitude scales to determine certain convictions held strongly by the subjects, others held less strongly. Then a law-of-effect experiment was arranged, in which multiple-choice answers were permitted to selected statements, and the subject was informed which choice was correct. The method of information was the ingenious one of using chemically prepared paper so that the correct response came out in color when it was marked by the instrument provided. This permitted the experiment to be done with groups. When the experiment was then repeated, it was possible to see which tendency was the greater, to repeat the response answered correctly or to change from the response answered incorrectly. The change was found to be correlated with the conviction represented by the answer. The better-established replies were more influenced by punishment, the less-well-established by reward.

There is a difficulty of interpretation in this experiment which may help to account for uncertainty in other experiments about the relative influence of reward and punishment. There is a logical difference between responding in the intelligent direction to *Right* and to *Wrong*. The intelligent response to *Right* is to do again what was last done. This makes possible immediate rehearsal; the task is clear. The intelligent response to *Wrong* is to do something different, but what to do is less clear. It is necessary both to remember what not to do and to form some sort of hypothesis as to what to do. Under time pressure this vagueness might well produce an asymmetry between responses following *Right* and *Wrong*. In the case of poorly established convictions, it may be harder to remember what was said that was called *Right* than in the case of well-established convictions to remember what was said that was called *Wrong*. If that were true, Stephens' results would follow. Anything which makes it easier to make the necessary discriminations in one case than in another will affect the relative potency of hearing *Right* or *Wrong*, and of modifying subsequent behavior accordingly. In other words, the situation is not nearly as mechanical and stupid as it appears; in fact, the results can be best understood on the assumption that the individual is doing his best to act intelligently under somewhat confusing circumstances.

The whole discussion of the effect of punishment in the Thorndike-type experiment is confused because of the complexity of the tasks set the subjects, the very small effects that have to be treated, and hence the very great importance of adopted baselines.

The experiment of Tilton, just cited, has been criticized on the grounds that serial position effects may have distorted the estimated "chance" level (Stone, 1950). Martens (1946), who sought "natural" associates between words and numbers as in the free-association experiment, found a higher baseline of repetition than Wallach and Henle (1941), whose method may have discouraged repetition (Postman and Adams, 1954). Obviously any arbitrariness about the baseline must lead to arbitrariness in the interpretation of positive and negative effects. Later experiments, seeking to do as well as possible in clearing up the baseline problem, have been little more successful. Thus Stone (1953) developed a design in which two groups were used, both treated exactly alike except that some critical responses were punished in one group and not in the other. The task set the subject was so confusing, however, that it is difficult to interpret the results. Subjects in a word-number experiment were randomly reinforced with "Right," "Wrong," and no response for the first and final 16 items of a 40-item list, so that there was no possibility of improvement with practice, even though the subject might remember perfectly what he did on each trial. The middle eight items were, however, more orderly. For one group no aftereffect occurred for these eight items, while for the other group the middle two items were reported "Wrong" no matter what the subject did. Under these somewhat confusing circumstances, the subject increasingly stereotyped the responses that went without aftereffect, and more often varied the ones that were punished (Figure 2-3). While the experiment has been used to support Thorndike's interpretation that punishment is not effective (Postman, 1962, page 367), to do so one has to ignore the gains made under the control condition. The experiment might better be used to support the importance of the law of exercise! If the design of the experiment is accepted as valid, the only appropriate interpretation is that punishment has reduced the responding below the level attained without it.

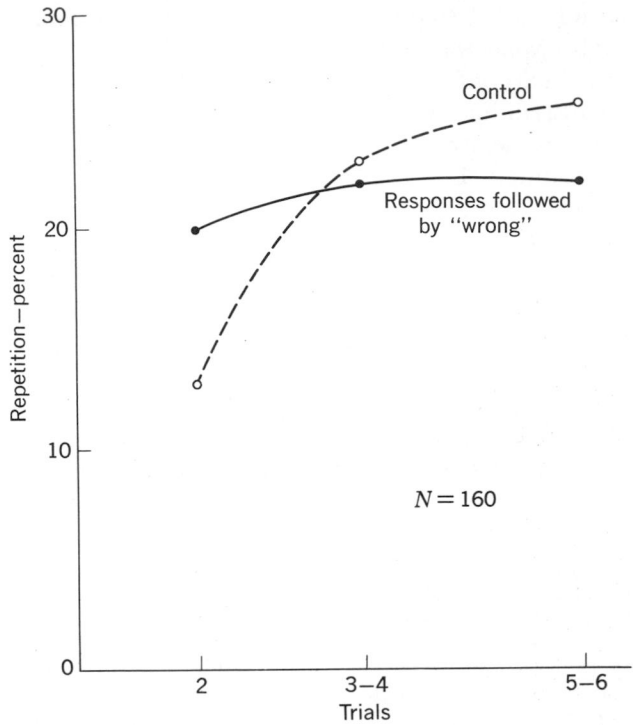

Figure 2-3   The rising curve of responses under control conditions means repetition of responses without specific aftereffects, possibly supporting a "law of exercise." With punishment (responses called "Wrong,") repetition is less frequent than under the control condition. Modified from Stone (1953, page 146).

The Theory of Discrete Connections Probably Faulty

The spread of effect as Thorndike describes it presupposes a series of stimulus–response connections with no other organization among them than succession in time. What is strengthened (or weakened) is the tendency for a stimulus to be followed by the response which accompanied it the last time. Other experimenters have given evidence that additional principles of organization do apply, and the automatic spread of the influence of reward to neighboring connections is either incorrect or a gross oversimplification.

Zirkle (1946a), by changing the order of stimulus words on successive trials, showed that what was repeated was a neighboring response, not a stimulus–response connection. That is, a tendency to repeat the response "five" given originally to the word "youthful" two steps removed from reward, was found on the next trial to be given to "supports" as the stimulus word in the corresponding position. There was no increase in the tendency to say "five" after "youthful" unless it appeared in its old place. Under the usual arrangements of the experiment on spread of effect, it would be impossible to distinguish between strengthening a response or a connection, but under the special circumstances of Zirkle's experiment it is clear that response is the more important beneficiary of the reward.

This suggestion by Zirkle that it is the response rather than the connection which enters prominently into spread-of-effect data received further support from the experiments of Jenkins and Sheffield (1946). They showed that guessing habits were important in the usual spread-of-effect experiments. Guessing habits refer to patterns of response, not to isolated stimulus–response preferences. They found that if a rewarded response was repeated, other responses following it were also repeated; if a rewarded response was not repeated, other responses in its neighborhood were not repeated beyond chance levels. Hence the repetition of a rewarded response appears to be more important than the fact of reward. The major effect of reward is to lead to repetition of the correct response; once this success is achieved, the repetition of responses after the reward depends upon guessing habits.[5]

A related but supplementary suggestion was made and verified by M. H. Smith, Jr. (1949). In what he called the "probability-bias hypothesis," he pointed out that subjects in attempting to respond with a random series of digits tend to avoid using the same digit over again until most of the digits have been used up. In a chance series, the digit has an equal chance of coming up on each trial; its appearance on any one trial is not influenced by the fact that it may have occurred on the preceding one. Intervals between two occurrences of the same digit in a "random" series are plotted in Figure 2-4 along with the intervals between two occurrences in a "subjectively random" series. The striking difference between the curves arises because the subjects, in attempting to produce a random series, postpone the recurrence of a digit once used. How can this bias against repetition produce a spread of effect? The chance of repeating a digit used on the preceding trial following a correct (*Right*) response is enhanced by the *avoidance* of the digit just used as the "correct" response. While this effect is slight, so is the amount of the spread of effect as commonly found. A consistent slight bias of this kind is enough to produce statistically significant results.

There are thus seen to be organizational factors in the spread of effect not described simply by remoteness of connections from rewards.

[5] The guessing sequence hypothesis was amply supported through additional work by the same authors, their collaborators, and others: e.g., Jenkins and Cunningham (1949), Sheffield (1949b), Fagan and North (1951), Sheffield and Jenkins (1952). Doubts have been raised, however, about the sufficiency of this explanation of the spread of effect (e.g., Marx, 1956, Postman, 1962).

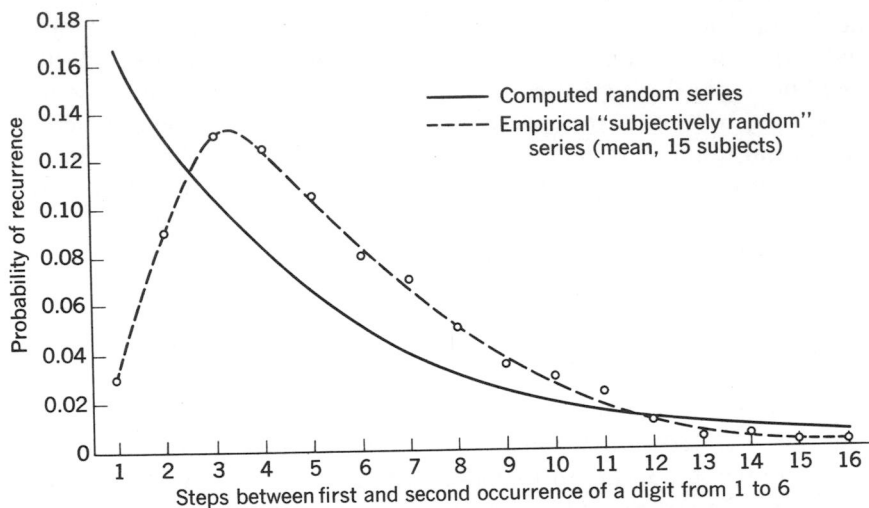

Figure 2-4   **Distribution of steps from the first to the second occurrence of a digit from "one" through "six" in a random series and in a "subjectively random" series produced by 15 subjects. Note that the subjects typically avoid using the same digit a second time until other digits have been used. From Smith (1949, page 360).**

Is "Reward" the Basis for the Enhancement Effect?

The presumption is made in Thorndike's experiments that the repetition of the response called *Right* results directly from reward. That this may not be the case was shown in the experiments of Wallach and Henle (1941, 1942). The subject believed himself to be in an experiment on extrasensory perception, so that as he went through a list he was trying to assign the number which had been assigned by someone else for that particular trial. Hence a response called *Right* on one trial might be incorrect on the next trial. There was thus no intent to learn the *Right* responses, and in fact the hearing of the word *Right* did nothing to improve the repetition of either the rewarded responses or its near neighbors. It appears that what the subject is trying to do is more important than one would suppose from Thorndike's insistence on the automaticity of the effect of reward.

Another experiment by Zirkle (1946b) bears importantly on the question of what causes the repetition of the response called *Right*. Influenced by the possibility that something like a figure–ground relationship may be effective in these situations, Zirkle arranged to have three degrees of isolation of the response called *Right*. It was his conjecture that with greater isolation there would be greater repetition of this response, and perhaps

of its near neighbors also. The degrees of isolation were obtained by insert-
ing within a list of black lower-case words as the words to be called *Right*
(a) a nonsense syllable in red capital letters, the highest degree of isolation,
(b) a word in black capital letters, the next degree of isolation, and (c) a
word printed the same as all the other words, in black lower-case letters,
but isolated solely by being called *Right* in the midst of consecutive words
called *Wrong*. The results are plotted from Zirkle's data in Figure 2-5. His

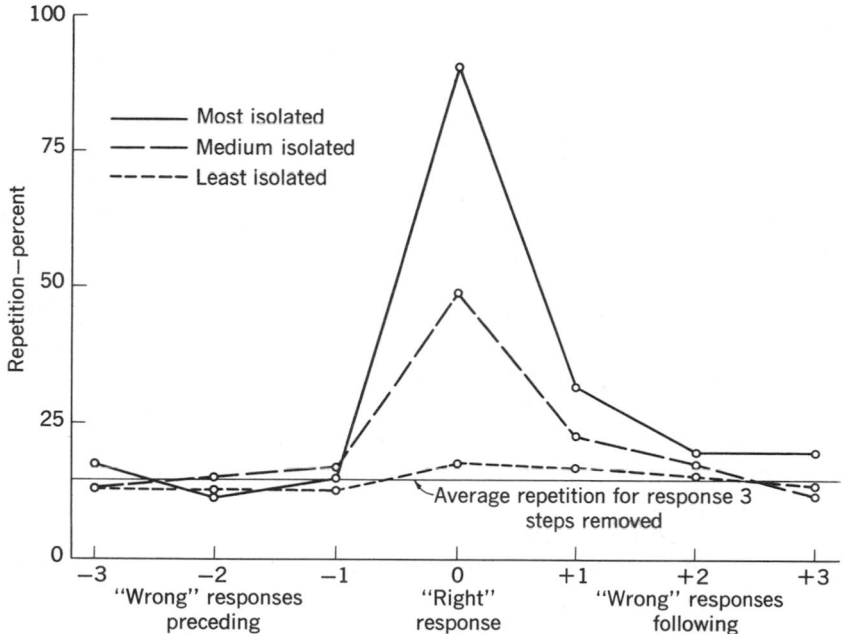

Figure 2-5   Gradient of effect around *Right* responses with three degrees of isolation. All isolated responses called *Right*, all contiguous responses
between called *Wrong*. The differences among the three curves depend upon the degree of isolation (or contrast) of the *Right* and
Wrong items. These degrees are "most isolated," red capital letters;
"medium isolated," black capital letters; "least isolated," black
lower-case letters, like items called *Wrong*, and isolated only by position among several contiguous *Wrong* items. Plotted from Zirkle
(1946b).

prediction was fully confirmed. Not only was the most isolated response
most regularly repeated, but its repetition was followed by the enhanced
repetition of the words immediately following. Because the spread of effect was not demonstrated for the words immediately preceding the isolated word, it is probable that isolation led to the repetition of the isolated word, and that guessing habits then produced the after-gradient.

This conjecture was indirectly supported by the experiments of Jenkins and Postman (1948), in which they found no gradient around an isolated stimulus when guessing sequences were eliminated.

In his experiment on spread of effect when there was neither reward nor opportunity for learning, Sheffield (1949b) found the typical "spread," but the level of repetition was lower than in the usual Thorndike experiment. While Thorndike (1933b) had found the average percent of repetition for the position following reward to be 20.4, the corresponding percent in Sheffield's experiment was 13.3. Was there after all some effect of "reward," or can the difference in level be accounted for on other grounds?

Sheffield and Jenkins (1952) set out to determine whether or not the reward was responsible for the enhancement in Thorndike's experiments. They continued to use Sheffield's procedure of having subjects assign numbers at random, without any statement of *Right* or *Wrong* or any instructions to attempt to repeat. But the numbers were assigned while the subject was engaged in irrelevant learning tasks, approximating the kinds of tasks used in Thorndike's experiments. Depending upon the task used, percentages of repetition equal to and greater than those found by Thorndike could be produced—all without reward and any learning related to the number sequences. A few of the results are summarized graphically in Figure 2-6. A change in instructions, and the concealing of the record of previous replies, raised the level of repetition, without any new task being introduced; when an irrelevant learning task was used, with a fixed order of stimulus presentation (typical of Thorndike's practice), the repetition of other ordered stimuli led to an enhanced repetition of the supposedly random numbers; finally, a paired-associates task in which the assigning of a random number followed the attempt to recall the response member of the associated pair led to the highest level of repetition of numbers on succeeding trials. These experiments lend further support to the guessing-sequence hypothesis, and appear to make unnecessary the attributing of the spread of effect to a control by way of reward.

Despite the bulk of negative evidence, a few experimenters have found results favorable to the spread of effect. Aware of the many criticisms of the spread of effect, Duncan (1951) designed an experiment in which the *stimulus*-member of the associated items would again be important. (It must be remembered that most of the criticisms center around the fact that the spread of effect is generated by response-habits having little to do with the nature of the stimuli presented.) To this end he used two sets of stimulus words. One set consisted of unrelated adjectives ("ancient," "downcast," "mutual") while the other consisted of adjectives very similar in meaning ("superb," "choice," "unique"). Duncan suggested that saying *Right* to a number assigned to one of the similar adjectives might very well lead to a repetition of a number assigned to another similar adjective. In other words, the generalization tendencies might lead to an enhancement of the spread of effect, through uncertainty as to the exact locus of the reward. By the use of the control adjectives of dissimilar meanings, presumably guessing tendencies and the like would be balanced out. His results were largely ambiguous, but the one statistically significant difference he found favored his hypothesis and thus gave some slight support to Thorndike's position.

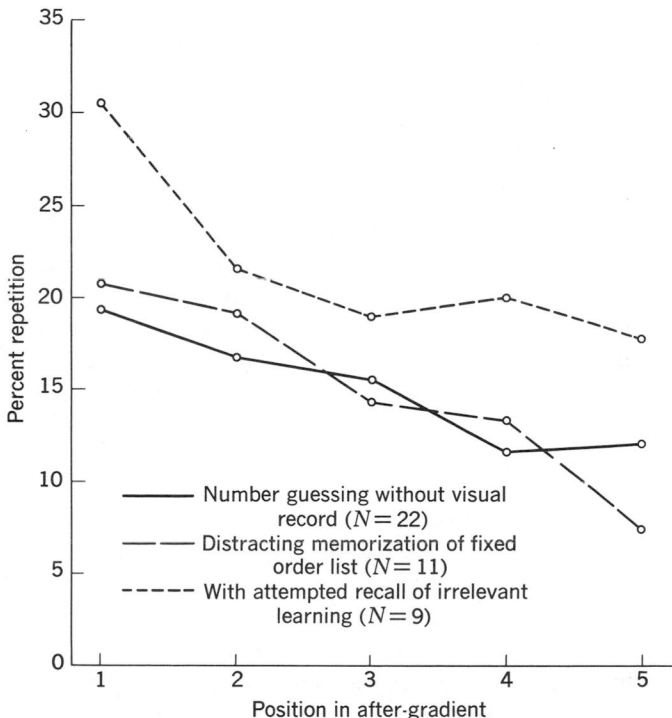

Figure 2-6 **Modified conditions of experimentation raising the level of repetition in a "spread-of-effect" type of experiment without reward or relevant learning. Plotted from the data of Sheffield and Jenkins (1952).**

The suggestion from Duncan's experiment that uncertainty as to what was rewarded may have something to do with the spread of effect receives indirect confirmation from experiments by Nuttin (1949, 1953). The subject was given a list of 40 well-known stimulus words. Each word was followed by five two-syllable words of an "unknown language" (actually artificially constructed nonsense words). He was asked to choose the word that was the exact translation of the stimulus-word, and then told whether he was *Right* or *Wrong*. The rights and wrongs were assigned in a prearranged manner. The list was then repeated a second time, but now the subject was asked to repeat the reply he had given the first time, adding whether the choice had been called *Right* or *Wrong*. Nuttin found that wrong items next to ones called *Right* were remembered as having been called *Right* more often than those farther removed. There is thus some subjective uncertainty as to the locus of the experimenter's assigned *Rights* and *Wrongs*. (Correct responses in the neighborhood of a *Wrong* were also often remembered as having been called *Wrong*.)

Two additional experiments may be cited as illustrative of those which have kept the spread of effect alive as an experimental and theoretical problem.

The first of these is an experiment by Marx and Goodson (1956) in which the possibility of influence by guessing sequences was carefully considered. Marx (1957a) proposed a theory of serial response–response reinforcement, that is, that in serial learning the rewarding of one response tends to strengthen the nonrewarded responses that follow it. This is the same as the spread of effect, except that it attempts to account only for the after-gradient, the fore-gradient appearing so seldom in better controlled experiments that there is perhaps nothing to explain. In a test of this hypothesis, Marx and Goodson used fifth- and sixth-grade school children, working individually with multiple-choice boxes in which the task was to find the hole among 12 in a row through which a stylus could be punched all the way down; the remaining holes were blocked. There were 27 rows of such holes. Experimental subjects were successful ("reinforced") on one, two, or three of their 27 attempts in the first two trials; control subjects were never successful. On the basis of these data, key responses were selected as those on which the same hole of a row was chosen on the two trials. For the experimental subjects this was a reinforced response; for the control subjects it was of course one not reinforced. It is assumed that this controls for the guessing-sequence hypothesis, because measurements in both cases are taken from a successful repetition of a response. For example, if after having punched the seventh hole there is a tendency to avoid another seventh hole, or to prefer the fifth hole, this should apply to both groups. Instead, a gradient was found following the reinforced responses of the experimental group, and not following the responses of the control group (Figure 2-7). No fore-gradient was found, so that, at best, only part of the spread of effect was demonstrated.

The psychological situation for the subject in these experiments is always a complex one, and it is of interest to compare this experiment with Zirkle's (1946b) isolation experiment. In a multiple-choice box of the kind used in the Marx and Goodson experiment, the holes form a visual display, and it is not too difficult to remember those one, two, or three holes through which the stylus went all the way down, for those are the holes being looked for. In any case, those successfully repeated (and perhaps remembered) holes are the ones from which all gradient measure-

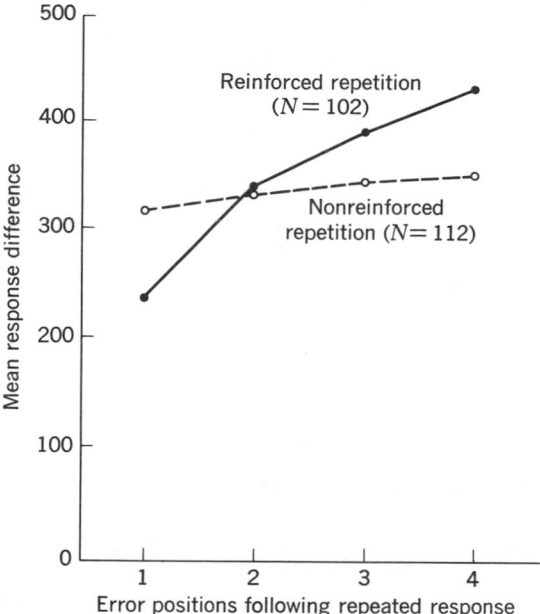

Figure 2-7   An after-gradient of effect for repetition of a motor response by school children. The gradients called "reinforced repetition" were measured from the repetition of a reinforced response, the "non-reinforced repetition" from a nonreinforced but repeated response in the same position. The somewhat awkward measure used (mean response difference) is smaller when a response is repeated. After Marx and Goodson (1956, page 423), with permission from the American Psychological Association.

ments are made. By contrast, there is no sign of any sort to tell the control subjects that they have repeated a response on the board; the items from which *their* gradients are measured have no psychological meaning for them. If the remembered, "stylus-all-the-way-down" holes are considered emphasized or isolated, in Zirkle's sense, the findings parallel his. Guessing sequences, when anchored in this way, might operate more uniformly than when not so anchored. In fact, there were some gradients found for *nonrepeated* reinforced responses (Marx, 1956, page 154), which conforms with the anchorage hypothesis.

Another experiment favorable to the spread of effect is that of Postman (1961a). By using both an immediate and a delayed test he showed that the after-gradient persisted, even though there was a substantial drop in the repetition of rewarded responses after an interval of twenty minutes. He thus argued that the after-gradient does not depend on repetition of the rewarded response; because such dependence is implied in the guessing-sequence hypothesis, he interpreted his experiment as refuting that hypothesis. When he sorted out those tests following immediately after original learning he found the same thing, that is, that the after-gradient remained whether or not the rewarded response was repeated.

Postman's argument appears entirely sound, and any application of the guessing-sequence hypothesis cannot therefore rely on the repetition of the rewarded response for initiating the sequence in recall. Explanations other than the guessing-sequence hypothesis remain open. For example, there is some uncertainty about which stimulus-response pair was rewarded, as shown by a gradient of repetition of the rewarded response around the correct position. This uncertainty, here concerning which *stimulus* was involved, might also affect which *response* was involved, thus leading to a repetition of responses in the neighborhood of the rewarded one.

Some Methodological Lessons from the Spread-of-Effect Experiments

The spread-of-effect experiments stand as a warning of the many pitfalls confronting the experimenter seeking conscientiously to design experiments relevant to theory. The spread-of-effect experiment epitomized Thorndike's final system: discrete connections, automatic ("biological") influence of rewards, ascendancy of reward over punishment. The experimental results were objective, quantitative, reproducible by others. Thorndike was so pleased with these experiments as a proof of the validity of his system that he turned a deaf ear to the critics. In preparing the collection of his papers for his final book he inserted this comment regarding the criticisms of the spread-of-effect experiments: "There are a few recent dissenters, but if they will repeat the original experiments in full I prophesy that they will be convinced" (Thorndike, 1949, page 27).

The causal factors in any learning experiment are complex. The positive contribution of the experiments critical of Thorndike has been to call attention to a number of these factors that he either overlooked or slighted in his description and explanation of the spread phenomenon. Some of these are:

1. The phenomena are influenced by the set or instructions that determine what the subject is trying to do (Wallach and Henle, 1941; Postman and Adams, 1954).

2. The learning task undertaken may be irrelevant to the spread phenomena, yet influence the level of repetition (Sheffield and Jenkins, 1952).

3. An isolation or emphasis effect is as important as reward in determining which response is most frequently repeated (Zirkle, 1946b; but note Postman and Adams, 1955).

4. Guessing habits result in a gradient of response around the focal response that is repeated for any reason whatever (Jenkins and Sheffield, 1946).[6]

5. A probability bias operates so that a subject repeats a digit at less than chance frequency when attempting to respond in random fashion. This avoidance of one or more previously used digits leads to a beyond-chance repetition of the remaining digits (Smith, 1949).

6. Integration of serial acts through anticipatory responses, remote associations, etc., produces types of gradient superficially similar to, but not causally identifiable with, the spread of effect (Jenkins, 1943).[7]

If errors enter because of these six causal factors, they are errors in explanation or interpretation. They do not in themselves imply poor experimentation, for the factors may themselves be systematically varied and their effects studied.

There are, in addition, errors in the treating of data that led to systematic distortions of the results as these results were reported from many of the earlier experiments on spread of effect that attempted to do just what Thorndike recommended, that is, to repeat his experiments in full. Three of these are worth noting:

1. A faulty baseline of chance was selected, on the assumption that empirical chance levels are equal to computed random levels. This error led to an underestimation of the influence of punishment (saying *Wrong*).

2. Improper weighting of steps in the gradient by scoring responses between two rewarded responses (*Rights*) as both preceding and following a *Right*. This error led to a greater symmetry in the "before" and "after" gradients than has been found in later experiments avoiding this error. Nearly all find only an after-gradient.

3. Repeating lists many times in the same order, thus increasing the proportion of *Right* responses through learning and reducing both the prevalence of *Wrong* responses and their distance from the nearest *Right*. As a consequence the *Wrong* responses that remain are predominantly those which (for any reason) are stereotyped and resistant to chance. Because late in practice these are necessarily near to *Right* responses, it will appear statistically (but spuriously) that *Wrong* responses are repeated because of their proximity to *Right* ones.

---

[6] The suggestion was earlier made by Tolman (1936), in a review of one of Thorndike's books, but he did not follow it up.

[7] Jenkins found data apparently supporting the spread of effect in a maze experiment with rats, but anticipatory and perseverative tendencies make unsuitable an interpretation in terms of spread of effect to discrete connections. We shall later meet other gradients, such as the gradient of reinforcement, which have only a family resemblance to spread of effect. For a review of spread-of-effect experiments with animals, see Marx (1957b).

It is seldom that a single variety of experiment is as crucial to a systematic theoretical position as the spread-of-effect experiment was to Thorndike's. For that reason its criticisms have been more pertinent than the criticisms of less important experiments.

ESTIMATE OF THORNDIKE'S POSITION

Before proceeding to an appraisal of the contemporary significance of Thorndike's position, his answers to the standard problems of learning will be summarized. By attempting such a summary for each of the several leading learning theorists it will be easier to keep perspective on their similarities and differences.

Thorndike's Position on Typical Problems of Learning

Thorndike's answers are briefly summarized according to the six typical problems discussed in the first chapter.

1. Capacity.   Learning capacity depends upon the number of bonds and their availability. The differences between bright and dull are quantitative rather than qualitative, although intelligence has dimensions of altitude as well as of breadth (Thorndike and others, 1927). The theory of intelligence is consonant with the identical-elements theory of transfer.

2. Practice.   Repetition of situations does not in itself modify connections. Repetition of connections leads to a negligible increase in strength, unless the connections are rewarded. Practice is important because it permits rewards to act upon connections.

3. Motivation.   Reward acts directly on neighboring connections to strengthen them; punishment has no corresponding direct weakening effect. Punishment may work indirectly, however, through making the learner do something else which may confront him with a reward. "Ideas" need not intervene; connections may be strengthened directly, without awareness.

4. Understanding.   The role of understanding is minimized, not because it is undemonstrable, but because it grows out of earlier habits. The best way to get understanding is to build a body of connections appropriate to that understanding. When situations are understood at once it is a matter of transfer or assimilation, that is, there are enough elements in common with old situations to permit old habits to act acceptably.

5. Transfer.   The theory of identical elements is espoused. Reaction to new situations benefits by the identity of these new situations, in part, with old situations, and also by a principle of analogy described as assimilation.

6. Forgetting.   The original law of disuse assumed forgetting to take place without practice in accordance with the empirical findings of studies such as those of Ebbinghaus. Later books did not deal with the problem in any detail; the law of disuse was not mentioned, but some decay with no practice was still implied.

The flavor of Thorndike's theory was all along that of the automatic strengthening of specific connections—directly, without intervening ideas or conscious influences. While Thorndike was not an avowed behaviorist, and was willing occasionally to use subjective terms, his emphasis was certainly behavioral. It would be unfair to leave the discussion of Thorndike without referring again to his insistence on measurement, and through that insistence his contribution to the improvement of the learning of skills in the schools. There was an energetic empiricism about Thorndike's experimenting and theorizing which compensated for their lack of systematic elegance.

The Specificity Doctrine a Source Both of Strength and of Weakness

Thorndike gave great impetus to what has sometimes been called the scientific movement in education—the movement which suggests that educational practices be regulated according to verified outcomes of specific practices. His tremendous drive led to enormous output in fields as varied as handwriting scales, dictionary-writing, methods in teaching arithmetic and spelling, intelligence tests, and vocational guidance. But the secret of his output was not only energy: the output stemmed also from his matter-of-fact conception of science, that in order to do something about anything you have to know specifically what you are about.

The specificity doctrine helps you to roll up your sleeves and get to work. Consider, for example, all the complications involved in the teaching of reading. What is it that the child is to be taught? Philology? Grammar? Semantics? It took a Thorndike to give the simple answer: "Words." With that answer he proceeded to count the frequency with which each word occurs in English, by tabulating millions of printed words from all manner of sources. He then arrived at the most common words. These are the words which must surely be understood. He made available lists and dictionaries to facilitate teaching the most needed words. A specificity theory like Thorndike's tells the educator where to look and how to measure in a baffling field such as schoolroom practices.

The specificity doctrine is also a source of weakness, and it has been the target of the most severe attacks upon Thorndike. The illustration above shows the kinds of criticisms which Thorndike invites. Is language no more than words? Are the most frequent words really what we wish to teach? Perhaps we need to think of language as a means of expression, as logic in action, and must therefore equip the child with the minimum set of tools necessary for adequate communication. That this approach is a possible one has been shown by the development of Basic English, wherein the central vocabulary of 850 words overlaps only in part with Thorndike's most frequent words.[8] The approach of Basic English takes into account the organized character of language as an instrument of meaning. Thorndike, true to association tradition, tended to think of language as a collection of words, which he set out to treat quantitatively.

In Thorndike the analytical emphasis of all association theory also pervaded the conception of rewards and punishments, and weakened somewhat the analysis of these phenomena. The notion that the law of effect works mechanically on all connections in the neighborhood of the rewarded one makes of reward something extrinsic to the activity in question, something pinned on adventitiously. In showing that the law of effect may work this way, he slighted the internal relationships between success and what the individual is trying to do, goals which satisfy aroused motives or needs. Again, texts may be cited in proof of the fact that Thorndike knew all this—he early quoted the "interest series" as we have shown and later added the notion of "belongingness"—but that does not alter the conclusion that his scientific preoccupations led him away from the internal relations of effort and success to the external relationship of any satisfying state of affairs strengthening any connection which happened to be near it.

Perhaps more heat has been generated over Thorndike's subordination of insight and understanding to drill and habit than over any other aspect of his writings. While he thought insight very rare in animals—perhaps rarer than it actually is—he did not deny insight in man. He was not awed by it, and thought it best understood by the same associative laws applying in other situations. Just as erroneous inferences are made because of habitual associations which throw the learner off his course, so the insights of the genius are made by appropriate habitual associations and analogies. He had this to say of reaction to novel situations:

There is no arbitrary hocus pocus whereby man's nature acts in an unpredictable spasm when he is confronted with a new situation. His habits do not then retire to some convenient distance while some new and mysterious entities direct his behavior. On the contrary, nowhere are the bonds acquired with old situations more surely revealed in action than when a new situation appears (1913b, page 29).

---

[8] See Richards (1943). The basic list of 850 words includes some words in the seventh thousand of Thorndike's count, such as *advertisement* and *sneeze*.

Although this comment is true enough, Thorndike's failure to give real concern to the way in which past habits are utilized in problem solution, to consider what arrangement makes a problem hard, what easy, when the same essential bonds are involved, is a genuine limitation. The difference is a real one for school practice. It is possible to teach number combinations first (establish the "bonds"), then expect some glimmer of understanding later, or it is possible to achieve some understanding of what numbers are for, to comprehend the situation as a problem, and then to learn the combinations in this context. In the end you come out at the same place, knowing the tables and knowing how to use them, but it is not a foregone conclusion that the one method of teaching will be more efficient than the other, either for knowing precisely what has been taught or for being able to apply it in new situations. Thorndike's preoccupation with bonds has insured that we turn to others, not Thorndike's followers, for a more careful appraisal of the role of meaning and understanding.

SUPPLEMENTARY READINGS

Thorndike was a prolific writer. His bibliography appears in two parts in the *Teachers College Record:* for the years 1898 to 1940 in volume 41 (1940), pages 699-725; for the years 1940 to 1949 in volume 51 (1949), pages 42-45. The total comes to more than 500 items.

The following books contain his major contributions to learning theory, with much supporting experimental data:

THORNDIKE, E. L. (1911) *Animal intelligence.*

THORNDIKE, E. L. (1913b) *The psychology of learning (Educational psychology,* Vol. II).

THORNDIKE, E. L. (1922) *The psychology of arithmetic.*

THORNDIKE, E. L. and others (1928) *Adult learning.*

THORNDIKE, E. L. (1932a) *The fundamentals of learning.*

THORNDIKE, E. L. (1935) *The psychology of wants, interests, and attitudes.*

THORNDIKE, E. L. (1949) *Selected writings from a connectionist's psychology.*

The following reviews bear importantly on the law of effect as a central feature of Thorndike's system:

MARX, M. H. (1956) Spread of effect: A critical review. *Genet. Psychol. Monogr.,* 53, 119-186.

MEEHL, P. E. (1950) On the circularity of the law of effect. *Psychol. Bull.,* 47, 52-75.

NUTTIN, J. (1953) *Tâche, réussite et échec.* Especially Chapter V, pages 247-304.

POSTMAN, L. (1947) The history and present status of the Law of Effect. *Psychol. Bull.,* 44, 489-563.

POSTMAN, L. (1962) Rewards and punishments in human learning. In Postman, L. (Editor) *Psychology in the making,* 331-401.

Pavlov's Classical Conditioning

One cannot mention conditioned reflexes without thinking of the distinguished Russian physiologist, Ivan Petrovich Pavlov (1849-1936) who gave them their name, and, although not beginning his investigations of them until he was 50 years of age, spent the rest of his long life in laboratory investigations of them, eventually with a research staff that numbered well over one hundred professionals and assistants. His influence upon learning theory has been very great outside the Soviet Union (as well as within it); the prominent place of conditioned reflex concepts in American theories will become abundantly clear in the next chapters presenting the views of Guthrie, Skinner, and Hull.

The classical experiment is by now familiar to every schoolboy. When meat powder is placed in a dog's mouth, salivation takes place; the food is the *unconditioned stimulus* and the salivation the *unconditioned reflex*. Then some arbitrary stimulus, such as a light, is combined with the presentation of the food. Eventually, after repetition and if time relationships are right, the light will evoke salivation independent of the food; the light is the *conditioned stimulus* and the response to it is the *conditioned reflex*. American psychologists have tended to use the words *conditioned response* instead of *conditioned reflex,* on the grounds that all that gets conditioned is not reflex, but the differences in terms are not very important.

Pavlov began his scientific career with investigations of circulation and the heart, then turned to the study of the physiology of digestion, for which he was awarded the Nobel Prize in 1904. This came as something of a surprise to him, for he had not felt that his book *The work of the digestive glands* (Russian, 1897; German, 1898; English, 1902) had been very enthusiastically received. The main work on conditioned reflexes began in 1899 with the publication of Wolfson's thesis done under Pavlov's direction entitled "Observations upon salivary secretion" (Pavlov, 1927, p. 412). The newly discovered reflexes were then called "psychic secretions" to distinguish them from the unlearned physiological reactions. The term which has come to be translated *conditioned reflex*[1] was first used in print by Tolochinov, one of Pavlov's associates, in a report to the Congress of Natural Sciences in Helsingfors in 1903, based on investigations begun in 1901. Pavlov wrote two books on the work of the next quarter of a century, translated into English under the titles *Conditioned reflexes* (1927), and *Lectures on conditioned reflexes* (1928). At the time these books were written Pavlov was already seventy-five, but he now became interested in psychiatry, and in the remaining years of his life spent a good deal of time making observations in mental hospitals and attempting to parallel some of his observations with experiments upon dogs in his laboratory. The final papers were collected by Gantt, translated, and published in a volume entitled *Conditioned reflexes and psychiatry* (1941), although it may be noted that many other topics are covered in the translated lectures. The Russians themselves, in later years, translated some of his Wednesday lectures, as they were called; some of these appear with other papers in a volume called *Selected works* (1955). In addition to secondary accounts of Pavlov's work, of which there are a number (e.g., Frolov, 1937; Babkin, 1949), there is one other collection in English of Pavlov's own writings, entitled *Experimental psychology and other essays* (1957). Although this chapter is being written nearly 30 years after his death, it is evident that Pavlov's scientific influence is still current; we are fortunate that most of what he had to say about conditioned reflexes is available to us in English.

ANTICIPATIONS OF CONDITIONING[2]

Modern experimental psychology developed under the influence of association theory which had its origins in the philosophical school of Eng-

[1] A better translation of the Russian would doubtless have been condition*al* reflexes, that is, reflexes that are found only under special conditions. Professor Konorski has suggested to us that the form current in English doubtless came about through translating the German *bedingte Reflex*, in which *bedingte* in German means conditional, but its word-form is more readily translated into English as conditioned.

[2] Much of what follows is adapted from Hilgard and Marquis (1940) and Kimble (1961).

lish empiricism: Locke, Hobbes, Berkeley, Hume, Hartley, and the Mills. Ever since Aristotle the laws of association tended to be stated as those of contiguity, similarity, and contrast, although later associationists, such as Thomas Brown (1820), designated these as primary or qualitative laws, and added a number of secondary or quantitative laws. When the laws were stated in quantitative form (effects of frequency, etc.) there came a strong tendency to emphasize contiguity above the principles of similarity and contrast. Physiological explanations tended to rest primarily on contiguity:

> When two elementary brain-processes have been active together or in immediate succession, one of them, on reoccurring, tends to propagate its excitement into the other (James, 1890, I, p. 566).

If, as in this statement from William James, we emphasize contiguous events, and state their association as one between brain states, we are not far from Pavlov's conditioned reflex.

The fundamental facts of conditioning were known before anyone attempted to do what Pavlov did, that is, to study exactly what happened, and to vary the parameters that controlled the events.

Whytt (1763) recognized "psychic secretion" over a century before Pavlov:

> We consider . . . that the remembrance or *idea* of substances formerly applied to different parts of the body produces almost the same effect as if these substances were really present. Thus the sight, or even the recalled *idea* of grateful food, causes an uncommon flow of spittle into the mouth of a hungry person; and the seeing of a lemon can produce the same effect in many people (1763, p. 280, as quoted by Rosenzweig, 1962).

There must have been many related observations. Twitmyer, for example, working in an American psychological laboratory in 1902, noted a conditioned knee jerk (though he did not call it that), but like earlier observers he did not follow up his discovery with later experiments.

Pavlov's own work was greatly influenced by Sechenov, known as the father of Russian physiology, whose book on *Reflexes of the brain* was published in journal form in 1863, and as a book in 1866; selections are available in English (Sechenov, 1935). He freely used the expression "psychic reflexes" and interpreted man's voluntary behavior in reflex terms. Pavlov acknowledged the importance of having read Sechenov as he began to study psychic processes by physiological means.

Pavlov was apparently in some conflict during the years 1899–1902, not yet having turned his back on the study of gastrointestinal function, but becoming more interested in the physiological approaches to psychic functioning. Apparently he resolved this conflict around 1903, when he lectured on experimental psychology and psychopathology in animals, defended the study of psychic reactions by physiological means, and discussed the conditioned reflexes to which he was thereafter to devote his exclusive attention (Pavlov, 1928, pp. 47-60).

PAVLOV'S EXPERIMENTS AND THEORIES

Some Empirical Relationships

Pavlov's contribution rests not so much on his discovery of the conditioned reflex, or even on his theorizing about it, as in the care with which he explored numerous empirical relationships, and thus determined the essential parameters, and provided the background and the terminology for countless succeeding experiments by others as well as by his own colleagues and disciples.

Reinforcement, extinction, spontaneous recovery. The history of a simple conditioned reflex begins with its acquisition with repeated *reinforcement,* that is, following the conditioned stimulus repeatedly by the unconditioned stimulus and response at appropriate time intervals. Pavlov presented data from often-conditioned dogs, so that the course of

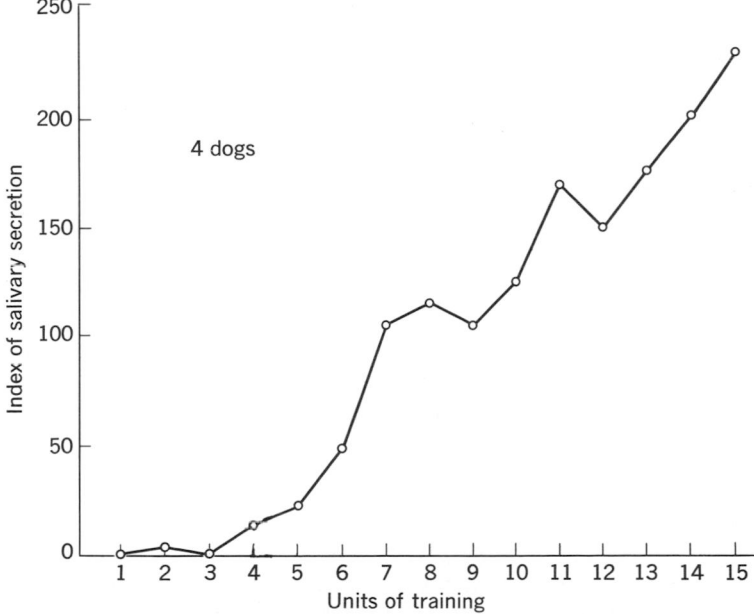

Figure 3-1   The course of acquisition of a conditioned salivary response. The salivation anticipated injection of morphine in four dogs. Plotted by Hull (1934b, page 425) from the data of Kleitman and Crisler (1927).

original acquisition is not commonly available from his data, but comparable experiments show some tendency for an S-shaped curve, an initial portion with little or no response, then a rapid increase, then some falling off in rate of increase. The curve of Figure 3-1 shows the initial acceleration, but the experiment was not continued long enough for the slowing down to occur.

When reinforcement is discontinued and the conditioned stimulus is presented alone, unaccompanied by the unconditioned stimulus, the conditioned response gradually diminishes and disappears, a process that is called *experimental extinction*. Pavlov gave numerous small tables showing such extinction; the data from one of them are plotted in Figure 3-2. Note, however, that after elapsed time without further repetition of any kind the conditioned salivation has returned; this is called *spontaneous recovery*.

Pavlov's explanation of these effects will be discussed later.

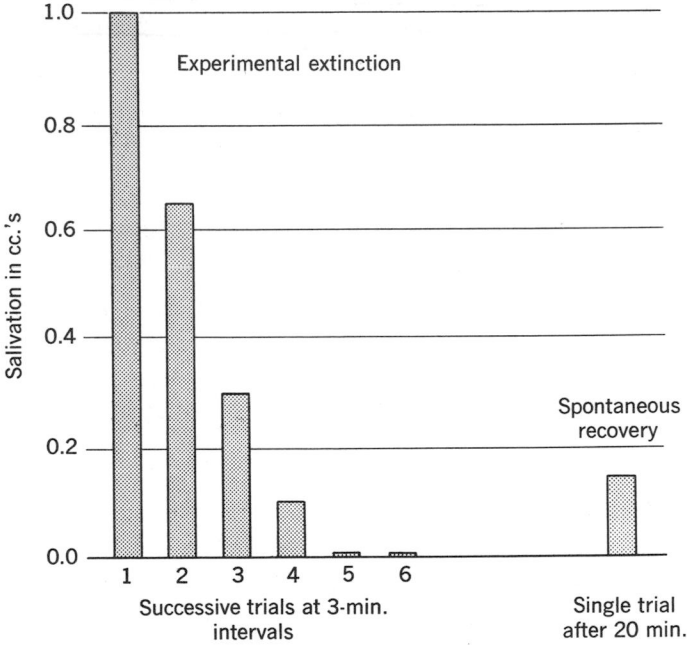

Figure 3-2   The course of extinction and of spontaneous recovery. The decreasing heights of the bars at the left indicate the fall off in conditioned salivation as the conditioned stimulus (the sight of meat powder) was repeated without reinforcement. The bar at the right shows spontaneous recovery after a rest of 20 minutes. Data from Pavlov (1927, page 58).

Generalization and differentiation. The first complication to be considered is that a conditioned reflex evoked to one stimulus can also be elicited by other adventitious stimuli, not necessarily very similar to the first. Thus a conditioned response conditioned to a tactile stimulus may be given to either a thermal stimulus or a tone, as shown in Table 3-1, from Pavlov.

If conditioned reflexes are to facilitate adaptation to the environment, the complementary process to generalization is needed, that is, *differentiation.* Pavlov went on to demonstrate that the initial generalization could be overcome by the method of contrasts in which one of a pair of stimuli is regularly reinforced, the other not reinforced. In the end, after some fluctuations, the conditioned reflex occurs only to the positive (reinforced) stimulus, and not to the negative (nonreinforced) one.

We shall see later how the process of generalization is explained by an underlying *irradiation* of excitation in the cortex, and differentiation by a corresponding *concentration* of excitation. But first we must consider some other empirical relationships.

Table 3-1   **Elicitation of a Conditioned Salivary Reflex Established to a Tactile Stimulus by a Thermal Stimulus and a Tonal Stimulus through Generalization (Pavlov, 1927, page 114).**

Time	Stimulus applied during one minute; interval of one minute before reinforcement	Salivary secretion in drops during successive minutes from the beginning of the conditioned stimulus	Remarks
	Experiment of 6th February, 1909		
11.39 a.m.	Tactile	0, 3	Reinforced by introduction of acid
11.55 a.m.	Tactile	0, 7	
12.06 p.m.	Thermal at 0°C	1, 4, 7, 7	Not reinforced by acid
12.22 p.m.	Tactile	0, 4	Reinforced
	Experiment of 7th February, 1909		
2.36 p.m.	Tactile	0, 9	Reinforced by introduction of acid
2.45 p.m.	Tactile	0, 15	
2.54 p.m.	Tone	0, 3, 4, 5, 2, 0	Not reinforced
3.02 p.m.	Tactile	0, 0	Reinforced by introduction of acid
3.10 p.m.	Tactile	0, 1	
3.22 p.m.	Tactile	0, 6	

Favorable and unfavorable time relationships between conditioned and unconditioned stimuli. The temporal relations within conditioning, as defined and discussed by Pavlov, were summarized as follows by Hilgard and Marquis (1940, pp. 44-45):

A. Conditioned and unconditioned stimuli overlap temporally.
  1. *Simultaneous conditioned response.* The conditioned stimulus begins from a fraction of a second to 5 seconds before the unconditioned stimulus, and continues until the latter occurs. The conditioned response tends to follow the beginning of the conditioned stimulus almost immediately.
  2. *Delayed conditioned response.* The conditioned stimulus begins from 5 seconds to several minutes before the unconditioned stimulus, and continues until the latter occurs. Although the conditioned response begins before the unconditioned stimulus, it follows the onset of the conditioned stimulus by a delay proportional to the length of the interval between the two stimuli. Delayed conditioned responses are difficult to form unless a simultaneous conditioned response has already been established.
B. Conditioned and unconditioned stimuli do not overlap temporally.
  3. *Short-trace conditioned response.* The conditioned stimulus is removed for a few seconds before the unconditioned stimulus begins.
  4. *Long-trace conditioned response.* The interval between the cessation of the conditioned stimulus and the beginning of the unconditioned stimulus is 1 minute or more. The conditioned response does not begin at the onset of the conditioned stimulus, nor at its cessation, but after an interval proportional to the time elapsing before the presentation of the unconditioned stimulus. Long-trace conditioned responses are formed with greater difficulty than delayed conditioned responses.
  5. *Backward conditioned response.* The conditioned stimulus does not begin to act until after the cessation of the unconditioned stimulus.
C. Time interval functions as the conditioned stimulus.
  6. *Temporal conditioned response.* An unconditioned stimulus is presented at regular intervals of time. If it is now omitted, a conditioned response will occur at approximately the usual interval. Intervals as long as 30 minutes have been used successfully with dogs.

American experimenters have tended to follow Pavlov's classificatory scheme, except that simultaneity for them does not have as much duration as it had for Pavlov, and many of the studies of the effect of stimulus interval have been made, usually with a maximum of but two to four seconds, well within what Pavlov considered "simultaneous" conditioning. These studies have been summarized by Kimble (1961, pp. 155-160).

Varieties of inhibition.   The inhibitory phenomena within conditioning, first described in connection with extinction, became of great interest to Pavlov, and a classification of various types of empirical manifestations of inhibition was arrived at. The summary by Hilgard and Marquis of these types of inhibition follows:

A. External inhibition.

Temporary decrement of a conditioned response due to an extraneous stimulus, as when a loud sound reduces conditioned salivation to a light.

B. Internal inhibition.

Internal inhibition develops slowly and progressively, when a conditioned stimulus is repeatedly presented under one of the following conditions:

1. *Experimental extinction.* The weakening of response to a conditioned stimulus which is repeated a number of times without reinforcement.

2. *Differential inhibition.* A conditioned response given originally to either of two stimuli is restricted to one of them through the reinforcement of one and the nonreinforcement of the other. The nonreinforced negative stimulus becomes inhibitory.

3. *Conditioned inhibition.* A combination of stimuli is rendered ineffective through nonreinforcement, although the combination includes a stimulus which alone continues to evoke the conditioned response. The other stimuli in the combination are conditioned inhibitors.

4. *Inhibition of delay.* If a regular interval of sufficient duration elapses between the commencement of a conditioned stimulus and its reinforcement, during the early portion of its isolated action the conditioned stimulus becomes not only ineffective, but actively inhibitory of other intercurrent activities. (There may be temporary disinhibition at the onset of the conditioned stimulus, so that there is a slight conditioned response before the inhibition is manifested.)

C. Disinhibition.

Temporary reappearance of an inhibited conditioned response due to an extraneous stimulus. This may be considered as an external inhibition of an internal inhibition.

Irradiation and concentration apply to inhibition as well as to excitation. These are matters of theory, and to these theories we now turn.

Pavlov's Cerebral Physiology

Pavlov commonly talked of the "higher nervous activity," by which he meant the physiological processes going on within the cerebral cortex. An early experiment in which conditioning was attempted in a decerebrate dog (by Zeliony in 1912), convinced Pavlov that conditioned reflexes could not be formed in the absence of the cerebral cortex.

Although many extirpation experiments were conducted and some anatomical localization of function was recognized, the main physiological processes described by Pavlov are inferences from behavior, not the result of direct studies of particular centers. When the "visual analyzer" or the "auditory analyzer" are mentioned there are assigned vague anatomical localizations, but they are primarily inferred from the kinds of visual or auditory discriminations of which the animal is capable. The same is true of "pathological cortical cells" or other references to quasi-anatomical portions of the brain. Contemporary Russian neurophysiologists, although followers of Pavlov, use modern electrophysiological, pharmacological, and other techniques for direct study of the brain, but at this point we are considering the theories as Pavlov enunciated them.

Association. The connection between the excitation produced by the conditioned stimulus and the center aroused by the unconditioned stimulus is a result of a kind of attraction or drainage of impulses from the first aroused center to the second, similar to the suggestion quoted above from William James. Presumably the direction of attraction is both a matter of time order (the conditioned stimulus arriving first and serving a signalling function) and of relative intensity, the unconditioned center normally being more highly excited. Pavlov is clear that what he calls conditioning is what psychologists have called association:

Thus, the temporary nervous connection is the most universal physiological phenomenon, both in the animal world and in ourselves. At the same time it is a psychological phenomenon—that which the psychologists call association, whether it be combinations derived from all manner of actions or impressions, or combinations derived from letters, words, and thoughts. Are there any grounds for differentiation, for distinguishing between that which the physiologist calls the temporary connection and that which the psychologist terms association? They are fully identical; they merge and absorb each other (Pavlov, 1955, p. 251; original date, 1934).

Irradiation, concentration, and reciprocal induction. Two fundamental nervous processes, excitation and inhibition, manifest themselves in various ways; their interactions provide the essential basis for the operation of the cerebral hemispheres. Incoming impulses by way of afferent nerves and the lower centers finally reach some special cells of the cortex appropriate to the sensory system (analyzer) to which the afferent nerves belong. From these special cells the excitatory process *irradiates* to various other cells over a greater or lesser area. It is this irradiation that provides the basis for generalization, through the overlap of the fields of excitation produced by differing stimuli. Hence, in addition to the association or coupling of excitations, we need the notion of irradiation. However, finer analysis would be destroyed if irradiation were not corrected by *concentration* of excitation back to the original special cells. This comes about most promptly if aided by *inhibition*. Thus differentiation by the methods of contrasts, in which the positive stimulus is reinforced, the negative one not, develops an inhibitory process in relation to the negative stimulus that reduces the irradiation of excitation from the positive stimulus, and concentrates it where it belongs. The inhibition irradiates also, which can be demonstrated by showing that immediately after presenting the negative stimulus the response to the positive one is also weakened. This is true in the early stages of the establishment of a differentiation; later, when both excitation and inhibition have been concentrated, *reciprocal induction* takes place. Now the effect of the positive conditioned stimulus becomes stronger when applied immediately or shortly after the concentrated inhibitory stimulus; the effect of the inhibiting stimulus likewise proves to be more exact when it follows the concentrated positive one. Thus the eventual cortical patterns are determined by the interplay of excitation and inhibition through irradiation, concentration, and reciprocal induction.

There are a number of complications about the operation of irradiation. For one thing, it is said to be related to the *strengths* of the processes involved (whether excitation or inhibition). Thus weak excitation (or inhibition) irradiates; medium strengths concentrate; strong excitation (or inhibition) again irradiate. Furthermore, there is presumably a temporal course, a wavelike flow of irradiation and concentration. Some of Pavlov's data yielding evidence for the irradiation and concentration of inhibition as a function of time are plotted in Figure 3-3. The conditioned reflex was established to a low tone of 132 cycles, then extinguished, and the amount of generalized extinction tested with other stimuli after various intervals of time. The curves of Figure 3-3 plot the decrease in amplitude of the original and generalized conditioned responses as a function both of the stimulus and the time following the extinction. Two features may be noted. First, the curves fall in the order, from top to bottom, most inhibition with the 132-cycle tone (the one actually extinguished), then the 1161-cycle tone, presumably somewhat similar as a tonal stimulus, then the hissing sound, less similar because it is a noisy stimulus. This reveals one characteristic of generalization, that it follows a gradient of similarity. Second, the time functions are orderly, in that the maximum of inhibition is approached most quickly with the tone originally extinguished, and followed by the other two in order, although all three seem to have a common maximum at about 5 or 6 minutes after extinction. This phase is called by Pavlov *irradiation,* because the generalization (in this case of inhibition as a consequence of extinction) spreads

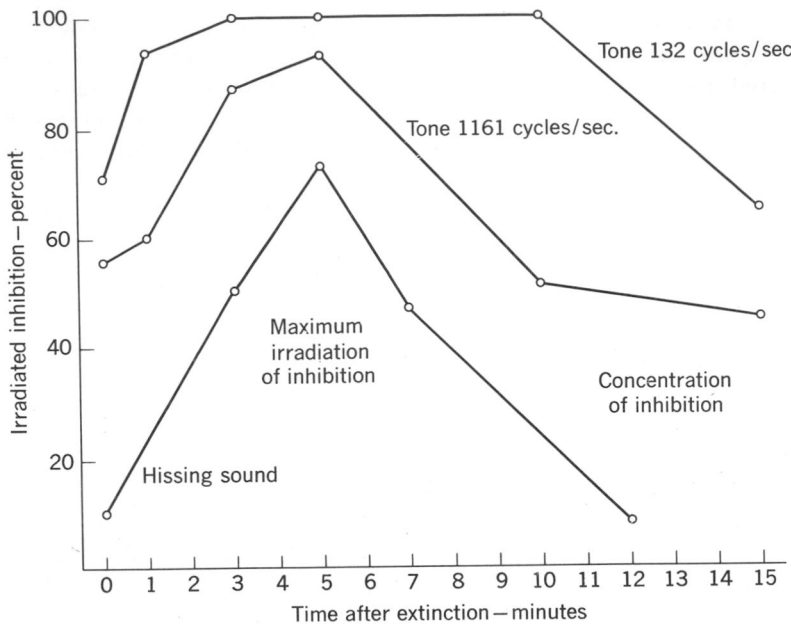

Figure 3-3   Irradiation as a function of stimulus similarity and of time. The top curve represents the temporal course of extinction following non-reinforcement of the originally reinforced tone of 132 cycles. The next two curves show the temporal course for stimuli with two degrees of similarity, the tone of 1161 cycles presumably more similar to 132 cycles than the hissing sound. Rising curves represent spread of inhibition (irradiation) and falling curves represent concentration, to the extent that the original response is the one most inhibited. Data from Pavlov (1927, page 166).

out in time to neighboring stimuli. The irradiation phase is followed by a phase of *concentration,* in which the original stimulus (132 cycles) shows much more inhibition than the more remote stimuli. This appears to be particularly evident at about 10 to 12 minutes from the beginning of extinction. By 15 minutes there is some spontaneous recovery from the inhibition. Were these processes entirely lawful and predictable, they would be important in making inferences from conditioning to other forms of learning, as in transfer of training, where generalization may be the significant principle in common between conditioning and more complex learning.[3]

---

[3] Loucks (1933), carefully examining the original evidence, failed to find support for the contention that irradiation and concentration follow the wavelike form proposed by Pavlov. Actually less was made of the temporal aspects of irradiation and concentration in later writings, with more attention given to the effects of intensity of excitation and inhibition.

It may be noted that the evidence used in support of irradiation is entirely behavioral, and the shift from an explanation in terms of generalization to one in terms of irradiation is an inference from behavior, and not a result of measuring cortical processes.

Hypnosis and sleep. The irradiation of weak inhibitory processes over the cortex produces a state of partial sleep that is called by Pavlov hypnosis, and related by him to hypnotic phenomena familiar in man.[4] There are some peculiarities in the behavior of conditioned responses when a dog is in this state of irradiated weak inhibition. Three *phases* are associated with the condition:

1. *Equalization phase:* all conditioned stimuli are equal in effect, regardless of intensity.
2. *Paradoxical phase:* weak stimuli yield more secretion than strong ones.
3. *Ultraparadoxical phase:* positive conditioned stimuli are ineffective; negative stimuli now produce secretion.

If the irradiation of inhibition is more widespread, and the inhibition more intense, then sleep ensues. Experiments on conditioned reflexes were often made difficult, early in the history of conditioning, because of the drowsy states into which the dogs fell; instead of considering this a troublesome irrelevancy, sleep became an important topic of study in Pavlov's laboratory.

Another source of sleep, beyond irradiated inhibition, was reported in some later experiments from another laboratory, in which it was found that if vision, hearing, and olfaction were all destroyed at once through damaging the sense organs without injuring the central nervous system, the dog would sleep as much as 23 hours per day (Pavlov, 1955, page 376; original date, 1935). Pavlov explained this as due to the withdrawal of varied sources of stimulation, so that the remaining stimulation (chiefly tactual, from the quiet lying position) would itself tend to lead to inhibition. Although Pavlov knew of evidence cited by others for a sleep center in the hypothalamus (e.g., Hess, 1929) he argued against any subcortical theory of sleep.

The cortical mosaic and dynamic stereotypy. Pavlov conceived of the cortex as a mosaic of points with varying degrees of strength of their excitatory and inhibitory states. These are mobile states, for the most part, and account for the adjustive potential of the cortex. However, with repeated conditioning to various stimuli in fixed orders there appears what Pavlov called a *dynamic stereotype* or systematization, easily maintained,

---

[4] In his classical book on hypnosis, dealing largely with case studies of therapy using hypnosis, Platonov (1959) seeks the explanation for all the phenomena in terms of Pavlov's theory.

but eventually inert and little susceptible to change. This corresponds, in a way, to James' fixity of habit (Pavlov, 1955, page 448; original date, 1932).

> It seems to me that the painful senses[5] which often accompany change in the habitual mode of life, an interruption of customary work, loss of close relations or friends, to say nothing of a mental crisis and collapse of beliefs, are, to a considerable degree, physiologically caused precisely by the change, the disturbance of the old dynamic stereotype and the difficulty of elaborating a new one (Pavlov, 1955, page 452).

Types of nervous system. Pavlov recognized four types of genotypical nervous system, based on the strengths of excitatory and inhibitory processes, their equilibrium and mobility. These types turned out to be coordinated with the ancient classification of temperaments that has come down from Hippocrates. Where excitation and inhibition are both strong, but equilibrated, two types arise. If the states are labile, the *sanguine* temperament results; if they are inert, then the *phlegmatic* temperament is found. If, however, excitation overbalances inhibition, so that the processes are unequilibrated, then the temperament is *choleric.* Finally, when both excitation and inhibition are weak, whether the states are labile or inert, a *melancholic* temperament ensues.

While each animal belongs to one or another of these temperament classes, his actual character (the phenotype) depends upon his experiences with the environment so that character is "an alloy of the characteristics of type and the changes produced by external environment" (Pavlov, 1955, page 260; original date, 1934). Pavlov was dissatisfied by Kretschmer's typology (Kretschmer, German, 1921; English, 1925) for several reasons: it was too simple (two types only), it was based on pathology, and it failed to distinguish between genotype and phenotype (Pavlov, 1955, pages 616-619; original date, 1935).

Second signal system. While in his own work Pavlov made little of the point, he recognized that the ability to speak greatly enlarged man's potentialities, and later Soviet scientists have made much of this. The conditioned reflex mechanisms that man shares with lower animals are grouped together as the *first signal system;* speech in man provides a *second signal system.*

> When the developing world reached the stage of man, an extremely important addition was made to the mechanisms of nervous activity . . . speech constitutes a second signalling system of reality which is peculiarly ours, being the signal of the first signals. On the one hand, numerous speech stimulations have

[5] The translation of the Russian is not a good one; the meaning of "painful senses" is something like annoyance or anxiety.

removed us from reality, and we must remember this in order not to distort our attitude toward reality. On the other hand, it is precisely speech which has made us human, a subject on which I need not dwell in detail here. However, it cannot be doubted that the fundamental laws governing the activity of the first signalling system must also govern that of the second, because it, too, is activity of the same nervous tissue (Pavlov, 1955, p. 262; original date, 1934).

Pavlov speculates that the frontal lobes play an essential part in the operation of the second signal system (Pavlov, 1955, page 285; original date, 1932).

Pathological states. The discovery of the "experimental neurosis" in Pavlov's laboratory, and Pavlov's concern with psychiatric patients late in life, led Liddell repeatedly to refer to Pavlov as "the psychiatrist of the future" (Liddell, 1936, 1961). Whether or not this view is justified, as recently as 1964 American psychiatrists were assessing the contributions made to psychiatry by Pavlovian conditioning (Group for the Advancement of Psychiatry, 1964).[6]

This is not the place to go into Pavlov's views with respect to pathology in any detail. He felt that the experimental neuroses in his animals were similar to neurasthenia in man, that persecution delusions corresponded to the ultraparadoxical phase in hynotic states in the dog, that catatonic schizophrenia was a hypnoticlike state of *protective inhibition*,[7] that manic-depressive reactions represented a derangement of the normal relations between excitatory and inhibitory processes. Obsessional neuroses and paranoia he felt must be due to a pathological inertness of the excitatory processes of different motor cells.

On the whole the leap from his speculative brain physiology to confident statements about neuroses and psychoses appears much too pat to be taken seriously as scientific explanation, although doubtless some psychiatrists have been led to interesting hypotheses on the basis of his conjectures.

In summary, then, we find Pavlov accounting for a myriad of relationships on the basis of a clash of excitation and inhibition in the cerebral hemispheres, their irradiation and concentration, plus some characteristics of cortical cells, including their occasional inertness or pathological excitability.

---

[6] The report referred to is thought by Reese, Dykman, and Peters (1964) to underplay the role of Pavlovian conditioning in American psychiatry. They cite a number of pertinent references not mentioned in the GAP Symposium.

[7] When a conditioned stimulus exceeds a certain strength, instead of the expected increase in response with increasing strength there follows a decrease in response, to which Pavlov gave the name *protective inhibition*. He believed that this mechanism protected the organism from overstimulation. This is part of the rationale for "sleep therapy" as used by the Russians (Gantt, 1965, page 135f.).

POST-PAVLOVIAN DEVELOPMENTS IN CONDITIONED REFLEX EXPERIMENTATION AND THEORY

Although in the early post-revolution days Pavlov was openly antagonistic to the new Soviet regime, he was treated very well under Lenin and beyond, and later became much friendlier to what he considered the social experiment that the Soviet Union represented. A laboratory was built for him outside Leningrad at a village called Koltushy. On his eightieth birthday he was honored by having the street leading to his Institute of Experimental Medicine named for him and the village in which his laboratories was located was renamed Pavlovo. The support of the Pavlovian laboratories was increased from one million rubles in 1936 (the year of his death) to two and one-half million in 1939; the number of workers increased from 172 in 1937 to 357 in 1938, according to official statements cited by Gantt (Pavlov, 1941, page 31).

There was a period in which Pavlov's work was continued by the Russian physiologists, while Russian psychologists paid little attention to it. After 1950, however, there was a "Pavlovianization" of Russian psychology, and from then on the psychologists began to quote Pavlov extensively (Razran, 1957). They found much in Pavlov that permitted them to work along familiar lines, particularly the "second signal system" which permitted studies of human behavior that involved language: child development, concept formation, hypnosis, and so on. Even so, the major work on conditioned reflexes continued within the physiological laboratories, manned by the senior workers who had been with Pavlov: Bykov, Ivanov-Smolensky, Asratyan, Anokhin, and others.

The physiological work has succeeded in subjecting some of Pavlov's ideas to study through more direct work on the brain, rather than relying so much on inferences from behavior. A group of Russian workers were invited to what was called the *Pavlovian Conference on Higher Nervous Activity,* meeting with a number of American workers in New York in 1960. The senior members of the Russian delegation included P. S. Kupalov, P. K. Anokhin, and E. A. Asratyan, all of whom had worked with Pavlov. Their reports (Kline, 1961) show the advances that have been made in the Pavlovian tradition. Anokhin, for example, makes a good deal of the cortico–subcortical relations in conditioned reflexes, a relationship neglected by Pavlov. While Asratyan reports that he is now turning to electrophysiological methods, his ingenious experiments, within the Pavlovian framework and conducted without the aid of direct study of the brain, caused him to propose an interpretation of the locus of inhibition slightly different from that of Pavlov. He presents the diagram reproduced as Figure 3-4. In Pavlovian fashion, he designates a focal center for the conditioned stimulus in the cortex (CS) and one for the unconditional stimulus (US) and a conditioned connection (CC). He points out that Pavlov believed inhibition to be initiated in the cortical cells of the focus of the conditioned stimulus; he and others, including Anokhin, believe that it is initiated in the conditioned connection (CC). This is inferred from experiments in "trans-switching" in which a single indifferent stimulus becomes the signal for different outcomes in different rooms.

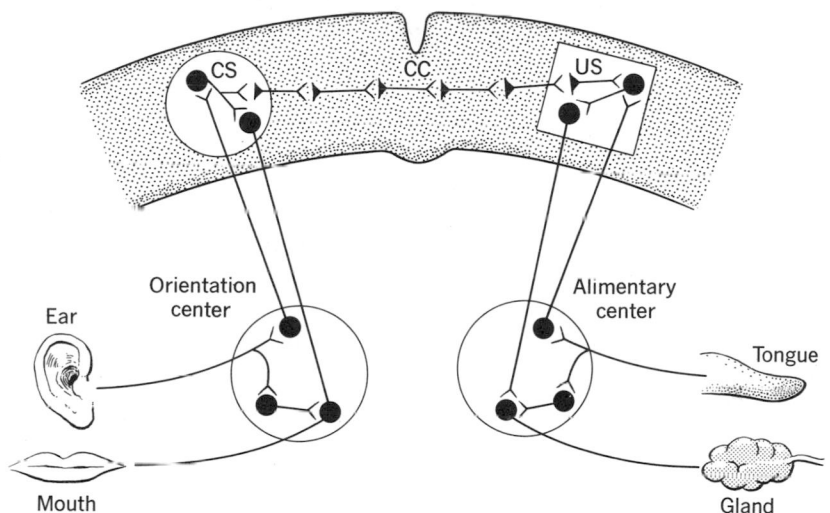

Figure 3-4 **Scheme of the conditioned reflex arc. Of the various possibilities for the locus of inhibition, Asratyan places it in the conditioned connection (CC). Key: CS, conditioned stimulus; US, unconditioned stimulus; CC, conditioned connection. From Asratyan (1961, page 1142).**

For example, a positive-conditioned salivary response to a tone may be established in one room, and a withdrawal-conditioned motor response to electric shock established to the same tone in another room. Now either one of these can be subjected to inhibition (as by extinction through nonreinforcement) without affecting the other. If the inhibition were in the brain center aroused by the conditioned stimulus one would not expect the two conditioned responses to be so independent of each other. By a corresponding argument he shows that inhibition cannot be localized in the center for the unconditioned stimulus either; hence it must lie in the conditioned connection.

For our purposes, however, it is somewhat more profitable to turn away from the strictly Pavlovian research to consider some other developments relevant to learning theory as it has developed outside the USSR.

Classical and Instrumental Conditioning

Although many writers, especially physiologists, imply that learning and Pavlovian conditioning are essentially synonymous, this position is no longer generally held among psychologists. One kind of distinction that has arisen is between conditioning of the type studied by Pavlov, which has come to be called *classical conditioning,* and another variety that has come to be called *instrumental conditioning,* or, within the arrangements studied by Skinner, *operant conditioning.* Actually much of the work within the Soviet Union also follows the paradigm of instrumental conditioning, so that it is appropriate to call attention to the distinction between classical and instrumental conditioning.

Konorski's two types of conditioned response. Working in Warsaw, Miller and Konorski (1928) began studying a kind of conditioned reflex which they felt to be a second type, Pavlov's salivary conditioning being the first type. The experiments were repeated in Pavlov's laboratory, with his approval. A typical experiment was that in which the dog was trained to lift its paw to a conditioned stimulus. The leg was passively flexed after a signal, and then the dog was fed. This "reward" type of training soon led to conditioned leg flexion at the signal. This type of conditioning was called "instrumental conditioning" by Hilgard and Marquis (1940) because the leg flexion was "instrumental" to the receiving of the reinforcement; the same term was applied by them to the operant conditioning of Skinner (1938). Konorski (1964) later adopted the terms classical and instrumental conditioning when writing in English, and has continued to show in what respects the two types of conditioned reflex differ. The two types have provided the basis for a good deal of Russian experimentation (Razran, 1961c).

Classes of conditioned reflex according to American psychologists. The distinction between two classes of conditioned reflex, as first proposed by Miller and Konorski (1928) has had a number of reflections in classifi-

Table 3-2   Twofold Classifications of Learning proposed by Different Authors (from Kimble, 1961, page 66).

Author(s)	*Term for Classical Conditioning*	*Term for Instrumental Conditioning*
Thorndike (1911)	Associative shifting	Trial-and-error learning
Miller and Konorski (1928); Konorski and Miller (1937a, 1937b)	Type I	Type II
Skinner (1937a)	Type S, or Respondent	Type R, or Operant
Schlosberg (1937)	Conditioning	Success learning
Hilgard and Marquis (1940)	Classical conditioning	Instrumental conditioning
Mowrer (1947)	Conditioning	Problem solving

Table 3-3 **Subclasses of Classical Conditioning (Based on discussion by Grant, 1964, pages 3-8).**

Subclass	Characteristic Features
1. Pavlovian A Conditioning	Typical salivary conditioning to an indifferent stimulus followed by food. Only the salivary component is measured, thus guaranteeing the similarity between conditioned and unconditioned responses. Importance of hunger and subsequent food ingestion not part of data.
2. Pavlovian B Conditioning	Conditioned nausea to the approach of the needle used in morphine injection. Here the full unconditioned response is described, and the conditioned stimulus apparently produces substantial fractions of it. Much interoceptive conditioning (Bykov, 1957) follows this paradigm. Motivational state less important than in Pavlovian A conditioning.
3. Anticipatory Instructed Conditioning	Typical experiment is voluntary squeezing of a rubber bulb in response to a sound stimulus. An incidental stimulus, e.g., a light, may then serve as a conditioned stimulus, following the practice of Ivanov-Smolensky (1927). Great care is needed to preserve uniformity in instructions to the subject.
4. Sensory Preconditioning	In the preconditioning phase two conditioned stimuli become associated through their concurrence, even though no overt response is involved. Later one of them becomes a conditioned stimulus; after that, the second one also elicits the conditioned response without any reinforcement (Brogden, 1939).

catory schemes by American psychologists. Kimble (1961) has drawn up a table showing a number of these twofold classifications of learning (Table 3-2).

More careful studies of the taxonomy of conditioning suggest, however, that these twofold schemes may not be enough to encompass the varieties of experiment actually undertaken. Thus Grant (1964) has listed four kinds of arrangements for classical conditioning, as shown in Table 3-3. The point is made that the assumed simplicity of conditioning is somewhat illusory, no matter how convenient conditioning experiments may be for some purposes.[8]

The Second Signal System: The Differences That Words Make

It has already been indicated that, toward the end of his life, Pavlov had things to say about the importance of words to man, and about some of the differences between the first and second signalling sys-

[8] There are also a number of arrangements of instrumental conditioning, of which Grant (1964) lists eight. Because this is a chapter about Pavlov, it does not seem appropriate to go into further detail regarding these arrangements, many of which would have been far outside his experimental interests.

tem. It is worth commenting somewhat further on this matter, because the psychologists within the Soviet Union have found this a permissive way in which to state a great many facts about child development and human psychology generally without violating the current Pavlovian theories.

A distinction should be made between those experiments concerned with the genuine difference between the organization of verbal and other behavior and those which treat verbal responses merely as an alternate form of response. The ordinary arrangments of classical conditioning are followed in many of the experiments on *semantic conditioning;* some of these, for example, study the generalization from objective stimuli to their verbal equivalents (or study the equivalence of one word to another as conditioned stimuli). While some characteristics of language arise from such studies, they do not necessarily reflect the unique properties of language behavior. A review of a good deal of the Russian experimentation along these lines can be found in Razran (1961a), who, working in America, originated the term semantic conditioning (Razran, 1939). Another form, known as *verbal conditioning,* attempts to influence the words that a subject uses by reinforcing certain of his utterances and extinguishing others. This practice has become incorporated into some forms of psychotherapy (Krasner, 1965). Neither *semantic conditioning,* as such, nor *verbal conditioning* gets at the full flavor of the differences between the first and second signalling systems as they have been studied, for example, by Luria and his associates (Luria, 1961).

Luria's interest has been in the development of the child, particularly in the development of voluntary control, and here he finds language of central importance.

The tie to classical conditioning is by way of an experiment originally designed by Ivanov-Smolensky (1927), and listed as the third subclass of classical conditioning by Grant (1964), as shown earlier in Table 3-3, page 65. A child is instructed to press a rubber bulb whenever a given signal comes on; this is equivalent to an unconditioned response. Some second signal, say a colored light, is now regularly associated with the appearance of the original signal, and a conditioned bulb-pressing response is made to this new or conditioned stimulus. The usual rules about reinforcement, extinction, discrimination, apply. Actually the experiment is transitional to instrumental conditioning, but no point is made of this by Luria or those who work with him. For them anything that is learned is conditioned, and they are interested in how learning is controlled rather than in the purity of the conditioned reflex paradigm. The main point lies in what goes on inside the human organism as he relates himself to the environment. Luria points out that the laws that Pavlov discovered for the gradual development of conditioned reflexes and for their resistance to change are fundamental ones, but they do not apply in full force to the human learner because of speech—the *second signalling system.* Speech makes possible a new *information system* which modifies considerably the laws according to which new responses are learned by man. For one thing, new responses in man are not usually acquired gradually but instead are incorporated at once into some existing category and regulated by a rule that can be stated in words. Learned behavior no longer requires reinforcement to sustain it, because it is sustained by a behavior rule, and behavior thus becomes self-regulating.

Let us consider four stages in the development of the child's control of behavior through language, and see what kinds of experimental evidence bear on each stage. These are, according to Luria (1961):

1. Speech has first an *impellant* or *initiating* function. This is easily demonstrated in the child of eighteen months. Say "Clap hands," and the action follows.

2. The *inhibitory* function of speech develops later. At first it is not possible to alter an action once it gets started, for example, by asking the child to take his stockings *off* while he is pulling them *on;* he finishes what he starts.

3. The *regulatory* function of speech then develops, as in following the instruction, "When you see the light squeeze the balloon."

4. *Self-regulation* follows, as gradually *internal* speech develops.

A number of very ingenious experiments show how different the motor and the speech systems operate in the child between the ages, say, of eighteen and thirty-six months. Some illustrative observations follow.

If a child of eighteen months is told to squeeze a rubber balloon, he is likely to respond, and to continue to respond, even if told "Stop" or "That's enough." The inhibitory statements may even lead to further intensification of squeezing. It is possible to teach the child of this age (or a little older) to master a "stopping" technique ("When there is no light don't squeeze") by using the principle of conflicting positive actions to produce the necessary inhibition. Thus the child is easily taught to do *two* things when the light comes on: to squeeze the bulb briefly and then to place his hand on his knee. Having learned to terminate the squeezing, it is possible to shorten the distance the hand moves from the bulb (to the table-top instead of to the knee) and gradually to eliminate the second act. Now the child is able to squeeze only when the light is on, and to inhibit the tendency to keep on squeezing when it is off.

The regulatory function of speech shows many interesting complexities. For example, children of three or four who could not follow the self-instruction "I shall press twice!" readily pressed twice to their self-repeated "Go!" "Go!". (The "Go!" "Go!" instructions failed at age two and a half.)

Luria believes that the original control through speech is based more on impulse control than on significance, but it is worth noting that the speech control is more adaptable, even at this age, than motor control. The limits of control through significance is illustrated by modifying the "Go!" "Go!" experiment to one in which following a positive signal the child is to say "Press!" and then press, while following a negative signal he is to say "Don't press!" and resist pressing. This is too much for him; he tends to press while saying "Don't press." If he keeps *quiet* at the negative signal, the task becomes an easy one for him.

The ultimate control through significance, and through internal speech comes more gradually; then we have the highest form of self-regulation.

These observations provide a warning against too literal an extension of Pavlovian classical conditioning principles to human learning. It is of interest that those closest to Pavlov have been the ones to sound the warning most clearly.

The Orientation Reflex

Pavlov early talked about the "what-is-it reflex" or the "reflex of curiosity," and this came to be called the *orientation reflex* in his laboratory. It referred to the tendency to orient toward (or pay attention to) any novel stimulus, without regard to its significance. This tendency was found to interfere with conditioned reflexes (illustrating external inhibition), but as the conditioned reflexes became stronger the orientation reflex tended to disappear.

The orientation reflex has in late years become a matter of major interest in the Soviet Union, with numerous investigators concerned with its physiological and behavioral manifestations. Interest in America has been furthered through the overlap between the functioning of orientation and arousal, as controlled to some extent by the reticular formation in the brain stem.

The *physiological* indicators that have been most used in the study of the orientation reflex have been EEG activity, plethysmographic responses, and galvanic skin responses (GSRs). The behavioral correlates are adjustments of the sense organs, head turning, pricking up ears, modification of thresholds (Berlyne, 1960; Sokolov, 1963).

The *adaptive* significance of the orientation response is twofold, first, in preparing for environmental events that may call for swift action ("emergency reactions"), and second, through habituation, to avoid wasteful energy in resisting meaningless distractions. In general, the orientation response extinguishes quite promptly to repeated meaningless stimuli, but if the stimuli have meaning (e.g., have to be reacted to or counted), then it resists extinction.

The emphasis upon the orienting reflex illustrates how something, at first merely a source of trouble in experimentation (accounting for Pavlov's sound-shielded laboratories), may become of interest in its own right. It illustrates also how topics such as "attention" which in the early days of objective psychology seemed too subjective, gradually return to their rightful places.

ESTIMATE OF PAVLOV'S CONTRIBUTION TO LEARNING THEORY

How the Theory Bears on the Typical Problems of Learning

As in the other chapters, we may see what Pavlov's theory has to say about the various questions that are put to each of the theories.

1. Capacity. The capacity to form conditioned reflexes is in part a matter of the type of nervous system, hence there are some congenital differences in learning ability. Such capacity differences between normal and retarded children have interested Luria, who has studied them particularly in relationship to language development (the second signal system) and the orientation reflex; little is made of anything resembling Pavlov's types, however.

2. Practice. In general, conditioned reflexes are strengthened with repetition under reinforcement, but care always has to be taken to avoid the accumulation of inhibition, for inhibition may appear even within repeated reinforcement.

3. Motivation. In the usual alimentary reflexes, in which salivation is reinforced by food, the animal has to be hungry; drive is particularly important in the case of instrumental responses (Konorski). Because of the "signalling" function of conditioned stimuli, it is presumed that some sort of drive-reduction is usually involved; mere contiguous stimulation does not appear to be the basis for learning, although there is some lack of clarity on this point.

4. Understanding. Subjective terms are to be avoided, so that Pavlov finds no use for terms such as understanding or insight. Yet his conception of reflex activity is so broad that he does not hesitate to say such things as:

When a connection, or an association, is formed, this undoubtedly represents the knowledge of the matter, knowledge of definite relations existing in the external world; but when you make use of them the next time, this is what is called insight. In other words, it means utilization of knowledge, utilization of the acquired connections (Pavlov, 1955, page 575; original date, 1934).

This is the characteristic associationist view of understanding: the utilization of past experience through some kind of transfer. The problem of novelty is not raised.

Razran (1961b) in somewhat ironical fashion has discussed the behavior of the ape Raphael observed by Pavlov. The ape gave all the evidences of insight characteristic of Köhler's apes, but Pavlov dismissed it all as without any evidence of "ideational" behavior.

5. *Transfer*. Transfer is best considered to be the result of generalization (irradiation) whereby one stimulus serves to evoke the conditioned reflex learned to another. Particularly in the language system, words substitute readily one for another, and thus permit wide generalization.

6. *Forgetting*. Pavlov did not deal systematically with the retention or forgetting of conditioned reflexes over time, partly because the same animals were used over and over again, their conditioned reflexes were greatly over-learned, and forgetting was not a laboratory problem. The decline of conditioned reflexes through experimental extinction, or other forms of inhibition, was always recognized, and he always spoke of conditioned reflexes as temporary. It is important to distinguish between extinction and forgetting, however, for there is spontaneous recovery following extinction, and a weakened conditioned reflex is not therefore a forgotten one.

Some Residues from Pavlov's Work Important for Contemporary Learning Theory

Razran (1965) has summarized Pavlov's influence in the form of six summary paragraphs, which may be paraphrased as follows:

1. Pavlov stimulated an enormous number of experimental investigations using the paired-stimulus method, with all kinds of organisms, throughout the life span, and with a great variety of stimuli and responses. Razran estimates that there have been some 6,000 experiments using his exact paradigm (i.e., classical conditioning), reported in at least 29 different languages, predominantly Russian and English.

2. Pavlov converted the general notion of associative learning by way of conditioning into a highly parametric area of study, that is, the quantitative influences upon conditioning interested him from the beginning. One illustration of this is the persistence of his terms to define the significant variables. In Kimble's (1961) glossary of terms relevant to conditioning and learning, 31 terms are attributed to Pavlov, and 21 others to all American and western psychologists combined.

3. Pavlov succeeded in getting the conditioned reflex adopted as the most convenient basic unit for all of learning. While the desirability of this is a matter of some dispute, and other units compete with it (while

some authorities question that there *is* any such basic unit at all), there is no doubt that it has taken a leading place in this respect.

4. By introducing the notion of the second signal system, unique to man, Pavlov prevented the system from being frozen at an unprofitable reductionist level, in which no distinction would be made between animal and human learning. Oddly enough, he accused the American psychologists of oversimplifying, and of not being in tune with the complexity of actual events.

5. Pavlov's continuing interest in psychopathology, beginning in 1903, but evidenced particularly in his later years, opened up fruitful rapprochements between learning theory and psychiatry, including such functional matters as sleep and drug therapy. Razran notes that of the six volumes in Russian reporting his Wednesday seminars, three volumes, comprising 1,716 pages, are reports of clinical demonstrations in which he participated.

6. Even when a second paradigm of conditioning was introduced by Miller and Konorski (1928) and Skinner (1935), it was found that most of the parameters held. While there are some differences, as has been pointed out, the basic facts of reinforcement, extinction, generalization, and so on, are found to hold. Skinner, scarcely a Pavlovian, has found it possible to use many of Pavlov's terms in describing the functional relations within his variety of operant conditioning. While he went much farther than Pavlov on schedules of reinforcement, the first experiments on intermittent reinforcement were indeed done in Pavlov's laboratory. Because rewarded learning, fitting the instrumental paradigm more nearly than the classical one, were characteristic of American studies of animal learning, it made Pavlov's work more acceptable when it was found that most of the principles held within instrumental conditioning.

Pavlov's Attitude Toward Psychologists

Pavlov, in trying to make his studies purely objective, anticipated American behaviorism, and later contributed to the behaviorist tradition in America. While he remained strictly within physiology, as he understood it, he was not unaware that he was dealing with essentially psychological problems, and in his Wednesday seminars he made a good many references to the writings of psychologists which he had read. A few of his remarks on psychologists are worth noting.

He thought particularly well of E. L. Thorndike, and felt that in some respects his work had anticipated his own. He mentioned the problem-box experiments of Thorndike (1898) as being used for the study of associations between stimuli and the locomotor apparatus; his own work was started at about the same time, in ignorance of what Thorndike had done (Pavlov, 1927, page 6).

While he had earlier carried on some correspondence with Yerkes, and approved of his work, he later attacked both Yerkes and Köhler for their "insight" doctrines (Pavlov, 1955: Wednesdays of May 16, 1934, pages 551-557; September 12, 1934, pages 558-562; January 9, 1935, pages 592-599; January 23, 1935, pages 599-605).

Therefore, basing myself on the study of apes, I affirm now that their somewhat complex behavior is a combination of association and analysis, which I consider to be the foundation of the higher nervous activity. So far we have seen nothing else in their behavior. The same can be said of our thinking. Beyond association there is nothing more in it (Pavlov, 1955, page 557; original date, 1934).

He also criticized other members of the Gestalt school notably Koffka and Lewin, objecting chiefly to their arguments against the concept of association (Pavlov, 1955; Wednesday meeting of November 29, 1934, pages 569-576; Wednesday, December 5, 1934, pages 576-588). Some of this discussion was based upon his reading of Woodworth's *Contemporary schools of psychology* (1931).

He also took occasion to criticize Janet's book on the sources of the intellect (Janet, 1935), stating that he was against Janet as a psychologist, but fascinated by him as a neurologist (Pavlov, 1955; February 20, 1935, pages 606-610). He likewise attacked the Swiss psychologist Claparède's monograph on the genesis of hypotheses (Claparède, 1934) (Pavlov, 1955; March 27, 1935, pages 611-616). In the course of his criticism he had some disparaging things to say about Warren's *Dictionary of psychology* (1934). Psychological thought, according to Pavlov, "is quite a peculiar matter; it does not regard words as signs and does not observe the principle that in using words one must always remember the reality implied by them" (Pavlov, 1955, page 616; original date, 1935).

There are two points to be made about these selected references from the Pavlov Wednesdays:

1. Although well into his late 80's he was still reviewing new books on psychology as they came to his attention, and,

2. The fact that he bothered to consider them and to refute them was evidence that he thought he was in some sense remaking psychology as a physiological science.

As far as influence upon American psychology is concerned, by testimony of the American psychologists themselves, Pavlov ranks with Freud and Wundt as a major influence (Coan and Zagona, 1962). It therefore behooves the student of learning theory to know something about the man who is responsible for so many of the concepts of contemporary psychology, especially in the field of learning.

SUPPLEMENTARY READINGS

The following English sources cover most of Pavlov's major writings:
PAVLOV, I. P. (1927) *Conditioned reflexes* (Anrep translation).
PAVLOV, I. P. (1928) *Lectures on conditioned reflexes* (Gantt translation).
PAVLOV, I. P. (1941) *Conditioned reflexes and psychiatry* (Gantt translation).
PAVLOV, I. P. (1955) *Selected works* (Edited by Koshtoyants and translated by Belsky).
PAVLOV, I. P. (1957) *Experimental psychology and other essays.*

For shorter introductions to Pavlov's work, the interested reader can do no better than to read some of Pavlov's own summaries. His very early essay (1903) on "Experimental psychology and psychopathology in animals" gives much of the later flavor; it can be found in Pavlov (1928), pages 47-60, and in Pavlov (1955), pages 245-270. A chapter by a devoted follower is Gantt, W. H. (1965) Pavlov's system. In Wolman, B. B., and Nagel, E. (Editors) *Scientific psychology,* pages 127-149.

Some books that carry on the experimental tradition started by Pavlov, but make their own contributions, include:
BYKOV, K. M. (1957) *The cerebral cortex and the internal organs.*
GRAY, J. A. (Editor) (1964) *Pavlov's typology.*
KONORSKI, J. (1948) *Conditioned reflexes and neuron organization.*
LURIA, A. R. (1965) *Higher cerebral processes in man.*
For biographical material on Pavlov:
BABKIN, B. P. (1949) *Pavlov, a biography.*
FROLOV, Y. P. (1937) *Pavlov and his school.*
While much of the experimentation in American laboratories has departed from the classical conditioning paradigm, that there is still vigorous interest in it is shown by the following books:
GEIS, G. L., STEBBINS, W. C., and LUNDIN, R. W. (1965a) *Reflexes and conditioned reflexes: a Basic Systems program.*
KIMBLE, G. A. (1961) *Hilgard and Marquis' conditioning and learning* (second edition)
PROKASY, W. F. (Editor) (1965a) *Classical conditioning: A symposium.*

Guthrie's Contiguous Conditioning

In some respects the system proposed by Edwin R. Guthrie (1886-1959) follows naturally from those of Thorndike and Pavlov. It is a stimulus–response association psychology, objective, and uses the conditioned response terms coming from Pavlov, while being practical and relevant in the spirit of Thorndike. But in other respects the interpretations of learning are very different. It is such similarities and differences which pose problems for learning theory.

GUTHRIE, THORNDIKE, PAVLOV, AND BEHAVIORISM

Thorndike accepted two kinds of learning: selecting and connecting (under the law of effect), and associative shifting. For him associative shifting was originally the fifth of some subsidiary principles, and by far the major burden was carried by selecting and connecting. For Guthrie, on the contrary, a conception very like associative shifting became the cornerstone of his system, and trial-and-error learning became for him secondary and derivative. Guthrie did not accept the law of effect in Thorndike's sense, and this was the basic cleavage between their systems.

Guthrie was an early behaviorist. Behaviorism as a "school" of psychology is usually thought of as originating with John B. Watson (1878-1958) who in 1913 announced the behaviorist position, and became thereafter its most vigorous spokesman. There were other varieties of behaviorism, however, and Guthrie was led to his position by way of the philosopher Singer (1911), with whom he had studied. The behaviorists, then and now, had and have in common the conviction that a science of psychology must be based upon a study of that which is overtly observable: physical stimuli, the muscular movements and glandular secretions which they arouse, and the environmental products that ensue. The behaviorists have differed among themselves as to what may be inferred in addition to what is measured, but they all exclude self-observation (introspection) as a legitimate scientific method (except that, if studied as verbal behavior, much formerly called introspection can be saved for science). Partly as a protection against an indirect use of introspection, behaviorists have tended to prefer experimentation on animals and infants.

Watson's *Behavior: An introduction to comparative psychology* (1914) was the first book to follow the announcement of his new position. In it occurred his attempted refutation of Thorndike's law of effect and the substitution of the laws of frequency and recency. He believed that animal learning, as in the maze or problem-box, could be explained according to what the animal had most often been led to do in the situation, with the most recent act favored in recall. Because the successful act was both most frequent and most recent, its recurrence could be explained without recourse to an added principle of effect. This denial of effect was part of his program of getting rid of the residual subjectivity which he felt was implied in Thorndike's concepts of satisfiers and annoyers. While the frequency–recency theory did not survive its criticisms (Peterson, 1922; Gengerelli, 1928), it serves to point up Watson's desire to find objective laws to substitute for those with even a tinge of subjective flavor.

The behaviorist knows that other events intervene between measured stimuli and the responses to them. In order to preserve a systematically coherent position, these intervening events are posited to be much like the observed ones, that is, *implicit* or *covert* stimulus–response sequences. In his early studies on the control of the maze habit, Watson (1907) had attributed great importance to kinesthetic stimuli as integrators of the habits involved. Because kinesthetic stimuli are aroused as a result of the organism's movements, they fit well into a behavioral or reaction psychology. Even the unobserved processes inferred to be going on between stimuli and responses are said to be comprised of movements and movement-produced stimuli. This emphasis upon kinesthesis as the integrator of animal learning served Watson well when he became puzzled about human thought processes. He decided that thought was merely implicit speech, that is, talking to oneself. Sensitive enough instruments, he conjectured, would detect tongue movements or other movement accompaniments of thinking. He was thus able to hold to his consistent behaviorist position without denying that thinking goes on.

It was somewhat later that Watson discovered that the conditioned reflex of Pavlov and Bekhterev might serve as a useful paradigm for learning (Watson, 1916). Because it grew out of the objective tradition that had happened to develop within Russian physiology, it fitted his temper and he adopted it enthusiastically. In Watson's later writings the conditioned reflex was central to learning, as the unit out of which habits are built.

Watson's general textbook, *Psychology from the standpoint of a behaviorist,* appeared in 1919. It was soon followed by other books written from an avowedly behavioristic standpoint. Among these was Smith and Guthrie's *General psychology in terms of behavior* (1921). Like Watson's book, it treated all of psychology from a behavioral viewpoint and made use of conditioning principles. It, too, laid great stress upon movement-produced stimuli. Hence there is a family relationship between the two books, although they differ greatly in expository style. Watson laid far more stress upon the details of physiology and anatomy, and upon appropriate methods for the behavioral study of psychological relationships. Smith and Guthrie showed less concern for experimental and neurophysiological detail, but instead gave a plausible interpretation of ordinary experience as described consistently from the new standpoint. Guthrie's later writings preserved the flavor of the Smith and Guthrie book. Despite their similarities, Guthrie's point of view must be considered as something other than a working out of Watson's position.

Doubtless influenced by Watson, Guthrie began to use the language of conditioning in his behavioristic psychology, but he chose to use what was learned from conditioned reflexes in a manner very different from Watson. Watson used the Pavlov experiment as a paradigm of learning, and made of the conditioned reflex the unit of habit, building his whole system eventually on that foundation. Guthrie, unlike Watson, started with a principle of conditioning or associative learning, a principle which is not dependent strictly on the Pavlov kind of experiment. Pavlov, in fact, criticized Guthrie for his emphasis on the one principle of contiguity, without sufficient concern for the many complexities within conditioning (Pavlov, 1932). Guthrie (1934) stuck to his guns in a reply, implying that Pavlov's was a highly artificial form of learning, and what was found to occur within Pavlov's experiments needed explanation according to more general principles.

CONTIGUITY OF CUE AND RESPONSE: THE ONE LAW OF ASSOCIATION

The Lowest Common Denominator of Learning

Guthrie's one law of learning, from which all else about learning is made comprehensible, was stated by Guthrie as follows: "A combination of stimuli which has accompanied a movement will on its recurrence tend to be followed by that movement" (1935, page 26).[1]

There is an elegant simplicity about the statement, which avoids mention of drives, of successive repetitions, of rewards or of punishments. Stimuli and movements in combination: that is all. This one principle serves as the basis for a very ingenious and intriguing theory of learning.

A second statement is needed to complete the basic postulate about learning: "A stimulus pattern gains its full associative strength on the occasion of its first pairing with a response" (1942, page 30).

This somewhat paradoxical statement, in view of undeniable improvement with practice, is a very necessary adjunct to the theory, because it makes possible a number of derivative statements about learning and forgetting. It can be thought of as a kind of *recency principle,* for if learning occurs completely in one trial, that which was last done in the presence of a stimulus combination will be that which will be done when the stimulus combination next recurs.[2]

How could Guthrie demonstrate that more complicated forms of learning conform to these simple principles? As in the case of other sophisticated theorists, he did not proceed by denying familiar forms of learning. His problem was that of showing that learning as we know it can, in fact, be shown not to contradict these basic principles. He did not deny that there is learning which may be described as insightful or purposive or problem-solving. It was Guthrie's task to show that each of these forms requires no new principles of explanation beyond the primary law of association by contiguity.

Why Strict Contiguity of Measured Stimulus and Response is Not Essential

One of the standard experiments in the literature of conditioning is that showing the importance of the time interval between the conditioned stimulus and unconditioned response. The empirical results suggest a gradient, with a most favorable interval and less favorable intervals on either side of this optimal interval (Kimble, 1961, pages 155-160).

Guthrie was able to defend strict simultaneity of cue and response in the face of these data by proposing that the true cue being conditioned is not the stimulus as measured. An external stimulus may give rise to movements of the organism. These movements in turn produce stimuli. When associations appear to be made between stimuli and responses

---

[1] Where the quotations from Guthrie remain unchanged between the 1935 and 1952 editions of his book, the earlier only will be cited.

[2] Because it refers to the last response of a succession rather than to recency in time, Voeks (1948, 1950) suggested that it be called the *principle of postremity.*

separated in time, it is because these intervening movements fill in the gap. The true association is between simultaneous events.

There is a strong preference for *movement-produced stimuli* as the true conditioners in Guthrie's system. They permit the integration of habits within a wide range of environmental change in stimulation, because these stimuli are carried around by the organism. It appears that some of this preference dates from the early emphasis of Watson (1907) on kinesthesis as the basis of control of the maze habit, a position no longer tenable.[3] Such covert movement-produced stimuli provide ever-present explanations for conduct which cannot be inferred from external stimulus–response relationships.

Why Repetition Brings Improvement

The reason that practice brings improvement is that improvement, and other forms of success, refer to acts, to outcomes of learnings, rather than to *movements*. Guthrie believed that his interest in movements, and the prediction of movements, was almost unique among learning theorists; others, he says, are interested in goal achievements, and results of one sort or another. One difference between him and Thorndike was that Thorndike was concerned with scores on tasks, with items learned, pages typed, or correct responses attained. Guthrie was concerned only with the movements of the organism, regardless of whether they led to error or success.

A skill, such as getting the ball into the basket in a game of basketball, is not one act but many. It does not depend upon a single muscular movement, but upon a number of movements made under a number of different circumstances. Any one movement may be learned in any one trial, but to learn all the movements demanded by the complicated skill calls for practice in all the different situations: while near the basket and far away, on one side and on the other, with and without a guard nearby. Practice is necessary; but it produces its consequences, not in accordance with a law of frequency, but according to the simple principle of the attachment of cues to movements. The more varied the movements called for in a given act of skill, and the more varied the cues which must become assimilated to these movements, the more practice is required. There is no mystery about the length of time it takes to learn to operate a typewriter: there are so many keys in so many combinations, calling for the attachment of a great many cues to a great many responses. It is concomitantly necessary to get rid of the faulty associations which lead to what, from a product point of view, is an error. This is done by having the correct behavior occur to the cue which previously

[3] Honzik (1936) found kinesthesis to be one of the least useful of several sensory controls of the maze habit.

gave rise to the faulty behavior. When finally all the cues lead to acceptable behavior, the task is mastered. The apparent contradiction of single-trial learning with the actual experience of painstaking fumbling before achieved success is resolved when the skilled task is seen to be composed of a large number of habits.

Associative Inhibition, Forgetting, and the Breaking of Habits

The fact of extinction is one of the findings of conditioning experiments that is in need of explanation. Because cues should remain faithful to their responses, Guthrie could not agree to extinction as a decay due to mere nonreinforced repetition. According to him, extinction always occurs as associative inhibition, that is, through the learning of an incompatible response. His is an interference theory and hence requires no new principles, because the original learning and the interfering learning follow the same rules.

He explained forgetting in the same way. If there were no interference with old learning there would be no forgetting. It has been shown, for example, that conditioned responses, even though in some respects they appear fragile, are actually quite resistant to forgetting (e.g., Hilgard and Campbell, 1936; Wendt, 1937; Skinner, 1950). The long-lasting character of these conditioned responses is to be understood because they represent learning highly specific to cues not confronted in daily life. If the learners lived in the laboratory, their responses would be subject to more interferences. Guthrie's position is but an extreme form of the retroactive inhibition theory of forgetting, to be discussed in greater detail later.

If it is desired to break a habit (that is, to accelerate its forgetting), it is only necessary to cause other movements to occur in the presence of the cues to the habit. The problem of locating the cues and substituting other behavior often takes time, because many cues may lead to the undesirable habit.

Drinking or smoking after years of practice are action systems which can be started by thousands of reminders. . . . I had once a caller to whom I was explaining that the apple I had just finished was a splendid device for avoiding a smoke. The caller pointed out that I was at that moment smoking. The habit of lighting a cigarette was so attached to the finish of eating that smoking had started automatically (1935, page 139).

Guthrie suggested three ways in which activities are commonly weakened:[4]

1. The first method is to introduce the stimulus that you wish to have disregarded, but only in such faint degree that it will not call out its re-

[4] Paraphrased from Guthrie (1935), pages 70-73.

sponse. This is the method of training a horse to the saddle by starting with a light blanket, and gradually working up to full equipment, at no time permitting the horse to become so startled that it plunges or struggles.

2. The second method is to repeat the signal until the original response is fatigued, and then continuing it, so that new responses are learned to the signal. The "bronco-busting" of the western ranches followed essentially this technique.

3. The third method is to present the stimulus when other features in the situation inhibit the undesirable response. One illustration given by Guthrie is that of training a dog not to catch and eat chickens by tying a dead chicken about its neck. As it struggles to get rid of the corpse it develops an avoidance response to chickens at close quarters. Another example, illustrating undesirable learning, is the disobedience learned by the child whose mother calls him when he is too occupied with what he is doing to obey.

SOME DERIVATIVE EXPLANATIONS AND APPLICATIONS

In his two main books *The psychology of learning* (1935, 1952) and *The psychology of human conflict* (1938), Guthrie found it unnecessary to make any formal additions to the basic principles of learning in order to apply his theory to practical learning problems and to the handling of personality disorders.[5] While the basic principles remain, there are some ingeniously derived supplementations which, once accounted for, play an important role in the further discussions. Among these are explanations of the place of motives, the action of reward and punishment, and the origin of anticipatory responses as important substitutes for ideas and intentions.

Motives

The motivational state of the organism, its hunger, thirst, or state of comfort or discomfort, has no formal place in Guthrie's learning theory; the motivational state is important only because it determines the presence and vigor of movements that may enter into associative connection. The motive[6] is important only for the stimulus–response sequences that occur. The movements that occur get associated; if a hungry cat acts differently from a well-fed cat, her movements are different and so her learning may be different. She learns what she does; what she does

[5] The same comments apply to his collaborative books as well: Smith and Guthrie (1921), Guthrie and Horton (1946), Guthrie and Edwards (1949), Guthrie and Powers (1950).

[6] For a related treatment of motivation, see Estes (1958).

is more important than what her motivational state happens to be. In the Guthrie and Horton (1946) experiments to be described later, the cat often did not eat the salmon provided in the dish outside the cage. This did not matter, for *leaving the cage* was the important behavior.

Motives are, however, important in one of the derivations from the basic theory of contiguous association: they are important in providing *maintaining stimuli,* keeping the organism active until a goal is reached. The goal removes these maintaining stimuli, and brings the activity to an end (1942, page 18). We shall see how these maintaining stimuli, along with movement-produced stimuli, tend to keep a series of acts integrated, and account for anticipation, for behavior characterized by intent.

Reward

While Guthrie believed as everyone else does that rewards influence outcomes, his rejection of the law of effect and of the principle of reinforcement in conditioning was based on the position that nothing new is added to associative learning by reward except a mechanical arrangement. This mechanical arrangement, which places reward at the end of a series of acts, removes the organism from the stimuli acting just prior to the reward. Hence, being removed from the stimuli, the behavior to these stimuli is preserved intact. Instead of behavior being strengthened by reward, reward preserves it from disintegration. It was just as strong before the reward occurred, but, if there had been no reward, behavior in the same situation would have been changed. The act leading to the reward, being the last act in the problematic situation, is the one favored when the situation next repeats itself. Guthrie was very explicit about this. Of an animal's escape from a problem-box he said:

The position taken in this paper is that the animal learns to escape with its first escape. This learning is protected from forgetting because the escape removes the animal from the situation which has then no chance to acquire new associations.

(Of latch-opening followed by food.) *What encountering the food does is not to intensify a previous item of behavior but to protect that item from being unlearned.* The whole situation and action of the animal is so changed by the food that the pre-food situation is shielded from new associations. These new associations can not be established in the absence of the box interior, and in the absence of the behavior that preceded latch-opening (1940, pages 144-145).

Although this is the fundamental position with respect to reward, and frequently reiterated in refutation of the law of effect and related interpretations, the action of reward is found to be somewhat more complicated when one examines the totality of Guthrie's system. The first (and primary) role of reward is to remove the animal from the problem and thus prevent unlearning. But by the principle of association the animal also learns the activity that he carries on in the presence of the reward (chewing and salivating to food, for example), and this behavior tends to be invoked by renewed hunger and by any of the cues from the problem that may have persisted while the rewarded behavior was going on.

. . . There is one act, however, to which hunger may remain a faithful conditioner. That is the act of eating; and the faithfulness of hunger to this association derives from the fact that hunger dies when eating occurs. As Stevenson Smith and I pointed out in our *General Psychology,* elements of the consummatory response tend to be present throughout a series of actions driven by a maintaining stimulus (1935, pages 151-152).

Not only do general movements of eating tend to be aroused by hunger contractions, but the specific movements demanded by the particular nature of the food are possibly in evidence. Hence when the rat runs the maze he is ready for whatever reward has been received in the past, sunflower seed or bran mash. This readiness is an actual muscular readiness . . . (1935, page 173).

A theoretical problem arises when Guthrie held at once (*a*) that the reward removes the learner from all the cues prior to the reward, and (*b*) that these prior cues are somehow reward-attached. He could have resolved this dilemma in one of two ways. He could have retreated from the all-or-nothing removal of cues by reward: perhaps reward acts by *changing* the situation somewhat, even though not entirely. Or he could have defined the "true" reward as coming at a stage later than eating, perhaps consummation through food digestion. The animal is still hungry while eating, hence hunger produces anticipatory eating responses. Then, however, the act of eating does not remove the animal from the cues to which he has been exposed, because he has been exposed to eating-response cues all along. What finally changes the situation and brings the end of hunger (and presumably other cues) is satiation. Although this sounds like something of a quibble, the distinction between the theory of contiguous association and the theory of reinforcement is so slight that only the utmost clarity of statement can permit a choice between them.

One illustration may serve to show how important it is to know exactly what the theory states. The experiment of Sheffield and Roby (1950) shows that the nonnutritive taste of saccharin may serve as a reward. The result is used as a refutation of the need-satiation theory of reinforcement and as support for the theory of contiguous association. The empirical support for Guthrie derives from the fact that the rat's behavior changes strikingly after the saccharin is ingested. The authors conclude:

It is suggested that elicitation of the consummatory response appears to be a more critical *primary* reinforcing factor in instrumental learning than the drive reduction subsequently achieved (Sheffield and Roby, 1950, page 481).

While this consummatory response is the final one in a series, it has not yet taken the learner out of the situation. It must itself be part of the series, otherwise there could be no anticipatory responses reflecting it. What *really* takes the animal out of the situation? What is *really* reinforcing? Is it the new behavior that takes place after the consummatory response is over? But if it is this new behavior, does that not occur *after* some sort of stimulus-reduction has taken place?

Guthrie's general standpoint is clear enough: reward does not strengthen prior behavior, it merely protects it from unlearning. But the more precise questions about the relation of this position to his interpretation of anticipatory response remained unanswered.

Punishment

The primary interpretation of punishment was for Guthrie that of all associative learning: you tend to do what you did under the same circumstances:

. . . Sitting on tacks does not discourage learning. It encourages one in learning to do something else than sit. It is not the feeling caused by punishment, but the specific action caused by punishment that determines what will be learned. To train a dog to jump through a hoop, the effectiveness of punishment depends on where it is applied, front or rear. It is what the punishment makes the dog do that counts or what it makes a man do, not what it makes him feel (1935, page 158).

What we can predict is that the influence of stimuli acting at the time of either satisfaction or annoyance will be to re-establish whatever behavior was in evidence at the time (1935, page 154).

If Guthrie had stopped with statements such as these, it would appear that he treated reward and punishment in a symmetrical fashion. Certainly punishment changes a situation very strikingly, as reward does. Hence one might infer that all antecedent behavior would remain intact, being protected from new learning by the altered conditions of punishment as much as by the altered conditions of reward. Sometimes this does actually appear to be the case. Running responses leading to charged grills, with safety beyond, may prove resistant to extinction (Gwinn, 1949; F. D. Sheffield, 1949a).

The symmetry in treatment of reward and punishment, as implied in the foregoing quotations, is somewhat illusory, for "doing what you last did" refers to very different parts of the behavior cycle when the reference is to reward than when the reference is to punishment. "What you last did" that remains in your behavior repertory because of reward is what you did *just before* the reward appeared; "what you last did" in the case of punishment refers to what you did *just after* the punishment, leading to escape. Punishment produces "maintaining stimuli" relieved by a later movement that brings relief:

> . . . An animal on a charged grid, a barefoot boy on a hot pavement, a man sitting on a tack have as their goals mere escape from the intense stimulation that causes general tension and restlessness as well as specific movement. These stimuli continue to act as what Stevenson Smith and I called maintaining stimuli until some movement carries the subject away from the source of stimulation, or the source of stimulation away from the subject (1935, page 165).

When these stimuli are removed, we have the circumstances defining reward, and so, if that were the whole story, the prior behavior should remain intact. This kind of relief from punishment has come to be known as *escape learning* to distinguish it from *avoidance learning*. To move from escape learning to avoidance learning we require an anticipatory response, conditioned to some cue, so that the punishment is circumvented. As we saw in relation to reward, Guthrie's system makes provision for anticipatory responses, and these can, of course, be used to explain avoidance learning. The animal merely makes the escape to some cue present at the time of punishment—a cue which, fortunately, makes its appearance before the threatened punishment. Hence what happens at the end of a sequence of acts leading to punishment does something *in addition to* and *other than* removing the organism from the scene: it also sets up some conditioned anticipatory responses.

Noxious stimuli may lead not only to escape and avoidance learning but to a third subvariety, more properly called punishment, that is, to the inhibiting of otherwise rewarded behavior. We may try to stop the child's doing something he enjoys; we may try to break a "bad habit." Punishment of this kind always involves conflict.

Guthrie's position with respect to this subvariety of punishment has been aptly summarized by Sheffield:

> (a) Punishment works only if the last response to the punished situation is incompatible with the response that brought on the punishment.
> (b) Punishment works only if the cues present when the incompatible response is performed are present when the punished response is performed.
> (c) Punishment that produces only emotional excitement will tend to fixate the punished response (F. D. Sheffield, 1949b).

The main point is that punishment is effective in conflict situations where incompatible responses have a tendency to occur. The statement about the presence of cues is not as decisive as it sounds, in view of Guthrie's acceptance of anticipatory responses and movement-produced stimuli as cues. In other words, there are always plenty of cues, if one needs them. The third point is a useful one: In some cases, what appears to be punishing to the trainer may not be punishing to the learner; in other cases, punishment, even though annoying, may accentuate stereotyped behavior.

Intentions

Conduct is organized into sequences in which people make plans and carry them out, or at least start to carry them out. Guthrie was aware of this and devoted a chapter to learning with and without intention (1935, pages 202-211).

He and Smith had earlier followed the lead of Sherrington and Woodworth in considering sequences of behavior as composed of precurrent or preparatory responses and consummatory responses (Smith and Guthrie, 1921; Sherrington, 1906; Woodworth, 1918). Such acts appear from the outside to be intentional, for the earlier adjustments clearly are in readiness for the consequences that are to follow. These anticipatory responses or readiness reactions are said to be conditioned to maintaining stimuli.

The typical case is that of the hungry rat running down an alleyway to food at the end. The activity is maintained by the internal stimuli aroused by food deprivation to which running and eating behavior have been conditioned in the past. That is, the rat found food at some previous time after running while hungry. These internal stimuli, plus the stimuli from the runway (if it has been previously a path to food), maintain the running of the animal against competing responses, such as stopping to explore. Anticipatory salivation or chewing movements give directional character to the behavior. All this food anticipation is fulfilled if there is food at the end of the maze. Because the stimuli of hunger and anticipation are now removed, and the animal is out of the maze, all the learning is intact for a new trial at a later time. This is about as complex a description as Guthrie ever indulged in, and the details were not taken as seriously as Hull, for example, would have taken them. But the paradigm provides a way of talking about human intentions and purposes also.

The essence of an intention is a body of maintaining stimuli which may or may not include sources of unrest like thirst or hunger but always includes action tendencies conditioned during a past experience—a readiness to speak, a readiness to go, a readiness to read, and in each case a readiness not only for the act but also for the previously rehearsed consequences of the act. These readinesses are not complete acts but they consist in tensions of the muscles that will take part in the complete act (1935, pages 205-206).

This statement goes a long way toward the point of view which those with very different theories of learning accept. The only feature which keeps it within the bounds of Guthrie's theory is that all the readinesses, including the readiness for the "previously rehearsed consequences of the act," are said to consist in tensions in the muscles. This assumption, characteristic of the behaviorist position, remains in the realm of conjecture rather than of demonstration.

The Control of the Learning Process

It is part of the charm of Guthrie's writing that it was closely in touch with life and provided amusing but cogent suggestions for meeting the problems of animal training, child-rearing, and pedagogy. This practicality is not a necessary characteristic of the system, for if one seriously attempted to provide evidence for the theory he would be buried in the midst of the precise movement correlates of measurable stimuli and the muscular tension accompaniments of preparatory adjustments. But the system was not intended to be taken seriously in that sense. As long as a convenient way of talking about things can be found without seeming to contradict the system, quantitative precision is not essential. It was Guthrie's conviction that scientific laws to be useful must be approximately true, but they must also be stated coarsely enough to be teachable to freshmen (1936a).

Most of the practical advice which Guthrie gave was good advice, and he succeeded in making it flow from the theory. Consider the following example:

The mother of a ten-year-old girl complained to a psychologist that for two years her daughter had annoyed her by a habit of tossing coat and hat on the floor as she entered the house. On a hundred occasions the mother had insisted that the girl pick up the clothing and hang it in its place. These wild ways were changed only after the mother, on advice, began to insist not that the girl pick up the fallen garments from the floor, but that she put them on, return to the street, and re-enter the house, this time removing the coat and hanging it properly (1935, page 21).

Why was this advice given? Behavior is in response to stimuli. Hanging up the coat and hat was in response to her mother's pleading and the sight of the clothing on the floor. In order to attach the desired behavior to its proper cues, it was necessary to go outside and come into the house, so that entering the house became the cue for hanging up the coat and hat.

The following statements represent the kind of suggestions which recur in Guthrie's writings:

1. If you wish to encourage a particular kind of behavior or discourage another, discover the cues leading to the behavior in question. In the one

case, arrange the situation so that the desired behavior occurs when those cues are present; in the other case, arrange it so that the undesired behavior does not occur in the presence of the cues. This is all that is involved in the skillful use of reward and punishment. A student does not learn what was in a lecture or a book. He learns only what the lecture or book caused him to do (1942, page 55).

2. Use as many stimulus supports for desired behavior as possible, because any ordinary behavior is a complex of movements to a complex of stimuli. The more stimuli there are associated with the desired behavior, the less likely that distracting stimuli and competing behavior will upset the desirable behavior. There would be fewer lines confused in amateur theatricals if there were more dress rehearsals, since the cues from the stage and the actors are part of the situation to which the actor responds. Another way of putting this is to rule that we should practice in the precise form later to be demanded of us.

EXPERIMENTS ON THE PUZZLE-BOX

One of the serious lacks in the early history of Guthrie's proposals was the failure to set convincing experiments. Such an experiment was completed by Guthrie and Horton (1946) between the two editions of Guthrie's book on learning and provides a much more tangible ground on which to come to grips with both the strengths and the weaknesses of Guthrie's position.

It is fitting that Guthrie and Horton should have chosen as a characteristic experiment the behavior of the cat in escaping from a puzzle-box, because this situation had already been the occasion for both experiment and theory. Thorndike's classical experiment has already been cited (page 16). This gave the send-off to Thorndike's theory by convincing him that little of the cat's behavior was mediated by ideas and much of it controlled by the influence of rewards.

The Guthrie and Horton Experiment

Because of their wish to record details of movement rather than to score achievement in some other manner, a special problem-box was designed which permitted the cat to be fully observed during the period prior to solution and its exact posture to be recorded photographically at the moment it activated the release. The release mechanism was a small pole set in the midst of the floor of a cage with a glass exit door in the glass front. The animal entered through a starting box and tunnel at the rear. If it touched the pole in any manner at all, the front door was opened and the animal could escape into the room. A camera was operated as the door was opening, so that a photograph of the animal was obtained at the moment of release, while it was still in contact with the pole.

In each of three preliminary trials the animal entered the box through the tunnel and made its way out the front door, which was left ajar, to find a bit of salmon on the table top in front of the box. The first of the regular trials followed. During the regular trials, the experimenters kept notes of the animal's behavior as it entered the box through the tunnel at the rear, and the camera recorded the exact time and position when it struck the release mechanism.

The results are remarkable for the amount of repetitiousness in each cat's successive release. A cat which bites the pole may do so time after time; one which has escaped by backing into the pole may back almost endlessly in its efforts to escape by the same movement. Others use front paws or hind paws, or roll against the pole. The cat, in full agreement with the theory, learns the method of escape in the first trial and then repeats what is essentially the same solution time after time. Some cats have several modes of escape which they use at different times, or they have one type of escape for a long time and then shift to another. These exceptions to the principle of doing what was done the last time are ac-counted for on the basis of a different entrance, which changes the stimu-lating conditions; the result of accidental distractions; or, having been in the box a long time and failing to operate the release by a familiar method, some new method may have superseded the familiar one. The fact that the last movement—the movement at the time of release—is the most stereotyped is in agreement with the principle that such an act will remain intact because nothing can interfere with it, the cat leaving the situation as soon as he strikes the release mechanism. The fact that the food reward is inconsequential is shown by the cat's often failing to eat the fish or to lick the milk provided for it.

Guthrie and Horton say that they have seen in the behavior of their cats all that Thorndike reported. But they have also seen a degree of stereotypy which points strongly to the tendency for behavior to repeat itself under similar conditions. Some of the tracings of photographs of Guthrie and Horton's cats are shown in Figure 4-1.

This behavior is so convincing that it has to be acknowledged. It is coherent with all that Guthrie had been proposing in his theory. That is surely as much as could be wished for by a theorist from a series of ex-periments.

Why did these cats learn so much more easily than Thorndike's? The answer given is plausible. These cats always found the release mechanism available in exactly the same form, and readily operable. Thorndike's re-lease mechanism was more difficult to operate and was probably not al-ways in precisely the same position. Hence Thorndike's cats had to learn a series of habits rather than a single habit. When Guthrie and Horton's

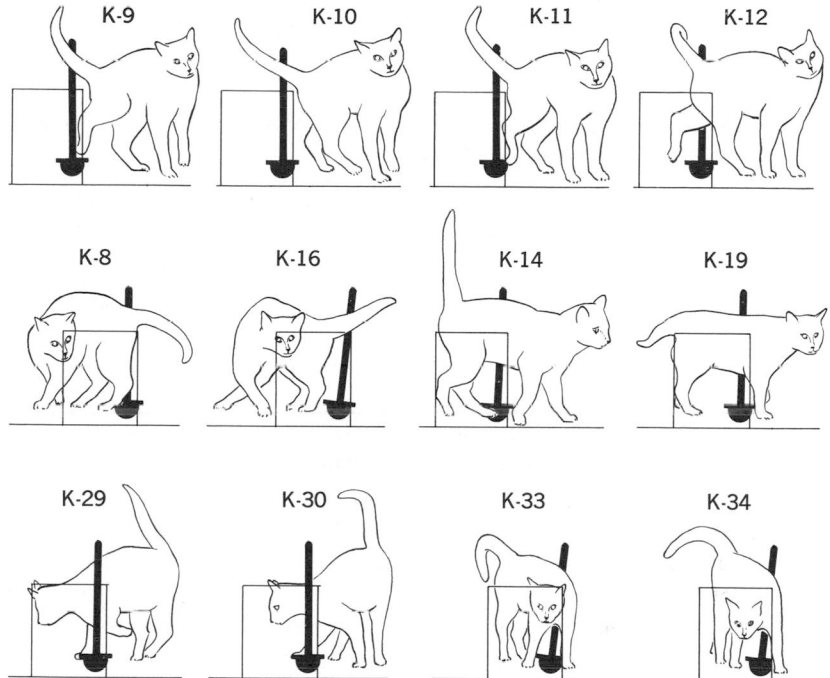

Figure 4-1   **Alternative stereotyped responses of a single cat escaping from the puzzle box by touching the pole. Responses K-9 through K-12 illustrate one type of response used frequently by cat K. The remaining pictures show four other response types used by the same cat. Reproduced from tracings of photographs taken automatically at the time of release. From Guthrie and Horton (1946).**

cats failed to operate the mechanism by a familiar method they, too, adopted a new method. Stereotypy was shown because stereotypy worked.

Guthrie and Horton are clear that they are not proposing a test of the cat's intelligence. They could easily have devised an experiment in which there would have been much less stereotypy. But the point is that as far as the learning of movements is concerned, the animal tends to do what it last did in the situation. If the situation forces it to do something else, it will do something else. Cats do not jump at the place where a bird was previously caught if there is no bird there, though they may lie in wait at the same spot.

The experiments were accepted by the authors as fully justifying the theory which Guthrie had all along expounded:

It has been our conclusion from our observation of this series of experiments that the prediction of what any animal would do at any moment is most securely based on a record of what the animal was observed to do *in that situation at its last occurrence.* This is obviously prediction in terms of association (Guthrie and Horton, 1946, page 42).

Some Objections to the Guthrie and Horton Experiments as Representative of Animal Learning

The experiments of Guthrie and Horton are appropriate ones for showing that, under limiting conditions, learned responses may show a high degee of stereotypy. To go beyond this and assume that these experiments provide the typical case for animal learning is misleading.

According to the authors themselves, varied behavior supervenes if the response of the animal does not release it from the box fairly quickly. The stereotypy appears to result in part at least because the problem is an easy one. It may be mastered in a single trial, and the later trials are then merely the repeated performances of a learned act. There is little remarkable about easy learning taking place promptly, or about its being repeated when there is nothing to block it and reward to sustain it.

Some critics have argued that the restrictions on the photographs violate Guthrie's insistence that learned behavior should not be defined by outcome or effect, because the moment at which the picture was snapped was defined by the consequences of the activity: releasing the door.

The effect of this restriction in picture taking could be seen more clearly in an experiment that required the animal to stand on his hind legs and reach out of the upper corner of the cage in order to press a button to release the door and take the picture. In this way we further restrict the set of possible responses and achieve added stereotypy. On the other hand, other experimental situations could be constructed, which would reduce stereotypy. In either case, however, what is procured are data concerning responses defined in terms of effect (Mueller and Schoenfeld, 1954, page 358).

It is not quite clear how much Guthrie and Horton wished to make of the amount of stereotypy they observed. Commenting on an earlier and related experiment done with guinea pigs by Muenzinger, Koerner, and Irey (1929), Guthrie wrote:

These authors conclude that the mechanization of habitual movement "is still accompanied by variability of its pattern . . ." and that accessory movements, "while on the whole exhibiting much plasticity, show some mechanization of a brief and unstable kind."

The account given by Muenzinger, Koerner, and Irey is quite consistent with what Horton and I observed in our cats. We were interested in the routinizing, they in the exceptions and new behavior. We were convinced that whole segments of movement appear and are repeated all-or-none on succeeding trials (1952, pages 271-272).

Guthrie and Horton certainly succeeded in showing a considerable amount of repetitiveness and stereotypy in learned behavior. This led them to conclude, as indicated in the earlier quotation, that prediction is best made on the basis of the last prior occurrence, and that such a prediction is obviously one in terms of association. We may question this last conclusion. To prophesy that a man who owns and wears only blue ties will wear a blue tie tomorrow is an actuarial prediction pure and simple, with no theory in it. It is logically similar to the prediction of an insurance company that a given percentage of people will die at a given age. The only assumption is a certain uniformity of events when taken *en masse*—an assumption scarcely attributable to associationism.

To account for learning, rather than for the repetition of learned acts, one has to account not for uniformity but for change. Upon learning in this sense the Guthrie and Horton experiments throw little light. Most of the change in behavior took place in the neglected early trials in which the cats learned to find their way out of the box through the glass door. There was, to be sure, the supplementary learning to use the pole to open the door. A harder but possibly clearer problem, of the type used in "insight" experiments, perhaps would be solved by fewer animals, but those which solved it could use the solution in novel situations. Thus the chosen learning situation has a great deal to do with what aspects of behavior will be revealed. The problem-box of Guthrie and Horton, which at first blush appears to lay bare the primitive nature of learning, may in fact be a highly specialized situation poorly designed to show the behavior of the cat as it would solve a problem which, while harder for it, was more appropriate to it in clarity of cue-response relationships.

GUTHRIE'S FINAL REFLECTIONS UPON HIS THEORY

Shortly before his death, Guthrie was invited to prepare a chapter giving the background, orienting attitudes, and general systematic characteristics of his learning theory. This he did, and the chapter appeared in his last year (Guthrie, 1959).

He repeats his arguments for the need for simplicity. Thus in the statement of scientific laws, or rules for regularities in nature, the requirement that these must be communicable and teachable makes simplicity desirable (1959, page 162). He denies that nature was set up in a pattern of simple laws, waiting to be discovered—the requirement of simplicity is a human requirement. "It is men that are simple, not nature" (page 162).

This orientation implies that psychology must choose an appropriate level for its categories of stimulus and response. Guthrie notes that human behavior is highly predictable in our daily interactions, and that our lives would be intolerable if this were not so. It is therefore rather remarkable that we have been so unsuccessful as psychologists in formulating general rules of behavior. Perhaps we have been going at it the wrong way. When we describe behavior changes that are predictable we do so according to the presence or absence of specific stimuli and responses observed, not according to their intensity or degree. In our scientific efforts, however, we often try to abstract measurable attributes of response like latency, vigor, or time to extinction. These measurements, Guthrie notes, fail to agree, the only promising one being probability of occurrence. He cites Estes' (1950) development of a probabilistic theory, which, in favoring association by contiguity, is in some respects like his own. Yet he objects strongly to two of Estes' assumptions: first, that the elements that make up a situation have independent probabilities, and, second, that the effects of elements are additive (Guthrie, 1959, page 167).

Although his is an S–R theory, Guthrie resists any effort to make a kind of laboratory game out of the theory, as he finds others doing:

A system may be productive of research, but research has no value in itself. It is knowledge that we are after rather than research, and the test of a system is the light that it throws on an area, and in psychology, not just the amount of prediction that it makes possible, but the ability to predict what is worth knowing. Practically all research results in prediction, but if it is merely the prediction of how rats will behave under certain complicated conditions found only in a number of psychological laboratories, we have not furthered knowledge or science (1959, page 173).

The Revised Law of Association

The main supplement to his earlier formulations was an emphasis upon the role played by the organism's own activity in selecting the physical stimuli to which it would attend. There is a certain amount of "scanning" that goes on before association takes place. The new rule can be succinctly stated:

What is being noticed becomes the signal for what is being done (1959, page 186).

Guthrie went on to list eight assumptions concerning what goes on in associative learning, although he denied these the status of formal postulates (1959, pages 187-189):[7]

1. Patterning of physical stimuli is effective as such, as distinct from the effects of degrees of intensity or the summation of the effects of stimulus elements.

[7] These have been somewhat abbreviated and paraphrased.

2. A given pattern of physical stimuli is accepted by the observer to be a cue for the observed organism only on the basis of supplementary data available to the observer, either data from the past history of the organism or from present observation of the perceptual response to the cue.

3. The effectiveness of physical stimuli is governed by a class of responses called attention.

4. When two cues that have been associated with incompatible movement patterns are both present, action is withheld and the movements involved in attention become pronounced, including behavior which may be called scanning.

5. At any moment the class of movement responses possible is limited by the ongoing action.

6. Rules which do not take into account what the animal is doing when stimulated will not be descriptive of the phenomena of association.

7. The complexity of the determiners of action requires that prediction allow for high degrees of error.

8. What is being noticed, as a response is elicited, becomes a potential cue for that response.

What this amounts to is, in the first place, a warning against defining effective stimuli in physical terms. Of course stimuli can be analyzed into physical changes taking place, but these are only changes that the observer *expects* to become stimuli until he has some evidence of the organism's reaction to them. Hence the attention (scanning) behavior becomes important because it in some sense converts the physical patterns into stimuli for the organism. In the second place, the law of association by contiguity, of single-trial association, is modestly reaffirmed.

STEPS TOWARD FORMALIZATION AND ADDITIONAL EXPERIMENTAL TESTING

Some of Guthrie's students have undertaken the task of clarifying and formalizing his theory, and of designing new experiments crucially related to it. The theory has gained support also from other quarters, and it remains a serious contender among contemporary learning theories.

Voeks's Postulates

Guthrie's statements were collected and cast into postulational form by Voeks (1950). She went on to state eight theorems open to experimental test, and provided some confirming experimental results. Her four basic postulates are here quoted verbatim:

Postulate 1: Principle of Association
   (a) Any stimulus-pattern which once accompanies a response, and/or im-

mediately precedes it (by $\frac{1}{2}$ seconds or less), becomes a full strength direct cue for that response. (b) This is the only way in which stimulus-patterns not now cues for a particular response can become direct cues for that response.

Postulate 2: Principle of Postremity
(a) A stimulus which has accompanied or immediately preceded two or more incompatible responses is a conditioned stimulus for only the last response made while that stimulus was present. (b) This is the only way in which a stimulus now a cue for a particular response can cease being a cue for that response.

Postulate 3: Principle of Response Probability[8]
The probability of any particular response's occurring (P) at some specified time is an increasing monotonic function (x) of the proportion (N) of the stimuli present which are at that time cues for that response $(P = N^x)$.

Postulate 4: Principle of Dynamic Situations
The stimulus-pattern of a situation is not static but from time to time is modified, due to such changes as result from the subject's making a response, accumulation of fatigue products, visceral changes and other internal processes of the subject, introduction of controlled or uncontrolled variations in the stimuli present.

These four postulates (and the theorems related to them) deal with isolated responses as the essential core of Guthrie's theory. Unfortunately Voeks's theorem system was not extended to deal systematically with the puzzling problems posed by various arrangements of reward and punishment, with anticipatory responses, with the integration of acts through movement-produced stimuli. Nevertheless, the start made by Voeks is a very useful one, and her experimental tests are cogent.

Her first experimental test (Voeks, 1948) (completed before the system was formalized, but consistent with the formalization) deals with the prediction of behavior in a maze. She studied the individual responses at each choice-point of 57 human subjects learning a raised relief finger maze and a punchboard maze. She tested which of two predictions was the more accurate: (1) prediction based on the *frequency* of prior choices at the point of choice, and (2) prediction based on *postremity* (i.e., the last choice that was made). Postremity won out easily. The success of prediction by postremity was most striking when the prediction disagreed with that on the basis of frequency. For 56 of the 57 subjects, postremity predicted better than frequency for those choices in which the predictions disagreed. The difference was statistically highly significant. These results are, of course, in agreement with Guthrie's theory, especially as stated in Voeks's Postulate 2.

The major puzzle is why the maze was learned at all. Why was not the last trial chiefly a repetition of the first, with some minor fluctuations

[8] Some of the subscripts have been omitted from the symbols in Postulate 3 as unnecessary here.

according to Postulate 4? The explanation is not very difficult for the high-relief maze, for the last response was always leaving the choice-point by the true path. The explanation is more difficult for the punchboard maze, because a "noncorrection" method was used. That is, if the "wrong" hole was punched, this was signalled to the subject, but he went on to the next choice without punching the "right" hole. Let us look at Voeks's explanation of the learning of the punchboard maze:

> . . . Now, in the learning of the punch-board maze, S may insert his stylus into the wrong hole of a pair, e.g., pair 8. A stimulus then is presented (the sound of the buzzer in our experiment, E saying "wrong" in others, etc.) which may cause S to withdraw his stylus and make additional responses on that trial to that choice point. These responses may involve, for instance, the S's saying to himself "Eight, not this hole, that one is right," or even making incipient or possibly overt movements toward the correct hole while looking at the pair. If this has been the case, the next time S comes to the pair of holes, he will say "Eight" (as instructed), and it is expected he will start toward the incorrect hole, draw his stylus back, say "No, not this hole; that one is right," and then make the previously established conditioned response to the stimulus "That-is-right," i.e., the response of inserting his stylus into the hole at which he has just looked and said "That is right." Thus another error may be eliminated. This again is in accordance with the principle of postremity (1948, page 505).

In fairness to the experimenter it must be pointed out that this change of response would have been *recorded* as a failure of prediction by postremity, although on the basis of her theoretical analysis it was no failure at all. Hence her successful predictions by postremity are on the conservative side. The explanation offered for the actual learning (the elimination of an error) seems to come very near to an explanation according to knowledge of results or effect, and gives somewhat specialized meaning to the concept of "doing what you last did."

The second experiment (Voeks, 1954) studied conditioned eyelid responses of human subjects, measuring both the occurrence of the responses and their amplitudes. The question asked was this: "Is a stimulus–response connection gradually strengthened by reinforcement, or is a stimulus–response connection established suddenly, in all-or-none fashion?" Hull is said to favor gradual strengthening, Guthrie all-or-none appearance of responses, according to Voeks's postulates 1 and 2.

Two tests were made of the theory of gradual strengthening, the first studying amplitude, the second frequency. Beginning with the first conditioned response (CR), succeeding responses for each subject were divided into fourths. For only 6 of 32 subjects was there a progressive increase in *amplitude* of CR from quarter to quarter. In general, increases from quarter to quarter were not statistically significant, although for 25 of the 32 subjects the last CR was larger than the first (a significant difference). Amplitude changes thus gave little support to Hull's theory of gradual increase in strength with repeated reinforcement. The *frequency* results were more strikingly in Guthrie's favor, because a response was required in all-or-none fashion. No subject showed an increase in frequency of CR from quarter to quarter following his first CR. Half the subjects gave CR's on every trial after their first one, and there were only a few lapses for the others.

How do Voeks's results compare with the many acquisition curves published for CR's? It is well known that curves for groups of subjects show characteristics very different from curves for individual subjects. Voeks has very convincingly shown that response acquisition may be all-or-none, and yet a group learning curve will show a gradual slope. The accompanying learning curve (Figure 4-2) results, for example, when the prob-

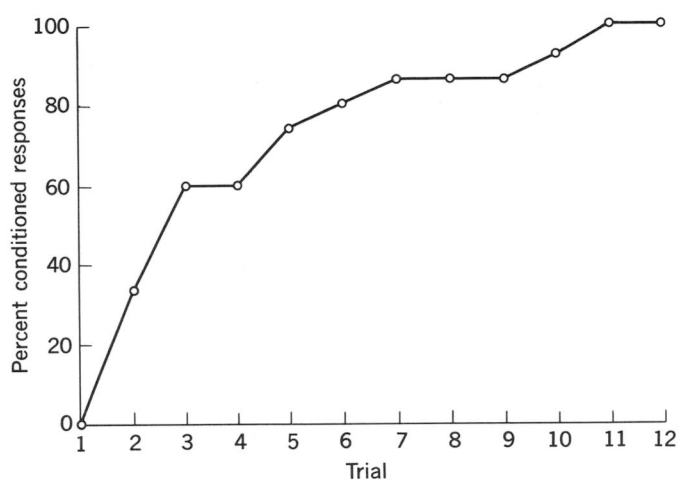

Figure 4-2   Misleading effect of combining individual learning curves. The group curve results from combining the curves of 15 subjects all of whom had jumpwise curves, i.e., a run of no responses followed by consistent responding. After Voeks (1954, page 145).

ability of response is plotted as a group function for 15 subjects all of whom had jumpwise curves, that is, all of whom responded consistently with CR's after the first CR was made. The form of the curve is determined solely by the trial on which the first CR happened to appear for different subjects.[9]

Voeks predicted jumpwise curves of learning under the very uniform

[9] Not all individual conditioning curves are of Voek's jumpwise type. Many acquisition curves showing gradual acquisition have been published for single learners: dogs, rats, human subjects. For individual curves of eyelid conditioning (the response Voeks studied) see Hilgard (1931), page 14; Cohen, Hilgard, and Wendt (1933), page 64.

conditions of stimulation that she arranged to produce, and her predictions were well borne out. A jumpwise curve is, of course, ideal for a test of the postremity principle: if there is an unbroken run of no responses, the prediction by postremity is perfect during the course of this run; if this is followed by an unbroken run of conditioned responses, prediction by postremity is perfect then, too. The prediction fails for only one trial (that on which the conditioning occurs!). By the test of postremity prediction, Guthrie's theory was beautifully confirmed. Of the total predictions made, 84.6 percent were correct.

What are we to do with the fact that an unconditioned response of the eyelid *did* occur (within $\frac{1}{2}$ second of the conditioned stimulus) on every trial from the beginning? Does not Voeks's Postulate 1 lead us to expect a conditioned response right away? Why does the CR wait for several trials (as many as 10) before it makes its appearance? Perhaps there is something to the group curve after all, showing that the probability of giving the *first* CR increases with the number of reinforcements. The postremity principle cannot predict when the first CR appears, because its appearance *always* violates the principle (at least, so far as *recorded* responses are concerned).

This leads us to consider another postulate. There is a frequency principle in Guthrie's system, stated in Voeks's Postulate 3. It is the principle that cues are assimilated to a response with practice, and, conversely, cues are alienated during forgetting. According to Guthrie:

The strengthening of an S–R connection with repetition may very possibly be the result of the enlistment of increasing numbers of stimuli as conditioners (1930, page 420).

But why should practice make the effect increasingly certain? Is it not quite possible that on successive practice periods more and more conditioners are enlisted, so that after twenty periods there is a high probability that the cue will have enough support to be effective? (1935, page 100).

Although this interpretation is very plausible, it makes it difficult to find a crucial test of Guthrie's theory. If one-trial learning suffices, then either the basic principle of association, or the related principle of postremity, is confirmed; if learning is gradual, then the principle of probability is confirmed. Only as the principles are made more precise will it be possible to find exceptions and hence improve the theory. Estes (1950) has given a more precise statement of Guthrie's probability principle and worked it out in a form suitable for critical testing. He regards a stimulus, or stimulating situation, as a finite population of relatively small, independent, environmental events, of which only a sample is effective at any given time. Each occurrence produces conditioning of the momentary effective sample of stimulus elements. Estes acknowledges that the line of argument is the one developed by Guthrie (Estes, 1950, page

100). We shall return to the details of Estes' theory later, as we consider other mathematical and probabilistic theories.

The work of Voeks and of Estes well illustrates the steps needed to make Guthrie's theory more suitable for experimental testing. While the theory was undergoing formalization, a number of aspects of it were undergoing experimental tests. It is difficult to summarize these briefly, because most of the experiments require, in addition to the presentation of their data, the elaboration of an argument to show how the data lead to a preference for one interpretation over another. A few representative studies are listed in Table 4-1 merely to indicate the kind of work that has gone on, and to provide a "search-pattern" for those who wish to seek out the newer studies that are appearing right along.

SHEFFIELD'S EXTENSION OF CONTIGUOUS CONDITIONING TO PERCEPTUAL RESPONSES

Those influenced by Guthrie's theories are not limited, of course, to the formalizing and testing of what Guthrie said, but they are free to extend the theory through making use of its orientation in novel ways. An interesting and important extension was made by F. D. Sheffield (1961) in developing a theory to explain the learning of complex sequential tasks from demonstrations and practice.[10]

The faithfulness of Sheffield's general orientation to that of Guthrie is clear:

A fundamental assumption underlying all of the theoretical considerations is that learning *per se* requires only association by contiguity. This process will usually be referred to as "conditioning" (1961, page 14).

An important additional assumption is that *sensory responses* exist which are completely central in locus and need not have any motor components. These responses are, in their substance, un-Guthrian (since Guthrie's behaviorism allowed only for movements and secretions as responses) but in their functional relationships they are completely Guthrian:

Such sensory responses are assumed to be subject to the learning principles of association by contiguity and are assumed to have cue properties as well as response properties. That is, a sensory response can not only be connected to a

[10] The bearing of Sheffield's theory on practical aspects of instruction will be considered in Chapter 15. For the present it may be noted that not only Sheffield, but Lumsdaine, the editor of the volume in which Sheffield's paper appeared, and Maccoby, a collaborator with Sheffield in some of the experimentation, were all Guthrie's students as undergraduates; although each took his Ph.D. degree elsewhere, the theoretical orientation of each of these three men has remained close to this original imprinting.

Table 4-1   Some Experimental Results Bearing on Guthrie's Theory

Experimenter and Date of Report	General Nature of Experiment and Findings	Relationship to Guthrie's Theory as Stated by Experimenter
Seward (1942)	Rats learned to press a bar more readily when rewarded by food than when merely removed after pressing the bar.	"The superiority of the rewarded animals was marked. . . . In this respect Guthrie's theory appears inadequate."
Seward, Dill, and Holland (1944)	Human subjects given task of finding a correct button in response to each of a series of colors. Some colors shown twice paired with different buttons. In recall, with new order of stimuli, subjects more often responded with first response than with second (postextreme) response.	". . . These findings challenge the general validity of Guthrie's proposition and call for an examination of the conditions under which it does or does not hold."
V. F. Sheffield (1949)	In alley experiment with rats, after massed training resistance to extinction was greater for 50 percent reinforcement group than for 100 percent; groups did not differ, however, after spaced training.	"These results verify a prediction from a hypothesis utilizing stimulus–response learning concepts" ("such as those used by Guthrie and Hull").
Kimball and Kendall (1953)	Rats learned to avoid shock by turning a wheel when a light came on preceding the shock. Extinction was either by a "toleration" method, in which the conditioned stimulus came on gradually, or by the usual "exhaustion" method, with nonreinforcement of conditioned stimulus presented at full strength. Extinction was more rapid by toleration method.	"This result confirms one of Guthrie's theoretical ideas and necessitates a reformulation of Hull's theory of extinction."
Zeaman and Radner (1953)	Rat learns response that turns light off but not one that turns light on.	"Guthrie's theory as formalized by Voeks is not directly confirmed. The crucialness of the data for Guthrie's theory is seen to be dependent upon the outcome of further research on the nature of the rat's unlearned response to light."
Wickens and Platt (1954)	Finger withdrawal for one group conditioned to tone that ceased when .450 sec shock began; for other group tone continued with shock. Difference in conditioning not significant.	"The results of this experiment would seem to be predicted more readily by the type of theory advanced by Mowrer than by Guthrie's strict contiguity theory. . . . It is likely, however, that Guthrie's theory could handle the results through the use of the concept of movement-produced stimuli."

cue, but also is a cue to which other responses can be connected (1961, page 14).

The position taken here is that what is usually called "perception" refers to cases in which the immediate sensory stimulation is not only eliciting its innate sensory responses, but is also eliciting other sensory responses which have been conditioned to the immediate stimulation in past experience (1961, page 15).

What consequences flow from the introduction of these sensory responses? For one thing, they allow for the occurrence and utilization of what historically have been called memory images. Thus perceptual responses commonly give a full representation of a distinctive stimulus *object,* even in the absence of that object, or when the given stimuli incompletely represent it.

[A] wristwatch is completely "transparent" to a skilled watch repairman. From the outside he can note the distinctive brand and model; this is sufficient for him to "fill in" all the internal parts—their sizes, shapes, arrangements, and so forth. When he takes the watch apart, he is completely prepared for everything he sees because his anticipatory conditioned sensory responses correspond with immediate unconditioned sensory responses when he opens it and makes the inner works visible (1961, page 16).

This manner of speaking frees this kind of behaviorism from the necessity of finding movement intermediaries for sensing and thinking, and makes it simpler to deal with the problems of patterned perception than it was when behaviorism required that such patterns be carried by speech mechanisms or other movements.

Some of the implications of introducing sensory or perceptual responses follow (1961, pages 16-25):

1. Because sensory responses have both cue and response properties, the various responses associated with an object become "cross-conditioned" so that as soon as one sensory response is elicited by an object, the total perceptual response appropriate to that object tends to be aroused. Such a response was earlier called a redintegrated response (e.g., Hollingworth, 1928). This relatively stable patterned response also serves as a cue, as for example, in eliciting the name "orange" from the olfactory orange as well as from the visual orange.

2. In addition to the formation of stable perceptual patterns through experience, sensory conditioning provides also for the integration of response sequences or chains. All those later portions of a sequence which can occur simultaneously with earlier portions tend to move forward, so that the sequence is more highly patterned and stable than it would be if events were simply chained in an a-b-c order. Such integration of sequences applies both to well-coordinated motor habits and to perceptual sequences whose responses are presumably central.

3. Supraordinate sequences may be formed in which the subordinate sequences are themselves "natural units" which serve as "elements" in the new sequence. A "natural unit" has a common and distinctive context, different from other parts of the task. Thus in the game of golf, "putting" is in the context of the putting green, whereas "driving" is in the context of tees, fairways, and the rough. "Learning to play golf" is therefore divisible into at least the two "natural units" of putting and driving. A sensible solution of the part–whole problem requires the identification of such "natural units."

4. Some perceptual mediation occurs without the formation of an overt serial chain, that is, without requiring the acquisition of a perceptual sequence. Learning from demonstrations is often of this sort in which *perceptual "blueprints"* are formed and followed in reconstructing the called-for responses. Sheffield recognized the similarity here to the "cognitive maps" of Tolman (1948b). It may be noted that "natural units" facilitate perceptual "blueprinting."

Sheffield lists a number of related hypotheses (1961, pages 25-30), but the four listed principles suffice to illustrate the flavor of his supplement to Guthrie.

The two main points to be noted are (1) the many references·to the possibility that sensory responses may be central, without movement, and (2) the emphasis upon "perceptual patterning" and "natural units." While the Gestalt-like nature of these references is recognized, Sheffield believes that, by contrast with Gestalt theory, he has not *assumed* perceptual structure, but has *deduced* it from such principles as cross-conditioning (1961, page 18).

It is unimportant whether or not Sheffield's emendations of Guthrie's theory have made concessions to other theories, such as those of Tolman and the Gestalt theorists. In any case, he has brought the theory into contact with important aspects of learning with which the theory had not dealt earlier in any such detail.

ESTIMATE OF GUTHRIE'S POSITION

Guthrie's Position on Typical Problems of Learning

By way of comparative summary, how Guthrie stood on the several representative problems of learning will be briefly stated.

1. Capacity. Problems of capacity are not formally treated, although species differences are recognized and allowance is made for maturation as a determiner of many classes of acts (1935, pages 18, 38). Presumably any response which the organism can make can become associated with any stimulus to which he is sensitive—a generalization about the possibility of learning which is reminiscent of what Thorndike says about associative shifting. If pressed, Guthrie could find a basis for differences in capacity both in the differentiation of movement and in the discrimination among proprioceptive cues. All animals are not equally versatile and equally equipped with receptors.

2. Practice. Practice assimilates and alienates cues, until a whole family of stimulus combinations comes to evoke a whole family of responses which lead to the outcome socially described as successful performance. Because skill represents a population of habits, learning appears to accumulate with repetition, although basically each individual habit is learned at full strength in a single repetition.

3. Motivation. Motivation affects learning indirectly through what it causes the animal to do. Reward is a secondary or derivative principle, not a primary one as in Thorndike's system. Reward works because it removes the animal from the stimulating situation in which the "correct" response has been made. It does not strengthen the "correct" response, but prevents its weakening because no new response can become attached to the cues which led to the correct response. Thus there is a relative strengthening, because responses to other cues get alienated.

Punishment does at once several different things. In general, its effects for learning are determined by what it causes the organism to do, according to the principle that the best predictor of learning is the response in the situation that last occurred. We may distinguish four cases:

a. Mild punishment may be merely exciting, and enchance ongoing behavior without disrupting it.

b. More intense punishment may break up a prior habit by leading to incompatible behavior in the presence of the cues for the earlier habit.

c. Continuing punishment acts like a drive, producing maintaining stimuli that keep the organism active until it finds relief. Then the consequence for learning is really that of reward: the act that leads to safety is rewarding because it terminates the punishment and by removing the maintaining stimuli protects from unlearning the activities carried on in the presence of those stimuli.

d. Stimuli that have previously accompanied the punishment produce behavior that formerly occurred following the punishment itself. Here we have an illustration of anticipatory response, essential to avoidance behavior. The cues to avoidance must earlier have been present at the time of punishment for this anticipation to occur.

4. Understanding. Concepts like "insight" are handled in a derisive manner, although it is recognized that learning with foresight of its consequences may occur. The tendency is to talk down such learning, however, just as Thorndike did, and to emphasize the mechanical and repetitious nature of most human as well as animal learning. Such learning with intention and foresight as does occur is explained on the basis of conditioned anticipatory or readiness reactions, based upon past experience and hence not contradicting association principles.

5. *Transfer.* Learning transfers to new situations because of common elements within the old and new. In this the position is rather like Thorndike's. Stress is laid, however, on the identity being carried by way of common responses evoked, the proprioceptive stimuli being sufficiently similar from responses to a variety of stimuli to evoke common conditioned responses. The emphasis upon movement-produced stimuli thus represents Guthrie's supplementation to Thorndike.

Because of his principle of responses being conditioned to all adventitious contiguous stimuli, Guthrie expects rather little transfer and is, in fact, rather extreme about it. The only way to be sure to get desired behavior in a new situation is to practice in that new situation as well. To be able to perform in a variety of situations, you have to practice in a variety of situations.

6. *Forgetting.* Learning is said to be permanent unless interfered with by new learning. Hence all forgetting is due to the learning of new responses which replace the old responses. It may take place gradually for the same reason that skills may be acquired gradually: remembering depends upon many habits to many cues, and subhabits may drop out gradually as subcues become attached to new responses.

In contrast to Thorndike, Guthrie was an avowed behaviorist who made it a matter of some importance to get rid of subjective terms, to refer, for example, to inner speech instead of to thinking. The emphasis upon movement-produced stimuli was part of the older behaviorist tradition which Guthrie carried into the present. While an orthodox behaviorist in these respects, his was an informal behaviorism, with little of the brittleness of earlier Watsonianism. We have already seen how it permitted itself in Sheffield's hands to adapt itself to nonmovement response learning.

Invulnerability of the Theory a Cause for Skepticism

The uncertainty that exists in practically all learning experimentation makes the fact-minded psychologist suspicious of a finished system at this stage of our knowledge. While scientific truth must eventually have exceptionless validity—if its laws are truly lawful—the history of our most advanced sciences shows that their theories move by successive approximations, and the most advanced theories do not emerge full blown from the head of the theorist. Even as loose a system as Thorndike's went through revisions on the basis of evidence regarding the effects of punishment; Hull's system was continuously being revamped to meet experimental fact. One of the sources of uneasiness about Guthrie's system lies in its assured answers to the problems of learning—answers that remained unchanged through more than a quarter of a century of the most active psychological experimentation we have ever known. Experimental controversies finally get resolved as we learn more about the independent variables that modify the measured consequences. No matter how these issues get resolved, Guthrie's system remains unchanged. Either the theory is a miraculously inspired one or it is not stated very precisely, and hence is not very sensitive to experimental data.

Criticism of Guthrie's position is rendered somewhat difficult by the nature of the task which he set himself. It is not quite clear whether he believed his system to have any responsibility with respect to details.

The principle of association or conditioning is not an explanation of any instance of behavior. It is merely a tool by which explanation is furthered. A tool is not true or false; it is useful or useless (1935, page 232).

The paradox of the theory lies in the kind of sophistication implied in this statement, combined with a casualness which baffles the critic. It is not unfair to ask of the position that it substantiate its claims, which are, indeed, far-reaching and are competitive with the claims of others.

Of the opposing points of view to which he objected, Guthrie generously admitted that their phenomena and the terms used to describe them were correct and useful for certain purposes.[11] What he said in essence is that what they do is all right for limited purposes, but it is not very helpful so far as understanding ordinary learning is concerned. All other writers were said to be concerned with outcomes, in the form of success of goal achievement. Under their theories, he said, the teacher must be a mere passive element in the situation and cannot be told how to influence the outcome (1942, page 47). This *non sequitur* indicated a failure to take opposing claims seriously. Insight, he said, if not predicted on the basis of past experience, must be in the category of luck, and hence lies outside of science (1935, page 25). While many of Guthrie's observations were astute, a cavalier handling of serious alternatives to his own gave an impression of immutability inappropriate in a growing science.

[11] See Guthrie's comments on Tolman, Hull, Skinner and others, Guthrie (1952), pages 189-252. These pages were new to the revised edition of his book on learning, although the orientation was unchanged from views expressed much earlier, e.g., Guthrie (1942), page 57.

The Simplicity of the Theory May Be Illusory

Certainly much of the fascination of Guthrie's theory rests upon his ability to deduce a wide range of phenomena from the single principle of one-trial contiguous association. Parsimonious scientific theories are attractive, and this is the ultimate in reductionist theories. Although Voeks found it convenient to state four postulates, with proper definitions of the stimuli and responses entering into association, she could have found one to be enough, with the other three as corollaries.

A painstaking search through Guthrie's writings for careful definition of stimulus and response, for distinctions between observables and constructs, for statements taking the form of predictions and those taking the form of *a posteriori* explanations, led critics to conclude:

> While the principles of conditioning which he expands seem to have a parsimony that would be desirable in a theoretical formulation of behavior, a closer analysis reveals that a formidable set of additional assumptions and constructs are required if his theory is to possess any real applicability to experimental data (Mueller and Schoenfeld, 1954, page 377).

> It is undoubtedly true that many reviews of Guthrie in the literature have mistaken incompleteness for simplicity (Mueller and Schoenfeld, 1954, page 368).

GUTHRIE'S LASTING CONTRIBUTIONS

Despite his formal concern with the more hard-boiled aspects of scientific observation and scientific logic, Guthrie was without a peer in the use of anecdote and illustration to make pertinent comments about the activities of everyday life, including the symptoms found in the psychological clinic. This complicated material he talked about in dramatically simple terms, and his theory makes this kind of talk possible. The difference between plausibility and proof is one of the differences that hounds psychological science, and a theory that is not sensitive to experimental data will not be sensitive either to those clinical patients who do not get well following good advice. Nevertheless, there is something to be learned from Guthrie's type of psychologizing, and it is not a sufficient explanation to remark that he was a wise and experienced person, a shrewd observer of human beings. His kind of psychologizing is appealing enough to have led many promising young men and women to enter upon productive careers in psychology—a contribution to the field not to be overlooked.

At the experimental level, Guthrie's greatest contribution was to call attention to the large element of repetitiveness and stereotypy in behavior when the opportunities are favorable to such monotonous behavior. The tendency toward smugness is easily overlooked, especially by those who choose to study the changes in behavior called learning.

There are enough well-trained younger psychologists friendly to Guthrie's ideas to continue the task of increasing the rigor of his system beyond that yet attained. The promise of the system is great enough to make the effort worthwhile.

SUPPLEMENTARY READINGS

The two following books, available also in more recent paperbound editions, give Guthrie's own theory:

GUTHRIE, E. R. (1935) (1952) *The psychology of learning.*

GUTHRIE, E. R. (1938) *The psychology of human conflict.*

His own shorter summaries, which show how little the theory changed over the years, can be found in the following three accounts:

GUTHRIE, E. R. (1930) Conditioning as a principle of learning. *Psychol. Rev.,* 37, 412-428.

GUTHRIE, E. R. (1942) Conditioning: A theory of learning in terms of stimulus, response and association. Chapter 1 in *The psychology of learning.* Natl. Soc. Stud. Educ., 41st Yearbook, Part II, 17-60.

GUTHRIE, E. R. (1959) Association by contiguity. In Koch, S. (Editor) *Psychology, a study of a science,* Vol. 2, 158-195.

For a critical review of Guthrie's contributions from the point of view of the logic of science and system-making, see:

MUELLER, C. G., JR., and SCHOENFELD, W. N. (1954) Edwin R. Guthrie. In W. K. Estes and others. *Modern learning theory,* 345-379.

For another evaluation of Guthrie's contribution, and of the changes made by his followers, see:

HILL, W. F. (1964) Contemporary developments within stimulus–response learning theory. Chapter II in *Theories of learning and instruction.* Natl. Soc. Stud. Educ., 63rd Yearbook, Part I, 27-53, esp. 40-46.

For the manner in which Guthrie's theory has evolved in the hands of Fred D. Sheffield, see his two papers, Sheffield (1966a, 1966b).

5

Skinner's Operant Conditioning

In a series of papers beginning in 1930, B. F. Skinner (b. 1904) proposed a formulation of behavior which arose out of observations of animal performance in a type of experiment that he invented: the bar-pressing activity of a rat in a specially designed box called (by others) the Skinner box. The experiments and theories were first brought together in book form in his *Behavior of organisms* (1938). Experimentation has continued, much of it using a new organism (the pigeon) and a new equivalent of bar-pressing (the pigeon's pecking at a spot). The principles have become the basis for two textbooks of general psychology, Keller and Schoenfeld's *Principles of psychology* (1950), Skinner's *Science and human behavior* (1953a), and a programed textbook, Holland and Skinner's *The analysis of behavior* (1961). As an avowed behaviorism making use of conditioning principles, the system can be understood as a development of the ground broken by Thorndike, just as Guthrie's system can be so understood. But if Guthrie's theory is thought of as a development of Thorndike's associative shifting, Skinner's operant conditioning is a development more along the lines of Thorndike's learning by selecting and connecting under the law of effect. As we shall see, Skinner acknowledges two kinds of learning, just as Thorndike did, but, unlike Guthrie, he places more emphasis upon that kind of learning which is under the control of its consequences.

RESPONDENT AND OPERANT BEHAVIOR

The greatest break with conventional stimulus–response psychology within Skinner's system is the distinction between respondent and operant behavior. Conventional stimulus–response psychology enforced the dictum "no stimulus, no response" by assuming the presence of stimuli when a response occurred though no stimuli were identifiable. Although it was often convenient to talk about "random" or "spontaneous" responses, it was not doubted that stimuli were present to elicit them, if the experimenter only had means of detecting them. Skinner finds this method of forcing facts both undesirable and unnecessary. He proposes that two classes of response be distinguished, a class of *elicited* responses and a class of *emitted* responses.

Respondent and Operant Distinguished

Responses which are elicited by known stimuli are classified as *respondents*. Pupillary constriction to light and the knee jerk to a blow on the patellar tendon serve as convenient illustrations. There is a second class of responses which need not be correlated with any known stimuli. These *emitted* responses are designated *operants,* to distinguish them from respondents. While the conventional treatment of such responses is to consider them as respondents with unknown stimuli, Skinner holds the conviction that the stimulus conditions, if any, are irrelevant to the understanding of operant behavior. Because operant behavior is not elicited by recognized stimuli, its strength cannot be measured according to the usual laws of the reflex, which are all stated as functions of stimuli. Instead, rate of response is used as a measure of operant strength.

An operant may, and usually does, acquire a relation to prior stimulation. In that case it becomes a *discriminated operant;* the stimulus becomes an occasion for the operant behavior, but is not an eliciting stimulus as in the case of a true reflex. Skinner formerly extended the term "reflex" to cover the operant, although this proved somewhat awkward because several of the laws of the reflex do not apply. A simple illustration of an operant coordinated with a stimulus would be a reaction-time experiment as commonly conducted in the psychological laboratory. The correlation between stimulus and response may easily be changed, as by instructions to depress the key instead of lifting the finger from it. The relationship of latency of response to changes in stimulus intensity is very different for a discriminated operant from what it is for an elicited response, say the lid reflex to sound—a respondent. Such a comparison between a discriminated operant and a respondent was made by Peak

(1933). Although the characteristics of voluntary and reflex eyelid responses both were changed in response to sounds differing in loudness, the magnitudes of changes differed for the two kinds of response.

𝑥 Most human behavior is operant in character. The behavior of eating a meal, driving a car, writing a letter, shows but little of respondent character. The emphasis which Skinner places upon operant behavior is appropriate if he is going to have something to say that applies in principle to the commonest forms of human (and animal) behavior.

Two Types of Conditioning

Related to the two types of response there are said to be two types of conditioning.

The conditioning of respondent behavior is assigned to Type S, because reinforcement is correlated with stimuli. The conditioned stimulus (e.g., a tone) is presented together with the unconditioned stimulus (e.g., food) and thus comes to elicit the response (e.g., salivation). The reinforcing event that interests Skinner is the presentation of the unconditioned stimulus, not the response to it. Pavlov's classical conditioning experiment is said to be of Type S. Its two laws are the Law of Conditioning of Type S, and the Law of Extinction of Type S (1938, pages 18-19). The law of conditioning makes such conditioning depend upon the approximate simultaneity of stimuli. The evidence for the existence of Type S conditioning is actually quite slim, because much that by experimental arrangement conforms to classical conditioning is better understood as a consequence of factors other than contiguity of stimulus and response. Hull, as we shall see, denied the existence of conditioning of Type S; Skinner admits that it does not appear experimentally in pure form (1938, page 238). But Skinner does not attribute much importance to Type S in any case. Whether or not there is such conditioning (i.e., contiguous conditioning with no operant reinforcement) does not matter too much to his system.

Type R he believes to be much the more important. This is the conditioning of operant behavior, and the letter R is used to call attention to the important term in the correlation with reinforcement. In this case it is a *response* which is correlated with reinforcement. The experimental example which he originally used was lever-pressing. This response may be strengthened by following it with food. It is not the *sight* of the lever which is important; it is the *pressing* of the lever. The conditioned response does not resemble the response to the reinforcing stimulus; its relationship to the reinforcing stimulus is that it causes it to appear. In operant conditioning, conditioning of Type R, reinforcement cannot follow unless the conditioned response appears; reinforcement is *contingent upon response*. Two of the laws of Type R are not unlike those of Type S, including a law of conditioning and a law of extinction. The law of conditioning of Type R may be compared to Thorndike's law of effect: *If the occurrence of an operant is followed by presentation of a reinforcing stimulus, the strength is increased* (1938, page 21). Note that the reinforcing situation is defined by its stimulus; nothing is said about satisfying aftereffects or about drive reduction. What gets strengthened is not a stimulus–response connection, because the operant requires no stimulus; this statement by Skinner is unlike Thorndike:

This dependence upon the posterior reinforcing stimulus gives the term operant its significance. . . . The operant . . . becomes significant for behavior and takes on an identifiable form when it acts upon the environment in such a way that a reinforcing stimulus is produced (1938, page 22).

The mechanical arrangement under which Type R conditioning is usually demonstrated is that suggested by the quotation, a situation in which the response of the organism produces the reinforcing agent. This is what came to be called instrumental conditioning to distinguish it from the arrangements of classical conditioning (Hilgard and Marquis, 1940, pages 51-74).[1]

One suggestion offered quite tentatively by Skinner (1938, page 112) is that conditioning of Type S may be limited to autonomic responses, Type R to skeletal behavior. The crucial question is whether Type S occurs at all; if it does, it may well be limited to autonomic responses. That Type R occurs is evident, and most skeletal responses, including those obtained under the arrangements of classical conditioning, can easily be shown to conform to the pattern of discriminated operants. Actual experiments in which autonomic conditioning takes place (salivation, galvanic response) are full of indirect accompaniments of Type R. When the circumstances seem almost ideal for demonstrating Type S conditioning, as in attempts to condition pupillary constriction by presenting a tone along with a light, it is extremely difficult to obtain any conditioning at all.[2]

REINFORCEMENT OF AN OPERANT

In order to get at the quantitative relationships within operant conditioning, Skinner designed a special apparatus suitable for use with white rats. It consists essentially of a darkened sound-resisting box in which the

[1] See also Chapter 3, pages 63-65.

[2] As pointed out by Kimble (1961, footnote 2, page 51), success in pupillary conditioning has been found almost exclusively in experiments in which the unconditioned reflex was elicited by shock; when light has been used as the unconditioned stimulus, experiments have been notably unsuccessful. This gives some support to Skinner's conjecture that Type S is limited to autonomic responses, but since the pupillary response is autonomic in any case, something more has to be said about when Type S is to be expected.

rat is placed. There is a small brass lever within the compartment which, if pressed, delivers a pellet of food. The lever is connected with a recording system which produces a graphical tracing of the number of lever pressings plotted against the length of time that the rat is in the box. By a carefully controlled handling of the animals, remarkably consistent and "lawful" results can be obtained. Modifications of the experiment can be introduced so that food is not delivered every time the lever is depressed. The consequences of doing this and of making other changes in the situation have been systematically reported. The "pigeon-box" is a corresponding arrangement for obtaining a response record as a pigeon pecks at a spot and is reinforced by receiving grain.

The evident consequence of the reinforcement of an operant is to increase the rate with which the operant response is emitted. This increase in rate of responding is an indicator of the increased probability of response, which is an appropriate measure of *operant strength;* other measures, such as amplitude and latency, are more appropriate for measuring the strength of a respondent. While the expression *reflex strength* was originally used for both respondent and operant behavior (1938, page 20), in Skinner's later writings he tends to restrict the word "reflex" to its ordinary meaning of elicited reflexes (salivation, knee-jerk), and to conditioned reflexes based on them, that is, to respondent behavior (1938, pages 45-59).

Extinction as a Measure of Operant Strength

When an operant is regularly reinforced, the rate of responding is interrupted by the activity of eating. Because the time-consuming act of eating does not occur during extinction, responses within extinction serve better than responses during conditioning as measures of the consequences of reinforcement. Two measures of responses within extinction are commonly used: *rate of responding,* and the *total number of responses* before responding returns to its normal rate prior to conditioning. The total number of responses during extinction, now often described as resistance to extinction, was formerly called the *reflex reserve* (1938, page 26), a figure of speech to describe a kind of reservoir of responses ready to be emitted during extinction. Skinner no longer believes the concept of a reflex reserve to be very useful, although he appears to reject it because of his later interpretation of appropriate scientific concepts rather than because of any change in the factual relationships described (1950, page 203).

A single reinforcement suffices to produce a number of conditioned operant responses in extinction. After receiving a single pellet of food following one pressing of the bar, a rat may respond 50 or more times, yielding a typical extinction curve. Additional reinforcements add slowly to the number of responses during extinction. An extinction curve following a single reinforcement and one following 250 reinforcements are reproduced in Figure 5-1. The curves are cumulative ones, not to be confused with learning curves as usually plotted. As the curve levels off it means that responses have stopped; as the curve is constructed it is not possible for it to fall.

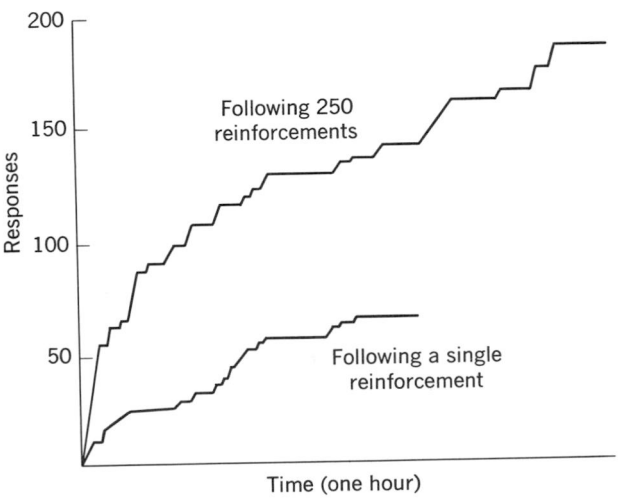

Time (one hour)

Figure 5-1   **Extinction of level-pressing by rats following a single reinforcement and following 250 reinforcements. Although several times as many responses are emitted after 250 reinforcements as after a single reinforcement, it is evident that the total number of responses does not increase in direct proportion to the number of reinforcements. Data from Skinner (1933) and F. S. Keller and A. Kerr (unpublished data) replotted from Skinner (1938, pages 87 and 91). Both curves have been moved back so that time is here shown as measured from the first response.**

The considerable influence of a single reinforcement leads Skinner to conjecture that, if we were able to isolate a single operant, we might find an instantaneous change to a maximum probability (1953a, page 68). This conjecture, we may note, is very similar to that of Guthrie with respect to one-trial learning. The further conjecture that actual conditioning is found to be gradual because several component operants are involved is also not unlike Guthrie. The residual difference is that the single event for Skinner is a reinforcement, whereas for Guthrie it was a mere occurrence.

The importance of single reinforcements ("one-trial learning") is brought out in two arrangements which have come to prominence in Skinner's later work. The first of these is the development of "superstitious" behavior. The second is the control of behavior through successive approximations.

If there is only an accidental connection between the response and the appearance of a reinforcer, the behavior is called "superstitious." We may demonstrate this in the pigeon by accumulating the effect of several accidental contingencies. Suppose we give a pigeon a small amount of food every fifteen seconds regardless of what it is doing. When the food is first given, the pigeon will be behaving in some way—if only standing still—and conditioning will take place. It is then more probable that the same behavior will be in progress when the food is given again. If this proves to be the case, the "operant" will be further strengthened. If not, some other behavior will be strengthened. Eventually a given bit of behavior reaches a frequency at which it is often reinforced. It then becomes a permanent part of the repertoire of the bird, even though the food has been given by a clock which is unrelated to the bird's behavior. Conspicuous responses which have been established in this way include turning sharply to one side, hopping from one foot to the other and back, bowing and scraping, turning around, strutting, and raising the head. The topography of the behavior may continue to drift with further reinforcements, since slight modifications in the form of response may coincide with the receipt of food (1953a, page 85).

If, for example, three reinforcements were always required in order to change the probability of a response, superstitious behavior would be unlikely. It is only because organisms have reached the point at which a single contingency makes a substantial change that they are vulnerable to coincidences (1953a, page 87).

Positive and Negative Primary Reinforcers

A reinforcer is defined by its effects. Any stimulus is a reinforcer if it increases the probability of a response. The stimuli that happen to act as reinforcers fall into two classes (1953a, page 73):

1. A *positive reinforcer* is a stimulus which, when added to a situation, strengthens the probability of an operant response. Food, water, sexual contact, classify as positive reinforcers.

2. A *negative reinforcer* is a stimulus which, when removed from a situation, strengthens the probability of an operant response. A loud noise, a very bright light, extreme heat or cold, electric shock, classify as negative reinforcers.

Notice that the effect of reinforcement is always to *increase* the probability of response. Punishment is something other than negative reinforcement as here defined. While a reinforcer is defined by its effects, this is not true for punishment. Punishment, according to Skinner and his followers, is defined as an experimental arrangement whose effects remain to be investigated empirically. The *arrangement* is the opposite of reinforcement (although the *effects* are not opposite), so that two main cases arise: (1)

the presentation of a negative reinforcer, and (2) the removal of a positive reinforcer. We shall return later to a consideration of the consequences of punishment.

Other psychologists have been interested in the question, Why is a reinforcer reinforcing?, but this question has not been of much interest to Skinner. He is interested in why behavior changes, and finds reinforcers importantly involved.

He rather tentatively accepts an explanation of reinforcement in terms of evolutionary biology, but he does not find it of much help in the detailed functional analysis of what actually occurs (1953a, pages 81-84).

Schedules of Reinforcement

The reinforcement of operant behavior in ordinary life is not regular and uniform. The fisherman does not hook a fish with every cast of the line, and the farmer does not always receive a harvest from his planting, yet they continue to fish and to plant. Hence the problem of maintaining or strengthening a response through *intermittent reinforcement* is more than a laboratory curiosity.[3] Skinner has explored extensively two main classes of intermittent reinforcement, now called *interval reinforcement* and *ratio reinforcement.*

By *fixed-interval reinforcement* he means reinforcement given at standard intervals of time, every 3 minutes or every 10 minutes, at the discretion of the experimenter. In the experiment itself this means the reinforcement of the first response that occurs after that interval of time, so there is actually some slight variation in the time of reinforcement depending upon the activity of the learner. This arrangement, earlier called periodic reconditioning, or periodic reinforcement, delivers a standard amount of reinforcement per hour. It results in lawful rates of responding, the rate being proportional to the interval between reinforcements, the shorter intervals yielding more rapid response rates. Under standard conditions of experimentation and drive, for example, Skinner found in the rat about 18 to 20 responses per reinforcement, over a considerable range of intervals. The uniformity of rates of responding is illustrated in Figures 5-2 and 5-3.

The uniform number of responses per reinforcement is called the *extinction ratio,* that is, the ratio of unreinforced to reinforced responses. The size of the ratio does not change much from one length of interval to another, provided drive remains constant.

Although curves drawn in the scale of Figures 5-2 and 5-3 appear uniform, there is actually a stepwise character to response when reinforce-

---

[3] The expression "intermittent reinforcement" is a better descriptive term than "partial reinforcement," an earlier name for the same arrangement (Hilgard and Marquis, 1940, page 347).

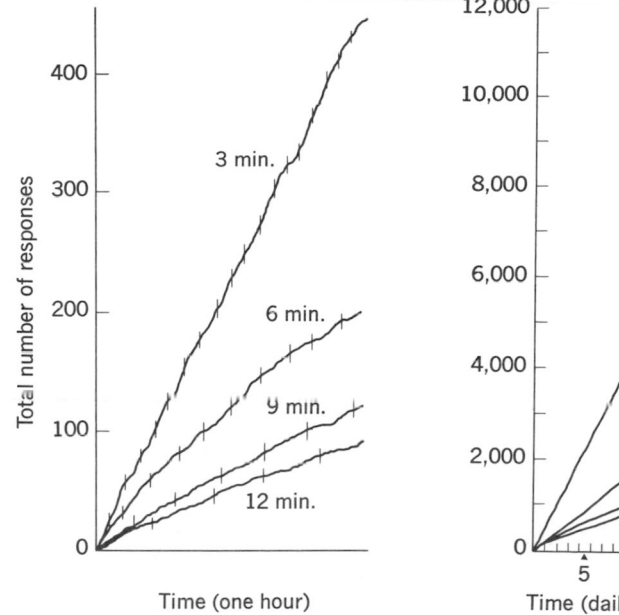

Figure 5-2   Responses within one session of fixed-interval reinforcement. A pellet was delivered every 3, 6, 9, and 12 minutes, respectively. The more frequent the reinforcement, the more rapid the rate of responding, although each rate is relatively uniform. After Skinner (1938), as reproduced by Hilgard and Marquis (1940, page 151).

Figure 5-3   Responses within repeated sessions of fixed-interval reinforcement. Responses of the same rats whose records are given in Figure 5-2 are here accumulated for successive daily sessions. The uniformity of rate persists throughout. When expressed as number of responses per reinforcement this rate is described as the "extinction ratio." After Skinner (1938), as reproduced by Hilgard and Marquis (1940, page 151).

ment is given at regular intervals. This follows because a response is never reinforced shortly after a prior reinforcement, and so, after a time, the rate of responding is low following a reinforcement. This minor fluctuation or scalloping of the curves can be abolished by a modification known as *variable-interval reinforcement* (called aperiodic reinforcement). Under this arrangement, an *average* interval is substituted for a fixed interval, so that, while a response may be reinforced every 5 minutes on the average, in some cases the second reinforcement follows immediately upon an earlier reinforcement, and at other times it is longer delayed. Under such a schedule, performance is remarkably stable and uniform, and highly resistant to extinction. An illustration is found in Figure 5-4. A pigeon has given as many as 10,000 unreinforced responses in extinction following such variable-interval reinforcement.

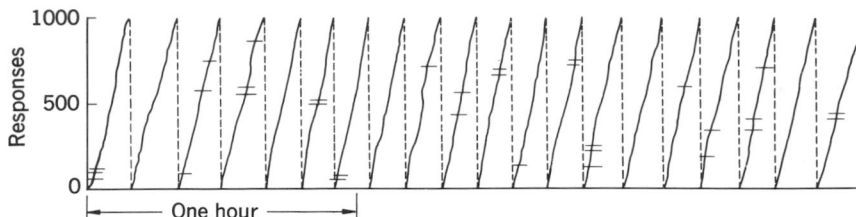

Figure 5-4   Responses within variable-interval reinforcement. The curves are of the pecking responses of an individual pigeon reinforced at intervals ranging from 10 seconds to 21 minutes, but averaging 5 minutes. Each of the sloping lines represents 1,000 responses; the pen resets to zero after each 1,000. The whole record represents some 20,000 responses in about 3 hours, with an average of 12 reinforcements per hour. Each reinforcement is represented by a horizontal dash. From Skinner (1950, page 208).

The results under intermittent reinforcement show how input and output change under different schedules of reinforcement. While the constancy of the extinction ratio under conditions of interval reinforcement suggests a standard input–output ratio, something very different happens under another arrangement of intermittent reinforcement, that known as ratio reinforcement.

In *fixed-ratio reinforcement,* instead of delivering a pellet of food at standard intervals of time, a pellet is delivered after a standard number of responses. In one study they were delivered after 16, 24, 32, 48, 64, 96, or 192 responses. These ratios have to be approached gradually, for such

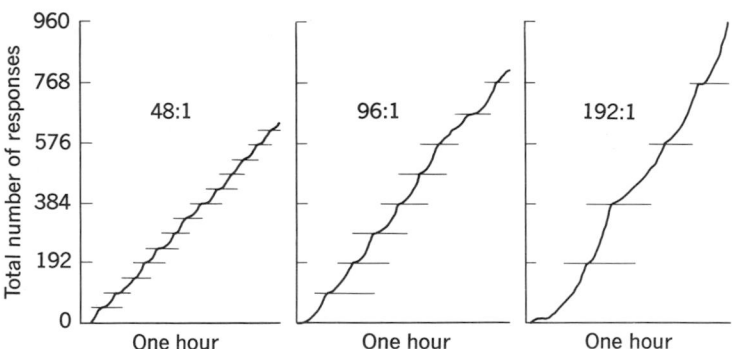

Figure 5-5   Responses within ratio reinforcement. Responses from individual rats reinforced every 48, 96, and 192 responses, as indicated by the horizontal lines. Under these circumstances very high rates of responding develop, the highest rate being found with the lowest frequency of reinforcement. After Skinner (1938), as reproduced by Hilgard and Marquis (1940, page 152).

occasional reinforcements can maintain responses only if responses are already being emitted at a rapid rate. The end-products of such training are shown in Figure 5-5. The somewhat paradoxical finding now is that the less frequent the reinforcement, the more rapid the response! The extinction ratio has changed from the order of 20:1 under interval reinforcement to 200:1 under ratio reinforcement.

The steplike character of performance, mentioned in connection with reinforcement at fixed intervals, is pronounced with reinforcement at large fixed ratios. After the burst of responding just before reinforcement there follows a period of very slow responding just after reinforcement. If the ratio is made too high, there develop long periods of no response following reinforcement, a condition likened by Skinner to "abulia," the inability to expend effort. He points out the analogy with the student who has finished a term paper, perhaps in a burst of speed as the deadline approaches, and then finds it difficult to start work on a new assignment (1953a, page 104).

The pause after reinforcement may be eliminated by adopting *variable-ratio reinforcement,* that is, using a range of ratios around a mean value. Because the probability of reinforcement at any moment remains approximately constant, a uniform rate of responding ensues; because this probability is increased with rapid responding, the rate tends to be high. A pigeon may respond as rapidly as five times per second and keep up this rate for many hours. (This rate corresponds to that of the ticking of a watch.)

Schedules can also be brought under multiple control. For example, by selecting one of three colors to be projected on the key that the pigeon pecks, the pigeon can be put on fixed-interval for one color, fixed-ratio for another, or variable-interval reinforcement for a third, and will behave as it has learned to behave under each of these schedules alone. Skinner has trained a pigeon up to nine different performances under nine different conditions of stimulation.

The possibilities within various schedules of reinforcement are almost unlimited, as Ferster and Skinner (1957) have shown in a large book concerned exclusively with variations on the themes of ratio reinforcement, interval reinforcement, and mixed schedules. They have, in fact, outlined 16 chief classes of schedule, within which there are of course many individual arrangements. These, with their code designations, are as shown in Table 5-1.[4] There are over 900 figures in the Ferster and Skinner book reproducing individual cumulative records obtained under various schedules. The variety is so overwhelming and the descriptions so meticulously

[4] The followers of Skinner have become a fairly large in-group in psychology, with a primary journal (*Journal of the Experimental Analysis of Behavior,* annual volumes beginning in 1958), and a special division of the American Psychological Association. Because of the common tradition, they not infrequently use the coded designations of reinforcement schedules, hence some purpose is served by having a list available.

Table 5-1   Schedules of Reinforcement (After Ferster and Skinner, 1957, pages 3-7; also Chapter 13)

Name and Code Abbreviation	Characterization of Program of Reinforcement
I. *Nonintermittent schedules*	
1. Continuous reinforcement (crf)	Every emitted response reinforced
2. Extinction (ext)	No response reinforced
II. *Schedules of intermittent reinforcement*	
3. Fixed-ratio (FR)	A given ratio of responses to reinforcements is indicated by the addition of a number to the letters FR. Thus in FR 100 the one-hundredth response after the preceding reinforcement is reinforced.
4. Variable-ratio (VR)	A random series of ratios lying between arbitrary values with a fixed mean (as in VR 100).
5. Fixed-interval (FI)	The first response occurring after a given interval of time since the preceding reinforcement is reinforced. The designation, as in FI 5, is normally in minutes.
6. Variable-interval (VI)	A random series of intervals lying between arbitrary values and with a fixed mean, as in VI 5, expressed in minutes.
7. Alternative (alt)	Reinforcement is delivered according to a fixed ratio or fixed interval schedule, whichever is satisfied first; designated as in alt FI 5 FR 300. If 300 responses occur before 5 minutes is over, reinforcement will occur; if not, reinforcement will occur when 5 minutes have elapsed
8. Conjunctive (conj)	The requirements of both the fixed ratio and the fixed interval must be satisfied, e.g., in conj FI 5 FR 300, reinforcement is contingent on at least 5 minutes of time and at least 300 responses.
9. Interlocking (interlock)	This is a decreasing ratio program in which the number of responses required per reinforcement decreases steadily with time after each reinforcement. The organism is, in effect, penalized for responding rapidly enough to be reinforced early, for then more responses are required for reinforcement than if his responses are spread out in time.
10. Tandem (tand)	A single reinforcement is contingent upon the successive completion of two units, each of which would have been reinforced according to a single schedule. Thus in FI 10 FR 5, reinforcement depends upon a response after 10 minutes have passed, followed by 5 additional responses, whatever their spacing.

Table 1 (continued)

Name and Code Abbreviation	Characterization of Program of Reinforcement
11. Chained (chain)	In a tandem schedule there is no change in the stimulus when one of the programs is completed, while in chaining a conspicuous change is introduced. Thus the color of the spot being pecked may change after the FI requirement has been satisfied, but reinforcement is delayed until the FR component has been satisfied.
12. Adjusting (adj)	The value of the interval or the ratio changes systematically as a consequence of reinforcement. (Distinguished from an interlocking schedule because there the change occurs according to responding *between* reinforcements.)
13. Multiple (mult)	Reinforcement is programed by two or more schedules, usually alternating at random. Change from one schedule to another is signalled by a change in the stimulus that endures as long as the schedule is in force.
14. Mixed (mix)	Similar to multiple, except that no stimuli are correlated with the schedules; the shift from one schedule to another has to be detected from the pattern of reinforcement.
15. Interpolated (inter)	A small block of one schedule may be introduced into a background of another schedule, substituting for that other schedule for a few minutes within, say, a 6-hour period under other standard conditions.
16. Concurrent (conc)	Two or more schedules independently arranged but operating at the same time, reinforcements being set up by both.

empirical that it is almost impossible to make summarizing statements that are pertinent. An illustration of the results of a mixed FI–FR schedule will serve to show the kinds of results obtained and how they are presented and discussed. Consider Figure 5-6. In the mixed schedule that determines these results, the bird is reinforced (as shown by the small marks on the rising curves) *either* after its first response following a 10-minute interval (when FI 10 is in force) or after responding 27 times (when FR 27 is in force). Because the schedule may remain the same or may change at any time at the whim of the experimenter, the performance cannot be uniform, though it may develop a fairly stable pattern. A characteristic feature of the pattern is the interval scallop, that is, the fairly flat portion of the curve which indicates almost no responding during the first portion of the 10-minute interval, followed by very rapid responding as the time of reinforcement nears. Rapid responding continues during the period of FR 27, but (in this record) this program is never in force for more than two reinforcements.

The characteristic stable performance is thus described by Skinner:

The bird runs off a number of responses at a high rate. If the current schedule is a ratio schedule, it will then be reinforced. If it is, however, an interval schedule, the bird will run somewhat past the number reinforced as a ratio and then will break suddenly to a zero rate of responding from which emerges a smooth interval scallop extending over the rest of the 15-minute period. That is, the bird "tests" the schedule by running off a number of responses sufficient to achieve reinforcement if the schedule is a ratio; if no reinforcement is forthcoming, the performance "primes" the bird into the interval scallop (Private communication dated December 28, 1954).

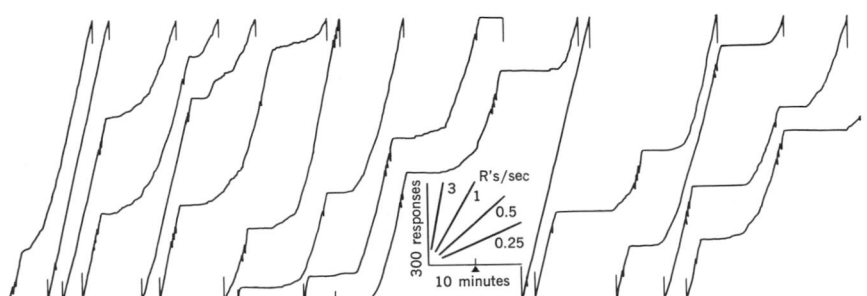

Figure 5-6   Responding under a mixed schedule. The schedule is defined as mix FI 10 FR 27, and the record was obtained from a pigeon after 95 hours of responding by pecking at an orange key. Marks on the curves show when reinforcements were delivered. See text. (Ferster and Skinner, 1957, Figure 787, page 622).

Ferster and Skinner introduced some complications into stimulus arrangements which incorporated the stimuli in new ways into the already complex schedules. Two of these are called the counter and the clock.

A *counter* is a stimulus presented to the behaving organism having some dimension which varies with the number of responses emitted after some anchoring event, such as the last reinforcement. Thus in a fixed-ratio experiment, a visible slit may grow wider and wider as more responses are emitted, reinforcement occurring at the greatest width (continuous counter), or the light may change color as certain milestone frequencies are passed (block counter). The information yielded by the counter affects performance in complex ways not easily stated as a generalization.

A *clock* is available to the learner as a counter is, but it changes with time instead of with responses, and hence is better correlated with fixed-interval programs. With a clock the pigeon tends to postpone response until very near the end of the interval, and then responds rapidly as reinforcement time approaches.

The above discussion does not exhaust the arrangements. For example, there are also schedules differentially reinforcing low rates of responding (drl) or differentially reinforcing high rates (drh).

The more recent experiments, while belonging to the same general family of experiments as those reported in *The behavior of organisms* (1938), show a shift of emphasis. Earlier Skinner's attention was directed to the general course of a change in behavior over an experimental period or through a series of experimental sessions. His primary concern later moved to the moment-to-moment behavior, or as he puts it, to the "fine grain" of the records rather than the over-all course of changes. With this change of emphasis the fundamental measure of response strength became *the momentary probability of responding,* rather than a more global "habit strength" or "reflex reserve." In order to determine a momentary probability, it is of course necessary to study frequency of response over more extended periods of time. Skinner's emphasis upon frequency of response has persisted from his earliest writings, and he has ably defended his choice of this measure (Skinner, 1953b).

Secondary Reinforcement

The principle of secondary reinforcement is simply this:

A stimulus that is not originally a reinforcing one . . . can become reinforcing through repeated association with one that is (Keller and Schoenfeld, 1950, page 232).

That is, through conditioning, a stimulus acquires the power to condition. Consider, for example, the acquisition of reinforcing power by the light in the following experiment. When a rat presses a bar, a light comes on. After one second a pellet of food falls into the tray, reinforcing the bar-pressing. The light remains on for two seconds after the food appears. Several groups of animals are conditioned in this way, for 10, 20, 40, 80, and 120 reinforcements, respectively. After conditioning, the rate of responding is reduced to a low level by extinction in the dark. Then pressing the bar again turns on the light for one second, but does not deliver food. Under these circumstances responses again appear, showing that the light has acquired reinforcing properties. The number of responses emitted in a 45-minute period increased with the number of prior pairings of light and food (Bersh, 1951).

Other experiments suggest that the light will acquire secondary reinforcing properties only if it appears *before* the reinforcing stimulus, and is thus either part of a chain or a discriminative stimulus (Schoenfeld, Antonitis, and Bersh, 1950; Webb and Nolan, 1953).

The following summary of secondary reinforcement shows its systematic importance in operant behavior:

1. A stimulus that occasions or accompanies a reinforcement acquires thereby reinforcing value of its own, and may be called a conditioned, secondary, or

derived reinforcement. A secondary reinforcement may be extinguished when repeatedly applied to a response for which there is no ultimate primary reinforcement.

2. A secondary reinforcement is positive when the reinforcement with which it is correlated is positive, and negative when the latter is negative.

3. Once established, a secondary reinforcement is independent and nonspecific; it will not only strengthen the same response which produced the original reinforcement, but it will also condition a new and unrelated response. Moreover, it will do so even in the presence of a different motive.

4. Through generalization, many stimuli besides the one correlated with reinforcement acquire reinforcing value—positive or negative (Keller and Schoenfeld, 1950, page 260).

One of the most important consequences of the development of secondary reinforcement is the emergence of a class of *generalized reinforcers* (Skinner, 1953a, pages 77-81). This generalization comes about because some secondary reinforcers tend to accompany a variety of primary reinforcers. Money is a convenient illustration, because money provides access to food, drink, shelter, entertainment, and thus becomes a generalized reinforcer for a variety of activities. The so-called needs (need for attention, need for affection, need for approval) lead to the kinds of persistent behavior best understood as a consequence of intermittent reinforcement, and the kinds of reinforcement sought are the generalized ones implied in the words "attention," "affection," and "approval." Language behavior, such as calling objects by their correct names, tends to be reinforced by the generalized reinforcement from the listeners, who show in indirect ways whether or not they understand and approve. According to Skinner, eventually generalized reinforcers are effective even though the primary reinforcers on which they are based no longer accompany them (1953a, page 81). This is close to the functional autonomy of motives, as proposed by Allport (1937).[5]

OTHER INFLUENCES AFFECTING OPERANT STRENGTH

In the effort to remain descriptive and positivistic, Skinner has attempted to avoid the postulating of intermediaries not observed in his experiments, and to deal instead with a procedure that he calls *functional analysis*. A functional analysis is concerned with the lawfulness of relationships and the manner in which these relationships fluctuate under specified conditions. We have just reviewed one very important class of events in the functional analysis of behavior: reinforcements, as they affect operant strength. Two other classes of events are significantly correlated with responses in the problems that Skinner studies. These are the classes known as *drive* and *emotion*.

[5] Note also its relation to Pavlov's second signalling system, Chapter 3, pages 65-68.

Drive

Hours of food deprivation are important in determining the rate of responding in a Skinner box. The variable actually plotted is exactly that: hours of deprivation. Is it necessary to say anything further? Is it important to talk about physiological needs, or hunger? Let us first cite some typical experimental results and then return to these questions.

Eight rats learned to press a lever under interval reinforcement. They practiced daily but received the main portion of their rations on alternate days. The correlation between responding and hours of deprivation showed up in high and low rates on successive days. Two subgroups were created, matched according to their response rates during conditioning. They were now extinguished on alternate days, one group when hunger was high, the other when hunger was low. The high hunger group yielded nearly double the responses of the low group on successive daily periods, although the two extinction curves show similar curvature (1950, pages 201-202).

Does deprivation affect the amount of contribution of each reinforcement, or does it merely affect the rate of responding during extinction? In a test of these relationships, rats were reinforced after different amounts of food deprivation, from ½ hour to 47 hours. Various subgroups of animals received 1, 10, and 30 reinforcements, respectively. Then the strength of conditioning was tested by resistance to extinction, at a common level of deprivation (23 hours). Resistance to extinction was throughout correlated with the number of prior reinforcements, but *not* with the level of deprivation within reinforcement (Strassburger, 1950).

These two studies suffice to illustrate the kinds of relationships between drive and operant conditioning that are open to investigation. In a narrative account of the results we tend to move back and forth between describing the rats as "deprived of food" or as "hungry." The two expressions are operationally equivalent, though when we assign the results to "hunger" instead of to "hours without food" we tend to imply a theory. This leads us back to the problem of the status of "drive" as a concept.

Skinner is quite clear that he means by "drive" merely a set of operations (such as the withholding of food for a certain number of hours), which operations have an effect upon rate of responding. He is interested in the lawfulness of these effects under various circumstances. He objects to most of the current psychological uses of "drive" by supporting the following assertions (1953a, pages 144-146):

A drive is not a stimulus.
A drive is not a physiological state.
A drive is not a psychic state.
A drive is not simply a state of strength.

By these negatives he makes it clear that he does not accept the stimuli from stomach contractions as the prototype of drives, nor does he accept physiological needs, or pleasures or pains, or desires or wishes. For the purposes of the systematic study of behavior, the word "drive" is used only to acknowledge certain classes of operation which affect behavior in ways other than the ways by which reinforcement affects it. He does not believe inference to an intermediary (intervening variable or hypothetical construct) to be necessary in order to carry out the functional analysis.

Emotion and Punishment

Just as drives are inappropriately classified as stimuli, so, according to Skinner, emotions are often unwisely classified as responses. Weeping at a bruised shin or over the loss of a game is ordinarily said to be an emotional response, but weeping because of a cinder in the eye is not. This way of treating emotion is rejected in favor of referring it to a set of operations, in many ways like drive. Its importance arises because of the accompanying or ensuing changes in response.

The effects of punishment are often emotional by this definition. Punishment might act dynamically as negative conditioning, as though reinforcement were being subtracted, but in fact it does not serve in this way. If at the beginning of extinction the rat is slapped on its feet when it presses the lever, its rate of responding is depressed, but it eventually recovers. The total responses to extinction have not been reduced by the punishment, as they should be if the punishment were negative conditioning (1938, page 154). Such a temporary effect upon rate but not upon total resistance to extinction is emotional. There is here some support for Thorndike's belief that punishments do not act opposite to rewards.

Because of the importance of the problem of punishment, Estes' (1944) study, carrying further Skinner's earlier explorations, will be reviewed later as an exemplification of Skinner's system.

DISCRIMINATION AND DIFFERENTIATION

In situations which require more than a change in rate of responding, two features stand out. One is the discrimination between stimuli, so that a given response may be made to one of a pair of stimuli and not to the other member of the pair. A second feature is differentiation of response, so that response form or topography is altered or adjusted appropriately to the situation. The complexities of behavior can be understood according to discriminations and differentiations arranged into appropriate chains or patterns.

Discrimination of Stimuli

The standard lever-pressing experiment may serve the purposes of discriminatory conditioning if the lever-pressing delivers a pellet of food in the presence of a positive, supporting stimulus (e.g., a 3 candlepower light) and fails to deliver in the absence of this discriminative stimulus. The rat learns to respond only when the light is on, but the light does not actually elicit the response. The difference between a discriminative stimulus as an occasion for a response and actually eliciting a response is clarified by an example. I reach for a pencil lying on the desk, but I reach only when the pencil is there, and I do not reach for it just *because* it is there. While the pencil does not *elicit* reaching, it has something to do with my reaching. If it were dark and there were no pencil there, I might grope for it because the discriminative stimuli would be lacking. The pencil does not elicit reaching in the light any more than in the dark. It is only the occasion for reaching (1938, page 178).

When the food is delivered only in the presence of the light, the situation is a sort of controlled intermittent reinforcement, for lever-pressing is reinforced only part of the time. Eventually response occurs almost exclusively when the light is on, so that nearly every response is reinforced. The resistance to extinction that is built up at this stage is not that of interval reinforcement, but that of ordinary every-trial reinforcement. There are two operants with the same form of response, one with the light on, one with the light off; they are selectively reinforced and extinguished. There is an interaction called *induction* by Skinner which corresponds to Hull's generalization; whatever happens to one operant affects the other to some extent.

The following statements are offered to clarify this somewhat complex situation (1938, page 229):

1. Responses accumulated in the presence of the positive stimulus are available in the presence of the negative stimulus. This is the principle of inductive conditioning or generalization.

2. Responses emitted in the presence of the negative stimulus are no longer available under the positive stimulus. This is the principle of inductive extinction.

3. Selective reinforcement and extinction increase the number of responses available chiefly in the presence of the positive stimulus. This is the positive half of the principle of discrimination.

4. Responses acquired in the presence of the positive stimulus may become less readily available under the negative stimulus. This is the negative half of the principle of discrimination—the breakdown of induction.

The discrimination experiment is always complicated by an additional fact of importance. The positive stimulus which acts as the occasion for the response and for the reinforcement becomes itself a secondary reinforcing agent.

Skinner believes that his arrangement for obtaining discrimination is superior to that usually used, in which a choice of responses confronts the animal. His rats may either respond to the lever or not respond. They do not have to choose between two levers, or between a right and a left turn. He believes that the discrimination box is a "crude instrument" for studying the nature of the process (1938, page 231), and finds Tolman's (1938) dependence upon choice-point behavior a severe limitation (1938, page 437). The objection is that in the choice situation no measure of strength is obtained—only a measure of relative strength.

Differentiation of a Response: Shaping

Among a number of novel and useful distinctions made by Skinner is that between discrimination of stimuli and differentiation of response. In operant conditioning, reinforcement can be made contingent on either (a) the properties of accompanying stimuli (when the result is a discrimination), or (b) the properties of the response (when the result is a differentiation).

The rat may be taught, for example, to press the lever with a given force, or to hold it down for a given duration, in order for the pellet to be delivered. He can be trained to press rapidly or slowly. The basic rule of operant conditioning applies: the response must occur before it can be reinforced. Extreme forms or values may be obtained by successive approximations; the process has come to be called *shaping* the behavior. Operant responses are emitted with an original range of form or intensity (Hull's response oscillation). If only the more extreme values are reinforced, the whole distribution shifts, so that higher and higher values may be obtained. Through successive approximations the shaping method permits the finally learned behavior to be very different from that originally emitted.

Animal trainers are well versed in this method. As a sort of *tour de force* I have trained a rat to execute an elaborate series of responses suggested by recent work on anthropoid apes. The behavior consists of pulling a string to obtain a marble from a rack, picking the marble up with the forepaws, carrying it to a tube projecting two inches above the floor of the cage, and dropping it inside. Every step in the process had to be worked out through a series of approximations, since the component responses were not in the original repertoire of the rat (1938, pages 339-340).[6]

[6] For other accounts of animal training, see Breland and Breland (1951), Skinner (1951).

Response novelty is one of the features rather badly accounted for in most stimulus–response systems. Thorndike's law of assimilation, Guthrie's principle of compromise movements, and Skinner's shaping through differentiation are all attempts to deal with the problem. The concept of emitted behavior has advantages over that of elicited behavior. It has always been embarrassing for theories of the conditioning type to try to find original stimuli to produce the responses called for in singing a song or writing a poem. Such stimuli need not be specified for emitted behavior, which can be brought under the control of the most varied stimuli.

THE SEARCH FOR A UNIT OF BEHAVIOR

In the foregoing account of some of the kinds of data which Skinner has collected and of the concepts used in describing them, his more general theory has been implied rather than made explicit. Skinner has been definitely interested in supporting a scientific theory of a specific kind. He favors what he calls a purely descriptive system, and a frankly analytical one. How he has gone about system-making is well illustrated in his early discussion of the *reflex* and its laws.

Early Reliance on the Reflex as the Unit

Skinner believes that a purely descriptive system, in order to be scientific and not a mere "botanizing" of behavior, must be based upon an appropriate natural unit of behavior. A real unit will not be an artificial bit of behavior taken improperly out of context, nor will it be something too complex to enter into orderly relations as a descriptive unit. The level of specification found to be necessary is not something *a priori*, but is the level found in experience "marked by the orderliness of dynamic changes." What this means, essentially, is that we are interested in events that cause changes in behavior, and the analysis must take these essentially causal relationships into account. Such relationships are the ones that scientists (who often object to the word "cause") prefer to state as lawful ones. Skinner thought that the *reflex*, as he defined it, was an appropriate unit for the analysis of behavior.

By a reflex Skinner means a lawful correlation between a class of stimuli and a class of responses. The reflex is not to be identified with the spinal reflex, which is defined topographically; its reference is solely to behavior and not to anatomy or neurology. What a stimulus is, what a response is, what a reflex is, can be defined only through the lawful relationships discovered in experiments.

The reflex as an analytical unit is actually obtained in *practice*. The unit is a fact, and its validity and the validity of the laws describing its changes do not depend upon the correctness of analytical assumptions or the possibility of a later synthesis of more complex behavior (1938, page 29).

The Functional Unit Studied Is Not Necessarily the "Atom" of Behavior

While Skinner later continued to search for the appropriate unit of analysis, the basic datum, he appeared no longer confident that he had found the unit either in the reflex or in the components of the measured operant: the discriminative stimulus that is the occasion for the response, the response, and the reinforcement. The "same" response is not the "same" operant if correlated with different stimuli or with different reinforcers. The operant under study is perhaps not a "single" operant.

A somewhat modified suggestion as to an "element" of behavior emerged in the following passage which followed a discussion of the problem of transfer:

This leads us to identify the element rather than the response as the unit of behavior. It is a sort of behavioral atom, which may never appear by itself upon any single occasion but is the essential ingredient or component of all instances. The reinforcement of a response increases the probability of all responses containing the same elements (1953a, page 94).

We lack adequate tools to deal with the continuity of behavior or with the interaction among operants attributable to common atomic units. The operant represents a valid level of analysis, however, because the properties which define a response are observable data. A given set of properties may be given a functional unity. *Although methods must eventually be developed which will not emphasize units at this level,* they are not necessary to our understanding of the principal dynamic properties of behavior (1953a, page 95. Emphasis added).

These quotations suggest that Skinner believed at the time he wrote that we were still at a very preliminary stage in the development of behavioral science. Perhaps his objection to theory (as theory is used by others) arises because of his strong conviction that we need to discard old concepts and make a fresh start. We may not be far enough along this new road to begin the more detailed analysis called for in matured theory.

Chained Responses as Illustrative of Functional Units

What is the practical meaning of assigning "functional unity" to a given set of properties? Some light can be thrown on this by an analysis of chaining, for actual behavior as we know it comes in sequences larger than those of bar-pressing or spot-pecking.

Even the bar-pressing operant is in reality a chain:

The use of a chain cannot be avoided in operant behavior because the very act of reinforcement implies it (1938, page 43).

In their discussion of chaining, Keller and Schoenfeld (1950, pages 197-208) gave a lucid account of the problem of determining the degree of analysis desirable in order to remain at the level of experimental specification. They began with six distinct operants describing what the rat actually does in a Skinner box:

Operant Number	Discriminative Stimulus	Response of the Rat
1	Bar-location	Approach of rat to front of box
2	Visual bar	Rising on hind legs; placing paws on bar
3	Tactual bar	Pressing of bar, thus activating food-magazine
4	Apparatus noise	Lowering foreparts to food-tray
5	Visual pellet	Seizing of pellet by teeth and paws
6	Pellet-in-mouth	Chewing of pellet

It would be possible, as they suggest, to lengthen this list, including the several responses making up the approach from the door to the bar-location, and the several ingestion responses that follow upon the chewing of food. Instead, however, they find it equally legitimate to reduce the list, as follows:

Operant Number	Discriminative Stimulus	Response of the Rat
1	Visual bar	Rising
2	Tactual bar	Pressing
3	Apparatus noise	Lowering
4	Visual pellet	Seizing

The advantage of this reduction lies in the clearly observable and regularly recurring sequence or chain of responses, with identifiable (and controllable) stimuli. In this chain each response produces the discriminative stimulus for the next response.

Does the chain operate as a unit? The well-conditioned rat makes the transitions so smoothly that it seems to be giving one response, not four. But the independence of the units of the chain can be tested experimentally.

1. If we eliminate only the stimulus for the final unit of the chain (the pellet), as in extinction, the first three links of the chain are gradually weakened, but the last is unaffected. The rat will seize and eat a pellet exactly as before.

2. If we now eliminate both the third and fourth links in the chain (the apparatus noise as well as the pellet), and carry out extinction, we can find out more about the chain. Reintroducing the noise after extinction is well along again reinforces bar-pressing. Hence, during conditioning, the third link had become a secondary reinforcer. Furthermore, the

extinction of the preceding two links in the chain did not extinguish the reinforcing properties of the third link.

This kind of functional and experimental study isolates units of the chain which preserve some independence in the whole. These units are part of a chain, and their distinctiveness as units is not entirely arbitrary. It would be possible to record the separate responses, and not only the final one. It is suggested not only that future investigations will undoubtedly employ such procedures, but that exploratory attempts are reported to have already been made (Keller and Schoenfeld, 1950, page 203).

The unit appropriate for experimental study turns out, in fact, to have a measure of arbitrariness about it. If it is a matter of convenience whether to measure one response of the chain, or four responses, or many more than that, there is evidently some selectivity exercised by the experimenter. This is always true: *all* description is partial description. The nature of events is such that description of them cannot be exhaustive. The functional unit, for Skinner, as for other experimenters, is not given completely by the processes under investigation. Sometimes the functional unit is a simple response, sometimes a complex act, sometimes a rate of responding. The unit no longer has the clean dimensions of a correlation between a class of stimuli and a class of responses as implied in the original concept of a reflex. The atom of behavior proves to be evasive.

EXTENSION AND APPLICATION OF OPERANT CONDITIONING

The generality of Skinner's approach to problems of behavior is suggested by the titles chosen for his books: *The behavior of organisms* (1938) and *Science and human behavior* (1953a). Neither title betrays that the precise data derive largely from experiments on rats and pigeons. Although the data are now being supplemented by experiments with human subjects, both children and adults, normal and disturbed, in these books the extension of the theory is by analogy rather than by experimentation. From a scientific point of view (using the word "science" as Skinner uses it) the extensions merely explore the kinds of variables which may eventually be brought under scientific control. The ultimate possibilities, as Skinner envisages them, are boundless: one chapter he includes is entitled "Designing a culture." We are not here concerned with the larger political and ethical aspects of the society he presents. Instead, our problem is to see the steps by which laboratory learning is extended to encompass learning in a larger context. For our purposes we may therefore select some typical problem areas and see how they are handled. Four such problem areas are laboratory technology, programed learning, verbal behavior, and psychotherapy.

Laboratory Technology

What is the source of substantive principles in one area of scientific knowledge may become a method or technology for another. Thus the transistor is of interest to the physicist for what it tells about solid state physics, but it is a technological assist to the person constructing hearing aids or pocket-sized radios. Operant conditioning, similarly, is of interest for what it tells about learning, but it is also very useful for many whose interests are not primarily in learning at all.

One use that interests experimental psychologists is in animal psychophysics. It is possible, by using operant methods, to produce visual sensitivity curves for pigeons that show the course of adaptation to darkness with all the precision of experimentation with trained human subjects (Blough, 1961).

Another widespread use has been in the testing of drugs. Because the cumulative response curves that are recorded in the standard Skinner apparatus are very sensitive to the influence of drugs, these methods become useful for calibration experiments in pharmacology. The methods are so widely used that a number of commercial firms now market animal cages equipped with cumulative recorders and accessory equipment to be used for such purposes.

The wide applicability of the technologies associated with the recording of operant behavior is recognized by many who are testing theories departing widely from those of Skinner. Thus much of the work of Hull and his students, to be discussed in the next chapter, made use of the Skinner box. A recent summary (Honig, 1966) shows the many uses that have been made of the method in the study of a variety of psychological and physiological topics. It is a fair statement that the Skinner box, for rats and pigeons, has displaced the maze as the favorite apparatus among American students of animal behavior.

Programed Instruction

Skinner in 1954 announced and embarked upon a series of investigations and inventions designed to increasing the efficiency of teaching arithmetic, reading, spelling, and other school subjects, by using a mechanical device expected to do some things much better than the usual teacher can do them, while saving the teacher for tasks that the teacher can do better. An early form of the device presented number combinations for the teaching of addition. The child punches the correct answer in a kind of adding-machine keyboard; if the answer is correct, "reinforcement" occurs by having the machine move on to the next problem. Skinner early pointed out that no teacher can be as skilled a reinforcer as the machine, for the teacher cannot be with every child at once, commending proper responses and correcting erroneous ones. Furthermore, the teacher cannot be as skilled in determining the proper order and rate of presentation of problems.

Skinner's devices, and others modeled after them, soon came to be called *teaching machines* or *autoinstructional devices,* and the materials that became the basis for instruction came to be called *programs.* Some of them began to appear as programed books (e.g., Holland and Skinner, 1961).

An important summary paper by Skinner in *Science* in 1958 catalyzed the interest that had been mounting, and *programed instruction* presently became a major educational and commercial enterprise.

While Skinner believed that the rationale for his proposals was derivable from the principles of operant conditioning, his theoretical interpretations have been the subject of some controversy.[7] Whatever the verdict may be with regard to the essence of programed instruction, there is no doubt that the upsurge of interest in the 1950's was due to him, and there is no doubt either but that he arrived at his methods through an attempt to generalize to education what he had learned through the study of operant conditioning in rats and pigeons.

Verbal Behavior

Language most clearly distinguishes human behavior from that of other mammals. Knowledge of how we acquire language, and how we use it, is essential to an understanding of human learning. Skinner has long been interested in verbal behavior. As early as 1936 he produced a phonograph record composed of chance groupings of speech sound, which because they were chance were inherently meaningless. The record, called a "verbal summator," was used to study the words "read into" sounds by the listener. It was a kind of projective technique, similar in the auditory field to the ink-blots used in the visual field (Skinner, 1936). Within the next few years Skinner reported studies of word association, alliteration, and other kinds of sound patterning.[8] His William James Lectures, delivered at Harvard University in 1948, appeared in revised form as a volume entitled *Verbal behavior* (1957). We can see that verbal behavior has been taken seriously as an empirical problem.

The main point of the analysis is that speech sounds are emitted (and reinforced) as any other bits of behavior. Some speech utterances make demands upon the hearer and get reinforced as the hearer complies. This function (called the "mand" function) appears early in the language be-

[7] Programed learning is discussed in greater detail in Chapter 15.
[8] Skinner (1937b), Cook and Skinner (1939), Skinner (1939, 1941).

havior of the child. A second function is concerned largely with naming (the "tact" function). The tact function leads to the richness and versatility of language. Its reinforcement by the hearer is more general than mand reinforcement. The reciprocal relationship between the speaker and the hearer, involving mutual reinforcement, is complex, but subject to straightforward analysis. The analysis calls for no new principles, however, beyond those familiar in operant conditioning.

A third term introduced by Skinner is that of *autoclitic* behavior, intended to suggest verbal behavior that is based upon or depends upon other verbal behavior (1957, page 315). The speaker is commonly talking in part about his own role when he emits autoclitic behavior: "I was about to say . . ." "I hesitate to say that he is a liar."

In essence, our verbal behavior is "shaped" by the reinforcement contingencies of the verbal communities in which we live.

The book on *Verbal behavior,* while certainly a serious effort, has not proved to be very influential. This may have come about because it was not well received by the professional linguists, whose rapidly developing linguistic science has made great strides by means of analyses different from Skinner's, (e.g., Chomsky, 1959). Or it may be that the interest in programed learning, coming to a head about the time when this book appeared (1957), siphoned off the interest and debate that the book might otherwise have provoked. If that should prove to be the case, we may some day see a revived interest in the book.[9]

Psychotherapy

Skinner (1953a, page 359-383) has said that the need for psychotherapy results from the by-products of excessive control by other people (especially through punishment), whereby the individual is either incapacitated or rendered dangerous to himself or to others. Excessive control has by-products that are either emotional (fear, anxiety, anger or rage, depression) or revealed in operant behavior (drug addiction, excessively vigorous or restrained behavior, defective discrimination of stimuli, defective selfknowledge, aversive self-stimulation) .

The patient turns to the therapist because any relief (or promise of relief) is positively reinforcing. Psychoanalytic therapy can be characterized most simply, according to Skinner, as follows: the therapist constitutes himself a nonpunishing audience. Under these circumstances, responses repressed by punishment tend to return. Forgotten experiences may be recovered, the patient may act aggressively (or at least verbalize aggressive impulses), and he may exhibit strong emotion. The appearance

[9] For a treatment of Skinner's ideas on verbal behavior in the context of meaning, see Carroll (1964b), pages 36-39.

of previously punished behavior in the presence of the nonpunishing therapist makes possible the extinction of some of the effects of punishment. This Skinner believes to be the principal result of such therapy.

This plausible account calls for no "explanatory fictions"—no id, ego, or superego, inhabiting a psychic or mental world.

What is "wrong" with the individual who displays these by-products of punishment is easily stated. A particular personal history has produced an organism whose behavior is disadvantageous or dangerous. In what sense it is disadvantageous or dangerous must be specified in each case by noting the consequences both to the individual himself and to others. The task of the therapist is to supplement a personal history in such a way that behavior no longer has these characteristics (1953a, page 372).

Psychotherapy rests on the direct investigation and redirection of behavior itself. Behavior is itself the subject matter of therapy; the behavior is not the symptom of some other subject matter.

These conjectures are based on analogies between human behavior and experimental studies largely on lower forms. The methods were extended, however, to the study of human patients hospitalized with psychoses. Early results showed that vending machines with candy or cigarettes or pictures as reinforcing stimuli could sustain operant behavior over long periods of experimentation lasting an hour a day. Periods of psychotic activity within the experimental hour appear reduced in frequency and duration, at least for some patients (Lindsley, 1960).

Two developments have furthered the application of operant methods to psychotherapy. The first of these resulted from a growing interest in verbal conditioning, that is, the shaping of verbal behavior by the therapist through signs of approval (as reinforcement) or ignoring (as extinction). Numerous studies appeared after some early work of Greenspoon (1955).[10] A second development was a lessening of interest in psychoanalytically oriented therapy (insight or depth therapy) in favor of what has come to be known as behavior therapy (symptom treatment or action therapy). While some of the origins of behavior therapy were unrelated to Skinner's teachings, the interest in behavior modification is shared with operant conditioning, and it is not surprising that operant methods have been tried increasingly, once symptom management became popular again (e.g., Sidman, 1962).

The foregoing discussion of laboratory applications, programed learning, verbal behavior, and psychotherapy suffices to show the flavor of

[10] The development of interest in verbal conditioning, particularly in its relationship to psychotherapy, was well underway before *Verbal behavior* (Skinner, 1957) appeared. It is of interest that the ideas in the book affected what was later done in verbal conditioning very little, except, perhaps for identifying verbal behavior as a response. For reviews of verbal conditioning in clinical psychology, see Krasner (1958, 1965), Salzinger (1959), and Greenspoon (1962).

Skinner's theory as applied to a broader range of problems. The steps from the present knowledge of behavior to these broader fields are largely matters of technique and engineering, rather than of the discovery of new scientific principles. Skinner would expect nothing new in the way of dynamic principles to emerge as the broader subject matter is investigated.

THE CONSEQUENCES OF PUNISHMENT AS ILLUSTRATIVE OF EXPERIMENTS WITH OPERANT BEHAVIOR

Some of the suggestions about the action of punishment which Skinner had earlier made were more extensively studied by Estes (1944) under his direction. Estes' work serves as a convenient example of the experimental approach to a problem by an investigator adopting Skinner's general point of view. Estes chose a more conventional terminology than Skinner, avoiding words like "operant" or "reflex" or "emitted," but the experiments could have been described in Skinner's words. It is of some interest that Estes found the more usual vocabulary satisfactorily precise for his purposes.

On the assumption that punishment does have effects, the two chief possibilities are that it weakens the habit or that it merely suppresses response. If the habit is weakened, punishment acts as a negative reinforcement, or as an agent hastening extinction. If the response is merely suppressed, the response has not been eliminated from the organism's repertory. Skinner's preliminary experiments favored the latter alternative, that punishment suppresses the rate of responding without eliminating responses from the total of responses to appear in extinction. Estes points out that the alternatives are genuine ones in the light of clinical experience. It is familiar that behavior may be repressed, and not overtly expressed, although the tendencies continue to exist at considerable strength.

Punishment Does Not Act as a Negative Reinforcement

In agreement with Skinner (and the later Thorndike), Estes finds that punishment does not lead to a reduction in the total number of responses given during extinction, even though there is temporary suppression of response following the punishment. Some characteristic findings are shown in Figure 5-7.

On the basis of additional experiments in the series, Estes concludes that the total number of elicitations of the response necessary for extinction may be reduced somewhat by punishment, but the time required for complete extinction of the response will not be affected by the punishment. More generally, the conclusion is reached that a response cannot be eliminated from an organism's repertory by the action of punishment alone.

Punishment More Importantly Associated with Stimuli Than with Responses

If punishment were a reinforcing agent similar to reward, it would act on responses, in accordance with Skinner's principle of Type R conditioning. That its more significant correlation is with discriminative stimuli is pointed out by Estes on the basis of several kinds of evidence.

In one experiment (1944, Experiment I) the animals of the experimental group were shocked at intervals of approximately 30 seconds, care being taken not to shock them during or immediately after a response to

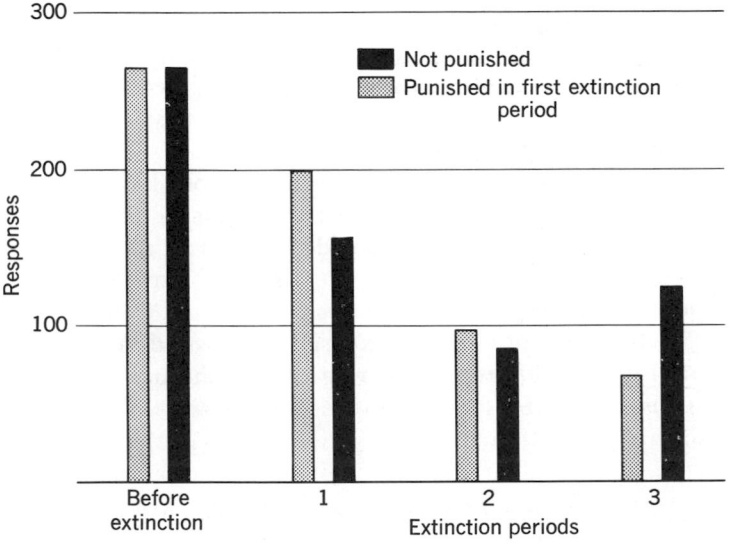

Figure 5-7   Evidence that punishment depresses rate of responding without decreasing the total responses within extinction. Responses of two groups of 8 rats each are compared. While the groups were not alike in their response frequency prior to extinction, their rates have been equated, and other comparisons are based upon this adjustment. Within the first extinction period one group of rats received an average of 9 punishments (electric shocks while pressing the lever). This punishment reduced the number of responses on the first day, and perhaps on the second, but by the third day there was a compensatory increase in the number of responses so that the total responses of the group punished on the first day and of the group not punished are the same over the three days of extinction. Data from Estes (1944, Experiment A, corrected for differences prior to extinction).

the lever. Recovery from the effects of punishment follows the same course (i.e., fits the same mathematical function) as that following punishment of the response itself. It is argued therefore that the effect must be due to the contiguity of the disturbing stimuli with stimuli in the box which normally act as occasions for lever pressing.

This conjecture was tested in another experiment (1944, Experiment II) in which the rat was left in the box for an adaptation period following punishment. During this time the lever was withdrawn, so that response to it was impossible. The effects of the short period of severe punishment were almost completely dispelled, confirming the interpretation that punishment was related to the stimulating situation rather than specifically to the response.

Intermittent Punishment More Effective Than Punishment at Every Occurrence

If punishment is delivered every time the response is made, the rate of responding is seriously depressed. While it is not depressed as much if punishment is given only occasionally, the effects of punishment persist longer in the latter case.[11] This is shown in two experiments: in one the test is made by simple extinction, in the other the extinction follows an adaptation period. The results are most striking following adaptation. Adaptation does not bring recovery after intermittent punishment as it does after every-trial punishment. The results are shown in Figure 5-8.

Estes offers some conjectures in explanation of these results. He accepts a twofold theory of the effect of punishment. One principle, already referred to, is that punishment creates an emotional state which depresses operant responses while the state is aroused. The second principle is one congruent with Hull's interpretation of punishment, that is, an interpretation of the cessation of shock as reinforcing. Estes believes that the withdrawal responses are positively conditioned by the termination of the shock delivered by the lever. He believes, further, that such withdrawal responses are conditioned more strongly through intermittent reinforcement than through ordinary continuous reinforcement, consistent with Skinner's findings for conditioning in general.

Punishment in the Practical Control of Behavior

Estes suggests several practical implications of his study.

The main finding is that a response cannot be eliminated from the organism's repertory more rapidly with the aid of punishment than with-

---

11 Estes (1944), Experiments E and K. The average number of punishments received by each rat turns out to be about the same for both groups. Hence it is legitimate to compare the long-time effects of the two types of punishment.

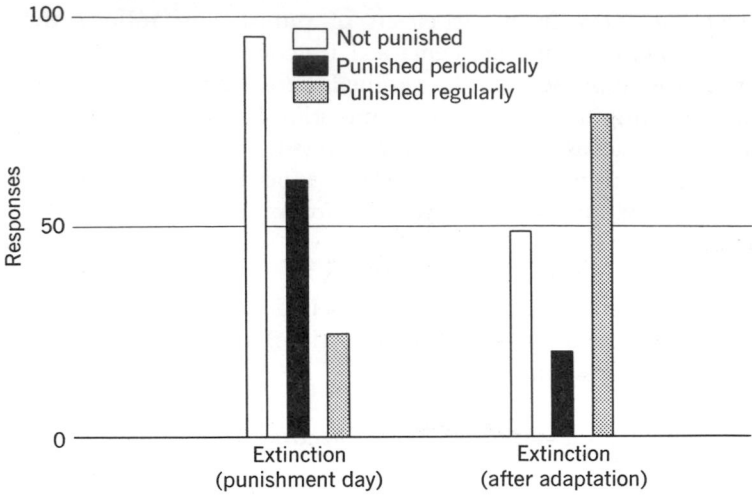

Figure 5-8   Evidence that intermittent punishment is more effective than regular punishment. The mean numbers of responses of three groups are shown, a control group extinguished in the usual manner, a group punished for responding whenever response occurred, and a group punished periodically, for responses occurring within every fourth minute of the 40-minute extinction period. Following the experimental day there were two adaptation days, when the animals were placed in the boxes with the levers retracted. The results for extinction are for the first day with the exposed lever, after these adaptation days. The adaptation period has almost completely eradicated the results of regular punishment, but the consequences of periodic punishment persist. Each group consisted of 6 rats. Data from Estes (1944, Experiment K, corrected for differences prior to extinction).

out it. Permanent weakening comes about only by nonreinforced elicitation—and this weakening process may be prevented if punishment suppresses the response. This is in line with clinical finding about forms of aggressive or hostile responses which have come under parental or other social punishment. They are not eliminated until they can be brought to free expression, when the behavior can be appropriately redirected.

Another disadvantage of punishment lies in the concomitant emotional state which is aroused. This state will suppress other responses in addition to the one punished. The lack of specificity of its target is a weakness of punishment.

On the positive side, there are several "rules" which serve to show when and how punishment may be useful:

1.   Punishment may be used to hold a response at low strength. Under these circumstances, punishment has to continue indefinitely, as it does

not eliminate the response. The continuing punishment is equally or more effective if administered occasionally than if it is given every time the objectionable behavior occurs.

2. It is possible to take advantage of the period of suppressed response following punishment in order to strengthen some other response by reinforcement.

3. It is important that punishment be given in the presence of the discriminative cues for the response. Delayed punishment is likely to prove ineffective because it is given at a time when the discriminative stimuli leading to the undesired conduct are absent.

The series of experiments by Estes, with their interpretations, show how, within the experimental and theoretical framework of Skinner's system, it is possible to experiment upon problems genuinely relevant to the practical control of learning situations. The challenging difficulty is finding appropriate ways to test the implications in a social context.

ESTIMATE OF SKINNER'S SYSTEM

Skinner's Position on Typical Problems of Learning

The existence of general textbooks written from the standpoint of Skinner's position makes possible a summary in relation to problems that do not fit directly into his conceptual scheme.

1. Capacity. In a descriptive system, it is to be expected that the laws will contain empirical constants differing for various species and for different members of each species. The eating rate, for example, cannot be expected to remain the same for young and old animals, and for animals unlike in their food preferences. Because *lawfulness* rather than *laws* is what the systematist insists upon, differences in capacity are not of central importance. There is no suggestion that at higher capacity levels the laws are essentially any different; verbal behavior in man, for example, is said to conform to the general principles of operant behavior.

Skinner argues against the usefulness of a "trait" description in studying individual differences. A trait-name does not refer to any unit of behavior suitable for study through the functional analysis that he recommends (1953a, pages 194-203).

2. Practice. Something like a simple law of exercise (practice under conditions of contiguity of stimulus and response) is accepted for Type S conditioning. The conditioning that occurs under Type R depends upon repeated reinforcement. The possibility is favored that maximum reinforcement may occur in a single trial for the single operant, but the single operant is not achieved experimentally. In the usual case, the accumulation of strength with repeated reinforcement depends upon a population of discriminated stimuli and the related operants, more or less after the manner of Guthrie's explanation of the interpretation of the acquisition of skill with practice.

The effect of a single reinforcement is greatly enhanced by the secondary reinforcement deriving from it. Hence there is no direct correspondence between the number of responses yielded in extinction and the number of responses reinforced. The schedule of reinforcements is very important, with the greatest yields in the way of resistance to extinction coming from intermittent reinforcement (interval or ratio reinforcement).

3. Motivation.   In agreement with Thorndike, reward is found to increase operant strength, while punishment has no corresponding weakening influence. Although there are several ways in which punishment enters, one is to create the variable called emotion, which reduces the rate of responding without reducing the number of responses yielded in extinction.

Drive level (determined by degree of deprivation) affects the rate of responding, but its level does not influence the effectiveness of a reinforcing stimulus in producing resistance to extinction. There is an unresolved problem of a lower limit here, for there must be enough drive to maintain responding and to make the reinforcer relevant.[12]

4. Understanding.   The word "insight" does not occur in the indexes of Skinner's books. Keller and Schoenfeld identify insight with rapid learning, and then explain it on the basis of (1) *similarity* of the present problem to one earlier solved, or (2) the *simplicity* of the problem (1950, page 60).

Because solving a problem means only the appearance of a solution in the form of a response, Skinner believes that the technique of problem-solving is merely that of manipulating variables which may lead to the emission of the response. No new factor of originality is involved. This makes it possible to teach a child to think (1953a, pages 252-256).

5. Transfer.   Skinner prefers to use the term "induction" for what is commonly called generalization in the literature of conditioning. Such induction is the basis of transfer. The reinforcement of a response increases the probability of all responses containing the same elements. Similarly, the control acquired by a stimulus is shared by other stimuli with common properties. This interpretation of transfer is, in spirit, very similar to Thorndike's.

[12] We shall meet this same problem in the next chapter, when Hull's interpretation of reinforcement is under consideration.

6. Forgetting. There is no special theory of forgetting proposed, although the distinction between extinction and forgetting is carefully maintained. Conditioning is long retained. A pigeon showed sizable extinction curves six years after the response had been last reinforced. Extinction, too, is retained. Spontaneous recovery does not mean that extinction is forgotten, for successive extinctions show the results of earlier ones.

True forgetting appears to be a slow process of decay with time. Other kinds of response decrement are better subsumed under extinction or interference by incompatible responses. The latter interpretation applies to so-called Freudian forgetting.

The Reflex No Longer a Satisfactory Unit

When he first committed himself to the reflex as his unit (Skinner, 1931), he referred to the correlation between a class of stimuli and a class of responses. If this correlation was lawful, he believed the term "reflex" to be appropriate. A case could be made for his position, but the consequence was no more than to discover as his unit what Thorndike had earlier named the "connection" or "bond." Thorndike, too, accepted the correlation between situations and responses as the basis for his unit.

When Skinner developed the notion of emitted behavior, his earlier unit was no longer appropriate. The discriminated operant, which is the basis of experiment and theory in the newer writing, he early referred to as a *pseudoreflex* (1935). He pointed out that it would be a great mistake to suppose that the correlation established between a discriminated stimulus and an operant followed the laws of the reflex. Thus the systematic correlation between stimuli and responses, a legitimate extension of the historical term "reflex," was no longer appropriate in dealing with operants. The terms which enter a reflex relationship should be those of "stimulus" and "response." Skinner's concern has appropriately shifted to mere lawfulness of behavior. The reflex proper (the basis for respondent behavior) is limited to autonomic and postural responses; the operant can just as well run under its own name, and not be confused with these reflexes. Instead of insisting on the analysis into reflex units, Skinner now appears somewhat less sure about the ultimate unit, and is temporarily satisfied with a functional analysis at the level of experimental convenience.

Coordination with Other Systematic Viewpoints

Skinner's "fresh start" approach to psychology has made it difficult for him to use the data collected by others, and, on principle, he rejects their concepts. His role in reference to the theories of others—insofar as he has paid any attention to their claims—has been chiefly that of a trenchant critic. He has felt no responsibility for the task of inter-investigator coordination. In his book *Science and human behavior* (1953a), written as a textbook, he used no literature citations, and he mentions by name, among writers with some place in learning theory, only Thorndike, Pavlov, and Freud.

That some coordination is possible is shown by Keller and Schoenfeld (1950), who made a serious effort to bridge the gap between the data collected by Skinner and his followers and by others interested in learning. They were able to find much that they could use, even though they remained within the conceptual structure of Skinner's system.

The almost exclusive preoccupation with animal experiments (except for the studies of verbal behavior, programed learning, and work with abnormal human subjects carried out in the spirit of technology rather than of scientific inquiry) raises some interesting questions. Presumably a functional, descriptive psychology of this kind must ultimately design experiments at the level at which scientific statements are to be made. As Verplanck points out, it is somewhat anomalous that a systematist who refuses to predict what a rat or pigeon will do—because such prediction does not belong in a scientific study of behavior—was willing to make confident assertions about the most complex forms of human behavior, economic, political, religious (Verplanck, 1954, page 311). The intervening steps are, to be sure, being filled out within the newer technological applications.

The Anti-Theory Argument

Skinner's espousal of a descriptive, positivistic position and his opposition to a hypothetico-deductive system have frequently been reasserted, nowhere more clearly than in his presidential address before the Midwestern Psychological Association, entitled: "Are theories of learning necessary?" (1950).

The theories he opposes are of at least two kinds. One kind is that which would find its explanations at a different level of discourse, using, for example, a physiological explanation for psychological events. There is no real objection to such a theory, unless it is overly insisted upon. The independence of the behavioral subject matter must be permitted, and explanatory mechanisms, especially explanatory fictions, are to be avoided. He challenges another kind of theory, commonly called hypothetico-deductive, which stresses the formulation of hypotheses and their testing. This kind of theory Skinner objects to as a futile and extravagant exercise. The argument can be stated simply enough. The end result of scientific investigation, whether the investigation is descriptive or an effort to confirm a theory, is a described functional relationship demonstrated in the data. Because the end result is the same, the only point at issue is really which method more efficiently directs the inquiry. Skinner is firmly of the opinion that theories are wasteful and misleading. They usually send the investigator down the wrong paths, and even if the scientific logic makes them self-correcting, the paths back are strewn with discarded theories. Once the data are in order, the theories tend to drop out. "If the theories have played no part in the design of the experiment, we need not be sorry to see them go."

Criticism of existing hypothetico-deductive systems in psychology is easy. This does not mean that their scientific logic is wrong. It may mean that some particular efforts have been premature or misdirected. Perhaps Skinner is right in criticizing unripe theorizing, but surely he is wrong if he means that we should return to a Baconian conception of science. The power achieved by other sciences through theoretical formulation is too convincing for such formulation not to serve at least as a long-range goal for those trying to create a science of behavior. That Skinner's approach is a fruitful one need not lead to the conclusion that other approaches are futile.

One of the next steps for a science, after lawful relationships have been discovered and appreciable amounts of data collected, is to represent the data in a kind of shorthand summary, using a minimal number of terms, and mathematical representation. This kind of systematic science Skinner can support, because it does not call for inferences alien to the data of observation. But he says of it:

> We do not seem to be ready for a theory in this sense. At the moment we make little use of empirical, let alone rational, equations. A few of the present curves could have been fairly closely fitted. But the most elementary preliminary survey shows that there are many relevant variables, and until their importance has been experimentally determined, an equation that allows for them will have so many arbitrary constants that a good fit will be a matter of course and cause for very little satisfaction (1950, page 216).

It is not surprising that a critic well familiar with the system found it appropriate to remark that Skinner's is "a highly formal, but not a highly formalized, theory" (Verplanck, 1954, page 295).

Success of the System

Two major achievements give the system a firm place in contemporary psychology.

At the level of data, the most novel and interesting data are those deriving from the various schedules of intermittent reinforcement (Ferster and Skinner, 1957). Only the sketchiest of experiments have been done by other workers in this fascinating field,[13] and the kind of operant behavior studied by Skinner has lent itself beautifully to this kind of investigation. It is a far cry from pointing out that rewards influence learning to achieving the kind of control whereby several thousands of responses are yielded at a uniform rate during extinction following a particular pattern of rewarding.

At the level of practical behavior the most striking results have been obtained in animal training and in programed instruction. While the animal stunts have not been of very great theoretical interest, it is not wise to dismiss them as merely signs of cleverness on the part of the trainers. These practical demonstrations serve as important empirical supports for certain aspects of the system—a kind of support very much needed for learning theories, and notably lacking thus far. No other learning theorist has been able to train an animal before an audience in a prompt and predictable manner, while at the same time epitomizing the principles of his theory. There have long been public demonstrations of learned behavior—of conditioned responses, of maze learning, of discrimination—but these demonstrations have usually relied upon exhibiting the results of earlier training. By contrast, Skinner's pigeons can be brought before a class and taught various tricks before the eyes of the students. The empirical demonstration that learning is under the experimenter's control is important, and if what happens can be described in terms of the system, so much the better for the system. The programed learning work has opened up important avenues of instructional advance in both schools and industry.

The practical use of the system is based on the complementary principles of control through presenting and withholding reward. The supplementary principles of stimulus discrimination and response differentiation suffice to inaugurate shaping through the method of successive approximations. Beyond that, all that is needed is the experimenter's ingenuity. It is not necessary to worry about anything precise in the way either of experimental data or of correlated principles. From the point of view of a theoretical achievement this is really a pretty modest extension of Thorndike's law of effect. Just how far one can go in controlling human affairs through operant conditioning is a matter of ingenuity and empirical demonstration. The theory does not propose to predict!

SUPPLEMENTARY READINGS

The following books contain Skinner's own accounts of his work:
SKINNER, B. F. (1938) *The behavior of organisms.*
SKINNER, B. F. (1953a) *Science and human behavior.*

[13] For a critical review of the literature, see Jenkins and Stanley (1950).

SKINNER, B. F. (1957) *Verbal behavior.*
FERSTER, C. B., and SKINNER, B. F. (1957) *Schedules of reinforcement.*
HOLLAND, J. G., and SKINNER, B. F. (1961) *The analysis of behavior: A program for self-instruction.*

A collection of his experimental and theoretical papers, selected by him as most representative of his contributions is found in:
SKINNER, B. F. (1961) *Cumulative record.*

Skinner's novel *Walden Two* (1948), also available as a paperback, is worth reading along with *Science and human behavior* (1953a) for a comparison between the scientific system and its imaginary application in an experimental Utopia. The ethical implications of Skinner's proposals for social control was the subject of a debate between him and Carl Rogers (Rogers and Skinner, 1956).

For the methodological implications of Skinner's system, a book by a disciple is Sidman, M. (1960) *Tactics of scientific research.* For illustrations of various applications, a useful source is Honig, W. K. (Editor) (1966) *Operant behavior: Areas of research and application.* Note also Verhave, T. (Editor) (1966) *The experimental analysis of behavior: selected readings;* Geis, G. L., Stebbins, W. C., and Lundin, R. W. (1965b) *Reflex and operant conditioning: a Basic Systems program.*

Hull's Systematic Behavior Theory

Clark L. Hull (1884-1952), greatly impressed by the appearance of Pavlov's *Conditioned reflexes* (1927), began thereafter a long series of theoretical and experimental studies that in their totality comprise the best example of hypothetico-deductive system-making in psychology to appear during the first half of the century. The system is a behaviorism, and as such falls into the family of theories which also includes those of Guthrie and Skinner. Each of these three systems represents in its own way a fulfillment of the behavioristic program originally proposed by Watson. Like Watson's, Hull's theory is avowedly mechanistic and studiously avoids reference to consciousness. Its central concept is habit, and it derives most of its information about habit from experiments with conditioned responses. Complex behavior, furthermore, is derived step by step from what is known about more elementary forms of learning. In these respects the theories of Watson and Hull are alike, but in other respects Hull's system represents a great advance over Watson's. Hull took the detailed findings of conditioning experiments much more seriously than Watson, who was satisfied to make use of the general paradigm provided by conditioned responses. Hull adopted (and adapted) Thorndike's law of effect, whereas Watson rejected it. For Watson's policy of denials and negations, Hull substituted a positive program of trying to explain purposes, insights, and other phenomena difficult for a behaviorism to encompass.

THE BASIC ORIENTATION

Before turning to the more formal system, expressed in postulates, corollaries, and theorems, we may do well to examine the broad framework within which the system operates.

Intervening Variables and Their Anchorage in Observables

In the first revision (1929) of his widely used textbook Woodworth suggested that we substitute the formula S–O–R for the earlier recommended S R formula. The stimulus (S) affects the organism (O), and what happens as a consequence, the response (R), depends upon O as well as upon S. Hull's system may be thought of as a herculean elaboration of this S–O–R formula (Spence, 1952, page 646).

In experiments we measure environmental influences upon the organism (the input), and then measure the organism's responses (the output). These measures provide firm anchorage for the data in the environment, where objectivity can be achieved and maintained. Input and output are not comprised exclusively of the experimentally studied stimuli and responses. Other influences upon the organism can be treated as experimental variables, such as prior history of training, deprivation schedules, injection of drugs, and these influences can be described as objectively as stimuli and responses. What goes on within the organism we have to infer, and in the course of making these inferences we postulate certain *intervening variables* or *symbolic constructs*. If we tie these inferences firmly to the input-output terms by way of quantitative mathematical statements, we lose nothing in objectivity, and gain something in convenience, understanding, and fertility of deducing new phenomena. This is the basic logic of the system.

Reinforcement the Primary Condition for Habit Formation

In his choice among the three major possibilities (contiguity alone, reinforcement alone, or a dual theory), Hull stood firmly for a reinforcement theory. As early as 1935 he suggested that the Pavlov experiment might be considered a special case under Thorndike's law of effect, and in 1937 he published a formal derivation of Pavlovian conditioning on the basis of a reinforcement principle (Hull, 1935a; 1937). Although some modifications were made in his interpretation of reinforcement, he held to the end to the one principle as central to learning.

Reinforcement theory of the kind Hull espoused requires, in the specification of a primary reinforcing state of affairs, either drive reduction, as in need satisfaction, or drive-stimulus reduction, as in the satisfaction of a craving rather than a need. Hull earlier held to the drive-reduction theory, most clearly exemplified in escape from a continuing noxious stimulus, such as an electrically charged grid. The activity that terminates the noxious stimulus is reinforced because the need to escape injury is satisfied in the escape. Later, under the influence of the Miller–Dollard (1941) theory of drive-stimulus reduction, Hull went over to the drive-stimulus reduction theory and abandoned the drive-reduction interpretation of reinforcement. The example of escape from a noxious stimulus was equally cogent, though now the reduction in pain (the consequence of stimulation) is theoretically the basis for reinforcement instead of the escape from injury (the underlying need). In primary reinforcement the two events (drive and drive-stimulus) are so closely associated that it does not matter very much which is assumed to be reduced. But needs may require time for their satisfaction (as in the time required to digest food) whereas incentives (including food) work promptly as reinforcers, more as stimuli might be expected to work. Furthermore, as secondary reinforcement came into greater and greater prominence in reinforcement theories, the stimulus-reduction theory became even more attractive. This follows because secondary reinforcement is a function of stimuli rather than of needs.

Integration of Behavior Sequences Through Anticipatory Responses

Most of the primary behavioral laws in Hull's system were derived from either classical or instrumental conditioning (both interpreted as illustrations of learning under the control of reinforcement). But the appeal of the system rests upon the comprehensive explanation that it provides of many phenomena of learning in experiments not classifiable as simple conditioning: more complex trial-and-error and discriminatory learning, maze learning, rote memorization, tool-using, and so on. In order to make these further deductions, Hull proposed a number of intermediate mechanisms, derivable from the basic laws of his system, but, once derived, of very wide applicability. At this point the intent is merely to give something of the flavor of these intermediaries; more detailed illustrations will be presented later in this chapter.

Many of the stimuli present at the time the goal is reached are also present earlier. These include the stimuli from the drive (what Guthrie called maintaining stimuli), environmental stimuli present both earlier and during reinforcement, traces from earlier stimuli persisting to the goal, as well as stimuli aroused by the animal's own movements. Hence in repeating a sequence of acts leading to a goal, as in running through a maze, there are always enough of these stimuli conditioned to the goal response to elicit fractions of the goal response prior to reaching the goal. These fractional antedating goal-response (r_G's) are very important integrators in Hull's system, and he made very ingenious use of them. While they were prominent all along in Guthrie's system, Guthrie never did formalize their use as Hull did.

The fractional anticipatory responses give rise to stimuli (s_G). These stimuli sometimes serve as surrogates for directing ideas. In that case the r_G is a "pure-stimulus act," that is, an act that serves functionally merely to produce a stimulus that maintains a steering role in behavior (Hull, 1931).

These same stimuli (s_G) are very important in secondary reinforcement, permitting reinforcement originating in food at the end of the maze to move back and reinforce turns far from the goal (Hull, 1952a, page 14).

Furthermore, it is these same stimuli (s_G) that generate the *gradient of reinforcement* and the *habit-family hierarchy*, important intermediate mechanisms, which we shall meet later on.

Thus, on the basis of primary behavioral postulates, Hull deduced types of mechanism that led to wide generality in his deductions.

The Requirements for a Quantitative, Deductive System

Hull knew very clearly what he wanted in the way of a formal system. Such a system should begin with adequately defined terms, and then state a few (as few as possible) basic postulates. These postulates may either be very general empirical findings, and thus independently verifiable, or, if not directly testable, they must be subject to indirect verification. Their purpose is to relate the fundamental intervening variables by strict logic (and quantifiable mathematical equations) to each other and to their anchorages in environmental events. These postulates, taken together with the definitions, will generate new testable deductions or predictions. These are the corollaries and the theorems of the system.

The progress of science comes about through the experimental testing of theorems. When agreement is found, the postulate system generating the theorem remains in the running; when disagreement is found, a search is made for the faulty postulate, if such there be, and the postulate is then revised. Possibly, if no faulty postulate can be found, a new postulate may have to be added. Thus the system is self-correcting, and only those features survive that have stood the scrutiny of meticulous experimental testing.

Systems of this kind begin as "miniature" ones. That is, they encompass at first only a limited range of data. Even these limited data put the early system under strain, and the next steps consist in trying to secure a better fit between the theory and these data. Then additional data are incorporated through extensions of the system. Sometimes two or more "miniature systems" may be combined as appropriate bridging concepts are developed. There may be major shifts in the systematic formulations, as when, in physics, Newtonian theory became a special case under Einstein's more general theory. Thus theory construction proceeds by successive approximations, and finality in a theory is often a sign that the theory is faulty.

Did Hull succeed in producing a good system, according to these criteria? A satisfactory answer may perhaps have to wait for the verdict of history. If a generally acceptable theory of learning eventually emerges with convincing evidence of its ancestry in Hull's earlier formulations, he will have succeeded. If the direction in which he moved turns out to have been a blind alley, and greater success comes from a fresh start in new directions, then his succees will not have been as great. Even so he will have done a profoundly valuable service in showing what a mature system might look like, and in insisting that it was not too early to attempt to systematize psychology in rigorous fashion.

EARLIER SETS OF POSTULATES

Hull's theoretical system evolved gradually. He habitually wrote down various conjectures and plans for experiments in bound notebooks, seventy-three notebooks between 1902 and 1952.[1] Many of his later publications were foreshadowed in these notes and in the frequent mimeographed memoranda that he circulated. His first paper addressed specifically to the subject matter of his final system was in 1929, entitled "A functional interpretation of the conditioned reflex" (Hull, 1929). In it he acknowledged his great indebtedness to Pavlov and began on an informal basis to make the kinds of deductions he later sought to formalize. Another important influence upon his later theorizing arose out of a summer's teaching at Harvard in 1930, when he was invited to lecture on aptitude testing because of the favorable reception of his recent book on that topic (1928). There he met C. I. Lewis and other philosophers, and asked them why philosophers had neglected his doctoral dissertation on concept formation (Hull, 1920). Their answers are no longer available to us, but in any case he added to his library, and read, Newton's *Principia,* and Whitehead and Russell's *Principia Mathematica.* These raised his sights as to the kind of theory to which he might aspire. The first formal system, using definitions, postulates, and theorems, appeared in 1935 (Hull, 1935a). It was what he called a "miniature system" concerned with rote learning, to be elaborately worked over later in the most detailed of Hull's formal systematic efforts, the collaborative book entitled *Mathematico-deductive theory of rote learning* (Hull and others, 1940).

---

[1] He mentioned these in Hull (1951), page 120. A number of excerpts from these notebooks have been published, and they provide an interesting glimpse into the private thinking of a scientist (Hull, 1962).

The true ancestor of the later postulate sets, however, was contained in Hull's presidential address before the American Psychological Association at Dartmouth in 1936 (Hull, 1937). This new "miniature system" was concerned with adaptive behavior of the kinds reflected in the later postulate sets in *Principles of behavior* (1943), *Essentials of behavior* (1951), and *A behavior system* (1952a). The final book was completed only a few weeks before Hull's death and appeared posthumously. It was written while he was suffering from a heart condition and could work only a few hours a day. It is a tribute to his devotion to his work that it was finished at all. Some of the changes in the latest version may very well turn out not to have been improvements. The system was by no means a finished one, and Hull was the first to acknowledge this. The promised books on individual differences and on social behavior did not get written, and the final book is full of qualifications and reservations.

THE 1940 THEORY OF ROTE LEARNING

In a thoroughgoing study with the forbidding title *Mathematico-deductive theory of rote learning: A study in scientific methodology,* Hull and his collaborators attempted a rigorous systematization of rote memorization, in which interrelated hypotheses would be subjected to empirical testing (Hull, Hovland, Ross, Hall, Perkins, and Fitch, 1940). The book is so ponderous that it is little referred to, although, within its own area, it is doubtless the most careful systematic attempt since the original work of Ebbinghaus (1885).

It is called a mathematico-deductive theory to indicate not only that it uses the hypothetico-deductive method, but that it uses it in a strictly quantitative way. The approach is very formal, beginning with undefined concepts and definitions, and proceeding to postulates, corollaries, theorems and problems. There are 18 postulates with 10 corollaries, followed by 54 theorems with 110 corollaries and 8 problems. The postulates are stated first in verbal form, including familiar mathematics, then restated in the notation of symbolic logic, and finally explained with experimental illustrations. The theorems are stated, then proven by mathematical derivation from the definitions and postulates, then subjected, where possible, to experimental test. For an ambitious system of this kind, and one in its early stages, the success was substantial. Of 71 corollaries which could be subjected to test by available data, the corollary was clearly supported in 39 cases (55 percent), ambiguous in 20 cases (28 percent), and in disagreement with the prediction in the rest, 12 cases (17 percent) as computed by Hilgard (1940).

The book covers three main bodies of factual material: (1) serial position effects, having to do with the ordinal position of a nonsense syllable in a list being memorized; (2) reminiscence and forgetting, relating the initial rise in the curve of retention to other factors, such as distributed practice, serial position, and length of list; and (3) reaction thresholds and the course of memorization. The formal structure of the book interfered with orderly topical exposition and made it difficult to locate the treatment of these topics; hence Table 6-1 is provided as a guide.

Table 6-1 **Topics of Mathematico-Deductive Theory of Rote Learning, Related Theorems and Postulates (Modified from Hilgard, 1940).**

Topic	*Theorems*	*Essential Postulates*
1. Serial Position Effects	1—9, 16—17, 20—34, 54	1—11
2. Reminiscence and Forgetting	10—11, 35—44	12—13
a. As related to distribution of practice	12—15, 54	
b. As related to serial position	45—50	
c. As related to length of list	51—53	
3. Reaction Thresholds and the Course of Memorization	16—19	14—17

One illustration of the kind of theoretical result predicted by the system, with its empirical testing, is given in a formulation of the curve of rote learning (memorization), when plotted in a particular way. In the formal derivation, which need not concern us here, the derivation is linked to other aspects of the system by way of three constants, ΔE, the increment of excitation due to each repetition, ΔK, the amount of inhibition generated by each repetition of each syllable, and L, the reaction threshold. Another constant, σ_L represents the oscillation of the threshold. The empirical fact of response oscillation was first noted in a memorization experiment by Hull (1917), when he observed that a syllable correctly given on one trial was often failed on succeeding trials until finally it was completely mastered, so that it could be counted upon trial after trial. This led him to both a theory of acquisition and a way of plotting the curve to test the theory.

The theory predicts that the form of the curve of acquisition *for all syllables which required the same number of trials to reach mastery*, will be in the form of an ogive. Oscillation of the threshold from moment to moment in a chance manner would result in such a curve if the underlying excitatory strength were increasing linearly with repetition. Syllables requiring the same number of trials to master are pooled for this purpose because they are presumed to be about equally difficult. The prediction is that the approach to the threshold and the post-threshold portions of the curve should combine to take ogival form. In Figure 6-1 are shown the empirical results for syllables requiring 8 trials to mastery. The form of the curve is roughly ogival in agreement with the theory. The data on which the curve of Figure 6-1 is based are as empirical as any; yet this form of plotting would be unlikely to be used were it not for the theory which led to it. This is one illustration of the fertility of such system-building.

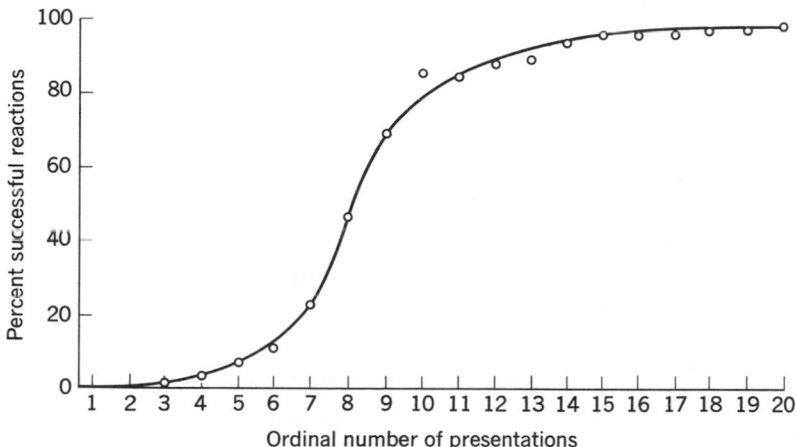

Ordinal number of presentations

Figure 6-1   **Empirical learning curve for nonsense syllables equally difficult to master. From a number of sessions in which nonsense syllables were memorized, data were chosen for those syllables for which final mastery was preceded by eight failures. The curve represents the percentage of successful responses per trial for 163 such syllables. According to the prediction, a curve plotted in this manner should be in the form of an ogive. Reproduced from Hull and others (1940, page 162).**

Why, despite Hull's prominence and influence in other directions, this theory did not assume importance, is a matter of speculation. It appeared just before the United States entered World War II, and the attention of psychologists turned largely in other directions. There was also a certain *ad hoc* quality about the postulate system, so that, despite its elegance and precision, it was not as generalizable as the later systems. Still it must be noted that rote verbal learning has remained a topic of general interest to psychologists, and there are many pertinent ideas in this book which have been largely neglected.

THE 1943 POSTULATE SYSTEM

In his *Principles of behavior* (1943) Hull's general system was presented at the height of his confidence in it, and many of his followers continue to refer to this book when comparing their views to his.

The general plan is straightforward. The complete behavioral event begins with stimulation provided by the external world and ends by a response, also part of the interplay with the environment. Everything else lies within the organism, influencing in one way or another what response will occur, if any, following the onset of the stimulus. The set of intervening processes, which are scientific constructs rather than observables, are anchored, as Hull says, at both ends—at the stimulus-end and at the response-end.

The Postulates

In order to make it easier to grasp the system as a whole, in what follows the postulates have been paraphrased and assigned titles. The more exact statement can be found in the pages of Hull (1943) to which reference is made in each case.

A. *The external cues which guide behavior, and their neural representation.*

Postulate 1. *Afferent neural impulses and the perseverative stimulus trace.*

Stimuli impinging upon a receptor give rise to afferent neural impulses which rise quickly to a maximum intensity and then diminish gradually. After the termination of the stimulus, the activity of the afferent nervous impulse continues in the central nervous system for some seconds (1943, page 47).

Postulate 2. *Afferent neural interaction.*

Afferent neural impulses interact with other concurrent afferent neural impulses in a manner to change each into something partially different. The manner of change varies with every impulse or combination of impulses (1943, page 47).

B. *Responses to need; reinforcement and habit strength.*

Postulate 3. *Innate responses to need.*

Organisms at birth possess a hierarchy of need-terminating responses which are aroused under conditions of stimulation and drive. The responses activated by a given need are not a random selection of the organism's responses, but are those more likely to terminate the need (1943, page 66).

Postulate 4. *Reinforcement and habit strength.*

Habit strength increases when receptor and effector activities occur in close temporal contiguity, provided their approximately contiguous occurrence is associated with primary or secondary reinforcement (1943, page 178).

C. *Stimulus equivalence.*

Postulate 5. *Generalization.*

The effective habit strength aroused by a stimulus other than the one originally entering into conditioning depends upon the remoteness of the second stimulus from the first on a continuum in units of discrimination thresholds (just noticeable differences) (1943, page 199).

D. *Drives as activators of response.*

Postulate 6. *Drive stimulus.*

Associated with every drive is a characteristic drive stimulus whose intensity increases with strength of drive (1943, page 253).

Postulate 7. *Reaction potential aroused by drive.*

Habit strength is sensitized into reaction potential by the primary drives active at a given time (1943, page 253).

E. *Barriers to response.*

Postulate 8. *Reactive inhibition.*

The evocation of any reaction generates reactive inhibition. Reactive inhibition is spontaneously dissipated in time (1943, page 300).

Postulate 9. *Conditioned inhibition.*

Stimuli associated with the cessation of a response become conditioned inhibitors (1943, page 300).

Postulate 10. *Oscillation of inhibition.*

The inhibitory potential associated with every reaction potential oscillates in amount from instant to instant (1943, page 319).

F. *Response evocation*

Postulate 11. *Reaction threshold.*

The momentary effective reaction potential must exceed the reaction threshold before a stimulus will evoke a reaction (1943, page 344).

Postulate 12. *Probability of reaction above the threshold.*

The probability of response in striate muscle is a normal (ogival) function of the extent to which the effective reaction potential exceeds the reaction threshold (1943, page 344).

Postulate 13. *Latency.*

The more the effective reaction potential exceeds the reaction threshold, the shorter the latency of response in striate muscle (1943, page 344).

Postulate 14. *Resistance to extinction.*

The greater the effective reaction potential, the more unreinforced responses of striate muscle occur before extinction (1943, page 344).

Postulate 15. *Amplitude of response.*

The amplitude of responses mediated by the autonomic nervous system increases directly with the strength of the effective reaction potential (1943, page 344).

Postulate 16. *Incompatible responses.*

When reaction potentials to two or more incompatible responses occur in an organism at the same time, only the reaction whose effective reaction potential is greatest will be evoked (1943, page 344).

These sixteen postulates summarize in verbal form the exposition that requires upwards of 300 pages of text, and cannot therefore give any hint of the effort that went into stating them in precise mathematical form, and in their empirical justification. In order to write equations, Hull adopted a special notation which has been omitted in the statement of the postulates. The chief symbols that he used are given and defined in Figure 6-2.

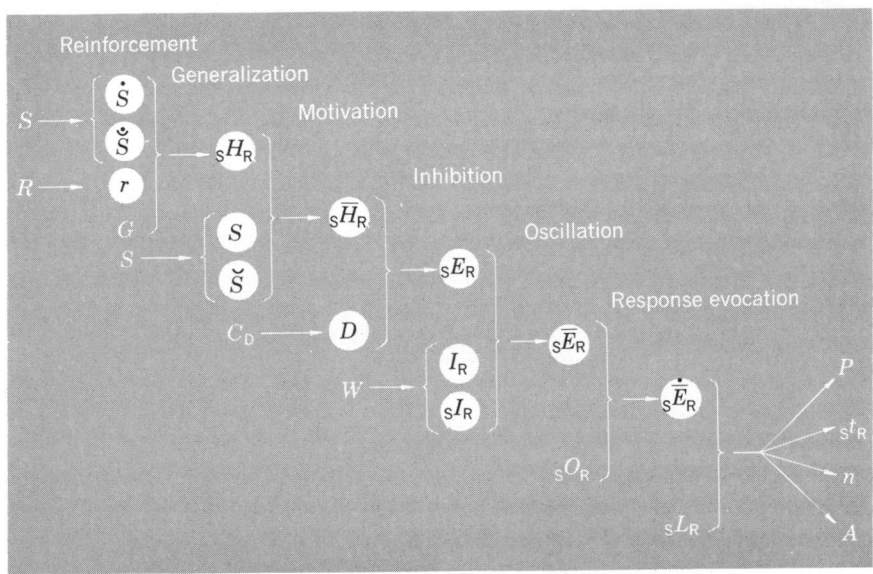

Figure 6-2   **Diagram summarizing the major symbolic constructs in Hull's system of behavior. After Hull (1943a, page 383).**

A, amplitude of reaction

$\dot{S}$, the physical stimulus energy

R, the organism's reaction

$\dot{s}$, the neural result of the stimulus

$\check{s}$, the neural interaction arising from two or more stimulus components

r, the efferent impulse leading to reaction

G, occurrence of reinforcing state of affairs

$_sH_R$, habit strength

S, evocation stimulus on same stimulus continuum as S

s, the neural result of S

$\check{s}$, neural interaction

$_s\overline{H}_R$, the generalized habit strength

C_D, the objectively observable phenomena determining the drive

D, the physiological strength of the drive

$_sE_R$, the reaction potential

W, the work involved in evoked reaction

I_R, reactive inhibition

$_sI_R$, conditioned inhibition

$_s\overline{E}_R$, effective reaction potential

$_sO_R$, oscillation

$_s\dot{\overline{E}}_R$, momentary effective reaction potential

$_sL_R$, reaction threshold

p, probability of response evocation

$_st_R$, latency of reaction evocation

n, number of unreinforced reactions to extinction

The System as a Chain of Symbolic Constructs

The diagram in Figure 6-2 may be read from left to right as a chain of six major processes going on when a learned response is evoked; some of these are processes guided by environmental events; mostly the processes are inferred intervening variables.

1. Reinforcement.   Habit strength $(_sH_R)$ is the result of a reinforcement of stimulus–response connections in accordance with their proximity to need reduction. (Postulates 3 and 4)

2. Generalization.   Generalized habit strength $(_s\overline{H}_R)$ depends both upon direct reinforcement and upon generalization from other reinforcements. (Postulate 5)

3. Motivation.   Reaction potential $(_sE_R)$ depends upon the interaction of habit strength and drive. (Postulates 6 and 7)

4. Inhibition.   Effective reaction potential $(_s\overline{E}_R)$ is reaction potential as reduced by reactive inhibition and conditioned inhibition. (Postulates 8 and 9)

5. Oscillation.   Momentary effective reaction potential $(_s\dot{\overline{E}}_R)$ is effective reaction potential as modified from instant to instant by the oscillating inhibitory factor associated with it. (Postulate 10)

6. Response evocation.   Responses are evoked if the momentary effective reaction potential is above the threshold of reaction. Such responses may be measured according to the probability of reaction, latency of reaction, resistance to extinction, or amplitude. (Postulates 11-16).

We thus see how the system fulfilled Hull's desire for an inferential system firmly anchored to the physical world. It is anchored to antecedent observable events in the physical environment and the organism, and, on the consequent side, to observable and measurable reactions. This anchorage makes possible the systematic manipulation of the logical constructs in mediating valid deductions. A system may be rooted in empirical fact even though its variables are constructs and not observables.

Habit Strength $(_sH_R)$ and Influences Upon It

Paraphrasing Hull's postulates in the foregoing account has necessarily lost much of their detail and elegance. The fourth postulate, concerning reinforcement and habit strength, was stated by him as follows:

Whenever an effector activity ($r \longrightarrow R$) and a receptor activity ($S \longrightarrow s$) occur in close temporal contiguity ($_sC_r$), and this $_sC_r$ is closely and consistently associated with the diminution of a need (G) or with a stimulus which has been closely and consistently associated with the diminution of a need ($\dot{G}$), there will result an increment to a tendency (Δ_sH_R) for that afferent impulse on later occasions to evoke that reaction. The increments from successive reinforcements summate in a manner which yields a combined habit strength ($_sH_R$) which is a simple positive growth function of the number of reinforcements (N). The upper limit (m) of this curve of learning is the product of (1) a positive growth function of the magnitude of need reduction which is involved in primary, or which is associated with secondary, reinforcement; (2) a negative growth function of the delay (t) in reinforcement; and (3) (a) a negative growth function of the degree of asynchronism (t') of $\dot{S}$ and R when both are of brief duration, or (b), in case the action of $\dot{S}$ is prolonged so as to overlap the beginning of R, a negative growth function of the duration (t'') of the continuous action of $\dot{S}$ on the receptor when R begins (Hull, 1943, page 178).

In this postulate, and the developments growing out of it, we have the essence of the learning theory: the fundamental operation of rewards, the effects of repetition, and the gradients of reinforcement. To restate what it implies requires at least the following three statements:

1. Learning depends upon contiguity of stimulus and response closely associated with reinforcement defined as need reduction (or, in secondary reinforcement, associated with a stimulus that itself has been associated with need reduction). This is essentially a restatement of Thorndike's law of effect, with reward specified in terms of need reduction.

2. The course of learning described as a simple growth function is based on the implied assumption that the increment of habit strength with each reinforcement is *a constant fraction of the amount remaining to be learned*. Because more remains to be acquired early in learning and little remains late in learning, the result is a curve of decreasing gains, very familiar in laboratory studies of learning.

3. The upper limit of learning tends to be at a maximum when need reduction is great, when delay between response and reinforcement is short, and when there is little separation between the conditioned stimulus and the response to be acquired. This statement has within it some of the aspects of Thorndike's spread of effect, insofar as a gradient is generated by separation of the response from its reinforcement.

Because in many experiments everything is kept constant but the number of reinforcements, the form of learning curve equation that has remained familiar from the 1943 book is as follows:

$$_sH_R = M - Me^{-iN} \qquad \text{(1943, page 119).}$$

Since $M = 100$ habs (an arbitrary scale for stating the maximum possible learning), and $e = 10$, a numerical constant,[2] we may rewrite the equation

$$sH_R = 100\ (1 - 10^{-iN}),$$

where $N =$ number reinforced repetitions, and $i =$ a constant related numerically to F, the fraction of the amount remaining to be learned that is acquired with each reinforcement.

The relation between i and F is given by the equation:

$$i = \log \frac{1}{1 - F} \qquad (1943,\ \text{page } 119).$$

This equation has no particular importance in itself, except that it assists in the transformation of the basic equation to one in which F appears directly and permits comparison with more rationally derived equations, such as those of Estes (1950).

The Role of Drive

The concept of drive was very important in Hull's theorizing. It had three distinct functions, all implied in Postulates 6 and 7:

1. Without drive there could be no primary reinforcement, because primary reinforcement requires the rapid diminution of D. There could, of course, be no secondary reinforcement, either, for secondary reinforcement originates in the association of a stimulus with primary reinforcement, producing a conditioned S_D to be reduced in secondary reinforcement.

2. Without drive there could be no response, for drive activates habit strength into reaction potential. Drive is the basic multiplier of sH_R.

3. Without the distinctiveness of the drive stimulus S_D there could be no regulation of habits by the need state of the organism, no way to learn to go one place for water when thirsty, another place for food when hungry.

The first and third of these functions determine *which* incentive is reinforcing, as well as *why* it is reinforcing; the second function is also that of a goad to action in the direction of need satisfaction; the third gives drive a discriminative or steering role.

The equation that expresses the relationships among reaction potential, habit strength, and drive, is based on the assumption that drive interacts with habit strength in some multiplicative fashion to produce reaction potential:

$$sE_R = f\,(sH_R) \times f\,(D) \qquad (1943,\ \text{page } 242).$$

[2] Hull took this liberty with e, which is properly 2.7183....

If the *effective* habit strength $(_s\bar{H}_R)$ and the effective drive $(\bar{D})$ are entered into the equation, it is assumed that a simple multiplication suffices, and the equation becomes

$$_sE_R = \frac{_s\bar{H}_R \times \bar{D}}{100} \qquad \text{(1943, page 245)}.$$

The reason for the division by 100 is to keep everything in a centrigrade scale, with the maximum of habits being 100 *habs*, of drive 100 *motes*, and of reaction potential 100 *wats* (named for Watson). These named units have not survived, and are now of historical interest only.[3]

Hull recognized that the drive state of the organism was based not only on the relevant drive (D), such as hunger drive with food reinforcement, but on contributions from irrelevant drives $(\dot{D})$, which might also alert the organism. Hence he worked out the following formula, in order to keep the maximum drive at 100 (the assumed maximum for D alone):

$$\bar{D} = 100\frac{\dot{D} + D}{\dot{D} + 100} \qquad \text{(1943, page 245)},$$

where $\bar{D}$ is the effective drive, $\dot{D}$ the contribution of alien drives, and D the relevant drive.

It takes little mathematical sophistication to see that such a formula of convenience (designed merely to keep a common maximum for the combined drives) has implications for drive interaction that were by no means derived from the theory. Thus if the irrelevant drive is at the maximum, and the relevant drive is zero, the maximum effective drive is 50. Perhaps this is reasonable, but it is not the kind of consideration upon which the equation was derived.

It is to Hull's credit, however, that he always found some sort of equation that permitted him to plunge ahead, the equations being subject to later refinements. There are many more such equations in the book, the successes in matching empirical data with derived functions being great enough to give the whole a flavor of great optimism with respect to the future of quantitative psychology.

THE FINAL BEHAVIOR SYSTEM (1952)

The book *Principles of behavior* (1943) was intended as an exposition of the most basic aspects of the system, and stopped short of the kinds of derivations of more complex behavior of which Hull was very fond, and at which he was very skillful. He began immediately thereafter to work on

---

[3] The unit of inhibitory potential (I_R) was named the *pav*, honoring Pavlov.

a more thorough quantification of the postulated processes, revising the postulates as necessary, and then returned again to the derivations of other kinds of behavior on the basis of these basic principles. The quantitative program in which he took most satisfaction was an elaborate effort to arrive at a measurement of habit strength.[4] The revised postulates were published first in 1950, again in 1951, and finally in *A behavior system* in 1952 (Hull, 1950, 1951, 1952a). The final book, appearing just after Hull's death, contains not only the new postulates with evidence related to them, but many derivations of other behavior familiar in the writings of Hull from 1929 on.

The differences between the 1943 and 1952 books are readily apparent. The whole of the 1943 book (or nearly all of it) is concerned with developing the system of postulates and corollaries, while these are condensed into the first chapter of the 1952 book. The remainder of the final book is devoted to applying the principles to a wide variety of more complex behavior, such as trial-and-error learning, discrimination learning, maze learning, and problem-solving.

Rather than review the new postulates in detail, some differences between the 1943 and 1952 sets will be noted, and then attention will be directed to some of the derivations.[5]

Changes in the Postulates Between 1943 and 1952

While there are a number of minor changes in detail, such as the inclusion of mathematical statements within the postulates themselves, only a few changes that represent major theoretical alterations will be noted here.

The first change is in the conception of primary reinforcement. While in the 1943 postulates primary reinforcement depended upon need reduction (hence reduction in D), it came in 1952 to depend chiefly on the reduction of drive-produced stimuli (S_D), or on the decrease of the goal stimulus (s_G) produced by the fractional anticipatory goal response (r_G). While favoring drive-stimulus reduction, Hull left the matter somewhat open, having vacillated between drive-reduction and drive-stimulus reduction as essential to reinforcement (1952a, page 153).

The second important change is that the quantitative aspects of reinforcement have no influence upon habit strength, provided there is some unspecified minimum amount; what counts is only the frequency with

[4] The pertinent papers are: Hull, Felsinger, Gladstone, and Yamaguchi (1947), Felsinger, Gladstone, Yamaguchi, and Hull (1947), Gladstone, Yamaguchi, Hull, and Felsinger (1947), and Yamaguchi, Hull, Felsinger, and Gladstone (1948).

[5] A critical exposition of the postulates can be found in the second edition of this book (Hilgard, 1956, pages 127-150). Hull's own treatment of them is more thorough in his *Essentials of behavior* (1951) than in *A behavior system* (1952a), although the reader must be warned that there were a few modifications between 1951 and 1952.

which reinforced trials have occurred. The basic formula for the relationship between habit strength and number of reinforcements remains structurally the same, though now the postulate includes a more empirical type of equation,

$$_sH_R = 1 - 10^{-0.0305\dot{N}}$$ (1952a, page 6),

where $\dot{N}$ is the number of reinforcements from the absolute zero of reaction potential. The constant (-0.0305) is obviously one derived from particular experiments with white rats. The centigrade scale (habs) has been abandoned, and the maximum of $_sH_R$ is now 1.00.

The third important change is the addition of a number of nonassociative factors affecting reaction potential. While some of these were recognized in the 1943 book, they are now incorporated in a different manner, all as multipliers affecting reaction potential through the multiplication of habit strength. The constitution of reaction potential now becomes

$$_sE_R = {_sH_R} \times D \times V \times K$$ (1952a, page 7),

where V is the stimulus-intensity dynamism of the evoking stimulus, and K is the incentive motivation based on the weight of the food or quantity of other incentive given as reinforcement.

The new roles for stimulus intensity (V) and for the amount of incentive (K) deserve a little discussion. Because all associative learning is based solely on the number of reinforcements (and not on the amount of drive reduction involved in any one reinforcement) all the nonassociative factors now become equivalent to drive as multipliers of habit strength. In the 1943 version, the amount of incentive (there designated w) entered into an equation limiting the maximum amount of habit strength that could be acquired under given incentive conditions; in 1952, the amount of food reinforcement on the prior trial determines the vigor of response (reaction potential) on the next trial, while not affecting habit strength. The same applies to the newcomer, stimulus intensity dynamism (V) which states merely that a stronger stimulus will evoke a greater response, habit strength remaining equal.

A fourth modification, arising out of adopting the standard deviation as the unit according to which $_sE_R$ was quantified, is a new role for oscillation. The history of oscillation in Hull's system throws some light on the problems of system-making in relation to empirical evidence.

1. In 1940 it was the response threshold that oscillated. Hence a given reaction potential might suffice to bring a response above threshold on one trial, and then (without change in the reaction potential) the response might fall below the oscillating threshold on the next.

2. In 1943 behavioral oscillation became an inhibitory appendage to reaction potential. Thus the amount of $_sO_R$ present at the moment of responding was always *subtracted* from the $_sE_R$ present at that moment. The distribution of $_sO_R$ was assumed to be normal, that is, Gaussian.

3. By 1952, the oscillation was incorporated into reaction potential, and (while the symbol $_sO_R$ was retained) no systematic reason existed any longer for the symbol, oscillation having become simply the standard deviation of $_sE_R$, and, incidentally, the unit according to which reaction potential was quantified. The detailed efforts to quantify reaction potential led to several of the refinements reflected in the appropriate postulate, notably (*a*) the statement that the distribution of $_sE_R$ is leptokurtic rather than Gaussian, and (*b*) the discovery that the dispersion of $_sO_R$ is not constant, but changes with the number of reinforcements.

The deductive use of the concept of behavioral oscillation was also extended in 1952 to account for alternation cycles in trial-and-error learning. We shall return to this deduction later in this chapter.

While other changes in detail occurred, one more is worth citing because it reflects a change in interpretation: this is the conception of the influence of delay in reinforcement. In the first place, delay in reinforcement now produces less reaction potential ($_sE_R$), while earlier it produced less habit strength ($_sH_R$). But also the time intervals have shrunk, so that the primary gradient for a single reinforced response extended up to perhaps 60 seconds earlier (1943, page 145), while later it extended not more than 5 seconds (1952a, page 131). The shortening of the gradient came about as secondary reinforcement gained more prominence in the generation of the longer gradients. Hull was influenced by Spence's (1947) suggestion that all gradients may be generated through secondary reinforcements or other intermediate mechanisms.

The Final System Summarized

The set of postulates and corollaries became somewhat formidable, and in places somewhat fragmented as Hull attempted to work into the basic principles not only all manner of quantitative relationships found to hold in classical and instrumental conditioning, but other kinds of phenomena needed to deal with types of problems beyond these reference experiments. Even so, it is possible to cut through some of the specific detail, and to summarize the system in rather direct fashion as a chain of anchored constructs beginning with the antecedent conditions (input), moving through the intervening variables to response (output). Such a summary is given in Figure 6-3, to be compared with Figure 6-2, page 156.

In Column 1 we have input conditions, all except $_sH_R$ defined by objective experimental conditions. ($\dot{s}H_R$ is habit strength from a related habit, to become expressed as generalized habit strength, $s\bar{H}_R$.)

In Column 2 we find the intervening variables most closely tied to the antecedent conditions. In Column 3 we assemble, in an intermediate step, the consequences of the simultaneous presence of the variables in Column 2. We are now (in Column 4) close to response evocation, but we

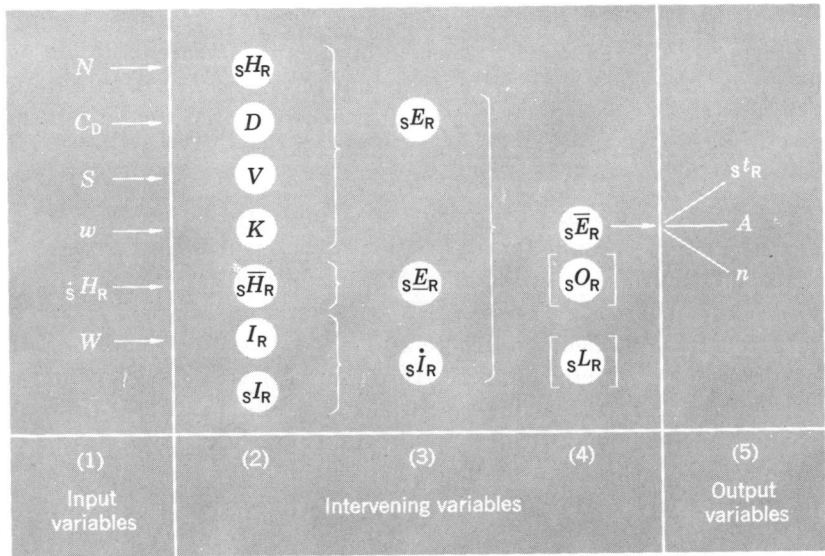

Figure 6-3   Summary of Hull's final system. The input and output variables, and the intervening variables, are symbolized as follows in the figure:

Column (1)

N, number of prior reinforcements
C_D, drive condition
S, stimulus intensity
w, amount (weight) of reward
$\dot{s}H_R$, strength of a habit based on same response conditioned to another stimulus
W, work required in responding

Column (2)

sH_R, habit strength
D, drive
V, stimulus-intensity dynamism
K, incentive motivation
$s\bar{H}_R$, generalized habit strength from related habit
I_R, reactive inhibition
sI_R, conditioned inhibition

Column (3)

$\dot{s}E_R$, reaction potential
$s\underline{E}_R$, generalized reaction potential
$s\dot{I}_R$, aggregate inhibitory potential

Column (4)

$s\bar{E}_R$, net reaction potential
sO_R, oscillation of reaction potential
sL_R, reaction threshold

Column (5)

$s{}^tR$, reaction latency
A, reaction amplitude
n, number of nonreinforced responses to extinction

must first take into account the oscillation of reaction potential $(_sO_R)$ and the threshold of response $(_sL_R)$. Finally (in Column 5) the response emerges, with the measurable characteristics of latency $(_st_R)$, amplitude (A), or number of nonreinforced evocations to extinction (n). Formerly, probability of response was also used as a response measure, but in the final system the probability measure was felt by Hull to be appropriate only when conflicting responses were involved, and hence probability is inappropriate as a measure from which to infer $_sE_R$.

The diagram falls short in not listing the several important stimulus components making up the complex of traces present when a response is evoked, important among which are the drive stimulus (S_D), and the fractional antedating goal stimulus (s_G). The kinds of items serving as components of the stimulus trace are listed in Table 6-2. Because these components are not all contemporary in origin, some of them representing the subsiding residues of just prior stimulation, others (on the basis of acquired antedating responses) representing events still to come, the complex pattern of stimuli makes possible the linking together of response patterns covering large segments of time and space. The stimulus complex contains traces that both activate behavior and guide it.

Table 6-2 **The Components of a Stimulus Trace.**

Origin of Stimulus-Trace Component, with Symbol		Resulting Component of the Stimulus Trace
Environmental stimulus S	s	Molar afferent impulse
Compound stimuli $S_1, S_2, \ldots$	$\breve{s}$	Molar afferent impulse modified by afferent interaction
Drive D	S_D	Drive stimulus
Response R	s_R	Proprioceptive consequence of response
Fractional antedating goal response r_G	s_G	Fractional antedating goal stimulus

DERIVED INTERMEDIATE MECHANISMS

Hull's system was characterized by him as molar, by which he meant non-physiological. That is, the inferences to intervening variables do not depend upon the discovery of the physiological substratum which is causal in a "molecular" way. The assertions about molar stimulus traces, or afferent interaction, need not include specification in terms of the constitution of nerve bundles or the characteristics of the nervous impulse. Hull vacillated somewhat by including physiological *language* in his postulates. In any case, Hull's system classifies as a *reductive* system, in that more complex phenomena are deduced on the basis of presumably simpler, more basic phenomena and relationships. In this sense the more complex are "reduced" to the simpler through analysis. It is characteristic of all systems of this kind *that they intend to explain behavior that is superficially unlike the behavior from which the postulates are derived.* In other words, Hull did not intend merely to systematize the account of rat lever-pressing, from which most of the data for his later set of postulates derived. He intended to arrive at the basic laws of behavior, at least the laws of the behavior of mammalian organisms, including the social behavior of man.

In order to bridge the gap between the simple laboratory experiments furnishing the constants in the postulates and corollaries, and the more familiar behavior of organisms adapting to a complex environment, he derived *intermediate mechanisms.* Once these mechanisms were available, they opened the way to the explanation of many more varieties of behavior. We shall consider two of these mechanisms: the gradient of reinforcement (originally the goal gradient), and the habit-family hierarchy.

We have to distinguish between the historical and the logical order of postulates and intermediate mechanisms. Many of Hull's most brilliant deductive accounts of complex phenomena were made in early papers, prior to the postulate systems.[6] Many of these accounts were essentially unchanged when they were reworked for the 1952 book, even though in the meantime the postulate system underwent substantial revision. From a logical point of view, however, once the system has been constructed, the postulates take priority. The same applies, of course, to predictions. An experimental fact may be "predicted" by a system, even though the fact has long been known. The only advantage in predicting new (unknown) facts is that, in predicting them, there is less temptation to include the facts in the postulates used as a basis for their prediction.

The Gradient of Reinforcement (the Goal Gradient)

There are two chief kinds of time gradients involved in conditioning experiments. The first (found primarily in classical conditioning) is based on the time between the conditioned stimulus and the unconditioned stimulus, short forward intervals being found most satisfactory. Hull took this interval into account in developing a postulate regarding the stimulus trace. The assumption is that conditioning is actually simultaneous, but the gradient is produced by a rising and falling molar trace set into motion by the external stimulus. The second kind of time gradient (found chiefly in instrumental conditioning) is based on the time between the response to be strengthened and the reinforcement. This second gradient is considered in a corollary concerned with delay in rein-

---

[6] For an introduction to the deductions available before 1940, see the summaries in Hilgard and Marquis (1940): maze learning, 216-221; serial verbal learning, 221-226; reasoning experiments, 236-241; circumventing a barrier, 242-243.

forcement. As pointed out earlier, the simple gradient (a single response reinforced) is assumed to extend for about 5 seconds; if a reinforcement is delayed more than 5 seconds, its effectiveness must depend upon other mechanisms.

The measurement of the gradient of reinforcement depends upon experiments of the instrumental conditioning type, in which an act such as pushing a lever or running down an alley leads to the goal-object and reinforcement. Delay may be introduced between the act to be rewarded and the goal-object which provides the reinforcing state of affairs. Thus the delivery of the pellet of food which is the reward for lever-pressing may be postponed for an arbitrary number of seconds in order to study the effect upon rat learning of such a delay. The gradient of reinforcement is derived from such delayed reinforcement experiments, as distinguished from the stimulus–response separation experiments of classical conditioning. Hull at first believed, on the basis of a delayed reinforcement experiment done with rats in the lever-pressing box, that the basic gradient of reinforcement was fairly short, in the case of the rat, "possibly no more than thirty seconds and very probably less than sixty seconds."

Other experiments on the effect of delayed reward, such as those of Wolfe (1934), show that in a simple alley maze the reward is effective for learning with much longer delays, at least as long as 20 minutes, the longest delay tested. A gradient is shown here, also, with the longer intervals less effective for learning than the shorter ones.

Let us see how these gradients are related. The final theory somewhat unclearly implied four steps.

1. The influence of reinforcement is solely upon the immediately concurrent stimulus and response units. There is no genuine primary gradient of reinforcement. In this Hull follows Spence (1947), and he has eliminated delay in reinforcement from his postulate set.

2. For a single stimulus–response conjunction followed by delayed reinforcement there is a short nonprimary gradient of reinforcement, extending about 5 seconds. This short gradient is derived on the basis of r_G and its s_G, especially via the secondary reinforcement role of s_G.

3. For links in a chain of responses, with terminal reinforcement, the links farther removed from reinforcement are less strongly reinforced. This is a longer gradient than that for the unchained single response, and it depends upon the secondary reinforcement provided by the environment and by the organism's own movements. This is the principle to account for the gradients in *minutes* rather than in *seconds*. It is described qualitatively in a corollary, but is not derived. While later it is treated quantitatively, the quantities are assigned *on the assumption that the gradient exists in appropriate magnitudes.* Nowhere is it linked quantitatively with the 5-second gradient of the other corollary.

4. In any actual chain of responses as observed and recorded, the gradients of reinforcement affecting individual links in the chain summate in complex fashion to produce *empirical gradients*[7] bearing little resemblance to any single inferred underlying gradient of reinforcement.

While the gradient of reinforcement did not remain the primary one it was earlier considered to be, it continued as a derivative or intermediate principle, which, once established, again served its former purposes in the explanation of more complex learning. The original application was to the maze. The principle mediated the deduction that responses nearer to the goal would be more strongly conditioned than those farther removed, so that short paths would be preferred to longer ones, blinds near the goal would be eliminated more readily than blinds farther away, longer blinds would be more readily eliminated than shorter ones, and so on (Hull, 1932). The goal gradient principle was later applied to field-force problems as studied by Lewin (Hull, 1938; also 1952a, pages 262-268). For example, in experiments involving the circumventing of barriers between the learner and a visible goal, Hull proposed that the reaction to the perceived goal-object should behave in accordance with the goal gradient. That is, the nearer the learner came to the goal, the stronger should be its response-evoking power. Thus Hull, by way of the gradient of reinforcement, came to conclusions similar to those described by Lewin as goal-attraction in relation to distance.

The Habit-Family Hierarchy

A second derived principle is that of the habit-family hierarchy. This is not included among the postulates because, like the gradient of reinforcement, it is a principle at intermediate level, being itself derived from more basic principles. It carries great weight, however, in the deduction of further behavioral phenomena.

Because there are multiple routes between a starting point and a goal, the organism learns alternative ways of moving from a common starting point to a common goal-position where it finds need satisfaction. These alternatives constitute a habit family because of an inferred integrating mechanism. The integration into a family is by way of the *fractional antedating goal reaction,* present as each alternative is active. The fractional antedating goal reaction provides a stimulus (s_G) to which all overt responses are conditioned. Through the differential action of the

---

[7] The term "empirical gradient" is a convenient term for the gradients actually found. At one time the distinction was made between the gradient of reinforcement as the gradient of habit strengthening, and the goal gradient as the effect upon performance, a distinction first suggested by Miller and Miles (1935). But when the gradient of reinforcement came itself to be derived rather than basic, the former distinction between it and the goal gradient was no longer maintained by Hull.

derived gradients of reinforcement, some responses are less strongly conditioned to s_G than others. The starting responses of longer routes, for example, are more remote from reinforcement than the starting responses of shorter routes. Hence the latter are more strongly reinforced, and more strongly conditioned to s_G. As a consequence, the alternative behavior patterns are arranged in a preferred order. The less favored routes are chosen only when the more favored are blocked. It is this set of alternative habits, integrated by a common goal-stimulus, and arranged in preferential order, that constitutes a *habit-family hierarchy*.

It is further deduced by Hull that if one member of a habit-family hierarchy is reinforced in a new situation, all other members of the family share at once in the tendency to be evoked as reactions in that situation (Hull, 1937). This makes possible the explanation of response equivalences and other appropriate reactions in novel or problematic situations, such as those found in insight and reasoning experiments.

The principle was first applied to maze learning (Hull, 1934a), serving chiefly to explain the tendency for the rat to enter goal-pointing blinds, even though such blinds may not have been entered previously and so had never been reinforced in the maze situation. Goal orientation was taken to represent an inappropriate transfer of spatial habits acquired in free space. Another application was in relation to the detour experiments (Hull, 1938). The difficulty of turning away from a perceived goal beyond a barrier depends on the presence of habit-family hierarchies as well as upon goal gradients. In the usual experience of free space, the favored path is the straight line between the learner and the goal. The next-favored starting response is that making least angle with the goal. The greater the angle, the less favored is the starting response in that family of habits built up in previous experience. Hence, when blocked, the learner prefers a path which goes off at a right angle to one which requires that he turn his back on the goal. In some objective situations he may come to choose a longer path to a shorter one, if the habit-family hierarchy proves to be misleading.

SOME REPRESENTATIVE DEDUCTIONS AND THEIR EXPERIMENTAL TESTS

Hull's system commanded its initial attention because of his ingenuity in carrying out computations in a variety of fields of experimentation, as in predicting maze behavior, rote learning, and behavior in free fields.[8] A number of these early deductions were repeated in the final book, with moderate changes to conform to the new system. The three illustrations

[8] Amsel (1965) believes that the early theorizing of the 1930's is actually more influential in the 1960's than the more formal theorizing of 1943 and later.

chosen for discussion in what follows are, in substance, new to the final book (behavior chains, latent learning, and adient-abient conflict). Although they represent but a small sample of the total available deductions in the final system, they will serve to demonstrate Hull's method of deriving new phenomena with the help of familiar postulates.

A Simple Behavior Chain

This is our first illustration, in any detail, of how Hull proceeded to use an intermediate mechanism in accounting for concrete behavior in a complex situation. Beginning with the assumption of a long gradient of reinforcement, the problem is to account for the actual latencies of response at each step of a four-response chain, the steps leading to reinforcement at the end.

Let us begin with the empirical data that we wish to derive. They come from an experiment by Arnold (1947). A rat learns to press a button presented outside the window of its restraining cage, whenever the shutter is opened. Pressing the button is rewarded by a pellet of food. Now the experiment proper begins. A clever device presents to the rat a chain of four stimulus-response possibilities by means of a car running by his window on a track. In this experiment, there are four parts of the car, all alike, all with buttons exactly like the one he already learned to press. When the shutter is opened, button B_1 is presented. He presses it, and starts the car in motion, though no pellet appears. Three seconds later the second button B_2 has come into view as the car stops with it before the window. He presses it; now button B_3 appears. In three more seconds he has the opportunity of pressing B_4. Because the response was well learned, there is not enough extinction in these few nonreinforced trials to prevent the response. Having made the four responses in order, the shutter falls, and the food reward appears, giving terminal reinforcement to the whole linked series. The series of events is presented once a day, and a measure of reaction latency taken at each button. The results for trials 2–10 are shown in Figure 6-4. While there is a kind of gradient of reinforcement, with latency getting shorter nearer to the goal, there is a striking upturn at B_4. The theoretical problem is to derive this empirical gradient from the overlap of gradients, all of which fall off from the point of reinforcement.

The steps involved are as follows:

1. On the basis of prior learning, before the car is introduced there is the original $_sE_R$ available equally to B_1, B_2, B_3, and B_4. Some initial value must be assumed. (Hull arbitrarily assumed 2.0 σ.)

2. The general form of the gradient of reinforcement with time after the car is introduced is assumed. Both its form and the number of trials

required to generate it are arbitrary, though the form is consistent with empirical gradients of generalization. The resulting increments of reaction potential at each of the stimuli turn out to be: B_1, 0.234; B_2, 0.380; B_3, 0.617; B_4, 1.000 σ. This conforms to our expectation of greater gains nearer to reinforcement, because reinforcement follows B_4.

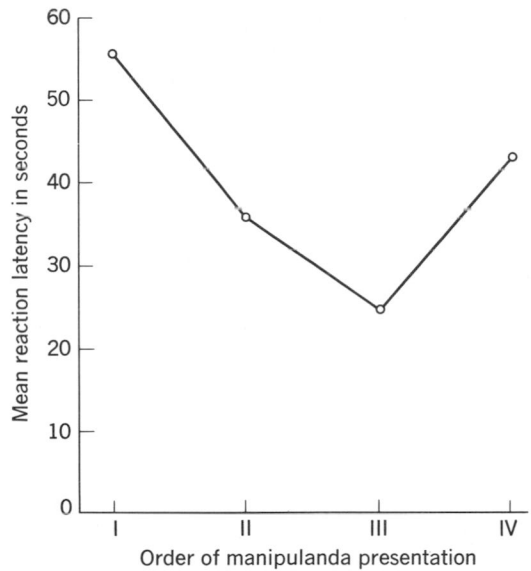

Figure 6-4   Reaction latency of responses to each of the four stimuli in a behavior chain with terminal reinforcement. Adapted from Arnold (1947, page 356), and Hull (1952a, page 164).

3. The original $_sE_R$ (2 σ) and the increment through reinforcement must be added for each link in the chain, according to the principle by which reaction potentials are combined. The sum will, of course, be less than the arithmetical sum. The result turns out to be: B_1, 2.16; B_2, 2.25; B_3, 2.41; B_4, 2.67. These values Hull calls the *gradient-of-reinforcement* values in this context, because they are the values at each link before we consider the interaction of the different links.

4. We must now take into account the fact that a stimulus does not cease to operate when it is withdrawn, but its trace persists. Hence that persisting stimulus trace will derive reinforcement from each of the subsequent secondary reinforcements along the route to the goal, and through generalization the effect will be felt at the next onset of the stimulus. Similarly, each response along the way contributes strength to the links preceding it (whose traces are represented when it is being reinforced) and to the responses following it (because its stimulus trace will be part of the stimulus complex when these succeeding responses occur). This

two-way contribution of each link to the others is computed, again through arbitrary formulas whose exponents have no relationship quantitatively to those given in the postulates, though the form of the equations is as postulated. The results are given in Table 6-3.

Table 6-3   **Steps Used by Hull in Computing the Theoretical Mean Reaction Latencies at the Response Points of a Four-Link Response Chain. The Gradient of Reinforcement values, from which the remaining values in the table are generalized, are shown in bold type. See Text. From Hull (1952a, page 162).**

	Components of Reaction Potential ($_sE_R$)			
Assumed d values (in j.n.d.'s)	4	2	1	
Response number	B_1	B_2	B_3	B_4
Values based on delay in reinforcement				
9 seconds delay	**2.16**	.14	.03	.02
6 seconds delay	.57	**2.25**	.57	.28
3 seconds delay	.30	1.21	**2.41**	1.21
0 seconds delay	.24	.95	1.89	**2.67**
Behavior sums ($\dot{+}$) of $_sE_R$	2.82σ	3.54σ	3.78σ	3.46σ
Reaction latencies ($_st_R$)	3.51 sec.	2.19 sec.	1.91 sec.	2.30 sec.

5. Now we add up the various components of reaction potential at each link in the chain. The addition is again by formula, and not straight arithmetic. The sums are given in the row second from the bottom of Table 6-3.

6. The final step is to convert these $_sE_R$'s to latencies ($_st_R$'s). Here again an arbitrary formula, with new constants but familiar form, is used, and the latencies computed, as shown in the bottom row of Table 6-3. This is the end of the determination, and the results are plotted in Figure 6-5, for comparison with Figure 6-4.

The general agreement between the two figures is striking enough to indicate Hull's ingenuity. There is some disagreement in the absolute magnitudes, however, and this led Hull to assert:

This degree of agreement between experiment and theory is, perhaps, as close as may reasonably be expected in the present early stage of the science (1952a, page 165).

The agreement lies in the form of the function. The failure lies in the latency measure—a matter of really great importance to the system because of the reliance on latency for quantifying $_sE_R$. Hull had earlier, in choosing the equation for the computation of latency, multiplied the values derived from Postulate 14 by an arbitrary constant ($3\dot{+}$) because

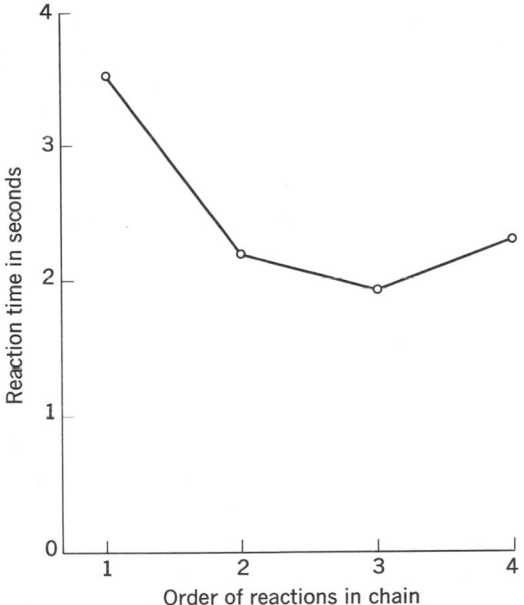

Figure 6-5   **Theoretical reaction latency of responses to each of the four stimuli in a behavior chain with terminal reinforcement. Compare with the empirical results shown in Figure 6-4. Adapted from Hull (1952a, page 163).**

he noted that the values would otherwise have been too small, then two pages later he noted that he had not boosted the latency enough (1952a, pages 163, 165). He could easily have chosen a constant to make the values correspond much more closely, by multiplying by 50 instead of multiplying by 3. Possibly he worked the matter out independently, and then felt it would be deceptive to work backwards from the result, or thought a 50-fold correction was too great. Because the constants are arbitrary anyhow, he might as well have worked backwards, and achieved as good a fit as possible. Had the constants been independently determined, there would have been some point in seeing how much discrepancy remained. As it stands, the prediction of the form of the function is an achievement. Everything else is arbitrary.[9]

The main point of this detail with respect to the derivation of the gradient for a chain of responses has been to point out how the derivation depends primarily upon the intermediate mechanism (the gradient of reinforcement), but then uses other principles (e.g., generalization, summation of reaction potentials, conversion of reaction potential to latency) to achieve a predicted result, an empirical curve that bears little resemblance to the principles used in its deduction, but corresponds closely in form to the results of a complex learning experiment. The deduction

[9] For a much more precise derivation of serial learning results, see Bower (1959b).

points out also how deceptive is the apparent quantitative rigor of the system. The quantities in the postulates are mere illustrations of quantities, and are not, in fact, made use of in any consistent manner in later derivations.

Latent Learning

Sometimes, when a new incentive is introduced, animals performing at a very mediocre level without the incentive make sudden gains, bringing them abreast of animals trained all along with the favored incentive. Because the new incentive seems to bring out concealed or unused learning, experiments of this kind, when successful, are said to reveal *latent learning*. Such experiments were formerly a source of controversy between reinforcement theorists and cognitive theorists. The cognitive theorists cited these experiments in support of their position and pointed out the difficulties for the reinforcement theorist. In the type of theory Hull held in 1943 they were indeed difficult to account for, because $_sH_R$ then depended upon the magnitude of the reinforcement. With the change in emphasis from $_sH_R$ to $_sE_R$, Hull no longer had difficulty with latent-learning experiments and proceeded to deduce their results as consequences of his new theory.

It is doubtful that Hull deliberately shifted his system in order to account for latent learning, for the facts of latent learning were at the time very much in doubt, and his followers were still very critical of the results of earlier latent-learning experiments. Another possibility is that the shift from $_sH_R$ to $_sE_R$ occurred because of Hull's preoccupation with quantification. He found that he could quantify $_sE_R$, but was far from quantifying $_sH_R$. Hence it was preferable to write more equations in terms of $_sE_R$.[10]

The method by which Hull derived latent learning is simplicity itself. So long as there exists a modicum of reinforcement, $_sH_R$ builds up as a function of the number of trials. The revealed $_sE_R$ will be small, and the revealed learning slight, because one of the multipliers (K, the incentive reinforcement) is small. Now when K is made large, through the introd-duction of the major incentive, we have a new multiplier, and the amount of $_sE_R$ (for the same $_sH_R$) will be much greater. This is largely what is meant by latent learning: a sudden gain in $_sE_R$ with the introduction of incentive.

Hull's deduced latent learning is shown schematically in Figure 6-6. Shifts of incentive, either upwards or downwards, within a few trials place the organism on the learning curve characteristic of animals trained all along with the new incentive. Hull accepts the familiar latent-learning data of Tolman and Honzik (1930b) as supporting his prediction.[11]

[10] This is also Koch's interpretation, Koch (1954), page 106, footnote 29.
[11] We shall meet latent learning again in the next chapter.

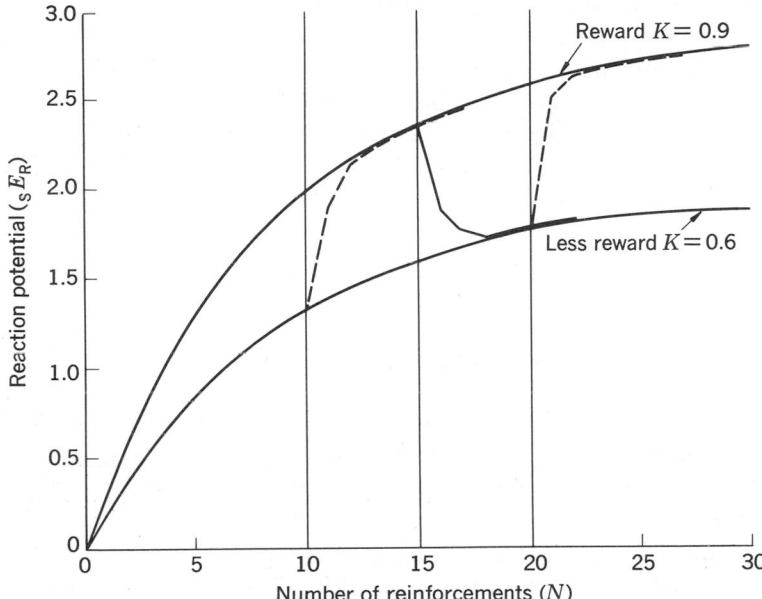

Figure 6-6   Hull's theoretical prediction of latent learning. The upper curve represents the course of learning with a large incentive (K = .9) throughout. The lower curve shows the course of learning with a smaller incentive (K = .6) The first curve that crosses between the two predicts what will happen if the incentive is increased at trial 10 for animals previously trained with the smaller incentive (the typical latent learning result). The next two crossings represent the result of a decrease in incentive at trial 15, and an increase at trial 20. After Hull (1952a, page 144).

Adient-Abient Conflict

The postulates and corollaries include references to anticipatory goal responses and to a factor (K) having to do with the magnitude of incentives used in prior reinforcements. They assert nothing, however, about *perceived* incentives. Hence Hull saved the problems of perceived incentives to be treated through theorems derived from the more basic postulates.

Perceived incentives are very important in ordinary behavior. Consider a cat lying in wait to pounce upon a bird, or a buzzard circling in search of carrion, or a male dog attracted by a female in heat. The ongoing behavior is very much influenced by the perceived incentive.

Perceived incentives are of two kinds: those, such as food, which invite approach; and those, such as noxious stimuli, which invite avoidance. Hull, selecting some older terms, called approach behavior *adience* or *adient behavior,* and withdrawal *abience* or *abient behavior.*

Hull takes the major steps from the postulates to the basic theorems of adient and abient behavior informally, that is, without quantitative reference to the postulates (except for similarities in the forms of function chosen). In the first step, he accepts it as plausible that approach responses to an attractive incentive near at hand have been conditioned according to familiar principles. The same is implied, but in reverse, for withdrawal responses. At a distance, an incentive object, whether adient or abient, will produce a stimulus pattern resembling the one close to the object, so that responses conditioned to the object itself will be conditioned to the object at a distance, at an intensity corresponding to the difference between the stimulus patterns for the near and far object. Thus the familiar generalization gradient applies. It is further assumed, on the basis of these considerations, and because locomotion is itself a highly generalized kind of behavior, that both adient and abient behavior will be highly generalized in respect to both direction and distance. Through these informal steps, largely by analogy with matters dealt with in the postulates and corollaries, Hull succeeded in providing for the kinds of conflicts in free space that Lewin treated under his concepts of "valence," an adient goal being (for Lewin) positively valenced, and an abient goal being negatively valenced.

Now we come to the quantitative portion of the deduction. For this purpose we take a special problem of adient–abient conflict, best illustrated in the experiments of J. S. Brown (1942, 1948) and the related experiments as reported by N. E. Miller (1944).[12] Brown determined two points on a gradient of adient behavior, as illustrated in Figure 6-7. A hungry rat ran down an alley to receive food at the end, the food location being distinctively marked with a light. The animals wore a little harness attached to a cord. The harness did not restrain them during their learning, but in testing they could be restrained by the cord, and the strength of pull measured. This is the pull in grams as recorded in Figure 6-7 at the two points of the approach gradient. Other animals, instead of receiving food at the end of the alley, received electric shock. When restrained near the point of shock, they pulled hard to get away from the shock zone, but if restrained at a distance they pulled away only slightly. These two points make up the avoidance gradient, which is seen to be much steeper than the approach gradient. Miller and his associates predicted that if animals were both fed and shocked at the end of the alley, they would be placed in conflict. When placed at the end of the alley farthest from the ambivalent goal, they should approach part way and then stop, the point of stopping being related to the point at which the two gradients cross, because here the opposite pulls are equal. By strengthening the hunger or weakening the shock, the animals could be made to

[12] The important evidence for the theorem under study is from an unpublished study by Miller, Brown, and Lipofsky (1943), discussed by N. E. Miller (1944), page 437.

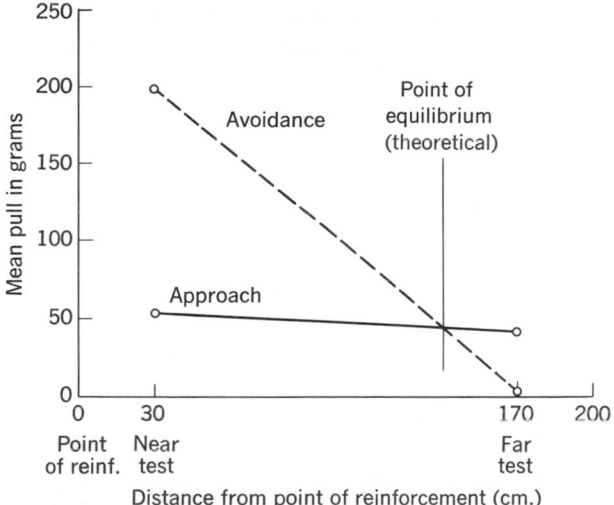

Figure 6-7   Empirical form of approach and avoidance gradients. The straight-line gradients are based on two points determined by J. S. Brown for each gradient separately, as reproduced by Miller (1944, page 434). The theoretical point of equilibrium has been added.

approach nearer to the goal before stopping. Hence the experimental results agreed with the interpretation that the two independent gradients measured by Brown would interact when both food and shock occurred together.

Now let us see how Hull, with these facts before him, ties them into his system. This is a good illustration of prediction after-the-fact, but such prediction is, with proper caution, entirely permissible in a deductive system.

The theorem which Hull advanced is stated as follows (1952a, pages 249-250):

Theorem 86. Other things equal, with moderately sophisticated subjects, when an adient object and an abient object occupy nearly the same point in space and the maximum abient reaction potential is greater than the maximum adient potential, there will be a point of stable equilibrium at a j.n.d. distance from the adient–abient object amounting to

$$d = \frac{\log_{10} \dfrac{_sE'_R}{_sE_R}}{j' - j}.$$

Miller's conclusion is thus given a precise mathematical form. The derivation here will serve to provide a step-by-step illustration of the method Hull used much more generally.

First, for the straight-line gradients of Figure 6-7, Hull substituted the curved gradients of Figure 6-8, in order to use curves of the same form that he used in generalization gradients. The adience exponent he made half that of the abience exponent, simply because Brown and Miller had found the two gradients to differ in slope.

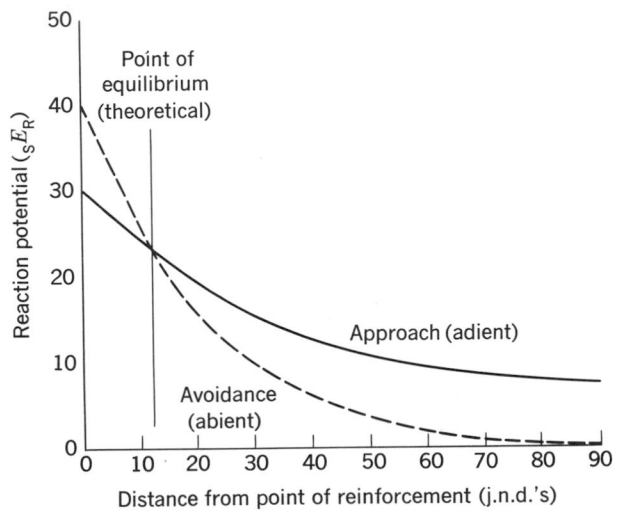

Figure 6-8   **Theoretical adient and abient gradients used by Hull in predicting the point of equilibrium in an adient–abient conflict. Compare with the empirical results of Figure 6-7. Replotted from Hull (1952a) to conform with the conventions of Figure 6-7.**

This tampering with the exponents, in order to force agreement with the results of experiments, is allowable, but it should follow some of the rules of the system. In strict logic, because Hull does not *deduce* these differences in exponents, he must *postulate* them. Therefore he has added a new but unacknowledged postulate to his system at this point (until such time as the differences are derived from more fundamental principles).

The point of equilibrium in Figure 6-8, like that in Figure 6-7, is the point at which the two curves cross. What Theorem 86 states is merely the algebraic solution of the problem solved graphically in Figure 6-8.

For adient behavior, we assume the gradient to be of the form

$$_s\underline{E}_R = {}_sE_R \times 10^{-jd}, \tag{1}$$

where $_s\underline{E}_R$ is the generalized reaction potential at any point on the gradient at a distance d in j.n.d.'s from the point of reinforcement.

The corresponding gradient for abience is

$$_s\underline{E}'_R = {}_sE'_R \times 10^{-j'd}. \tag{2}$$

To derive the equation required for the theorem we find that value of d at which the two gradients will balance each other, where $s\underline{E}_R = s\underline{E}'_R$. This is a matter of simple algebra, which looks more forbidding than it is partly because the subscripts S and R are appendages which serve only as labels.

We know that, at the value of d which we seek

$$s\underline{E}_R = s\underline{E}'_R. \tag{3}$$

Hence, from (1) and (2)

$$sE_R \times 10^{-jd} = sE'_R \times 10^{-j'd}. \tag{4}$$

Eliminating the negative exponents, we may write

$$\frac{sE_R}{10^{jd}} = \frac{sE'_R}{10^{j'd}}. \tag{5}$$

Transposing terms, we have

$$\frac{10^{j'd}}{10^{jd}} = \frac{sE'_R}{sE_R}. \tag{6}$$

Taking the logarithm of both sides,

$$j'd - jd = \log_{10} \frac{sE'_R}{sE_R}. \tag{7}$$

Solving for d, the value we are interested in,

$$d = \frac{\log_{10} \dfrac{sE'_R}{sE_R}}{j' - j}. \tag{8}$$

Equation (8) is the one appearing in the theorem. It results solely from selecting as the form of the gradient the form earlier adopted for generalization gradients, with the added assumption (similar to Miller's) that there is an equilibrium point where the two gradients coincide.

To prepare a plot as in Figure 6-8, it is necessary to make computations, using actual values for the terms entering into Equation (8). Let us see how Hull did this. He assumed the following values, which, while arbitrary, are of an order of magnitude used elsewhere in the system:

$sE'_R = 4\sigma$ The greater magnitude of the abient reaction potential sE'_R
$sE_R = 3\sigma$ is assumed in Theorem 86.

$j' = 0.02$ The greater steepness of the abient gradient $(j' > j)$ is as-
$j\ = 0.01$ sumed to be a fundamental characteristic.

Substituting these values in Equation (8), we have

$$d = \frac{\log \dfrac{4\sigma}{3\sigma}}{0.02 - 0.01} = \frac{\log 1.333}{0.01}$$

Looking up the value of log 1.333 in a table of logarithms, we find log 1.333 = 0.1248, hence

$$d = \frac{0.1248}{0.01} = 12.48 \text{ j.n.d.'s.}$$

By examining Figure 6-8, we see that the algebraic and graphical solutions agree (as indeed they should!).

What do we learn from these computations? When we follow Hull's computational technique, we find that very often the results are obtained, as in this example, through assigning equations to simultaneous functions, and then solving the simultaneous equations. The tie-in with the total system is often very slight. In this case, the forms of the gradients are the same as those used in generalization gradients, and the constants are similar in meaning. But the accuracy of the deductions does not depend upon these similarities, and, in fact, some of the correspondence between the system and the deductions is purely gratuitous. For example, no operational meaning is given to difference in j.n.d.'s along a gradient of this kind, so that there is no check whatever on the use of these units. An accurate use of empirically defined j.n.d. units might very well change the slope of the gradient. Furthermore, the puzzling problems of the relative effectiveness of reward and punishment, which ought to be dealt with as central features of a reinforcement theory, are here glossed over by the very molar assumption that the exponent for the gradient of abience is double that for adience. For a genuinely precise deduction it would be necessary also to show that strength of pull when restrained has a determinate relationship to reaction potential as quantified in the system. Despite the appearance of precision, and of tie-in with his system, Hull's deduction is by no means rigorous and represents little, if any, advance over the simpler presentation of Figure 6-7.

Proceeding in somewhat similar manner, now that the general principles of adience and abience were accepted and in some sense justified, Hull was able to combine the principle of the habit-family hierarchy with that of the gradient of reinforcement to explain the attraction of goals beyond barriers, and of the paths taken around such barriers. These are the kinds of problems in open space emphasized in field theories such as

Lewin's. Hull was willing to go so far as to borrow portions of the physical analogies used by the field theorists:

Assuming as a first approximation that behavioral vectors in quite naive subjects operate roughly as physical vectors, even a slight movement to one side of the line will unbalance the otherwise completely opposed reaction tendencies . . . (1952a, page 242).

Because adience and abience operate in two-dimensional space, Hull acknowledged that he had developed a field theory of sorts:

The theory of adient and abient behavior thus involves examples of bona fide field theory, though this theory must not be confused with physical field theories, from which the present theory differs in most respects (1952a, page 269).

Hull referred to two chief differences between his kind of field theory and physical field theory: first, the organism is not propelled, as a physical particle is, by external forces from the field, but the energy for its movements comes primarily from the food it eats; second, the distances important in physics are actual distances (centimeters or meters) while the distances in his system are in j.n.d.'s, hence defined according to the organism's reactions. The residual difference between Hull and Lewin on these points appears to be almost purely linguistic, for Lewin would not have objected to the substance of either of Hull's two points.

Success in Prediction

Eventually a self-correcting hypothetico-deductive system must be judged by its successes, that is, the agreements between predictions and observed events, and by its adjustments to its failures.

On any kind of tabulation, Hull's several postulate systems have fared very well. The successes represent a substantial achievement, but the failures, too, are achievements, in that they show Hull's statements to have been made clearly enough that data could contradict them.

Hull presented his own summary of successes in prediction in the final book (1952a, 351-353). He classified the evidence bearing on 121 of 178 theoretical propositions in that book. Of these, he found 106 (87 percent) substantially validated, 14 (12 percent) probably valid, but uncertain, and only one (1 percent) definitely invalid.

This very high agreement is somewhat disturbing at this stage in science, even though the ultimate aim is exceptionless validity. Too-high agreement, when the system is as unfinished as this one, suggests either (1) low standards with respect to what constitutes agreement, or (2) too great reliance on working backward from data, with *ad hoc* assumptions to guarantee agreement. Guaranteed agreements should not be tabulated as verifications. Working backwards is not, in itself, a defect in a theoretical system. In fact, there is no real alternative, for the improvement in a system comes precisely through "working backwards" to obtain better agreement with reality. But there are rules by which the deductions remain coherent and internally consistent, and these are often difficult to apply. As Hull pointed out, the 55 predictions in his book not covered by known relevant evidence could provide a good test of the fertility of his system, because they are free of the charge of working backward from the known.

ESTIMATE OF HULL'S POSITION

Hull's Position on Typical Problems

Because he was willing to face the problems of learning posed by others as well as those which he set himself, it is possible to assign Hull a position on the representative problems chosen as the basis for comparing the different points of view.

1. Capacity. A volume on individual differences on which Hull had been working was not completed by the time of his death. He published but a single paper on the problem (1945), and did not carry the analysis much further in his final book. Individual differences in capacity will be reflected in the constants that appear in the behavioral laws. Once these are under control, it will be possible to make fundamental attacks on such problems as that of the relationship between learning and persistent individual differences.

2. Practice. Mere contiguous repetition does nothing but generate inhibition; all improvement depends upon reinforcement. Hull is in this respect in agreement with Thorndike and Skinner, and opposed to Guthrie. Because the *amount* of reinforcement does not affect habit strength, provided some minimum amount is present, the number of reinforcements is the basic variable in acquiring habit strength.

3. Motivation. The basic paradigm for reinforcement lies in need reduction, as when food relieves the body's need for sustenance, or when escape saves the organism from injury. Thus the primary reinforcing quality of reward and of punishment is the same: food reward relieves hunger tension, escape from shock reduces shock tension. While these are the underlying biological facts, the reinforcement itself is mediated by stimulus reduction, that is, by reducing the stimuli associated with the drive, rather than by satisfying the drive itself. Secondary reinforcement can be provided by any stimulus regularly associated with primary reinforcement.

Drive is complexly related to learning: (1) it provides the basis for both primary and secondary reinforcement, (2) it activates habit strength into reaction potential, and (3) it provides differential internal stimuli that guide behavior.

More complicated relationships involving anxiety, avoidance, expectation, frustration, conflict, may be derived from the more primitive principles of primary and secondary reinforcement. Important intermediate derivations include adient (approach) behavior to perceived positive incentives and abient (withdrawal) behavior to perceived negative incentives.

4. Understanding. The organism's own responses furnishes the surrogates for ideas. The fractional antedating goal response (r_G) provides stimuli (s_G) whose sole function, in some instances, is to guide behavior. Responses that provide such stimuli are called "pure stimulus acts." Ideas thus have the substantive quality that Guthrie also assigns to them. Two intermediate mechanisms emerge as important in meeting the problems of behavior in space, and in problem-solving generally. These are the principle of the gradient of reinforcement, extended to include objects perceived at a distance, and the habit-family hierarchy, which permits the maximum utilization of past experience in the solving of present problems. Both principles depend for their effectiveness upon aroused fractional antedating responses, and upon discriminations among the stimuli that these responses produce.

5. Transfer. There are two aspects to transfer: equivalence of stimuli and equivalence of responses. Hull explains equivalence of stimuli either on the basis of generalization, or via intermediate reactions. Equivalence of responses depends in part upon response oscillation, and the generalization there involved; it depends also on the organization of responses into hierarchies by way of the habit-family hierarchy. All responses in the hierarchy have in the past led to the same goal, so that they are in that respect equivalent.

6. Forgetting. In the volume on rote learning, the decay of excitation is postulated by Hull and his associates to occur according to a kind of law of disuse, making forgetting a function of time. He reaffirmed this position in one of the corollaries of the 1943 book, but did not provide for it in his postulate set (1943, page 296). There is no reference to forgetting as such in the 1952 book, the only references being to the *rise* in the curve of reminiscence, without discussion of the subsequent fall. The only acquired function that decays systematically with the passage of time is reactive inhibition (I_R).

It is pertinent to refer here to Hull's own summary of the basic principles as he perceived them, after completing the system reported in his final book. He listed and described eight *automatic adaptive behavior mechanisms* (1952a, pages 347-350):

1. Inborn responses tendencies ($_sU_R$) provide the first automatic mechanisms for adapting to emergency situations.

2. The primitive capacity to learn is the second mechanism, "a slightly slower means of adaptation to less acute situations."

3. The antedating defense reaction, arising through learning combined with stimulus generalization, provides the third adaptive mechanism.

4. The extinction of useless acts, negative response learning, is the fourth mechanism.

5. Trial-and-error learning is the fifth mechanism.

6. Discrimination learning is the sixth mechanism.

7. A second type of antedating defense reaction, depending upon the persistence of stimulus traces (rather than upon generalization, as in the case of a perceived dangerous object), is the seventh mechanism.

8. The fractional antedating reaction (r_G) with its proprioceptive stimulus correlate (s_G), provides for the "automatic (stimulus) guidance of organismic behavior to goals." This eighth and final mechanism is the crowning achievement of the system.

Further study of this major automatic device presumably will lead to the detailed behavioral understanding of thought and reasoning, which constitute the highest attainment of organic evolution. Indeed the $r_G \longrightarrow s_G$ mechanism leads in a strictly logical manner into what was formerly regarded as the very heart of the psychic: interest, planning, foresight, foreknowledge, expectancy, purpose, and so on (1952a, page 350).

The Status of Hull's Final Reinforcement Theory

Hull's theory is not a highly integrated one, so that no one concept is truly central to it. If one accepts Hull's own summary, according to the foregoing eight mechanisms, the fact of learning is important, but the particular mechanism of learning is not crucial. Perhaps the most crucial concept is that of the r_G–s_G mechanism, which has only a tangential relationship to reinforcement theory. Nevertheless, the most controversial issue among the S–R theories concerns the status of reinforcement.

Hull's vacillation between the items to be reduced in primary reinforcement led him to reject D, to turn to S_D, then to add s_G as an afterthought. There was no finality to his interpretation of primary reinforcement.

He was also quite unclear as to what lay beneath secondary reinforcement, although he was clear as to its importance. A stimulus associated with primary reinforcement became at once (1) a conditioner of secondary drive, hence a producer of S_D, and (2) a secondary reinforcer, and hence the equivalent of reduced S_D. Hull was not really clear about this, because he seems not to have thought about both secondary drive and secondary reinforcement at the same time. His thinking was particular, not general. When he thought of secondary drive, he thought of what Miller and Mowrer talked about as fear or anxiety. When he thought of secondary reinforcement, he thought of such things as distinctive end-boxes, or tokens substituting for food. But when he wrote his formal propositions, they implied that a stimulus associated with reinforcement could become at once *both* a drive and a reinforcing agent, for the conditions necessary to become a secondary drive appeared to be the same as the conditions for becoming a secondary reinforcing agent.

Hence these fundamental matters—the nature of primary and secondary reinforcement—he really left for others to settle.

How Satisfactory a System Did Hull Leave?

Hull's system had many points of superiority over other contemporary psychological systems. It was at once comprehensive and detailed, theoretical, yet empirically quantitative. It is easy to locate faults within it because it is so carefully worked out, so explicit and mathematical that its errors of incompleteness or inconsistency are easily brought into focus. A theory expressed solely in the ordinary literary language may sound very plausible because the gaps in the theory are glossed over through cogent illustrations. A theory such as Hull's calls attention to itself whenever it jumps a gap. In criticizing Hull's theory we must not lose sight of the fact that, with all its weaknesses, it was a major achievement.

We do well to think of Hull's system as really twofold. On the one hand, he embarked upon a bold and comprehensive theory of behavior, a theory he hoped would serve as a basis for much of social science. On the other hand, he was experimenting with a very precise miniature system, with determinate constants based upon controlled experimentation. He attempted to combine these two enterprises at once, and was not very skilled at distinguishing between what he accomplished on a large scale and on a small scale, for he wanted the whole to be one system.

On a large scale, when dealing with behavior in free space, problem-solving, and ideas, Hull made skillful use of peripheral mechanisms, particularly the hypothesized r_G–s_G sequence. By interlocking these goal anticipations into other features of his system, particularly through the gradient of reinforcement and the habit-family hierarchy, he was able to make large-scale deductions of familiar forms of behavior. When moving on this large-scale level, the theory was very "molar" indeed, and almost no efforts were made to pin down precisely the kinds of anticipatory movements (chewing movements, bodily postures) that would serve as the tangible base for the important fractional antedating response. The choice of this mechanism was made (as a surrogate for ideas) because it was ponderable, and hence, in principle, at least, subject to measurement. One can easily think of possible experiments to test aspects of the r_G mechanism, especially the grosser aspects (e.g., N.E. Miller, 1935). If experiments cannot be designed to test the subtler r_G mechanisms, then one might as well deal with "ideas" as with "pure-stimulus acts." The argument that the characteristics of these acts can be inferred, if not measured, has some appeal, but it is possible to infer discriminations between ideas or engrams, too. Perhaps r_G need have no more tangible reality than $_sH_R$, but the system always implies that it is a genuine response, with proprioceptive consequences. It may be noted also that the large-scale deductions, built on r_G, do not require any one special theory of learning, so long as goal anticipation can be achieved by that theory.

When Hull was operating on a smaller scale, and attempting to become precise and quantitative, he became highly particularistic, confining many of the later postulates and corollaries to the results of single experiments done with rat bar-pressing in a Skinner box modified so that a latency measure could be secured. Hull became so preoccupied with this quantification that he failed to distinguish between this exercise in miniature-system construction and the larger task on which he was simultaneously engaged. He therefore began to write into his *basic postulates* what were really *exercises in quantification*. Surely a set of laws of mammalian behavior ought not reflect in the constants of its basic postulates such specialized information as was contained in some of the 1952 postulates: the most favorable interval for human eyelid conditioning (Postulate 2), how many days without food weaken a rat (Postulate 5), the weight in grams of food needed to condition a rat (Postulate 7), a rat's reaction time (Postulate 13), or the amplitude in millimeters of galvanometer deflection in human conditioning (Postulate 15). Surely it is preposterous to assert that these quantities hold for all responses of all species; yet this is the implication of including them in a postulate set.

It would have been preferable to distinguish between the tentative generalization and then separately to offer the quantitative evidence as illustrative. An alternative would have been to limit the miniature system to the rat in the bar-pressing box, with every effort to be systematic and to make the various constants interchangeable, to make a determined effort to measure intervening variables within this one limited universe. Then the particularistic postulates would have been appropriate, as other postulates were appropriate to human rote learning.

The source of these deficiences in the system cannot easily be specified. It is difficult to distinguish between weaknesses inherent in the system, and problems that were Hull's as a theorist and system-maker. We have two illustrations in his career of systems beginning with a large sweep and then, after heroic quantitative effort, ending so particularistic as to be much less inviting than they were before the effort was made. The first was the rote-learning theory, which, in its grosser form (1935a) appeared more inviting than its better worked-out form (Hull *et al.,* 1940). So many *ad hoc* assumptions had to be made in the more precise formulation that little has been heard from the rote-learning theory since. Now we find a similar progression in the theory of adaptive behavior. The early papers, in the 1930's, gave a new outlook upon the systematic prediction of behavior in a great variety of situations. The postulates were based largely upon the interpretation of maze behavior, simple trial and error, and serial learning. As the system became more precise, these larger predictions were mostly carried over from the past; the new postulates in both 1943 and 1952 became so tied to a limited kind of experiment (chiefly rat bar-pressing) that they are little likely to survive. It may be that particularism is an inevitable consequence of seeking precise quantitative prediction in the present stage of behavioral science. If so, it means that the theorist, at least for a time, will have to be modest in what he attempts to do, and may have to be satisfied to remain within a miniature system. If particularism is not the inevitable result of the scientific logic used, then it may be that something was wrong with the kind of concepts employed. The additional possibility is that some limitation in Hull as a systematist led him to particularism. Whatever the reason, Hull's followers will undoubtedly be able to build on his foundation to produce a more satisfactory postulate set than he left.

It must be acknowledged that Hull's system, for its time, was the best there was—not necessarily the one nearest to psychological reality, not necessarily the one whose generalizations were the most likely to endure —but the one worked out in the greatest detail, with the most conscientious effort to be quantitative throughout and at all points closely in touch with empirical tests. Furthermore, it may well be said to have been the most influential of the theories between 1930 and 1950, judging from the experimental and theoretical studies engendered by it, whether in its defense, its amendment, or its refutation. Its primary contribution may turn out to lie not in its substance at all, but rather in the ideal it set for a genuinely systematic and quantitative psychological system far different from the "schools" which so long plagued psychology.

Influence Upon Others

For some 20 years Hull was a very important person in the Institute of Human Relations at Yale University, where he influenced not only successive generations of graduate students in psychology, but also left his mark upon colleagues in the other fields of behavioral science, particularly anthropology and psychiatry. The richness of his contributions is not fully represented in his published papers and books, for in his seminars, digested in the form of mimeographed Memoranda (1934-1950), some of which are still available in a few libraries,[13] the interests ranged widely and his catalytic role was great. This influence extended to his colleagues through a Monday-Night Group which he regularly attended, and in which he occasionally took leadership.[14] A bound set of abstracts of meetings of this group during that year called *S–R Sessions* exists for the year 1938–1939. Among those who made more or less formal presentations, in addition to Hull himself, were Robert R. Sears, Neal E. Miller, Carl I. Hovland, O. Hobart Mowrer, Donald G. Marquis (all considering fairly basic principles), and P. H. French on political science, G. P. Murdock and J. W. M. Whiting on incest in cross-cultural perspective, and Mark A. May on applications to educational psychology.

Hull's seminar in 1935–1936 was devoted to an examination of psychoanalysis, leading to one published paper in this area (Hull, 1939); by 1936–1937 there were included considerations of law and political science; in October 1937 Hull presented his seminar with an outline of a systematic approach to an integration of the social sciences, with fifty-nine topics to be harmonized through the eventual postulate system. The effort to achieve a systematic integration of the social sciences continued in the year 1938–1939. The productive work that went into these seminars is largely lost because in view of his failing health Hull did well to complete the programs that were already better established.

A tribute to the tone set by his seminars was made by a visitor present in the sessions of 1939:

> C an we anticipate the truth by taking thought,
> L eaning on postulates and theorems clear?
> A re not deductions only to be sought
> R ather than SUMMAE that to SAINTS are dear?
> K nit closely, then, the experimental woof:
>
> L ast, but conclusively, we'll bring the proof.
>
> H appy the man who Logic's rules can use
> U ntil experiment shall show the flaws.
> L et fools with faith their postulates confuse,
> L eaving to us both MINIATURES and laws![15]

---

[13] At Yale University, University of Chicago, University of Iowa, University of North Carolina, Oberlin College.

[14] It was out of this group that a multiple-author volume *Frustration and aggression* was developed (Dollard and others, 1939). While this enterprise was not inspired by Hull, his influence can be detected in some of its S–R formulations.

[15] By O. A. Oeser, University of Melbourne, Australia, and quoted by permission.

Various objective estimates exist of Hull's influence upon psychology. For example, during the decade of 1941–1950 in the *Journal of Experimental Psychology* and the *Journal of Comparative and Physiological Psychology*, 40% of all experimental studies and 70% of those in the areas of learning and motivation referred to one or more of Hull's books or papers (Spence, 1952), while in the *Journal of Abnormal and Social Psychology* during the years 1949–1952 there were 105 citations of Hull's *Principles of Behavior,* and the next most frequently cited book was mentioned but 25 times (Ruja, 1956).

Among those influenced more or less directly by Hull who have continued to write in the field of learning theory, Miller (1959) and Mowrer (1960) have adopted styles of their own, and although remaining essentially within the S–R tradition they never did use Hull's more formal mathematical approach. The one who has carried on more directly is Spence, who with his students best represents a continuation of what Hull began. Spence, at the University of Iowa, and later at the University of Texas, has been concerned with quantitative theorizing in the general style of Hull, although he has departed considerably from Hull in the developing of his own position. His point of view is best presented in two books, the Silliman Lectures entitled *Behavior theory and conditioning* (1956) and a volume of collected papers, *Behavior theory and learning* (1960b).

There was a reciprocal influence between Spence and Hull. Actually Hull gained much from Spence through personal contact and correspondence; for example, it was Spence who introduced Hull to the intervening variable approach, earlier used by Tolman, and adopted by Hull in his 1943 book. Because of the common tradition represented by Hull and Spence, the general standpoint is sometimes referred to as the Hull-Spence position (Logan, 1959).

The newer mathematical models of learning, as we shall see (Chapter 11), differ in many respects from Hull's style of mathematical presentation, yet there are affiliations which should not be overlooked. His influence is in the background, if in no other way than through the effect of his persistent insistence upon the possibility of a strictly quantitative approach to psychological systematization.

SUPPLEMENTARY READINGS

The four books which represent Hull's behavior theory are:

HULL, C. L., HOVLAND, C. I., ROSS, R. T., HALL, M., PERKINS, D. T., and FITCH, F. B. (1940) *Mathematico-deductive theory of rote learning.*

HULL, C. L. (1943) *Principles of behavior.*

HULL, C. L. (1951) *Essentials of behavior.*

HULL, C. L. (1952) *A behavior system.*

For a detailed and searching criticism of Hull's system from the standpoint of the logic of science, see:

KOCH, S. (1954) Clark L. Hull. In W. K. Estes and others. *Modern Learning theory*, 1-176.

A rare opportunity exists to follow the course of Hull's thinking through excerpts from the 73 "idea books" that he left. The first of these was begun in October, 1902, at the age of 18, and the last entry was made on April 21, 1952, eighteen days before he died. These were intensely personal, and not intended for publication; as Ammons (1962) points out, it is instructive to compare the passages with the autobiographical sketch, which was of course intended to be read. The pertinent references are[16]:

HULL, C. L. (1952b) Autobiography. In H. S. Langfeld and others. *A history of psychology in autobiography*. Vol. 4, pages 143-162.

AMMONS, R. B. (1962) Psychology of the scientist: II. Clark L. Hull and his "Idea books." *Percept. Motor Skills,* 15, 800-802.

HAYS, RUTH (1962) Psychology of the scientist: III. Introduction to "Passages from the 'Idea books' of Clark L. Hull." *Percept. Motor Skills,* 15, 803-806.

HULL, C. L. (1962) Psychology of the scientist: IV. Passages from the "Idea books" of Clark L. Hull. *Percept. Motor Skills,* 15, 807-882.

[16] The articles listed by Ammons (1962), Hays (1962) and Hull (1962) are also available as Monograph Supplement 9-V 15 to *Perceptual and Motor Skills.*

Tolman's Sign Learning

The theory of Edward C. Tolman (1886–1959) was called purposive behaviorism in his major systematic work, *Purposive behavior in animals and men* (1932b). Later he (and others) called it a sign-gestalt theory, a sign-significate theory, or an expectancy theory. These later terms all emphasize the *cognitive* nature of the theory, which distinguishes it in certain respects from the stimulus–response theories of Thorndike, Guthrie, Skinner, and Hull. The designation *sign learning* provides a satisfactory short name, abbreviating sign-gestalt and sign-significate, while calling attention to the cognitive reference within the theory.

Tolman acknowledged the complex affiliations of his system—with Watson's behaviorism, McDougall's hormic psychology, Woodworth's dynamic psychology, and gestalt psychology (in both classical and Lewin's forms). He later recognized a number of parallels between his system and the probabilistic functionalism developed independently by Brunswik (Tolman and Brunswik, 1935). Still later, the influence of psychoanalysis began to be noticeable (1942, 1943). Because of these complex affiliations it is appropriate to consider his system following the treatment of other behaviorisms, and before turning to the nonbehavioristic theories.

Despite some shifts in vocabulary, Tolman held firm to his main tenets during the twenty-seven years between the time his book appeared and his death.

1. His system was a genuine *behaviorism,* and as such rigidly rejected introspection as a method and "raw feels" as data for psychological sci-

ence. When he made reference to consciousness, to inventive ideation, and the like, he was talking about interpretations of observed behavior. He did not accept "verbal report" as a dodge by which to smuggle consciousness in through the back door.

2. The system was a *molar*, rather than a *molecular*, behaviorism. An act of behavior has distinctive properties all its own, to be identified and described irrespective of whatever muscular, glandular, or neural processes underlie it. The molecular facts of physics and physiology upon which behavior rests have identifying properties of their own, which are not the properties of behavior as molar. This meant for Tolman an independence from physiology, a characteristic which he shared with several of the writers whom we have considered.

3. The system was a *purposivism*, but of a sort to avoid the implications of a teleological metaphysics. It was a purposivism because it recognized that behavior is regulated in accordance with objectively determinable ends. It was not mentalistic; purposes are not those of a self-conscious mind. It is not in agreement with teleological points of view which make effects take precedence over and determine their causes.

The strongest rejection was of American structuralism, because structuralism was dependent upon introspection of the most offensive sort, that known as Beschreibung. Watsonian behaviorism was almost as vigorously rejected, because it was not only molecular but tended to neglect the problems of goal-seeking behavior.

THE SYSTEMATIC POSITION

Behavior as Molar

The descriptive properties of molar behavior are the most general characteristics of behavior which would impress themselves upon an intelligent onlooker without presuppositions and before any attempt to explain how the behavior comes about.

First, behavior is goal-directed. It is always a getting-toward something, or a getting-away from something. The most significant description of any behavior is what the organism is doing, what it is up to, where it is going. The cat is trying to get out of the box, the carpenter is building a house (or earning a living), the musician is seeking acclaim for his virtuosity. The particular movements involved are less descriptive of the molar behavior than is the goal toward which or away from which the movements lead. This feature characterizes molar behavior as *purposive*.

Second, the behavior makes use of environmental supports as means-objects toward the goal. The world in which behavior goes on is a world of paths and tools, obstacles, and by-paths with which the organism has commerce. The manner in which the organism makes use of paths and tools in relation to its goals characterizes molar behavior as *cognitive* as well as purposive.

Third, there is a selective preference for short or easy means-activities as against long or difficult ones, called the *principle of least effort*.

Fourth, behavior, if it is molar, is *docile*. That is, molar behavior is characterized by teachableness. If it is mechanical and stereotyped, like a spinal reflex, it belongs at the molecular level. Docility is said to be a mark of purpose.[1]

Intervening Variables

The complete act of behavior is initiated by environmental stimuli and physiological states. Certain processes intervene, and behavior emerges. Programmatically, this is the formula which Hull took over from Tolman. The problem of psychological analysis at the molar level is to infer the processes which intervene between the initiation of action in the world of physics and physiology and the resulting observable consequences, again in the world of physics and physiology. Because all of the data are rooted in this world, the system remains a behaviorism.

In spite of his methodological behaviorism, Tolman was clearly bent on making a "psychological" as against a "physiological" analysis. The intervening variables include such processes as cognitions and purposes, so that, on one side of its ancestry, Tolman's position belongs with the gestalt psychologists who have been characterized as "centralists," rather than with the stimulus-response psychologists characterized as "peripheralists."

The precise variables entering into behavior determination did not remain fixed in Tolman's later discussions, but his logic of system-making remained the same. The set of terms used in his presidential address before the American Psychological Association in 1937 (Tolman, 1938) may serve as illustrative.

The background of physiology and physics with which choice-point behavior begins is defined by environmental and individual difference variables:

I. Environmental Variables
    M   Maintenance schedule
    G   Appropriateness of goal object
    S   Types and modes of stimuli provided
    R   Types of motor response required

---

[1] In this Tolman follows Perry (1918).

Σ (OBO)   Cumulative nature and number of trials[2]

P   Pattern of preceding and succeeding maze units

II. Individual Difference Variables

H   Heredity

A   Age

T   Previous training

E   Special endocrine, drug or vitamin conditions

It is possible to study the effect of such variables on resulting behavior. The usual learning curve is a plot of the functional relationship under stated conditions. These are the behavioral "facts" about learning. It is the effort to explain the facts which leads to theories.

Tolman's explanation rests on *intervening variables*. These are inferred processes between the independent variables (stimuli, etc.) and the dependent variables (responses, etc.). The preliminary list as presented coordinates one intervening variable with each of the environmental variables.

Intervening Variable		*Environmental Variable*
Demand	correlated with	Maintenance schedule
Appetite	correlated with	Appropriateness of goal object
Differentiation	correlated with	Types and modes of stimuli provided
Motor skill	correlated with	Types of motor response required
Hypotheses	correlated with	Cumulative nature and number of trials
Biases	correlated with	Pattern of preceding and succeeding maze units

Although the intervening variables may sound subjective, in principle each can be given objective definition and measurement through a defining experiment in which everything else is held constant except the correlative environmental variable while that one is systematically varied. Demand, for example, may be expected to increase with the number of hours since feeding, but the relationship between food deprivation and demand is not a simple one. It must be studied empirically. The same holds for each of the intervening variables.

Having thus established a basis for inferring the value of the intervening variable from the antecedent conditions, the next stage in theory construction is to find the equations relating intervening variables to behav-

---

[2] Σ (OBO) is a shorthand formula which means some consequence or summation of previous experiences in which one occasion (O) has led through behavior (B) to another occasion (O). The occasions are such features as a choice-point, a goal at the left, and so on.

ioral outcomes, as these intervening variables simultaneously take on different values.

In spite of the clear outline of what a systematic theory ought to be, Tolman nowhere attempted quantitative predictions paralleling those of Hull, so that his conjectures have not in that sense been put to the test.[3] This does not mean that his experiments were unrelated to his theory. There were, in fact, many predictions, but they assert that one path will be preferred to another, that under one set of circumstances the problem will be easier than under another set, and so on. The dimensional analysis which completes the function was not provided, and Hull's conscientious efforts are instructive in showing how difficult that task proves to be.

SIGN LEARNING

Sign Learning as an Alternative to Response Learning

Stimulus–response theories, while stated with different degrees of sophistication, imply that the organism is goaded along a path by internal and external stimuli, learning the correct movement sequences so that they are released under appropriate conditions of drive and environmental stimulation. The alternative possibility is that the learner is following signs to a goal, is learning his way about, is following a sort of map—in other words, is learning not movements but meanings. This is the contention of Tolman's theory of sign learning. The organism learns signsignificate relations; it learns a behavior route, not a movement pattern. Many learning situations do not permit a clear distinction between these two possibilities. If there is a single path with food at the end and the organism runs faster at each opportunity, there is no way of telling whether his responses are being stamped in by reinforcement or whether he is guided by his immanent purposes and cognitions.

Because both stimulus–response and sign learning so often predict the same behavioral outcome, it is necessary to design special experiments in which it is possible to favor one theory over the other. Three situations give strong support to the sign-learning alternative. These are experiments on reward expectancy, on place learning, and on latent learning.

1. Reward expectancy. One of the earliest and most striking observations on reward expectancy was that of Tinklepaugh (1928). In his experiment, food was placed under one of two containers while the monkey was looking but prevented from immediate access to the cans and food. Later the monkey was permitted to choose between the containers and

---

[3] Some starts were made, e.g., Tolman (1939, 1941).

showed skill in choosing correctly. The behavior which is pertinent here occurred when, after a banana had been hidden under one of the cups, the experimenter substituted for it a lettuce leaf (a less preferred food). The monkey rejected the lettuce leaf and engaged in definite searching behavior. Somewhat the same sort of behavior was found by Elliott (1928) when the food in the goal-box of a rat maze experiment was changed from bran mash to sunflower seed. More systematic experiments were carried out later with chimpanzees (Cowles and Nissen, 1937). There is little doubt that animals have some sort of precognition or expectancy of specific goal objects. Under those circumstances, other goal-objects produce signs of behavior disruption. Such behavior means that the sign-learning theory is appropriate; it does not, of course, mean that other theories may not attempt to deduce the behavior from other principles.

2. *Place learning.*   Experiments on place learning are designed to show that the learner is not moving from start to goal according to a fixed sequence of movements, such as would be predicted from reinforcement theories, but is capable of behavior which is varied appropriately to changed conditions, as though he "knows" where the goal is. There are three subtypes of these experiments.

The first subtype of the place-learning alternative to response learning leaves the form of the path intact but interferes with the movement sequences in getting from start to goal. In one experiment, rats that had learned to run a maze straight on were unable to run the maze except in circles after surgically produced cerebellar damage; but they were still able to run without error (Lashley and Ball, 1929). They could not have been repeating the earlier learned sequences of kinesthetic habits. In another, rats were able to demonstrate what they had learned by swimming the correct path after having been trained in wading it (Macfarlane, 1930).

The second subtype of place-learning experiment sets a movement habit against a spatial habit and determines which is the more readily learned. Tolman and his collaborators (Tolman, Ritchie, and Kalish, 1946, 1947) arranged an elevated maze in the form of a cross, as shown in Figure 7-1. The response-learning group was started in random alternation from either S_1 or S_2, always finding food by turning to the right. That is, food was at F_1 when the start was S_1 and at F_2 when the start was S_2. The place-learning group, by contrast, always went to the same place for food. This meant that if running to F_1, a right turn would be required when starting from S_1, and a left turn when starting from S_2. The place-learning group was much the more successful. The eight rats of the place-learning group all learned within 8 trials, so that the next 10 trials were without error. None of the eight rats of the response-learning group learned this quickly, and five of them did not reach the criterion in 72 trials. Under the circumstances of an elevated maze with many extra-maze cues, it is clearly demonstrated that place learning is simpler than response learning.[4]

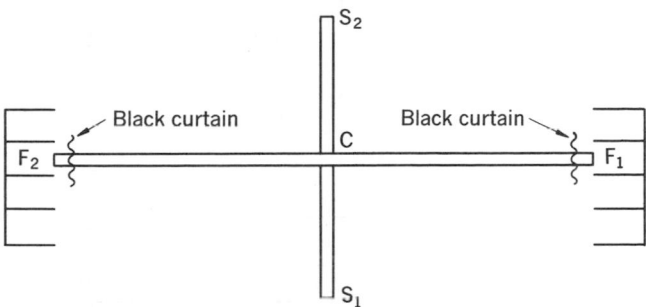

Figure 7-1   Maze used to test the relative ease of learning either a response which brings reward or the place at which reward is found. By starting irregularly at S_1 and S_2, but finding reward at the same food box each time, one group of rats turns now to the right, now to the left, to find food always at the same location. These are the place learners. By starting at either S_1 or S_2, but always finding food as a result of turning the same way (right or left), another group is taught always to make the same response, but to find food at different places, depending upon the starting point. Place learning, under the conditions of the experiment, is found to be easier than response learning. From Tolman, Ritchie, and Kalish (1946, page 223).

The third subtype of place-learning experiment involves the use of alternative paths when a practiced path is blocked. An early form of the blocked-path experiment is that of Tolman and Honzik (1930a) which is said to demonstrate inferential expectation, or insight. The main features of the arrangement are as follows. There are three paths (1, 2, and 3), in that order of length from shortest to longest, and hence in that order of preference (Figure 7-2). In preliminary training, when path 1 was blocked, a preference was established between paths 2 and 3 for the shorter of these paths. Only when path 2 was blocked also, did they run by path 3. We may somewhat oversimplify by saying that a familiarity with all paths and a preference for them in the order 1, 2, 3 was established in preliminary training. An important feature of the maze design, crucial for the test, was that paths 1 and 2 had a common segment leading to the goal. Previously the block in path 1 had been placed before this

[4] The importance of the extra-maze cues has been demonstrated by Blodgett and McCutchan (1947, 1948), who have other criticisms of the experiment cited. See the experimental reply, Ritchie, Aeschliman, and Peirce (1950). For other criticisms of space-learning experiments see Gentry, Brown, and Kaplan (1947).

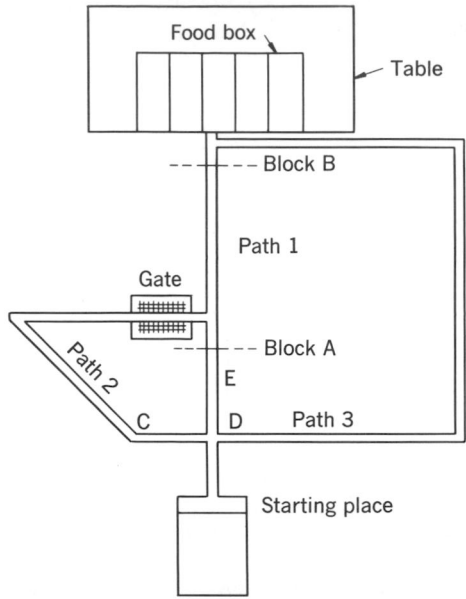

Figure 7-2   Maze used to test insight in rats. The paths become established as
                    a hierarchy according to length, Path 1 preferred to Path 2, Path 2
                    to Path 3. If Path 1 is closed by Block A, the rats run by Path 2. If
                    Path 1 is closed by Block B, the rats run by Path 3 if they have "in-
                    sight" that the barrier closes Path 2 as well as Path 1. From Tol-
                    man and Honzik (1930a, page 223).

common path; then the rat, after backing up from the block, ran to path
2. Now in the test the block was placed farther along path 1, so that it fell
in the common path. Would the rat in backing out again run by the
second preference, path 2, and be frustrated, or would it "see" that path
2 was also blocked? What the rats did, predominantly, was to avoid
path 2, and to take the path ordinarily least preferred, the long path 3,
but the only one open. Again the hypothesis is supported that the rat
acted in accordance with some sort of "map" of the situation, and not
according to blind habit, or according to the automatic performance of
habits in hierarchical order.[5]

One of the several later experiments using blocked paths also involved
rotation of the starting table through 180° on test trials, as illustrated in

[5] The Tolman and Honzik experiment was criticized by other experimenters who
showed that the results, while reproducible, were easily disturbed by the manipulation
of experimental variables such as alley width which would not be expected to make
insight impossible. See Evans (1936), Harsh (1937), Keller and Hill (1936), Kuo (1937). A
successful repetition was reported in an alley maze by Caldwell and Jones (1954). An
ingenious variation was introduced by Deutsch and Clarkson (1959), to which further
reference will be made.

Figure 7-3 (Ritchie, 1948). The original T-maze used in training is dia-
gramed at the left. From the tabletop A the F_1 rats learned to turn left,
in the direction of the light L_2. The figure on the right shows how the
table was moved from the test trials. It was not only moved, but provided
with 10 radiating paths, in addition to the original straight-ahead path,
now blocked. You would predict from a naive place-theory that the rats,
knowing their way around, would take that path leading most directly
toward the light where they had been fed. With rare exceptions they
failed to choose the direct path. They did, however, show a direction reversal, the F_1 rats now predominantly turning right rather than left, the
F_2 rats turning left rather than right. They responded to the rotation of
the starting point all right, but they tended to choose the extreme paths
running most directly toward the appropriate wall rather than directly to
the place where they had been fed. While the results thus lend some support to a directional-orientation theory, they show that a rat's "cognitive
map" (if it exists) does not correspond in any simple or direct manner
to the rat's experienced spatial reality.

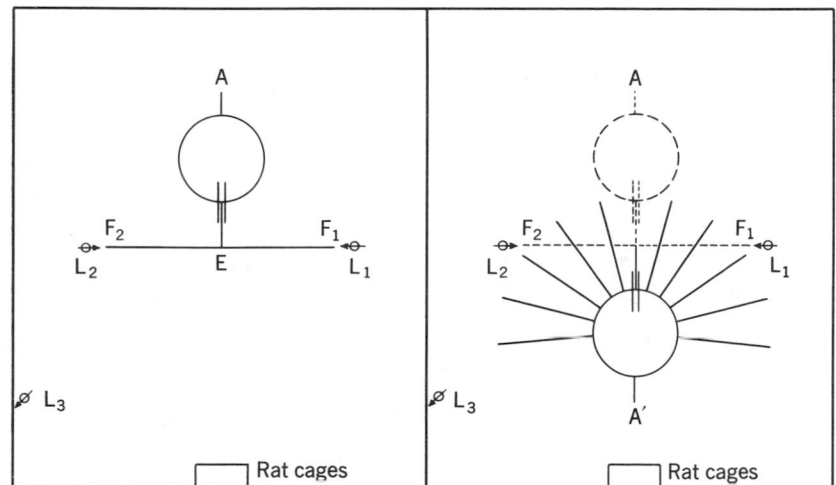

Figure 7-3   Place orientation in the rat. The dotted figure on the right shows
                 the T-maze used in training, the solid figure the rotated maze, with
                 radiating paths as used in testing. In testing, the direct path from
                 the table-top to the original choice-point was blocked. After Ritchie
                 (1948, page 664).

3. Latent learning. In addition to the experiments on reward expectancy and on space learning, a third variety of experiment bears importantly on sign learning: the latent-learning experiments. The latent-
learning experiments show that an animal can learn by exploring the

maze, without food reward, so that, when reward is later introduced, performance is better than that of rats without this exposure, and sometimes as good as that of rats with many previously rewarded trials. The "latent learning" consists of knowledge of the maze, not revealed in choice of the shortest path from entrance to exit until the rat is motivated to make that choice. The experiments, beginning with those of Blodgett (1929), have been interpreted as critical of reinforcement explanations of learning, although, as we have seen, the issue has been somewhat dulled by changes in Hull's interpretation of reinforcement.

Following up the work started by Blodgett (1929), Tolman and Honzik (1930b) studied the effect of introduction of reward in a rat-maze experiment after the animals had run several days without food. The control group, fed each day in the maze, reduced their error and time scores much more rapidly than the nonfed group, but when food was introduced for the latter group, error scores and time scores abruptly became alike for both groups. Thus the nonfed group had apparently profited as much by its earlier trials as the fed group. Since this profiting did not show in performance, the learning taking place is said to be "latent." The results for error elimination are shown in Figure 7-4.

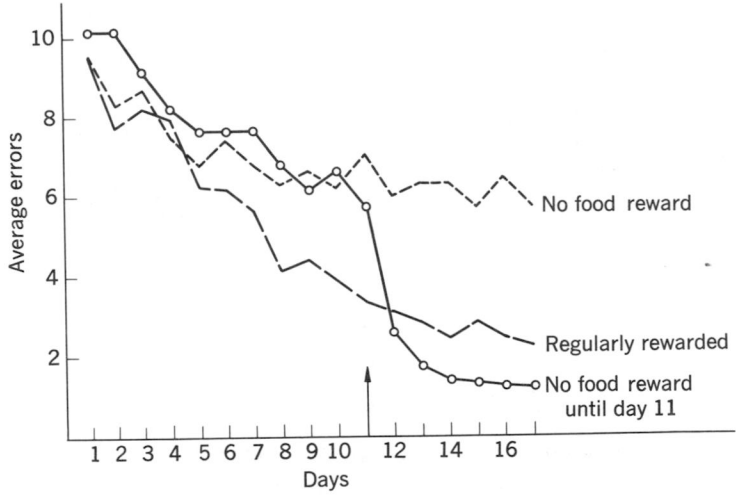

Figure 7-4   Evidence for latent learning in the maze. With no food reward there is some reduction in errors, but not as great a reduction as with regular food reward. Despite the higher error scores prior to the introduction of food, the group rewarded only from the 11th trial immediately begins to do as well as the group that had been regularly rewarded. The interpretation is that some learning went on within the first 10 trials which did not show in performance until the food incentive activated it. After Tolman and Honzik (1930b).

There were three groups: two control groups, one rewarded throughout, the other nonrewarded throughout; and the experimental group, nonrewarded until the eleventh trial. On the twelfth day, the experimental group, having been fed but once in the maze, made as few errors as the group which had received food in the maze each of the preceding days.

There are several comments to be made on this situation, in its bearing on other theories as well as Tolman's. The maze used was a 14-unit one of multiple-T type (Stone and Nyswander, 1927), arranged with doors between each unit to prevent retracing. The rat without food at the end still progressed through the maze, so that, according to such a theory as Guthrie's, learning conditions were ideal. The rat had no opportunity to unlearn what it last did in each segment, which was of course to go through the door to the next one. The results are critical of Guthrie's theory not because the rat shows latent learning but because it does not show *enough* learning when there is no food at the end of the maze. (It is to be recalled that the Guthrie and Horton cats often did not eat when they left the problem-box; their behavior was said to be fixed because they left the box.) The Guthrie explanation is not sufficient, because the fed rats learned much better than the unfed ones.

Reinforcement theories, in their older form, were at a loss to explain latent learning. In the older forms of "law of effect" theory, the presumption was that reinforcement worked directly upon response strength, so that all that was learned should be revealed in performance. Reinforcement theorists usually made much of the decrease in errors during nonrewarded trials in latent-learning experiments as evidence that *some* reinforcement was present before reward was introduced. But they could really only account for *that much* gain by reinforcement, any previously concealed gain, shown when reward was introduced, being unaccounted for. In Hull's later theory, however, in which habit strength ($_sH_R$) is acquired independently of the magnitude of reinforcement, this difficulty no longer holds. Under minimum values of incentive magnitude K (such incentives as are present without food reward, including exploration, return to home cage, etc.) habit strength will be practically "latent," to be revealed in reaction potential when large values of K are created by introducing the food reward.

Tolman's explanation is that the nonreward situation was a good one for learning the spatial relations of the maze. Every unit had one dead end and another end with a door. The last thing done in each case was to go through the door. Recency (which is accepted as favoring sign-gestalts) would strengthen the cognition that the door was the way from one segment to the next, though under nonreward conditions there were no reasons for the rat to show what it "knew." The substitution of the food at the end of the maze, a highly demanded goal-object, led the rat to use its cognitive map, to take the turns which led from one unit to the next. Hence the sudden reduction in errors. That the group with later introduction of reward had a tendency to do even better than the regularly rewarded group may conceivably have been due to a more thorough exploration of the maze in the early trials by the nonrewarded group, with consequent better orientation when finally running toward the goal.

An upsurge of interest in the issues opened up by the latent learning experiments led to a great many experimental reports, chiefly in the 1940's and 1950's. These were reviewed by Thistlethwaite (1951) and again by MacCorquodale and Meehl (1954, pages 199-213).[6] While different varieties of latent-learning experiment led to somewhat different scores, of the 48 studies reviewed by MacCorquodale and Meehl, 30 were reported as positive, 18 as negative. There is little doubt that, under appropriate circumstances, latent learning is demonstrable.

Following their review of the latent-learning literature, MacCorquodale and Meehl concluded:

> In spite of the preceding difficulties of interpretation, it seems safe to say that the current state of the evidence is at least encouraging to the theorist oriented to some form of expectancy theory. We were, frankly, somewhat more impressed by the overall trend of the evidence than we had expected to be (1954, page 213).

In his own summarization of the experimental work supporting his theory, Tolman (1948b) listed two additional varieties as significant: the experiments on "hypotheses" in rats (Krechevsky, 1932a) and the experiments on vicarious trial and error (VTE) (Muenzinger, 1938; Tolman, 1939; Geier, Levin, and Tolman, 1941; Jackson, 1943). The experiments on hypotheses led to the conclusion that in a four-choice maze the animals adopted systematic modes of solution, such a choice being somewhat tentative, so that one mode would be rejected for another. These experiments furnished the background for a controversy over "continuity" and "discontinuity" in discrimination learning, the hypothesis experiments furnishing support for the "discontinuity" interpretation. Vicarious trial and error refers to the vacillation at a choice-point before the animal is "committed" to one or the other choice. This active comparing of stimuli appeared to Tolman to support his viewpoint that perceptual or cognitive processes are prominent in controlling behavior at a choice point.

---

[6] A review was also presented in the second edition of this book (Hilgard, 1956, pages 211-215). Thistlethwaite's early review was considered to be too friendly to latent learning by Kendler (1952) and Maltzman (1952). For his reply to their criticisms see Thistlethwaite (1952).

Expectancy versus Habit

Can a more precise formulation be made of the sign-learning theory—the theory to which the results of all of these experiments are said to conform? It has sometimes been characterized as a theory of "what leads to what," a theory of signs, significates, and behavior routes. There are really two central problems in a theory of this kind: first, how is the expectation acquired that a given sign will lead to its significate, and, second, how is this expectation translated into action? We begin with the problem of acquiring the expectation.

The theory is that with repeated experience of a sequence of events leading to a goal the probability that the given behavior will eventuate in the expected end result becomes learned. The result (for behavior) is faster running and blind-alley elimination, exactly as if a habit were being strengthened by reward. Hence some ingenuity is required to isolate circumstances in which the expectancy interpretation is more appropriate than the habit-strengthening one. While the foregoing account of experiments gives qualitative support to a cognitive interpretation of learning, if expectancies conform to probabilities, a more quantitative approach should be possible. In a very stimulating paper Tolman and Brunswik (1935) proposed that the causal texture of the environment is not such as to permit firm expectations but that predictions must often be made on the basis of probabilities. In an experimental test of the proposal, Brunswik (1939) presented his rats with such a contingent environment, in which food might sometimes be found on the right, sometimes on the left. He found that there was some measure of agreement between the choices of the rat and the probability that food would be where he went for it.

An important supplementary finding in Brunswik's experiment was that the nature of the goal provides an emphasis that makes a great difference in the behavioral response to the discriminated probability. He found, for example, that rats rewarded on one side of a T-maze in 100 percent of their runs to that side, and on the other side in 50 percent of their runs to that side, showed a preference for the two sides in roughly the 2:1 ratio of these reward schedules. This preference was tested during the last eight trials of training. During these trials, the rats ran to the 100 percent rewarded side in 72 percent of the runs, and to the 50 percent rewarded side in 28 percent of the runs. If, however, the partial reward side was also "dangerous" on half the trials (a shock being used instead of nonreward), this cancelled the effect of the intermittent reward, and learning was equivalent to that in a conventional T-maze experiment in which one side only was rewarded. This, and related results, led Brunswik to state:

Discrimination of probabilities tends to increase with the rate of the probability of *emphasis* on the two sides of the probability discrimination problem (1939, page 185).

Common experience amply justifies this supplementation to a simple probability theory. One might walk into a store to try to make an unusual purchase even though the probability was only 1:10 that the store carried the merchandise sought. But one would not buy a ticket on an airline where the probability of a crash was 1:10. Discriminated probabilities are *weighted* before they emerge in action.

In order to compare an expectancy theory with a reinforcement theory, Humphreys performed several experiments of the conditioned-response type. In human eyelid conditioning, it had already been shown that conditioned discrimination was more rapid when subjects knew which stimulus of a pair was to be positive, which negative, than when the probabilities had to be established through experience with the stimuli (Hilgard, R. K. Campbell, and W. N. Sears, 1938). The conjecture that the subjects were responding according to their expectations was a plausible one. Humphreys (1939a) went on to show that random alternation of reinforcement and nonreinforcement led not only to as much conditioning as reinforcement every trial, but was followed also by greater resistance to extinction. During extinction, responses increased in frequency at first, and then fell off. This would be anticipated on an expectancy theory because the likelihood of reinforcement was great after a nonreinforcement during the body of the experiment, and greater still after two nonreinforcements because there were never more than two successive nonreinforcements during the training sessions. But even after this high point, extinction was gradual. Humphreys conjectured that a shift from intermittent reinforcement to uniform nonreinforcement must have led with difficulty to the hypothesis of uniform nonreinforcement. Because the experiment was done with human subjects, a direct test was possible on the verbal level, and Humphreys (1939b) designed and carried out a simple experiment which confirmed his conjecture.

For the study of verbal expectations, two lights were arranged on a board. When one of these lights was turned on, the subject was asked to guess whether or not it would be followed by the other light. Half the subjects were "trained" with the second light invariably following the first. They came gradually to guess in a high percentage of the cases that the first light would be followed by the second, in agreement with their experience. The other half had the second light turned on only in random alternation, so that half the time it did not appear. They guessed at chance level. Within the conditioning experiment, the intermittent-reinforcement group performed like the group uniformly reinforced; but in the verbal experiment, the groups behaved entirely unlike. Does this difference not invalidate the comparison? On the contrary, it is an essential part of it, because it is necessary to distinguish between performance and expectation. In the conditioning experiment, uncertainty leads to conditioned responses as well as certainty because it is a "danger" situation; blinking is as easy as refraining from blinking, and there is no penalty for an "erroneous" response, that is, for blinking to the conditioned stimulus alone. In the verbal experiment, response is more nearly representative of "pure" expectation, because a false guess is subjectively interpreted as a mistake in a way in which a false conditioned response is not.

The crucial portion of the experiment is that in which extinction is simulated, that is, in which the first light is never again followed by the second. Humphrey's results are plotted in Figure 7-5. It is seen that the group which had been trained on the every-trial "reinforcement" quickly developed the hypothesis of uniform nonreinforcement, and ceased to expect the second light. The group trained with intermittent "reinforce-

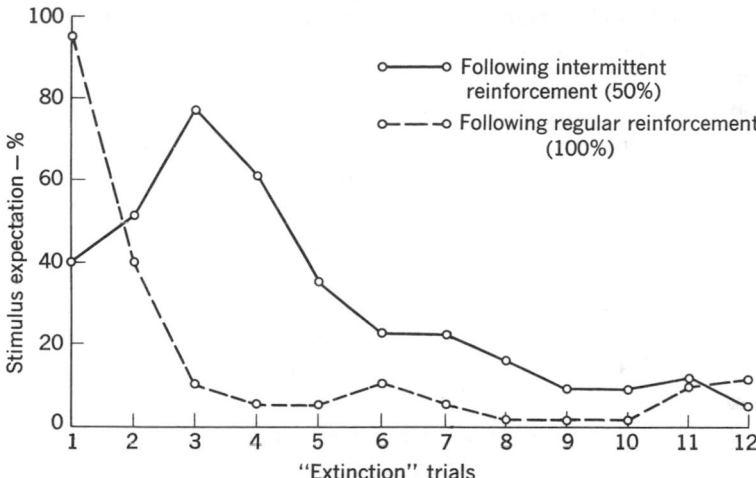

Figure 7-5   A phenomenon like extinction in an experiment on verbal expectation. Prior to yielding the data in this figure, one group had regularly experienced a second light following a signal light, and had developed the expectation that a second light would regularly follow. This condition simulates 100 percent reinforcement in a conditioning situation. For the second group, the signal light had been followed by the "expected" light only half the time. This condition is like 50 percent reinforcement in conditioning, and leads to uncertainty as to whether or not the signal will be followed by a second light. Beginning with the trials shown in the figure, the signal light was never followed by a second light, thus simulating extinction. What is recorded is the percentage of subjects guessing on each trial that the second light would occur. Following regular reinforcement the change to the expectation of regular nonreinforcement occurs more readily than following intermittent reinforcement. After Humphreys (1939b).

ment" showed the rise in expectation which the theory demands, and the slow acceptance of the hypothesis that there would be no more second lights.[7]

A provisional expectancy is an hypothesis. When a situation is not yet structured so that path-goal relationships become clear, behavior in relationship to the situation may either be "random" or "systematic." If it is systematic, it may be said to accord with an hypothesis. Score averages from groups of animals tend to conceal the differences between chance approaches and more orderly approaches, because one animal's responses cancel another's unless they happen to correspond to the experimenter's plan as to what will be counted correct. By studying the presolution behavior of individual animals, systematic attempts at solution can often be discovered, solutions of the order: "turn right," "alternate," "go to the dark." These are not mere fixed preferences, because after one pattern has been used for a while, the animal learner may shift to another one. Krech named such systematic attempts at solution "hypotheses," and studied them under a number of conditions (Krechevsky, 1932a, 1932b, 1933a, 1933b).

The full-fledged conception of expectancy thus includes at least the following aspects: (1) The organism brings to a problematic situation various systematic modes of attack, based largely on prior experiences. (2) The cognitive field is provisionally organized according to the hypotheses of the learner, the hypotheses which survive being those which best correspond with reality, that is, with the causal texture of the environment. These hypotheses or expectancies are confirmed by successes in goal achievement. (3) A clearly established cognitive structure is available for use under altered conditions, as when a frequently used path is blocked.

Most of the discussion thus far has been concerned with acquiring an expectation, and with the nature of expectancy. The second question posed earlier was how an expectancy was translated into action. The answer is by no means self-evident, and, in fact, Guthrie accused Tolman of leaving the rat "buried in thought" (Guthrie, 1952, page 143). This problem is common to all information-processing theories, but their answers are also similar. When there is some sort of demand or motive to be satisfied, the organism will make use of its available information in action. This is the basis for the distinction between learning and performance, as implied in the latent learning experiments. Hence as we turn now to a discussion of confirmation versus reinforcement we are examining Tolman's reply to this second question.

[7] The results of intermittent reinforcement, both within conditioning experiments and within verbal experiments, have proved to be of considerable theoretical interest, and the experimental literature is now sizable. For a useful summary, see Jenkins and Stanley (1950). On verbal experiments similar to Humphreys', see Grant, Hake, and Hornseth (1951).

Confirmation versus Reinforcement

Because Tolman was at such pains to protest against the law of effect and the principle of reinforcement as essential to learning, it is in order to inquire what role he assigned motivation in learning.

One role assigned to motivation was in relation to performance. Learning is *used* when drives are active. When drives are aroused, a state of tension ensues, leading to demands for goal-objects.[8] These tensions lead to activity, guided by the expectancies or cognitive structures available. In this role, then, motivation is not really a factor in learning at all. It is related to performance, not to acquisition. Because this role of motivation is made much of in Tolman's criticisms of reinforcement theories, the impression is given that learning, the acquiring of cognitive structures, is independent of motivation. This is not true in fact, nor is it true in Tolman's theory.

The second role of motivation is in the acquisition of cognitive structures. In one of the experiments critical of the law of effect, the suggestion was made that what appeared to be the principle of effect might better be considered the influence of *emphasis* (Tolman, Hall, and Bretnall, 1932). That is, motivation determines which features of the environment shall interest the learner, and those to which he pays attention. Such factors are influential in perceptual acquisitions, which are the genuine substance of place learning. Causal sequences of the environment are not all spatial. Some are temporal; some are logical or systematic or arbitrary. The goal-object, by its presence or absence, verifies or refutes hypotheses. Hence the goal-object is essential for the establishment of some features of cognitive structure. Latent learning, which dramatizes a relatively unmotivated, incidental type of learning, is an extreme instance of the relationship of goal-behavior to learning and is probably not a typical case.

The importance of something like emphasis is well brought out in the series of experiments by Muenzinger and his associates between 1934 and 1952 (e.g., 1935, 1952) in which punishment or obstacles to be overcome, even on the side of the correct choice, aid learning. Whether or not punishment will be an aid to learning thus depends upon what influence it has on the cognitions of the learner. It may be helpful as an emphasizer or harmful as a distractor.

The principle in Tolman's system that most nearly replaces reinforcement is the principle of *confirmation*. If an expectancy is confirmed, its probability value is increased; if an expectancy is not confirmed, its probability value is decreased (i.e., it undergoes extinction). Tolman distin-

---

[8] The parallel may be noted with Hull's interpretation of drive as activating habit strength into reaction potential.

guished between confirmation and reinforcement in a passage describing the building up of preferences for one restaurant over another:

Such learning takes place, I believe, not primarily through reinforcement in the Hullian sense but merely by the *repeated "confirming"* experiences of finding what restaurants lead to what foods by what costs and with what degrees of gratification (1952, page 396).

The regulatory role of reward is not very different in Hull's system from this role in Tolman's, though the interpretations differ. According to Tolman, the learner acquires knowledge of a means-end relationship; according to reinforcement theory, he learns behavior which is followed by reward. In any case, it would be most misleading to interpret Tolman's position as if reward influenced performance only, and not learning. All that he insisted upon was that learning and performance cannot be equated, and the role of motivation in learning differs in some respects from its role in performance. This conclusion, originally proposed by Lashley (1929), can scarcely be doubted.

VARIETIES OF LEARNING AND THEIR LAWS

The 1932 Version

Learning theorists commonly select one kind of learning problem or situation as typical and then proceed to develop a theory appropriate to this reference situation. Having constructed a set of principles in this way, they attempt to show by a logical process that other kinds of learning are really at base like the typical one, and hence explicable in the same terms. Recognizing this tendency, Tolman selected for review three kinds of learning experiments, with their three corresponding doctrines. These were conditioned-reflex learning (Pavlov), trial-and-error learning (Thorndike), and inventive learning (Köhler). He then gave a sign-gestalt interpretation of each of the three kinds of learning as alternative to the usual theory associated with each. He found it useful to preserve the typical experiments, which represent a kind of hierarchy from stupidity to intelligence. The laws applicable to the more stupid situations have to be supplemented by additional laws for the higher forms of learning.

In the 1932 version there were three groups of laws: capacity laws, laws relative to the nature of the material, and laws relative to the manner of presentation.

1. Capacity laws. Only organisms can learn. It is evident, therefore, that what the organism can learn must depend on what kind of an organism it is. That is the reason for capacity laws.

The list of capacity laws is as follows (1932b, pages 376-377):

a. Formal means-end-capacities
b. Discriminating and manipulating capacities
c. Retentivity
d. Means-end-capacities needed for alternative routes, detours, etc.
e. Ideational capacities
f. Creative instability

In order to learn conditioned reflexes, the learner must have the necessary capacities to form and act in accordance with "sign-gestalt-expectations." That is, the conditioned stimulus serves as a sign that the unconditioned stimulus is about to appear and the conditioned behavior is appropriate to the sign. This capacity is named a "means-end-capacity." In his later writings, Tolman dropped a number of the hyphenated terms which made his book clear, entertaining, but also somewhat forbidding. In the list of laws which we have given above, his terms have been freely paraphrased to make for easier reading, although there may be some loss involved. In addition to the general capacity for sign learning, conditioning requires special capacities for discriminating and manipulating features of the environment. Finally retentivity is implied, if the results of earlier conditioning trials are to influence later ones. Only capacity laws a, b, and c apply to conditioning.

The capacities needed for trial-and-error learning are the same as those required for conditioning (a, b, c) except that additional means-end-capacities (d) are needed because more alternatives are open to the learner. The field relationships of alternate routes, detours, final common paths, are involved. Additional capacities of ideational sort (e), permitting comparison of alternates (a mental "running-back-and-forth"), are probably helpful in trial-and-error learning.

Inventive learning requires all the capacities of the other varieties of learning plus *creative instability* (f). This is a capacity to break out into new lines of activity which have never occurred to the learner before.

The need for capacity laws seems evident enough, once they are proposed, though they have been neglected in most learning theories. Even Thorndike, strongly identified with the study of individual differences, neglects capacity laws in his learning theory. Such a statement as "Any response of which the organism is capable can become attached to any stimulus to which it is sensitive" (Thorndike, 1913b, page 15) implies only sensitivity capacity and response capacity, and neglects any capacity to establish relations between them. It would be grossly unfair to say that Thorndike did not recognize differences in learning ability, but it is true that he slighted the different kinds of capacities needed for different kinds of learning, because all learning was merely the forming of bonds. Hull, who also in one of his earlier research interests contributed to the psychology of individual differences (Hull, 1928), only late in his career began to consider individuality as something to enter into his learning theory (Hull, 1945).

2. Laws relating to the nature of the material.   In Tolman's discussion of these topics, he called attention to certain "gestalt-inducing-conditions" and suggested that they are of the sorts emphasized in gestalt studies of perception.

The list follows (Tolman, 1932b, pages 378-385):

    a. Togetherness
    b. Fusibility
    c. Other gestalt-like laws
    d. Interrelations among the spatial, temporal, and other characters of the alternatives
    e. Characters in the material favoring new closures and expansions of the field.

In relation to conditioned-reflex learning, these laws suggest that there must be a "togetherness" of essential signs and their means-end-relationship to the thing signified (*a*). Tolman states that this is about what Thorndike called "belongingness." Tolman adds a somewhat similar law of fusibility of sign, significate, and signified means-end-relationship (*b*), by which he means a certain naturalness about the situation which makes it easier to form a gestalt of the whole. He provides in a third law for the possibility of new discoveries (*c*). He adds one law (*d*) for trial-and-error learning and one for inventive learning (*e*), to suggest that some arrangements must be easier than others. He points to Köhler's observation that the ape could learn to use the stick more easily to rake in the food if the stick and food were perceived together.

These laws show great catholicity, but there is no ordering principle among them. "Spatial, temporal, and other" can scarcely be said to arrange things dimensionally. They do make a definite bow to the important fact that perceptual principles must be understood if the relative ease or difficulty of problematic situations is to be made comprehensible.

3. Laws relative to the manner of presentation.   These are the laws inherited largely from association psychology, the ones for which abundant evidence can be found recorded in McGeoch and Irion's book (1952).

The list is as follows (Tolman, 1932b, pages 385-389):

    a. Frequency, recency
    b. Revival after extinction, primacy, distributed repetition, etc.
    c. Motivation
    d. Not "effect" but "emphasis"

    e. Temporal orders and sequences in the presentation of alternatives

    f. Temporal relations between the presentations of certain of the already given alternatives and the true solution.

Of these, the first four belong to conditioned-reflex learning, the first five to trial-and-error learning, and all six to inventive learning.

The principles of frequency and recency are accepted in the following form: "The more frequently and more recently the actual sequence of sign, means-end-relation and significate have been presented, the stronger, other things being equal, this resulting sign-gestalt will tend to be" (1932b, page 386). That is, only in a situation favorable to sign-gestalt formation will frequency be effective. The other laws provide opportunity again to raise the question of the law of effect, and to make some observations descriptive of favorable conditions in trial-and-error and multiple-choice experiments.

As a set, the laws are rather disappointing. They serve as a useful reminder of the main tenets of the point of view and of its criticisms of prevailing doctrines. They leave much to be asked for on the positive side in their lack of sufficient precision of statement so that they can be called true or false.

Leaving the laws in this form makes everything a matter of correlations between situation and behavior and does not get at the formal problem of rigorous definition and measurement of intervening variables. This lack was never made up, in spite of later reworkings of the list of laws.

The 1949 Version

New sets of laws were proposed by Tolman from time to time. The "laws" do not have the centrality within his system that Hull's postulates have within his, so the revision of the list of laws requires little reinterpretation of earlier experimentation. For purposes of understanding the restatement of the theory, however, it is useful to review one of these later revisions. The one selected for review appeared 17 years after the first (Tolman, 1949).

In this later paper, Tolman distinguished six "types of connections or relations" that get learned, and then proceeded to indicate what was known about the "laws" applying to each.

1. Cathexes. Tolman borrowed the word "cathexis" (plural, cathexes) from psychoanalytic theory, where it refers metaphorically to the energy charge with which an activity is invested. He gives it a related but more restricted meaning, almost equivalent to Lewin's valence. A cathexis is an acquired relationship between a drive and an object. If a hungry child wants a banana, you know that the child has a learned cathexis between its hunger drive and a banana as a preferred goal-object. This is a positive cathexis, for the child is led to seek bananas. A negative cathexis works the other way. If a burned child fears a hot stove his fear is connected, as a negative cathexis, to the stove, and the cathexis is negative because he shuns the stove.

Tolman believes that drive reduction (reinforcement) is probably valid as an explanation for the acquiring of cathexes, but he believes we need more experimental evidence.

Both positive and negative cathexes, he believes, are very resistant to forgetting.

2. Equivalence beliefs. This is Tolman's substitute for secondary reinforcement, whereby an organism reacts to a subgoal (or a subdisturbance, in the case of negative cathexes), as it would in the presence of the goal or actual disturbance. In social behavior, and especially in the psychological clinic, we see evidences of faulty equivalence beliefs. These are often engendered by traumatic experiences. Hence Tolman concludes that the reinforcement principle is valid for equivalence beliefs as for cathexes, but it needs to be supplemented by an awareness of the importance of traumatic experience.

3. Field expectancies. These are the rechristened sign-gestalt-expectations of the earlier system. They permit the organism to take shortcuts and roundabout routes, and make possible latent learning. Tolman reasserts his contention that reinforcement *per se* is not valid in the explanation of field expectancies, although he acknowledges the importance of motivation.

The presence of reinforcement in a particular locus makes the locus a goal which determines what performance will take place but it does not stamp in S–R connections though it probably does give a special vividness to that locus in the total field expectancy (1949, page 151).

Although we know little at present about laws of the formation of field expectancies, when we do work them out we shall have to take into account perceptual sensitivity, memory, and inference abilities.

The forgetting of field expectancies is probably more rapid than the forgetting of cathexes and equivalence beliefs. Such forgetting, Tolman believes, probably follows the sorts of laws the gestalt psychologists have uncovered.

4. Field-cognition modes. These modes are of higher order than the field expectancies. A field-cognition mode makes a given expectancy-formation possible. The mode is based in part upon innate capacities and in part on previously established field expectancies. Hence a field-cog-

nition mode represents a disposition or readiness to acquire field expectancies of one of three varieties: perceptual, memorial, or inferential.

Tolman has no laws to suggest. Such laws will arise out of at present
nonexistent types of transfer experiment.

5. *Drive discriminations.*   Tolman here refers to experiments such as
those of Hull (1933) and Leeper (1935a), in which the animal learned to
go one way when hungry, another way when thirsty. Tolman has no
laws to suggest.

6. *Motor patterns.*   Because his behaviorism was not of the stimulus-
response variety, Tolman recognized that he needed some special principles governing the acquisition of motor patterns. For these, Tolman
was in 1949 prepared to accept Guthrie's simple conditioning explanation.

It is evident that these laws did not move toward precision over the
initial set. Tolman stated his own estimate of what he had done here:

> And, although, as usual, I have been merely programmatic and have not at-
> tempted to set up, at this date, any precise system of postulates and deduced
> theorems, I *have* made some specific suggestions as to some of the conditions and
> laws for the acquisition, de-acquisition, and forgetting of these relationships
> (1949, page 154).

While Tolman made very thoughtful observations on learning, and
was responsible for much original experimentation, he did not propose
a system clearly enough defined so that successive approximations succeeded in making it more exact and testable. We find, in this statement
of six kinds of learned relationships, two explained by reinforcement
(Hull, Skinner), one explained by simple conditioning (Guthrie), and
three not explained at all. This is characteristic of Tolman's role. In addition to making concessions to other interpretations, he consistently
pointed out relationships difficult for stimulus–response theorists to explain, without himself being able to offer much in the way of detailed
explanation for these discovered relationships.

A Final Statement

Shortly before his death Tolman accepted the invitation to review his system, and his account appeared in a chapter the year he died
(Tolman, 1959).

The most formal portion of this chapter describes five learning paradigms according to *independent variables* (from the past, and some operating in the present), *intervening variables* (two classes: means-end

readinesses; expectations, perceptions, representations, valences), and *dependent variables* (performances, VTE's).

The five paradigms are:

1. Approach learning (as in approaching and eating food).
2. Escape learning (as in escaping from electric shock).
3. Avoidance learning (by not doing something, pain is avoided).
4. Choice-point learning (one alternative leads to a positive goal-stimulus, the other to a negative goal-stimulus).
5. Latent learning (at an early stage, all choices are equally "good," but when food is introduced reduces to Paradigm 4).

Each of these is described by a complex diagram of many subequations, representing relationships of the following kinds:

$S_1 \rightarrow S_p$ (a stimulus S_1 has in the past been associated with pain, S_p).

$S_1 R_1 \rightarrow S_2$ (making the response R_1 to S_1 leads to a new stimulus S_2).

While means-end readinesses or beliefs are symbolized by lower-case letters, they too are made up of s's and r's, but these have special meanings:

$s_1 r_1 \rightarrow s_f$ (a type of stimulus s if manipulated by a *type* of response r will lead to a food stimulus of the *type s_f*).

Because such equations have so many references ("surplus meanings") beyond their mathematical properties, the diagrams prove not to be very helpful, and it is doubtful that they will survive as significant features of Tolman's theorizing.

Tolman remained concerned about the extent to which he could substantiate his claims that he was presenting a behaviorism, so that everything important could be specified by public operations, or, as he chose to call them, "pointer readings." That is, stimuli and responses can be specified by their status as events in the physical world, hours of food deprivation serve as "pointer readings" for food drive, and head movements (or vacillating body movements) provide "pointer readings" for vicarious trial and error (VTE) behavior. He expressed some doubts about appropriate pointer readings for means-end readinesses (beliefs) and at one stage tried to get along without them (Tolman, 1955), but he finally decided that a means-end readiness is a more enduring disposition than an expectancy. In order to preserve the distinction he returned to the means-end readiness in the final paper. He hoped that perhaps through *transfer experiments* means-end readinesses could be better specified. Correspondingly, he thought perhaps *disruption experiments* could help to specify perceptions, expectations, representations, and valences. He also detected the need to determine *work* involved in performance (for there is a drive against effort), and *uncertainty*, which also reduces performance. He made his characteristic apology:

In order to draw the teeth of possible critics I am ready to admit that this matter of pointer readings for intervening variables . . . is the weakest part of my theory. I would like to suggest again, however, that the hypothetical little r_g's and s_g's of the Hullians are almost equally difficult of empirical verification (1959, page 114, footnote).

With respect to the laws of learning, he reasserted his acceptance of the principle of "exercise" as strengthening, not habit, but means-end readinesses or beliefs. These of course lead usually to performances, which he, like others, tends to call responses. Performance is the preferred term, however, because what is done becomes a matter of *organism-environment rearrangements*, not a matter of specific muscular or glandular activities.

He had now come to see that "effect" was more important than he had earlier supposed it to be. The evidence led him "to believe that 'effect,' in the sense of final positive or negative values attached to a terminal stimulus, does always play some part in favoring the acquisition of beliefs" (1959, page 125).

The modifications in the final statement were not many; the original book of 1932 represents the system at the height of his confidence in it, and the essential flavor of that book survives through all the changes.

ESTIMATE OF TOLMAN'S SIGN LEARNING

Tolman's Position on the Typical Problems of Learning

Because it is a system with some aspirations toward completeness, there are statements within Tolman's writings relevant to most of the problems raised by other writers.

1. Capacity. Tolman recognized the need for capacity laws. The matter interested him chiefly because of the possible gradation of learning tasks from those requiring least to those requiring most intelligence. It is natural that one who makes predictions about what animals will do in problem-solving situations is confronted with the limitations of one organism as compared with another. Tolman believed that the high degree of specificity of capacities in the rat is due to the lack of influence of a culture which prizes certain behaviors over others. Hence one of the contributions of animal studies may be to show processes at a subcultural level (1945).

2. Practice. The law of exercise is accepted in the sense of the frequency with which the sign, the significate, and the behavioral relation between the two have been presented. Exercise is not the cause of the initial selection of the right response. Mere frequency without "belonging" does not establish a connection. After a response has been learned, overexercise tends to fix it, making it unduly resistant to change (Krechevsky and Honzik, 1932).

3. Motivation. Rewards and punishment tend to regulate performance, rather than acquisition, although they are related to acquisition also because they serve as "emphasizers" and because goal-objects confirm or refute hypotheses. Because of the demonstration of latent learning, the law of effect in its usual sense (reward as a strengthener of response tendencies) is not accepted, although a few concessions were made by Tolman later on.

4. Understanding. Cognitive processes are of the very essence of molar behavior and learning. Hence Tolman was friendly to learning by creative inference, inventive ideation, and so on. He repeatedly stated, however, that he did not wish to imply "introspectively get-at-able conscious contents." The prototype of learning is sensible, reasonable adjustment according to the requirements of the situation; stupid learning occurs as a limiting case when the problem is unsuited to the learner's capacities or is set up in inaccessible form. Insightful learning is not limited to the primates; it is characteristic of rat behavior as well.

5. Transfer. The problem of transfer of training as such has been of relatively slight interest to those experimenting with animals. To some extent all of the experiments on change of reward, change of drive, place learning, and latent learning are experiments on problems related to transfer, that is, the ability to use something learned in one situation in relation to another. All cognitive theories expect a large measure of transfer, provided the essential relationships of the situation are open to the observation of the learner.

6. Forgetting. Having earlier experimented in the field of retroactive inhibition (1917), it is probable that Tolman was friendly toward some theory of retroactive inhibition, and he indicated that he accepted the Freudian mechanism of repression (1942, pages 63-64). These conceptions were not prominent in his writings on learning theory, although, in the 1949 version (see pages 211-213) he speculated about the relative permanence of various subvarieties of learning.

Thus he asserted the resistance of cathexes and equivalence beliefs to forgetting, and the susceptibility of field expectations to the kind of forgetting emphasized by gestalt psychologists.

Molar Behavior as a Field Concept

The student of molar behavior contends that there can be a psychological science or behavioral science in its own right, not waiting for its progress upon advances in other sciences. While there is some controversy about this, it is a position which was defended in the 1930's and 1940's by both stimulus–response and cognition psychologists. Hull too was able to adopt a concept of molar behavior by this definition.

Beyond the matter of level of discourse there lies the question as to whether molar behavior is essentially a field concept. The question might be put another way. To what extent is Tolman's sign-gestalt theory a true gestalt psychology? Koffka (1933), in his review of Tolman's book, welcomed the friendliness to gestalt, but deplored some limitations which he detected in Tolman's variety of gestalt. He believed that the distinction between molar and molecular did not go far enough, because Tolman acknowledged the reality of the molecular. Koffka would wish field principles applied to physiology as well as to psychology, so that all explanatory concepts should be molar. Furthermore, Tolman's preoccupation with behavior sequences and historical interpretations makes sign-gestalts only a limited illustration of the variety of possible gestalts.

This disadvantage, from Koffka's point of view, makes it easier to compare Tolman's experiments with those done under the influence of other theories. Since the experiments were done with rats in mazes and discrimination situations, they are directly comparable to the experiments in the typical American animal laboratory. Therefore Tolman challenged prevailing conceptions such as those of Thorndike and Guthrie and Hull more vividly than did the more orthodox gestalt writers, whose situations were often so different as to be incommensurate.

Tolman made so many generous acknowledgments to Lewin that there is no doubt of the affiliations between their systems, as third parties have made clear (e.g., White, 1943). Their differences became adjusted in a brief and friendly controversy.[9]

The conception of molar behavior is consonant with prevailing conceptions of science, in which some degree of arbitrariness is recognized in the abstractions to be made from the totality of natural events for the purposes of any given science. Natural laws can be formulated in many different ways to cover aspects of occurrences. Tolman undoubtedly did a service to psychology in joining with those who saw the importance of a "psychological" psychology, that is, one whose concepts are appropriate to the level of its descriptions and predictions.

[9] Tolman, 1932a; Lewin, 1933. For his appreciation of Lewin, see Tolman (1948a).

The Status of Intervening Variables

The distinction between performance and learning, which must be accepted in one form or another, requires that learning be inferred from performance. These inferences are always being made, in even the most "objective" sorts of observations, because only "relevant" physical or physiological occurrences are recorded. There is nothing especially new about Tolman's intervening variable, except that he pointed out clearly and insistently that the intervening variable is there, and is not out of place in a behavioral science. The logical mistake is easily made of supposing that the physical and physiological terms to which the intervening variables are anchored are themselves independent of theories, which they are not. The kinds of experiments which are performed, the kinds of measurements which are taken, always involve selection by the experimenter. The data, even though reproducible, are not "pure" facts of nature. The question may therefore be raised whether the intervening variables are going to be anything not found in the experimental relationships directly. It is doubtful whether a satisfactory answer can be given until the intervening variables are identified with quantities. If there are derived constants, interchangeable from one situation to another, then the intervening variable becomes a scientific construct of some importance (Seward, 1955).

As previously pointed out, Hull adopted the intervening variable also, so that the logic is common to the differing points of view. The remaining difference lies in the sorts of intervening variables chosen.

A distinction was made by MacCorquodale and Meehl (1948) between two kinds of symbolic intermediaries: "intervening variables" and "hypothetical constructs." A pure "intervening variable" is a mere convenience in system-making, and has no properties or dimensions other than those specified in the equations that define it. A "hypothetical construct" is an entity with properties attributed to it beyond those of the functional equations in which it appears. Hull's r_G is an example of a hypothetical construct because it has all the properties of a muscular response and is said to give rise to proprioceptive stimuli (s_G) as any muscular response does. While it is hypothesized, rather than observed, it is potentially observable and need not always have the status of a metaphor. Although Tolman's system appears to be built around "intervening variables" in the MacCorquodale and Meehl sense (demands, cognitions, etc.), Tolman denied this and asserted not only that all theories use both types of intermediary, but that hypothetical constructs are desirable.[10]

The distinction made by MacCorquodale and Meehl is a useful one, but

[10] Tolman (1951b), pages 282-283. For a further discussion of the isssues, see Marx (1951), Ginsberg (1954), Maze (1954), Hilgard (1958), Deutsch (1960, pages 1-16).

it is a mistake to jump to the conclusion (which they did not suggest) that one of the types of intermediary is invariably preferable to the other. Possibly what we need is a clearer specification of the rules under which each should be used. Consider the gene theory in biology. If the gene is believed to be "a something" that has its place on the chromosome, it is a hypothetical construct, and its added properties are such as may be revealed eventually under the microscope or by chemical analysis. If it were merely a pawn to be used in the study of the statistics of unit characters and their genetic transmission, the gene would be a pure intervening variable. In this case, the status of hypothetical construct has seemed to be a useful one, as one considers chromosome maps, crossovers, and so on. The parameter (g) commonly appearing in the law of falling bodies is another kind of intervening variable, for it is merely a constant defining the acceleration of a free-falling body under specified conditions, with no other status beyond that. It is a convenience in harmonizing free-falling bodies, balls rolling down inclined planes, and the period of a pendulum, and as such justifies itself even though it has no independent existence as an entity. Precisely what kinds of intervening variables prove useful in psychology will depend upon what we can do with them. The test comes in their clarity, specificity, and fertility in system-making. If a hypothetical construct is used, its surplus meanings should be reasonable, and ideally a search should go on for its independent verification.

What Kind of Behaviorism?

When Tolman announced his purposive behaviorism (Tolman, 1922), ten years before his major book appeared, American psychology was still excited over the new behaviorism of Watson. It was Tolman's contribution then to show that a sophisticated behaviorism can be cognizant of all the richness and variety of psychological events, and need not be constrained by an effort to build an engineer's model of the learning machine.

With the diversification of behaviorism under the influence of Tolman and others, the old brittleness of Watsonian behaviorism has largely disappeared, and what virtues there are in the behavioristic position have now become part of the underlying assumptions of most American psychologists—without most of them thinking of themselves as behaviorists at all.

Tolman's catholicity and his friendliness to new ideas prevented his developing a "tight" or "elegant" system, even though he all along made suggestions as to what such a system would be like. He kept his prominent place in the forefront of learning theorists by his sensitivity to important problems, by his inventiveness in experimentation, and by keeping others on their mettle.

THE RESIDUE FROM TOLMAN'S THEORY

Tolman left no "crown prince" to carry on his theorizing. He deeply influenced those who worked with him, and they revere him, but they go their own ways. Hence we have to seek in the general culture of contemporary psychology for those whose work has been influenced by Tolman, even though that work is done by those who were not his students and do not even think of themselves as his followers.

Attempted Quantification of Expectancy Theory

Because of its more precise formal structure, stimulus–response theory has guided more research and theory construction in recent years than cognitive theory. Many of the *problems* set for stimulus–response psychologists, however, were posed by those from the other camp: for example, the distinction between learning and performance, latent learning, transposition, systematic modes of problem solution, secondary reinforcement (in the form of sign learning), incentive motivation (the valence of perceived incentives). As stimulus–response experimentation and theorizing have become more developed many of the challenging problems which cognitive theorists first called attention to have taken on new interest for the stimulus–response theorists. For example, instead of denying latent learning, new stimulus–response derivations are required to account for it; instead of denying relational discrimination, earlier theories are modified to include it. This is entirely wholesome, and in the end may lead to the kind of unification of psychological theory that we all wish to see.

A few psychologists, many of them trained in stimulus–response approaches, have become increasingly aware that the cognitive theorists were talking about psychological reality, even though their formalization of certain phenomena was inadequate. Some of them have turned their attention to the formalization of cognitive theories in a manner more nearly consonant with the kind of systematic treatment that stimulus–response theories have been getting.

Osgood (1950), acknowledging a preference for stimulus–response theories, tried his hand at applying Tolman's theory to avoidance learning. He suggested four postulates consonant with Tolman's theory, and believed that they could be used satisfactorily to derive avoidance learning.

Olds (1954) set up a neural model for Tolman's theory, based on Hebb's (1949) discussion of cell assemblies. The model was sufficiently precise to allow for experimental testing, and one experimental study based on it was reported (Olds, 1953), before Olds turned to other matters.

Rotter (1954) in a book designed to provide a theory for clinical psychology evolved an expectancy-reinforcement theory, with some points of contact with Tolman's views. His basic formula for *behavioral potential* (B.P.) makes it a function of *expectancy of reinforcement* (E) and the *reinforcement value* of the expected reinforcement. The expectancy of reinforcement is close to Tolman's means-end-readiness, and the reinforcement value corresponds roughly to valence.

Bower (1962b) has shown that it is quite feasible to make a mathematical model for VTE behavior in which the empirical data fit very well a probabilistic model. No doubt Tolman could have found a congenial way of talking about his results.

MacCorquodale and Meehl's Postulate System

The most careful attempt to date to develop a Hull-like set of postulates for a Tolman-like expectancy theory is that of MacCorquodale and Meehl (1953, 1954). Without arguing its truth-value they have taken the task of making explicit what expectancy theory would be like were it formalized.

To begin with, an expectancy is said always to have three terms: (1) something initially perceived, called an *elicitor* of the expectancy (S_1); (2) something to be done following this perception, a response (R_1); and then something that will be perceived, as the goal of the expectancy, the *expectandum* (S_2). The process can be symbolized as S_1–R_1–S_2 in the defining of an expectancy just as the process S–R is used to define an association. The best way to remember the process is to think of some ordinary sentence, such as: "When this *button* (S_1) is *pressed* (R_1), I expect to hear the *ringing doorbell* (S_2)." This total process, prior to doing anything to the button right now, is the expectancy. If ringing the doorbell becomes a goal (becomes *valenced*), then the expectancy is *activated*. I *push* the button only if I want to ring the doorbell; I may have the expectancy $(S_1R_1S_2)$ without doing anything about it.

Capital letters are used to describe the significant environmental events S_1–R_1–S_2, and the same letters may be used for the inferred construct, the expectancy $(S_1R_1S_2)$. The letters are enclosed in parentheses when reference is to the construct rather than to events themselves. But whenever capital letters are used, whether in describing events or the inferred expectancy, it is appropriate to use physical-stimulus language. That is, S_1 and S_2 are objects in the environment, with their ordinary characteristics, and R_1 is a physical response. The specification of the terms of an expectancy in physical language permits not only objective verification, but also clear statements about confirmed and unconfirmed expectancies.

(The logic of the physical language is no different from that used in assigning dimensions to Hull's $_sH_R$.) [11]

Twelve postulates are stated, often with guesses as to the form of mathematical function involved. For a briefer introduction to the flavor of the system, the postulates are here paraphrased, with much of the quantitative detail omitted.

1. *Mnemonization.* The occurrence of the sequence S_1–R_1–S_2 results in an increase in the strength of an expectancy $(S_1R_1S_2)$. The *rate* of growth increases with the valence of S_2. The *limit* of growth depends on the probability (P) with which S_2 regularly follows S_1–R_1. That is, growth approaches P as a limit.

This is the basic acquisition postulate. It is a contiguity theory, in that mere occurrence of the sequences presumably leads to increase in expectancy. But it is also a kind of reinforcement theory, because the expectancy is influenced by the valence of the terminal item (S_2) in the sequence. It is not, however, a stimulus–response theory in the usual sense. MacCorquodale and Meehl point out that by their accepting specified parameters for rate and limit of growth they have not made concessions to some form of nonexpectancy theory.

2. *Extinction.* The occurrence of a sequence S_1–R_1, if not followed by S_2, tends to produce a decrement in the expectancy.

Two cases have to be distinguished. If P has been 1.00 (that is, S_1–R_1, always followed by S_2) a single omission of S_2 will lead to a prompt decrement, depending both on the current strength of $(S_1R_1S_2)$ and the valence of S_2. If, however, P has been less than 1.00, the course of decrement will be slower, and, if P′, the expectancy will approach the new value of P′ as an asymptote.[12]

3. *Primary-stimulus generalization.* When an expectancy $(S_1R_1S_2)$ has been strengthened, other expectancies $(S'_1R_1S_2)$ will also have received some strength, depending upon the similarity of the elicitors S'_1 and S_1.

Similarity gradients are an empirical matter, and there is no point in trying to distinguish the functions from those used by stimulus–response

---

[11] MacCorquodale and Meehl allow for a central state called *the expectant* $(s_1r_1s_2)$, but they make no use of it in their preliminary formalization. Presumably if one were to turn to neurophysiological explanations there would be some translations between the neurophysiological language of $(s_1r_1s_2)$ and the physical language of $(S_1R_1S_2)$.

[12] We know from Humphreys' (1939b) experiment that following a P of .50 there may be an increasing level of $(S_1R_1S_2)$ for a few trials if S_2 is regularly omitted. The MacCorquodale-Meehl postulate is incomplete, as they were the first to admit. Yet it is a few points, such as this increase in response in the first few trials of extinction, that provide some of the greatest support for an expectancy interpretation over other interpretations.

psychologists. Tolman (1939) recognized this when he built Spence's (1937) gradients into his "schematic sowbug."

4. *Inference.* When an expectancy $(S_1R_1S_2)$ exists at some strength, the presence of a valenced object S^* in close contiguity with S_2 gives rise to a new expectancy $(S_1R_1S^*)$.

5. *Generalized inference.* Even though $(S_1E_1S_2)$ is originally of zero strength, the occurrence of a valenced object S^* in close contiguity with S_2 may give rise to a new expectancy $(S_1R_1S^*)$, provided $(S_1R_1S'_2)$ is of some strength, and S'_2 is similar to S_2.

These are the kinds of postulates said by MacCorquodale and Meehl to contribute heavily to the identification of an expectancy theory. They give the basis for latent learning and for the interpretation of experiments modeled after Maier's reasoning experiments.

The next six postulates have to do with motivation, described according to needs, cathexes, and valences. They have been renumbered for expository purposes. They can easily be identified in the original source because their titles are unchanged. The three following postulates state the fundamental position with respect to motivation.[13]

6. *Cathexis.* The Cathexis (C^*) of a valenced stimulus situation (S^*) is a function of the number of contiguous occurrences between it and the consummatory response.

7. *Need strength.* The need (D) for a cathected stimulus (S^*) is an increasing function of the time interval since satiation for it.

8. *Valence.* The valence of a stimulus S^* is a multiplicative function of the correlated need D and the cathexis C^* attached to S^*.

Postulates 6 to 8 imply a fairly complex theory of motivation, generated (as Spence's theory was) by the problems of latent learning (Spence, 1956). The *sight* of food leads to food-seeking because of the correlation of sight of food with consummatory response (eating). This is the meaning of cathexis. Food thus gains a certain attractiveness (*cathexis*) through prior experiences of eating, but its present pulling power as an incentive (its *valence*) depends also on how hungry the organism is (its *need* level). Need is a function of deprivation; cathexis is a function of experienced satisfactions in the past; valence is a product of both. There is a striking parallel with Hull and Spence's *D* and *K*, which act together (as a product or as a sum) to influence reaction potential.

Now we are ready for some postulates (actually earlier in the original list) concerning some further relationships between experience and cathexis.

---

[13] The treatment covers rewarding (appetitive) motivation only. Pain and avoidance are not treated.

9. *Secondary cathexis.* The contiguity of S_2 and S^* (a valenced stimulus) increases the cathexis of S_2.

This is a kind of "secondary reinforcement" or acquired incentive value, whereby the valence of one expectandum is given to a contiguous expectandum.

10. *Induced elicitor-cathexis.* The acquisition of valence by an expectandum S_2 belonging to an existing expectancy $(S_1 R_1 S_2)$, induces a cathexis in the elicitor S_1.

11. *Confirmed elicitor-cathexis.* The confirmation of an expectancy $(S_1 R_1 S_2)$, when S_2 has a positive valence, increases the cathexis of S_1.

These two postulates mean that an elicitor, as a discriminative stimulus, comes to have reinforcing power. It is easily demonstrated that cues at a choice-point, if similar to cues in the goal-box, facilitate learning. While usually interpreted according to secondary reinforcement, the notion of acquired elicitor cathexis is roughly equivalent.[14]

The difference between "induction" and "confirmation" is that between introducing food after satiated runs, and learning while hungry.

12. *Activation.* The reaction potential $_sE_R$ of a response R_1 in the presence of S_1 is a multiplicative function of the strength of the expectancy $(S_1 R_1 S_2)$ and the valence of the expectandum.

This final postulate gets around the jibe of Guthrie (1952, page 143) that Tolman leaves the rat buried in thought. The parallel with the Hull-Spence basic formulation is striking:

$$Hull\text{-}Spence:\ {}_sE_R = f\ ({}_sH_R) \times f\ (\mathbf{D}, \mathbf{K})$$

$$MacCorquodale\text{-}Meehl:\ {}_sE_R = f\ (S_1 R_1 S_2) \times f\ (\mathbf{D}, \mathbf{C^*})$$

As one goes on to specify in more detail the relations between reaction potential and response, there remain the problems of thresholds, oscillation, and the like. MacCorquodale and Meehl point out that there is no reason to handle these further matters differently in the expectancy model and the stimulus–response model.

How successful are these postulates in deducing the experimental phenomena of learning? MacCorquodale and Meehl (1953) illustrate the procedure by deducing the phenomena from several experiments representing sub-varieties of latent learning.[15] They succeed reasonably well in accounting for the data through manipulation of the postulates.

[14] Bauer and Lawrence (1953) show that the problem of choice-point cues and goal cues is complex. Conditioned inhibition may turn out to be as relevant as secondary reinforcement.

[15] The experiments are those of Kendler (1946), Meehl and MacCorquodale (1948), and Tolman and Gleitman (1949).

The postulate set is avowedly weak on some matters that have been of particular interest to expectancy or cognitive theorists, such as the problems of multiple paths, systematic modes of solution ("hypotheses"), perceptual patterning. The authors believe that they have chosen a course more fruitful than that of Tolman himself in his emphasis on "maps" and "perceptions." It is a useful beginning in showing, first, how a theory of this kind can be made explicit, including notational reference to response within an expectancy setting, and second, when made explicit, that there are large areas of agreement between a theory of this kind and stimulus–response theory.

Related Systematic Ideas

As intellectual climates change ideas formerly expressed in one form tend to turn up in others, and may be unrecognized.

Thus *decision processes* have become very interesting in contemporary psychology, growing out of the theory of games as proposed by von Neumann and Morgenstern (1944). As the theory has been adapted by psychologists (Edwards, 1954, 1962) increasing interest arises in *subjective expected utility* (SEU), a term very similar in meaning to Tolman's means-end readiness, but a similarity not readily detected. The importance of both probabilities and of risk was explicit in the paper by Tolman and Brunswick (1935), in which their separate views were harmonized. Pointing this out does not mean that the ideas in decision theory came historically from Tolman and Brunswik. It is rather that if related ideas appear in new forms, with appropriate experimental and mathematical procedures, there is no special point in pushing for the earlier ideas, except to point out that they had a measure of validity.

The *structural model* proposed by Deutsch (1960) and used in connection with a great variety of experiments appears a far cry from Tolman, yet in many respects it represents a kind of thinking about psychological problems quite consonant with that of Tolman. Even though Deutsch proposes a "machine" type of model, when such a machine has a memory storage and feedback mechanisms, it can show insightful behavior of the order of Tolman's rats (Deutsch, 1954). In fact, one of the more ingenious experiments is a repetition with changes of the Tolman and Honzik (1930a) experiment, as reported by Deutsch and Clarkson (1959).

As in the Tolman and Honzik experiment (see Figure 7-2) the maze was arranged with longer and shorter alleys, and the various portions could be blocked. The pattern is shown in Figure 7-6. Three problems were set, problems A, B, and C, but only after the rats were familiar with the maze, and had found food in both goal boxes whenever they reached them.

In problem A the near goal box (Goal Box 1) was left empty. Nearly all the rats ran to the near goal box first. Now, having found it empty, the rat could return by the same short route, take the alternate short route, or take the long route. What the rat did, in agreement with the "insightful" interpretation, was to take the long path to Goal Box 2; 9 of 12 rats made this choice, and in view of oft-repeated habits of running to the near box via the short path the result is highly significant statistically.

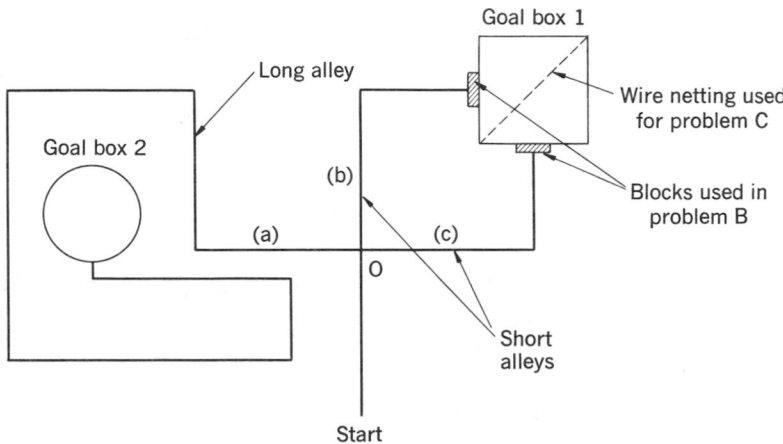

Figure 7-6   **A reasoning experiment. The maze is actually an alley maze, but has been diagrammed for simplicity. For explanation, see text. Modified from Deutsch and Clarkson (1959).**

In problem B, one of the short paths was blocked as shown. (Actually both paths were blocked, but the rat had no way of knowing this). Now the rat has the choice of taking the other short path or the long one. In this case, 9 of 12 rats chose the other short path, rather than the long one as in problem A. The results for both problems A and B support Tolman's interpretation, as well as the predictions (made on other grounds) by Deutsch and Clarkson.

Problem C is really the crucial one, for here the Deutsch-Clarkson prediction does violence to common sense. A wire-mesh barrier was placed within the near box (diagonal broken line in Goal Box 1 in Figure 7-6). No blocks were used. The animal entered the box by way of one of the short paths, and perceived food beyond the wire netting, but could not eat it. The rat was observed while in the box and was not removed until it had made distinct attempts to thrust its snout through the wire mesh. Now common sense (and the latent learning predictions of Tolman) would predict that the rat, knowing the maze and knowing where the food was, would take the other short path the next time. But Deutsch and Clarkson predicted that this would not take place. The reasoning is that the food-seekings via the two short paths are very closely linked.

When the block occurs prior to any commerce with food, the linkages are not involved as they are when there has been some commerce with food, even though frustrating, as in problem C. This frustration now affects both the short-path behaviors, and raises the potency of the long path. Hence the long path will be chosen in preference to the alternate short path. This turned out to be the case, again with 9 of 12 rats choosing the long path.

The theory proposed by Deutsch is more complex than this short description suggests, but the point being made here is that we have a very Tolman-like experiment, critical of S–R reinforcement theory, yet guided by a theory that predicts results somewhat different from those that Tolman would predict. This is exactly the kind of development to be expected in an experimental science, except that one might hope eventually for fewer discontinuities between the theories that accompany related experiments.

Some experiments with a Tolman-like interpretation (though not designed particularly in relation to his theory) were presented by Lawrence and Festinger (1962) to test predictions based on Festinger's concept of cognitive dissonance (Festinger, 1957), a type of motivational theory deriving from the level of aspiration experiments of Lewin, with which Festinger had been earlier associated (Festinger, 1942). The interpretation can be thought of as Tolman-like because of the inference to cognitive processes in rats. The findings of the Lawrence and Festinger experiments are that with insufficient rewards (requiring excessive effort, appearing infrequently, or being of small size) running habits in rats become very resistant to extinction, provided the minimal reward has been enough to keep them working. The interpretation is that some "added attractions" must develop in these relatively nongratifying experiences in order to justify the expended effort, just as a man, stuck with a low-paying job, may stay with it because he "likes the work," or "is getting good experience." These added attractions reduce the equivalent in rats of the discrepancies between beliefs and actions which cause man to make such maneuvers to reduce his dissonance.

While it is true that in the early 1960's there were very few experiments showing their direct origin in Tolman's theory, many of the basic ideas are still pertinent, as these several illustrations show. What kind of contribution by a scientist is likely to endure? A global system, unless it is very successful in grouping together a number of well-established empirical facts (Newton's laws, or Einstein's relativity theory) is less likely to endure than a single well-established relationship (Archimedes' principle, Ohm's law, the Weber-Fechner law). Tolman's system was not tight enough to endure, and there is no Tolman law to give him immortality; perhaps the latent learning experiment is as uniquely his as the nonsense syllable was uniquely Ebbinghaus's. Some of these less dramatic contributions, as they work their ways into the stream of science, may be enough to win a rightful place in the history of science for the man who made them.

The hope, however, is for something more than this, and that is for the march of science (in our case, psychological science) to be evident either in firm factual relationships upon which future theories are built, or in the convulsions of new paradigms which give science a fresh look, as emphasized by Kuhn (1962). It is quite possible that in retrospect Tolman's contribution may have been of this latter kind, giving a new cast to behaviorism by insisting that it be open to the problems created by cognitive processes, problem solving, and inventive ideation.

SUPPLEMENTARY READINGS

The only major book on Tolman's system is:
TOLMAN, E. C. (1932b) *Purposive behavior in animals and men.*

Fortunately, his shorter writings have been assembled in book form:
TOLMAN, E. C. (1951a) *Collected papers in psychology.*

An interesting little book, which started out to be a book on motivation, but was retitled because of World War II (and remains a book on motivation despite its title) is:
TOLMAN, E. C. (1942) *Drives toward war.*

For a thorough review of Tolman's position, with some suggestions as to possible steps in systematization, see:
MACCORQUODALE, K., and MEEHL, P. E. (1954) Edward C. Tolman. In W. K. Estes and others. *Modern learning theory,* 177-266.

Gestalt Theory

During the first quarter of the century in America the quarrels within academic psychology lay chiefly inside the framework of association psychology. Structuralism, functionalism, and behaviorism were all members of the association family. A few dissident voices, such as Freud and McDougall, got little hearing. This complacency was disturbed by the new gestalt doctrine which influenced American learning theories chiefly through the appearance in English of Wolfgang Köhler's *Mentality of apes* (1925) and Kurt Koffka's *Growth of the mind* (1924). The theory had been developing in Germany since it was first announced by Max Wertheimer in 1912, but these books, and the visits of Köhler and Koffka to America about the time of their publication, brought the new theory vividly to the attention of American psychologists.

Koffka's book had an important effect upon American learning theory because of its detailed criticism of trial-and-error learning as conceived by Thorndike—a thrust at the very heart of the currently popular theory. The vigorous attack on Thorndike (and upon behaviorism, although Thorndike was not, strictly speaking, a member of the school) was supported by Köhler's well-known experiments on apes, described in detail in his book which appeared close in time to Koffka's. Köhler's book brought the notion of insightful learning into the foreground, as an alternative to trial and error. He showed how apes could obtain rewards without going through the laborious processes of stamping out incorrect responses and stamping in correct ones, as implied in Thorndike's theories and as displayed in the learning curves of Thorndike's cats. Apes could use sticks and boxes as tools; they could turn away from the end of the activity toward a means to the end.

Köhler's experiments with apes were done in the year 1913–1917, on the island of Tenerife off the coast of Africa. His book about these experiments (Köhler, 1917) appeared in English a few years later and immediately was widely read and quoted. Two main series of experiments interested the American psychological public in the problems of insight. These were the box problems and the stick problems.

In the single-box situation, a lure, such as a banana, is attached to the top of the chimpanzee's cage. The lure is out of reach but can be obtained by climbing upon and jumping from a box which is available in the cage. The problem is a difficult one for the chimpanzee. Only Sultan (Köhler's most intelligent ape) solved it without assistance, though six others mastered the problem after first being helped either by having the box placed beneath the food or by watching others using the box. The problem was not solved by direct imitation of others. What watching others use the box did was to lead the observer to attempt to use the box as a leaping platform, but sometimes without making any effort whatsoever to bring it near the lure. When the problem was mastered, a chimpanzee alone in a cage with box and banana would turn away from the goal in order to seek the box and to move it into position. This "detour" character of insightful behavior is, according to Köhler, one of its important features.

The box-stacking problem, requiring that a second box be placed upon the first before the banana can be reached, is much more difficult. It requires both the incorporation of the second box into the pattern of solution, and a mastery of the gravitational problem of building a stable two-box structure. While the emphasis in secondary accounts of Köhler's work is usually upon the intelligence which his apes displayed, he himself was at pains to account for the amount of apparent stupidity. In the box-stacking experiment, for example, he believed that the apes had shown insight into the relationship of "one-box-upon-another," but not into the nature of a stable two-box structure. Such physical stability as was achieved in later structures was essentially a matter of trial and error.

The stick problems required the use of one or more sticks as tools with which to rake in food out of reach beyond the bars of the cage. The beginning of insight occurs as the stick is brought into play, although often unsuccessfully, as when it is thrown at the banana and lost. Once it has been used successfully, it is sought after by the chimpanzee and used promptly. The most dramatic of the stick-using experiments was in a problem mastered by Sultan, in which eventually two sticks were joined together after the manner of a jointed fishing pole in order to obtain a banana which could not be reached with either stick alone. The process was a slow one, and the first placing of the sticks together appeared to be more or less accidental. Once having seen the sticks in this relationship, however, Sultan was able to "get the idea" and to repeat the insertion of one stick into the end of the other over and over again.

Although the attack by Köhler and Koffka was chiefly upon Thorndike, it came at a time when American psychology was in the grips of a confident but somewhat sterile behaviorism. It is hard to see at this distance why such a common-sense and familiar notion as insight in learning should have created such a stir. But at the time Watsonian behaviorism had, in fact, won support for a fairly "hard-boiled" view of learning, according to which the organism was played upon by the pushes and pulls of the environment and reacted in ways essentially stupid. Lloyd Morgan's canon which had seriously undercut the attributing of higher mental processes to animals had fairly well succeeded via behaviorism in excising them from man also. Therefore the return to a more balanced view, represented by the insight experiments, gave new hope to teachers and others who saw thinking and understanding returned to respectability. Insight was not a new discovery—it was a return to a conception laymen had never abandoned. Nobody uninfluenced by peculiar doctrines would ever have denied insight as a fact—yet it took Köhler to restore it as a fact in American psychology. It was, in some respects, time for a change, and Köhler's experiments dramatized release from the negatives of Thorndikian and Watsonian thinking.

That the more enthusiastic reception for the new learning theories should have come first from the educators is not surprising.[1] There had already been a rift growing between Thorndike and the more progressive group within education, who, under Dewey's leadership, had made much more than he of the capacity of the individual for setting and solving his own problems. The new insight doctrine fitted nicely their slogan of freeing intelligence for creative activity.

Animal psychologists like Yerkes, who had never espoused behaviorism, welcomed the new movement as a natural development. Yerkes himself had done experiments on insightful learning independent of gestalt influences (e.g., Yerkes 1916), and the intelligence demonstrated by Köhler's apes did not surprise him. Curiously enough, insightful learning in subhuman animals was less threatening to theorists than learning by understanding in man, chiefly because it was still the rather rare and unusual behavior among animals. Rats still learned mazes, it was thought, without insight. So the animal experimenters added insight experiments to their list and continued both old and new experiments. But if the insight doctrine were to be accepted in human learning, the field would be wide open for destroying all the familiar laws of learning as they applied to

[1] It was an educator-psychologist, R. M. Ogden, who translated Koffka (1924).

man. It is not surprising that those who were at the time concerned more largely with human learning, such as Thorndike, Robinson, and Guthrie, should all have been cool to the insight concept.

The visible opposition between Köhler and Thorndike was over insight and trial and error, that is, over intelligent learning as contrasted with blind fumbling. But the opposition between gestalt psychology and association psychology goes much deeper. In order to understand this opposition, it will be necessary to examine the gestalt views in greater detail.

There are a number of variants within the gestalt movement and among those strongly influenced by gestalt conceptions. Köhler and Koffka were closest to Wertheimer, the official founder of the school. This chapter is devoted to their treatment of learning. Lewin, while originally from Berlin and definitely within the ranks, broke new ground. All four of these men, originally German, eventually settled in America, where three of them (Koffka, Lewin, and Wertheimer) have since died. They are the leaders of what is historically gestalt psychology.

Their views were picked up and considerably modified by Wheeler (1929, 1932, 1940) under the name of *organismic psychology,* but his position deviated too much from the classical gestalt psychology for him to be counted within the core group.[2]

The fullest and most systematic treatment of the problems of learning from the gestalt viewpoint is found in Koffka's *Principles of gestalt psychology* (1935). It was written after a period of acclimatization to America, and so meshes somewhat better than earlier writings with the concerns of American psychologists. Most of the direct references will be made to this source.

THE LAWS OF ORGANIZATION

Gestalt psychology had its start and has achieved its greatest success in the field of perception. Its demonstrations of the role of background and organization upon phenomenally perceived processes are so convincing that only an unusually stubborn opponent will discredit the achievement. The primary attack upon association theory was an attack on the "bundle hypothesis" sensation theory—the theory that a percept is made up of sensationlike elements, bound together by association.

When the gestalt psychologists turned later to the problems of learning, the equipment brought to the study of learning was that which had

[2] Wheeler's views were elaborated, with Perkins, in a widely used textbook on educational psychology, Wheeler and Perkins (1932). For an account of the organismic position, see the first edition of this book, Hilgard (1948), page 234-260. Because Wheeler's theory is no longer influential, the chapter was dropped from later editions despite some provocative ideas contained in the theory.

succeeded in the field of perception, and the arguments previously used against the sensation were turned against the reflex. In spite of the attention which Köhler's ape experiments received, gestalt psychologists can be fairly said to have been only moderately interested in learning. This does not mean that their few experiments are without significance; it means only that they have considered the problems of learning secondary to the problems of perception. Perhaps in America the shoe is on the other foot, and in preoccupation with learning we have too long neglected the relationship between the two fields.[3]

The starting point for Koffka's treatment of learning is the assumption that the laws of organization in perception are applicable to learning. This applicability is enhanced because of the prominence in learning given in his theory to the initial adjustment, to the discovery of the correct response in the first place. Since this discovery depends upon the structuring of the field as it is open to the observation of the learner, the ease or difficulty of the problem is largely a matter of perception. In some sense, Köhler's apes were presented with perceptual problems; if they literally "saw" the situation correctly, they had "insight."

The application of the laws of organization to learning problems is done too casually by Koffka to be very convincing, but if he had been more systematic about it, the development of the argument might have gone along the following lines. There would be a guiding principle (the Law of Prägnanz) and four laws of organization subordinate to it: the laws of similarity, proximity, closure, and good continuation.

The Law of Prägnanz

The law of *Prägnanz*[4] suggests the direction of events. Psychological organization tends to move in one general direction rather than in other directions, always toward the state of Prägnanz, toward the "good" gestalt. The organization will be as "good" as prevailing conditions allow. A "good" gestalt has such properties as regularity, simplicity, stability, and so on.

Because of the dynamic properties of "fields," the conditions of equilibrium are necessarily important. In physics, processes which terminate in stationary distributions are characterized by certain maxima and minima, as by a minimum of energy capable of doing work. This minimum for the whole sometimes requires a part to absorb a maximum of energy. The law of *Prägnanz* is a law of equilibrium like the principles of the maximum or minimum in physics. It ought to correspond to them in reality, since it is the phenomenal representation of physiological proc-

---

[3] The point was made some years ago by Leeper (1935b).

[4] The German word is inadequately translated as "pregnancy." It has the meaning of *"knapp, und doch vielsagend"* (compact but significant).

esses which obey physical laws. In effect, however, it is used as an analogy. When organization moves toward a minimum, it is characterized phenomenally by the simplicity of uniformity; when it moves toward a maximum, it is characterized by the simplicity of perfect articulation (Koffka, 1935, pages 171-174). "We might say, sacrificing a great deal of the precision of the physical proposition, that in psychological organization either as much or as little will happen as the prevailing conditions permit" (1935, page 108).

Learning situations are problematical. They therefore give rise to tensions and to disequilibria. Some such principle as the law of Prägnanz becomes appropriate to them, although Koffka does not develop the point, except by way of the other laws, each of which, in its own way, is an illustration of the more general principle.

1. The law of similarity.   The law of similarity or of equality is the counterpart of associationist's law of similarity. This and the other laws all derive from Wertheimer (1923). He used it as a principle determining the formation of groups in perception, such as groups of lines or dots. Similar items (e.g., alike in form or color) or similar transitions (e.g., alike in the steps separating them) tend to form groups in perception. In a series of experiments with nonsense syllables, two-place numbers, and nonsense two-dimensional figures, Köhler (1941) showed quite conclusively that similar (homogeneous) pairs were much more readily learned than dissimilar (heterogeneous) ones. Homogeneous pairs illustrate the law of similarity. He denied that his results supported simple association theory, preferring instead to attribute the results to "interaction" producing a unitary trace rather than a "connection" between similar items.

The law of similarity was applied by Koffka to the selection of a memory trace by a process active at the time of recall. That trace will be selected by an excitatory process which possesses the same wholeness character. The meaning of trace selection will be considered later. The meaning is conveyed sufficiently by the process of recognition, where a face present now recalls the same one seen earlier and results in the feeling of familiarity.

2. The law of proximity.   Perceptual groups are favored according to the nearness of the parts. Thus if several parallel lines are spaced unevenly on a page, those nearer together will tend to form groups against a background of empty space. Because whatever favors organization will also favor learning, retention, and recall, the law of proximity becomes the gestalt equivalent of association by contiguity. Patterning through proximity holds also within audition, as in the grouping of successive clicks. Then the proximity is a temporal one. As it applies to memory, the law of proximity becomes also a law of recency. Old impressions are less well recognized and recalled than new ones because the recent trace is nearer in time to the present active process (1935, page 464).

3. The law of closure. Closed areas are more stable than unclosed ones and therefore more readily form figures in perception. As applied to learning, closure is an alternative to the law of effect. The direction of behavior is toward an end-situation which brings closure with it. It is in this manner that rewards influence learning.

So long as activity is incomplete, every new situation created by it is still to the animal a transitional situation; whereas when the animal has attained his goal, he has arrived at a situation which is to him an end situation.[5]

In a problematic situation the whole is seen as incomplete and a tension is set up toward completion. This strain to complete is an aid to learning, and to achieve closure is satisfying. This is the meaning of the above quotation, and shows how closure is an alternative to effect.

4. The law of good continuation. This is the last of Wertheimer's principles taken over by Koffka, although Wedtheimer had several more. Organization in perception tends to occur in such a manner that a straight line appears to continue as a straight line, a part circle as a circle, and so on, even though many other kinds of perceptual structuring would be possible. Closure and continuation are aspects to articulate organization. Organization applies to learning as well as to perception.

Köhler (1941) demonstrated, for example, that the learning of paired figures was facilitated when the figures "fitted," that is, when the cue and response items formed a regular pair. Pairs fitting less well were harder to learn.

In each of the foregoing laws we have a principle from perception applied to learning.

THE SPECIAL PROBLEMS OF LEARNING

The general point of view of gestalt psychology is expressed in the statement that the laws of organization apply equally to perception and to learning. There are, however, special problems within learning to which Koffka devoted considerable discussion. Because of his antiempiricist[6]

---

[5] Koffka (1924), page 102. From *The growth of the mind* by K. Koffka, Kegan Paul, Trench, Trubner & Co., Ltd., London, 1924.

[6] Koffka was *antiempiricist,* objecting to an explanation of present perception solely on the basis of past experience. This did not make him a *nativist,* however, for he believed that gestalt laws of organization provided a *third* solution to the problem of space perception. See Koffka (1935), pages 160–161; Luchins (1951), pages 83–86.

position, he had to find some way of dealing with the evident influence of earlier experiences on present performance. The problem is best approached via memory, in which the past is represented somehow in the present. A second problem concerns the gradual transformation which takes place as skills of the trial-and-error sort are mastered. Finally, of course, there is the problem of restructuring the present field, as implied in insightful learning and in productive thinking.

The Role of Past Experience: the Trace Theory

Because modification by and through experience is part of the very definition of learning, the gestalt attitude toward experience is important.

The gestalt preference is distinctly for conceiving psychological processes as the function of the present field, and the explanatory role of past experience is denied in situation after situation in which to others it seems to be important. Examples include the perceptual constancies whereby a man looks man-size at a distance, a red coat looks equally red in sunshine and shadow. The illusions of movement and perception of third dimension are also included. Koffka, in spite of a vigorous objection to empiricism, took a moderate view toward the role of past experience in learning.

It will not be necessary to point out that an anti-empiristic attitude does not mean the denial of the enormous value of experience. Not *that* it makes use of experience causes our objection to empiricism, but *how* it makes use of it (1935, page 639n).

A favorite experiment repeatedly cited by gestalt psychologists in order to disprove the role of experience is that of Gottschaldt (1926). For example, if a picture of a letter E is presented 1000 times, and then a church window is exposed, are you any more likely to notice that some of the leaded lines in the windows could form a letter E than if E had been presented only once? We may doubt if a jury of association psychologists or anyone else would expect experience to tear down a percept into the thousand and one possible parts unless there were some kind of search involved. If you looked for the hidden part, and found it, the finding would be easier the next time. Gottschaldt accepts this conclusion, and had evidence that the results of previous discovery were evident in later tests. In the newspaper puzzles with faces hidden in the trees, once the face has been found it is more easily found again. Gottschaldt's experiment reduces to the demonstration that camouflage hides familiar objects as effectively as it hides unfamiliar ones—provided we have no reason to be looking for the familiar objects. Gottschaldt's experiments are cited by gestalt psychologists as very damaging to associationist or empiricist positions. Because of the difference in conception as to what is important, the experiment has not impressed association psychologists as being a crucial refutation of their position.[7]

By the very nature of the case, it is not as easy for the gestalt psychologist to dismiss the role of experience in memory as it is to dismiss its role in perception. Memory so obviously depends upon prior experience that it would be foolhardy to deny it. Koffka is as puzzled as a non-gestalt psychologist over Wheeler's attempt to get rid of memory traces (e.g., Wheeler, 1932, pages 167-169). Koffka believes some trace theory essential and proceeds to consider how the traces of past experiences can be reactivated by present processes.

The trace hypothesis is an involved one, and its full exposition requires over 100 pages of text (Koffka, 1935, pages 423–528). The essential features of the theory are (1) a trace is assumed which persists from a prior experience, so that it represents the past in the present; (2) a present process is also posited, one which can select, reactivate, or in some manner communicate with the trace; and (3) there is a resulting new process of recall or recognition. The process and the trace are to be distinguished; they are localized in different parts of the brain. The trace system is organized according to the same laws applying in other fields, and the communication between process and trace follows these laws.

The trace concept was further elaborated by Köhler (1938) and by Katona (1940). Katona made a distinction between *individual* traces, referring to specific items, and *structural* traces, derived from the wholeness character of a process. The structural traces are said to be more adaptable and flexible, to be formed more quickly, and to persist longer than individual traces (Katona, 1940, pages 194-195).

By way of the doctrine of traces, the gestalt psychologist is able to represent a past event in the present. That is, of course, all that the association psychologist proposes to do. But the trace system, if it is a system organized under gestalt laws, must undergo changes according to the law of *Prägnanz*. If these changes are of a systematic sort it will be evidence against a theory of mere connections weakening in time or inhibited by new learning.

The experiments of Wulf (1922) and later experiments following up his suggestions will be reviewed among the illustrative experiments. The main point is that perceived figures are reproduced differently from the original model, and that the differences are systematic and progressive rather than random. The changes with successive reproduction correspond to the laws of organization, and move toward the "good" gestalt. A circle with a small break in it tends to become more symmetrical in a drawing of it from memory. There are two chief tendencies noted by Wulf: *leveling* and *sharpening*. The leveling tendency is that already de-

[7] Moore (1930), Braly (1933), and Henle (1942) dispute Gottschaldt's interpretations.

scribed, a tendency to move according to the intrinsic character of the figure into symmetry and uniform relations of parts. Sharpening consists in the accentuating of details which serve as the discriminatory features of the pattern. For example, a saw-toothed figure may be reproduced with deeper and more striking teeth. Against the theory that memory leads to decay and fuzziness, the gestalt theory is that it leads to change but in the direction of greater clarity. A third tendency pointed out by Wulf is called *normalizing*. A figure which looks something like a familiar object tends on reproduction to be drawn more like such an object. All these changes (leveling, sharpening, and normalizing) are in the direction of a "good" gestalt.

To the extent that these systematic changes occur in the trace, there is a real addition which gestalt theory makes to other theories of memorial change.

New Learning: the Formation of Traces

What happens as new traces get formed? It is to be recalled that Koffka distinguished between the process and the trace. The process is that which goes on because of the present stimulating situation; the trace is the result of earlier processes.

1. Some processes are directly dependent upon stimuli. When such stimuli are presented a second time, the processes differ from those present the first time because the stimuli have been reacted to before. For example, the second exposure may be recognized as "familiar." This difference suffices to show that learning took place with the first exposure. His illustrations are limited to perceptual ones, and it is apparently perceptual responses to which Koffka refers when he speaks of processes directly dependent upon stimuli (1935, pages 549-550).

2. Processes may undergo transformation within a single sustained presentation. For example, when a series of sentences about mathematics is finally "understood" as a demonstration or proof, such a transformation has occurred. The insight experiments also illustrate such transformations (1935, pages 555-556).

3. Some processes are transformed by their consequences. This amounts to an acceptance by Koffka of the empirical "law of effect," but the explanation differs from Thorndike's. The transformation of process is at base the same as in the insight experiments, but it often occurs piecemeal as a consequence of the experimental arrangements. In the insight experiments all the data necessary for the transformation of process are present simultaneously, so that restructuring can take place at once. In the typical trial-and-error experiment, by contrast, the situation cannot be understood until the animal's activity has itself led to consequences—to food,

to freedom, and so on. Once success is achieved, the process leading to success is transformed. It has a new meaning, a new role in the goal-directed activity (1935, page 552).

The Effects of Repetition: the Consolidation of Trace Systems

The aggregate trace system resulting from repetition is always being transformed. With each repetition the trace organization left from preceding processes interacts with the present process to create something new. According to the principle of retroactive inhibition (which Koffka accepted), preceding individual traces are disrupted by the new learning. Repetition can still be beneficial, however, because the trace system becomes consolidated even while individual traces are destroyed. As the trace system becomes more fixed, it becomes preeminent over process and exerts more influence on future processes than such processes affect it. Such a trace system is said to become increasingly available; that is, it corresponds to what associationists think of as a habit system ready to function. A precaution is needed in the interpretation of availability, for conditions which make a trace more and more available for mere repetitions of one process may make it less available for other processes (1935, page 547). This is one of the dangers of too much drill in the school subjects, because drill may have a narrowing or "blinding" influence (Luchins, 1942).

The treatment of the acquisition of skill by Koffka is sketchy and conjectural, for the problem has not been experimentally attacked by members of the gestalt group. But skill is made coherent with the process-trace theory through a line of thought somewhat as follows. The trace, as part of the field of a process, exerts an influence on the process in the direction of making it similar to the process which originally produced the trace (1935, page 553). This is close to Guthrie's statement that we tend to do what we last did in the same situation. Highly perfected skills can be repeated after periods of disuse because the process communicates with a stable trace system to which it then conforms. While the skill is being learned the trace is less stable. Through the interaction of trace and process, greater stability is achieved. This achievement of greater stability is what is meant by improvement in the skill. Because the trace system, obeying dynamic laws, also undergoes stabilizing changes over a period of no practice, the greater improvement with distributed practice than with massed practice is explained.

Restructuring the Present Field: Insight

The contrast between trial and error and insight is a subject of some misunderstanding because there are empirical facts on the one hand

and theories about these facts on the other. So far as empirical situations are concerned, there are experiments which demonstrate a maximum of fumbling, with gradual improvements and little understanding of how improvement takes place. These may be classified as experiments in which learning is by trial and error, without prejudging the processes to be invoked in explaining the learning. There are also experiments in which the learner obviously perceives a relationship which leads to a problem solution, and the experiment may be classified as an insight experiment. And there are situations which fall between where there is partial insight combined with rather blind trial and error. The empirical grading of situations does not mean that the interpretations have to be so graded, that is, that the trial-and-error behavior must be explained by a trial-and-error theory, insight by an insight theory, and mixed behavior by appropriate mixtures of the theories. This impression is occasionally given by writers taking a middle-of-the-road position. The theorist, recognizing these empirical differences, tries to account for the differences on the basis of a unified set of principles.

Descriptive Characteristics of Insightful Learning

We may distinguish between what goes on in an actual experiment investigating insightful learning and the distinctive criteria of insight, for what goes on is by no means limited to insight, and overlaps greatly with other forms of learning. The overlap is illustrated in the following four characteristics:

1. A more intelligent organism is more likely to achieve insight, just as it is more likely to be successful at other forms of complex learning. Thus older children are more successful at insight problems than younger ones (e.g., Richardson, 1932), and apes more successful than guinea pigs.

2. An experienced organism is more likely to achieve insightful solution than a less experienced one (e.g., Birch, 1945). To some extent insight depends on past experience, as other forms of learning do. Thus a child cannot get insight into a mathematics problem stated symbolically unless he understands the conventional signs, even if the problem is otherwise suited to his capacity.

The difference between association theories and gestalt theories lies in the implication of association theories that the possession of the necessary past experience somehow guarantees the solution. While gestalt theorists would agree that past experience will facilitate solution, they object to explanations in terms of previous experience without taking organization into account. More is needed than the necessary amount of information. Just knowing enough words does not cause you to write a poem. The necessary experience alone does not solve the problem. In one of his early experiments, Maier (1930) provided his subjects with all the experience necessary for solving a problem, but only one of the thirty-seven solved it. The past experience had to be used appropriately before solution would occur.

Harlow (1949) thought he had discredited the insight interpretation because he had shown the importance of "learning how to learn" in the acquisition of what he called "learning sets." He found in experiments with monkeys that, after practice, discrimination reversals could be made in a single trial. Using single-trial learning as a mark of insight, he believed that he had shown insight to depend on prior experience. He wrote:

> The field theorists, unlike the Neo-behaviorists, have stressed insight and hypothesis in their description of learning. The impression these theorists give is that these phenomena are properties of the innate organization of the individual. If such phenomena appear independently of a gradual learning history, we have not found them in the primate order (1949, page 65).

This statement of Harlow's, while empirically correct, distorts the insight problem, which has to do with how experience is utilized rather than with the nonnecessity of experience; he is at fault in accepting one-trial learning in a highly practiced situation as a sufficient criterion of insight.

3. Some experimental arrangements are more favorable than others for the elicitation of insightful solution. Organization is contributed both by processes inherent in the organism and by structural patterning in the environment, and, of course, basically through the interaction of organism and environment. Insight is possible only if the learning situation is so arranged that all necessary aspects are open to observation. If a needed tool is hidden, its use in solution is made unlikely, or at least more difficult. In one form of the puzzle-box it is necessary for the rat to dig through a sawdust floor to discover a concealed tunnel which permits exit. Because the entrance to the tunnel is concealed beneath a uniform bed of sawdust, insight is impossible, and the first solution necessarily occurs almost by chance—being aided only by the fact that sawdust-digging is within the rat's habitual action pattern. The parts which need to be brought into relationship for solution are assembled more easily if they are simultaneously present in perception; for example, it is harder for an ape to learn to use a stick which lies on the side of the cage opposite the food than one which lies on the same side as the food (Jackson, 1942).

Skilled teachers are well aware of differences between situations in which understanding is arrived at easily and those in which it is achieved with difficulty—even though the same ultimate steps are involved and the same end stage reached. In the favored arrangement the problem is so structured that significant features are perceived in proper relationship, and distracting or confusing features are subordinated. Some mathematics teachers make problem solution difficult to grasp because they go through derivations step by step without an overview of where the steps are leading or what the articulating principles are. They teach the necessary operations, but the final insight eludes the students because of the manner in which the proof is arranged.

4. Trial-and-error behavior is present in the course of achieving insightful solution. In the presolution period the learner may make many false starts and be engaged in activity which can be characterized as trial and error. When insight will come (if it does come) is not predictable. These two features (initial fumbling and lack of predictability) have been used by opponents of insight either to assimilate it to associative learning because trial and error occurs, or to characterize it as mystical, nonscientific, or accidental because the moment of solution cannot be predicted.

The reply to those who find trial and error in insight experiments, and therefore wish to make insightful solution continuous with ordinary associative learning, is that fumbling in problem-solving is not *mere* trial and error. Even those who tend to favor trial-and-error interpretations have come to speak in terms of approximation and correction (Dodge, 1931) or in other ways to indicate that the "try" is a real try and not just any old action in the behavior repertory. In the case of adult insight experiments, the "try" is often a plausible hypothesis which has to be rejected. A succession of such hypotheses may be tried before the appropriate one is hit upon. The more intelligent reasoner may actually take longer to solve a given problem because he commands a greater variety of hypotheses to bring to its solution. There is a theoretical distinction which ought to be made between blind fumbling and intelligent searching. Merely varied behavior is one thing; behavior testing hypotheses is varied also, but according to a different type of organization.

That random behavior and luck may further solution is illustrated by some behavior which was observed one summer in Yerkes' laboratory during an insight experiment with a young chimpanzee. The problem set the animal was to obtain a banana from a long hollow box, open at both ends.[8] The box, essentially a rectangular tube, was firmly fastened to the floor of a large cage. The banana was inserted through a trap door in the middle of the box under the watchful eye of the animal, then the trap door was padlocked. The chimpanzee, after a number of unsuccessful efforts to obtain the banana by direct attack—reaching in either end of the tube with hands and with feet, attempting to lift the tube from the floor— seemed to give up temporarily, or, as gestalt psychologists say, to "go out of the field." This extraneous behavior took the form of playful cavort-

[8] The box is illustrated in Yerkes (1943).

ing. In this mood the animal incorporated into her play the hoe handle which was standing in the corner of the room, climbing it, and throwing it. Once the handle fell with its end near the open tunnel. The chimpanzee stopped her play, became calm, looked reflective, and, for the first time in her history used the pole as a tool to push the banana out of the far end of the tube.

The lucky position of the hoe handle structured the situation perceptually to make solution easier. It brought the hoe handle in as a possibility and gave direction to the problem-solving behavior. It did not add to the chimpanzee's past experience, but it made it easier to assemble the experiences appropriate to solution. Out of what was superfluous activity there thus developed a "hint" as to the direction of solution. An illustration of the way in which direct hints may aid solution is provided by Maier's (1930) experiment previously referred to. By giving a few "hints," in addition to the necessary past experience, solutions were obtained to the same problem by a much larger fraction of his subjects.

The objection to insight that it is unpredictable and therefore outside of science is lacking in force. The moment of insight is not the important feature in any case. Other features, such as reproducibility of the behavior and applicability of new situations are more important. But even though the moment of insight for a given animal confronted with a given problem is not predictable, it is possible to arrange problems in an order of difficulty so that the *degree of probability* that insight will occur is predictable. To assume that all predictions based on past occurrences (empirical probabilities) imply associative learning[9] is to make of association a term so broad as to be meaningless.

The four characteristics described (effects of capacity, prior experience, experimental arrangements, and trial and error) are not distinctive for insight, although in the course of discussion certain suggestions were made of differences in interpretation when the solution is viewed in stimulus–response or association terms and when it is viewed as the achievement of insight.

Distinctive Criteria of Insight

Because of the overlap of what happens in trial and error and in insightful learning, can we specify a few defining criteria by which insight can be clearly differentiated from other kinds of problem solution?

An early list of evidences of insight was provided by Yerkes (1927), based upon his analysis of photographic records of the problem-solving of a young gorilla, following upon earlier experiences with the orangutan and chimpanzee.

[9] The assumption was made by Guthrie (1935), page 193, and by Guthrie and Horton (1946), page 42.

In acts which by us are performed with insight or understanding of relations of means to ends, we are familiar with certain characteristics which are important, if not differential. The following is a partial list of features of such behavior. It is presented here with the thought that the comparative study of behavior with insight, in different organisms, may reveal common characteristics.

(1) Survey, inspection, or persistent examination of problematic situation. (2) Hesitation, pause, attitude of concentrated attention. (3) Trial of more or less adequate mode of response. (4) In case initial mode of response proves inadequate, trial of some other mode of response, the transition from the one method to the other being sharp and often sudden. (5) Persistent or frequently recurrent attention to the objective or goal and motivation thereby. (6) Appearance of critical point at which the organism suddenly, directly, and definitely performs the required adaptive act. (7) Ready repetition of adaptive response after once performed. (8) Notable ability to discover and attend to the essential aspect or relation in the problematic situation and to neglect, relatively, variations in non-essentials (Yerkes, 1927, page 156).[10]

On the basis of his observations of the young gorilla Congo, Yerkes went on to say that these observations confirmed his suspicion "that the conventional formula for habit-formation is incomplete, and the process of 'trial and error' wholly inadequate as an account of anthropoid adaptations."

The three types of evidence for insight most convincing to the experimenter seem to us to be three: *First,* the interruption of movement for a period, referred to by Yerkes as one of survey, inspection, attention, followed by the critical solution. This combines Yerkes' points (1), (2), (5) and (6). In the chimpanzee experiment described above, this stage was initiated following the "lucky" fall of the hoe handle near to the opening of the box. *Second,* the ready repetition of the solution after a single critical solution. This is Yerkes' point (7). The ape in the illustration given was returned to the experimental room on the following day. Everything was arranged as before. When the banana was locked into position and the chimpanzee released, there was a single flip of the lock (it *might* have been unfastened!) and then the animal went directly for the hoe handle, carried it over a shoulder in a manner very different from the day before, and proceeded to use it appropriately as a tool. There was no byplay, no dropping it on the floor. This was convincing to the experimenters as evidence that the previous day's solution was accompanied by insight. (There might be some argument as to *when* the insight came, whether *before* or *after* the previous day's success, although the pause before solution of the first day strongly suggested that insight came before the first solution.) *Third,* solution with insight should be generalized to new situations that require mediation by common principles or awareness of common relationships. While this is not specified in Yerkes' list, it is implied in the multiple-choice experiment, a kind of

[10] For other criteria of insight, see Pechstein and Brown (1939).

insight experiment that Yerkes invented. Here insight is indicated by a perceived relationship such as "the middle one of the open doors," "the second from the right of the open door." In human subjects these generalizations are often put into words when the problem is solved.

These three types of evidence are not entirely clear-cut and unambiguous, but they serve reasonably well when the whole context of the problem is considered. A rat pauses, too, before making a jump in the Lashley discrimination apparatus. How, one may ask, do you distinguish this pause from the kind Yerkes speaks of? The answer lies partly in the greater freedom of Yerkes' animals to move about and to do other things. Interrupted behavior is more readily observed when the possibilities of varied behavior are rich. So too the repetition of a first solution can be made without insight, as shown by the Guthrie and Horton cats. However, when the release pole was moved a few inches they were unable to use their prior pole-pushing habits, thus failing to live up to the third kind of evidence for insight (Guthrie and Horton, 1946, page 17). But a chimpanzee or gorilla that has learned to obtain a banana with a stick will *search* for a stick when a banana is out of reach, or will improvise a stick substitute out of bundled straw. Having reacted to the more abstract relationship of stick-as-a-tool-to-obtain-banana, it is not disturbed by a slight change in the environment.

Such applications of a perceived relationship to another situation in which it is applicable is the equivalent of transfer of training. The gestalt writers prefer to speak of it as *transposition,* on the pattern of a transposed melody. What is transferred is a relationship or a generalization, although the contents in the two situations may be entirely changed.

Stimulus–response psychologists recognize a corresponding application of old learning to new problems through stimulus generalization. While there is some overlap between the theories at all points (hesitation, repeated solution, transposed solution) there is no denying that, descriptively, behavior characterized as insightful occurs. The residual differences between the two theories lie more in their theoretical interpretations of what happens than in the descriptive overlap between the simpler forms of trial-and-error learning and the more convincing illustrations of insight. At the level of observation, insight is not the *explanation* of problem solution for a gestalt psychologist any more than for a stimulus–response psychologist.

Köhler complains about the misinterpretations to which his book on apes led:

When I once used this expression (insight) in a description of the intelligent behavior of apes, an unfortunate misunderstanding was, it seems, not entirely prevented. Sometimes the animals were found to be capable of achievements which we had not expected to occur below the human level. It was then stated that such accomplishments clearly involved insight. Apparently, some readers interpreted this formulation as though it referred to a mysterious agent or faculty which was made responsible for the apes' behavior. Actually, nothing of this sort was intended when I wrote my report. . . . No question of inventions or other outstanding intellectual achievements is here involved, and, far from referring to a mental faculty, the concept is used in a strictly descriptive fashion (Köhler, 1947, pages 341-342).

To the gestalt psychologist, insight exemplifies rather more clearly than other forms of learning the applicability of the laws of organization. It is these laws that explain insight, and it is the gestalt contention that the same laws explain other forms of learning. Only in that sense is insight for them the typical or characteristic kind of learning.

Productive Thinking

Wertheimer had lectured on thought processes for many years, but had published only a few fragmentary papers during his lifetime. He had, however, completed the manuscript of a small book just before his death. This was edited by his friends and appeared under the title *Productive thinking* (1945, 1959). In it a number of his experimental studies are summarized in his characteristic way, with penetrating qualitative analysis of simple situations serving to illustrate the differences between his approach and other approaches to which he was objecting.

The two chief competing alternatives to adopting the gestalt approach to thinking and problem-solving are said to be formal logic on the one hand and association theory on the other. Both of these alternatives are believed to be too limited to encompass what actually happens when an individual confronted with a problem finds a sensible solution.

The distinction is made throughout between a blind solution in which the learner applies a formula, and a sensible solution in which the learner understands what he is doing in relation to the essential structure of the situation. The blind solution is often an unsuccessful application of the formula to a situation not seen to be inappropriate. Experiments are cited, for example, in which school children are taught to find the area of a parallelogram by dropping lines from two corners perpendicular to the base, thus converting the figure to a rectangle, whose area can be found. Children who could do the examples perfectly were baffled, however, when a parallelogram was presented in a new orientation, so that the "correct" steps of the procedure led to confusing results. They had learned the solution according to a blind procedure. By contrast, the solution of a five-and-one-half-year-old child is reported.

Given the parallelogram problem, after she had been shown briefly how to get at the area of the rectangle, she said, "I certainly don't know how to do *that.*" Then after a moment of silence: "This is *no good here,*" pointing to the region at the left end; "and *no good here,*" pointing to the region at the right. [Figure 8-1.]

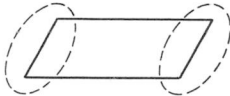

Figure 8-1 **Troublesome parts in child's attempt to apply rectangle theory to parallelogram. After Wertheimer (1945, page 48).**

"It's troublesome, here and there." Hesitatingly she said: "I could make it right here . . . but . . ." Suddenly she cried out, "May I have a scissors? What is bad there is just what is needed here. It fits." She took the scissors, cut vertically, and placed the left end at the right (Wertheimer, 1945, page 48). [Figure 8-2.]

Figure 8-2 **Child's solution of parallelogram problem with a scissors. After Wertheimer (1945, page 48).**

Another child, given a long parallelogram cut out of a piece of paper, remarked early that the whole middle was all right, but the ends—. She suddenly took the paper and made it into a ring. She saw that it was all right now, since it could be cut vertically anywhere and made into a rectangle.

In cases such as these the solutions appear in an orderly way, in line with the true "structure" of the situation. It is this structural approach which Wertheimer emphasizes.

Children readily grasp such "structural" solutions unless they are badly taught in an atmosphere of blind repetitive drill. Given figures such as those on the left in Figure 8-3 and those on the right, they can easily sort out the unsolvable ones from the solvables ones. It is futile to argue, says Wertheimer, that these distinctions are made on the basis of familiarity, as the associationist seems to believe. Children make the distinctions because they know the essential nature of the solution. The structural features and requirements of the situation itself set up strains and stresses which lead in the direction of improving the situation, that is to say, to solving the problem.

The implications of Wertheimer's point of view for teaching are fairly clear. It is always preferable to proceed in a manner which favors discovery of the essential nature of the problematic situation, of the gaps which require filling in, so that, even at the cost of elegance or brevity, the proof is "organic" rather than "mechanical" (Duncker, 1945, page 45).

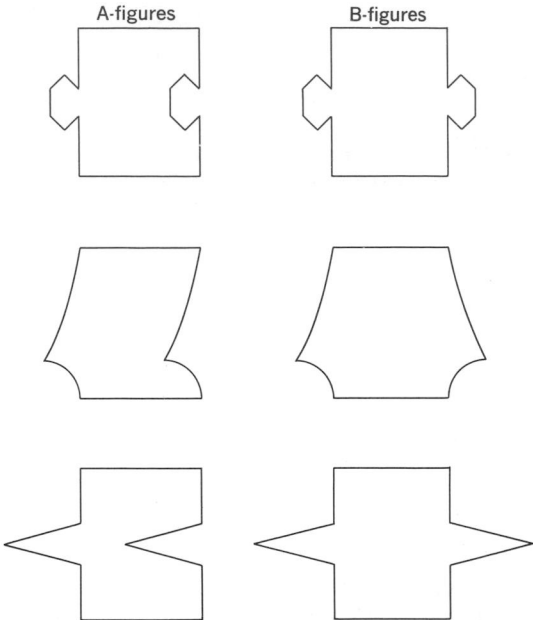

Figure 8-3 Applicability of solution of parallelogram problem to new figures. It is possible to change the A-figures sensibly so that they form rectangles. It is not possible to change the B-figures in this way. The ability of school children to solve the A-figures and to reject the B-figures is said to depend on something other than the familiarity of the figures. From Wertheimer (1945, page 20).

EXPERIMENTS ILLUSTRATIVE OF GESTALT THEORY OF LEARNING

Three sets of experiments have been selected as representative of the topics stemming from the interests of Köhler, Koffka, and Wertheimer. These are: (1) experiments devised to test the hypothesis that memory traces change in a systematic manner with time, (2) experiments contrasting organization with association in retroactive inhibition and related phenomena, and (3) experiments testing the relative roles of understanding and rote learning in memorization, retention, and transfer. The familiar insight experiments have already been referred to.

Does the Memory Trace Undergo Systematic Change?

The position first advanced by Wulf (1922), that memory traces change according to the dynamic principles of organization, received early support from the experiments of Allport (1930) and Perkins (1932). Gibson (1929) found verbal factors a strong influence in producing what Wulf called normalizing, that is, each reproduction's becoming more like a real object on successive attempts to reconstruct what was seen. He therefore was somewhat critical of the theory of intrinsic factors within the memory trace producing the change.[11]

There is no doubt but that reproductions are often inaccurate and often exhibit the kinds of changes that Wulf suggested. But these changes are often found in the very first reproduction, so that the change may belong more to *perception* than to *memory*. The crux of the matter lies in the finding of progressive changes with lapse of time.

Most of the experiments that have shown changes demanded by the theory have used the method of successive reproductions, which introduces the disturbing factor that the second reproduction is affected by the first, the third by the second, and so on. An extreme illustration of changes which can be made from one reproduction to another is that shown in Figure 8-4, where each person made one reproduction based on perceiving what the person before him had drawn. Mere lapse of time between seeing the original and reproducing it would scarcely have resulted in, say, the tenth reproduction.

In order to remedy the defect that experiments testing the theory used successive reproduction predominantly, Hanawalt (1937, 1952) had different subjects reproduce the same figures after various intervals of time, with but a single time interval for any one subject. Under these conditions, no progressive change was found. Such changes as occurred were commonly present on the first reproduction, and even might be present when the subject copies the figure present before him.

Hebb and Foord (1945), in a carefully controlled experiment, used the method of recognition rather than that of reproduction, asking the subject to select from a series of figures the one that had been originally presented. There was only one retest for each figure learned by a subject, but the retest was made after a lapse of time differing from one subject to another. The objects presented visually were a circle with a small portion of its circumference incomplete and an arrowhead figure. Presumably there would be a change either toward closure (leveling) or toward emphasizing the broken part (sharpening). The circle may be used for illustration. Testing was done by selecting from a series of broken circles the one which was said to have been seen before. Although there was some variability, the trends were not in support of Wulf's theory, and there were no progressive changes evident with the passing of time.

The conclusions to be reached from these experiments are certainly damaging to the gestalt interpretation of spontaneous changes in the memory trace. They do not deny the gestalt interpretation of changes in perception, or of progressive changes in successive reproduction, where successive perception is involved.

Bartlett's (1932) experiments on repeating stories over long intervals

[11] Gibson's results were extended and confirmed by Carmichael, Hogan, and Walter (1932), Brown (1935).

Original Reproduction 1 Reproduction 2

Reproduction 3 Reproduction 8 Reproduction 9

Reproduction 10 Reproduction 15 Reproduction 18

Figure 8-4 Changes in figures within the method of serial reproduction. Each person views the reproduction by the person preceding him, and then passes his reproduction to the next person. There are progressive changes and elaborations, as in the series illustrated. From Bartlett (1932, pages 180, 181), by permission Cambridge University Press, England, and The Macmillan Company, N.Y.

are perhaps more instructive in some ways than the experiments repeating line drawings. They reveal rather striking tendencies toward structuring the story so that it "makes sense," and as the story grows older it also got shorter and irrelevant details dropped out. This led Bartlett to speak of the *productive* nature of memory as contrasted with its *reproductive* nature. However, the gestalt claim with respect to changes in the trace was based on the experiments of Wulf, and the refutations have been based on experiments using very similar materials. A common-sense use of Wulf's classification of changes into leveling, sharpening, and normalizing has been made by social psychologists (e.g., Allport and Postman, 1947), but these uses probably do not require confirmation of spontaneous changes in the trace. Krech and Crutchfield state, for example, that successive reproduction is characteristic of "real life," that is, "an occasional recall (without checking on the accuracy of the recall) of an event that has occurred in the past" (Krech and Crutchfield, 1948, page 127, footnote).

These experiments illustrate how a theory leads to a particular variety of experiment not suggested by other theories. Despite the negative results, the experiments are useful. Experimentation is not intended merely to confirm theories; an equally important role is to refute, to correct, and to delimit the claims of a theory. The by-products have given some support for gestalt perceptual theory while almost invariably refuting the claims respecting the nature of spontaneous changes in the memory trace over time.

The methodological possibilities have not yet been exhausted. Osgood (1953, pages 590–591) points out a failure to use figures whose perceptual dynamics are known on the basis of actual perceptual experiments (afterimages, interpretation of the figure in dim light, etc.). Whether reproduction or recognition tests should be used cannot be given an easy answer. Using several figures at once causes a number of confusions in reproduction, not attributable to the spontaneous changes in a single trace. Possibly more subtle methods should be used in testing individual subjects repeatedly; one suggestion made by Osgood is the use of hypnosis.

Organization versus Associative Interference in Retention

In a series of experiments published between 1933 and 1937, Köhler and his associates found results interpreted by them as interactions implying a field relation between a particular process and a particular trace.[12]

In her first study, von Restorff (1933) showed a relationship between perceptual laws and the recall of nonsense materials. She showed that in the recall of nonsense material, part of the difficulty lies in the homogeneity of the material. If lists of paired associates are constructed so that one pair is of very heterogeneous material, this pair will be retained much better than the pairs of items representing materials more frequently repeated within the list. The interpretation is that the heterogeneous items stand out like a figure on the ground, exactly as in perception. This favorable structuring in perception turns out to be favorable also for recall. Müller (1937) went on to show that the recall of isolated or unique material was favored even when the unique items were dis-

---

[12] von Restorff (1933), Köhler and von Restorff (1935), Bartel (1937), Müller (1937). Aspects of these experiments were reviewed by Köhler (1938, 1940).

tributed over eight separately learned and recalled lists. The final task was the unexpected recall of whatever could be remembered from the eight lists. Six of the eight lists contained one kind of unique item, while two of the lists contained another kind of unique item. Recall favored the rarer unique items found only in two of the eight lists.

In the study of Köhler and von Restorff (1935) an ingenious arrangement was used to test "spontaneous recall" when there was a minimum of induced "set" to recall. The laws of dynamics are best revealed when the results of process-trace interaction emerge naturally, without any special instruction to "search" for relationships.

All subjects first worked on the following computational problem:

$$x = 21 \ (91/7 + 6) + 14.$$

Most subjects went through the usual steps:

$$\text{First, } 91/7 = 13.$$

Therefore,

$$x = 21 \ (13 + 6) + 14$$
$$= 21 \ (19) + 14.$$

Performing the major multiplication:

$$
\begin{array}{r}
21 \\
\times 19 \\
\hline
189 \\
21 \\
\hline
399
\end{array}
$$

Hence,

$$x = 399 + 14 = 413.$$

At this point the experimenter pointed out, somewhat casually, that the subjects might have noticed a somewhat easier way of multiplying 21×19, using the formula $(20 + 1) \ (20 - 1) = 20^2 - 1 = 400 - 1 = 399$. The later retention test required recalling the pertinence of the principle that $(a + b) (a - b) = a^2 - b^2$.

After this exercise in computation, and the casual suggestion of another solution, half the subjects went on to do problems in arithmetical computation, while the other half worked on matchstick problems. Then both groups were again assigned a problem related to the one outlined above. The prediction was that the new problem would be detected as similar to the first one more frequently by those working on matchsticks than by those who had continued to work on arithmetic. That is, the computation problem would be more distinctive for those for whom it had been the *only* computation problem, and the new process would therefore be more likely to communicate with the memory traces from the first problem.

The prediction was borne out. The "short-cut" method was used more frequently by those whose intervening activity was with matches than by those whose intervening activity was additional arithmetic. (See Table 8-1.) Upon questioning, the other subjects could easily remember having

Table 8-1   **Spontaneous Recall as Affected by Homogeneous and Heterogeneous Intervening Activity (Kohler and von Restorff, 1935, page 79).**

	Continued with Arithmetic (Homogeneous Activity)	*Worked with Matchsticks (Heterogenous Activity)*	*Total Subjects*
Recalled short cut	9	27	36
Failed to recall short cut	25	10	35
Total subjects	34	37	71

Chi square $= 15.3$
P less than .001

been told about the short cut. This bears out the importance of arranging the experiment so as to test *spontaneous* recall if the dynamics of the process are to be exposed. Bartel (1937) continued with related experiments, with consonant results.

Müller (1937) also studied a problem familiar in the history of retroactive-inhibition experiments, the problem of the point in the interval between learning and recall at which the interpolated material produces the greatest amount of interference. Müller's findings supported the view that retroactive inhibition was at a maximum near the point of reproduction, suggesting that the action was really proactive rather than retroactive.

All of these experiments show a resemblance in design to experiments done in the tradition of associative learning. What is unique about them, or about the theories used to explain them?

First, the experiments commonly employ both homogeneous and heterogeneous materials, in order to point to principles of organization from perception as applying also to retention and recall. Added cogency is given to these arguments by later experiments of Werner (1947), where he showed that boundary phenomena which, in perception, prevent the confusion of forms, also operate in proactive inhibition. Material that was strongly "bounded" did not intrude as erroneous responses in a second list, and produced less interference with the retention of the second list.

Second, the conception of process-trace interaction is said to differ from explanations according to associative connections. Köhler notes, for example, that in the usual retroactive-inhibition experiment traces are poorly distinguished and are densely crowded, so that they no longer function according to their intrinsic natures. Köhler points out that the experiments on spontaneous recall do not have these objections, for they permit the traces to function more normally, with results as predicted from principles of organization (1940, page 155).

Drill versus Understanding in Memorization and Retention

In his book on *Organizing and memorizing* (1940), Katona reported a number of experiments inspired by Wertheimer, who contributed the foreword to the book.

Katona attempts experimentally to define and characterize two types of processes leading to recall: rote memorizing and understanding. When a list of nonsense syllables is memorized, the learner is forced to use the former process, because there are no organizing principles which will permit understanding to help. On the other hand, there are many kinds of problems which illustrate principles; in such cases learning by understanding will have advantages. Simple and ingenious experiments were designed in which it was possible to commit the same material to memory with or without understanding, and then to test the results on new learning.

One experiment consisted in the teaching of simple match tricks of the kind illustrated in Figure 8-5. The problem is to move 3 lines and in so doing to have only 4 squares left. The possible solutions are shown in the figure. There is a simple principle involved in all solutions, which is that no side must be used for more than one square. (There are 16 matches making the original 5 squares; because these 16 matches are now to make 4 squares it is evident that each side can be used but once.) A number of different tasks were used, all bringing changes on the same general pattern.

In his Experiment A, three groups were used, a control group, a memorization group, and a group practiced on examples. No preliminary practice was given the control group. The memorization group was shown the first problem (that of Figure 8-5.) with one of its solutions. Then this same problem was presented in rotated form and the same solution shown. The memorization group was thus shown essentially the same solution four times, with the problem very slightly rearranged geomet-

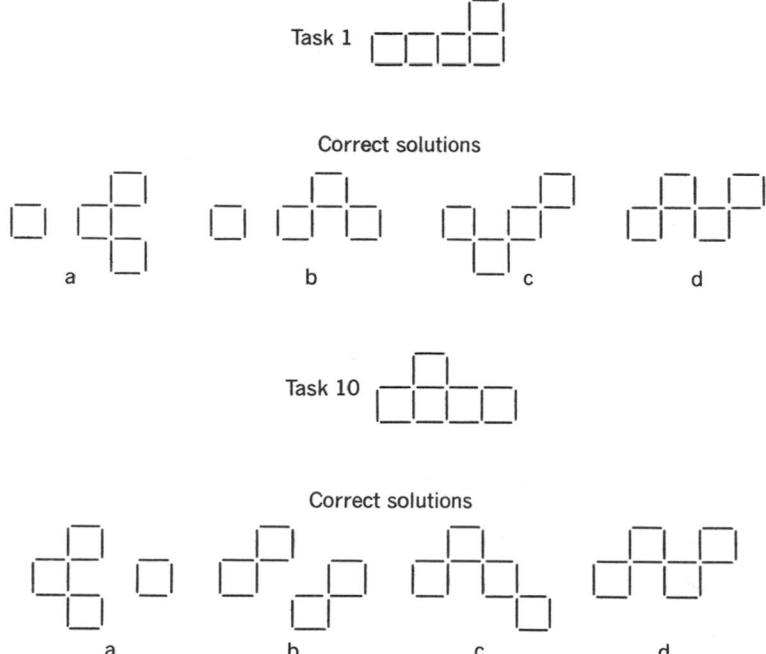

Figure 8-5   Match-stick problems. The assigned problem is to make 4 squares instead of 5 by moving 3 matches (all matches to be used in the solution). Four solutions are shown for each of two tasks. From Katona (1940, page 120).

rically. The group which had practiced on examples experienced six different transitions from one situation to another in their preliminary practice period, although no general principle was enunciated. Following this preliminary practice, each of the three groups was given four tasks to solve; these were all new to the control group, but one of the four tasks was familiar to the memorization and examples group. There was a retest four weeks later, with a new control group. In this retest three new tasks were presented along with one of the originally practiced tasks. Successes on the practiced task were about alike for the two groups, in spite of the fact that the practiced task for the examples group was only one of three tasks practiced, while the memorization group had spent all of its practice period on this one task. The advantage of the examples group was more pronounced on new tasks, as shown in Table 8-2.

Why was the group practiced on examples superior? Presumably because the more varied experience had produced some measure of understanding. Verbal reports showed that this understanding was fragmentary, taking such forms as "filling up holes increases the number of squares"; "spreading it out decreases the number of squares." In any case, the method produced a more varied attack, and alternative solutions to the familiar problems were used in a way not true for the memorization group. Memorization sometimes tends to narrow rather than to increase the range of problem-solving.

Table 8-2   Comparison of Scores* on New Tasks of Groups Practiced in Different Ways (Katona, 1940, page 86)

	Immediate Test	*Retest After 4 Weeks*
Control Group	1.06	2.20
Memorization Group	1.79	2.84
Group Practiced on Examples	3.92	6.24

* Weighted scores, with possible score of 10. The differences between the examples group and the others are statistically significant.

Katona concludes that learning with understanding not only improves retention of that which is learned, but better qualifies the learner to move forward to new learning. Thus understanding is important for transfer. Some of Katona's conclusions were critized by Melton (1941b) on statistical grounds, but Melton accepted as demonstrated the following points on transfer following learning by understanding:

1. A group which has learned by rote memorization is little better than an unpracticed control group in the learning of new tasks, while a group which has learned with understanding learns new tasks much more readily.

2. When tasks have been learned with understanding, repeated tests with new tasks result in progressive improvement in performance. By contrast, if the repeated tests are done with practiced tasks, the efficiency of performance on new tasks is reduced.

Katona concludes from all this that there is a real difference in what happens when meaningless memorization goes on and when learning takes place with understanding. He believes that the two kinds of learning are genuine and should be distinguished. This does not mean that he believes that there are two fundamental prototypes of learning, corresponding to the two types of arrangement under which learning takes place. According to him, the underlying factor is organization. Only when better organization fails do you get the extreme picture of rote learning, which is itself a special form of organization resorted to with comparatively incoherent materials. The distinction in kind is not one of ease or of difficulty, for it is sometimes easier to learn by rote than to learn by understanding. The advantages of learning by understanding are that

meaningful learning is applicable to new situations and is more enduring.[13]

ESTIMATE OF GESTALT THEORY OF LEARNING

Gestalt Theory and the Typical Problems of Learning

The gestalt psychologists find a somewhat distorted emphasis in
conventional treatments of learning, so that the problems typically emphasized are not the most natural selection of problems from their standpoint. In order to maintain the symmetry of comparative study of the
different positions, however, the same list will be followed which was used
to summarize the stimulus–response positions.

1. Capacity. Because learning requires differentiation and restructuring
of fields, the higher forms of learning depend very much upon natural
capacities for reacting in these ways. Poor methods of instruction, however, may be responsible for some inability to face new situations, for a
"blindness" which might be confused with stupidity.

2. Practice. Changes go on within repetition, not as a result of repetition. Practically all psychologists now agree that this is so, but they differ
with regard to the pertinent processes which go on within the repetitions.
From the gestalt point of view, repetitions are successive exposures, bringing to light relationships to enter into restructurization. To Koffka, they
also make possible the consolidation of trace systems, which is as near as
any gestalt psychologist comes to saying that responses become fixed by
repetition.

3. Motivation. Goals represent end-situations, and as such modify learning through the principle of closure. The processes leading to the successes or failures get transformed by their consequences. The empirical
law of effect is accepted, but Thorndike's interpretation of the blind
action of effect is denied.

4. Understanding. The perceiving of relationships, awareness of the
relationships between parts and whole, of means to consequences, are
emphasized by the gestalt writers. Problems are to be solved sensibly,
structurally, organically, rather than mechanically, stupidly, or by the
running off of prior habits. Insightful learning is thus more typical of appropriately presented learning tasks than is trial-and-error.

[13] For his reply to Melton's criticisms, see Katona (1942). Some features of Katona's
experiments were satisfactorily repeated and extended by Hilgard, Irvine, and Whipple
(1953), Hilgard, Edgren, and Irvine (1954).

5. Transfer. The gestalt concept most like that of transfer is *transposition*. A pattern of dynamic relationships discovered or understood in one situation may be applicable to another. This is in some respects like Judd's generalization theory of transfer (Judd, 1908). There is something in common between the earlier learning and the situation in which transfer is found, but what exists in common is not identical piecemeal elements but common patterns, configurations, or relationships. One of the advantages of learning by understanding rather than by rote process is that understanding is transposable to wider ranges of situations, and less often leads to erroneous applications of old learning.

6. Forgetting. Koffka relates forgetting to the course of changes in the trace. Traces may disappear either through gradual decay (a possibility hard to prove or disprove), through destruction because of being part of a chaotic, ill-structured field, or through assimilation to new traces or processes. The last possibility is familiar as a form of theory of retroactive inhibition. Traces which continue to exist may at a given moment be unavailable. While little is known about this, Koffka believes it must have something to do with ego organization (1935, pages 525-527). Finally, there are instances of forgetting in which a process fails to communicate with an otherwise available trace. The forgetting of an intention (Birenbaum, 1930) would presumably classify here. This is also an ego problem.

In addition to such forgetting, there are the dynamic changes which take place in recall, so that what is reproduced is not earlier learning with some parts missing, but a modified trace which is productive as well as reproductive.

General Aspects of Gestalt Theory

In discussing gestalt psychology solely as a theory of learning, some of its more general features have been sidestepped, especially its philosophical orientation and its relation to biology.

The objection to association theory of learning is part of the *holistic* emphasis within the general theory, and coherent with the opposition to "atomistic" explanations according to connections between parts. The objection to sensations as elements of perception ("the bundle hypothesis") is carried over in the objection to stimulus–response connections as elements of habits.

The *phenomenological* standpoint, often stated by gestalt psychologists as opposed to the prevailing *positivistic* position, is not easy to characterize satisfactorily in limited space. Phenomenal observation is more "subjective" than behaviorism, but less sophisticated and specially trained than the introspection recommended by Titchener. The recommended variety of observation is natural and childlike, appreciative rather than analytical. For example, Köhler's later accounts of insight depended upon such a phenomenological description of events. Insight in this context includes such everyday experiences as enjoying a cool drink. We refer the pleasures we feel to the taste of the drink and to our thirst, through a natural "requiredness" of the relationships. We do not attribute our pleasure to accidental accompaniments, "not, for instance, to the spider on the wall, nor to the size of the chair before me, nor to the thousands of other things in my environment" (Köhler, 1947, page 346). These everyday experiences of the determination of events, here called insight, are said to refute the theory of chance contiguous associations.

The interpretation of gestalt psychology as a *field theory* rests largely on the evidence assembled by Köhler in his *Physischen Gestalten* (1920), showing the relationship between gestalt laws of organization and well-established principles in physics and biology. The biological emphasis within gestalt was carried forward by Gelb and Goldstein.[14]

Köhler all along held *isomorphism* to be central to the understanding of gestalt psychology. This is the principle that the underlying brain fields correspond in their dynamic aspects to phenomenal experience. If there is perceived separation in space there will be separation in centers of excitation in the brain; if there is perceived movement, there will be some sort of movement of excitation patterns in the brain. It is not a "copy" theory; that is, the representation need not be direct, but it must be dynamically equivalent. In the experiments conducted late in his career, before retiring from the laboratory, Köhler appeared to find some physiological support for his theories. Working with amplifiers that could record resting potentials or slowly varying ones, he and his collaborators detected some changes at the surface of the skull corresponding in some ways to the patterns of movement of visual stimuli (Köhler and Held, 1949; Köhler, Held, and O'Connell, 1952).[15]

Köhler believed psychophysical isomorphism followed from the principles of evolution, so that mental events are not alien to physical events, but are rooted in the laws of nature:

[14] The collaboration between Gelb and Goldstein began in the study of brain-injured soldiers of World War I (Gelb and Goldstein, 1918). Goldstein's matured views were presented in book form in Goldstein (1939, 1940, 1948). Wheeler's organismic psychology picked up and extended the biological emphasis, and assimilated embryological studies, but it must be considered an offshoot of gestalt psychology rather than part of the central core of development. So, too, many gestalt-affiliations can be found in Werner (1948), but he was not, strictly speaking, one of the gestalt group.

[15] The theory that the experiments supported was criticized experimentally by Lashley, Chow, and Semmes (1951), who placed silver foil on the cortex, thus short-circuiting such "fields" as might exist, without thereby destroying the discrimination that, according to the theory, should have depended upon these fields.

Some fundamental properties of nature rather than any special arrangements in the organism are, I believe, the counterparts of essential mental facts (Köhler, 1938, page 400).

The Interrelationship Between Perception and Learning

Any estimate of the gestalt position would be incomplete which did not appraise the success with which the basic thesis has been defended that the dynamic laws of perception and of learning are alike. For the most part, these conjectures have been programmatic rather than worked out in convincing experiments. The point of view has been helpful to the extent that it has brought emphasis upon organization, meaningfulness, and understanding, and has called attention to the importance of the structure of the problematic situation. The laws of similarity (or equality), of proximity, of closure, and of good continuation, are not very convincing as laws of learning, and the attempts made by Koffka to summarize his point of view of learning in terms of them is not very successful. As we saw in the review of Tolman's position, the reintroduction of cognitive features into learning has been important, whatever one's judgment of the importance of the laws of organization may be.

Insight as an Alternative to Trial and Error

It is implied in gestalt theory that a learner acts as intelligently as he can under the circumstances which confront him, so that insightful solution of problems is the typical solution, if the problem is not too difficult and the essentials are open to inspection. Fumbling and trial and error are resorted to only when the problem is too difficult, either intrinsically, or because of the way in which it is presented to the learner. This reverses the associationist position that trial and error is the typical method of attack and that reasoning is essentially "mental" trial and error. The empirical facts of insight are as satisfactory as the empirical facts of trial and error. Learning theorists are not yet in agreement on one of the three possibilities: (1) that all learning is of one kind, basically like trial and error, from which insightful learning can be derived; (2) that all learning is basically of one kind, like insightful learning, with trial and error a derivative form; or (3) that more than one kind of learning occurs, of which trial and error and insight are two illustrative examples. A strong case can be made for the gestalt point of view that blind learning is not the prototype of all learning. But this is one of the unresolved issues, to face us in succeeding chapters of this book.

In any case, the gestalt psychologists have sharpened the lines of cleavage in thinking about problems of learning, and by questioning most of what was conventionally accepted they have been of real service, regardless of whatever verdicts or compromises the future may produce.

GESTALT PSYCHOLOGY IN THE 1960'S

The excitement created by the introduction of gestalt psychology to America in the late 1920's and early 1930's had largely subsided by the 1950's. As the substance of this chapter indicates, there is much that is valid in what the gestalt psychologists taught, and an interesting problem in the history of ideas exists as one views the decline of interest in the gestalt position.[16]

According to Boring, it was success that made the gestalt position lose its identity:

The movement has produced much new important research, but it is no longer profitable to label it as Gestalt psychology. Had Gestalt psychology resisted the inclusion of behavioral data in psychology, there might have been a long war over the question whether psychology is or is not principally the study of direct experience. As it was, Köhler's chimpanzees were admitted as data from the start. The result is that Gestalt psychology has already passed its peak and is now dying of success by being absorbed into what is Psychology.[17]

Kendler, in reviewing learning theory in the months before 1959 concluded:

Cognitive learning theory of the sort Tolman espoused, as well as the Gestalt variety, is either asleep or dying. This seems to be the only conclusion to draw from the limited amount of activity each has generated over the past year (1959, page 73).

Four hypotheses may be examined with respect to the recent history of gestalt theory: (1) that it has been found false, (2) that it is neglected because of shifts of interest, (3) that it is neglected because its good ideas were imbedded in inacceptable theories, and (4) that transformations have taken place so that its good ideas are persistent, but not recognizable as gestalt psychology.

The first of these hypotheses may be rejected. While there are areas of difficulty in the gestalt position, this is equally true of its competitors, and there are many cogent ideas within gestalt psychology that have not been disproved. The second is also not a reasonable interpretation, in view of the very great contemporary interest in the cognitive processes generally, in problem-solving, and in creativity. If anything, current interests could be moving closer to the kinds of learning problems with which the gestalt psychologists dealt than to the standard S–R problems of conditioning, motor skills, and rote learning. This then leaves the last two hypotheses to be examined.

[16] What is said here is based in part upon Hilgard (1946c, pages 54-77).
[17] Boring (1950), page 600.

There is no doubt that some of the imbeddedness of the experiments has militated against their acceptance in American psychology. Köhler turned from an acceptable view of insight in the book on apes to the rather mystical one in his later book (Köhler, 1947). Wertheimer's examples of productive thinking have the same freshness today as when they were written, yet one of his former students and followers felt that the book was too little worked out in a systematic way (MacLeod, 1962). The excesses in Wheeler's version of organismic psychology diverted attention away from some of his useful empirical ideas, such as those on *pacing,* a concept which suggests a natural learning rate within limits of stimulation. It was doubtless the failure of Lewin's theoretical structure (Leeper, 1943; Estes, 1954) that took him out of the competition as a learning theorist, although he is still very influential within social psychology.[18]

While therefore it is in part a rejection of the gestalt psychologists that has led to a rejection of their more fertile ideas, the fourth hypothesis, that the ideas persist, but in new transformations, deserves some attention.

1. The critique of stimulus–response associationism, initiated strongly by the gestalt psychologists, has continued in other hands, as, for example, by Miller, Galanter, and Pribram (1960). These authors attempt to introduce a new unit into psychology, the TOTE (Test-Operate-Test-Exit) schema. This is a rejection of the reflex arc as the paradigm, and the assertion of the need for a more cognitive type of unit.

2. The development of many new "Centers for Cognitive Studies" under various names and at various universities, attests to the current interest in cognition. While there are other roots than gestalt psychology, any pertinent ideas from Wertheimer and others of the group will not be neglected (along with information theory, cybernetics, computer simulation, the work of Piaget, and psychoanalysis). This is one way in which transformation of ideas takes place.

3. Piecemeal assimilation (or rediscovery) takes place all along. Thus a study emphasizing *inherent organization* in a task as an essential feature to be considered in efficient learning has been conducted by Sheffield and Maccoby (1961). These authors, under the influence of Guthrie's association theory, would be surprised to learn that they are serving as examples of those who are keeping alive principles of gestalt psychology.

There are, of course, direct lines from earlier gestalt. Thus the book by Luchins and Luchins (1959) continued the earlier experiments of Luchins (1942), and a chapter on the applicability of gestalt principles to audio-visual aids has appeared (Luchins, 1961). But those who are self-

---

[18] A chapter on Lewin's views in the earlier editions of this book has been omitted in this edition because of lack of current interest. It may be noted that one of Lewin's followers, in summarizing his total contribution, omitted reference to the one article in which Lewin was explicit about learning (Cartwright, 1959; Lewin, 1942).

consciously within the gestalt tradition have not more generally kept alive the interest in learning; in a book collecting papers that have appeared within gestalt psychology chiefly since 1950, there is no section on learning, and under "cognitive processes" nothing directly on either learning or problem-solving (Henle, 1961).

Without the challenges to other viewpoints which arise from those actively committed to a particular theoretical position, that position is likely to lose prominence. The lack of gestalt psychologists interested in learning at the present time weakens the challenges to current alternatives. This lack of identifiability of the gestalt position in the present is unfortunate, in that some of the important ideas therefore lose out through lack of dramatic impact; in the end, however, what is most valuable for the understanding of learning is bound to reappear and eventually to survive.

In his presidential address before the American Psychological Association Köhler (1958) complained not of the successful assimilation of gestalt psychology, but of the continued rejection of some of its basic ideas, such as the appropriateness of using what has been learned from modern field physics. We shall have to await future developments to find out the extent to which he proves to have been correct.

SUPPLEMENTARY READINGS

The books by the "big three" of gestalt psychology are as follows:

KOFFKA, K. (1924) *Growth of the mind.*

KOFFKA, K. (1935) *Principles of gestalt psychology.*

KÖHLER, W. (1925) *The mentality of apes.*

KÖHLER, W. (1929) (1947) *Gestalt psychology.*

KÖHLER, W. (1940) *Dynamics in psychology.*

WERTHEIMER, M. (1945) (1959) *Productive thinking.*

Although not treated in this chapter, the most relevant book by Lewin is:

LEWIN, K. (1935) *A dynamic theory of personality.*

His chapter most directly concerned with learning is:

LEWIN, K. (1942) Field theory and learning. Chapter 4 in *The psychology of learning.* Natl. Soc. Stud. Educ., 41st Yearbook, Part II, 215-242.

For a sympathetic, yet critical, account of gestalt psychology, the following is pertinent:

PRENTICE, W. C. H. (1959) The systematic psychology of Wolfgang Köhler. In Koch, S. (Editor) *Psychology: A study of a science,* Vol. I, pages 427-455.

The following thoughtful summary treats the major issues in terms of the contrast between cognition and stimulus–response theories:

SCHEERER, M. (1954) Cognitive theory. In G. Lindzey (Editor) *Handbook of social psychology,* 91-137.

Freud's Psychodynamics

Sigmund Freud (1856-1939) so influenced psychological thinking that a summary of theoretical viewpoints, even in a specialized field such as the psychology of learning, is incomplete without reference to him. In the context of the history of psychology, Boring has this to say of Freud's place:

It was Freud who put the dynamic conception of psychology where psychologists could see it and take it. They took it, slowly and with hesitation, accepting some principles while rejecting many of the trimmings. It is not likely that the history of psychology can be written in the next three centuries without mention of Freud's name and still claim to be a general history of psychology (Boring, 1950, page 707).

It is no simple task to extract a theory of learning from Freud's writings, for while he was interested in individual development and the kind of reeducation that goes on in psychotherapy, the problems whose answers he tried to formulate were not those with which theorists in the field of learning have been chiefly concerned. Psychoanalytic theory is too complex and, at least at the present time, too little formalized, for it to be presented as a set of propositions subject to experimental testing. Therefore, instead of attempting an orderly exposition of a psychodynamic theory of learning, we shall rest content with examining in somewhat piecemeal fashion suggestions from psychoanalysis that bear upon learning. Some of the suggestions have already influenced experimentation in learning, and some of them may be more influential in the years ahead.

PARALLELS BETWEEN PSYCHOANALYTIC THEORY AND CONVENTIONAL INTERPRETATIONS OF LEARNING

One can find in Freud's writings a number of statements that parallel very closely statements made by contemporary learning theorists little influenced by him. The common topics within psychoanalysis and learning theory serve usefully to show how relevant psychoanalysis is to learning.

The Pleasure Principle and the Law of Effect

Hedonistic theories—that man seeks pleasure and avoids pain—are among the oldest interpretations of human conduct, and any theory of learning must come to grips with the facts to which they refer. There is no doubt that we can control learning by way of reward and punishment. The details sometimes elude us, but the gross facts cannot be doubted.

Freud's pleasure principle is in accord with these facts, and his interpretation of the pleasure principle represents one of the first points of correspondence between his views and those of learning theorists. The corresponding principle in contemporary learning theory is more likely to go under the names of the *law of effect* or *reinforcement theory*. The broad conception, common to both psychoanalysis and learning theory, is that a need state is a state of high tension. Whether we describe this in terms of instincts seeking gratification or of drives leading to consummatory responses, we are talking about the same sequence of events. What controls the direction of movement is a tendency to restore a kind of equilibrium, thus reducing tension. Freud talked about a return to a constant state, and the physiologists, after Cannon, refer to homeostasis. The principle goes back at least to Claude Bernard, but in any case it is shared by Freud and the learning theorists whose views have already been considered.

One of Freud's concise statements of this position is found in the introductory paragraph of his *Beyond the pleasure principle:*

In the theory of psychoanalysis we have no hesitation in assuming that the course taken by mental events is automatically regulated by the pleasure principle. We believe, that is to say, that the course of those events is invariably set in motion by an unpleasurable tension, and that it takes a direction such that its final outcome coincides with a lowering of that tension—that is, with an avoidance of unpleasure or a production of pleasure.[1]

[1] Freud (1920b), page 1. From *Beyond the pleasure principle* by Sigmund Freud, by permission of Liveright Publishers, New York.

Freud speculated about the relationship between pleasure and quantity of excitation. Unpleasure, he said, corresponded to an increase in excitation and pleasure to a *diminution,* although he allowed some importance to the *rate of change* of excitation. In this he followed a classical psychologist, Fechner, who wrote along the same lines much earlier (1873).

American psychologists at the height of the behaviorist era preferred to talk about tension and its reduction without bringing in the term "pleasure." In the 1950's and thereafter, however, attention again began to be paid to affectivity (e.g., Young, 1952). McClelland and his associates (1953) proposed a quantitative theory of pleasantness and unpleasantness, somewhat along the lines suggested by Freud. They proposed that a slight departure from the level of stimulation to which the organism is adapted is usually pleasurable, while an extreme departure is unpleasant or annoying. Thus if one adds salt to distilled water, small quantities make the taste more acceptable, but large quantities make it less acceptable. Freud suggested that this was a field open to experimentation, and indeed it is (1920b, page 2).

If we are to move to more sophisticated and refined theories of learning, it is imperative that we pay attention to the differences between proposals as well as to their similarities. There is an important aspect of Freud's tension-reduction theory less well represented in contemporary law-of-effect discussions. This is the basic principle that an aroused need that remains unsatisfied produces a fantasy of the goal-object that could satisfy the need. That is, tension reduction that is not accomplished through actual gratification is accomplished through *wish fulfillment,* in the form of a hallucination of the satisfying object. At the id level this fantasy is confused with reality, just as the thirsty man on the desert confuses the mirage with a true oasis. In the *primary process,* under the control of the pleasure principle, wish fulfillment is hallucinatory; the later, more realistic expectation of future events comes with the development of the *secondary process,* when memory images become substituted for hallucinations.

The problem of hallucinations has not been entirely neglected by learning theorists. Mowrer (1938) proposed the study of hallucinations as a means of investigating certain aspects of expectancy. Dollard and Miller, treating perception as a response, and a hallucination as a learned perception in the presence of minimal or ambiguous cues, accepted the fact that hallucinations are more likely if drives are strong. They cite evidence for their position.[2]

The first area of correspondence, then, between learning theories and psychoanalysis, is the family resemblance between the tension-reduction

[2] Dollard and Miller (1950), pages 178-181. The evidence is from McClelland and Atkinson (1948) that images are influenced by drives, and from Holmberg (1950) that hallucinatory images in dreams are influenced by motivation.

interpretation of the law of effect (reinforcement theory in one of its forms) and the pleasure principle, with the caution, however, that learning theories have not fully incorporated the fantasy-production feature of the Freudian principle.[3]

The Reality Principle and Trial-and-Error Learning

Freud's first supplementation of the pleasure principle was by way of the *reality principle,* whereby the organism instead of insisting upon immediate gratification takes the "long indirect road to pleasure" (1911). Because the pleasure is found at the end of the path, we may think of the psychologist's rat, winding its way through a tortuous maze, eliminating the blind alleys along the way, as being under the control of a reality principle.

There is some ambiguity here, for Freud's reality principle is bound up with the developing ego, and it would be a big jump to assign the rat an ego because it avoids blind alleys on the way to food.

Psychologists have been unclear in trying to find the correspondences between their principles and Freud's reality principle.

Dollard and Miller definitely related the pleasure principle to the law of effect, but they have no direct counterpart to the reality principle. Ego strength (related, of course, to mastery of reality) they treat in the familiar psychological terms of higher mental processes, learned drives and skills. Reality, they say, is elaborated according to the physical and social conditions of learning (1950, pages 9-10).

Mowrer took a different position. He believed that the law of effect was related to the pleasure principle, in agreement with Miller and Dollard, but he would relate trial-and-error problem solution to this principle also, rather than to the reality principle. He believed the reality principle to be appropriate instead to simple Pavlovian (classical) conditioning, because he believed Pavlov's dogs learn "not what is pleasurable and relieving, but what is actual, true, real." He went on to infer that such conditioning was limited to the autonomic nervous system, and thus led himself into what appears to be a most unusual position, namely, that reality learning is under the control of the autonomic system, whereas pleasure–pain learning is under the control of the central nervous system. To some it will seem more plausible to assign instinctive, impulsive functions to the autonomic system (though we would not go that far) and to assign reality-regulated functions, ego functions, to the cognitive apparatus: to the central nervous system and its related structures.

---

[3] Another point is that unresolved tension may dissolve in affective discharge, as in the upset crying of a young baby. The nearest we come to this in learning theory is the disruptive effect of too intense a drive (i.e., the Yerkes–Dodson law).

Let us return to animal learning as possibly representing the reality principle because there are many events intervening between the aroused tension and its ultimate resolution. A white rat can learn the true path in a maze, and in a discrimination apparatus it can learn to jump to a triangle and not to a circle. Thus it learns permitted and unpermitted behavior, much in the way a child learns to behave in accordance with the dictates of its culture as transmitted by those in authority over him. The rat can learn probabilities also. If rewarded more frequently on the right than on the left he learns to turn more often to the right, as though to equate the response-reinforcement ratio on both sides (Brunswik, 1939). This conforming of behavior to reality, even to a contingent reality, surely has some resemblance to the earliest ego functions. Learned discrimination always involves conflict, and the conflict is resolved through the weighting of the choices by reward and punishment. These weights become available through the accumulation of experiences with the environment. Sometimes, when discrimination is difficult, the rat mobilizes his experience through what Muenzinger and Tolman call "vicarious trial and error" (VTE), that is, a sampling of both choices by looking back or forth, or by making shorts runs first to one side and then to the other before the animal is committed to a choice. This appears to be a kind of symbolic reality-testing, an analogue of ego-type behavior.

Academic psychologists and psychoanalysts spend a good deal of their time studying the approach to and solution of reality problems. We may conclude that there is some gross correspondence in *topic* between what Freud calls the reality principle and the studies in which behavior is regulated largely by experienced success and failure. What is lacking in the coordination is a clear ego psychology in academic psychology to be coordinated with the ego theory in psychoanalysis. The ego psychology of psychoanalysis is itself only now undergoing clarification.[4]

Repetition-Compulsion in Relation to Theories of Habit Strength

In *Beyond the pleasure principle,* Freud introduced a number of highly speculative notions, with awareness that he was trying out ideas to which he did not wish to commit himself. One of the suggestions most closely bound to evidence from his clinical experience was that of a *repetition-compulsion.* These repetition-compulsions are believed to be beyond the pleasure principle, for Freud says:

> The greater part of what is re-experienced under the compulsion to repeat must cause the ego unpleasure, since it brings to light activities of repressed instinctual impulses . . . The compulsion to repeat also recalls from the past experiences which include no possibility of pleasure, and which can never, even

[4] For developments within psychoanalytic ego theory, see Hartmann (1958), Rapaport (1959), White (1963).

long ago, have brought satisfaction even to instinctual impulses which have since been repressed.[5]

Freud recognized that sometimes repeating unpleasant activities yields pleasure, possibly through the sense of mastery that is achieved. These cases he believed to be genuine, but they are still under the control of the pleasure principle, and are not what Freud meant by acts not under the control of the pleasure principle. He was not talking about secondary or derived pleasure; he referred to behavior that he believed to be independent of, and to disregard, the pleasure principle.

In the effort to understand these repetition-compulsions, especially as they appeared in traumatic neuroses, Freud was led to posit a destructive instinct ("death instinct," *Thanatos*) existing alongside of *Eros* (the "life instinct," comprising self-preservation, self-love, and object-love). This is one of the more controversial topics within psychoanalysis itself, and some relatively orthodox analysts found Freud's formulation unsatisfactory (e.g., Fenichel, 1945, pages 59-61).

This is not the place to enter into a detailed critique of psychoanalytic theory, and in relating the work of academic psychologists to Freudian theory we must be satisfied to review some of the points of correspondence. In general, academic psychologists who have discussed repetition-compulsion have confined themselves to the kinds of behavior resistant to the usual principles of extinction. Mowrer (1950), for example, noted the parallel between acts that do not extinguish and the repetition-compulsion, and he saw a relation between repetition-compulsion and functional autonomy. Dollard and Miller (1950) indicated that the repetition-compulsion is a result of cues provided by emotions that are themselves aroused by meaningless shreds of memories that recur in free association. Instrumental acts (the tendencies to repeat) are conditioned to these cues.

Learning theorists have offered three suggestions to explain acts unusually resistant to extinction:

1. All compulsions may conform to ordinary principles of tension-reduction learning. They may involve subtle forms of anxiety reduction as in the defense mechanism known as "undoing." It is admitted that available data are insufficient to demonstrate that this explanation holds in all cases (Mowrer, 1950, page 112).

2. Overlearned activities may be resistant to change, hence lead to excessive repetition. Rats trained to jump a gap in order to be rewarded, if they repeat the activity often enough, will fail to take a direct path when one is provided (Gilhousen, 1931). A kind of "canalization" takes place,

---

[5] Freud (1920b), page 21. From *Beyond the pleasure principle* by Sigmund Freud, by permission of Liveright Publishers, New York.

so that the familiar is preferred and the behavior remains stereotyped (Murphy, 1947). This has a family resemblance to compulsive behavior, but because the behavior was once a source of gratification it does not fit Freud's specifications for repetition-compulsion.

3. Behavior acquired under excessive frustration may become "abnormally fixated," and thus resistant to change. This suggestion was elaborated by Maier (1949) on the basis of extensive experiments conducted by him and his students and collaborators. If rats in the familiar Lashley jumping apparatus are rewarded for jumping to a cross and punished for jumping to a circle, they soon learn to jump to the correct figure, whether it is presented on the right or on the left, and the habit is flexible and can be reversed if reward and punishment are reversed. If, however, they are given an insoluble problem, with reward now on the right, now on the left, with no systematic relationship between the cards in the windows and the rewards and punishments, they develop highly stereotyped behavior, such as jumping to the left, no matter what happens. The response occasionally persists for hundreds of trials, even though every trial is punished. It appears that the response is no longer under control of the reality principle. Accessory evidence shows that the discrimination between the cards may be learned without affecting the fixated response. Even when the opposite window is left open with the food clearly in view, the rat, fixated on the left, will continue to jump to the left, bump its nose, and fall into the net. This is the nearest we come to an experimental analogue of compulsive behavior.

The experimental problem was reopened by Wilcoxon (1952), who repeated Maier's experiments with a number of controls. He found the main cause of the excessive fixation to be the learning of an act that was occasionally punished, occasionally rewarded, when the alternative was invariably punished. While he interpreted his results as conforming to ordinary principles of associative learning, the causal factors are complex.

Compulsive behavior is a profitable field for further investigation, apart from trying to test in detail Freud's hypotheses. Fenichel (1945) listed three types of compulsion. The first type rests on the periodicity of drive states (instincts), so that derivatives of these states may be expected also to occur periodically. He believed that manic-depressive phenomena fitted this type. The second type is a repetition due to the tendency of the repressed to find an outlet. In the so-called neuroses of destiny the patient periodically evokes or endures the same experience. The symptoms are sometimes set off by "anniversaries" of significant events (Josephine R. Hilgard, 1953). Compulsive rituals, such as compulsive counting, are said by Fenichel to fit this type. The third type consists in the repetition of traumatic events for the purpose of achieving a belated mastery. Children who have been the passive victims of frustration may seek in their games an active repetition of the event at a time of their own choosing, in order to gain comprehension and mastery. The dreams and repeated symptoms in traumatic neurosis fit this pattern.

It is evident that there are problems here that have not been fully represented in learning experiments, although again there is overlap in topic, that is, between repetition-compulsion and overlearning, abnormal fixation, and resistance to extinction.

These three principles from Freud (the pleasure principle, the reality principle, and repetition-compulsion) have been selected to show that there are at least some parallels between Freudian theory and the discussions by learning theorists. It would no doubt prove fruitful to try to achieve greater clarity with respect to these parallels, for the interrelationships are by no means obvious and direct.

PSYCHOANALYTIC CONCEPTIONS THAT HAVE INFLUENCED LEARNING EXPERIMENTS AND THEORIES

In the foregoing account of parallels between Freudian theory and the work of academic psychologists it should be evident that the two lines developed rather independently. That is, studies of the law of effect, of overlearning, and of problem-solving were not undertaken to test Freudian theory, and Freudian theory was not developed in order to "explain" the results obtained by experimental psychologists. There have been a number of topics within Freudian theory, however, that have definitely set problems for the experimental psychologist. We now turn to a review of some of these.

Anxiety as a Drive

Freud's views about anxiety evolved along with other aspects of his theory.[6] At first he thought that attacks of anxiety in his patients gave evidence of repressed instinctive (libidinal) excitation. That is, repressed libido, he thought, was transformed into anxiety (1920a, pages 347–349). Later, as he developed the theory of id, ego, and superego, he assigned anxiety production to the ego. When the ego perceives danger this perception arouses anxiety, and then steps are taken to reduce anxiety. Symptom formation may be one of these steps. Repression may also be one of the devices adopted by the ego, so that, instead of repression causing anxiety, we now have anxiety causing repression (1926).

Anxiety is closely related to fear, though fear usually has a real object, while anxiety may be a vague apprehension of unknown danger. Three

[6] A useful account of the changes in Freud's conceptions is given by R. May (1950), pages 112-127.

kinds of anxiety can be distinguished, of which the first is indistinguishable from fear:

1. *Objective anxiety* (also called real or true anxiety) depends upon real or anticipated danger whose source lies in the external world. To be afraid of a poisonous snake or a holdup man is to be anxious in this way. True anxiety implies a real known danger.

2. *Neurotic anxiety* is in regard to an unknown danger. Upon analysis it is found that the danger is, as Freud put it, an instinctual one. That is, a person is afraid of being overpowered by some impulse or thought that will prove harmful to him. Sometimes there is a real or threatened danger but the reaction to it is excessive, thus revealing the neurotic element in the anxiety (1926, pages 112-117).

3. *Moral anxiety* is aroused by a perception of danger from the conscience (superego). The fear is that of being punished (belittled, degraded) for doing or thinking something that is contrary to the ego ideal. Moral anxiety is experienced as feelings of *guilt* or *shame*.[7]

Anxiety in later life was said to have two modes of origin: one, involuntary and automatic, whenever a danger situation arose, the second "produced by the ego when such a situation merely threatened, in order to procure its avoidance" (Freud, 1926, page 109).

Mowrer (1939) was the first of the experimenters on learning to see the possibility of studying an analogue of anxiety in experiments on avoidance conditioning. He proceeded to show experimentally how rats that had experienced pain in the presence of certain cues could be led to make avoidance responses in the presence of those cues, that is, when the pain was merely threatened (1940b). Thus he believed the anxiety-fear response to be the conditioned form of the pain response. Just as pain can be used as a drive to produce learning through escape, so anxiety can be used to produce learning. The anxiety can be reduced by appropriate avoidance responses just as pain can be reduced by escape responses. Hence these anxiety-reducing responses are learned by the ordinary reinforcement principle of tension reduction. Conceivably defense reactions or neurotic symptoms might be acquired through this familiar learning pattern. This kind of acquired fear or anxiety has been extensively studied as a drive in animal learning, especially by N. E. Miller (1948a).

Mowrer's views changed somewhat as he began to consider those features of human behavior less represented in rat behavior, especially man's capacity to consider the future consequences of his acts (e.g., Mowrer and Ullman, 1945). He gradually arrived at his own position on anxiety, at variance with Freudian theory. He developed what he called a "guilt

[7] For a discussion of the three kinds of anxiety, see Hall (1954), pages 59-69. On shame and guilt, see Piers and Singer (1953).

theory" as contrasted with Freud's "impulse theory" (Mowrer, 1950, page 537).

The problems of anxiety, shame, and guilt lead far afield from present-day learning theory. The main point of contact at present is in the treatment of acquired fear as a drive. The importance of fear as a drive is thus summarized by Dollard and Miller:

> One of the most important drives of all is fear, or "anxiety" as it is often called when its source is vague or obscured by repression (Freud, 1926). There are three main reasons why fear is so important: because it can be so strong, because it can be attached to new cues so easily by learning, and because it is the motivation that produces the inhibiting responses in most conflicts (1950, page 190).

A somewhat different, yet related, use of the concept of anxiety in learning experiments was introduced by Taylor (1951), when she classified human subjects in an investigation of eyelid conditioning according to their scores on a verbal "anxiety scale" derived from the Minnesota Multiphasic Personality Inventory. She found that the more anxious subjects conditioned more rapidly than the less anxious ones, and interpreted anxiety as drive—as the multiplier D in Hull's theory. A number of additional experimenters have used her scale in testing various hypotheses about the relationship between anxiety and conditioning.[8]

Our review shows us that in the course of experimentation theories of anxiety have diverged from the testing of Freud's interpretations. But the original introduction of anxiety concepts into learning theory was by those who were interested in Freudian theory, and they indicated indebtedness to Freud's writings.

Unconscious Influences upon Word Associations

The free-association technique of psychoanalysis has found its representation in psychological experimentation chiefly through the diagnostic word-association test introduced by Jung. Many experiments have been done, acknowledging the importance of the emotional processes behind word associations, leading quantitatively to the recognition of a number of "complex indicators" (e.g., Hull and Lugoff, 1921). Although these have not had much influence within learning experiments, lawful relations can be found, as between the frequency of response words and the reaction times with which they are given (Schlosberg and Heineman, 1950).

Word recognition, which is also a form of associative reaction to the printed word, has been studied in relation to the affective significance of the words. These studies, often referred to as studies of perceptual de-

---

[8] For a valuable review of both experiment and theory, see Farber (1954). The scale itself is described in Taylor (1953).

fense, illustrate another influence of psychoanalysis upon the psychological laboratory.

Repression, Forgetting, and Recall

Ever since Ebbinghaus, psychologists have made quantitative study of memorization and recall part of their laboratory practice. It was natural, therefore, that Freudian interpretations of memory lapses should have been seized upon as appropriate for experimental testing. At first, psychologists grasped only the forgetting aspect of repression, failing to take into account the motivational aspects. This was due, in part, to the rejection of the psychoanalytic theory of instincts, in part to the absence of motivational concepts in prevailing studies of memory and forgetting.[9]

Freud distinguished between a *primal repression* and a second phase called repression proper (1915a). The primal repression consists in "a denial of entry into consciousness to the mental (ideational) presentation of the instinct." The ideational content then remains unaltered and the instinct remains attached to it. "The second phase of repression, *repression proper,* concerns mental derivatives of the repressed instinct-presentation, or such trains of thought as, originating elsewhere, have come into associative connection with it." The tendency to ward off these secondary derivatives is sometimes called *afterexpulsion.*

It is to be noted that repression proper assumes a primal repression, so that the pattern for all later repressions is set up early in life. Later events may be assimilated to these earlier ones. The activity of repression is not, however, over at the time something is repressed.

The process of repression is not to be regarded as something which takes place once and for all, the results of which are permanent, as when some living thing has been killed and from that time onward is dead; on the contrary, repression demands a constant expenditure of energy, and if this were discontinued the success of the repression would be jeopardized, so that a fresh act of repression would be necessary (Freud, 1915a, page 89).

Sears (1936) has summarized the characteristics of a repressed instinctual impulse, according to Freud, in six statements:

1. It is not represented in its true form in consciousness.
2. The instinct-presentation develops in a more luxuriant fashion than it would if it were conscious.
3. The resistance of consciousness against derivatives and associations of the instinct-presentation varies in inverse proportion to their remoteness from the ideas originally repressed.

[9] These points were made by Sears (1936) in an able review of Freud's theory of repression and the possibilities within experimentation.

4. Repression is highly specific to each idea and substitute idea.
5. Repression is very mobile.
6. The degree of repression varies with the strength of the instinctual impulse.

The feature of repression that has appealed most to psychologists is its relation to pleasure and pain. Freud says, for example, that in repression the avoidance of pain must have acquired more strength than the pleasure of gratification. Psychologists have often interpreted repression quite superficially to mean that pleasurable events will be remembered and distasteful ones forgotten. The first experiments used merely affectively pleasant or unpleasant materials, such as pleasant and unpleasant odors, words such as "sugar" (pleasant) and "quinine" (unpleasant), studying whether or not such materials could be easily memorized or retained.[10] Later studies have sought in one way or another to meet more squarely the demands of psychoanalytic theory. We shall return later to a consideration of some of them.

Fixation

Fixation has two closely related meanings in psychoanalytic theory. The first meaning is that of *arrested development,* so that an adult may be fixated at an infantile or adolescent level of psychological functioning. This usually implies an object-choice (the mother; a like-sexed person) appropriate to the level of fixation, and the statement is then made that the person is fixated *at* such-and-such a level and fixated *upon* such-and-such an object. The second meaning is that of *fixed habits* leading to preferred modes of solving personal problems, such as a fixation upon a particular mechanism of defense. The habit fixations discussed as forms of compulsion (pages 268-271) are fixations of this second kind. The two meanings are not clearly distinguished in psychoanalytic theory because the stage of arrested development is so intimately related to the style of life. That is, habitual modes of reacting as an adult are likely to be described in developmental terms, for example, the "anal character," the "oral character." [11]

In his review of objective studies bearing on psychoanalytic concepts, Sears (1943) treated fixation as habit strength, and listed a dozen circumstances shown experimentally to modify the strength of instrumental acts. While aware of the problem, he failed to treat in any detail the qualitative features of transition from one stage of development to the next. The transition depends not only on the strength of the earlier fixation but on the hazards involved in transition to the next stage. If the next stage is

[10] E.g., Gordon (1905, 1925), Tait (1913), Tolman (1917).
[11] Fenichel (1945), page 523, writes that neurotics "are not only fixated to certain levels of instinctive demands but also to certain mechanisms of defense." He also includes "character attitudes" among the items to which they are fixated.

attractive and nonthreatening, presumably the growing individual will enter upon it even though he showed strong attachments at the earlier stage. If some residue from the earlier stage makes entrance upon the later stage painful and anxiety-producing, arrested development may occur. Habits at the different levels are not all-or-nothing affairs, for an adult who is grown up in some habits may be infantile in others. Ultimately we require a quantitative theory to account for arrested development in some aspects of personality and progressive development in others.

Regression

Regression is related to fixation in that when an act is blocked or frustrated, some substitute will occur. The substitute is quite likely to be an act once strongly established in the individual's repertory. Such a substitution of an earlier habit for a contemporary one represents one kind of regression.

We may distinguish three kinds of regression:

1. Instrumental-act regression. When the organism is prevented from using one habit, an earlier learned habit is substituted. Many animal experiments have demonstrated this to occur.[12] These results provide an analogy to *object-regression* in Freudian theory, the kind of regression in which gratification is gained by relinquishing a present object and returning to an earlier one.

2. Age-regression. Under some circumstances the person returns to earlier modes of behavior and obliterates future events, in a kind of *revivification.*[13] If, for example, an adult who regressed under hypnosis to an early age began to speak in a language used in childhood but no longer available to him in his adult life, we could say that he had regressed (at least in this respect) to an earlier period in his own life. Experiments under hypnosis have led to somewhat ambiguous results. Occasionally the functioning at the suggested (regressed) age resembles very closely the known historical circumstances in the person's life. When regressed subjects take intelligence and personality tests, their performances differ from those of actual children at the age levels represented by the suggested regression. Hence there appears to be a certain amount of role-playing going on.

3. Primitivation. Even though the regressed individual may not return either to instrumental acts once in his inventory of habits or to person-

[12] E.g., Hamilton and Krechevsky (1933), Mowrer (1940a), O'Kelly (1940a) (1940b). Sears (1943), pages 89-96, has reviewed this literature.

[13] The term is used by Weitzenhoffer (1953), page 191, as one classification of regressive manifestations under hypnosis.

ality functioning characteristic of himself at some previous period, he may, under stress, show a kind of behavioral disorganization that can be characterized as more primitive. This kind of regression has been studied with young children subjected to mild frustration. Barker, Dembo, and Lewin (1941) showed regression by such indices as reduced constructiveness in play following the experienced frustration.

Psychoanalysts suggest that some psychotic manifestations are regressive, particularly schizophrenia. DuBois and Forbes (1934) found little return to the fetal posture during sleep. Cameron (1938a, 1938b) failed to find childish thought patterns in schizophrenic speech. Sears (1944) pointed out, however, that these studies are inadequate tests of regression because they do not bear adequately on the possible *affective* indicators of regression.

Aggression and Its Displacement

In his later years Freud became increasingly aware of aggression, hostility, and destructiveness. In discussing racial tensions and other intergroup antagonisms he said:

> We do not know why such sensitiveness should have been directed to just these details of differentiation; but it is unmistakable that in this whole connection men give evidence of a readiness for hatred, an aggressiveness, the source of which is unknown, and to which one is tempted to ascribe an elementary character (1921, page 56).

Freud recognized the importance of giving expression to hostility, rather than holding it back, and many contemporary analysts now give prominence to the role of repressed hostile impulses in neurosis.

While Freud thus paid increasing attention to aggressiveness in his later writings, as something inherent in man, he had earlier suggested that interference with instinctual satisfaction leads to a hostile attack upon the source of the frustration. Symptoms of neurotic illness may be so directed as to cause distress to someone in the environment who is perceived as the agent of frustration. Building upon these suggestions in Freud (1915b), Dollard and his collaborators formulated the *frustration-aggression hypothesis* in a manner to make possible quantitative testing.[14] The general principle stated was that frustration leads to aggressive action; it was necessary later to correct the implication that aggression was the only (or even an inevitable) consequence.[15] The experimental evidence gave abundant support to the hypothesized linkage between experienced frustration and subsequent aggressive, hostile, or destructive behavior.

[14] Dollard, Doob, Miller, Mowrer, Sears, Ford, Hovland and Sollenberger (1939).
[15] Miller (1941), Sears (1941). These two papers are part of a symposium on the effects of frustration. The other papers are Rosenzweig (1941), Bateson (1941), Levy (1941), G. W. Hartmann (1941), and Maslow (1941).

If the agent responsible for frustration is unknown or inaccessible as an object of attack (absent or protected through conflicting response tendencies), another object will be chosen. This is called *displaced aggression*. The object may be as innocent as the scapegoat which in the ancient Hebrew ritual was made to bear the nation's sins.[16] The word "scapegoat" has come into general use to refer to a victim of displaced aggression.

Neal Miller and his collaborators have succeeded in relating displacement to stimulus generalization in learning theory.[17] In his original experiment, Miller taught rats to strike each other, as in fighting, when an electric shock came on. When a second rat was not present, a rat would "displace" the aggression to a celluloid doll or other object in the environment. The gain to be expected from Miller's experimental arrangement is that certain quantitative predictions can be made about the occasions for displacement, the intensity of the reaction, and so on. Miller formulated eight specific deductions from his theory, of which the following three are illustrative:

When the direct response to the original stimulus is prevented by the absence of that stimulus, displaced responses will occur to other similar stimuli and the strongest displaced response will occur to the most similar stimulus present.

When the direct response to the original stimulus is prevented by conflict, the strongest displaced response will occur to stimuli which have an intermediate degree of similarity to the original one.

If the strength of the drive motivating the direct response to the original stimulus is increased, it will be possible for increasingly dissimilar stimuli to elicit displaced responses (Miller, 1948b, pages 168, 170).

While Miller's experiments on displacement have been with animal subjects, he shows how the principles suggested may apply to human behavior. In human beings, discriminations tend to take the form of words, so that we narrow our meanings and reduce our generalizations. The reverse holds true also, and we use words to generalize, to name classes of objects that belong together. At this point, however, we are interested in discrimination and how it breaks down. Suppose that Mr. Brown distinguishes among his new neighbors by calling them all by name. Because of a painful snub, he becomes very angry at Mr. Jones, one of these neighbors. Because Mr. Jones's social position is more secure than Mr. Brown's, and Mr. Brown is new to the neighborhood, Mr. Brown may repress his anger. (This fits the suggestion that the expression of hostility may be prevented by conflicting tendencies.) In Miller's interpretation, what he represses is the sentence: "I am angry at Mr. Jones." Because this sentence is re-

[16] The Old Testament account of the scapegoat is in Leviticus 16:22.
[17] Miller (1948b), Miller and Kraeling (1952), Miller and Murray (1952), Murray and Miller (1952).

pressed, the anger is no longer tied directly to Mr. Jones, and it is more likely to generalize to another neighbor because discrimination through names has broken down.

Miller recognizes that the displacement problem is actually more complex than this. He points out that the *name* of Mr. Jones is not repressed when it is not in a sentence referring to anger. So Mr. Brown recognizes the neighbor's dog and says to himself: "This is Mr. Jones's dog." Because the name of Mr. Jones is attached unconsciously to hostile tendencies, he may give the dog a swift kick, which he would not do if he recalled that he was really angry at Mr. Jones, not at his dog. Thus Miller has deduced some functional differences between consciously and unconsciously determined behavior. He has restated his deduction succinctly:

> To summarize, the repression of verbal responses specifying the source of the aggression may remove a basis for discrimination and allow the illogical generalization, or displacement, of that aggression to be mediated by a different verbal response which is not repressed (1948b, page 176).

Some closely related observations arise out of the study of doll play by young children. When attention is paid to aggressive behavior (fantasy aggression, in this case), the choice of object follows some of the principles of conflict outlined by Miller. That is, where anxiety is high, the object of aggression is chosen as one less similar to the person who is the source of aggression than when anxiety is low. Consequently, as children play repeatedly in a permissive environment, their choice of object gradually shifts toward the parents, who have commonly been the authority figures responsible for some of their frustration.[18]

We may conclude this section by pointing out that on these topics (anxiety, affectivity and verbal responses, repression and recall, fixation and regression, aggression and displacement) the theories of Freud provided a stimulus to research. At the empirical level this has led to a fruitful interaction between psychoanalysis and experimental psychology.

SUGGESTIONS FROM PSYCHOANALYSIS LITTLE REPRESENTED IN PSYCHOLOGICAL STUDIES OF LEARNING

One has the feeling that a good deal of rich material from psychoanalysis has eluded the academic psychologist. This, if true, might be due either to a certain obtuseness on his part, or because the richer material is too difficult to bring under experimental control. The problem has been discussed repeatedly. Thus Sears at one time came to the conclusion:

[18] P. S. Sears (1951), R. R. Sears (1951), R. R. Sears, Whiting, Nowlis, and P. S. Sears (1953).

It seems doubtful whether the sheer testing of psychoanalytic theory is an appropriate task for experimental psychology. Its general method is estimable but its available techniques are clumsy (Sears, 1944, page 329).[19]

Kris, in a very thoughtful discussion of techniques of verification of psychoanalytic propositions, felt that a limitation of the laboratory was that the laboratory cannot produce the real dangers or deal with the basic needs which the genetic propositions of psychoanalysis encompass:

The limitations of the laboratory to quasi needs (and quasi dangers) seriously restrict the area of propositions that can be experimentally verified. In fact, up to the present, experimental approaches have been more successful in dealing with propositions concerning substitution than they have been with propositions concerning repression (Kris, 1947, page 255).

Kubie, while eager to see research on psychoanalysis move forward, and even outlining a research institute in psychoanalytic psychology, deplored a certain triviality in many of the psychologists' experiments on psychoanalytic phenomena.

It is important that any experimentalist should first make himself thoroughly familiar with phenomena as these occur in nature, ascertaining what can be proved with the unaided eye and ear before deciding what to subject to experimental verification . . . Experimental facilities should not be wasted on issues which are already clearly proved, and to which human bias alone continues to blind us. The experimentalist should rather take up where the naturalist leaves off (Kubie, 1952, pages 64-65).

Learning as Related to Stages of Development

Writers on psychoanalysis often stress that it is a *genetic* as well as a dynamic theory (Hartmann and Kris, 1945). That is, continuities in the life of the individual deriving from the past must always be taken into account along with what is happening in the present. At many points the theory suggests that the very young child is unusually susceptible to influences which leave a permanent mark upon his personality, so that, for example, dreams throughout his life may be influenced by these earliest learnings. If this interpretation is true, it is important for a general psychology of learning, and the evidence needs to be specified.

While the problems have not been formulated clearly in terms of learning (i.e., why and in what way the results of childhood learning are more permanent than later learning) we are beginning to get kinds of evidence supporting the gross facts of adult consequences of early childhood experiences. Among the early experiments with animals, the best known

[19] The antecedent of "its" is experimental psychology.

are the experiments of Hunt (1941) on the effects of infant feeding frustration on adult hoarding in rats, and of Wolf (1943) on the effects of sensory deprivation in early life upon types of functioning under stress in later life, again with rats. While the results of these experiments are subject to some reservations, they are relevant to the genetic theory that early experiences may show their influences in the conflicts of later life. A considerable later literature has developed, not all, of course, motivated by psychoanalytic theory (e.g., Beach and Jaynes, 1954; Fiske and Maddi, 1961).

Some conjectures about child-training practices and personality in adult life were put to the test by Whiting and Child (1953). They went to the cross-cultural files, where anthropoligical reports on upwards of 200 cultures are summarized according to a great many categories. Then they asked certain questions about childhood practices and developed hypotheses about their consequences for adult experiences in those cultures. To take one illustration, they predicted that socialization anxiety established in early childhood should affect the interpretation of the causes of illness in adult life. Even in our own culture, with the emphasis upon the germ theory of disease, we have many subordinate interpretations of illness: "It must have been something I ate," "I've been working too hard," "You have to suffer for your sins." Our remedies, too, show something of the magical quality: indiscriminate prescriptions of cure by rest, by liquids, by bland foods, by cathartics, by play, by sun-tanning, by religious observances. If a "scientific" culture such as ours has all these magical residues, it is not too much to expect that primitive interpretations of illness might be related to deep-seated anxieties.

Whiting and Child specified five kinds of anxiety and developed criteria for rating these. These five were: oral, anal, sexual, dependence, and aggression. The assumption is that severity of training and severity of punishment for infraction in these areas, or failures of gratification, would lead to anxiety. A culture might be severe in one of these areas and permissive in the others. In addition, Whiting and Child classified primitive interpretations of illness as derivatives of these anxieties.

When the childhood experience was correlated with adult interpretations of illness, some striking correspondences turned up. For example, 46 cultures could be classified with respect to degree of oral anxiety in childhood, and interpretations of illness with oral aspects, such as food poisoning. Of 20 cultures high in producing oral anxiety in children, 17 used oral interpretations of illness. Correspondingly, of 19 cultures low in oral anxiety, only 6 used oral interpretations of illness. This kind of evidence does not prove a relationship between childhood anxiety and adult behavior, but it makes such a relationship plausible.

Another important suggestion from psychoanalysis is that of childhood amnesia. In later life we appear unable to recall events that must surely have impressed us at the time, and about which we must have talked. Because these events become secondarily linked with repression sequences, they too are repressed. Memories that are recalled are often trivial, and perhaps distorted, the so-called "screen-memories," probably serving some of the purposes of repression. This whole field has been touched hardly at all by academic psychologists, who ought to be able to explore it with children, and not have to depend upon the retrospective accounts of adult patients.[20] Studies of hypnotic susceptibility in children show that post-hypnotic amnesia is one of the suggestibility items whose frequency of occurrence is much higher in children than in young adults (Moore and Lauer, 1963). This is consistent with the Freudian suggestion that amnesia is prevalent in children, but the dynamic similarity between hypnotic amnesia and what Freud was talking about remains to be demonstrated.

A further aspect of the developmental sequence posited by psychoanalysis, and relevant for learning, is the *latency period,* for it has been related to readiness for schooling (at about the age of 6) when the oedipal problems are temporarily solved and the ego is ready to feast its curiosity about the external world. After a few years adolescence produces a new threat, and learning may again be disrupted.

Most of the attempts to study the latency period by nonpsychoanalysts have raised serious doubts about the existence of such a period. Blum (1953), in reviewing the evidence up to 1952, reported that "there has been a growing trend, both within and outside psychoanalytic circles, to doubt the existence of sexual latency" (pages 133-134). One very interesting experimental study later appeared, giving results consonant with an orthodox interpretation of latency (Friedman, 1952). The developmental assumption was that castration anxiety will be high early (before the age of 7) and late (as adolescent development begins in the teen years). Using the method of incomplete fables, Friedman found that between the ages of 7 to 12 his subjects more freely than younger or older children ended the stories with a strongly suggested dismemberment ending, showing reduced castration anxiety during this period. A supplementary finding was that latency by this criterion ends earlier for girls than for boys, a result that is plausible in view of the earlier onset of puberty among girls. Further material having to do with the sexual attachments of daughters for their fathers showed that from the ages of 7 to 11 the girls differed little from the boys, while from 11 onwards there was a definite increase in the kinds of fantasies interpreted as sexual feelings toward the father. A decline was possibly setting in at age 16.

While our topic is learning, not personality development, if the genetic

---

[20] For a discussion from the psychoanalyst's viewpoint, see A. Freud (1935), pages 9-37. What data there were on the problem at the time were reviewed by G. J. Dudycha and M. M. Dudycha (1941).

theory of psychoanalysis contains any truth, learning will show differences from one level to another. Hence developmental stages are of possible significance for learning.[21]

Obstacles to Learning

In case histories from child-guidance clinics we find many illustrations of obstacles to learning based on the personal history of the learner. The teacher as a parent figure may arouse false expectations or reinstate continuing battles; some symbols used in teaching may be so freighted with personal meanings as to be defended against; conflicts over authority may result in nonreading or in spelling handicaps, for no subject matter is clothed more with arbitrary authority than English pronunciation and spelling.[22]

There is little recognition within the learning laboratory of these matters so important for the kind of learning that takes place in the social environment of the home and school. At least one skilled teacher, Nathaniel Cantor (1946), recognized that social learning at the college level may be influenced by defense mechanisms. In his book on the dynamics of learning he devoted chapters to the roles of resistance, ambivalence, projection, and identification.

Psychodynamics of Thinking

The possibility of drawing upon psychoanalysis in studying the psychology of thinking was brought strongly to the fore by the appearance of a large volume assembling papers on the organization and pathology of thought (Rapaport, 1951). Especially important for the psychoanalytic influences are the sections devoted to symbolism (including experimentally produced dreams), to motivation of thinking, fantasy thinking, and pathology of thinking.

A fundamental distinction within psychoanalytic theory of thinking is that between *primary process* thinking which is impulse-driven and largely irrational, seeking immediate gratification at all costs, even by way of hallucinations, and *secondary process* thinking which is patient and logical, willing to postpone gratification for future gains. Adult thinking falls somewhere between these poles, either oscillating between the two modes of thinking, or combining them in some manner (Hilgard, 1962). Kris (1952) stressed the importance for creativity of "regression in the service of the ego" by which he meant a partial and reversible regression

[21] Interest in developmental stages as related to learning follows also upon the works of Piaget. For some relationships between Freud and Piaget, see Wolff (1960). For possible relevance of Piaget to learning, see Aebli (1951).

[22] Much of the relevant case material was reviewed by Mahler-Schoenberger (1942) and by Pearson (1952, 1954).

in which the freedom of primary process thinking was made use of for assembling the fantasy material that could then be sorted out and refined by way of secondary process thinking. A similar idea was made use of by Koestler (1964) in accounting for creativity through the process of *reculer pour mieux sortir* (withdrawing in order better to advance). These appear to be fertile ideas deserving of study in the psychological laboratory.

The study of character or personality syndromes may prove useful in determining why of two people, equally intelligent, one is creative, the other not (e.g., Stein and Meer, 1954). We have to be careful not to give pat answers, based on a stereotyped conception of "typical" personalities. For example, the compulsive dispositions associated with the "anal character" are not creative in essence, and may, in fact, produce mere hand-washing instead of productive effort. Yet there is a certain plodding quality about scientific data-gathering which may demand some of this same compulsiveness. Scientific objectivity, a valuable trait, is at the same time a form of dissociation or isolation between wish and intellect, and is perhaps achieved at some cost to the individual. Some papers by Kubie (1953, 1954) stressed the personal problems of the scientist.

In the current emphasis on general-education programs in our colleges and universities we hear much about the integrative role of the arts and music. Yet as we look at artists and musicians we see truth in the popular conception that they are somehow different, and occasionally classify as deviates. Hence the question recurs of the relationship between art and neuroticism. One form of putting it is this: Would the artist be less creative if he resolved his conflicts through psychoanalysis? Is not his neurosis precious to him? Possibly if we were successful in our mental hygiene programs we would develop a class of very uninteresting normal and contented people; perhaps we are saved from this by the ineffectiveness of our measures. There are more constructive possibilities. For one thing, artists and writers who come to analysis are those who find that they are afraid to practice their arts. For them, psychotherapy may give back their creativity. Again, the end of therapy is not necessarily to get rid of conflicts, but to find a way of living with them. The issues are too important to be resolved casually on the basis of a few case studies. Academic psychology has increasingly been taking its share of responsibility in the study of creativity at all levels (Stein and Heinze, 1960).

Therapy as Learning

Experimental psychology will always be cut off from some of the more important aspects of psychoanalysis if it insists upon methods lying outside the psychoanalytic process itself. Without free association, the handling of the transference, and the rest that goes on within psycho-analysis, some kinds of data are simply not available. From the point of view of learning theory it is important to know *in detail* how transference operates to straighten out the confusions between past and present, be-tween magical omnipotence and reality, so that the patient unlearns neurotic habits and acquires realistic and socially acceptable ones. To know these facts and relationships in detail is not easy, for the nonverbal communications between patient and analyst are important along with the words spoken and those subtle nuances of language that express doubt, belief, or encouragement. For a time it was thought that when Freud abandoned hypnosis he had also abandoned suggestion. As trans-ference came increasingly into prominence as part of therapy, Freud realized that the handling of transference involved suggestion, and he did not hesitate to use the word (1920b, page 18). But suggestion is a subtle process, and it is a question whether the most conscientious analyst can give an accurate retrospective account of just exactly what forms of sug-gestions he used with his patient, and how the patient reacted. Therefore the need of some sort of objective record is required. We probably need, in addition to the recorded interview, an immediately recorded statement from the analyst, giving what he thought he was doing, and something of his own free associations that remained unexpressed. Where the psychol-ogist comes in will be in the analysis and interpretation of the data the analyst provides.[23]

Perhaps the main conclusion to be drawn from recognizing the unex-plored areas in developmental aspects of learning, in psychodynamic ob-stacles to learning, in the study of thought processes and creativity, and in the understanding of the learning that goes on within psychotherapy, is that these problems can be solved only through cooperative effort. The division of labor between the academic psychologist and the psychoan-alyst is not an absolute one, with the analyst doing everything that can be done within psychoanalysis, and the psychologist doing only that which can be done in the laboratory. If we are to achieve the ultimate under-standing of the learning process not only in all its richness, but also in the form of verified propositions, there must be collaboration as well as division of labor.

EXPERIMENTS ON REPRESSION AS ILLUSTRATIVE OF THE LABORA-TORY USE OF PSYCHOANALYTIC CONCEPTS

Psychologists were quick to pick up the suggestion from Freud that affec-tive factors might influence recall. We shall consider the relation between

[23] On the use of the recorded psychoanalytic interview see Shakow (1960).

affect and ease of recall. These test the implication that unpleasant affect may hinder recall through events identified with or analogous to Freudian repression.

A review of the pertinent literature by Zeller (1950a) listed 93 references, enough to suggest how inviting this field has proved to be to investigators. We shall consider a few experimental reports typical of four approaches to the study of affective factors in recall.

1. *Recall of associates to affectively toned sensory stimuli.* The most satisfactory study, following upon several earlier ones, is that of Ratliff (1938). He had subjects rate the pleasantness and unpleasantness of odors, pitches, and colors. Then the subjects associated numbers with the affective items and later were tested for recall. The results with odors were against the hypothesis of the forgetting of the unpleasant, but with pitches and colors the recall of numbers associated with the pleasant items was superior to the recall of numbers associated with unpleasant ones. Because the pleasantness and unpleasantness of sensory stimuli has little personal relevance, such experiments are no longer considered very pertinent as tests of Freudian theory.

Despite the tenuousness of the relationship to the repression theory, it is of some interest to cast up the score on experiments dealing with the recall of pleasant and unpleasant items (including words as well as sensory stimuli). Of 51 studies of this kind, Zeller found 32 (63 percent) to favor more effective recall of the pleasant over the unpleasant, 14 (27 percent) to favor the reverse, and 5 (10 percent) with neutral or ambiguous results.

2. *Recall of memorized words with personal affective connotations.* In order to introduce some kind of ego threat into the laboratory-type experiment, Sharp (1938) went to the case records of neurotic subjects to find words that would be emotionally unacceptable to individual subjects, and words that for them would express gratifications. She then compared their retention of unacceptable and acceptable words, and found the unacceptable words less well recalled. Unfortunately, the only reported repetition of portions of her work did not yield confirmatory results (Heathers and Sears, 1943; see Sears, 1943).

In an ingeniously designed experiment, Keet (1948) selected critical words from a word-association test given to each subject. One of these words was imbedded in a list to be memorized. The recall of the list was then disrupted by retroactive inhibition through new learning interpolated between memorization and recall. The disruption presumably included repression, for the critical word was more difficult to recall than the other words. Counseling procedures were used to alleviate the anxiety associated with the forgotten word, to encourage its recall much as forgotten experiences are brought to awareness in psychoanalysis. Although Keet's results were striking, those who have tried to reproduce the memorization and retroactive inhibition portions of the experiment have thus far been unsuccessful. The general logic of his experiment has so much to commend it, however, that it is to be hoped that some reproducible variant of his experiment can be discovered or invented.

A study related to that of Keet was conducted by Clemes (1964), who showed the possibility of bringing repression somewhat under control through hypnosis. Following Keet's technique of finding words with personal reference by selecting critical and noncritical ones from a Kent–Rosanoff test, Clemes then constructed lists individually for his subjects, the list containing half critical and half noncritical words in random order. These were then memorized under hypnosis. Evidence is given that the critical words in a list of this kind are memorized as readily as noncritical ones. The crucial test was then a suggested partial amnesia, in which the subject was told that he would forget half the list. The hypothesis was that the critical words would be the most likely targets for amnesia. No therapy was involved; the words were recovered by means of a prearranged signal given within hypnosis. To be sure that the paradigm of repression was followed, the only words to be treated statistically were those that were forgotten in the amnesia test but recovered when the amnesia was lifted. Clemes found that the hypothesis was confirmed, in that the critical words were disproportionately the targets for amnesia following the suggestion that half the words would be forgotten.

These experiments are more relevant to Freudian theory than the other experiments on affective materials because they selected items with a history of personal affective loading in the life of the individual outside the laboratory. Then they brought these items into the laboratory for quantitative study.

3. *Recall of affectively toned life experiences.* In a somewhat different effort to achieve naturalness in experiments, experimenters have abandoned the memorizing of material under the artificial conditions of the laboratory and turned instead to study the recall of actual experiences met outside the laboratory.

Meltzer (1930) asked 77 college men and 55 college women to describe their Christmas vacation experiences. He had them list their experiences, and also asked them to rate the experiences as pleasant, unpleasant, or indifferent. Six weeks later he unexpectedly asked them to repeat the listing they had done on the day of their return. Not only did they list more pleasant than unpleasant memories immediately after returning from vacation, but after six weeks the predominance of pleasant over unpleasant memories increased. This finding is in accord with the interpretation of repression as an active process, continuing after the original event, though other interpretations are possible (e.g., Waters and Leeper, 1936).

A social-psychological bent was given to the naturalistic-setting recall experiment by Edwards (1941, 1942) who studied the retention of political statements by those differing in their political views. He found that his subjects tended to remember better material compatible with their political attitudes than material incompatible with them. Hence he emphasized the "frame of reference" in which remembering occurs, conflict with prevailing beliefs perhaps being more important than pleasantness and unpleasantness in controlling selective forgetting.

4. *Repression induced by experienced failure.* In a careful theoretical treatment of repression phenomena according to possibilities within stimulus–response theory, Sears (1936) suggested a possible paradigm for the initiation of repression, and then proceeded to test it experimentally (Sears, 1937). The essential feature is that an excitatory tendency moving along a stimulus–response chain towards a consummatory response will be blocked and fail of consummation if, prior to consummation, a competing tendency is also evoked. This competing tendency violates conscience or is a threat to self-esteem, and can arouse guilt or self-criticism. Thus the arousal of an anxiety response concomitantly with an anticipatory goal response may prevent the occurrence of the goal response. That is, in short, Sear's paradigm for repression. His own experiment introduced a failure task (card sorting) between two sessions of nonsense-syllable learning. The interference with the second list following failure was interpreted by Sears as an indication of repression.[24]

Discouragement induced by failure might lead to a lowering of effort and hence lead to poorer performance on a later task without any active repression. Hence, as Zeller (1950a) has pointed out, a complete test of repression ought to show recovery when the associated threat is alleviated. Several experimenters have attempted to demonstrate the two phases: induced repression followed by the lifting of the repression. One of the first of these was done under hypnosis (Huston, Shakow, and Erickson, 1934). Suggestions under hypnosis led to the attachment of guilt to certain words. In the waking state, while amnesic to the hypnotic experience, the subjects showed through word associations an influence on associations to the guilty words that might be interpreted as repression. Following removal of the suggestions under rehypnosis, the repressive effects disappeared. Diven (1937) used a conditioning method, following certain word pairs with shock. In the recall of the paired-associates, subjects did much better with the nonshocked than with the shocked pairs, as though recall

[24] There is a family resemblance between this experiment and the completed–incompleted task experiment initiated by Zeigarnik (1927), and repeated with many variations since.

of the "dangerous" words had been inhibited. After a "deconditioning" series, recall proved superior for the *shocked* words, hinting that an unconscious (repressed) integration may be a strong one. An attempted repetition of Diven's work has not been successful (Cannicott and Umberger, 1950). There are apparently subtleties in this kind of experiment, as suggested also by Sharp's and Keet's, that are not communicated in the description of the experimental procedures.

The initiation of repression through induced failure has been studied in an extension of Sears' type of experiment by Zeller (1950b, 1951), Russell (1952), and Aborn (1953). These experiments, with the exception of Russell's, found not only a disruption of recall, but some subsequent recovery when threat was alleviated.

Zeller used nonsense-syllable learning and retention as the basic task, interpolating success and failure experiences in imitative tapping of Knox cubes. His experimental design included two tests of retention prior to the initiation of "repression," then an immediate and a delayed (48 hour) test while "repression" was active, and finally an immediate and delayed test after removal of "repression." His results for both recall and relearning corresponded to predictions from Freudian theory, though he pointed out that alternative interpretations cannot be excluded. Zeller used four conditions, so that he was able to compare the inhibiting results of failure specific to a second task with the inhibiting results of failure on a second task that had become associated with the performance of a previously learned task. Repression was not found when the failure was highly specific, but it was found when failure on the irrelevant task became associated with performance on the earlier learned one.

Aborn (1953) added another dimension by comparing the results for intentional ("set") learning with those for incidental learning. His subjects, reading the colored numbers on cards selected from the Ishahara and Dvorine tests, thought they were taking a color-blindness test. Those "set" to learn were told to remember the numbers that appeared on the cards; the "incidental" learners received no such instructions. The "ego threat" was introduced for the experimental subjects by following the series of numbered cards with others on which no numbers appeared, thus implying that the subject was color weak because he could not distinguish a number against the background of colored dots. The threat was enhanced by having him fail on some presumably related perceptual tasks, stencil designs taken from the Arthur Performance Scale. As a test of memory, the subject wrote down the numbers remembered from the color test cards, then checked the numbers on a recognition test. The memory tests were unexpectedly repeated two days later. At this point the "threat" was removed by revealing the true nature of the experiment. The memory test was again given unexpectedly two days later and after three days.

The results for the incidental learners are given in Figure 9-1. For the control subjects there is progressive decline ("forgetting") with the passage of time. For the experimental subjects, however, there are reduced scores after failure, followed by recovery after removal of threat. The *higher* scores at the end, for the experimental subjects, correspond to Diven's finding, mentioned above. There were no differences of this kind for the subjects who had been given a set to learn; hence Aborn concludes that there are advantages in using incidental learning for this kind of study, and perhaps this fact helps to account for Russell's (1952) negative results.

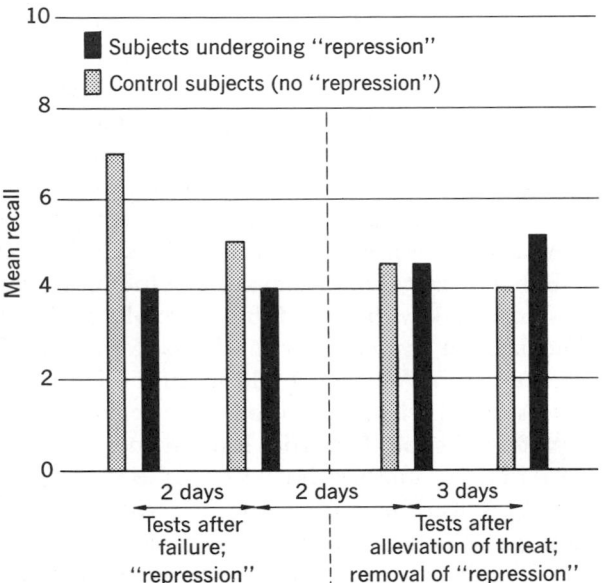

Figure 9-1   **Repression and recovery in incidental learning associated with ego threat. The recall scores are of numbers learned incidentally while taking a color-blindness test. Mean, 20 subjects in each group. Replotted from the data of Aborn (1953, page 228).**

Where do these studies lead us? The facts of amnesia, without additional experiments, make abundantly clear that repression occurs, and that memories once lost can be recovered without relearning.[25] While therefore experiments are not needed to establish the phenomena of repression, they may help us to delineate the precise circumstances under which repression occurs. Clarification of repression phenomena is today more important than establishing their genuineness.

[25] Cases of amnesia associated with combat neuroses may be found in Grinker and Spiegel (1945a, 1945b).

ESTIMATE OF FREUD'S CONTRIBUTION TO LEARNING

Freud's Position on the Typical Problems

The foregoing account shows many points at which Freudian theory has impinged upon the psychology of learning. A recapitulation is in order to summarize his views as they relate to the several problems with which learning theories deal.

1. Capacity. As a developmental psychology, Freud's theory implies that the very young infant is most impressionable,[26] so that primary repressions occur in the first years of childhood, and character syndromes find their origins in the conflicts over food, toilet training, sex, aggression. The resolution of these conflicts takes place according to fundamental themes or styles of response, and the rest of life is spent in playing out these early themes with the assimilation, of course, of new content. Fundamental changes in the structure of the personality do not take place through ordinary education; such changes require the special kind of reeducation provided by depth therapy. Alongside these modes of conduct determined by instinctual conflicts there are the conflict-free ego processes, which are the kinds dealt with in ordinary give-and-take with the real environment. At some stages of life the conflictual personal problems loom unusually large, and make difficult the adjustment to external reality implied in school learning. The easiest time for conflict-free learning should be during the "latency period," and after adolescent conflicts are resolved, but individual differences are to be expected throughout because some children do not outgrow their earlier fixations, and some conflicts remain active and disruptive at any age.

2. Practice. The repetition-compulsion is not a principle of learning-by-doing, for ordinarily the compulsive behavior is peculiarly resistant to change according to its consequences. The principle of learning through practice is better illustrated by "working through," that aspect of therapy in which the patient faces the same conflicts over and over again in the process of reeducation. Learning takes place in "working through" because the conflicts are faced from new angles, and the cues to faulty conduct become detected early enough so that the behavior can be deflected. Repetition is needed for learning, but for repetition to be effective it must be repetition with a difference.

3. Motivation. Freud's is chiefly a psychology of motivation, and he detected motivational control in kinds of behavior that others had thought

---

[26] This may possibly be related to "imprinting," as emphasized by the ethologists (e.g., Bowlby, 1958).

of as trivial or accidental, such as minor forgettings and slips of speech. The first serious effort to incorporate psychoanalytic theory into general psychology recognized the Freudian wish as providing a theory of motivation (Holt, 1915). The motivational concepts that have impinged most directly upon contemporary learning theory are *anxiety* (as a learned drive), and the consequences of various *ego threats,* as in the studies of regression, aggression, repression, and the defense mechanisms generally. The emphasis upon sex as a master drive has been less influential in learning theories than in other fields of personality study, although many of the ego-threatening situations used have included sexual conflicts.

4. Understanding. Despite Freud's preoccupation with the irrational in human behavior, his theory lays great stress upon the possibilities of cognitive control. We can even gain insight into our unconscious processes, if we work at it properly—no mean achievement for the intellect. The developing "ego psychology," playing up the "conflict-free ego sphere," allows even more room for rationality in the control of conduct.

The aim of psychoanalytic therapy is to get rid of self-deception and other blocks to rationality. To the extent that the methods are successful, they should provide some principles useful for learning and teaching.

5. Transfer. We must not permit verbal equivalences to lead us to assume identity where identity does not exist. "Transference" has a special meaning in psychoanalysis. It refers to the special role that the therapist plays for the patient as the therapist stands from time to time for important people in the patient's life, perhaps the mother, or father, or older brother. The patient reacts to the therapist with the emotions appropriate to these other people. Thus psychoanalytic transference does share with transfer of training the fact of generalization of responses learned in one situation to novel but related stimuli.

Problems of equivalence loom large in psychoanalysis. By way of symbols, something commonly stands for something else and provokes the responses (especially affective responses) appropriate to that something else. We have seen this process at work in displaced aggression. Other processes of symbolization and condensation are relevant to the manner in which earlier and later learning come into psychological relationship.

6. Forgetting. Freud long championed the view that registration of early experiences persists throughout life, that forgetting is therefore chiefly the result of repression. Forgetting is mostly a kind of amnesia, and under appropriate circumstances (as in dreams) the persistence of these memories may be detected, while under other circumstances (as in psychoanalysis) the repression may be lifted and the memories restored to waking consciousness. Although the most important repressions take place first in

early childhood, the repressive process continues throughout life, maintaining the original repressions, and adding new items to the unconscious
store.

Significance of Psychodynamics for Learning Theory

One influence of psychoanalytic thinking has been to broaden the
topical content studied within the field of learning. Psychoanalytical
thinking has helped to erase the boundaries between the neurotic and the
normal, so that what was once relegated to "abnormal psychology" now
becomes part of general psychology. Because there is a recognized continuum between the neurotic and the normal, the learning of symptoms
becomes continuous with the learning of mannerisms and the acquiring
of attitudes. Symbolism in night dreams makes us look for symbolism in
daydreams, and in other products of creative imagination and thought.
What we learn from unusual perceptual distortions, hallucinations, and
amnesias influences how we think about ordinary perception in relation
to the needs of the perceiver, and ordinary forgetting as related to motivation. Hence the range of topics that interest students of learning has been
extended to include perceptual distortion, repression, and symbolism, all
implying personal and idiosyncratic modes of expressing the results of
learning.

In one form or another the conception of *unconscious determination*
has made important changes in thinking about human motivation. Psychologists seeking to maintain the behavioristic orientation of the 1920's
were somewhat resistant to consciousness and even more so to an unconscious consciousness. But even Watson was influenced strongly by Freudian doctrine and accepted "the unverbalized" as a substitute for the unconscious (Watson, 1924). Thus the subjective–objective controversy did
not turn out to be a decisive one, so far as incorporating motives of which
the learner was unaware (or of which he could not speak). Freud can be
credited with being the first to propose that repression leads to the inability to verbalize:

> Now, too, we are in a position to state precisely what it is that repression de-
> nies to the rejected idea in the transference neuroses—namely, the translation of
> the idea into words which are to remain attached to the object (1915b, pages
> 133-134).

Any appraisal of psychoanalytic influences would be most incomplete if
it did not call attention to the emphasis upon unconscious processes and
their derivatives. This is the most obvious way in which to acknowledge
the dynamic contribution of psychoanalysis.

Finally, the genetic or developmental aspects of psychoanalysis have brought to the fore the need for an adequate *ego psychology*.[27] If we are to understand the learner as he sets his goals and works realistically toward them, or as he is torn by conflicts that prevent his using his abilities, or as he burns himself out in the quest for futile objectives, we need a theory of personality organization incorporated within our general theory of learning.

The goads from psychoanalysis to broaden the content studied within learning, to recognize the range of motivational determiners, including unconscious ones, and to build toward an ego psychology are acceptable ones, and the acceptance of these challenges has already proved rewarding. A word of warning is in order. Psychoanalytic thinking is very complex and loosely formulated, so that it is not easy to find out what is essential, what is dispensable, and what internal contradictions there are in it. We need a careful, critical systematization of what appears to be best substantiated through clinical experience and through other sources of scientific evidence, so that irrelevancies and contradictions are either discarded or stated in form for decisive testing. We need to locate the most pertinent issues, and then to do our best to get adequate evidence to resolve these issues. There is much in Freud that nearly everyone will reject, such as the inheritance of acquired characteristics, and some metaphorical statements about localization of function in the brain. The problem is not to guess what Freud "really" meant and then to defend or refute him. The problem is to find out what is true, regardless of who said it. Freud uncovered some interesting hypotheses. We need to state them as carefully as we can, and then put them to the test.

THE ANTI-FREUDIAN TENDENCY OF THE 1960'S

Styles change in psychology as in other fields of endeavor, and as this is being written there is a widespread coolness toward Freudian concepts relative to their enthusiastic acceptance in the years immediately following the second world war.

The attack began with a disparagement of the results of psychoanalytic therapy, with which this chapter is, of course, little concerned. Statistical results were said to show little efficacy in psychoanalytic treatment, despite its time-consuming and costly character (e.g., Eysenck, 1952). Hence in psychiatric circles attention began to turn to the new "wonder drugs," particularly the tranquilizers, and recognition was given to the new biochemistry, so successful in the realm of genetics, including molecular diseases. In clinical psychology, attention turned to the objective behavior therapies, drawing either on the more classical conditioning concepts of Wolpe (1958) or upon the operant conditioning methods deriving from

[27] For Freudian ego-psychology, see footnote 5, page 269.

Skinner, and finding expression not only in laboratory methods (Lindsley, 1963), but also in less formal "verbal conditioning" procedures (Krasner, 1965).

These attacks on the psychoanalytic method of treatment presently spread to attacks on psychoanalytic theory generally. These have turned out to be rather intemperate, seeking through debater's tactics to find flaws in psychoanalysis without making any effort to determine what there is to be learned from it (e.g., Bandura and Walters, 1963). Nothing that has been written in the foregoing account needs to be altered as a result of these attacks; it would be too bad if the generally negative attitudes were permitted to cause a neglect of the sound suggestions from psychoanalysis that have survived testing in the psychological laboratory.

The effort to attain objectivity in psychological science is all to the good, but it carries with it the dangers of easy and superficial answers to profound questions. We need to continue to face the kinds of questions that Freud called to our attention, no matter how we redefine them in our own terms.

The Need for Collaborative Research

If psychologists are to avoid working with pallid replicas of the events dealt with in psychoanalysis, some of their work will have to be carried on in collaboration with those experienced in depth therapy. The psychologist will have to gain such sophistication as he can through personal experience with the phenomena, while he also learns the necessary methods and controls required to do research with them. Some of the problems will elude him unless he works closely (at least some of the time) with those who are dealing intimately with the more extreme manifestations of the phenomena—with emotional panic instead of a comfortable rapport, with the unusual states created under drugs and hypnosis in addition to those created by a few hours of hunger. It may be that some research problems in this field can be solved only with types of facilities that are but now coming into being.[28]

SUPPLEMENTARY READINGS

The collected works of Freud appear in many volumes, but a few of the shorter books give the essence of his theories as they bear upon the topic of this chapter:

FREUD, S. (1920b) *Beyond the pleasure principle*. Translation, 1950.

FREUD, S. (1923) *The ego and the id*. Translation, 1927.

[28] For a sketch of a proposed Research Institute in Psychoanalytic Psychology, see Kubic (1952), pages 113-123.

FREUD, S. (1926) *The problem of anxiety*. Translation, 1936.

FREUD, S. (1940) *An outline of psychoanalysis*. Translation, 1949.

A variety of viewpoints about psychoanalysis in relation to psychology can be found in the following paperbound books:

SARASON, I. (Editor) (1965a) *Psychoanalysis and the study of behavior.*

SARASON, I. (Editor) (1965b) *Science and theory in psychoanalysis.*

A reflective account of what Freud has meant to American psychology can be found in:

SHAKOW, D., and RAPAPORT, D. (1964) The influence of Freud on American psychology. *Psychol. Issues,* 4, Monogr. 13.

Most of the bridges between psychoanalysis and learning theory have thus far been built by learning theorists who devise ways of predicting Freudian phenomena from their theories. There is no fully satisfactory learning account written from the other starting point, that is, beginning with psychoanalysis and then deriving theorems about learning. There are a number of essays and books of advice about learning from the psychoanalytic viewpoint, of which the following are representative:

CANTOR, N. (1946) *Dynamics of learning.*

FREUD, A. (1935) *Psychoanalysis for teachers and parents.*

PEARSON, G. H. J. (1954) *Psychoanalysis and the education of the child.*

Functionalism

The eight learning theories we have examined in the preceding chapters include one stimulus–response theory that antedated behaviorism (Thorndike), four varieties of stimulus–response behaviorism (Pavlov, Guthrie, Skinner, Hull), two cognitive-type theories (Tolman and gestalt), and a psychodynamic theory (Freud). For the final major position to review, we return to the one out of which behaviorism grew but which flourished alongside it and continues to be well represented in contemporary psychology. It is the loosely formulated position known as functionalism, appropriately treated last because of its eclectic character and because its supporters have been free to learn from all of the other theories of learning.

While the name "functionalism" arose in connection with the brand of psychology developed by Angell and Carr at the University of Chicago, the name is equally applicable to the dynamic psychology that Woodworth taught at Columbia. Boring considers Woodworth "perhaps the best representative of the broad functionalism that is characteristic of American psychology" (1950, page 722). Woodworth thought of functionalism as a middle-of-the-road position, not really a "school" of psychology (1948, page 255).

GENERAL CHARACTERISTICS OF FUNCTIONALISM

Functionalism in one form or another has a long history. In Europe such men as Galton, Binet, and Claparède could be classified as functionalists. In America, James, Hall, Ladd, Baldwin, Cattell, and Seashore were all functionalists in outlook. While we turn to the University of Chicago first because it was there that functionalism became defined, functionalism early in the century was "in the air" at Clark under Hall, at Columbia under Cattell and Woodworth, and at Yale under Ladd, Scripture, and Judd.

The Influence of John Dewey

John Dewey (1858-1952) is the "founder" of official functionalism. His famous paper on the reflex-arc concept in psychology (1896), through its clear opposition to prevailing elementarism, marked the beginning of the new protest. One might have expected him to direct his attack against sensationism, for sensation was the fundamental element in the Wundt–Titchener psychology. Instead the attack was on the reflex-arc concept, which, as Heidbreder has pointed out, was the very concept that had been introduced to move beyond a static description of elements of consciousness (Heidbreder, 1933, page 212).

There was, in fact, a controversy going on between Baldwin and Titchener over reaction time (involving the reflex arc) and the first experimental paper using Dewey's formulations was a study of reaction time by Angell and Moore (1896), mediating the Baldwin–Titchener controversy.

Dewey's main argument was that activity should not be thought of as starting with a stimulus, going through a central process, then emerging in a response. Instead, the activity is a complete cycle—a "reflex circuit" —in which the response may seek or "constitute" the stimulus. The relation of the response to the posterior stimulus may be as important as its relation to the anterior one.[1]

Functionalism was christened by Titchener (1898) when he attacked Dewey's position, contrasting functionalism with structuralism. The challenge was accepted by Dewey's younger colleague, James Rowland Angell (1869–1949), who became the leader of the new movement. We shall return to him presently.

Dewey turned from academic psychology to education before he left Chicago, and he went to Columbia in 1904 never again to concern himself directly with the problems of laboratory psychology. But he had already left his mark on the functional psychology that continued after he moved on. The animal laboratories and the studies of child development express the spirit of his Darwinism, with its emphasis upon the evolution of adaptive mechanisms (Dewey, 1920). Not much of his later writing appears in psychology textbooks; later references in them are chiefly to his *How we think* (1910), which gave a practical and teachable account of

---

[1] The same line of argument was picked up by a later Chicago psychologist, Thurstone (1923). There is a family resemblance between Dewey's position and Skinner's operant behavior, in which responses are coordinated with the stimuli to which they lead.

some steps in problem-solving modeled after the steps in scientific investigations.

It would be a mistake, however, to think of Dewey's influence upon the psychology of learning as limited to the work of those who developed functional psychology within the laboratories. At least three other lines of influence can be discerned, each bearing his imprint.

The most marked of these, for its relevance to the psychology of learning, is his influence upon ways of thinking about learning as the product of schoolroom practices. This influence began with his founding of the experimental elementary school at the University of Chicago,[2] and the subsequent development known in its heyday as progressive education. His emphasis upon interest and effort, upon the child's motivation to solve his own problems, represented a dynamic innovation for which the laboratory psychologists were not yet ready. Consequently Dewey's challenge was taken up by educational philosophers rather than by psychologists (e.g., Childs, 1931; Bode, 1940). It so happens that cousins may each resemble a common grandparent without resembling each other. Although Dewey's influence is clear in Carr's *Psychology* (1925), and in Kilpatrick's *Foundations of method* (1925), the detailed learning theories of these two books, the first a psychologist's and the second an educator's, have little in common. Progressive education, at its best, was an embodiment of the ideal of growth toward independence and self-control through interaction with an environment suited to the child's developmental level. The emphasis was upon intelligent problem-solving (*not* upon learning through play), in which each child solves his problems by selecting appropriate materials and methods and by learning to adapt these materials and methods to his ends. His interest sustains his effort as he experiments with his solutions by testing them in action. The kinds of problems solved are social as well as individual, for education is envisaged as a preparation for life in a democracy through democratic living here and now. How different this all sounds from the rules for memorizing a list of nonsense syllables in the minimum number of trials!

The second line of development, outside academic psychology, was upon sociological social psychology, by way of George Herbert Mead (1863–1931), who came with Dewey from Michigan to Chicago. Mead, whose views are very similar to those of Dewey, became the guiding spirit for developments in sociology paralleling those of Dewey in psychology and education. Mead is important for contemporary learning theory because he sponsored a form of self- or ego-psychology a whole generation before experimental psychologists were ready to take it up.[3] Mead's inter-

[2] For the early history of this school, with the point of view that infused it, see Mayhew and Edwards (1936).

[3] Mead's influence is discernible clearly in Cottrell and Gallagher (1941), and in Newcomb (1950). One learning theorist makes direct acknowledgment to him: Muenzinger (1942).

pretation of the self as arising out of social interaction is close to the spirit of Dewey the social philosopher and the defender of democratic values, who saw every act as the expression of a unified self seeking to resolve its conflicts through intelligent action in a world of objects and other selves.

Finally, we have Dewey the philosopher, carrying on the pragmatic tradition of Peirce and James in a form known as *instrumentalism* or *experimentalism*. Even late in life he continued to write upon logic (1938) and upon epistemology (with A. F. Bentley, 1949), always deferring to the scientific method as the one that has helped man to acquire his firmest knowledge. He insisted that ordinary mortals, without the scientist's equipment, could learn lessons from the method of science helpful in the conduct of their daily lives.[4]

A case could be made for bringing these diverging trends into a new synthesis that would have significance for the psychology of learning. Indeed, in ill-defined ways something of the sort may already be happening, as we meet new emphases within learning theory upon ego aspects of learning, upon searching behavior and intelligent problem-solving, upon learning in social contexts. These new emphases supplement a prior preoccupation with quantification and a somewhat constricted methodology. A new synthesis, strictly in the functionalist tradition, may legitimately acknowledge Dewey in its ancestry. History has a way of moving in cycles. Shortly before Dewey's death his interpretation of perception as a *transaction* between the organism and the environment (foreshadowed in the original paper on the reflex arc) began to find its way back into the literature of psychology (e.g., Kelley, 1947). Possibly the rediscovery of other useful ideas may cause a reevaluation of Dewey's place in the history of psychology.

Angell and His Successors

We return now to the main line of development of functional psychology, which went forward under Angell and his successors. Harvey Carr succeeded him at Chicago; Edward S. Robinson, a younger man, taught at Chicago before he went to Yale to carry on a similar program until accidental death cut short his career. Next to carry the mantle was John A. McGeoch, whose career, too, was ended by death at an early age. The students of Carr, Robinson, and McGeoch continue to be active, such men as Irion, McKinney, Melton, Waters, Underwood. Their students, in turn, keep the flavor of Chicago functionalism alive, although no one of those mentioned is now at Chicago, and most of them never were.

In an early clear statement of the functionalist position Angell (1907) made three points:

[4] For Dewey's philosophy, see Ratner (1939). A recent treatment of his influence upon educational psychology can be found in McDonald (1964).

1. Functionalism is interested in the *how* and *why* of mental operations as well as in the *what* (i.e., a descriptive content). It is a cause-and-effect psychology, or in modern terms, an input–output psychology, concerned with mental operations in their context.

2. Functionalism is essentially a psychology of the adjustment of the organism to its environment. Consciousness evolved to serve some biological purpose, to help the organism solve its problems especially when conflicts arise and habits no longer suffice. Once this position was taken, the way was open to welcome applied psychology: educational psychology, industrial psychology, mental hygiene.

3. Functionalism is interested in mind-in-body, and so studies the physiological substratum of mental events. The implied dualism is a purely practical one (as in current psychosomatic medicine) and does not imply a special position on the mind–body problem. The only position that must be rejected, if one is to stress the adaptive role of consciousness, is that known as epiphenomenalism, the view that consciousness is a useless by-product of neural activity.

Now that the quarrels within psychology have shifted somewhat, and the definition of psychology's province is no longer a matter to fight about, the word "function" has tended to return more nearly to its mathematical use, as in the expression, $y = f(x)$, ("y is a function of x"). This causes no great shift for the functionalist, for all he asked was to be free to study many sorts of contingencies, to find what depended on what, whether the dependency was upon age, species membership, prior practice, the ingestion of a drug, or accepting the experimenter's instructions. Nevertheless, the shift is away from the earlier emphasis upon adaptiveness, upon purposes served. While the functionalist is free to work on applied problems, the freedom is one of choice, and a functionalist may work with "pure" functions if he chooses. There is a kind of neutrality about the mathematical function that makes it particularly appealing to the scientist; like the correlation coefficient, it *expresses* a relationship without requiring anyone to claim that it *explains* the relationship. If it does lead to a kind of explanation, there need be nothing teleological about it; there is no implication, with Voltaire, that God must have given man a nose in order to have a support for his spectacles. If some noses support spectacles more readily than others, or if some kinds of spectacles fit more kinds of noses, that is all that the functionalist is interested in finding out.

The Background of Woodworth's Functionalism

Like Dewey, Woodworth (1869–1962) was influenced by William James and G. Stanley Hall, although he studied only with James. His functionalism derived in part from them, and from his early association with Thorndike, Cattell, Ladd, and Sherrington. Both Angell and Wood-worth became interested in imageless thought, and though they disagreed about it, the problems of imageless thought raised the question of meaning in relation to consciousness, a good functionalist topic.[5]

Woodworth's functionalism gave considerably more place to motivation than the earlier Chicago functionalism. The role of motivation was prominent in Woodworth's *Dynamic psychology* (1918), and much use was made of his suggestions when motivation was incorporated into Chicago functionalism by Carr (1925).

Apart, then, from their sharing ancestry in men like James and Hall, the developments at Chicago and at Columbia were not intimately related but were mutually congenial, and with the passing of time the differences between them have gradually faded so that we can treat the general outlook as one, particularly as that outlook is reflected in contemporary psychology.

The Flavor of Functionalism

Because contemporary functionalism is so loosely articulated, a point of view without acknowledged leadership and with few loyal and self-conscious adherents, it defies precise exposition. Hence we must be content to come to an appreciation of its flavor rather than to achieve final judgment about its principles.

1. The functionalist is tolerant but critical. The functionalist is free from self-imposed constraints that have shackled many other systematists. He uses the words from diverse vocabularies, borrowing words freely from other traditions. He is not forbidden the use of older words because today they sound subjective (e.g., "idea," "meaning," "purpose"), or because they have occasionally been given systematic connotations that he does not accept ("sensation," "image," "ego"). He does not believe that anything is gained by new terms, unless advance in knowledge justifies the further precision that new words can bring. For example, he believes it premature to call all thinking "implicit verbalization," for the objective terminology is not yet justified by what we know about thinking. Hence he holds to the older word. His definition of the field of psychology is also a tolerant one, and he is ready to accept information obtained by introspection, by objective observation, from case studies, from mental tests. He is tolerant as to method, and he is also tolerant as to content. The distinction between pure science and applied science seems to him trivial, so long as either is good science.

It is a mistake to confuse this broad tolerance with looseness, as though

[5] The functionalist Rahn (1914) pointed out that it was impossible to introspect a meaningless element. This was very damaging to the structuralist position of Titchener.

functionalism were merely an uncritical eclecticism. On the contrary, the functionalist is commonly a very astute critic. Because he has his eyes open for variables that may be ignored by more dogmatic systematists, he is not easily trapped into accepting "pat" systematic solutions for intricate problems. This critical attitude is expressed in a preference for *relativism* over *absolutism* (Carr, 1933). Recognizing the many determiners of psychological activities, Carr deplored what he called the quest for "constants," by which he meant one-to-one correspondences, or psychological laws stated without reference to all the influential variables.

2. *The functionalist prefers continuities over discontinuities or typologies.* The mathematical statement of a functional relationship usually implies a gradual transition between the values of the dependent variable correlated with the independent variable as it increases or decreases. While extremes may differ so markedly as to appear qualitatively unlike, the functionalist looks for connecting in-between cases. This continuity of function was made the basis for a *dimensional principle* by McGeoch, and the suggestion was elaborated by Melton.[6]

The two chief classes of variation recognized by Melton were those dependent upon experimental arrangements, which may be called *situational dimensions,* and those that depend upon the psychological functions involved, which may be called *process dimensions.*

The situational dimensions call attention to the differences between what the learner is called upon to do from one experiment to another. A very different problem is presented to the learner by a path through a maze, the rotating target of a pursuitmeter, a list of syllables on a memory drum, a reflex to be attached by conditioning to a new stimulus, and a mathematical problem to be solved by reasoning.

The process dimensions are correlated in a coarse way with the situational dimensions, but are distinguishable. They include such considerations as the amount of discovery required before the correct response is made (a distinction between *rote learning* and *problem-solving*), the involvement of motor or ideational responses (as between *motor skills* and *verbal memory*), and the relevancy of motivating conditions (*incidental learning* as against *intentional learning*).

Experiments have to be classified according to more than one dimension. Thus rote learning and reasoning experiments are alike on the dimensions verbal–nonverbal, but unlike with respect to the amount of discovery involved in the adequate response. It is important to recognize that the classification is not according to fixed types, but always according to scales that have intermediate values. Learning is not blind on the one hand and insightful on the other; there are degrees of understanding in-

[6] McGeoch (1936), Melton (1941a, 1950). The dimensional principle was applied earlier to a modern version of the attributes of sensation by Boring (1933).

volved from a minimum at one extreme to a maximum at the other, with most cases falling between these extremes.

Melton's abiding interest in classifications which reflect continuities may be found in the book that he edited on *Categories of human learning* (1964).

3. The functionalist is an experimentalist. In its modern form, functionalism is dedicated to the experimental method. The issues upon which the functionalist is so tolerant become a part of his science only when they are translated into experimentable form. He is free of constraint in his choice of dimensions, and may choose to set up a dimension of items graded for similarity or a dimension of tasks graded according to degree-of-understanding. He prefers to drive general issues back to specifics before he is led into controversy over them, for he believes that many linguistic difficulties fade when reference is made to the specific findings of experiments.

American psychology so generally accepts the three points which have been used to characterize functionalism that functionalism has become an almost unrecognized ground for mutual understanding.

4. The functionalist is biased toward associationism and environmentalism. There is, however, a lingering bias detectable among leading functionalists that tempers the judgment that functionalism is neutral in respect to the major quarrels among learning theorists. This is the bias toward association theory, and the environmentalism that so often accompanies association psychologies. The affiliation with historical association theory has been recognized by leading functionalists.[7] The preference for environmentalism shows up largely in the treatment of perception, where the issue associated with the differences between Helmholtz and Hering has been kept alive in differences between gestalt psychologists and associationists. The functionalist prefers to interpret perceptual discriminations as learned.[8] Although these biases are not absolute ones, when there is room for doubt (as in some aspects of size constancy) one can predict that the functionalist will be on the side of empiricism and against nativism.

In summary, we find the functionalist tolerant but critical, favoring continuities over discontinuities, seeking to translate his problems into experimentable form. Within the free, eclectic atmosphere, he nevertheless has a preference for interpretations coherent with historical association theory as against holistic or nativistic interpretations.

[7] Carr (1931), Robinson (1932a). Melton (1950) described his position as an "associationistic functionalism."

[8] E.g., Carr (1935). The favorite experiment quoted by functionalists has long been that of visual experiences with reversing lenses, Stratton (1896); its modern counterpart is Kohler (1963).

FUNCTIONAL ASPECTS OF THE LEARNING PROCESS

Because the functionalist does not have a highly articulated learning theory, we can best understand his approach by following a functionalist's analysis of the problems facing an experimental psychology of learning. In what follows we shall accept Melton's (1950) summary of learning as a representative functionalist statement, using his analysis of learning and his outline of topics.

Melton begins with Dashiell's diagram of the readjustive process (Figure 10-1). The diagram shows how a problem arises when ongoing activity

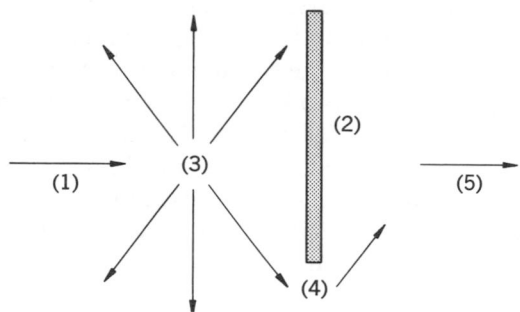

Figure 10-1   The readjustive process. After Dashiell (1949, page 26).

(1) is blocked by an obstacle (2). Eventually the organism through varied behavior (3) solves the problem (4) and proceeds on his way (5). If the process is repeated, the adequate response (4) recurs in less time, with less excess and irrelevant activity.

Thus the learning process is primarily a matter of the discovery of the adequate response to a problem situation and the fixation of the satisfying situation–response relationship (Melton, 1950, page 670).

From this analysis, Melton is led to state several major experimental problems of learning. Expressed as topics, these are:
1. Motivation
2. Initial discovery of the adequate response
3. Fixation and elimination
4. Factors determining the rate of learning
5. Transfer of training and retention

We can follow this outline in characterizing the functionalist approach to these topics.

1. Motivation.   Woodworth was the first functionalist to give a treatment of motivation in modern form, in a small book entitled *Dynamic psychology* (1918).

It was this book that gave currency to the term "drive" as alternative to "instinct." Woodworth set the stage for the prominence that drives and motives were presently to have within psychology.

The cycle between aroused activity and quiescence is discussed according to *preparatory* and *consummatory* reactions, Woodworth crediting Sherrington (1906) with the distinction. Consummatory reactions are those which satisfy basic drives or needs, activities such as eating or escaping from danger. They are directly of value to the organism. Their objective mark is that they terminate a series of acts, leading either to rest or to the turning by the organism to something else. A preparatory reaction is only indirectly or mediately of value to the organism, its value resting on the fact that it leads to or makes possible a consummatory reaction. The objective mark of the preparatory reaction is said to be that it occurs as a preliminary stage leading to the consummatory reaction.

Preparatory reactions are of two kinds. One kind represents alert attention, "a condition of readiness for a yet undetermined stimulus that may arouse further response." Another is the kind of preparatory adjustment evoked only "when the mechanism for a consummatory reaction has been aroused and is in activity." The latter sort of reaction is goal-directed, and evokes seeking behavior, as when a hunting dog, having lost a trail, explores about in order to get back on it.

A new conception introduced is that of ongoing activity as itself a drive —activity once under way leading to its own completion. Even if the original drive under which the activity started has ceased to operate, the activity, if incomplete, may continue. The distinction between drive and mechanism breaks down when it is asserted that the mechanism (i.e., the reaction under way) may become its own drive. Allport later (1937) proposed that motives may become *functionally autonomous,* that is, completely divorced from their primal sources in basic needs of the organism. Activity leading to further activity, and functional autonomy, are very similar conceptions. Both are related to the problem of secondary reinforcement. If stimuli associated with reinforcement themselves come to have reinforcing power, it may be that a system of derived rewards may be built up which will continue to have motivating power without recourse to the satisfaction of any basic need. The increasing importance attaching to secondary reinforcement in theories like Hull's and Skinner's shows Woodworth's perspicacity in being the first to recognize that the distinction between drive and mechanism becomes less sharp as activity gets under way.

In a book entitled *Dynamics of behavior* (1958) completed shortly before his death and a full 40 years after the *Dynamic psychology,* Woodworth went even further in emphasizing the role of the environment as against organic needs in his conception of motivation. He contrasted his new point of view, expressed as a *behavior-primacy theory,* with the need-primacy theories that he attributed to Freud and Hull. After discussing naturalistically how a dog pricks up his ears at a tone, sees that it is his master who calls, and then runs to him, he indicates that what the dog is doing is merely dealing with its environment: the whistle, the recognized master, his location in space, the terrain over which he must run.

Here we are making the claim that this direction of receptive and motor activity toward the environment is the fundamental tendency of animal and human behavior and that it is the all-pervasive primary motivation of behavior (1958, pages 123-125).

What [the theory] predicts is that the interaction of a capacity with the environment will generate a specific interest. It predicts that an individual who engages in a task will, unless distracted, find himself absorbed in that task, interested in it and motivated to bring it to completion (1958, page 133).

Another facet to Woodworth's motivational theory was the abiding interest that he showed in the concept of "set," dating from his early experiments on imageless thought. It was the new emphasis brought about by the imageless thought controversy that in the first decade of this century provided functionalism's supplementation to traditional association psychology. Although Angell and Woodworth were on opposite sides of the fence on some issues concerned with the introspective contents of thought, they were in agreement on the dynamic consequences of predisposing sets and intentions.[9]

The sets and intentions emphasized by the students of imageless thought, and the preparatory reactions oriented toward consummatory responses are concepts with a similar dynamic loading. They are both directional, they are both inferred from the manner in which behavior sequences are organized. In a later development of his conception of set, Woodworth introduced what he called the *situation-set* and the *goal-set* (1937). The situation-set refers to adjustments to environmental objects; the goal-set refers to the inner "steer" which gives unity to a series of varied but goal-directed activities.

The important suggestion in the concept of situation-set is that the environment must be brought into the psychological account in a manner not suggested by the usual stimulus–response psychology. Guthrie, for example, made much of the fact that he was interested in movements, not in outcomes. Woodworth took the opposite position. Movements were, to Woodworth, less important than the information about the environment to which these movements led. The rat in the maze learns spatial relationships, not running habits; in the problem-box the cat discovers the door-opening character of the button, not a sequence of manipulatory movements. As Woodworth put it: "The character of goodness attaches for the animal not to his movements in manipulating the button, but to the button as an object."

[9] See Woodworth (1906); Angell (1906).

It is to Woodworth's credit that his long history of espousing stimulus—response concepts did not so fix his thinking that he was unable to go outside this systematic framework as he felt it necessary. The conception of situation-set presents a kind of bridge to ways of looking at psychology that have been carried out more fully by others, notably by Tolman and Brunswik. Through the years, Woodworth's use of "set" and related concepts prevented his falling into a static system.

Carr's interpretation of motivation in his textbook (1925) was influenced by Woodworth's views, but he restated the preparatory-consummatory adjustment in new terms.

Carr accepted the principle that all behavior is initiated by stimuli, so that his point of view is similar to other stimulus–response psychologies, with the difference that responses may be ideational as well as motor. He is concerned with activities, not movements. An adaptive act is described as involving a motivating stimulus, a sensory situation, and a response that alters that situation in a way that satisfies the motivating conditions. The external object by which the organism satisfies its motives is called the incentive, or the immediate objective or goal of the response. (The more remote goal, such as maintaining the life of the organism by preventing starvation, does not enter directly into the control of the act). More specifically, a motive is described as a relatively persistent stimulus that dominates the behavior of an individual until he reacts in such a manner that he is no longer affected by it. This makes of a motive what Smith and Guthrie call a maintaining stimulus. The adaptive act is organized to obtain certain sensory consequences (i.e., the termination of the motivating stimuli) and the act can be interpreted as completed only when the consequences are attained. The interpretation of the end phase as a sensory change became Carr's way of talking about the empirical law of effect (1938).

Melton, accepting Carr's definition of motivation as a stimulating condition, pointed out that motivating conditions have three functions: (1) they energize the organism, making it active, (2) they direct the variable and persistent activity of the organism, and (3) they emphasize or select the activities that are repeated (fixated) and those that are not repeated (eliminated). Stated in this way, the functionalist's interpretation of motivation is consistent with Hull's, but it is coherent also with the position of Tolman.

2. Initial Discovery of the Adequate Response.   Melton noted that initial discovery may be the main problem in some kinds of learning (e.g., in the problem-box), while it plays little part in others (e.g., in serial rote memorization). The controversy between trial and error and insight in the interpretation of learning hinges in part on the nature of this initial discovery of the correct solution. The functionalist does not have to take sides: he waits for definitive experiments.

Melton saw that two other forms of initial discovery have played less systematic roles in learning theories, yet they should not be neglected. One of these is *guidance*. The discovery of the correct response can be facilitated by the teacher or trainer through appropriate manipulation of the environment or the learner. Hence guided learning is intermediate between rote learning (with no discovery) and problem-solving (with unguided discovery). An extensive research program on guided learning was carried out by Carr and his students and later summarized by him (1930). Such a program illustrates the freedom with which the functionalist selects his experimental variables.

The other form of initial discovery mentioned by Melton is *imitation*. He believed it could be subsumed under guidance, however, for it helps the learner to discover the solution by observing the solution by another organism.[10]

Melton, in common with other functionalists, was willing to accept the initial discovery of solutions with insight, but, in common with other associationists, preferred interpretations emphasizing past experience:

Insight is, however, not a term to conjure with even though it is a useful descriptive concept when employed within the framework of the major dimensions of analysis of the problem situation and the process of discovery of the correct response. In any event, the range, specific nature, and plasticity of the trial behavior of the organism seem to be most profitably related to the motivating condition of the organism and to the associative spread from previous learning (1950, page 676).

3. Fixation of Adequate Responses and Elimination of Inadequate Responses. Melton accepted the *empirical law of effect* as stated by McGeoch: "Other things being equal, acts leading to consequences which satisfy a motivating condition are selected and strengthened, while those leading to consequences which do not satisfy a motivating condition are eliminated" (McGeoch, 1942, page 574). When it came to explaining effect, Melton was cautious in choosing between a contiguity theory and a reinforcement theory:

Two alternatives seem to be available to the student at this time: (a) The issue of contiguity vs. effect will be decided at some distant time in terms of the over-all fruitfulness of one or the other postulate, as judged by the application of Hull's theoretical methodology; (b) It may be that *mere* contiguity and reinforcement are extremes of some as yet undefined dimension of the neurophysiology of the organism, such that associations may be formed through mere contiguity *or* through reinforcement. Meanwhile, it is necessary to recognize the experimental findings which make the complete generality of one or the other untenable, for these are actually the fruits of the research on this problem during the forty years (1950, page 677).

[10] The importance of imitation in learning has received a new impetus from the experiments of Bandura and others, as cited in Bandura and Walters (1963).

This quotation well illustrates the functionalist's unwillingness to prejudge the outcome of a controversy whose resolution ultimately must be determined by experiment.

4. Factors Determining the Rate of Learning.   Whatever may be the underlying principles of learning when learning is reduced to the barest essential relationships between stimulus and response, it is not difficult to arrange situations under which learning occurs. By long-established convention we plot performance scores against learning trials and come out with a "curve of learning." The search for a "typical" or "true" form of the learning curve has not proven profitable, but learning curves have helped in the search for the parameters of learning. Through a great many experiments we have learned much about the relationship between rate of learning and the amount of material to be learned, about the effects of length and distribution of practice periods, about how the characteristics of the learner affect the rate of progress. These problems have all been inviting ones to the functionalist who sets as his task the exploring of the many dimensions influencing learning.

Some guiding principles are needed to establish order in an empirical program of such vast scope as accounting for everything that affects all kinds of learning by all kinds of learners under all kinds of circumstances.

Some of these guiding principles were inherited from the pre-experimental association psychologists. A useful list had been provided by Thomas Brown as early as 1820. He had classified the *laws of association* (or laws of suggestion, as he called them) into *primary* or *qualitative* laws (the laws of similarity, contrast, and contiguity), and *secondary* or *quantitative* laws (frequency, vividness, emotional congruity, mental set, etc.). The primary laws represent the essential general conditions for associative formation or associative revival, whereas the secondary laws determine which of many possible associates is formed or recalled.

After Ebbinghaus (1885) had shown that associations could be studied experimentally, writers such as Müller (1911–1917) in Europe and Carr (1931) and Robinson (1932a) in America began to rewrite associative laws in quantitative form. Carr and Robinson were quite explicit that *all* associative laws could be made quantitative, and they gave lists of laws that they thought expressed our twentieth-century knowledge about associative learning.

Here is Robinson's list of laws (1932a, pages 62-122):

Law of contiguity
Law of assimilation
Law of frequency
Law of intensity
Law of duration
Law of context

Law of acquaintance
Law of composition
Law of individual differences

While some of Robinson's laws sound qualitative, he attempts to show how all qualitative distinctions can be subjected to a dimensional analysis. He himself raised the question whether or not in isolating these factors as important he had really stated "laws." He summarized his discussion of "laws" as follows:

> It is my firm conviction that the facility of associative fixation is a function of all of the factors enumerated. Probably several specific relationships are involved for each named factor and almost certainly there are other factors that have not been included in this list. But, if the assumption that these factors are important determiners of association be correct, then there are "laws" of these factors whether our knowledge of them is definite or not (1932a, page 124).

It turns out that Robinson's position is much like Skinner's, in that he points out the relevant variables and makes a claim for "lawfulness" rather than for "laws." Because of these limitations in the list of "laws," the Carr–Robinson laws did not catch on, even among their students, as a means of ordering the factors determining the rate of learning, although there are occasional mentions of isolated laws from the list. The issues expressed in the laws were somewhat too general. The empirical role of contiguity, for example, breaks down into the study of several varieties of time relationships between events, with their corresponding gradients. Thus the separation of a conditioned and unconditioned stimulus in classical conditioning yields one kind of empirical law of contiguity, while the delay of reward at the end of a maze yields another kind. We tend to name such relationships more concretely (e.g., gradient of reinforcement, spread of effect) rather than to refer them to a more general law of contiguity. So, too, the law of frequency, as a law of relative frequency, covers too many topics, including the form of the learning curve, the form of the work curve, the effects of distributed and massed practice, the consequences of degrees of overlearning. Frequency is only a general topic, within which a number of very different laws are discoverable.

Contemporary functionalist writers, instead of setting up basic laws of learning, tend to use classificatory schemes derived directly from experimental arrangements and results. Underwood, for example, used the following scheme to outline the factors determining the rate of learning:

a. Massed versus distributed practice
b. Type of material
  (1) Intra-list similarity
  (2) Meaningfulness

(3) Affectivity

c. Knowledge of performance

d. Miscellaneous (e.g., whole versus part learning; active recitation; sense modality; amount of material) (1949, pages 398-419).

While Underwood's treatment is part of a chapter in an introductory textbook on experimental psychology and is not intended to be exhaustive, his classification of variables bears a close resemblance to that used in other functionalist treatises on learning.[11] Such a classificatory scheme is not in itself a theory of learning, yet it suggests as well as the Carr–Robinson laws the kinds of variables with which functionalist systems deal.

5. *Transfer of Training and Retention.* Once something has been learned it can be used, provided it has not been forgotten and provided new situations recur in which the previously learned behavior is called forth. The study of the relative permanence of learning, when tested in situations essentially duplicating those of the original learning, is the study of *retention,* while the study of the effects of old learning in new situations is often discussed as *transfer of training.* Because recurring situations always recur with differences, there is obviously an intimacy between retention and transfer. Because transfer effects may be positive, negative, or indeterminate, one view of forgetting is that it is but an illustration of negative transfer.

Melton followed McGeoch (1932) in accepting two major laws of forgetting. The first is the *law of context* (one from Robinson's list), which asserts that the degree of retention, as measured by performance, is a function of the similarity between the original learning situation and the retention situation. The second is the *law of proactive and retroactive inhibition,* which asserts that retention is a function of activities occurring prior to and subsequent to the original learning. Proactive and retroactive inhibition have been major topics of research for several decades, ever since the problem was first opened up by Müller and Pilzecker (1900). A number of good summaries of the literature are available.[12]

The paradigm for retroactive inhibition is A-B-A, where the learning of B is interpolated between the learning and retention of A, and interferes with the retention of A. The paradigm for proactive inhibition is B-A-A, where the learning of B prior to the learning of A interferes with the later retention of A. Both retroactive and proactive interference with learning are readily demonstrable, and the empirical relationships have led to a number of hypotheses. Studying the development of one of these

---

[11] Major summaries of the literature handled functionally can be found in McGeoch and Irion (1952), Osgood (1953), Woodworth and Schlosberg (1954).

[12] A general summary can be found in McGeoch and Irion (1952, pages 404-447). Interest in the importance of proactive inhibition was furthered by Underwood's review (1957).

hypotheses about retroactive inhibition will help us to understand not only retroactive inhibition but the manner in which functionalists construct their theories.

One set of problems arises over the *similarity* between the interpolated material and the material originally learned. Robinson (1927), arguing from some earlier results of his own and of Skaggs (1925), formulated a hypothesis later christened by McGeoch as the Skaggs–Robinson hypothesis. With the usual functionalist preference for stating dimensions, Robinson, following Skaggs, proposed relating the amount of retroactive inhibition to the dimension of degree of similarity between the original and the interpolated material or activity.

With the similarity dimension in mind, Robinson argued that the interpolation of identical material (Material B the same as Material A) would simply provide additional practice on Material A, hence lead to increased retention on the test trials during which retroactive inhibition is usually shown. Because retroactive inhibition with dissimilar materials was already an established fact, the natural conjecture on the assumption of continuous variation is that starting with identity the amount of retroactive inhibition would increase gradually as dissimilarity was increased. Now, asks Robinson, what is likely to happen at the other end of the scale, as the original material (Material A) and the interpolated material (Material B) become *extremely* unlike? Presumably retroactive inhibition represents some sort of interference based on similarity between the original and interpolated activity. If there is very little similarity there should be very little retroactive inhibition. Putting all these considerations together, it is reasonable to expect a maximum of retroactive inhibition at some intermediate point of similarity between Materials A and B. Robinson formulated the whole generalization in words as follows: "As similarity between interpolation and original memorization is reduced from near identity, retention falls away to a minimum and then rises again, but with decreasing similarity it never reaches the level obtaining with maximum similarity." He expressed this graphically by the figure reproduced as Figure 10-2.

His own experimental test of the generalization was very simple. By the memory span method he studied the recall of the first four of a series of eight consonants as this recall was interfered with by the last four of the consonants. That is, the first four were considered to be Material A, the last four Material B, and the similarity and dissimilarity of Materials A and B were controlled. Similarity was defined as partial identity. Maximum similarity meant that the second four consonants were like the first four; maximum dissimilarity meant that all the last four differed from the first four.

The results confirmed the hypothesis only partially. Starting with near-identity, retroactive inhibition increased as the interpolated material be-

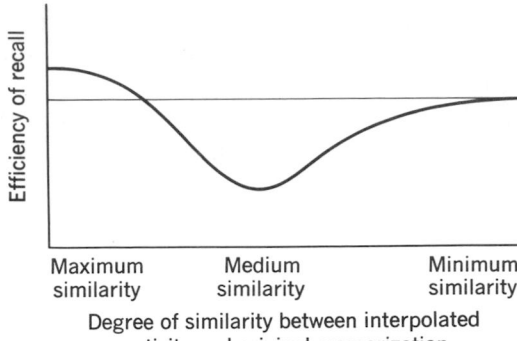

Degree of similarity between interpolated
activity and original memorization

Figure 10-2   Similarity as a factor in retroactive inhibition. The curve is intended to show that retroactive inhibition bears a quantitative relationship to the degree of similarity between the interpolated activity and the material originally memorized. With maximum similarity, the interpolated activity provides positive transfer, hence
increases the efficiency of recall. Maximum interference with recall is predicted to fall at some intermediate value of similarity.
After Robinson (1927, page 299).

came increasingly dissimilar. This was part of the conjecture. But the decrease in the amount of retroaction (increase in recall) with maximum
unlikeness was not found. In fact, with the materials totally dissimilar,
retroactive inhibition was at a maximum.

A number of other later experimenters attacked the problem, referring
back to Robinson's formulation.[13] Results gave partial confirmation, but
there was some incompleteness and minor contradictions in the data. The
results led Osgood (1949) to propose a more complex formulation of the
relationships involved. Osgood's solution of the similarity problem is dia-
gramed in the three-dimensional surface shown as Figure 10-3.

What Osgood's surface states is that the amount of transfer in positive
or negative directions is a function of shifts in similarity between learning
and retention of *both* the stimulus conditions *and* the response required.
Shifts in stimulus similarity are from front to rear as noted on the right-
hand margin, moving from identical stimuli (S_I) through similar stimuli (S_S) to neutral stimuli (S_N). Shifts in response similarity are represented from left to right, as noted along the back margin, with identical
responses (R_I) being at the left, and moving progressively through similar responses (R_S), neutral responses (R_N), partially opposite responses
(R_O) to directly antagonistic responses (R_A).

The best way to practice reading the diagram is to read its edges first.
The rear edge says that stimuli bearing *no* resemblance to those used in

[13] Mention should be made also of a more rational analysis of the form of the
Skagg-Robinson function by Boring (1941).

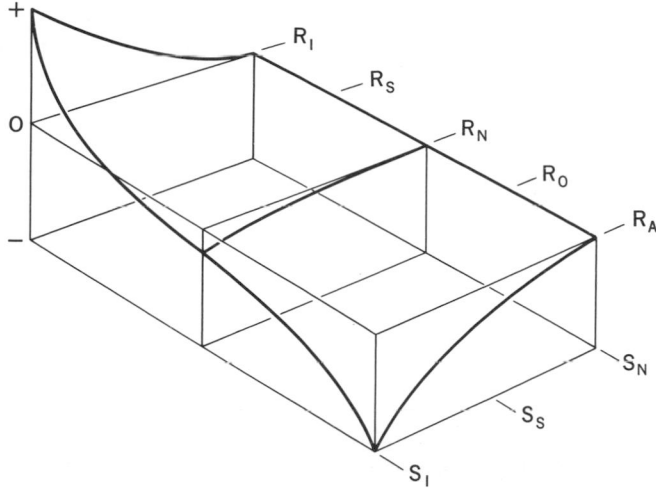

Figure 10-3 Osgood's transfer and retroaction surface (after Osgood, 1949). Vertical dimension, amount of transfer (+) or interference (−), with neutral zone represented by a plane (0). Left to right, amount of shift in response similarity between original task and new task, from identity (R_I) to antagonism (R_A). Front to rear, amount of shift in stimulus similarity between original and new task, from identity (S_I) to neutrality (S_N).

original learning lead to new responses without any transfer effect, positive or negative, regardless of the degree of resemblance between the required responses and responses that have been used in earlier experiments. The front edge says that with *identical* stimuli there will be maximum positive transfer with *identical* responses (for this is merely overlearning), whereas with directly *antagonistic* responses there will be maximum interference, for the earlier responses will have to be completely unlearned or overcome. The curve moves with two inflections between these extremes, but these inflections are not actually determinate from present data. The left edge says that, with identical responses, shifts in stimulus similarity from identity to neutrality will result in decreasing transfer, but no interference in new learning. The right edge says that, for antagonistic responses, shifts in stimulus similarity from identity to neutrality will produce decreasing interference, but no positive transfer. The diagram is a surface, and yields a curve wherever it is cut by a vertical plane.

In Robinson's kind of experiment the response called for varies with the stimulus, so if the stimulus changes the response also changes. (This is typically true in serial rote learning, because the response item is also a stimulus item for what follows.) Hence the Skaggs–Robinson diagram (Figure 10-2) can be approximated by making a diagonal slice across

Osgood's surface (Figure 10-3), from the near left-hand corner to the rear point marked R_N. The near left-hand corner represents the Skaggs–Robinson condition of maximum task similarity (identity of both stimuli and responses between learning and testing), while the rear point represents neutrality of both stimuli and response relative to the original task. Such a diagonal curve will be high at the left, dip down into a zone of interference, and return to the neutral point at the rear, thus having the essential characteristics of the Skaggs–Robinson curve, though with somewhat different inflections.

We may now trace the evolution of these models designed to account for the role of similarity. First we have the experiments that demonstrate the existence of retroactive inhibition, and then some that demonstrate the possible role of similarity as a factor. Next we have Robinson's somewhat crude dimensional hypothesis, leading to a series of experiments. Meanwhile a series of related experiments on transfer effects are being conducted, as though the two phenomena have little in common. Presently Osgood offers his new synthesis, covering the data that have accumulated since Robinson's hypothesis was announced, incorporating at once the retroactive inhibition and the transfer results. The Skaggs–Robinson hypothesis is seen to be a limited special case of a more complex set of relationships. This succession, with an interplay between data and theory, and a higher synthesis in dimensional terms, is exactly what might be expected in a maturing functional analysis. The next step, as Osgood points out, ought to be a quantitative (mathematically precise) model of his surface. While the surface now accounts in a general way for all of the available data, it is largely schematic, and nothing is known about the precise form it should take, or if, indeed, there is one form or a family of forms.[14]

The discussion of Melton's topics has led us somewhat afield from the content or conclusions of his own treatment of learning, but the outline served its purpose in providing the topics for an overview of the functionalist analysis of the problems of learning.

Does this emerge as a theory of learning? Melton emphasized in his summary that a dimensional analysis of learning, although scarcely qualifying as a theory, is not antitheoretical. Theoretical systems, he states, help to clarify problems and they lead to the discovery of new empirical relationships. But these relationships have to be firmly established if we are to have a science of learning. We need to standardize and calibrate valid and reliable methods of investigation in order to have better data for the theorist to manipulate.

[14] Further steps were taken by Bugelski and Cadwallader (1956) and Lindsay (1959) leading to modifications of interpretation rather than to mere quantification of Osgood's surface.

EFFECTS OF THE DISTRIBUTION OF PRACTICE AS ILLUSTRATIVE OF CURRENT FUNCTIONALISM

One of the best ways to study a scientific theory is to see it in action, that is, to note how those who hold to the theory select their topics and design their experiments and how they analyze and interpret their data. We have followed this procedure in reviewing the theories thus far discussed. We have had some introduction to the functionalist at work on the problem of retroactive inhibition. Now we are ready to examine further how functionalism works through giving more detailed consideration to some selected experimental problems.

How the General Orientation Contributes to the Planning of Experiments

When we attempt to determine how the theory directs the experiments that the functionalist chooses to perform we note two characteristics of his approach.

We discover, first, that the general theory provides only an orientation to experimentation, without providing a framework of crucial laws and postulates. The dimensional approach is a very broad frame of reference within which to work. It would be entirely unmanageable and cumbersome were it not for the guiding threads provided through years of experimentation by familiar methods upon familiar topics. Consider what would be involved in studying all the dimensions of massed and distributed practice. There are all the variables common to learning experiments (subjects, nature of materials, interrelationships within the materials, the kind of learning task), and there are the special variables specific to the problem of distribution (location of the interval between items, between trials, between banks of trials, between learning and retention, within relearning; length of the interval, whether uniform or variable; nature of the activities filling the interval). The combinations and permutations are staggering.

The second thing that we find out is that the experimenter typically narrows his task (within the broad dimensional orientation). He does this in two chief ways. First, he falls back on tasks that have familiarly been used in these studies, chiefly rote memorization and motor learning. He further restricts himself by addressing his attention to some of the "special theories" that are current or that he may himself invent. Hence the functionalist depends not only upon his general orientation but upon a body of experimental lore and a number of special theories that reduce his task to manageable proportions.

The Testing of Special Theories Related to Distributed Practice

In order to illustrate the foregoing interpretation of how the functionalist goes about his experiments, we shall examine a number of experiments studying distributed practice. A series of experimental reports, by Underwood and his associates, numbering over two dozen studies, well illustrates the nature of a systematic functionalist investigation. For our purposes we may rely on the summary report that followed the first twenty-one of these (Underwood, 1961). While these investigators appear to be making a strictly dimensional analysis, the papers are in fact guided largely by several special theories, and the dimensions chosen are by no means all that might have been selected. We turn now to some of these special theories—some tested by Underwood, and others with which he was not concerned.

1. The theory of differential forgetting. McGeoch (1942) stated that in the course of memorization or practice a subject learns erroneous (conflicting) responses that retard progress. Because these errors are less well learned than the correct responses, lapse of time will permit the errors to be forgotten more rapidly than the correct responses. Hence distributed practice will be advantageous over massed practice. In serial memorization some of these errors are remote associations (place-skipping tendencies). Because only the correct responses are repeatedly reinforced, the correct responses are probably better fixed than the errors. Experimenters who have looked for the forgetting of errors, as implied in McGeoch's theory, have been unable to find them. In one of the most careful direct studies of the problem, Wilson (1949) found no fewer errors in distributed than in massed practice, even though distributed practice resulted in more rapid learning, and he failed to find predicted effects in retention tests. Later studies, e.g., Underwood and Goad (1951) have also failed to substantiate McGeoch's theory.

2. The generalization-differentiation theory. Eleanor J. Gibson (1940, 1942) assumed that in the learning of a nonsense syllable the subject has to differentiate the individual syllables from nonsense-syllables-in-general. If the subject is making some correct responses and some erroneous ones, we may say, according to this interpretation, that the correct responses have been better differentiated from syllables-in-general, while the erroneous responses still suffer from too great generalization, that is, lack of discrimination. What will be the effect of a rest interval? Because differentiation (by analogy with what goes on in conditioning experiments) involves an inhibition of alternative responses, rest should bring "spontaneous recovery" of generalization. Hence the differences in the strengths of tendency to give correct and incorrect responses should be *reduced* after rest. Thus distributed practice should prove to be *dis*advantageous as compared with massed—an implication contrary to McGeoch's hypothesis.

Experimental results are more favorable to Gibson's theory than to McGeoch's. With distributed practice, erroneous responses commonly do show an increase over those in massed practice, especially during the early trials.[15]

How difficult it is to make predictions that are genuinely unambiguous! We assumed, in stating Gibson's theory, that distributed practice should be disadvantageous. This was not really a sound assumption. It has been found that with distributed practice there are more errors, as her theory predicts, but *learning may still be more rapid under conditions of distributed practice.* It is possible that more errors are associated with a heightened set to respond that is in turn associated with more rapid learning. Part of the mystery of the finding disappears if we remember that in addition to false responses there are other kinds of inadequate responses in a serial learning experiment, such as a failure to respond, not counted as an erroneous response.

Another aspect of Gibson's generalization hypothesis has to do with the intra-list similarity of items. If items in a list are very much like each other it will be harder to differentiate them. If the process of learning is one of differentiation, it should be harder to learn a list of similar (homogeneous) items than a list of heterogeneous ones. This implication of the theory can easily be confirmed experimentally.[16] A second implication is that forgetting will be more rapid with greater intra-list similarity because of the spontaneous recovery of interfering generalizations. The interfering generalizations will, of course, be more common with more similar items. This implication does *not* receive experimental support. Because of the support of Gibson's theory in the learning and relearning data, but not in the retention data, Underwood (1954b) was led to propose some supplements to her theory.

The results of four of Underwood's studies[17] (with both serial-syllable and paired-syllable lists) agreed substantially on the following three points: (1) The higher the intra-list similarity the more difficult the learning; (2) retention over a 24-hour interval is independent of the level of intra-list similarity; and (3) the higher the intra-list similarity the more difficult the relearning.

Underwood is called upon to account for the unexpected failure of

[15] Underwood and Goad (1951), Underwood (1951b, 1952b). But not all experiments agree with the theory, e.g., Underwood (1951a).

[16] When the items are in pairs, as in paired-associate learning, various kinds of stimulus and response similarity produce quite complex results, *e.g.*, Umemoto and Hilgard (1961), Umemoto (1962).

[17] The four studies are Underwood (1952b, 1953a, 1953b, 1953c).

intra-list similarity to have an effect upon retention (the second of the foregoing points) although it clearly affects both learning and relearning. He proposes that there may be two kinds of interference that do not reveal themselves in retention because they balance each other:

(1) If intra-list similarity is high, there is interference within the list, as predicted from Gibson's generalization hypothesis. Underwood's subjects learned and relearned three successive lists. His evidence shows a distinct trend for errors at recall to come from *within* the list when similarity of items within the list is high, and from *outside* the list when similarity within the list is low. Because some of these *outside* items came from previously learned lists, it is implied that there is *inter-list* interference when intra-list similarity is low.

(2) If intra-list similarity is high, the list being learned is more clearly differentiated from previously learned lists than if similarity is low. This accounts for less inter-list interference with high intra-list similarity.

Combining these two propositions we note that there is an inverse relationship between intra-list and inter-list interference with variations in intra-list similarity. Thus when intra-list similarity is high, the high *intra-list* interference is offset by low *inter-list* interference.[18] Provided these opposing tendencies balance each other, we have an explanation for the finding that recall is independent of the degree of intra-list similarity.

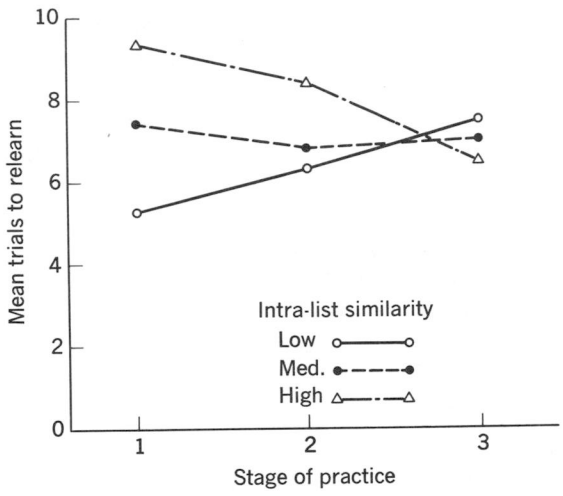

Figure 10-4   Relearning of paired-syllable lists as a function of stage of practice and intra-list similarity. Underwood (1954b, page 163).

Evidence supporting these conjectures is given in Figure 10-4. The curves are based on the learning of successive lists of paired associates.

[18] That better bounded material interferes less than loosely bounded material was shown earlier by Werner (1947).

Although early in practice the high-similarity lists are much harder to learn than the low-similarity lists, the curves converge with practice. High-similarity lists become relatively easier both because there is some learning-how-to-learn and because there is little inter-list interference. This accords with the hypothesis. Low-similarity lists become harder to learn, not because learning-how-to-learn is absent, but because there is increasing interference (proactive inhibition) from the learning of prior undifferentiated lists. (This, too, agrees with the hypothesis.)

The interpretation is that, as one of these interferences goes up the other goes down. Hence they may balance so that retention does not show any differential effects for high or low intra-list similarity. If these are balancing functions, it ought to be possible to give one a boost over the other. In one of Underwood's experiments in this series (1953c) it was found that with *extreme* similarity learning remained difficult, but retention was improved. This result, too, conforms to his hypothesis.

3. The theory of recovery from work decrement. A very plausible theory of the advantages of distributed practice has been proposed from time to time by those who noted that massed practice had some of the characteristics of a "work curve" as well as a "learning curve." This is particularly evident in motor learning. In Figure 10-5, for example, we have the performance curves of two groups on a pursuit rotor, one group of sub-

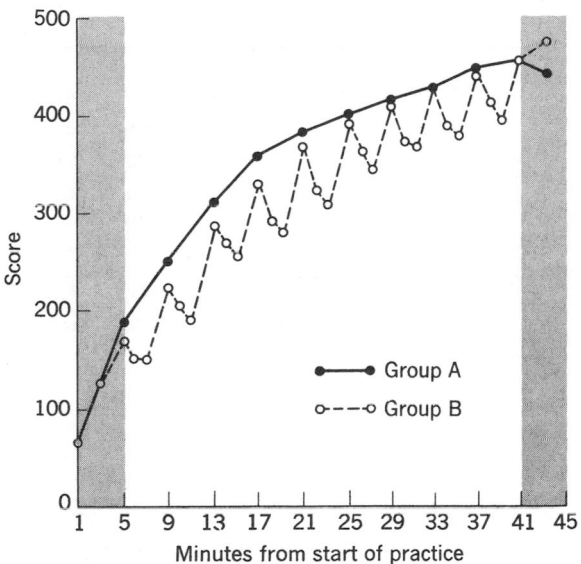

Figure 10-5   Distributed practice in pursuit learning. Group A practiced 1 minute and rested 3 minutes, while Group B practiced 3 minutes and rested 1 minute. Scores at each minute within the 3-minute trials show progressive work decrement. Doré and Hilgard (1937).

jects practicing for one minute and resting for three minutes (distributed practice), the other practicing for three minutes and resting for one minute (massed practice). Scores were recorded at the end of each minute of the 3-minute group, and these appear in the curve as a series of "work curves." The gain from practice shows as recovery over the 1-minute rests, but there is little advantage in the three times as much practice that this group has had. The kind of theory that these curves suggests, supplemented by "warm-up" phenomena, was given a more formal treatment by Ammons (1947), and works reasonably well for pursuit learning.[19]

The related theory for rote memorization was elaborated by Hull and others (1940), largely around the experimental work of Ward (1937) and Hovland (1938, 1939). Here it was assumed that interferences accumulating within learning are of the nature of inhibitions in conditioning, and thus recover with time. A number of conjectures were borne out in the data: that there should be reminiscence after a rest following learning, that the disadvantage for items near the middle of a list should be overcome somewhat with rest, that paired associate learning should show less benefit from rest than serial learning.

Theories of the work-interference type, whether expressed in terms of conditioned inhibition, or reactive inhibition, or in other language, are bound to have some place in the explanation of distributed practice. They account well for the similar effects found for such unlike tasks as nonsense syllable memorizing, pursuit learning, and concept formation. Direct tests were earlier made largely with motor tasks, but Hovland and Kurtz (1951) came up with an experiment in which the results of work are tested directly within a memorization experiment. If a subject does difficult mental work of another kind just before memorizing a list, more reminiscence for the list follows than if he either did not do the mental work or was permitted to rest between the mental work task and the memorization.

4. The consolidation theory. One of the earliest "special" theories bearing on distributed practice is that of Müller and Pilzecker (1900), known originally as the perseveration theory. The theory assumes that the benefits of practice continue for a while after practice ceases, and the results of learning are therefore not at their maximum until an appreciable time following the end of practice. Were the perseveration theory to hold, such phenomena as reminiscence and the advantages of distributed practice would be expected. Related forms of the theory attribute the consolidation effect to growth or maturation stimulated by practice (Snoddy, 1935; Wheeler and Perkins, 1932).

One hypothesis derived from the theory of stimulation-induced matura-

---

[19] Further work along closely related lines has been done by a number of others, e.g., Kimble and Horenstein (1948), and Irion (1949).

tion is that, within the wide limits of amount of practice, learning should proceed at a rate that is a function of the learner and of the task to be learned rather than a function of the number of trials or of the actual amount of time spent in practice. Too little practice (or, at the extreme, none at all) will fail to stimulate the growth underlying the skill, while too much practice will prove to be disruptive and inefficient.

Scores for the beginning and end of each of four days of practice under three widely different conditions of spacing are shown in Figure 10-6.

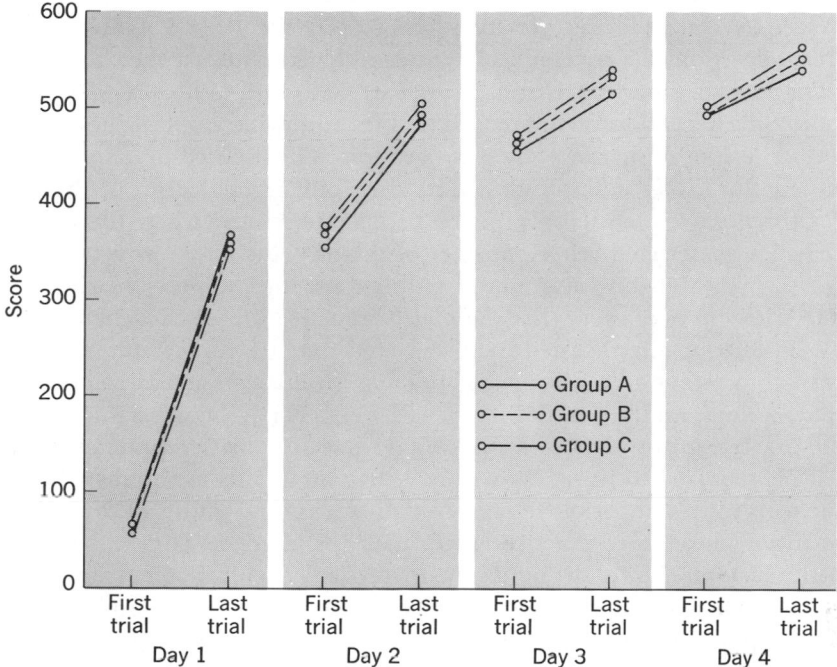

Figure 10-6   Similarity in trends with three distributions of practice in pursuit-learning. Group A by the end of the fourth day had practiced a total of 32 1-minute trials, Group B a total of 52 trials, and Group C a total of 72 trials. Data of Hilgard and Smith (1942) as plotted by Underwood (1949, page 406).

Whatever one's theory, it is pertinent to note that the gains within each day and the overnight losses are remarkably similar for the three groups despite the accumulated differences in the number of practice trials. The ordinary trial-by-trial plot would have shown striking advantage for distributed practice without calling attention to a uniformity that no other theory predicts.

Theories of consolidation have taken on new interest because of distinctions being made between short-term memory, which as its name implies fades rapidly, and long-term memory, which is more enduring. The possibility is that some process of fixing of the learned material occurs between them. The literature as of its date was reviewed by Glickman (1961). Some more recent evidence will be considered later.[20]

Other suggestions. It is characteristic of the functionalist to invent *ad hoc* theories to explain particular findings. This tendency in itself is neither good nor bad, although at some stages of knowledge it produces a great conglomeration of unrelated theories, with inconsistencies that may be hard to detect.

We may conclude this treatment of special theories by pointing out three suggestions not covered in the foregoing list of special theories.

The first of these suggestions is that of Cain and Willey (1939), who studied the retention of nonsense syllables following learning to a common criterion of mastery by two groups. The massed-practice group learned the list in a single day. The distributed-practice group learned over three days, each day's practice being interrupted when the subject reached a preselected criterion short of mastery, but progressively higher each day. By the third day the distributed-practice subjects reached the same criterion of mastery that the massed-practice subjects reached in one day. The group that learned by distributed practice turned out to be far superior in retention to the massed-practice group, as tested at intervals of 1 day, 3 days, and 7 days following learning. Partly because the distributed-practice group showed no advantage over the massed-practice group in trials required to learn, Cain and Willey argued from the distributed-practice group's superior retention that this group must have learned something the massed-practice group had not learned. This was to pick up the task on the following day where it had been left off many hours before, even when it had been poorly learned. In other words, the distributed-practice group had two days of practice at recalling after 24 hours that the massed-practice group did not have. While this is a plausible suggestion within the arrangements of this experiment, it is hardly suitable as a general interpretation of the advantages of distributed practice. It gives a warning, however, that qualitative changes occur when very long intervals are dealt with. It is always necessary to supplement mere scores by a psychological analysis of the activities going on.

A second suggestion was originally made and tested by Ericksen (1942). He proposed that massing of trials should lead to variability of response, through factors similar to the refractory phase that act as barriers to repetition. If this is the case, massing should be advantageous when the task is one calling for variability of attack. He found some evidence for this theory for human subjects solving a problem-box. Earlier work by Cook (1934) had found massed practice to be an advantage in early trials of puzzle-solving, a result coherent with Ericksen's hypothesis. A later

[20] In Chapter 14.

test by Riley (1952) failed to find benefit from massing in a task with many alternatives; distributed practice proved beneficial throughout.

A third suggestion comes from Underwood (1954a), calling attention to *individual differences* as a factor in the effects of distributed practice. He found that retention by slow learners tended to suffer from distributed practice as shown in Figure 10-7. While he believes these results to account

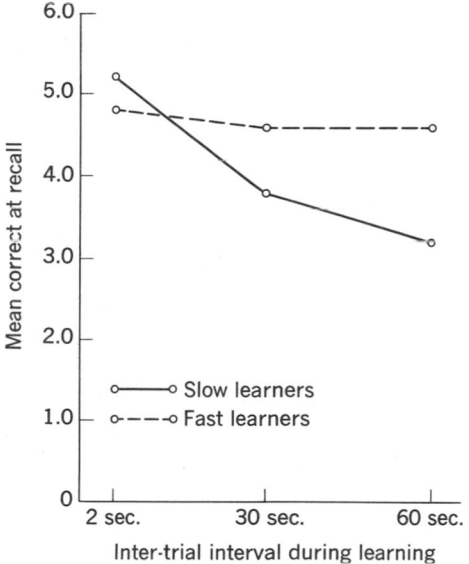

Figure 10-7   **Deleterious effects of distributed practice upon retention for slow learners compared with fast learners. Underwood (1954a, page 298).**

for some of the discrepant findings on the relation between distribution of practice and retention, the results do not suffice to account for all the discrepancies. The differences between the two kinds of learners are to be taken seriously, but the failure to find advantages with distributed practice even for the fast learners shows that something else is operative in these experiments.[21]

These suggestions (and they do not exhaust the possibilities) show how complex a dimensional approach would become if it were to take seriously the task of exploring in systematic variation all of the factors that have been shown by one or another experiment to be influential in experiments on the distribution of practice.

[21] One possibility is that the symbol cancellation task used to fill the interval has an interfering effect upon retention, and that this interference is more severe with the slow learners. The experiments that find more advantage for distribution have used chiefly color naming, shown to be somewhat facilitating as against symbol cancellation (Underwood, 1952a).

Concluding Comments on the Distribution of Practice

An examination of experiments and theories related to distributed practice has helped us to see some of the characteristics of functionalism at work. First, the general position provides an orientation towards dimensional experimentation. If intervals are important, then we explore an orderly series of intervals; if similarity is important, then we find a way of grading similarity and we explore the effects of several degrees of similarity. Second, however, the attack is always much more specific than the general orientation alone would suggest. Not *all* or *just any* dimensions are explored, for such an approach would be too cumbersome; instead, the methods and materials used tend to be restricted largely to familiar ones, and the particular dimensions chosen for investigation are usually related to one or more of the special theories that are current. The program is very much that of science in general. It is very similar to that proposed by Skinner, to the extent that it is dimensional and seeks lawfulness rather than laws; it is related to Hull in that the tests are commonly tests of hypotheses. It lies between these two positions in that the experimenters who are functionalists usually have more respect for hypotheses than Skinner has, and they are more cautious than Hull about general systematic formulations at this stage of knowledge.

Does the approach pay off in firm scientific knowledge? The answer, at least if we generalize from studies of distributed practice, is by no means unequivocal. We are left at present with a welter of special theories, mostly tested with undecisive results. What is the matter?

One embarrassment is the failure of later experimenters to agree in their findings with the results of earlier experimenters. If we cannot find reproducible experimental data, it is futile to try to reach agreement on theoretical predictions. Possibly these failures to repeat are due to slipshod experimental procedures, but this is unlikely. Most experimenters are careful in what they do and report their results accurately. A more plausible diagnosis of failure to come up with identical findings when experiments are repeated can be made along the following lines:

1. Experiments are seldom repeated without "small" or "trifling" changes. Strictly speaking, we are not interested in repeating earlier experiments *precisely,* for then we get no new information. Hence we introduce what we believe to be nonessential changes (such as a different task in rest intervals), hoping to reproduce the essential findings. If the same findings are indeed the outcome, no problem arises. But if we do *not* find the same results, then we do not know whether or not we *would have* found them had we not made the "trifling" changes. Because of the many difficulties in so-called repetition, it is essential that we be patient enough

to repeat *exactly* what other experimenters have done before we begin to make "small" changes.[22]

2. Experimental designs are permitted to become too complex, without prior psychological analysis of the processes under investigation. Experimental design is not solely a statistical problem. While of course results must be secured in a manner to make possible adequate statistical analysis, the subject's task must also be reckoned with. The counterbalancing of practice effects by using the same subjects in various cycles of an experiment is likely to prove *not* to be an economical procedure. Underwood's results as presented in both Figures 10-4 and 10-7 show how futile it is to try to equate effects at different stages of practice when subjects of different ability are used and when different kinds of tasks (e.g., paired associates versus serial learning) show very different effects early and late in practice. The simpler design, well represented in the experiment of Wilson (1949), in which each subject is used in but a single condition, gives all the advantages of applicability of modern analysis of variance statistics while permitting much better control of the psychological processes involved. It has the further advantage that new controls can be run without again going through an elaborate counterbalanced series in which one cannot fathom what confusion has been created for the subject.

These two suggestions are related. It is too costly to repeat *exactly* very involved counterbalanced designs. If simpler designs were used, it would be possible to repeat the particular cycle in which the next experimenter was interested, in order to show that under the original conditions the original results could be obtained. Then the experimenter is free to make any changes he wants, with some assurance that his changes bear upon the modified results that he obtains.

A second source of embarrassment (beyond failure to reproduce experimental findings) is that even the special theories appear to have a long life and seldom are disposed of by way of experimental evidence. The only special theory related to distributed practice that now seems ready to be dismissed is that of differential forgetting, for no experimenter has found the error items that he ought to find if the theory is true. The consolidation theory treated earlier as not very promising has recently taken on new life. The theories based on warm-up and recovery-from-work decrement satisfactorily explain some, but not all, of the results. So, too, Gibson's generalization—differentiation theory remains in the running

---

[22] Those not close to the experimental literature have no idea how serious this nonrepeatability of experimental results can become. A notable example is the Ward–Hovland reminiscence phenomenon, which led Buxton (1943) to ascribe to it the character of "now-you-see-it-now-you-don't." Underwood (1953d) found so little evidence for it in his review of later studies that he designated it as possibly "a prewar phenomenon."

with some substantial agreements between data and predictions, but some failures also.

In his summary of ten years of experimentation on distributed practice Underwood (1961) concluded that the amount of response interference and the length of the distribution interval are the two critical factors in determining whether or not distributed practice will facilitate learning. According to him, there are two phases in rote learning: a response-learning phase, and an associative or hook-up phase. The interferences occur primarily in the first of these, that is, in the response-learning phase.

It is perhaps to the functionalist's credit that he can tolerate this mass of material so loosely integrated, rather than blinding himself to some of it in order to make his theories sound more plausible. Yet it would be even more to his credit if he could invent a theory that would give a coherent account of the whole array of relationships. We may note a dilemma here. Special theories can be stated with great precision, and so they have that advantage over general theories, at least in early stages of experimentally established fact. But special theories can also be applicable more than one at a time. Hence it is almost impossible to find a crucial experiment to test a special theory. If the experiment agrees with the theory, that is fine, but we all know that you cannot prove theories through occasional agreements, but can only keep them in the running that way; if the experiment disagrees with the theory, the theory may still be true, but something else may be in conflict with it. There is no point in giving up any theory with which occasional agreement can be found until there is some more general theory that accounts for *all* the agreements. The hypothetico-deductive method is by no means as simple as at first blush it appears to be!

ESTIMATE OF FUNCTIONALISM

Current functionalism is not a unified theory such as those earlier discussed. What bonds of unity there are lie in a tolerant acceptance of a wide range of psychological phenomena and a conviction that the task before psychology is to subject the many variables to quantitative study. Such a methodological unity permits wide diversity in content.

The Functionalist Position on the Typical Problems of Learning

Within such an unstructured system there is no one clear answer to most problems of learning. The answer to be expected is that "it all depends on conditions." In practice the situation is not quite as free as this implies, for gradually there accumulate more commonly accepted generalizations.

1. Capacity. Robinson recognized individual and species differences in his laws of individual differences and of composition. It is in line with functional developments for McGeoch and Irion to include in their book a chapter on learning as a function of individual differences. They believe that the increase of learning ability with age is best accounted for on the basis of two hypotheses: first, organic maturation, second, changing psychological conditions (transfer, motivation, personality traits).

2. Practice. The law of frequency was to Robinson a law of relative frequency, which therefore recognizes the losses in score when practice is overcrowded, along with the gains when trials are more appropriately spaced. There is a tendency to emphasize the form of the learning curve and to seek the conditions under which one form rather than another is to be found. There is, however, no diatribe against a law of exercise.

3. Motivation. Woodworth's dynamic psychology placed motivation at its core. Carr accepted in principle the preparatory-consummatory sequence, assigning motivation the role of a continuing stimulus to be terminated by the goal-response. The concept of "set" enters into the more conventional experiments on memorization and skill as a motivational supplement to the more familiar laws of association. It was the preoccupation of the early functionalist with such tasks as the learning of rote verbal series which tended to place motivation in the background rather than the foreground of theories such as Robinson's.[23]

4. Understanding. While the functionalist recognizes that meaningful material is more readily learned than nonsense material, degree of meaning is but one of the dimensions upon which materials can be scaled. Hence he does not believe that problem-solving or insight require interpretations beyond ordinary associative learning. The organism uses what it has learned as appropriately as it can in a new situation. If the problem cannot be solved by analogy, the behavior has to be varied until the initial solution occurs. Insight is perhaps an extreme case of transfer of training (McGeoch and Irion, 1952, page 53).

A distaste for holistic or organization concepts (of which "understanding" is one) is evident in the treatment of meaningfulness by Underwood and Schulz (1960) in their book on *Meaningfulness and verbal learning.* They disavow concern for meaning in any ultimate sense:

More specifically, meaningfulness as used here should not be confused with the term "meaning." As is well known, meaning has been a focal point of argumentation for generations of philosophers and, in recent years, semanticists. It will be seen that there are no ultimates in the meaning ascribed to meaningful-

---

[23] For the same reason, Underwood (1959) much later found it appropriate to underplay the importance of motivation.

ness by the operations of the learning laboratory, and there need not, therefore, be any cause for confusion with philosophical problems of meaning (1960, page 5).

They also dissociate themselves from the "semantic differential" concept of meaning (Osgood, Suci, and Tannenbaum, 1957). Hence, when they arrive at a quantitative theory of meaningfulness (a frequency theory: those items are most readily associated which are most available because of their frequency of occurrence in the past), they have produced significant relationships in their laboratory exercises, without coming to grips with what to many would be the more interesting problems. Meanings in the real world have some kind of reference. It would be interesting to speculate how it comes about that meaningfulness in rote learning can be treated without regard to reference; may there not be something about significant referential meaning that lies behind this frequency relationship? By being strictly "operational," such interesting questions do not have to be raised at all, yet they remain interesting—and answerable.

5. *Transfer.* Following Thorndike, transfer falls chiefly under the law of assimilation. That is, transfer depends upon degree of likeness between the new situation and the old. Woodworth (1938) reinterpreted the theory of identical elements to mean only that transfer is always of concrete performances.

What the theory of identical elements demands is that transfer should be of concrete performances, whether simple or complex makes no difference to the theory (page 177) . . . Perhaps anything that can be learned can be transferred. But does not everything that can be learned have the concrete character of an act or way of acting? (page 207).

6. *Forgetting.* The favorite theory of forgetting is that of retroactive and proactive interference, but the functionalist does not insist that this is the whole story. There may be some forgetting according to passive decay through disuse, and there may be forgetting through repression, as pointed out by Freud (Robinson, 1932b, pages 113-118).

Has Functionalism a Systematic Theory of Learning?

Functionalism is empiricist rather than systematic. It eschews inference for established experimental relationships between demonstrable variables. Its laws are quantitative, directly descriptive of data. There is a healthy respect for data, and there is a commendable urge to state issues specifically in a form subject to test. The relativism brings with it a freedom from bigotry. Before his untimely death, Robinson had turned to social problems, with the conviction that the same methods would work there. So long as people were forced to think in terms of specifics he believed that they could often reach agreement, even though on larger issues they were swayed by prejudices and preconceptions (Robinson, 1935).

The disadvantage of an extreme empiricism and relativism lies in its lack of articulating principles to cut across empirical laws. What results is a collection of many "laws," without hierarchial structure. There is no economical multidimensional apparatus for fitting together the various two-dimensional functional relationships, each of which is necessarily cast in the form: "other things being equal." If the dimensional program of the functionalists were fulfilled we should have a large handbook of data, with each of the several laws illustrated by a number of graphs showing the variations of associative strength under specific conditions. Empirical multidimensionality would be achieved through experimental designs testing several variables at once, but unless some simplifying steps were taken, the possible combinations and permutations of conditions would mount fabulously. Dimensional analysis puts data in order for exposition and for verification, but in itself does not connect the data into an economical scientific system. Such a system has to be logically structured as well as empirically sound.

Functionalism is in some respects an eclectic position. It is eclectic on the problem of introspection versus behavioral description, by accepting both in the account of psychological activity. A favorite illustration is that less attention to details is required after a skill is mastered. Note that this assertion uses an introspective report about the representation of details in awareness, although the mastery of the skill may be studied by observation of the overt movements. Functionalism is eclectic on the problem of blind versus intelligent learning, accepting a continuum between these extremes, according to the dimensional analysis of McGeoch and Melton. Any point of view which is pragmatic and pluralistic can easily incorporate concepts from alien systems; hence functionalism is well suited to play the mediating role. Functionalism is, however, an eclecticism with a bias—the bias of associationism in favor of analytic units, historical causation, environmentalism. The bias has been more evident in Chicago functionalism than in that of Woodworth, who showed himself friendlier to less associationistic concepts. New data may be accepted but forced back into older concepts not fully appropriate. Thus some of the novelty of the observations made in insight experiments is lost when insight is treated as merely another illustration of the familiar transfer of training experiment. Similarly, what goes on in the reasoning process is not fully encompassed by treating reasoning as trial-and-error learning merely a little farther out on the dimension of explicit–implicit response. Those who disagree with the associationist position object to the functionalist's incorporating of new experimental findings without accepting the theoretical implications of these findings. This is a problem with which the eclectic always has to wrestle: how much can be taken over without incorporating its systematic context? The functionalist has not been greatly concerned about the inner consistency of his borrowings because he is less concerned than others about the inner consistency of his own concepts. What consistency there has been is provided by the framework of associationism within which the functionalist works.

Perhaps Melton's position is the best to take on the matter of functionalism's systematic position: the functionalist does not have an articulated system, but he would like to have one, and is not antitheoretical. His breadth and self-criticism prevent his embracing a comprehensive system until facts are better ordered.

Whatever the systematic limitations may be, it must be recognized that great energy for experimental study has been released within the functionalist group. The books of McGeoch and Irion (1952), Osgood (1953), Woodworth and Schlosberg (1954) amply attest to this. Out of the large number of research investigations on memory and skill, done largely within this group, there has come a rich body of data and factual relationships with which anyone interested in learning must be familiar.

Convergence Toward Functionalist Interpretations

Because there is so much room within functionalism, because it is an experimentalism, because it fits the American temper, it provides a kind of framework appropriate to much of American psychology. Many of the trends in contemporary theory and experiment, not explicitly related to functionalism as a school of psychology, nevertheless are in accord with its historical orientation.

1. The scientific logic of *operationalism,* whereby scientific facts and concepts are related to the concrete operations through which they are produced, has been widely espoused by psychologists of most divergent theoretical backgrounds (e.g., Stevens, 1939). To the functionalist, operationalism is a very natural development from James' pragmatism and Dewey's instrumentalism (e.g., Dewey, 1929, page 111).

2. Mathematical models that are "neutral" with respect to many historical controversies are essentially "functional" models, in the mathematical sense of function. This mathematical sense of function is coherent with the psychological meaning of function. Hence it is not surprising to find Skinner (1953a) writing about the need for a functional analysis (meaning essentially a dimensional analysis), or to find Brunswik (1955) describing his system as a "probabilistic functionalism." The mathematical models to be described in the next chapter can properly be described as functional ones.

3. Miniature systems, in which restricted realms of data are summarized

according to a few special theories, are also congenial to the functionalist. There is a heuristic pluralism involved in functionalism, not unrelated to James' pluralism. That is, in order to move forward in the interpretation of data it is sometimes necessary to accept provisional (heuristic) interpretations that permit you to move ahead with the analysis. A case in point is VTE ("vicarious trial and error") as proposed by Muenzinger and followed up by Tolman. This rather limited segment of behavior (vacillation at the point of choice) is given a name and its conditions studied. The many systematic questions (Is it vicarious? Is it trial and error?) can be postponed until some of the functional relationships are explored. At this stage there is a pluralism, because there exist *ad hoc* concepts not related by definition or equations to the fundamentals of an established system.

Contemporary psychology, to the extent that it is increasingly operational, and increasingly concerned with mathematical models and miniature systems, reflects the general outlook that, in one form or another, has all along characterized the functionalist.

SUPPLEMENTARY READINGS

The following books are functional in content, although only those by Robinson and Woodworth are designed to state systematic positions:

COFER, C. N. (Editor) (1961) *Verbal learning and verbal behavior.*
McGEOCH, J. A., and IRION, A. L. (1952) *The psychology of human learning.*
MELTON, A. W. (Editor) (1964) *Categories of human learning.*
OSGOOD, C. E. (1953) *Method and theory in experimental psychology.*
ROBINSON, E. S. (1932a) *Association theory today.*
UNDERWOOD, B. J. (1966) *Experimental psychology* (Revised edition).
WOODWORTH, R. S. (1958) *Dynamics of behavior.*
WOODWORTH, R. S., and SCHLOSBERG, H. (1954) *Experimental psychology.*

For Woodworth's position (including a complete bibliography of his writings), plus many other matters relevant to the content of this book, see:

WOODWORTH, R. S., and SHEEHAN, MARY R. (1964) *Contemporary schools of psychology* (Third edition).

Mathematical Learning Theory

Since the experimental method for the study of learning was first introduced, a tradition of quantitative methods for recording, processing, and describing behavioral data has been established. The common measures of response tendencies are numerical in nature: amplitude or latency of response or relative frequency of occurrence. Even the earliest experimental papers of Thorndike and Ebbinghaus reported learning functions and forgetting functions in which some quantitative behavioral measure, such as time to respond or percentage of items correctly recalled, was graphed against the independent variable, practice trials or time elapsed since learning. This tradition has survived and it is now standard practice to report the results of experiments in terms either of mathematical functions or of verbal descriptions of the general class of functions (e.g., "performance declines with an increase in x").

MATHEMATICAL MODELS AND MATHEMATICAL LEARNING THEORY

Since 1950, one trend in American psychology has been towards framing hypotheses regarding learning which take seriously the quantitative details of behavioral data. These *mathematical models* of learning seek to predict the exact numerical details of experimental results. A major historical impetus to this trend came from the writings and theoretical work of Clark Hull (cf. Chapter 6). Hull argued forcibly for the development of quantitative theories in learning. His own work in this respect was mainly programmatic and yielded few genuinely quantitative predictions of numerical data. However, the type of program for which Hull argued appeared in significant form in the work of Estes, Burke, Bush, and Mosteller after 1950 under the designation *stochastic learning models.* Since then it has become a small but prominent focus of theoretical activity in learning research.

In 1950, Estes published the initial theoretical paper on stimulus sampling theory (SST). Soon thereafter, Bush and Mosteller (1951) published their initial work on the linear learning model, which is closely similar to the central model used in SST (see below). Throughout the following years, Estes and Burke at Indiana University and Bush and Mosteller at Harvard University worked in close collaboration on experimental and mathematical analysis of the linear model for learning. Many of the early developments are reviewed by Bush and Mosteller (1955) and Estes (1959a).

One important point to stress at the outset is that there is really no such thing as "mathematical learning theory." This term denotes a particular kind of approach to theory construction rather than a single, particular set of postulates which could be properly called "the theory." The use of mathematics is freely available to theorists of all persuasions. The mathematics involved is indifferent to the content of the psychological ideas expressed by it. That is, a diversity of substantive hypotheses about learning and behavior can be stated and analyzed in mathematical terms. Mathematical learning theory as a field is occupied by a loose confederation of workers, with different substantive ideas, whose only common bond is their use of mathematics as a vehicle for precise statement and for testing their hypotheses against data.

In overview, work in mathematical learning theory has concentrated around the experimental situations exploited by Hull, Skinner, and the functionalist tradition, namely, classical and instrumental conditioning, selective learning, and a major emphasis on human learning under laboratory conditions. By and large, too, most of the theoretical work has been predominantly in the vein of "stimulus–response associationism." However, this primarily reflects the background and predilections of workers in the mathematical idiom, since "cognitive" hypotheses can be and often have been represented in mathematical form.

Perhaps the signal contribution of mathematical learning theory has been to make us aware of the richness of relationships existing in our data. In its more successful instances, it has shown how this rich network of relationships in data is all perfectly predictable from a very simple conception of what rules (laws) govern the subject's behavior. To take a simple example, consider the data gathered from successive trials of a group of rats learning to turn right in a T maze. For a given subject, the data consist of a trial-by-trial sequence of his errors and correct responses. Writing "C" for "Correct" and "E" for "Error," a particular protocol might be CEECCECEEECCCCECC . . . (all the rest C). We would have one such protocol for each of our N subjects. Reduced to its barest essentials, the job for an adequate theory is to describe and account for such sequences of C's and E's. The best job of description, of course, is simply to reproduce the original sequences. Theories as economical abstractions do not seek to do this. However, they can try to predict the general statistical characteristics of a sample of such sequences. A partial list of such characteristics (or statistics) might include the average total errors before learning, the average trial number of the first success, of the nth success, of the last error, the average number of runs of errors, the number of alternations of successes and failures, and so forth. There is an indefinitely large number of such descriptive statistics that one may calculate. Each statistic asks a slightly different question of the data, and each provides us with a slightly different perspective upon (or snapshot of) the mass of data. A mathematical learning model tries to paint a simple hypothetical picture of the learning process which will integrate into one these different snapshots of, or perspectives on, the data. The way it achieves this is by predicting, to within a hopefully small random error, the numerical value of any statistic you care to calculate from the data. When successful, such a model serves both as an economical description of the data and as an explanation of it. That is, the data are, in a sense, explained when we have expressed the rules of operation of a theoretical system (or machine) that produces results similar to those which we observe.

Practically all extant models treat learning and performance as a probabilistic (or stochastic) process. A stochastic process is simply a sequence of events that can be analyzed in probability terms. The main dependent variable of such theories is the probability of various responses of the subject at any point in time, given his particular learning history. For example, in our T-maze illustration, in the theory we would let p_1, p_2, p_3, . . . represent the subject's probability of making a correct response on trial 1, on trial 2, on trial 3, etc. The model might then consist of a set of assumptions about how this response probability changes from trial to trial as a result of the outcomes the subject experiences on each trial. Given this representation of learning and performance as a trial sequence of response probabilities, the business of predicting statistics of the data then consists only of mathematical work within the probability calculus, which itself has no psychological content or significance. Because frequent mathematical problems arise in making such derivations, a certain portion of the literature in the field is concerned with such purely mathematical problems and the techniques for solving them.

From the discussion above, it may be inferred that mathematical models are usually highly specific, local sets of assumptions designed to characterize learning in particular situations, and that different situations require somewhat different models. By and large, this is true. There are advantages and disadvantages in the specificity inherent in mathematical models. One advantage is that it allows a very close comparison between data and theory, so that more theoretical "mileage" is gained from a given set of data. A related advantage is that if the model is inadequate, comparison of its predictions with data is very likely to disclose its faults at once in a glaring way. Because of this, no model currently espoused goes for very long without being shown to be inadequate for some situation or other. Thus a model originally formulated to fit data from situation A is found to fail on B, to fit C well, D with partial success, and fail again on situation E. An alternative model may fail on A, fit B partially, succeed well on F and G, miss on D and be mediocre on situation C. And there are probably still more competitors in the market place.

Such mild cacophonies, conflicting patterns of fits and misfits of competing models, are commonplace occurrences in the field. No one theory dominates all others in all situations, for all have their failings and incompletenesses. It is characteristic that contemporary workers in the field have come to view this conflict with composure rather than alarm, as a to-be-expected state of affairs rather than an occasion for scientific revolution. The models are admittedly simplified, idealized, incomplete caricatures of the behaving organism, and once certain situational constraints are altered the incompleteness of any one caricature becomes evident. But being incomplete or overly idealized is not the same as being dead wrong, because the model may work extremely well in restricted cases. The hope is that eventually we shall have a powerful super-theory that will be generally dominant, essentially reducing to model 1 for those cases where model 1 fits, reducing to model 2 for cases where model 2 fits, and so on. Such a powerful theory is not to be found in the contemporary scene and very likely it will not be for some time to come. However, the theoretical activity on a lower level continues at a steady pace.

Stimulus sampling theory (SST; also called statistical learning theory) as developed by Estes and Burke was intended to be a high level theory in the sense discussed above. Starting from a general set of theoretical assumptions, amounting essentially to a "viewpoint," specific models were to be derived to handle specific situations when various special assumptions were added to the general framework. Such a program is so flexible that, in one sense, it is difficult to decide whether it has succeeded or failed, or if indeed such a question is at all relevant. This general approach has certainly led to a proliferation of specific models and to much experimental testing of them, and the stimulus sampling framework appears to give them all a common origin.

Stimulus sampling theory has operated at several levels throughout its history: these may be called the quasi-quantitative and the specific-quantitative levels. In the quasi-quantitative mode, exemplified, say, in Estes' theory of drive or spontaneous recovery, the aim is to show how SST can explain the correct general trends of the empirical functions observed in previous work, but no strong emphasis is laid upon precise validation of the mathematical description. Most of Clark Hull's theoretical work was quasi-quantitative in this same sense. In the specific-quantitative mode, however, it is intended that a specific model be put through the wringer of stringent tests, fitting many numerical aspects of a set of data, with attendant requirements that certain constants (parameters) of the model remain invariant as experimental conditions are varied that theoretically should not affect these parameters, and so on. Operation in this specific-quantitative mode can be a bone-crushing encounter for a plausible quasi-quantitative theory, and few will pass muster. In fact, only very few theories about learning are formulated with sufficient precision to even permit a test of this nature. One virtue of SST is that specific models derived from it can be put to this kind of test. Some of the models have passed these stringent tests with sufficient regularity to warrant discussing them in our review.

STIMULUS SAMPLING THEORY

In many respects, SST represents a formalization of Guthrie's approach to stimulus–response associationism (cf. Chapter 4). The stimulus situation is represented as a population of independently variable components or aspects of the total environment, called stimulus elements. At any moment (experimental trial), only a sample of elements from the total population is active or effective. The less variable the experimental conditions, the less variable are the successive trial samples of stimulus elements.

Two sources of random variation in stimulation may be identified: the first arises from incidental changes in the environment during the experiment (extraneous noises, temperature fluctuations, stray odors, etc.); and the second arises from changes in the subject, either from changing orientation of his receptors (what he is looking at or listening to), from changes in his posture or response-produced stimuli, or from fluctuations in his sensory transmission system (e.g., the temporal and spatial pattern of electrical activity in the auditory cortex evoked by the sound of a bell). There is no commitment to any fixed amount of such stimulus variability; that is to be estimated by the theory. Thus, in simple learning situations in which the experimenter is applying the "same" stimulus (say, the sound of a bell) at the onset of each trial, this may be represented simply as a potential population of N stimulus elements.

On each trial, only a sample of the N elements will be active or effective. If we think of the stimulus elements represented as N marbles in an urn, any particular sample represents a handful of marbles drawn from the urn. Various sampling schemes are possible, but two simple ones have been most widely employed in theoretical discussions. One scheme supposes that each stimulus element has probability θ of being sampled, independently of how many other elements are sampled. According to this scheme, the number of elements in the sample will randomly vary from one trial to the next, with the average sample size consisting of $N\theta$ elements. The second scheme supposes that a fixed number of elements are drawn at random without replacement from the N elements of the population. If we let s represent the fixed sample size, then each element has an overall probability of s/N of appearing in the sample. However, the samplings of any two elements are not independent in this scheme, but rather are negatively correlated; that is, sampling of one element may preclude sampling of another since only a fixed number are sampled. The special models obtained when it is assumed that $s = 1$ are called "pattern" models. They have been much investigated, and are reviewed later.

The Conditioning Assumptions

This much of the system tells us how the stimulus situation and trial sample are represented. To make contact with performance, the theory assumes that each stimulus element is conditioned to (connected to) one response. In a two-choice experiment, say, some elements would be connected to response alternative A_1 and some to the other alternative, A_2; in a free-operant situation, A_1 might be "pressing the lever" and A_2 would denote any behavior other than lever pressing. The procedure for identifying the relevant response alternatives is simply that commonly used by experimenters. It is supposed that the conditional connection between a stimulus element and a response is unitary and at full strength, not varying in degree. According to this approach, we can characterize the subject's dispositions at any moment in our situation by listing the various stimulus elements and the relevant response which is currently associated with each element. Such a listing is the theoretical "state of the system" as it applies to an individual at this time. Throughout the course of learning, the elements will be changing their associations for this subject; alternately, we would say that the state of the system is changing trial by trial.

Since the probabilities of the various responses depend on the state of the system, we have to calculate the state of the system as trials progress. Can we find a useful way to represent the state of the system so that these calculations can be simplified? Indeed we can, and the reason for this is that the sampling schemes mentioned above assign an *equal* sampling probability to each element. Because of this assumption, we do not need to know *which* elements are associated with which responses in order to predict response probability. All we really need to know is *what proportion* of the stimulus elements are associated with each response. For example, in a two-response experiment, we could let p denote the proportion of elements associated with response A_1 and $1 - p$ denote the remaining proportion of elements associated with response A_2. In this case, our description of the "state of the system" reduces to the single number, p. And calculations of this single number are considerably easier to follow than would be calculations on the changing listing of S–R associations.

Performance on any trial is determined by the elements which are experienced, or "sampled" on that trial. The probability of any response is equal to the proportion of sampled elements on that trial that are connected to that response. If a sample of size 10 contains 5 elements connected to A_1, 3 to A_2, and 2 to A_3, then the probabilities are 0.5, 0.3, and 0.2, respectively, that the response will be A_1, A_2, or A_3. If the number of elements is large so that the statistical "law of large numbers" applies, this performance rule has the effect of setting the probability of response A_1 equal to p, the proportion of A_1-connected elements in the population. It is usually assumed that this is the case.

Having drawn a stimulus sample and responded, the subject then receives some reinforcing outcome. It is these outcomes that change the conditional connections of the elements sampled on a trial, thus altering the state of the system. In theory, if r response classes have been identified, then $r + 1$ theoretical reinforcing events are defined, denoted E_0, E_1, E_2, . . . , E_r. It is supposed that exactly one of these reinforcing events occurs at the termination of the trial. Events E_1, E_2, . . . , E_r refer to reinforcement of responses A_1, A_2, . . . , A_r, whereas E_0 denotes that none of the responses was reinforced. If a trial terminates with reinforcing event E_k, then all elements sampled on that trial become conditioned to response A_k if they were not already so conditioned. For example, if an element connected to A_1 is sampled on a trial when reinforcement E_2 occurs, then this element switches its conditional connection from A_1 to A_2 in an all-or-none manner. Finally, E_0 denotes a null event; occurrence of E_0 means that none of the responses was reinforced, so no change occurs in the conditional connections of the sampled elements.

Let us comment upon these conditioning assumptions. First, these axioms presumably describe the dynamic changes in the state of the system over trials, and this is what learning is considered to be. By these rules, successive practice trials result in the attachment of the rewarded or "correct" response to progressively more stimulus elements sampled from the population, with the resultant detachment of "error" responses from these elements. The exact description of this process is given below. Second, we note that following Guthrie, SST assumes all-or-none conditioning of the sampled elements to the reinforced response. Conditioning of response A_1

is achieved at the expense of removing associations from alternative responses, and no special postulates regarding extinction are needed. Extinction is by "interference" in the sense that the probability of some reference response A_2 declines while the likelihood of a competing response A_1 increases.

This representation of reinforcing events is theoretically neutral. For particular applications, one must make substantive assumptions about the relationships between the hypothetical reinforcing events and the actual trial outcomes—food reward for turning left in a T maze, the unconditioned stimulus or its absence in classical conditioning, information about the correct answer in verbal learning, etc. Alternative interpretations are possible at this point. As a matter of personal preference, Estes and Burke have tried consistently to apply Guthrie's contiguity theory of reinforcement to interpreting the relationship between trial outcomes and the hypothetical reinforcing events. The Guthrian assumption is that the last response (overt or covert) to occur in the presence of the trial stimulus sample is the one that becomes associated with the elements of that sample. The effect of an empirical reinforcing operation is either (a) to insure that the appropriate response is evoked at the end of the trial (e.g., the US in classical conditioning evokes the response to be conditioned, information evokes rehearsal of the correct response in verbal learning, etc.) or (b) to delay or prevent the occurrence of competing reactions before the subject is removed from the trial stimulation (e.g., feeding a hungry rat in the goalbox of a straight alley). This contiguity interpretation of reinforcement is not a necessary adjunct of stimulus sampling theory. More often, the users of the theory simply employ a general law of effect: if the outcome of a particular trial has the effect of increasing the probability of response A_1, then this trial's outcome is identified as E_1 in the model. Secondly, this scheme for representing reinforcing events can accommodate the quantitative effects of variations in the traditional "reinforcement parameters" such as magnitude, quality, and delay of reinforcement. This consists of postulating particular probabilistic relationships between the particular trial outcome (e.g., the amount of food given as a reward to a hungry rat) and the hypothetical reinforcing events. For example, it might be assumed that the more food given following an A_1 response, the more likely it is that an E_1 rather than an E_0 event occurs on that trial. Later we show how this approach can be implemented.

Derivation of Basic Difference Equations

The state of the system, it will be recalled, is given by the fractions of stimulus elements conditioned to the various response alternatives. The assumptions of the theory permit us to derive how these proportions will change from trial to trial as a result of the reinforcing events. We will illustrate this for a two-alternative situation. Let p and $1 - p$ denote the proportions of elements connected to responses A_1 and A_2. Since these proportions will be changing over trials, we use a subscript to denote the trial number in question. Thus, p_n will denote the proportion of A_1-connected elements at the moment of evocation of the response on the nth trial. p_n may also be interpreted as (a) the probability that any randomly selected single element in the population is connected to A_1, and as (b) the probability that the response on trial n will be A_1.

Suppose that an E_1 reinforcing event occurs in trial n. We wish to calculate p_{n+1}, the probability that an element is conditioned to A_1 at the beginning of the next trial, $n + 1$. The equation may be written in two equivalent forms, where we recall that θ is the probability that a stimulus element is sampled on any given trial:

$$p_{n+1} = p_n + \theta (1 - p_n) \tag{1a}$$

$$p_{n+1} = (1 - \theta)\, p_n + \theta. \tag{1b}$$

Equation (1a) may be interpreted as follows: with probability p_n the element is already conditioned to A_1 and remains so conditioned when E_1 occurs on this trial; with probability $1 - p_n$ the element was formerly connected to A_2 but it switches to an A_1 connection if it is sampled (an event having probability θ) on this E_1 trial. Equation (1b), which is identical to Eq. (1a), is interpreted slightly differently: with probability $1 - \theta$ the element is not sampled, so its probability of being connected to A_1 remains at p_n; with probability θ the element is sampled, so the E_1 event conditions it to A_1 with certainty.

Let us note a few mathematical facts about Eq. 1 in either form. First, p_{n+1} will be greater than or equal to p_n, so an E_1 reinforcement increases the probability of an A_1 response. Second, p_{n+1} is a linear (straight line) function of p_n. From this fact comes the name "linear model," in reference to a system of such equations. Third, an E_1 event increases p to an eventual limit (or asymptote) of unity. That is, when $p_n = 1$, then Eq. 1 will give $p_{n+1} = 1$. In fact, the limit of any such equation may be generally defined as that value of p where $p_{n+1} = p_n$ (i.e., when p reaches its limiting value, it stops changing). If a consistent series of E_1 events were given, corresponding to repeated applications of Eq. 1, p would increase from some initial value and approach an asymptote of unity. Thus, Eq. 1 implies that consistent E_1 reinforcements would eventually lead to consistent occurrences of A_1 responses.

Suppose that an E_2 reinforcing event occurs on trial n. This should lower p_n and increase $1 - p_n$, the probability that an element is connected to A_2. Two equivalent versions of this equation are

$$p_{n+1} = (1 - \theta)\, p_n + \theta \cdot 0 = (1 - \theta)\, p_n \qquad (2a)$$

$$(1 - p_{n+1}) = (1 - \theta)\ (1 - p_n) + \theta. \qquad (2b)$$

The reader may prove for himself that these two equations are identical. To interpret (2a): with probability $1 - \theta$ the element is not sampled and so remains connected to A_1 with the same probability as before, namely p_n; with probability θ it is sampled and the E_2 event connects it to A_2 so that its connection to A_1 has probability zero. To interpret (2b): the probability, $1 - p_n$, of an A_2 response is increased by an E_2 event by exactly the same reasoning that led to Eq. (1b) whereby an E_1 event increased p_n. That is, the effect of E_1 on p_n is the same as the effect of E_2 on $1 - p_n$.

Examining Eq. (2a), it is seen that (a) p_{n+1} is less than or equal to p_n since $1 - \theta$ is a fraction (a probability), (b) p_{n+1} is a linear function of p_n, and (c) the limit of this equation is zero. That is, a succession of E_2 reinforcing events, with correspondingly repeated applications of Eq. (2a), would reduce p_n to zero, where A_1 responses would cease and A_2 responses would consistently occur.

Finally consider that a null E_0 event occurs on trial n. This null event produces no change in conditioning of the sampled elements. An equation which expresses this preservation of the status quo is simply $p_{n+1} = p_n$.

To collect the equations into summary form, we use $E_{i,n}$ to denote the event of E_i occurring on trial n. We have

$$p_{n+1} = \begin{cases} (1 - \theta)\, p_n + \theta & \text{if } E_{1,n} \\ (1 - \theta)\, p_n & \text{if } E_{2,n} \\ p_n & \text{if } E_{0,n} \end{cases} \qquad (3)$$

These equations constitute the core of the "linear model." We note that they are *difference equations*, expressing how a variable (p_n) changes its value from one discrete point in time (trial n) to the next point in time (trial $n + 1$).

These equations express the trial-by-trial incremental or decremental effects of reinforcing events. A learning curve consists of a plot of the performance probabilities $p_1, p_2, p_3, \ldots, p_n$ over the successive practice trials $1, 2, 3, \ldots, n$ of the experiment. If we wish to predict the learning curve, we simply trace out the trial-by-trial effect of applying Eq. 1 or 2 to the initial value p_1 from which the process begins on trial 1. Suppose that we have a consistent sequence of E_1 events; then we would repeatedly apply Eq. 1. That is, p_2 is calculated from p_1 by Eq. 1. Then p_3 is calculated from p_2 using Eq. 1 again, etc. The result of doing this is the following general expression:

$$p_n = 1 - (1 - p_1)(1 - \theta)^{n-1}. \tag{4}$$

This expression gives p_n as a "negatively accelerated" function of practice trials, n. The limit of p_n is 1 since the fraction $1 - \theta$ decreases to zero as it is raised to higher and higher powers. Some graphs of this function are shown in Figure 11-1. For these curves, $p_1 = 0.20$ and θ is 0.05, 0.10, and 0.20 for the three curves. The curve rises faster for larger values of θ. Recall that θ is the probability that a stimulus element is sampled; when θ is low, there will be much trial-to-trial variability in the composition of the stimulus sample; when θ is high, most elements will always be present so one sample will vary little from another. We see in Figure 11-1 how this stimulus variability affects the rate of learning. The retarding influence of increased stimulus variability upon learning was first noted by Pavlov (the phenomena of "external inhibition"). Later experiments by Wolfle (1936), Green (1956), and Burke, Estes, and Hellyer (1954) give results interpretable in terms of θ variations.

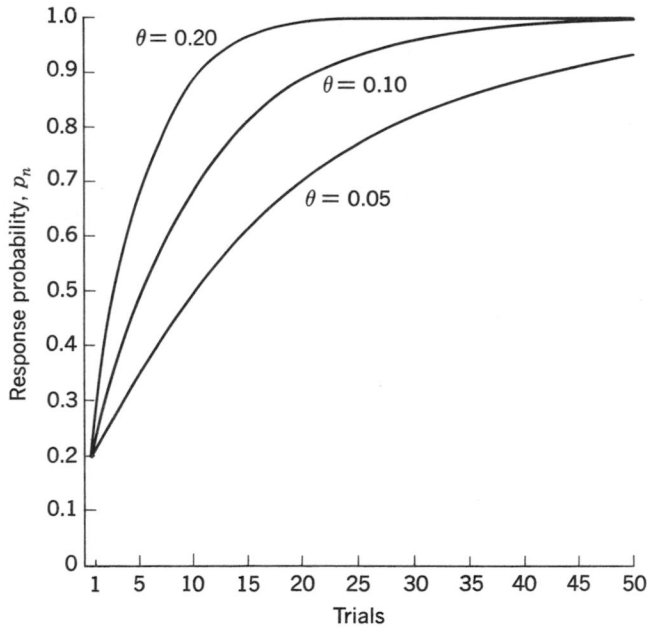

Figure 11-1   Graphs of the function p_n described by Eq. 4, where $p_1 = 0.20$ and the learning rate, θ, has the values of 0.05, 0.10, and 0.20 for the three curves.

Variations in Outcome Effectiveness

We digress briefly to show how the system might handle variations in rewarding outcomes provided to the subject. It will help to have a specific situation in mind, so let us consider the following: a hungry rat receives training in a T maze where he gets 0.5 grams of food reward for A_1 choices and 0.3 grams of food reward for A_2 choices. The two possible outcomes on a trial are A_1 and 0.5 grams, and A_2 and 0.3 grams, which we will denote as O_1 and O_2. In writing theoretical equations to represent this situation, we clearly want outcome O_1 to increase the probability of an A_1 response, p_n, and want O_2 to increase the probability of an A_2 response, or decrease p_n. Moreover, if we think that the larger amount of food reward is more effective, then we wish to indicate that the effect of O_1 upon p_n is larger than the corresponding effect of O_2 upon $1 - p_n$. The form of the equations we require is as follows:

$$p_{n+1} = \begin{cases} (1 - \theta_1)p_n + \theta_1 & \text{if } O_{1,n} & \text{(5a)} \\ (1 - \theta_2)p_n & \text{if } O_{2,n} & \text{(5b)} \end{cases}$$

The assumption that $\theta_1 > \theta_2$ will express the greater effectiveness of the larger reward; then the first linear equation would increase p_n more than the second equation increases $1 - p_n$.

A small inconsistency arises in SST, however, by the postulation of different θ values for different outcomes, since the stimulus sampling should occur at the choice point of the T maze before the choice and reward occurs. An alternative formulation which preserves consistency is to suppose that the different reward outcomes have different probabilities of producing an E_1, E_2, or E_0 reinforcing event. Let us assume, for example, that the 0.5 gram reward reinforces its response (produces an E_1 event) with some high probability b_1, but fails to reinforce (produces an E_0 event) with probability $1 - b_1$. In other words, we assume that on a fraction b_1 of the O_1 trials, event E_1 occurs, whereas on the remaining $1 - b_1$ proportion of the O_1 trials, event E_0 occurs. Similarly, assume that the 0.3 gram reward reinforces its response (E_2) with a lower probability b_2, and fails to do so with probability $1 - b_2$. The average effect of O_1 upon p_n may be obtained by averaging the appropriate parts of Eq. 3, namely,

$$p_{n+1} = b_1[(1 - \theta)p_n + \theta] + (1 - b_1)\,p_n = (1 - b_1\,\theta)p_n + b_1\,\theta$$
$$= (1 - \theta_1)p_n + \theta_1.$$

In the last line we have substituted $\theta_1 = b_1\,\theta$. We have thus arrived at an equation similar to Eq. (5a) for an O_1 event. A similar development will give us Eq. (5b) for an O_2 event. By this means then, we can represent differential effectiveness of outcomes in terms of the size of the learning parameter in the linear equations. A paper by Clayton (1964) shows how something like this scheme may be used to predict performance of animals in a differential reward situation.

APPLICATION OF SST TO SELECTED PROBLEMS

Response to Stimulus Compound

The question is whether we can predict the probabilities of the various responses to a compound of several stimuli given knowledge of how the individual elements of the compound are connected to the responses. If one set of elements, denoted S_1, is connected to response A_1, another set, denoted S_2, is connected to A_2, how are we to predict response probability to a compound or test pattern consisting of n_1 elements from S_1 and n_2 elements from S_2? The assumption of SST is that the response probabilities are determined by the proportions of stimulus elements in the sample connected to the various responses. In the test situation described above, the probability of response A_1 is expected to be $n_1/(n_1 + n_2)$, and of A_2, $n_2/(n_1 + n_2)$. Further, let S_3 be a third set of stimulus elements with a random one-half of the S_3 elements connected to A_1 and one-half of the elements connected to A_2. If the test compound consists of n_1 elements from S_1, n_2 from S_2, and n_3 from S_3, then the expected proportion of A_1 responses is

$$p = \frac{n_1 + \frac{1}{2}n_3}{n_1 + n_2 + n_3}.$$

The $\frac{1}{2} n_3$ term in the numerator is the expected number of A_1-connected elements of the n_3 drawn from the S_3 stimulus set.

An experiment by Schoeffler (1954) provides a test of these predictions. The three sets of stimulus elements were identified as different sets of 8 small jewel lamps in a 24-lamp display in front of the subject. Subjects were first trained to move a switch in one direction (A_1) when elements of the S_1 set were presented, and to move it in the opposite direction (A_2) when elements of the S_2 set were presented. The S_3 lamps never occurred during this preliminary training, and the theory presupposes that these elements start off (and remain) randomly connected, half to A_1 and half to A_2. Following this preliminary training, subjects were tested for their response to different combinations of the S_1, S_2, and S_3 elements (lamps). During the test series, subjects were told to respond as they thought appropriate and there was no information feedback concerning the "correct" response.

The test combinations used and the results obtained are shown in Table 11-1 along with the predictions from three different combination rules. To illustrate how Table 11-1 is to be interpreted, consider the fifth test pattern (row 5) consisting of 8 bulbs of the S_1 set, 4 randomly selected bulbs of the S_2 set, and all 8 bulbs of the S_3 set. To this combination, the average relative frequency of response A_1 for the group of subjects was 0.62.

Table 11-1 Proportions of A_1 responses, observed and predicted, to each of nine test patterns (rows). Composition of the test patterns is indicated by the column entries under S_1, S_2, S_3. See text for explanation of predictions. Data from Schoeffler (1954), with permission from the American Psychological Association.

Test Pattern	No. of elements from			Observed $p(A_1)$	Predicted by		
	S_1	S_2	S_3		Aver. Rule	Neutral Elements	Majority Rule
1	8	8	0	0.54	0.50	0.50	0.50
2	8	4	0	0.79	0.67	0.67	1.00
3	8	2	0	0.81	0.80	0.80	1.00
4	4	2	0	0.63	0.67	0.67	1.00
5	8	4	8	0.62	0.60	0.67	1.00
6	8	2	8	0.67	0.67	0.80	1.00
7	4	2	8	0.54	0.57	0.67	1.00
8	8	0	8	0.73	0.75	1.00	1.00
9	8	8	8	0.54	0.50	0.50	0.50

The column of predicted values labeled "averaging rule" uses the formula derived from SST above. For example, for test 6 consisting of 8, 2, and 8 elements from S_1, S_2, and S_3, respectively, the predicted value is

$$p_6 = \frac{8 + \frac{1}{2}\cdot 8}{8 + 2 + 8} = \frac{12}{18} = 0.67$$

This predicted value is identical with the 0.67 value observed. In fact, except for the second test pattern, the predictions of the averaging rule are uniformly close to the observed values.

The "neutral elements" rule, an alternative suggested by LaBerge's work (1959), applies the averaging rule with the exception that S_3 elements are presumed to be neutral and to contribute neither to A_1 nor A_2. For instance, in test 6, the neutral-elements hypothesis deletes the 8 S_3 elements and predicts $p = 8/(8 + 2) = 0.80$. From Table 11-1 it is seen that in tests 5 through 8 where the two sets of predictions differ, the neutral-elements rule is consistently inferior to the averaging rule.

The last hypothesis, labeled "majority rule" in Table 11-1, assumes that the response is determined by whichever conditioned elements are in the majority in the sample. This rule, which at first thought seems plausible, is discredited by these data.

There are many other sets of data of this general type, in which the averaging rule is tested by its predictions about response proportions to novel combinations of conditioned stimuli. By and large, the averaging rule has fared quite well throughout these various tests, and it seems an excellent working assumption to handle these kinds of problems.

Probability Learning

A considerable portion of the early experimental work in SST was carried out in the probability learning situation. In its simplest arrangement, the task for the subject is to predict on each trial which one of two events is going to occur. After he has made his predictive response, the actual event is shown. The common feature of these experiments is that the events occur in a random sequence and there is usually no information available to help the subject predict perfectly which event will occur. The label "probability learning" describes this fact about the situation.

We let A_1 and A_2 denote the subject's two predictive responses and E_1 and E_2 the two events, E_i meaning that response A_i was correct on a given trial. Suppose that π_n denotes the probability that the reinforcing event E_1 occurs on trial n, and $1 - \pi_n$ is the probability of an E_2 on trial n. If an E_1 event occurs, p_n is assumed to increase; if an E_2 event occurs, p_n is assumed to decrease. The average change in the A_1 response probability is obtained by weighting the two parts of Eq. 3 by π_n and $1 - \pi_n$ to obtain the following:

$$p_{n+1} = \pi_n[(1 - \theta)p_n + \theta] + (1 - \pi_n)[(1 - \theta)p_n] = (1 - \theta)p_n + \theta\,\pi_n. \tag{6}$$

There are a variety of procedures (or schedules) the experimenter can use to decide whether to show E_1 or E_2 on a given trial. To list a few examples, the probability of an E_1 on trial n might (a) be a constant π, (b) increase or decrease in some systematic manner as trials proceed, (c) vary depending on the response of trial n, (d) vary depending on the response or reinforcing event that occurred a few trials back in the sequence. Independently of how the sequence is generated, Eq. 6 makes the general prediction that the long-term average proportion of A_1 responses will eventually come to match (equal) the long-term average proportion of E_1 events. To show this, we take the average of both sides of Eq. 6 by summing over trials 1 to N, and dividing by N. The result is

$$\frac{1}{N}\sum_{n=1}^{N} p_{n+1} = (1 - \theta)\frac{1}{N}\sum_{n=1}^{N} p_n + \theta\,\frac{1}{N}\sum_{n=1}^{N} \pi_n$$

$$\frac{1}{N}\left[p_{N+1} - p_1 + \theta\sum_{n=1}^{N} p_n\right] = \frac{\theta}{N}\sum_{n=1}^{N} \pi_n.$$

To take the long-term average, we let the number of trials N become very large. In this case, the term $p_{N+1} - p_1$ divided by N becomes negligible (zero) and our final result is

$$\frac{1}{N}\sum_{n=1}^{N} p_n = \frac{1}{N}\sum_{n=1}^{N} \pi_n. \tag{7}$$

This equation says that the average proportion of A_1 responses over a large number of trials should be equal to the average proportion of E_1 events over those trials. This is called the "probability matching" theorem and it results from assuming that E_1 and E_2 have symmetric effects in increasing p_n and $1 - p_n$.

This matching prediction has been tested for a variety of reinforcement schedules. By and large, the prediction has been confirmed; moreover, the theory's predictions are usually fairly accurate regarding the shape of the learning curve under particular schedules (see Estes, 1959a). A paper by Estes (1964) reviews and systematically classifies those experiments which consistently yield matching results and those which yield results discrepant to some degree with matching. For example, it is known that the matching prediction is wrong when monetary payoffs and penalties are introduced for correct and incorrect predictions. Estes (1962) and Myers and Atkinson (1964) consider several generalizations of SST that will handle these discrepant cases.

To illustrate a few cases of predictive success of the simple model, let us return to Eq. 6 and consider the schedule where the probability of the E_1 event varies depending upon the response made on that trial. Specifically, let us suppose that the probability of E_1 is π_1 if response A_1 is made, and is π_2 if response A_2 is made; otherwise, an E_2 event occurs. For this schedule, the average probability of an E_1 on trial n is seen to be

$$\pi_n = p_n \pi_1 + (1 - p_n) \pi_2.$$

The first term represents the probability of an A_1 response followed by an E_1 reinforcing event; the second term represents the probability of an A_2 response following by an E_1 event. If we substitute this expression for π_n into Eq. 6 and simplify, we arrive at the following result:

$$p_{n+1} = [1 - \theta(1 - \pi_1 + \pi_2)]p_n + \theta \pi_2$$

or

$$p_{n+1} = p_n + \theta [\pi_2 - (1 - \pi_1 + \pi_2)p_n]. \tag{8}$$

For this case, we ask what is the limiting value attained when p stops changing? This limiting value is attained when the added term (inside the bracket) in Eq. 8 is zero, since at this value no more change in p occurs. Thus the asymptote is that value of p where

$$\pi_2 - (1 - \pi_1 + \pi_2)p = 0.$$

Hence, we have

$$p = \frac{\pi_2}{1 - \pi_1 + \pi_2}. \tag{9}$$

We note that, as in Eq. 7, the predicted asymptotic proportion of A_1 responses is independent of the learning rate θ. The asymptote depends on the relative "disconfirmation" probabilities: note that π_2 is the likelihood of an E_1 given an A_2 response, and the $1 - \pi_1$ term in the denominator is the likelihood of an E_2 given an A_1 response. An experiment by Suppes and Atkinson (1960) reports data relevant to these predictions. They ran three groups of 48 students on the π_1 and π_2 values specified in Table 11-2. The subjects were told to predict whether a left- or right-hand bulb would light on each trial. Each subject was run for 300 trials; the proportions shown in Table 11-2 are the group average proportion of A_1 responses over the last 100 trials, where performance was judged to have reached its limiting value. Examination of Table 11-2 shows the theoretical predictions from Eq. 9 were very accurate in this case.

Table 11-2 Average A_1 proportions at asymptote under response-contingent reinforcement schedules (data excerpted from Suppes and Atkinson, 1960, page 253).

π_1	π_2	Observed	Predicted
0.67	0.60	0.650	0.645
0.67	0.80	0.700	0.706
0.40	0.80	0.560	0.571

This probability matching result has been pursued in a variety of ways. Binder and Feldman (1960), for example, have shown that it predicts response frequencies on tests with single stimulus components which in previous training had been parts of stimulus patterns. To illustrate, suppose we let a, b, c represent three component elements. To the pattern ab we train response A_1; to the pattern cb we train response A_2. We unbalance the frequencies so that the ab pattern occurs, say, four times as frequently as the cb pattern. Binder and Feldman found that a later test to b alone resulted in approximately 80% A_1 responses and 20% A_2 responses. This result may be interpreted in SST by noting that when the b element occurred (within the training patterns), four out of five times response A_1 was reinforced. Hence, the probability that b is connected to A_1 would come to match this 4/5 relative frequency of E_1 to E_2 reinforcements.

Another line of work investigates probability matching in elementary "interaction" situations involving two subjects at once. The two subjects work concurrently on probability learning tasks in lock-step trials. On each trial, each subject makes one of two responses and receives reinforcement for one of these. The new wrinkle is that the probabilities of the reinforcing events on each trial depend upon the responses of both subjects on that trial. The reinforcement schedules for the two subjects are interactive in the sense that the probability of an E_1 event for subject A depends on B's response as well as A's. Special mathematical techniques are required to apply the model to such situations since both A's and B's behaviors are changing over trials. When applied to a variety of such interactive conditions, the asymptotic predictions come quite close to the obtained data (cf. Suppes and Atkinson, 1960). As before, the prediction is that both subjects will eventually match their A_1 response frequency to their E_1 event frequency. The only complication is the difficulty encountered in calculating this E_1 event probability in a given interactive situation.

A generalization of the probability learning experiment and theory has been investigated by Suppes and his coworkers (e.g., Suppes *et al.,* 1964). In their procedure, the subject's response and the reinforcing event can vary over an entire continuum on which there are, in principle, an infinite number of response alternatives. In the task employed, the subject tries to predict where a spot of light will appear on the edge of a large circle before him. Suppes' generalization of the linear model to this situation appears to do a fairly good job of accounting for the mean response distributions. Discussion of the nature of the model and data would take us too far afield for our present purposes.

Sequential Statistics

In the discussion above, we were interested in discovering whether the model would predict the mean learning curve and the limiting value of the average response proportions as trials increase. Part of the power of stochastic learning models is that they permit us to predict much more than just these mean response curves. In principle, predictions may be derived for any feature of the data we care to examine.

An important source of information about the learning process is provided by *sequential statistics.* These gauge the extent to which a subject's response on trial $n + 1$ is influenced by his responses and/or reinforcing events on one or more prior trials. The immediate history of events for a subject on trials $n, n - 1$, etc., have a large effect upon his response probability on trial $n + 1$. Sequential statistics enable us to examine these effects. The mean response curve is not informative on this score since in averaging over subjects we pool together subjects for whom different events occurred on trials $n, n - 1$, etc. In this sense, sequential statistics provide a more detailed examination of learning than does the classical "learning curve." Additionally, sequential statistics continue to yield useful measures of the incremental and decremental effects of single trial events long after the average response probability has reached its limiting value and has ceased to provide any new information.

To illustrate these matters, we consider a two-response experiment where E_1 occurs with a fixed probability π and we examine the process after a large number of trials, after the mean response proportions have ceased changing. We will be concerned with the probability of an A_1 response given that a particular response-and-reinforcement combination occurred on the previous trial, namely A_1E_1, A_1E_2, A_2E_1, and A_2E_2. We will write the conditional probability of A_1 given that A_1E_1 occurred on the previous trial as $P(A_1|A_1E_1)$; similarly for the other three combinations. It is possible to derive a theoretical expression for each of these quantities, and they depend upon θ and π. Once a numerical value of θ has been estimated, predictions of these sequential probabilities are possible. For derivational details the reader may consult Atkinson, Bower and Crothers (1965) or Suppes and Atkinson (1960).

To illustrate the results of this procedure, we may review the results of an experiment by Suppes and Atkinson (1960). Thirty college students were run 240 trials in a two-choice probability learning task with $\pi = 0.60$. Tabulation of response frequencies over the last 100 trials, when mean performance had ceased changing, gave the results displayed in Table 11-3. The first entry shows that the observed mean A_1-response probability came to approximate closely the probability matching value $\pi = 0.60$. The next four entries show the A_1 probability conditional upon the four response-reinforcement events on the prior trial. The last four entries give A_1 proportions conditional upon only the prior response or the prior reinforcing event.

Table 11-3 Observed and predicted sequential statistics for the Suppes–Atkinson experiment (1960). These show the conditional probability that an A_1 response occurs following the specified events of the preceding trial. For the predictions, the θ estimate is 0.185. The first entry and the last four are derivable from the four joint probabilities and the fact that $\pi = 0.60$. Hence they are not independent predictions once the joint probabilities have been predicted.

	Observed	Predicted
$P(A_1)$	0.596	0.600
$P(A_1|E_1A_1)$	0.715	0.708
$P(A_1|E_2A_1)$	0.535	0.524
$P(A_1|E_1A_2)$	0.603	0.624
$P(A_1|E_2A_2)$	0.413	0.439
$P(A_1|A_1)$	0.641	0.635
$P(A_1|A_2)$	0.532	0.550
$P(A_1|E_1)$	0.667	0.675
$P(A_1|E_2)$	0.488	0.490

It is noteworthy that these conditional probabilities vary over a wide range (from 0.413 to 0.715) even though the mean response probability is relatively constant near 0.60. Thus, there are powerful sequential effects from trial to trial in these data. To get an intuitive understanding of these sequential statistics, let us consider which events on the prior trial promote or demote the probability of A_1 on the current trial. First, an E_1 event will increase p_n whereas an E_2 event will decrease it; the bottom two lines show this difference. Second, when we select out those trials following the occurrence of A_1 on the prior trial, we will be selecting out those cases (trials and/or subjects) where the past history of reinforcing events has produced a higher than average bias towards the A_1 response. Other things being equal, we would thus expect that the probability of response A_1 will be higher for those subjects who make A_1 on the previous trial than for those who make A_2. This effect is shown in lines 6 and 7 of Table 11-3. The probability of A_1 following a given combination of the response and reinforcing event on the prior trial may be considered the result of these two effects adding together or canceling each other out, depending on whether the A and E are the same or different.

Comparison of the observed proportions with those predicted by the theory shows them to be in excellent agreement. The predictions from the theory depend upon getting a numerical estimate of θ from these various data. The estimate was $\theta = 0.185$. The linear model provides a very good fit to the details of these data. For more information on tests of the model in the probability learning situation, the reader is referred to papers by Estes (1964) and Friedman *et al.* (1964). Anderson (1964) provides a thoughtful analysis of the shortcomings of the model in this context. In Chapter 12, we discuss a computer simulation theory designed to deal with this probability learning situation.

Spontaneous Recovery and Forgetting

The phenomena of spontaneous recovery and forgetting have been recognized for a long time. Pavlov was the first to report facts regarding spontaneous recovery. Following experimental extinction of a conditioned response (CR), the CR showed some recovery if the dog was removed from the apparatus and allowed to sit in his home cage for a while before being returned to the experimental situation and tested. The CR had "spontaneously recovered" without any special reconditioning by the experimenter. Later studies have shown that the amount of recovery increases with the length of the rest interval between sessions. Pavlov and others have also performed experiments in which the CR is repeatedly extinguished over consecutive daily sessions. Their report is that the amount of recovery of the CR becomes progressively less as the extinction sessions proceed; eventually, the CR recovers not at all.

The salient facts about forgetting (spontaneous regressions) are markedly similar to those that characterize spontaneous recovery (e.g., Ebbinghaus, 1885). The amount forgotten increases with the time that has elapsed since the end of practice and the amount of session-to-session forgetting becomes progressively less as daily practice on a task continues. Apparently Estes (1955a) was the first to point out the apposition of spontaneous recovery and forgetting. Once it has been pointed out, the similarities of their functional laws are indeed apparent.

Estes (1955a) proposed to interpret these spontaneous changes in response probabilities as due, to some extent at least, to random changes in the stimulating environment from one experimental session to the next. In our previous discussion of stimulus sampling theory, it was assumed that the stimulus population was fixed and that random samples from this population were effective from trial to trial. Estes proposes now to expand this representation by assuming that at any given time only a subset of the total stimulus population is available for sampling, the remainder not being available at this point in time. Over time, different stimulus elements become effective or available for sampling, whereas previously available elements may become unavailable. The type of factors Estes presumably has in mind can be illustrated by day-to-day fluctuations in the temperature and humidity of the experimental room, changes in the subject's internal milieu, in his postural sets or attitudes, in the sensitivity of various receptors, and the like. Such fluctuations in subtle stimuli are practically beyond control. There need be no commitment in the theory regarding the magnitude of these changes; the amount of such change is to be estimated by inference from the change in behavior.

It is clear that if such random stimulus fluctuations do occur, then they help account for spontaneous changes in response probabilities between experimental testing sessions. Regression would occur if available elements conditioned to the response are replaced during a rest interval by elements, previously unavailable, which have not been connected to the response. Spontaneous recovery will occur if those elements to which the CR has been extinguished (by the end of an extinction session) are replaced by elements previously conditioned to the CR. These two schemes are illustrated in Figure 11-2 below, where the "available" and "unavailable" sets of cues at the end of session n and beginning of session $n + 1$ are shown.

To see some of the implications of this scheme, let us make the assumptions more explicit. The stimulus population is divided at any moment into a proportion J that are available for sampling and another proportion $1 - J$ that are temporarily unavailable. The elements in these two sets are assumed to be interchanged randomly at some fixed rate. The probability of the CR is given by the proportion of conditioned elements at that moment in the set available for sampling. Suppose that our ex-

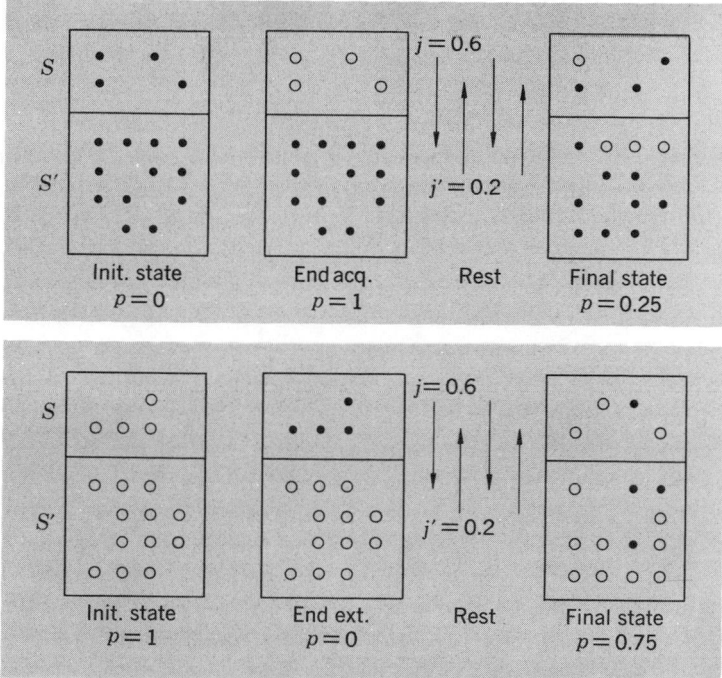

Figure 11-2   Hypothetical picture of stimulus fluctuation producing forgetting (top panel) or spontaneous recovery (bottom panel). The sets of available (S) and unavailable (S') elements are divided graphically into two boxes. Stimulus elements are represented as dots. Open dots indicate elements conditioned to some reference CR; filled dots indicate elements connected to incompatible behaviors. Reproduced from Estes (1955a).

perimental procedures during some session has brought the proportion of conditioned elements in the available set to p_0; let p_0' denote the proportion of conditioned elements in the set of stimuli that were unavailable during this session. We now impose a rest interval and let the fluctuation process go on for some time t, at which time we test the subject again. Let p_t denote the probability of the response to the set of stimulus elements available at time t. The equation Estes derives for this situation is as follows:

$$p_t = p_0[J + (1 - J)a^t] + p_0'(1 - J)(1 - a^t). \tag{10}$$

In this equation, J is the proportion of elements available from the total population, a is a fraction indexing the rate of interchange, and p_0 and p_0' are the proportions of conditioned available and unavailable elements of the beginning of the rest interval. We note that at time $t = 0$, $p_t = p_0$ since the a^t terms equal one when $t = 0$. As time goes on and t becomes very large, a^t goes to zero and we will have $p_t = p_0 J + p_0'(1 - J)$, which is the overall (population) proportion of conditioned elements. The effect of the fluctuation process is thus to modify the available set so that p_t changes over time from p_0 to the overall population mean. This diffusion causes a "homogenization" of effects of particular training, bringing the available and unavailable sets into equilibrium with respect to their proportions of conditioned elements. To give an analogy with diffusion, conditioning of the available set of elements is like introducing a concentrated dye into one of two solutions separated by a permeable membrane. With the passage of time, the added dye is diffused throughout both compartments, reaching stable equilibrium when the dye is equally concentrated in both compartments.

The cases of interest to us fall out as special cases of Eq. 10. If $p_0 > p_0'$, the p_t decreases over time to a lower value and we call it forgetting; if $p_0 < p_0'$, then p_t increases over time to a higher value and we call it spontaneous recovery. Figure 11-3a shows some theoretical forgetting curves plotted from Eq. 10; Figure 11-3b shows some recovery curves. Figure 11-3a shows, for example, that the amount of forgetting decreases as we increase p_0', the conditional strength of the elements unavailable during the previous session. These are the changes to be expected as the response is retrained over successive days. As the training sessions continue, it becomes more probable that every element in the population has been available at some time and been conditioned. Thus p_0' increases over sessions and progressively less response decrement (forgetting) occurs between one session and the next. A similar interpretation applies to progressive decreases in spontaneous recovery of extinguished responses (Figure 11-3b) except that we interchange the role of conditioned and unconditioned stimulus elements.

We thus see that the fluctuation theory accounts for the usual shapes of forgetting and recovery curves, and for their progressive changes as retraining or extinction is continued. Estes (1955a, 1955b) uses the theory to interpret a number of other facts related to recovery and regression. In addition, Estes (1959a) has shown how the theory applies to experiments on forgetting involving retroactive and proactive interference (see Chapter 14). In terms of the model, the interference studies are not very different from the study of spontaneous recovery of a CR that has been conditioned and then extinguished (i.e., elements connected to a response differing from the first one learned). Bower (1966a) gives more explicit illustrations of how some findings of interference studies may be interpreted in these terms. In summary, the concept of random stimulus fluctuation has been a very fruitful hypothesis, considering how many and diverse are the kinds of phenomena that it explains.

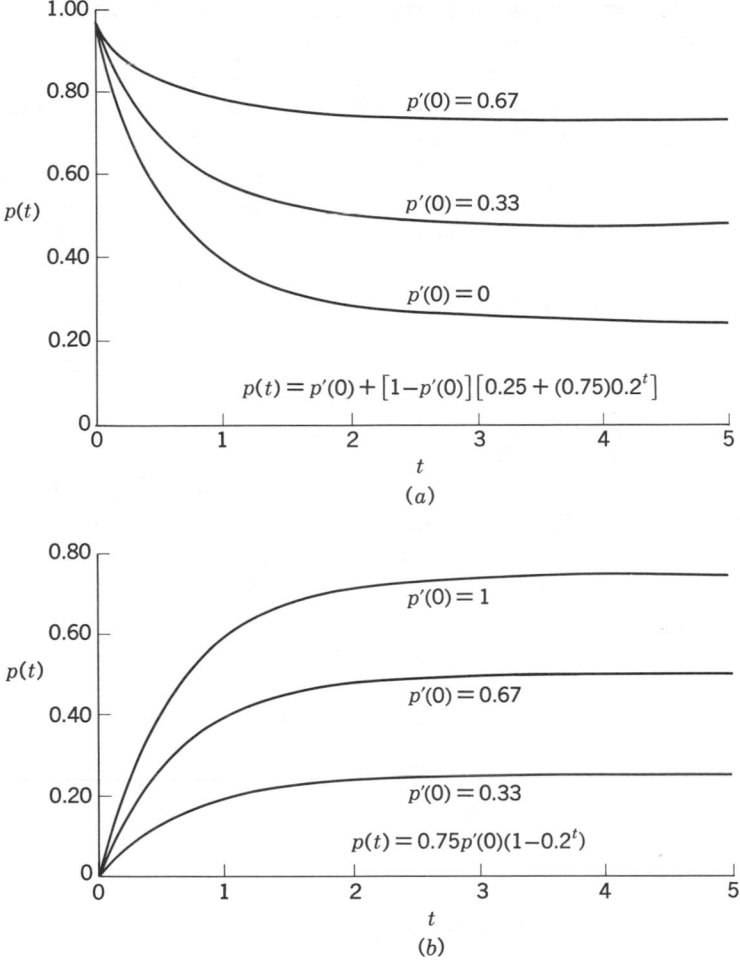

$$p(t) = p'(0) + [1-p'(0)][0.25 + (0.75)0.2^t]$$

(a)

$$p(t) = 0.75p'(0)(1-0.2^t)$$

(b)

Figure 11-3   (a) Families of forgetting curves. The proportion of conditioned elements in the available set at the end of the learning session is unity; the parameter differentiating the curves is the proportion of conditioned elements in the unavailable set (p'_o) at the end of the learning session. From Estes (1955a).

(b) Families of spontaneous recovery curves. The proportion of conditioned elements in s at time O is zero; the parameter of the curves is p', the proportion of conditioned elements in s' at the end of the extinction session. From Estes (1955a).

Other Response Measures

As we have seen, the sole dependent variable of SST is response probability. But experimenters frequently describe their subject's performance in terms of other measures such as response latency (or speed), response rate, or response amplitude. Much as Hull did with his $_sE_r$ construct, SST sets out to relate these other measures to its primary dependent variable, response probability. However, instead of simply postulating a particular relation between response probability and these other measures, the strategy in this case has been to derive this relationship by an auxiliary model of the response-emission process. By this means, it is possible to detach the assumptions about response-emission from the remaining assumptions about learning and so test them separately. At present writing, the response-models, while fairly good at the quasi-quantitative level, run into some difficulties at the specific-quantitative level of analysis.

Let us consider a very simple probability model for response latency. At the start of a trial, we present a signal, start a clock, and record the time elapsed before the subject performs some designated act. To be specific, suppose the act in question is getting a rat to run several steps down a straight alley (which has a food reward at the end) and interrupt a light beam outside the starting compartment. The latency measure is the time from the opening of the starting gate until the rat interrupts the light beam a few inches beyond the start box. An elementary model of this process supposes that in each small unit of time (of length h seconds, for example), the animal either performs the necessary act or does something else. We let p denote the probability that he performs the act in the next small unit of time if he has not already done so. The latency is then just the number of timed units of length h that pass before the act is performed. The probability that the latency is exactly $k \cdot h$ seconds is the likelihood that the subject lets $k - 1$ intervals go by and then responds in the kth interval. The probability of this sequence of $k - 1$ failures and then a success is

$$P(L = k \cdot h) = p(1 - p)^{k-1} \text{ for } k = 1, 2, 3, \ldots .$$

That is, with probability p he responds in the first interval; with probability $(1 - p)p$ he fails to respond in the first interval but responds in the second, and so forth. On the average, the response will occur in $1/p$ intervals, and so the average latency will be h/p.

This simple response model thus leads to a reciprocal relationship between average latency and response probability; as probability increases, latency decreases. In a learning experiment where we expect p_n to be changing over trials according to the learning function in Eq. 3, the average latency L_n will decline over trials. The equation would be:

$$L_n = \frac{h}{p_n} = \frac{h}{1 - (1 - p_1)(1 - \theta)^{n-1}}.$$

The two right-hand panels of Figure 11-4 show two empirical curves that were fitted by choosing the parameters h, p, and θ in this function. The bottom right curve is the average starting latency over trials of a group of rats learning to run down a runway for food reward. The top right is the average duration that rats held down a lever in a Skinner box when reward depended on pressing then releasing the lever.

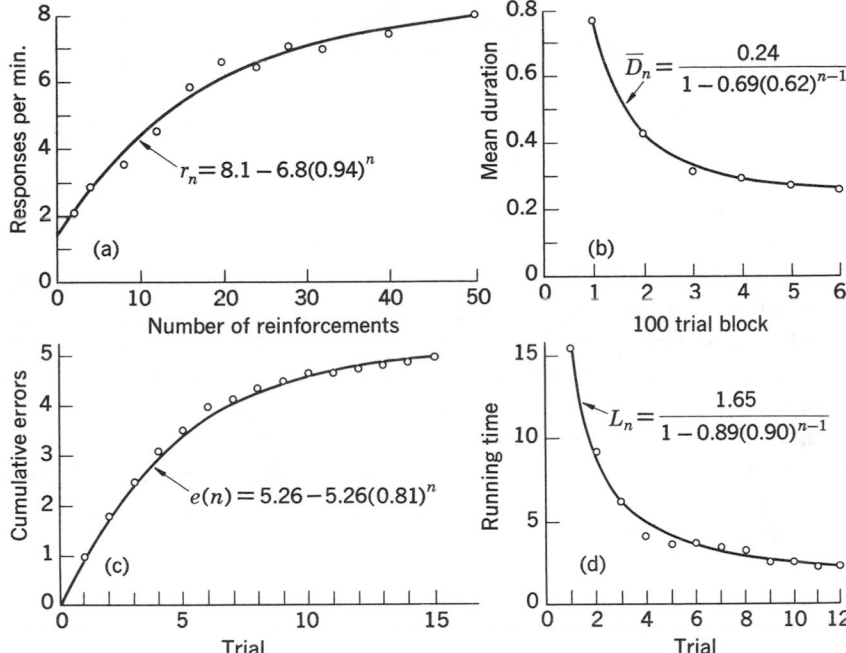

Figure 11-4 Four kinds of simple acquisition functions derived from statistical learning theory. Curves A, B, C, and D, respectively, represent rate of bar pressing versus number of reinforcements, mean bar-press duration per 100-trial block, mean cumulative errors versus trials in T-maze learning, and median running time versus trials in a runway experiment. From Estes (1959a).

The top left panel of Figure 11-4 gives the average rate of lever pressing (in responses per minute) of this same group of rats working for consistent reward in a free operant Skinner box. To interpret the free operant situation in terms of the response-emission model, assume that each response resets the clock to zero and that h/p is the average time until the next response. If the average time between responses is h/p, then the average *rate* of responding is the reciprocal, namely, p/h. Given the theoretical equation for p_n as a function of the number of reinforcements n, the curve in the upper left panel may be fitted to the data. In that equation, 8.1 is the estimate of $1/h$, so $h = 0.123$ minute.

We thus have seen how a probability theory can make contact with other measures of learned performance. Response amplitude has not been specifically considered in the literature of SST, although a model making amplitude proportional to p_n is easy to devise. In this case, learning curves of CR amplitude would be expected to look like the response rate curve in the upper left panel of Figure 11-4. In another vein, Bower (1959a, 1962a) has developed probability models to describe vicarious trial and error (VTE) behavior of subjects just before they make a choice. The role of this behavior in guiding the eventual choice was emphasized by Tolman (see Chapter 7).

Although the simple latency or rate models introduced above appear adequate for fitting mean response curves in simple acquisition, they are easily shown to be inadequate at a more detailed level of quantitative testing. For example, the elementary model implies that when p_n reaches unity, all responses occur in exactly time h, which is absurd. Moreover, the relative frequency histogram of observed latencies seldom has the shape implied by the simple model. Discussions by Bush and Mosteller (1955) and McGill (1963) show some of the detailed issues involved in predicting exact latency distributions. A fair amount of work in mathematical psychology is currently centered on this problem. A paper by Norman (1964) applies the linear learning model to inter-response times (in the free operant situation) with the added assumption that the subject is learning which inter-response times will produce reward. This model is related to Logan's "micromolar" approach discussed in Chapter 14.

Drive Effects

Experimentation on the influences of motivation upon learning and performance has been dominated by Hull's two-factor theory of drive. In Hull's theory, the prototypic drive-inducing operation consists in depriving an organism of some required commodity (usually food or water); his performance of responses rewarded by that commodity increases with the degree of deprivation. Hull emphasized two factors in accounting for drive effects: (a) an energizing factor, whereby strong drive states have the nonspecific effect of increasing reaction potentials of all responses, summarized in Hull's $E = H \times D$ formula; and (b) *drive stimulus,* a concept which accords recognition to a set of facts indicating that drive states have many of the properties ascribed to stimulation. Animals can learn a response discrimination where the only differential element is the nature or severity of the deprivation; for example, rats can be taught to turn left in a T maze when they are hungry and to turn right when thirsty, or to make one response while under severe deprivation and a different response while under moderate or low deprivation of the same commodity, and so on. Such experiments force upon us the interpretation that operations of deprivation and satiation act somewhat like the presentation and removal of particular sources of stimulation. In such cases, the drive stimuli are probably, to a large extent, intraorganismic, consisting of interoceptive stimulation from the load on the stomach and the gut, the dryness of the buccal membranes, the spontaneous firing rate of selectively sensitive chemoreceptors in the hypothalamus, the proprioceptive stimulation from changes in muscle tonus with deprivation, and so forth. As a class, these inferred sources of stimulation will be labeled "drive stimuli."

Estes (1958) has attempted to handle the effect of drive upon instrumental performance by assuming that the relative weight (number and/ or sampling probability) of the set of drive stimuli increases with time of deprivation. In describing the sources of stimulation present in a particular conditioning situation, Estes identifies three different sets: (a) the conditioned stimulus, (b) internal drive stimuli, and (c) random extraneous stimuli. Suppose that the average number of stimuli contributed to the trial sample from these three sources is C, D, and E; these contributions are determined jointly by the number of elements and sampling probabilities of the three sets of stimuli. Define w_C and w_D as the proportion of the trial sample that is contributed by the CS and drive stimuli, respectively. In simple conditioning situations it is presumed that the CS cues and the drive cues undergo conditioning to the reinforced response; additionally, it is presumed that particular extraneous stimuli so rarely recur that the E elements in the sample from this source may be presumed not to be connected to the reference CR. From these assumptions, Estes derives the following equation for CR probability on trial n:

$$p_n = w_C \, p_{C,n} + w_D \, p_{D,n} \tag{11a}$$

$$= w_C[1 - (1 - \theta_C)^{n-1}] + w_D[1 - (1 - \theta_D)^{n-1}]. \tag{11b}$$

Equation 11a uses the averaging rule for calculating p_n to a compound of several sources of stimulation; $p_{C,n}$ and $p_{D,n}$ denote the proportions of CS and drive stimuli conditioned by the beginning of trial n. In Eq. 11b the theoretical expressions for these probabilities have been substituted, assuming p_1 is zero.

Some graphs of Eq. 11b are drawn in Figure 11-5 for different D and θ_D values corresponding to subjects being trained under low, moderate, and high degrees of deprivation. What should be particularly noticed is that these performance curves approach higher asymptotes the higher the drive level, and that the rate of approach to the asymptote is faster under high drive. The curves diverge and, as training continues, they then converge somewhat.

Higher performance levels under high drive were interpreted by Hull in terms of the "energizing" component. However, in Estes' theory, the

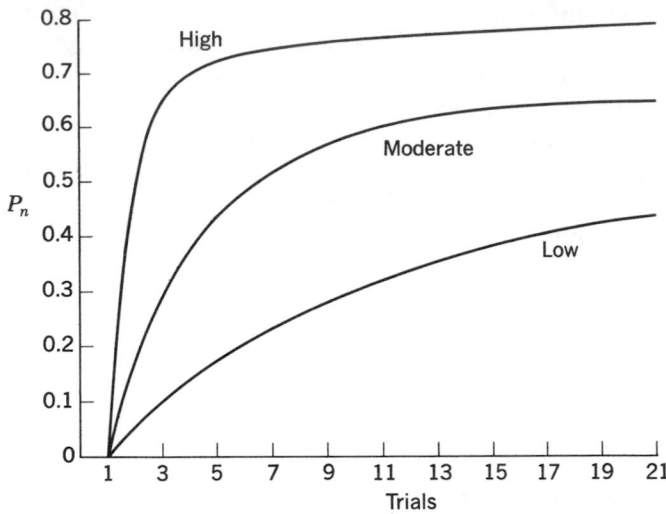

Figure 11-5   **Hypothetical curves depicting the improvement in performance with practice, where drive level (D and θ_D) varies among the three curves.**

energizing factor is accounted for on the assumption that the sampling probabilities of drive stimuli increase with deprivation. The effect of deprivation is seen as analogous to an amplification or increase in the salience of the conditioned stimuli, relative to random extraneous distraction. Estes handles CS-intensity effects upon performance in roughly the same way.

This stimulus theory of drive provides an easy interpretation of studies of drive discrimination. Each level of deprivation is represented as a characteristic set of stimulus elements, in which some members are shared with those of slightly higher or lower levels of deprivation. Figure 11-6 illustrates this representation. The number of elements shared between two sets of drive cues decreases with their difference in level. It is by virtue of these common drive stimulus elements (plus the CS cues) that a response conditioned at one drive level will transfer (generalize) to a different drive level, the amount of transfer varying with the degree of overlap between the two stimulus sets. From this stimulus representation, Estes (1958) attempts to fit the results of several experiments in which a subject's drive level is shifted between training and testing. By virtue of the elements unique to particular drive states, the theory leads us to expect that some degree of discrimination is possible on the basis of high vs low drive, or thirst vs hunger, etc.

Our illustrations have been of "internal" drives like hunger and thirst, involving deprivation of food or water. But it is clear that the theory applies just as well, if not better, to externally induced "drives" from

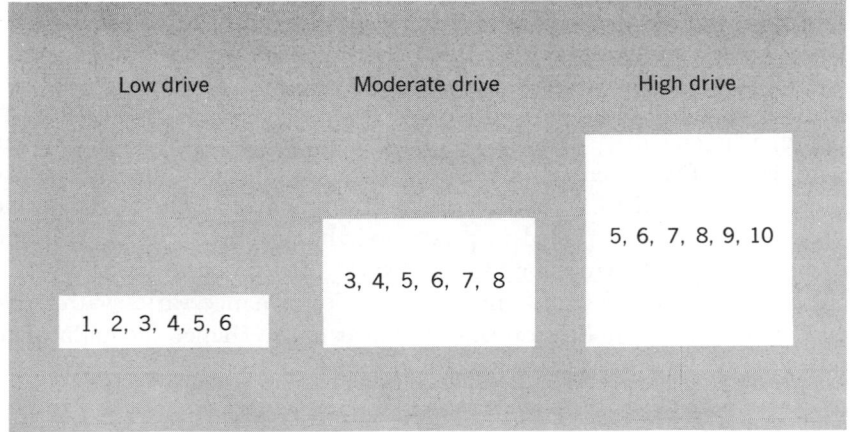

Figure 11-6   Representation of the change in drive stimuli going from a low to moderate to a high degree of deprivation. The numbers in the boxes are labels for particular stimulus elements; different drive levels share some elements in common. The height of the boxes represents the sampling probability for elements in the set.

noxious stimulation such as electric shock, loud noises, bright lights, temperature extremes, and the like. These are clearly instances in which the drive-inducing operation consists of increasing the intensity of a source of stimulation, which Estes interprets as an increase in the weight or sampling probabilities of conditioned elements. Estes is thus interpreting the internal drives, from deprivation, in a fashion analogous to our intuitive interpretation of such external drives.

In summary, Estes' theory explains the salient facts regarding drive and performance, and it does so without the energizing component of drive which Hull considered so essential. The key assumptions in Estes' account are (1) the relative weight of drive stimuli increases with deprivation, and (2) there exists a set of extraneous cues which have a persistent detrimental effect on performance. The postulated existence of extraneous cues which are not connected to the reference response, is clearly needed for the success of the explanatory enterprise. Without this assumption, Eq. 11a could not be derived. Two weak points in the theory may be noted: (1) no argument is provided to explain why the internal drive cues are activated and conditioned only on experimental trials. Since internal drive cues are present between CS trials, one might argue that they become connected to competing responses, thus leading to the inverse of the dynamism effect required by the data; (2) Estes' treatment neglects the fact that in appetitive conditioning, the probability and vigor of the consummatory response (to the rewarding substance) varies directly with drive level. A satiated animal will not eat readily, and so it is difficult to reinforce its responses with food. If a low drive level lowers the probability that a trial will terminate with an effective reinforcement, then the course of conditioning will be retarded for just this reason. This points out an intermediate link (viz., vigor of the consummatory response) whereby drive level may affect instrumental performance. The point is not fundamentally damaging to Estes' theory since the theory could be amended to take cognizance of this effect. That is, the drive theory could be first applied to predicting the amplitude of the consummatory response. Having done so, one could then go on to use this result and the theory to show how instrumental performance varies with drive level. The added complication would appear not to change the main qualitative predictions of the theory outlined above.

MARKOV MODELS

As we have seen, the earlier versions of SST represented the experimental situation as a very large set of N stimulus elements, only a sample of which affect the subject on any one trial. The assumption of all-or-none conditioning of the sampled elements leads to gradual change in the proportion of the population elements connected to the response. With N elements, the possible values of the A_1-response probability are 0, $1/N$, $2/N$, . . . , $(N-1)/N$, and 1. As the result of the reinforcing event on a trial, the response probability changes from one of these values to another. If N is large, then there are so many possible values of response probability that the "discreteness" of these changes cannot be detected by data analysis. In this case, one might as well represent learning as a change in a continuous variable p_n which can take on any possible value. This indeed is what is assumed once the linear model is used, and is the approach exemplified in Bush and Mosteller's work (1955).

Starting roughly in 1960 and thereafter, a major trend in mathematical learning theory has been one of increasing disenchantment with the continuous linear model (including its several variants) and an increasing pursuit of alternative models. This disenchantment, which is as yet by no means final or complete, has come about because of frequent failures of the simple linear model to deliver accurate numerical predictions in various experiments. And rightly or wrongly, the aim during these years has been to develop limited-scope models that do operate accurately at the specific-quantitative level for particular classes of experiments. As one result, the literature contains many instances in which a specific model fits a wealth of descriptive statistics of a single experiment with dumbfounding accuracy. These instances of very accurate fit of a model's predictions to data have had the effect of raising the general standards for assessing whether the fit of a model's predictions is good or bad. An unfortunate side-effect has been that a particular model is rather soon outdone by some alternative model, one perhaps contrived on the spot. This can lead to a proliferation of different models that are inadequately followed up with suitable experimental tests. And this proliferation may occur despite the fact that in a rough sense the fit of the first model to the data was really not all that bad. Later we will comment upon these aspects of the contemporary scene.

The current trend towards Markov models as alternatives to the continuous models probably got its initial impetus from another classic paper by Estes (1959b).[1] This paper was soon followed by the related work of Suppes and Atkinson (1960). Estes showed essentially that learning models of a different type follow from SST if one supposes that the number of stimulus elements, N, is small, say, 1 to 3 or so. When the number of elements is small, then the discreteness of the changes in response probability ought to be detectable by suitably sensitive data analyses. Moreover, it was found that many of the detailed predictions of data (e.g., sequential statistics) depended in a dramatic way upon the assumed number of stimulus elements. To put matters briefly, the main motivation behind recent work on "small-element" models springs from the fact that these finer analyses of data have yielded many instances in which the Markov models were clearly called for.

The N-Element Pattern Model

To exemplify the general approach, we discuss the axioms of the pattern model developed by Estes (1959b). The stimulus situation is represented by N patterns (functioning like the previous elements) exactly *one* of which is sampled randomly on each trial. The pattern is thought of as the total configuration of stimulation effective on a trial; different patterns may share some common components, but this fact is ignored in the simple version of the model. With probability c the sampled pattern becomes conditioned to the reinforced response in an all-or-none manner; with probability $1 - c$ the reinforcement is ineffective and the pattern remains connected as it was before. In a two-response situation, the state of this system is given by the number of patterns connected to A_1 instead of A_2. The state can change by $+1$ or -1, or possibly remain the same on each trial.

This system is best represented as a *Markov chain,* a class of probability processes that have been well analyzed by mathematicians. To characterize such processes here briefly, let us suppose that we observe a random process at spaced time intervals (trials) and that it occupies one of several different "states" at each trial. Then the process is a Markov chain if the

---

[1] The new directions were set off by the experiments of Rock (1957) which gave support to one-trial verbal learning.

state it occupies on the current trial depends only upon its state on the previous trial and is independent of the history of the process before it arrived at that state on the previous trial. A chain is characterized by its transition probabilities, which are the probabilities that the process will go from any given state to any other state on the next trial. It is a simple matter to derive these transition probabilities for the pattern model discussed above, where the possible transitions from state k (i.e., number of A_1 elements) are to $k + 1$, or to $k - 1$, or to remain at k from one trial to the next. A one-trial transition from state k to state $k + 1$ will occur if an A_2-conditioned pattern is sampled, an E_1 reinforcing event occurs, and the reinforcement is effective upon this occasion in conditioning response A_1 to the sampled pattern. This chain of events has probability $P(E_1) \cdot c \cdot (N - k)/N$. The other transition probabilities are similarly derived from the theory. This pattern model has been extensively tested in probability learning as well as other kinds of experiments. It fits such data as well, if not better, than the linear model.

A noteworthy general fact about the pattern models is that they imply an average learning curve that is identical with that of the linear model. For example, the equation for p_n following a consistent series of E_1 reinforcements is

$$p_n = 1 - (1 - p_1)(1 - c/N)^{n-1}. \tag{12}$$

If we interchange θ and c/N, we obtain Eq. 4 of the linear model. The parameters θ and c/N, mean roughly the same thing: both are the probability that any particular stimulus element (or pattern) will be sampled and effectively conditioned on a given trial.

The identicalness of the linear and Markov models in this respect is surprising. Imagine that $N = 2$ and that $p_1 = 0$. Then the pattern model says that there are only three possible values of A_1-response probability, namely, 0, $\frac{1}{2}$ or 1. The subject starts in state 0 (has $p = 0$), moves on some later trial into state 1 (has $p = \frac{1}{2}$), and moves on some later trial still into state 2 (has $p = 1$). How fast he traverses the states depends on c, the effectiveness of reinforcement. A schematic representation of the "learning curve" for an individual subject is shown in Figure 11-7. For the one-element model ($N = 1$), the individual "curve" is a step function, the step occurring on that random trial at which conditioning is finally effective. For the two-element model, the function consists of two discrete steps, from 0 to $\frac{1}{2}$ and from $\frac{1}{2}$ to 1. Despite these discrete steps in the individual curves, when we average together many subjects, having their steps at different trials, we get an average or mean p_n curve that is smooth and described by Eq. 12. However, if the appropriate analyses were done on individual data, we should be able to detect the discrete steps in the individual curves. For example, if the one-step function were appropriate, then we should find no improvement in performance prior to the trial

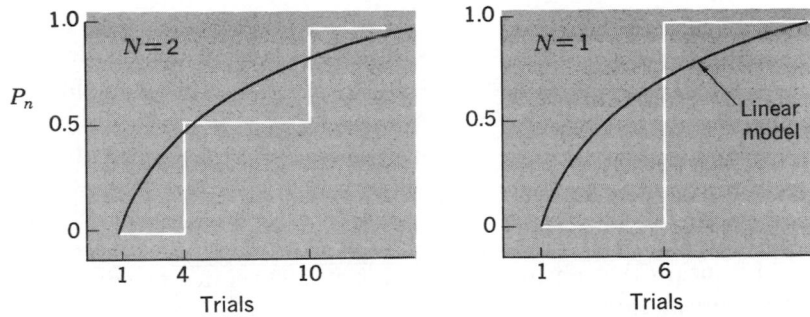

Figure 11-7 Examples of individual learning functions for the two-element and one-element models. The smooth curve is the learning function for the linear model.

of the last error. If the two-step function were appropriate, then we should find no improvement in performance over trials between the first correct response (state 0 has been left) and before the last error (state 2 not yet entered). Suppes and Ginsberg (1963) and Bower and Theios (1964) provide the rationale for these analyses and illustrate them with several sets of data that apparently show such step functions.

One-Element Model

To show the range of successful predictions that are possible with a simple model, let us apply the one-element model to an unpublished experiment by Bower on an elementary paired associates learning task. Thirty college students learned a list of 20 pairs where the stimulus member of the pair was a Greek letter and the response was the digit 1 or 2. Response 1 was assigned to 10 of the 20 stimuli selected at random. The 20 item list was gone through in random order until each subject gave three consecutive perfect recitations of the whole list of associates.

To represent this task in the model, we may consider the stimulus member of each pair as a single pattern that is always sampled when that stimulus is presented. The pattern is considered to be in one of two states: either connected to the correct response, or, prior to that, in a guessing state wherein the probability of a correct response is $p = 0.50$. On each trial, following the subject's response the experimenter shows the correct response. We assume that with probability c this reinforcement is effective in conditioning the correct response to the stimulus pattern if it is not already so conditioned; with probability $1 - c$ the reinforcement is ineffective and the state of the stimulus pattern remains as it was at the start of the trial. Items begin in the guessing state on trial 1 and stay there until their reinforcement is effective; once that happens, they remain conditioned so that the subject will respond correctly thereafter.

This model is to be applied to the trial-by-trial sequence of correct responses and errors that a subject gives to a particular stimulus item. With 30 subjects each learning 20 items, there are 600 such "subject-item" sequences of data. In principle, the theory could be applied by estimating a value of c for each of these 600 sequences. However, to reduce computational labor, we will assume that all sequences reflect the same value of c. Proceeding on this assumption, it is found that a good estimate of c is 0.20. This means that on the average, $1/c = 5.00$ reinforcements were required before an item was learned.

The observed and predicted results will be compared by means of two graphs and two tables of statistics. First, Figure 11-8 shows the mean proportion of correct responses over successive practice trials. The initial trial is a "pure guess" and the success rate starts at the a priori value of $\frac{1}{2}$. The theoretical curve fitted to the data in Figure 11-8 is Eq. 12, where

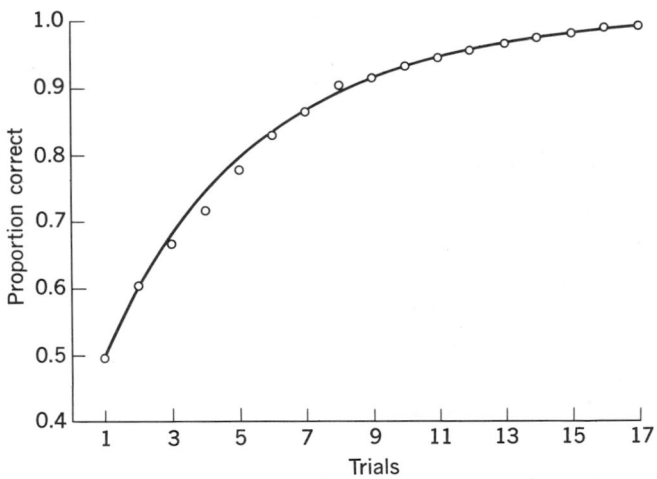

Figure 11-8 Observed and predicted mean proportions of correct responses over trials. Predictions derived from the one-element model. Data from Bower (unpublished).

$N = 1$, $p_1 = 0.50$, and $c = 0.20$. Figure 11-9 is a histogram of the relative frequency of the total errors per subject-item sequence before learning. It shows, for example, that 17.3 percent (104 cases) of the sequences had 0 errors, 25.0 percent (150 cases) had exactly 1 error, 18.2 percent (109 cases) had exactly 2 errors, and so on. Table 11-4 gives the proportions of sequences that have no errors following their kth success, for k running from 0 through 8. This proportion rises with k because the initial successes are likely to be guesses (followed by errors) whereas later successes are likely to be due to prior conditioning with the result that no

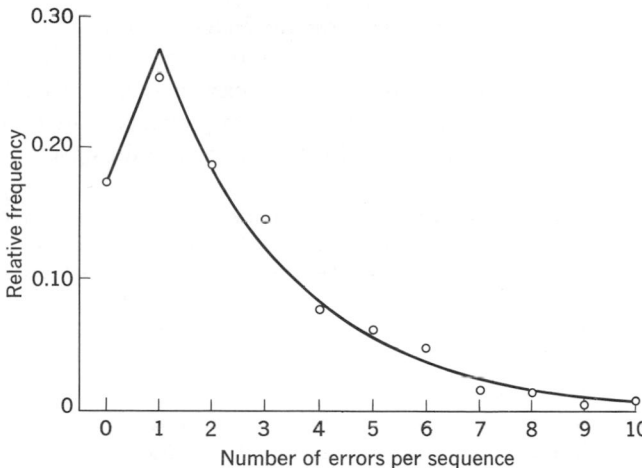

Figure 11-9   **Probability distribution of the number of errors per subject-item sequence before learning. Data from Bower (unpublished).**

errors will follow in the sequence. Finally, Table 11-5 gives a summary of various point predictions of the model. The last ten entries refer to sequential statistics. To explain two examples, a run of exactly two errors is counted once whenever a trial sequence of the form . . . CEEC . . . is encountered in a subject–item protocol. A pair of errors three trials apart (i.e., on trials n and $n + 3$) is counted once whenever a trial sequence of the form . . . EXXE . . . occurs where the X's may be correct or error responses.

Table 11-4 Proportion of sequences having no errors over those trials following their *k*th success for *k* = 0, 1, 2, . . ., 8. Data from Bower.

k	Observed	Predicted
0	0.17	0.17
1	0.43	0.44
2	0.62	0.63
3	0.76	0.75
4	0.83	0.83
5	0.90	0.89
6	0.93	0.93
7	0.95	0.95
8	0.97	0.97

The derivation of the theoretical predictions for such statistics is simple but lengthy and would serve no useful purpose here (see Atkinson, Bower, and Crothers, 1965; or Bower, 1961a). Though a variety of other statistics of the data could be calculated and predicted, the sample provided is sufficient to illustrate the accuracy of the model in this instance.

Comparison of the observed and predicted values reveals that the model is astonishingly accurate. In fact, the fit of the theory in this case is probably as close as psychologists can ever expect to get in studies of learning. This is the more impressive because only one parameter c had to be estimated from the data before the predictions could start.

Table 11-5 Mean values of various statistics for the paired associate experiment. The standard deviations refer to the statistic listed on the line above. Statistics calculated as mean per subject-item sequence.

Statistic	Observed	Predicted
Total errors	2.50	2.50
Standard deviation	2.34	2.50
Trial of first correct	1.92	1.84
Standard deviation	1.20	1.12
Trial of last error	4.18	4.17
Standard deviation	4.06	4.50
Pr. of error after an error	0.42	0.40
Total runs of errors	1.44	1.47
Runs of 1 error	0.85	0.87
Runs of 2 errors	0.33	0.35
Runs of 3 errors	0.13	0.15
Runs of 4 errors	0.08	0.06
No. pairs of errors:		
1 trial apart	1.06	1.03
2 trials apart	0.85	0.82
3 trials apart	0.65	0.65
4 trials apart	0.51	0.51

The close degree of correspondence between the obtained data and the predictions of a specific model as we have illustrated it above has come to be considered the attainable standard of success that we can hope for from an adequate model. Similar accurate fits of the one-element model to paired associates data have been reported in several publications (e.g., Kintsch, 1964; Keller *et al.*, 1965; Suppes and Ginsberg, 1962; Bower, 1961a, 1962b). In addition, analyses of response times in several experiments have shown results in line with this model; that is, (a) no differences in speeds of correct and incorrect responses, and relative constancy of these, over trials prior to the last error on an item, and (b) abrupt increases in speed of the correct response after the trial of the last error. These results are consonant with the assumption of a guessing state before conditioning occurs on or soon after the trial of the last error in a subject–item sequence. In related work, Restle (1962) and Bower and Trabasso (1964) have used a slightly modified version of the model to account for an elementary form of learning to identify concepts in a discrimination task. In that work, the subject was assumed to be testing out various hypotheses regarding the solution to the problem. The "guessing" state corresponds to the subject testing out irrelevant (incorrect) hypotheses, and the "conditioned" state corresponds to the subject using the correct hypothesis for classifying the stimuli. This work is related to the earlier ideas of Lashley and Krechevsky (see Chapter 7). The papers cited may be consulted for further details.

The results confirming the one-element model in paired associates learning have in common the fact that only two response alternatives are involved. Somewhat similar confirmatory results have been found in the case of recognition memory where the subject says whether or not he has seen a particular stimulus (e.g., nonsense syllable) before in the preceding series (e.g., Kintsch and Morris, 1964; Bernbach, 1965). The accuracy of predictions from the one-element model usually breaks down for paired associates learning involving more than two response alternatives. The reason for the breakdown is that performance improves somewhat over trials before the last error on an item. The one-element model supposes, instead, that the probability of a correct response will be constant over these trials. Various methods of testing by second-guesses, ranking of responses, confidence ratings, and so on (see Bower, 1966b) lead to the conclusion that the all-or-none description is probably wrong in these cases. That is, the performance is not always "all" or "none" but can be partial. In other words, as common sense would have it, something can be learned along the way before learning is complete.

Upon this state of affairs one can react in a variety of ways. One common interpretation is to say simply that the one-element model is wrong, that it fits the two-response data for irrelevant reasons, and that alternative conceptions should be pursued. This has been the predominant practice and possibly the correct one. An alternative reaction is to try to patch up the model, or to formulate it in a more general way, so that it covers, at least qualitatively, the main disconfirming results (cf. Greeno and Steiner, 1965; Polson and Greeno, 1965). A third alternative is to try seriously to discover why the model fits when it does and fails when it does; and from an understanding of this pattern, to develop a more general theory which essentially reduces to the one-element model in the former cases and accounts for the discrepancies in the latter cases. The degree of success of this latter undertaking has been limited to date. Prominent in this line of development, however, have been the two-stage or two-process Markov models, and the discussion of those is next on our agenda.

Two-Stage Models

We have seen that the simple all-or-none model often fails because performance may improve somewhat before learning is complete. One could interpret this as support for the linear model which assumes a gradual and continuous growth in response probability as training progresses. But the frequent poor quantitative fits of the linear model discourage us from accepting this interpretation too readily. Various alternative models must be considered. For example, it is clear that many "compromise" models must lie along the continuum extending from the one-step model to the continuous (infinite-step) model. Conceivably learning does consist of discrete stages or jumps between different levels of performance, but there may be more than the one-step envisaged by the one-element model. The simplest alternative would be a model which postulates that individual learning curves consists of two steps or stages.

By one or another psychological rationale, the various two-stage models come around to the idea that performance can be represented as a three-state Markov process wherein each state is identified with a different level of correct response probability. We let p_0, p_1, and p_2 be the three levels of response probability associated with the three states. In most applications, p_0 is some initial "guessing" probability of correct responses that can be achieved before the subject knows much of anything; p_2 is usually 1.00, the level attained when learning is complete; and p_1 is some level intermediate between p_0 and 1, wherein the subject knows something but not everything he needs if he is always to respond correctly. A diagram of the 3-state model is shown in Figure 11-10. The parameter a is the prob-

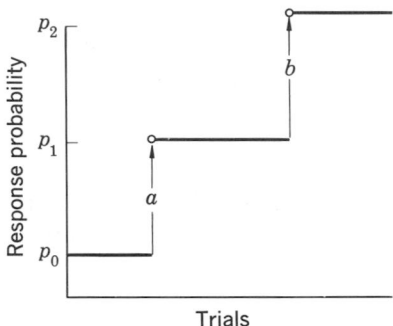

Trials

Figure 11-10   Diagram of 3-state learning model with response probabilities p_0, p_1, and p_2. The parameter a is the probability of a one-trial transition from the lower state to p_1; b is the probability of a one-trial transition from p_1 to the upper state.

ability that a subject moves from state 0 into state 1 as a result of one reinforcement; the parameter b is the likelihood of a one-trial move from state 1 to state 2. Once state 2 is entered, the process stays there and learning is complete. Various theories differ in the psychological constructs and assumptions they use to rationalize the 3-state representation and to interpret the learning parameters a and b. It is these theoretical backgrounds that give the model some rational plausibility, and that also lead to experiments which give presumptive evidence for a specific interpretation of the 3-state process. The theories differ in content, of course, depending upon the nature of the learning task being analyzed (e.g., paired associates with humans, avoidance conditioning with rats). We will briefly introduce a few of these ideas later, but first let us consider one feature of 3-state models considered as abstract descriptions of data protocols.

Bower and Theios (1964) noted that situations optimal for assessing the 3-state representation of performance are those in which response probability starts at zero and, with practice, asymptotically approaches unity. In the model, subjects would begin in the "$p_0 = 0$" state, remain there for a few trials and then shift either to the "$p_2 = 1$" state or to the intermediate p_1 state. Those who enter the p_1 state ultimately move into the "$p_2 = 1$" state because all subjects stop making errors eventually. Now consider those protocols wherein the first correct response occurs several trials before the last error. Then we know that during these trials, the subject has been in the intermediate state, because the first success signifies that he has left the "$p_0 = 0$" state and the later (last) error signifies that he has not yet entered the "$p_2 = 1$" state. For this reason we call these the "intermediate" trials or responses. If the 3-state representation is correct, then the proportion of correct responses over intermediate trials should be constant, reflecting no improvement in performance during these trials. During these intermediate trials, successive correct and incorrect responses should look like independent tosses of a biased coin that comes up heads (correct) with a probability near p_1 and tails (error) with a probability near $1 - p_1$.

Adopting this line of reasoning, Bower and Theios analyzed data from several diverse learning situations, including avoidance conditioning and escape choice-learning by rats, eyelid conditioning in human subjects, and four experiments on response-reversal in paired associate learning. In each case, the data supported the 3-state description of performance changes. Average response probabilities over trials between the first success and last error approximated a flat line. After estimating the transition parameters, a and b, for the 3-state model, they were able to predict statistics of each set of data with tolerable accuracy.[2]

Let us briefly mention just a few of the ideas that have led to the 3-state model in particular situations. Considering paired associates learning as have Atkinson and Crothers (1964) and Bernbach (1965), we can identify several processes that seem to be going on. One occurs when the subject learns to *recognize* each stimulus term of the list as one he remembers seeing before. We may suppose that this learning of an encoded label or tag for the stimulus goes on in an all-or-none manner. A second process occurs when he must recall the correct response to a recognized stimulus. We may suppose that he can recall for one of two reasons: one is because

---

[2] Later, Prokasy (1965b) reported eye-blink conditioning data at variance with the simple model. A slight generalization, allowing $p_0 > 0$ and $p_2 < 1$, appears better able to handle the eye-blink data (cf. Theios and Brelsford, 1965).

the association is in a relatively long-term or permanent storage system; the other, because the association is in a temporary short-term storage system from which it can be easily lost (see related discussions, pages 503–511 in chapter 14). When elaborated further (see references cited), these ideas lead to the 3-state model. State 0 characterizes the subject-item sequence before stimulus recognition learning. State 1 characterizes the process after recognition learning but before the correct association has entered into the permanent storage system. The intermediate response level, p_1, depends on the forgetting rate out of the short-term memory store. On this theory, the one-element model fits two-response data because the subject effectively converts the task into one of recognizing the A_1 stimuli, and such recognition learning is an all-or-none process.

Restle (1964a; see also Polson, Restle, and Polson, 1965) interpret the intermediate state in paired associates as due to stimulus confusion errors arising because of similarity among stimuli to which different responses are being associated. The intermediate state is entered from the initial guessing state by conditioning a response to nondiscriminating aspects of a stimulus (i.e., aspects that this stimulus shares with others). The intermediate state is either by-passed or escaped when the response becomes associated to a unique feature of the stimulus. Their data offer presumptive evidence that restricted confusions among similar stimuli produce the intermediate performance. On this theory, the one-element model describes paired associate learning either if (a) stimulus-confusion errors are minimized, or (b) there are two responses, in which case confusions and guesses cannot be distinguished.

In applying the 3-state model to the simple avoidance conditioning of animals, Theios and Brelsford (1966) assume that two associations are involved: one between the warning signal and the emotional fear reaction; the other, between the cues of being afraid and the response of running from the shock compartment into the safety compartment. The intermediate state is entered once the latter habit is learned but while the former (emotional) habit is still vacillating in strength. A series of experiments by Brelsford (1965) provides considerable evidence for this interpretation of the task.

Finally, Trabasso and Bower (1964) used the 3-state model to interpret learning to identify concept instances wherein two attributes (e.g., color and shape) had to be used for correct classification. The intermediate state was interpreted as one in which the subject has learned only one of the two relevant attributes so that his success rate improved above the chance level. Detailed internal analyses of the data plus subsidiary experiments established strong presumptive evidence for this interpretation of the learning.

These applications of Markov models utilize a common theoretical strategy first enunciated clearly by Restle (1964a). A given learning task is conceived to involve several stages, with each stage being a unit of learning which supposedly the subject acquires in an all-or-nothing fashion. When the simple all-or-none (one-element) process is used to describe each stage, then the multiprocess model conjoins end-to-end several all-or-none processes. The all-or-none process is used as a basic building block. The result of conjoining several all-or-none processes is to yield a model which, in its gross properties, resembles a "continuous improvement" notion of learning. However, in comparison with the continuous linear model, the Markov models generally are favored both in respect to their accuracy of fitting data and in the relative ease with which theoretical derivations can be carried through.

There is no way of knowing whether this strategy of using "all-or-none" building blocks will be successful in the long run. At present, several models of this kind seem to operate effectively. The question of validity always centers around the cogency and sharpness with which a theory identifies the various subparts of the task with their associated parameters, and how convincing the data are in supporting the proposed partitioning into subtasks. In some cases at least, specially designed experiments or data analyses can produce strong evidence favoring the task analysis proposed by a particular model.

THE LIMITATION OF GOODNESS-OF-FIT CRITERIA

During the years following 1959, the emphasis has increasingly been on fitting specific models to a large variety of descriptive statistics of each set of data. The theorists involved felt that it was important to demonstrate that detailed numerical accuracy in fitting a psychological theory was possible. The initial estimates of goodness-of-fit were only "ocular" tests; one simply looked at tables of predicted and observed statistics (like Table 11-5) and decided on some intuitive basis whether the overall fit was good, fair, or poor. This informal appraisal has in many instances been replaced by standard statistical tests of goodness of fit such as chi square.

Now we have gradually come to realize that a large experiment, with thousands of observations, will reject practically every model on the basis of such chi-square tests (Grant, 1962). The theory may predict the relevant data numbers with an average error of, say, 3 percent; but given sufficient observations, that 3 percent discrepancy can become statistically significant. Though statistically significant, the discrepancy may be trivial in a practical sense. All scientists are willing to admit that their theories are not literal truth, but rather ideal abstractions (models) that approximate the data more or less closely. And what "close" means in this context is a comparative judgment; the model is closer to the data than are competing theories, or its relative error is near the standard expected by the scientific fraternity for theories in this particular area of specialization. The goodness-of-fit tests are thus seen as really relevant only when several models are being compared on predicting the same data.

As the goal of relatively accurate fit is being achieved to a greater or less degree by most of the models on the current scene, goodness-of-fit as a theoretical decision strategy has begun to recede into its proper place. That is, relatively good fits to data are seen as an important though not overwhelming reason for favoring a particular model. This view has been forced upon us by the fact that some types of standard learning data are fitted fairly well by abstract models that have neither a sensible psychological rationale nor clear identifications with psychological processes. They are models in search of a rationale, in search of a psychological analysis that will lend some sense to the mathematics that provide an abstract description of the behavior involved.

There is some disagreement among workers in the field on this score (see Galanter, 1966). Some believe that we should characterize behavioral data mathematically, display the parameter values of the model, and then be silent—although admittedly neither aspect of this job is a simple matter. Others believe that we should attempt to formulate a relatively general (even speculative) theory from which particular models derive under various specific conditions, and that some stable identifications should exist for the psychological meaning of the parameters in the mathematical model. Psychologists of this persuasion are likely to conduct experiments which test a theory regarding a parameter in their model, or design experiments which get at a postulated process in a direct way or which show large qualitative differences. In this latter regard, the criteria for evaluating their theory is little different from the criteria by which qualitative theories have been generally evaluated throughout the history of psychology. The difference lies in their theory's potential for being translated into explicit models that operate accurately at the specific-quantitative level of prediction.

RANGE OF APPLICABILITY OF MATHEMATICAL LEARNING MODELS

Starting from a modest beginning in 1950, mathematical learning theories have been applied to an increasingly broader range of experiments. The specific ideas may vary from one application to another but a common method of theory-construction runs throughout. The range of behavioral phenomena investigated by these methods includes the traditional provinces of learning theory plus a few newly opened territories. We will list a sample of situations or phenomena for which mathematical models have been formulated and tested: classical conditioning, operant conditioning, stimulus generalization, mediated generalization, discrimination learning, rote serial learning, paired associate learning, free verbal recall, short-term or immediate memory, concept identification, probability learning, recognition memory, signal detection and recognition in psychophysics, imitation learning, avoidance conditioning, VTE and latency in choice situations, stimulus-compounding, paired-comparison choices, parametric investigations of drive, CS intensity, CS-US interval, and variations in reinforcement in conditioning situations, two-person interaction games, reaction time, spontaneous recovery and forgetting, retroactive interference experiments, and so forth. This list is representative but hardly exhaustive. Practically every domain of learning research has been infiltrated, at least to some degree, by quantitative theorizing.

The depth of the various applications differs considerably, some consisting only of a model for a single experiment, some amounting to a major line of continuing research. Some applications are of the quasi-quantitative variety wherein it is shown that derivations from some general assumptions account for the major qualitative trends observed. Frequently a mathematical model simply leads us to a reworking of data derived from some classical experimental situation, or leads to investigations of slight alterations of the standard situations. In its better moments, this reexamination of a familiar situation in terms of a mathematical model can bring to light new regularities in the data that had never before been suspected. For example, data analyses guided by the Markov learning models have shown the existence of performance plateaus or step-functions in situations where we have previously thought learning was a continuous and gradual improvement in performance.

A recent application of mathematical learning models is to the deciding of optimality questions about educational programs (see Restle, 1964b; Crothers, 1965; Dear and Atkinson, 1962). The types of questions investigated include (1) how best to allocate study-time to different independent materials in order to maximize the total amount learned in a fixed time, (2) the optimal rate for a teacher to present materials in a course in which understanding the nth unit requires that the student have learned the first $n - 1$ units, and (3) the best way in which to divide a large group of students into smaller tutorial classes so as to minimize the total cost (in teachers' plus students' time) of teaching particular material. When such problems are clearly formulated (often with simplifying conditions), a learning model can be used to calculate the value of different programs, and thereby tell us which programs teachers should use if they wish to optimize certain goals. This kind of work has just recently appeared and is small in substance; however, we may expect it to be a continuing concern of learning theorists.

Since psychology today consists of many areas of specialization, application of a model to a new area occasionally arouses a hornet's nest of criticism from the experts of the invaded province. In its initial application, a model may be shown to fit a specific situation, call it A. The criticisms in general point out the incompletenesses of the model if it were to be applied to situations B and C. Such criticisms are often informative and can lead to such alterations of a theory that henceforth it can handle all three situations adequately. But, of course, sometimes such a successful extension appears beyond practicable reach. In this case, the theorist may have to be content with accounting for situation A while leaving cases B and C for the future—all on the principle that half a loaf is better than no loaf at all. The research strategy involved here is controversial, for the evaluation of scientific gain is always a complex matter, and much inspired debate has centered about the merits of the strategy.

CONCLUDING COMMENTS

It is difficult to evaluate mathematical theory construction in psychology. It is a method or technique for formulating substantive theories, not a theory in its own right. Some of the uses are fitting and fruitful, some obviously are not, and each case has to be judged more or less on its own merits. In general terms, it is fair to say that mathematical models have guided psychologists into more intensive analyses of learning data. The models have shown us the rich information that can be gathered from learning data by carrying out more refined analyses. They have also demonstrated that valuable understanding sometimes arises from suitably sensitive comparisons of several well-formulated theories on data derived from very elementary experiments.

A therapeutic side-effect of the work in mathematical models has been the realization that such theories *can* yield predictions of data of an accuracy that is on a par with the accuracy of the best physical theories. The many instances now available demonstrate that numerical accuracy of a learning theory is possible. Such demonstrations are important in helping us to establish the standards which we can realistically hope for our theories to achieve.

The problems which beset work in mathematical learning theory appear generally characteristic of the contemporary scene in learning theory. Many small-scale models or local hypotheses seem to be spawned at a fast rate, and many are inadequately followed up with exacting tests or integrated with a more general body of theories. The observer gets an impression of clutter, of disjointedness and fragmentation, of particular theories whose range of experimental applications becomes more and more restricted and circumscribed. Another impression related to the above is that the developments are not cumulative, in the sense of building up strong evidence for or conviction in some particular view about learning. Changes certainly do occur yearly in the experimental situations studied and in the types of models used, but it is difficult to decide whether the changes represent progress towards anything in particular. One occasionally feels acutely the absence of any overall integrating scheme that guides these many efforts of mathematical model building. It is easy to deplore this state of affairs but such scorn is essentially ineffectual and will do little to change matters. Scientists remain dogged individualists who insist upon following whatever leads and openings satisfy their curiosity and interest, and moral exhortations to the contrary can just be damned.

At present, stimulus sampling theory appears to be the most versatile and comprehensive scheme for integrating the fragmented efforts in mathematical learning theory. However, even this general viewpoint is professed by an increasingly smaller proportion of the active contributors to the field. For example, although the initial developments of Markov learning models were inspired by Estes' original paper on these, most of the later work has used different theoretical rationales to justify the particular Markov model being used. This change in theoretical base was apparent in our discussion of the rationales provided for various applications of the two-stage Markov models. Many theorists simply find it more convenient to think in terms of various subprocesses or stages in learning, frequently using the "information processing" concepts current in computer simulation work (see Chapter 12); in any case, the stimulus sampling rationale is invoked less frequently.

Even on the basis of our selective review, it is clear that mathematical models have become thoroughly ingrained in many areas of learning research; they are definitely here to stay. We may expect that the contemporary models will soon be outmoded, but even so the enterprise as a whole can be expected to increase the quantity and quality of its products, because more students of psychology are being mathematically equipped to do this kind of theoretical work. Though not obviously the "wave of the future" in learning research, mathematical theorizing will nonetheless continue as a prominent current. Their influence throughout later generations of psychologists will serve as sufficient tribute to the small band of founders in this area—Estes, Burke, Bush, Mosteller, Luce, Suppes, Restle—whose early efforts provided enough momentum to convert an ideal into an expanding scientific movement.

SUPPLEMENTARY READINGS

ATKINSON, R. C. (Editor) (1964) *Studies in mathematical psychology.*
ATKINSON, R. C., BOWER, G. H., and CROTHERS, E. J. (1965) *Introduction to mathematical learning theory.*

Bush, R. R. (1960) A survey of mathematical learning theory. In Luce, R. D. (Editor) *Developments in mathematical psychology.*

Bush, R. R., and Estes, W. K. (Editors) (1959) *Studies in mathematical learning theory.*

Bush, R. R., and Mosteller, F. (1955) *Stochastic models for learning.*

Estes, W. K. (1959a) The statistical approach to learning theory. In Koch, S. (Editor) *Psychology: A study of a science.* Vol. 2.

Luce, R. D. (1959) *Individual choice behavior.*

Luce, R. D., Bush, R. R., and Galanter, E. (Editors) (1963a) *Handbook of mathematical psychology.* Vols. I and II.

Luce, R. D., Bush, R. R., and Galanter, E. (Editors) (1963b) *Readings in mathematical psychology.* Vol. I.

Luce, R. D., Bush, R. R., and Galanter, E. (Editors) (1965a) *Handbook of mathematical psychology.* Vol. III.

Luce, R. D., Bush, R. R., and Galanter, E. (Editors) (1956b) *Readings in mathematical psychology.* Vol. II.

Restle, F. (1961) *The psychology of judgment and choice.*

Information Processing Theories of Behavior

A recent technique in psychological theorizing is the formulation of theories in the format of *programs* that run on high-speed computers. The aim of the enterprise is to get such a programed computer to go through a series of "actions" which in some essential ways resemble or simulate the cognitive and/or behavioral actions of a real subject performing some task. This chapter explores and hopes to clarify this brief introductory statement; primarily we will be reviewing some of the theories and models that have been formulated in this manner.

The historical antecedents of this theoretical technique are diverse, although many of the modes of thinking have been imported into psychology from engineering. Perhaps an appropriate way to begin is with a discussion of the age-old art of robotology. Men have long been fascinated by the similarities between the "behavior" of machines and the behavior of living organisms. All the analogies are there, implicit in our natural-language descriptions of what machines do. Robotology consists in the deliberate design of machines which mimic the behavior of living organisms. From a leisurely and slow beginning, recent successful advances by mid-twentieth century have made this enterprise nothing short of spectacular. It is now widely recognized that machines can be designed to perform many sorts of tasks previously done exclusively by humans. Indeed, the machine may often exceed the performance capabilities of the man it replaces. The effect of this engineering feat is apparent in the present concern about automation and the possible obsolescence of the human worker of the future.

During the 1950's, a few behavioral scientists began to construct robots which were supposed to embody directly different principles about behavior. Included among these hardware models are Ashby's *homeostat* (1952) that seeks and maintains a favorable homeostasis of its "internal milieu," Walter's *Machina speculatrix* (1953) that imitates the actions of an animal foraging about its environment in search of food or shelter, Walter's (1953) and Deutsch's (1954) learning machines which mimic the maze learning of rats, Hoffman's machine (1962) that displays most of the phenomena of classical conditioning, and several others to be mentioned later.

One may ask whether these robots are to be considered seriously. What is their logical status? Are they to be viewed as serious explanations of behavior, or merely as amusing, but idle, curiosities? The prevailing consensus is that a machine which accurately simulates relevant aspects of some organism's behavior indeed constitutes a genuine explanation of that behavior. The idea is that the abstract principles involved in designing the machine—its functional components and their organization—could in fact be the same as those describing the design and functioning of the living organism. In designing and building a machine to simulate certain behaviors, one is in effect working out a physical embodiment of a theory about how that behavior is produced by that organism. Getting the machine to actually work and to simulate some interesting behavior is a way of demonstrating that the theory is internally consistent and that it has specified a sufficient set of mechanisms. Running the robot through one or another task is logically equivalent to deriving theorems about behavior from the theory that is modeled by the physical realization. Conversely, it is claimed that we have a fairly complete understanding of a piece of behavior when we know how to build a machine that would behave in just that way.

The distinction here between an abstract theory and a particular mechanical model of it is similar to the logician's distinction between an axiom system and various realizations of it. The theory or axiom system has the top logical priority; the particular physical realizations of it are secondary. In this sense, it is psychologically irrelevant what hardware is used to realize our robot, whether in terms of cog-wheels, relays, vacuum tubes, transistors, electrochemical processes, or actual neurons (although the neurophysiologist is concerned with the actual hardware). All proper realizations of the theory will carry out isomorphic behaviors, that is, they will display a parallelism or point-to-point correspondence in the behavioral path that they trace out over time. If two systems show this kind of functional parallelism, this point-to-point correspondence in critical features, then we shall say that one system is a *simulation* of the other.

If the correspondence is sufficiently extensive then we have some reason to believe that the two systems are different realizations of the same theory. In scientific practice, this means that a theory about behavior could be tested by constructing a machine designed in accordance with the theory, and then seeing whether this machine simulates the behavior of interest.

But having reached this point in the argument, we can begin dispensing with the actual hardware altogether. This paring away can be done simply by attending to what are the essential as opposed to the irrelevant features of the system to be simulated. This clearly is determined by one's goals. As an example, suppose that our goal were to simulate the behavior of a rat learning a maze. Then it is clearly immaterial whether our robot looks like a rat, or moves on wheels rather than legs, or for that matter merely informs us (by some means) what it would do if it had legs to run with. It would seem that all that a psychological explanation would require is that our robot be equipped with (a) a pseudo-sensory system whereby it receives stimulus information from its environment, possibly with additional elements sensitive to its "internal drive" states, (b) a central network of learning, storage, and decision-making mechanisms, (c) some way for the central mechanisms to deliver and/or sustain commands to a motor system (actual or imaginary), and (d) a means for relaying back to the sensory system the effects of its motoric actions. These components are essential; the rest of the rat's natural accouterments would appear to be just excess baggage from a logical point of view. Nonetheless, even agreeing to this functional caricature of the rat-as-learner does not carry us very far. The major work still lies ahead, in specifying the design and organization of these components, their "rules" of operation, and how they are interconnected.

But we may now dispense with the physical machinery entirely. The robot is just a physical embodiment of a particular explanatory theory; putting it through its paces corresponds to making various deductions from the theory. But there are alternate ways to make deductions from a theory. If the theory is simple enough, specifying only a few parts that perform simple functions, then deductions can be made either verbally, in symbolic logic, or with mathematics. But if the theory is complicated, then verbal deductions become tedious and error-laden whereas mathematical ones often cannot be pushed through at all. In these cases, we can have recourse to a high-speed computer.

By this approach, we would program a computer so that it goes through the same steps that we would if we were making a verbal deduction from the theory. The computer does the job for us in a short time and it makes no errors. When programed to operate according to our theory, the computer then becomes just another realization of that theory. It is, however, an inexpensive and efficient realization, since it saves us time and labor. But to realize a behavioral theory in the form of a computer program is not to imply that the theorist conceives of the organism as computerlike. The computer is being used here merely as a tool for making deductions. And the fact that a theory is realized as a computer program does not tell us what type of a theory it is, or lend any special credibility to it. Any theory that is sufficiently well specified can be realized as a computer program.

The foregoing passages outline some of the arguments for stating theories in the form of a computer program. The strategy itself is noncommital about the type of theory or concepts that are programed. It is a historical accident that most theories realized in this way have in fact had a distinctly "cognitive" bias. This results from the aims of the particular theorists involved; often those aims have been to simulate the "higher mental processes" of man, thinking and problem-solving. However, a good deal of work has been done also on programs to simulate learning. In this chapter we review some of the problem-solving programs as well as those directly concerned with learning. We have no hesitation in including discussion of the problem-solving programs since they illustrate important concepts common to the general approach, and they demonstrate how past learning can be utilized in novel and ingenious ways to solve problems.

INFORMATION PROCESSING CONCEPTS AND MODELS

Each new theoretical approach usually creates its own descriptive language, or jargon, and so it is too with the computer-simulation approach. The jargon is that of "information processing," and it derives from the ways computer scientists generally describe what their machines do. Stimuli, data, instructions—the generic name is "information"—are *input* or *read in* to the computer; after more or less whirling, the computer *outputs* (*reads out*) some particular end result, usually by printing it or displaying a picture on a cathode ray tube. Between the input and output, the computer is described as performing a series of instructed manipulations of the input data. These manipulations may consist of altering or transforming the mass of data, calculating something from it, comparing it to something else, using the result to search for something previously stored in the computer, evaluating what is found at intermediate stages, making decisions about it, and so on. Each of these manipulations may require a short series of instructions in the computer program, called a *subroutine*. It is convenient to refer to subroutines in terms of the functions they perform with the information input to them. And from this, it is an easy step to begin referring to the subroutine as representing an *information-processing mechanism*. Thus, the computer-simulation theories of behavior may be generally described as postulating the existence within the organism of an array of information-processing mechanisms, each of which performs a certain elementary function, and these processes are assumed to be organized and sequenced in some particular way.

It is perhaps apt to describe most research in the information-processing (IP) area as a concerted effort towards the experimental synthesis of complex human behaviors. Some typical sorts of behaviors that are simulated include the reasoning of a chess champion in selecting his next move in a chess game, the generation of hypotheses by a subject solving a concept formation task, the selection of stocks and other securities in which an investment broker can wisely invest his or his client's capital, and so forth. The models attempt to portray and understand the behavior of a man when he is using his rational capabilities to the utmost. Therefore, in conception and goals, IP models are separated by a wide gap from the traditional stimulus–response approach with its emphasis upon progressively finer analyses of simpler and smaller parcels of behavior. In revolt against this analytic tradition, the IP theorists have attempted to synthesize these complex behaviors, to construct models whose capabilities equal those of men.

To synthesize a complex piece of behavior (e.g., such as proving a theorem in symbolic logic), the theorist must specify many processes as well as a complex organization of all these processes; additionally, many conditional decision rules must be specified which stipulate how the model is to be switched one way or another in its search depending upon the outcome of previous calculations. How are we to gather information about the performance capabilities of such a complex system? As mentioned earlier, we could arduously follow through its operation step by step using paper and pencil. But to short-cut this, the system is programed as a sequence of instructions to be carried out by the computer. By running the program on a computer and having it print out its actions, we learn about its capabilities. First of all, we learn whether the system has been specified in sufficient completeness so that it will run at all; possibly more parts have to be specified or internal contradictions removed. Secondly, we can see whether the synthetic "behavior" it prints out displays the particular features we aimed to duplicate. Thirdly, we can determine from different runs how the behavior of the entire program changes when we modify selected parts of it.

Computers are programed by writing a usually long sequence of instructions which are to be carried out either on some input information or upon information stored in the "memory" banks of the machine. The total sequence of instructions is called a program. Such programs have to be written in a precise format using some standardized language that the computer can "understand." (For a discussion of interpretive languages, see Green, 1963.) The FORTRAN and ALGOL languages are in common use for programs that carry out ordinary numerical calculations. The flow chart of a simple program is shown in Figure 12-1. As data, we have the weights of 12 people; the program is to calculate their average weight. We let $x(I) = 1, 2, \ldots, 12$ represent the 12 numbers. These 12 numbers are punched into IBM cards and given to the computer. In the program, SUM is our label for a memory cell which we use as a temporary working space. The sequence of instructions is depicted in Figure 12-1. The main component is the "loop" which adds $x(I)$ to SUM and increases I by 1. This loop is executed 12 times, and then the program goes on to the division and print-out operations.

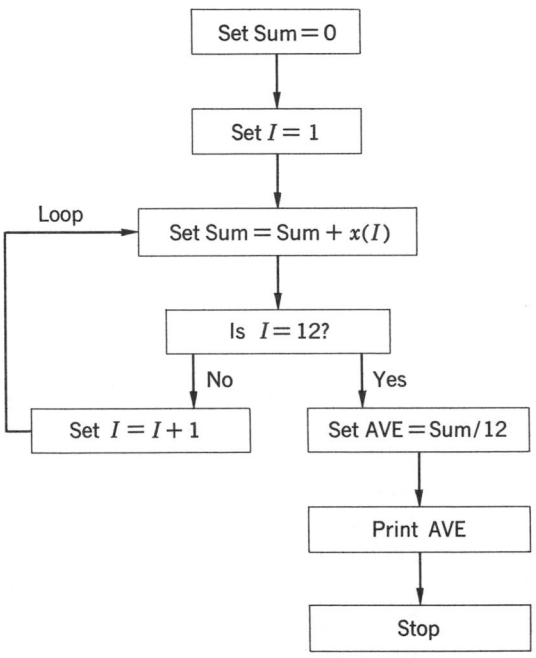

Figure 12-1　　**Flow chart depicting the steps involved in calculating the average of 12 numbers labeled x(1), x(2), . . ., x(12). A loop is used to calculate the sum of the numbers starting with x(1). On each pass through the loop the index I is increased by +1; after x(12) has been added to the sum, the program exits from the loop, calculates the average value and prints it out.**

Coincidentally with the development of IP models has been the growing recognition that the computer is not just a numerical calculator but a general-purpose symbol manipulating device. Mirroring this view, several "list processing" languages have been developed to serve as convenient vehicles for formulation and expression of IP ideas into computer programs. Of the several list-processing languages available, IPL-V (for Information Processing Language, version V—see Newell, 1961) is the one most often used in present IP work.

The basic objects of IPL-V are words (really, symbols) and names of lists of words. The operations that can be performed in IPL-V include adding or deleting a word on a particular list, reshuffling several lists, attaching a sublist onto another list, examining the words on a list to find matching words, describing the properties of a list and attaching this description-list onto the first list, erasing a list, copying a list, and so forth. Such basic processes presumably form a natural language for the IP programs. In themselves, such small-scale operations appear not to impute any intelligence to the basic machinery that does it. However, when tens of thousands of such small scale operations are cascaded within an organized program, the net performance characteristics of the machine change qualitatively into truly "intelligent" behavior, frequently of a variety unanticipated by the designer of the program.

Initial Developments

The years 1955–1960 marked the major beginnings of modern IP models. Near the start of this period, Newell, Shaw, and Simon (1958; Newell and Simon, 1956) were beginning their work on the Logic Theorist, a program which proves theorems in symbolic logic. At the same time a group of scientists at Massachusetts Institute of Technology began work on automatic pattern recognition. Personnel in the Carnegie Tech–MIT–RAND Corporation combine worked cooperatively and exchanged many ideas and techniques during this formative period.

It is probably fair to say that the Logic Theorist set the basic pattern for a large portion of the problem-solving programs that followed in the ensuing years, and that Selfridge's statement of the pattern recognition problem (1955, 1959) set forth the basic perplexities and tactics used to solve that problem. The Logic Theorist (LT) was designed to find proofs for theorems stated in the propositional calculus of symbolic logic. Such problems have a standard format. Some "givens," A, are provided, an end-statement or theorem, B, is conjectured, and the problem for the theorem-prover is to try to transform the givens into the end-statement. This has to be done by using the axioms of the system and the permissible transformation rules of the language (e.g., substitution, replacement, chaining, and detachment). As any student of logic can attest, theorem-proving is often a difficult and provocative task, and one in which failures are common. Since the axioms and transformation rules can be applied to the givens in a tremendous variety of sequential permutations, the problem is to select a path that leads to the given theorem.

A useful distinction may be made at this point between *algorithms* and *heuristic* methods of searching for an answer. An algorithm is a procedure or set of rules to follow that is guaranteed to lead eventually to the solution of a given kind of problem. Many algorithms exist in mathematics, e.g., rules for solving a set of linear equations, for inverting a matrix, for doing long division, etc. But there are many more problems for which no algorithm is known, and some efficient strategy is needed to guide the search for a solution to such problems. Proving theorems in mathematics or the propositional calculus are examples. To set out on a blind or even on a systematic search through all proper logical sequences that can be generated by the rules of the game, checking for one sequence that proves the theorem, would take a tremendously long time and be terribly inefficient. One could generate logical consequences of the givens for years in this manner without ever coming across a sequence that proves the theorem.

What obviously is needed is some means for directing the search towards a particular goal, one that has ways of detecting when it is getting close, and what must be done to move still closer to the answer. In the Logic Theorist program, Newell, Shaw, and Simon used some *heuristics* to aid and guide the search process. Heuristics are rules of thumb telling one how to search in ways that are probably fruitful or efficient. When successful, these can reduce the search time considerably, though there is no guarantee that they will always be successful. In LT the main heuristic was "working backwards" from the theorem to be proved. One or more propositions, A', are sought which imply the theorem B by a simple transformation of A'. A subproblem is then set up, to deduce one of these A' statements from the given, A, by a simple transformation. If it cannot do so directly, then it works backwards from A' to another proposition A" that implies A', and then tries to deduce A" from the given, A. A number of subproblems may be generated in moving backwards each step; these are stored on a list of subproblems to be worked on. They are then edited by special routines which delete those that look nonprovable and promote those that look simple to prove and that are "similar" in a special sense to the given. LT works on the subproblems in order, seeking a proof. If one subproblem fails to yield a proof within a time limit, it goes on to try the next. If it runs out of subproblems to work on and can generate no more, then it gives up and fails to solve the problem. A great deal more than this goes on in the LT program, and the papers cited should be consulted for the richness of detail needed.

In one experiment with LT, the first 52 theorems of *Principia Mathematica* (a standard classic in symbolic logic by Whitehead and Russell, 1925) were given to LT in the order they appeared. If LT proved a theorem, it was stored in its memory for possible later use. With this order of presentation, LT proved 38 (73%) of the 52 theorems. About half were solved with each of them requiring under a minute of computing time on the RAND JOHNIAC machine. Most of the remaining theorems took from 1 to 5 minutes each to solve. The time to prove a given theorem increased rapidly with the number of steps necessary to the proof. Other experiments showed that LT's ability to prove a given theorem depended upon the order in which the theorems were given to the program. Solutions to some easy theorems provided critical intermediate results for proving some of the more difficult theorems.

In discussing LT's performance as it was studied in several experiments, Newell, Shaw, and Simon (1958) point out numerous "human" characteristics of the model's problem-solving behavior. By way of summary, they say:

We have now reviewed the principal evidence that LT solves problems in a manner closely resembling that exhibited by humans dealing with the same problems. First, and perhaps most important, it is in fact capable of finding proofs for theorems—hence incorporates a system of processes that is sufficient for a problem-solving mechanism. Second, its ability to solve a particular problem depends on the sequence in which problems are presented to it in much the same way that a human subject's behavior depends on this sequence. Third, its behavior exhibits both preparatory and directional set. Fourth, it exhibits insight both in the sense of vicarious trial and error leading to "sudden" problem solution, and in the sense of employing heuristics to keep the total amount of trial and error within reasonable bounds. Fifth, it employs simple concepts to classify the expressions with which it deals. Sixth, its program exhibits a complex organized hierarchy of problems and subproblems (Newell, Shaw, and Simon, 1958, pp. 162).

It became clear very early that the advent of LT, more specifically the methodology, aims, and strategies involved in the LT program, heralded a new era of conceptualizations and theorizing about complex mental processes—thinking, problem solving, and the like. With rare exceptions (e.g., Duncker, 1945; DeGroot, 1946; Bruner, Goodnow, and Austin, 1956), previous psychological discussions of thinking and problem-solving had been characterized by serious vagueness and a baffling recognition of the incompleteness or insufficiency of any particular hypothesis, mechanism or theory to account for the multiple richness of the phenomena. The behavior of the LT program constituted a big step in the right direction: it was completely and precisely specified, and the sufficiency of its mechanisms was determinable. It brought a new technology for theory construction to the study of complex human behavior, an area, it should be remembered, that had been scarcely touched by the behaviorists.

Since the year 1955, there has been a fast proliferation of programs for models that perform a variety of intelligent tasks. Minsky provides a good review (1961a) and a descriptor-indexed bibliography to the literature (1961b). An excellent collection of basic papers has been edited by Feigenbaum and Feldman (1963). Students unfamiliar with computers will find the texts by Green (1963) and Borko (1962) especially helpful in explaining computers, computer languages, and their usages in the behavioral sciences. This chapter is necessarily a limited review of what is going on in this rapidly expanding field. We shall select for discussion some of the work on models for pattern recognition (perceptual learning), problem-solving, and learning. Each system we shall review is in fact a very long and complex set of detailed instructions in a functioning program. This means that a brief description of each can merely touch upon the highlights of what a particular model does and explain, in general terms, how it accomplishes this end.

A convenient, though frequently indefinite, classification of IP models is into those dealing with *simulation* and those dealing with *artificial intelligence*. The distinction hinges primarily upon the expressed intent of the theorist. If his intention is that the model should mimic step by step the processes he believes a person actually goes through in performing a task, then he is engaged in simulation of human behavior; if his intention is to design an efficient program that will perform some complex task, regardless of how a person might do it, then he is engaged in artificial-intelligence research. A radar-linked computer that calculates the trajectory of an approaching missile and fires off a countermissile to detonate it is an example of an artificially intelligent machine. What is wanted here is that the machine should outperform the man, not simulate his behavior exactly. This distinction between the two research areas is not always clearcut, however, and the principles used in constructing efficient automata are usually worth study, if only to see where or how a man falls short. Also, the principles incorporated in an artificially intelligent program to solve problems often derive from observation and introspection about how a man solves that problem. Man is far and away the most versatile, general purpose, problem-solver on this earth, so a model of man is often a good place from which to start in designing an artificially intelligent automaton. We may illustrate the problem of imitating man by considering pattern recognition.

Pattern Recognition

The problem is how to build a model, or write a program, or program a machine, that will display some of man's capabilities for classifying and discriminating the flux of environmental energies bombarding his sensors. To classify is to sort a series of things into separate classes, or what we may call "bins." Each bin has a name, and all things sorted to a given bin are given that name. The bin is an "equivalence" class: things sorted there must possess one or more features in common which constitute the criteria for equivalence though they may at the same time differ in a number of aspects irrelevant to the current classification. For example, in identifying printed and handwritten letters of the alphabet, a child in elementary school learns to give one name, "A," to all the objects in Figure 12-2. After perceptual learning, the identifying label is *invariant* under a variety of transformations in size, shape, orientation, and alteration by extraneous cues in the external stimulus. The problem is to get a machine to do the same good job of classifying these inputs that a competent and careful child can do.

Figure 12-2   **Sample of variations in handwriting of the capital letter A. The problem is to program a machine which discards irrelevant variations and identifies all these patterns as the letter A.**

In a trivial sense, the problem of pattern recognition is solved if the stimulus objects are reduced to a constant, standardized format before being given to the machine. For example, business machines are in use that "read" alphanumeric characters (the alphabetic letters plus the numerals 0-9) by a light-photocell scanning process. The scanner reads a character by matching the standardized input to one of a number of "templates" or character-prototypes that it has in store. The input is identified as that template which best matches it. But the input to such devices must be printed in a standardized type-font with a fixed orientation, size, and location. Such sensing machines are of practical use in banks (reading checks, account numbers, etc.), in business firms, and in post offices (for sorting mail). However, they have almost no significance as solutions to the invariance problem outlined above.

A beginning step towards solution of the invariance problem is to write a program that carries out some simple cleaning-up and preprocessing on the stimulus input before it is fed to the more central machinery of the pattern recognizer. Such crude preprocessing might consist of smoothing out local irregularities, filling in small holes, dropping off excess curlicues, centering the stimulus on the receiving display, changing it to a standard size and orientation, and so on. Following such preprocessing, we might then try out the template matching method in order to determine whether the whole system can now correctly identify all the stimuli. Figure 12-3 shows this method and illustrates one of its main disadvantages. The difficulty at this point is that even after preprocessing, a sample input may still match a wrong template better than the right template. In Figure 12-3, for example, the A template produces a better match to the input R sample than it does to the two A samples.

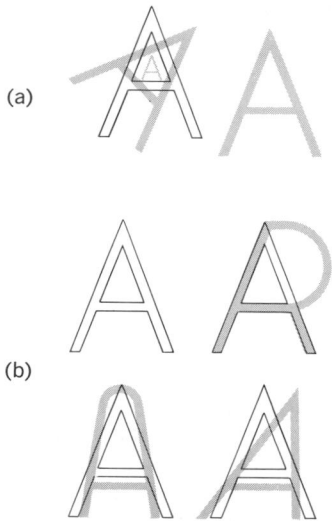

An alternative attack on these difficulties is to supplement the preprocessing with a variety of other information-extracting procedures which may be called "feature counting." For example, a capital A usually has two mostly vertical lines, and one mostly horizontal line, is generally concave at the bottom, and so on. Such features together identify A rather than some other element. The feature count gives a standardized profile of an input and decisions may be made on the basis of this profile. The number and nature of such features counted is usually stipulated in advance by the model builder.

Given a profile of features for the stimulus, there are two general schemes that can be used in coming to a decision about how to classify it: a *serial processor* and a *parallel processor*. To illustrate the serial processor, we use Selfridge and Neisser's (1960) example:

. . . a program to distinguish the letters A, H, V, and Y might decide among them on the basis of the presence or absence of three features: a concavity at the top, a crossbar, and a vertical line. The sequential process would ask first: "Is there a concavity at the top?" If no, the letter is A; if yes, then "Is there a cross-bar?" If yes, the letter is H; if no, then "Is there a vertical line?" If yes, the letter is Y; if no, V. (See Figure 12-4.) (From Selfridge and Neisser, 1960, p. 245.)

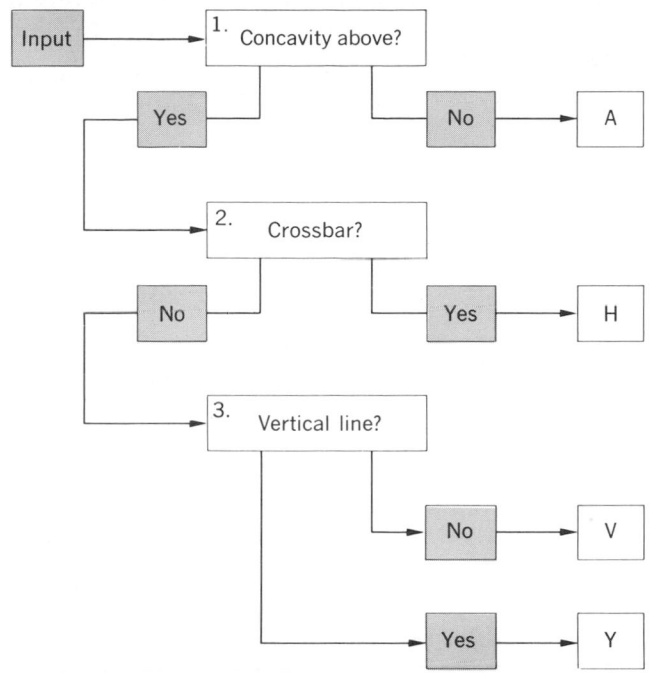

Figure 12-4   Sequential-processing program for distinguishing four letters, A, H, V, and Y, employs three test features: presence or absence of concavity above, crossbar, and a vertical line. The tests are applied in order, with each outcome determining the next step. From Pattern Recognition by Machine by O. Selfridge and U. Neisser. Copyright © 1960 by *Scientific American, Inc.* All rights reserved.

A serial processing system of this kind (called a "sorting tree") is very efficient if the decision at each node (question) of the tree is almost certain to be correct. But consider its behavior when the input data are noisy (sloppy) and each feature identifier is unreliable and uncertain in its output. If one feature is incorrectly identified, then the stimulus will be shunted off in the wrong direction through the sorting tree, and subsequent features that are correctly identified may not suffice to compensate for the misidentification of the initial features. The serial processor places too great a reliance upon the correctness of identifying each single feature. Perhaps a better decision process is one which pools together all of the feature-count information simultaneously; pooling many unreliable components may yield a total system whose reliability greatly exceeds that of any of its constituent parts. Parallel processors do just this.

In parallel processing all the questions would be asked at once, and all the answers presented simultaneously to the decision maker. (See Figure 12-5.) Different combinations identify the different letters. One might think of the various features as being inspected by little demons, all of whom shout the answers in concert to a decision making demon. From this concert comes the name "Pandemonium" for parallel processing (Selfridge and Neisser, 1960).

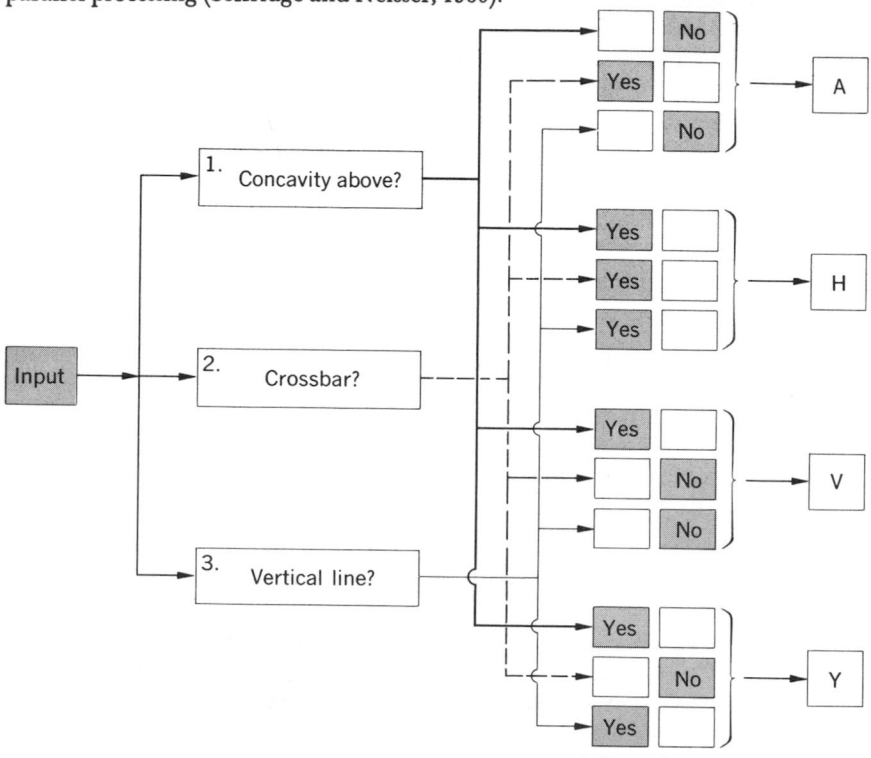

Figure 12-5   Parallel-processing program uses the same test features as does the sequential program in Figure 12-4, but applies all tests simultaneously and makes decisions on the basis of the combined outcomes. The input is a sample of the letters A, H, V, or Y. From Pattern Recognition by Machine by O. Selfridge and U. Neisser. Copyright © 1960 by *Scientific American, Inc.* All rights reserved.

A parallel processor of this nature is much less dependent upon the reliability of the separate feature counters. The combination of many unreliable components may still give an overall reliable performance. Additionally, an important aspect of the parallel processor is that the features contributing to a particular pattern can be differentially weighted (by "amplifiers"), determining how loud the feature-demons shout. Such differential weighting of the features by their importance cannot be done with a serial processor. For example, using the parallel processor, the weight of the "concavity above" feature to the A-pattern could be adjusted to make its absence three times as important as the absence of the "vertical line" feature. These weights can be adjusted in trial-and-error fashion with experience until a maximally effective combination of the weighted features is achieved. The process is little different from the way psychologists find the "best linear discriminant function" to predict a criterion variable (A or not A) from a linear combination of predictor variables. In the early programs, this trial-and-error adjustment of the feature weightings was not done intrinsically by the model; rather, the human theorist did the adjustments for the machine. An alternative weighting scheme assigns weights to features according to Bayesian probabilities calculated from past experience. That is, the weight assigned to a given feature in calculating its contribution to, say, the A-pattern hypothesis, is the probability that, over past instances, the correct answer was A when that feature appeared. The sum of the probabilities of features contributing to each pattern is taken, and that pattern name with the largest sum is chosen as the identification of the input.

A computer program employing such notions was used by Doyle (1960) to recognize 10 capital letters hand-printed by several different persons. Doyle's program used 28 different features of hand-printed letters and weighted these by the Bayesian probabilities determined from a "training set" of the handwritten characters. Its later performance on a test set showed it to make only about 10% more errors than did human judges (whose error rate was about 3%). This is an impressive performance, though one which can be improved by further refinements.

A different recognition task is illustrated by the program MAUDE (Gold, 1959) for automatic decoding of Morse code. Morse code is based entirely on discriminating the temporal durations of beeps and silent periods. In principle, a dash is to be three times as long as a dot; silent spaces between dashes or dots within a letter should be as long as a dot; silent spaces between letters should be three times as long; and silent spaces between words should be seven times as long as a dot. In practice, human code senders vary in producing these durations, and this variability is the source of confusion. The most difficult job in decoding is to separate the within-letter spaces from the between-letter spaces. MAUDE uses contextual information to decide this. Since no Morse character is more than five dots and/or dashes long, it is assumed that the longest of six consecutive spaces is a between-letter space and that the shortest is a within-letter space. The other four spaces of the six are classified according to whether they are above or below a threshold duration (continuously adjustable to the particular sender). If the tentative spacings do not make a permissible code letter in Morse, then the longest space is reclassified as a between-letter space. Similar processes are used to distinguish dots from dashes. In performance, MAUDE's error rate is only slightly higher than that of well-trained code receivers.

One of the failings of Doyle's model for visual pattern recognition described earlier is that the program-builder has to tell it what features to look at. It shows no perceptual learning in the sense of coming to extract those features from the samples which are particularly relevant to achieving a difficult discrimination. A fair amount of work on pattern recognition models has been concerned with the design of machines that construct their own feature counters, and that learn to keep good ones and discard poor ones, as well as to adjust the weightings of the features as they contribute to discriminating among the several patterns.

At present, the most successful program of this type was devised by Uhr and Vossler (1963). The input to the program is an array of "on" elements in a 20 × 20 square array of photocells: an excited receptor cell is given the value 1 and an unexcited cell is given the value 0. This simulacrum of a retina is often used in pattern recognition studies. A set of operators (similar to the former feature counters) is used to characterize the input. An *operator,* in the Uhr–Vossler system, is simply a 5 × 5 matrix, each cell of which contains one element (1, on; 0, off). The center of this matrix is moved cell by cell over the 20 × 20 display containing the sample to be recognized, much like a mask passing over the surface of a picture. At each point, a check is made for an exact match of 1's and 0's between the 5 × 5 mask and the display cells below. At the end of a sweeping over the entire display, we have a listing of the number and locations at which the mask matched subparts of the display. A number of such operators (masks) may be used by the program. The outputs from the operators may be considered as a list of characteristics of the shape displayed. These characteristics are then compared to the characteristics of patterns previously identified and stored in the machine's memory, and the name of the pattern most similar (in a complex sense) to the input is given as the response. Following the response, the environment feeds back information on the correct answer for the sample. The learning processes then take over: the operators are examined, and depending on whether they individually contributed to success or failure in the decision, their weighting (amplifier) is increased or decreased, respectively. If a particular operator is a poor one, it will eventually settle to a low weighting and will be discarded by the program and replaced by a newly generated operator. The new operators may be randomly generated or constructed within certain constraints.

One version of this model reported by Uhr and Vossler (1963) performed exceedingly well in discriminating several types of inputs which included hand-printed letters, outline pictures of faces and simple objects, random nonsense shapes, and the numbers "zero, one, two, three, four" spoken by different people. In this latter instance, the input to the program was a binary representation of the speech spectrogram which gives a moment by moment resolution of a complex speech sound into the amplitudes of the various frequency components.[1] In each case, the machine achieved very high discriminative performance (95–100%) after only a few trials with feedback ("reinforcement") through the set of training materials. On later transfer tests with new materials from the same sources, it correctly identified between 55% and 97% of the various types of materials. In an experimental comparison, the program learned to identify the random nonsense shapes much more rapidly than did college students. The performance of this system gives us some indication of the power of "self-improvement" computer programs that learn in the sense of trying out features (even random features) by trial and error and then evaluating and adjusting their weights according to their contribution towards a successful performance.

In summary, it is clear enough that most of the work on pattern recognition is not simulation but mainly artificial intelligence. The relatively successful program of Uhr–Vossler clearly does not extract the same kind of attribute-value information from the stimulus as the human eye and brain do. In terms of simulation, the challenge is to build a machine that not only manufactures its own feature counters (i.e., shows perceptual learning) but that also converges onto roughly the same ones that human beings obviously do. A more modest solution is to start off the machine with a potentially vast storehouse of feature counters (supplied by the builder) and let some learning process modify the weights of these counters, in the hope that they will eventually converge on the same features that people customarily use, if the latter are known. It is an arresting paradox that programing a machine to solve lengthy reasoning problems is relatively easier than programing it to recognize handwritten letters of the alphabet. For us, of course, the order of difficulty of the tasks is the reverse, for fine discriminations are effortlessly and immediately carried out in perception, whereas it is difficult to sustain a lengthy line of reasoning for very long without errors.

The example of pattern recognition has thus introduced us to the problems of simulation and of artificial intelligence. Just because a machine does intelligent work does not mean that it does it in the way in which we do; whether it is therefore a source of theories concerning human behavior depends upon criteria other than its successful outcome.

PROBLEM-SOLVING PROGRAMS

We now turn to several kinds of programs which come closer to the behavior of the human being as he solves problems: theorem-provers, game players, and special problem-solvers.

[1] See Forgie and Forgie (1959) for discussion of a speech recognition program. Their program distinguishes the vowel sounds in the spoken words *book, bit, bet, bot, bat, but, beet, boot, bought,* and *bert.*

Theorem-provers

Following the lead of the Logic Theorist discussed earlier, other programs were devised to help along the development of mechanical mathematics. Gelernter (1959) wrote a program which constructs proofs of plane geometry theorems. The givens and the theorem to be proved are given to the computer in the symbolic language of geometry, as line segments in various relations (e.g., parallel). A sample problem would be:

	Symbolic	Text
Given:	AB ‖ CD	line AB is parallel to line CD
	AD ‖ BC	line AD is parallel to line BC
	A–E–C	Form the line AEC
	B–E–D	Form the line BED
Prove:	AE = EC	length of line AE = length of line EC
	BE = ED	length of line BE = length of line ED

After performing syntactic and semantic analysis of the input, the program uses the givens, much as does the geometry student, to construct a diagram and to label the points and line segments. The diagram in Figure 12-6 is consistent with the givens. As does LT, the geometry machine

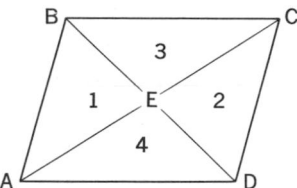

Figure 12-6   **A diagram constructed to be consistent with the givens of a geometry problem. The problem is to prove that line segments AE and EC are equal in length; also that BE and ED are equal in length.**

then tries to work backwards, looking for statements from which the theorem easily follows. In doing so, a number of subproblems may be generated as candidates to be worked on (e.g., prove that triangle 1 is congruent with triangle 2, and 3 is congruent with 4). A major heuristic of the program is to check out a subproblem by seeing whether it is true by measurement of the diagram. If it is, it is kept on the candidate list; if it is not true of the diagram, then it is discarded as a useless subgoal. Subproblems are further screened by a "similarity" analysis, and finally given to a subroutine that takes the input statements through a directed sequence of transformations permitted under the rules of plane geometry. In many respects, the program can be said to use the repertory of tricks taught to high-school students for solving geometry problems, and it came out with a good grade on the final examination.

A program that performs integration of symbolic (nonnumerical) expressions in the calculus has been written by Slagle (1963). The main job is first to "parse" and identify the basic form (syntax) of a mathematical expression to be integrated. This often requires substitution of new variables and some algebraic cleaning up. Once this is done, a "dictionary look-up" operation will often suffice to replace the standard form of the integrand by its indefinite integral. Of course, the program capable of achieving these ends is considerably more complicated than this brief description might suggest.

Game Players

The programing of a computer to play board games such as checkers or chess against an opponent shares many of the features found in programs that prove theorems. The arrangement of the pieces on the board at any moment constitutes the "givens." The objective is to transform the givens into a winning final position by a sequence of moves permitted by the rules of the game. The permissible moves of the game play the same role as do the rules of inference in constructing logical arguments. Of course, in games, the program plays against an adversary who must be assumed to be at least as rational as the program.

The basic unit for analysis is the individual move. The program, having an internal representation of the board and the location of all the pieces, looks ahead several moves—my move, his possible countermoves, my next move, his next possible countermoves to that, etc. How far ahead it looks is called the "depth" of its search. The "search tree" of possibilities can get very large if very many alternatives are considered at each move. The programs have to trade off the number of alternatives examined at each move for depth of search along particular branches of the tree. In general, programs that search deeply on a few "prosperous-looking" alternatives are more successful. Various heuristics are used to decide which alternatives one or two moves ahead warrant a deeper search.

Once a search tree of alternatives at a given move has been constructed, the program has to evaluate the various branches to discover their worth and to decide upon a move. The ultimate consequences of playing the entire game, to "win, lose, or draw," are usually too remote and too indeterminate to be of much help in evaluating a particular move. Thus, some *evaluation function* is needed that is sensitive to subgoals regarding a single, local move. Experts at the game can usually tell us a few generally desirable criteria to use in local evaluations in particular types of games, such as those that have a bearing on board control, piece advantage, king-piece exchange ratio, back row control, etc. In Samuel's checker-playing program (1959), a checker position was evaluated by computing a weighted average of the values of several such local characteristics. Each hypothetical position generated in a search tree was so evaluated.

In making a decision, the machine selects that move which has the highest value, where the value has been calculated by a "backwards mini-max" procedure. Reference to Figure 12-7 will illustrate **the procedure.**

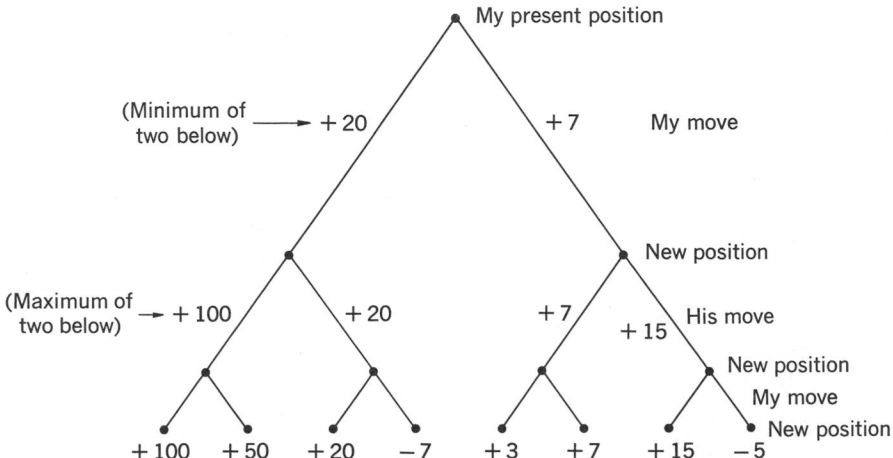

Figure 12-7　　A search tree of moves three levels deep, where only two moves are considered at each level. The positions at the deepest level searched are scored by the evaluation function. The score on a node at level 2 is the maximum of the scores on its two lower branches; the score on the level 1 node is the minimum of the score on its two lower branches.

This shows a very simple search tree involving only two moves at each level (the computer may consider 10 to 20 moves at each level) and a search going only three levels deep (my move, his countermove, my next move). Each node on the tree represents a hypothetical state of the game. At the deepest level, the 8 positions anticipated are scored by the evaluation function, with high positive scores indicating good positions for myself. Since I would choose the maximum scoring move on my second move, the value attached to the node above is the larger of the two lower scores. As to my opponent's move, we assume he would try to hold my gain to a minimum, so his choice would cause the minimum value to be attached to the node above. Backing up to my present position, the +20 branch is clearly a better move for me than the +7 branch, so that should be my choice.

This type of tree-search and minimax-backing-up analysis is done at every move of the game. Samuel's program for checker playing includes a variety of other features for improving the game it can play. Several are "learning" routines: one routine provides move-by-move feedback and correction of the weights assigned to the different subgoals in the evaluation function; the other involves a rote memory (on accessible magnetic tape) for all board positions previously encountered, searched and evaluated. This omnibus memory helps reduce the search tree at each step to just those few branches that should be searched in greater depth.

Samuel performed many explorations with this program, trying different heuristics and self-improvement learning routines. The machine was trained by having it play checkers against human players and against published championship games from checkers books. The program improved its performance remarkably, eventually to the point where it could usually beat its human opponent. In the summer of 1962, a match was arranged between a former checkers champion, Mr. Robert W. Nealey, and the program. The machine won handily. At the conclusion of the game, Mr. Nealey commented:

"Our game . . . did have its points. Up to the 31st move, all of our play had been previously published, except where I evaded "the book" several times in a vain effort to throw the computer's timing off. At the 32-27 loser and onwards, all the play is original with us, so far as I have been able to find. It is very interesting to me to note that the computer had to make several star moves in order to get the win, and that I had several opportunities to draw otherwise. That is why I kept the game going. The machine, therefore, played a perfect ending without one misstep. In the matter of the end game, I have not had such competition from any human being since 1954, when I lost my last game" (From Feigenbaum and Feldman, 1963, p. 104).

A variety of other theorem-provers and game-playing programs have been developed, but the ones reviewed suffice to characterize the undertaking in general. By and large, this is not simulation work and no one has seriously considered the programs as exact replicas of human thinking. The programs do have great intrinsic interest as fascinating, intellectual performers that frequently beat their designers. Since chess is a tremendously rich, complex, and challenging game, it is no wonder that a project is afoot to design a chess program capable of playing a top championship game. Several chess playing machines are already available, but as yet their performance is mediocre. The designing of a championship chess player can have little practical or even scientific significance, of course. Yet it would clearly constitute a major intellectual accomplishment on the part of the program writers. Fortunately, purely intellectual goals are highly esteemed and not at all rare in both mathematics and science.

Special Problem-solvers

Several programs have been written that have a bearing on various problems of special interest to psychologists. Research in problem solving (e.g., Duncker, 1945) has identified two areas of importance: the first, how a person sees, interprets, or represents a problem statement to himself and comes to understand what it is about; the second, the procedures he goes through in seeking a solution once he believes he understands the problem. The simulation models have bypassed the first, and in some ways more difficult, issue of how the problem gets interpreted by the subject; they have concentrated instead on the second issue. The problem is given to the program in a well-structured form and the programer ensures that the problem is interpreted correctly by the model before it is set to work on it.

The two programs to be discussed here, the first by Simon and Kotovsky (1963) and the second by Evans (1963), attack conceptual problems familiar to all of us from various IQ tests. The Simon and Kotovsky program attempts to infer the rule generating successive letters in a short series. In the Thurstone Letter Series Completion Test, the subject is shown a letter series and asked to supply the correct next letter of the series. Examples are cadaeafa_, atbataatbat_, and wxaxybyzczadab_. Such series vary in difficulty and some are sufficiently hard so that an appreciable proportion of college students fail them. The Simon–Kotovsky simulation program supposes that subjects solve such problems by developing a "pattern description" of the sequence and then using this description to generate the next member of the series. The model subject is assumed to have certain cognitive equipment to begin with, notably, the forwards alphabet, the backwards alphabet, the concept of "next successor" on a particular list, and the ability to detect and produce cycles through a list (e.g., in the simplest instances, repetitive cycling through the list b,a yields the series bababa . . .).

A standard format is used to state pattern descriptions, and the main job of the program is to discover a suitable pattern description. It first looks for periodicities in the sequence by looking for relations that repeat at regular intervals. For example, axbxcx has period 2 based on the "next" relation in the forwards alphabet starting at a; qxapxboxc has period 3 in which the first element of each triple uses the backwards alphabet starting at q and the third letter of each triple uses the forwards alphabet starting at a. The relation repeating at period 3 is "next successor" of the corresponding element in the prior triple. If this simple periodicity can not be found, then the program looks for a relation that is interrupted at regular intervals; for example, in aaabbbcccdd_, the relation "same letter" is interrupted in periods of 3. Once a basic periodicity has been found, the program makes a further analysis to uncover the details of the pattern, by detecting the relations—next successor or same—that hold between elements within a period or between corresponding elements in consecutive periods (as in the qxa . . . example above).

If such a generative rule is found, then it is used to extrapolate the next element. Several variants of the model differing in their power, i.e., in the richness of relations it can detect and use, were run and compared with the performance of college and high school students doing the same problems. A weak variant of the model did less well than the poorest subject, whereas a powerful variant did nearly as well as the best subject. There was considerable agreement between the subjects as a group and the program in ranking the problems in order of difficulty. Problem difficulty seemed correlated with the load on the subject's, and the model's, immediate memory. To solve the hard problems, the subject had to keep track in memory of his place on two separate lists (e.g., the forwards and backwards alphabet), while for all easy problems he needed to keep track of his place on only one list.

Another example of a program that performs a high-level intellectual task is one written by Evans (1963). Evans' program attempts to solve geometric-figure analogies of the type frequently encountered in various IQ tests. Two illustrative examples are shown in Figure 12-8 taken from tests prepared by the American Council on Education. The instructions to the subject (or program) are: "find the rule by which figure A has been changed to make figure B. Apply the rule to figure C. Select the resulting figure from figures 1–5." This task requires a considerable amount of information processing and transforming by human subjects, and it was of interest to Evans to see whether a heuristic program could be constructed which would arrive at the same answers that bright people do.

There are two main parts to Evans' program. The material given to the first part is a set of punched cards constructed by the experimenter giving a rather sketchy description of the outlined figures. For example, for panel A of Figure 12-8b it would identify a dot at a particular location in two-dimensional coordinates, a simple closed figure (triangle) with three vertices at specified locations, and another simple closed figure (square) with four vertices at specified locations. The first part of the program performs analyses on these descriptions of the figures. It first labels the objects and then, by various analytic geometry subroutines, provides various *relational* descriptions holding among parts of each figure. Thus, for panel A of Figure 12-8b it would find that the dot is *above* the triangle and the square, and that the square is *inside* the triangle. Finally, part 1 of the program performs a "similarity calculation" on pairs of objects within each figure and between two figures (e.g., panel A to B, and panel C to panels 1, 2, 3, 4, 5). The similarity calculations on a pair of objects is done by a topological matching process which tries to find a set of trans-

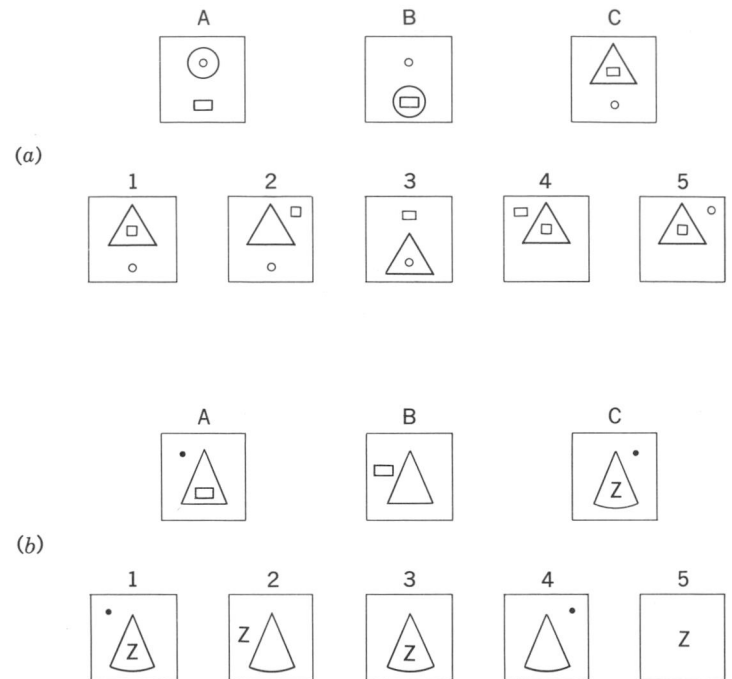

Figure 12-8   **Two illustrative problems solved by Evans' Geometric Analogies program. The question is: Figure A is to Figure B as Figure C is to which one of the five answer figures? For problem a, the answer is No. 3; for Problem b, the answer is No. 2.**

formations that take one object into another by horizontal or vertical reflection, rotation, translation, change of scale size, etc. Thus, in working on panels A and B of Figure 12-8b it would find that the triangle in A matches the triangle in B, the square in A matches the square in B, etc. The object list, relational sentences, and similarity calculations are punched out and form the input to part 2 of the program.

The job of part 2 of the program is to find the answer to the problem. The first step is for it to generate one or more rules which transform figure A into figure B. Such rules specify how objects in A are to be removed, added to, or altered in their properties and relations to other objects to generate figure B. Such a rule relating A to B in Figure 12-8b would be "delete the dot and move the square outside and to the left of the triangle." Each rule is generalized (if possible) so that it may be applied to figure C. It is performed on figure C and the program then checks to determine whether the transform of C matches one of figures 1–5. The method used deals generally with problems in which the number of objects added, removed, or altered in taking figure A into B is the same as the number of objects added, removed, or altered taking figure C into one of the answer figures. The routine may find two candidates for the answer. For example, several rules may be found taking figure A into B; more often the identification (or pairing) of A-objects with C-objects takes several forms (e.g., should we pair the Z with the rectangle or the triangle?), and depending on the pairings chosen, the rule formulated may transform C into something close to different answer figures. To select between answers (and identification pairings), the program selects (a) the rule that is the simplest in the sense of requiring the least alteration in the A → B rule to generalize it to the "C → some answer figure" rule, and (b) the rule which gives the better topological match of C-transforms to some answer figure. These decision rules in the program enable it to mimic quite well the accepted answers to these problems as envisaged by the test's constructors. Over a number of such problems, the program's selected answer agreed with the accepted answer practically all of the time. In some cases where it differed, one could see grounds for a legitimate argument against the prescribed answers. In other cases, failure was clearly due to a poor degree of figure decomposition in part 1 of Evans' initial program. For example, in Figure 12-9 below, the program decomposes it into a square and three small triangles, located at the top and two sides of the square. But human subjects alternately can see the pattern as a square superimposed in the foreground upon a large triangle in the background. This is an instance where the Gestalt rule of "good continuity" of figures describes the phenomenon. If this latter description of the pattern is useful in later comparisons and rule-generating, then the person may find an answer where the program fails. Canaday (1962) at the Massachusetts Institute of Technology has worked with a pattern recognition program that operates on and analyzes such Gestalt features of figures, so that it indeed sees Figure 12-9 as "a square on top of a triangle."

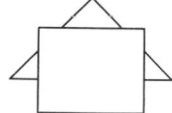

Figure 12-9   An ambiguous figure that can be seen as a square with three small triangles, or as a square superimposed upon one large triangle.

A related task of somewhat greater complexity would be to construct a program to handle the "word analogies" problem, another common IQ test. The format is the same as Evans' geometric analogies solver: *"horse* is to *buggy* as *locomotive* is to *(boxcar)."* One difficulty in simulating this task is to get long lists of associations into the machine's characterization of each concept (its various denotations, connotations, evaluative meanings, possible function usages, etc.).

By far the most ambitious program in this area is the General Problem-Solver (GPS) of Newell, Shaw, and Simon (1959; Newell and Simon, 1961). Their intent was to design a core set of processes that could work on and solve a variety of problems involving different subject matters (proving theorems in logic, proving trigonometric identities, solving word puzzles, etc.). In setting up its operation on any particular problem, a "task environment" is to be provided by specifying for the machine the objects to be encountered and the transformation rules (moves) of the particular game.

The premises and the goal must be stated in comparable terms so that GPS seeks to transform the premises (or starting point) into the goal. It uses means–ends analyses, generating subproblems to work on, and builds up a tree of subproblems. There are general routines for comparing two expressions and detecting differences between them. If differences are detected, it then seeks some transformation which reduces these differences. Figure 12-10 gives a summary of three goals (or subgoals) and the associated methods GPS uses for working on them. The goals often occur recursively within a loop. Starting with the goal of transforming object A (e.g., premise) into object B (conclusion), the program may find one or more differences. If so, it sets up the goal of reducing the most important difference. This then goes to the goal of finding an operator (allowable transformation) which can be applied to the premises. If it can not be so applied, then it sees whether A can be transformed into something to which the first operator can be applied. Part of the task-environment supplied to GPS with the problem is an operator-difference table giving the permissible transformations that are relevant to reducing particular kinds of differences.

Because pursuit of each goal often leads to a proliferation of subgoals within subgoals, the GPS program has an executive routine that monitors the generation of new subgoals, evaluates them on multiple criteria, and then discards them or decides the order in which they will be worked on.

GPS involves considerably more processes and heuristics than this brief description conveys. In many respects, it is the most sophisticated of the simulation programs. It proves theorems, of course. Of perhaps greater interest to psychologists is the attempt by Newell and Simon to fit "thinking aloud" protocols taken from subjects who are encountering and solving logic problems for the first time, after only minimal training on the rules of the game. The subject is asked to think aloud, to say what he is looking for or considering at every step of the way while proving a theorem. Similarly, the internal workings (reasonings) of the computer program are printed out as it proceeds step by step to solve the problem. Turning to the few protocols published to date, the authors point out a number of similarities in what the program and the subject are doing at various points along the construction of the proof. More of this research is

Goal I: Transform object A into object B

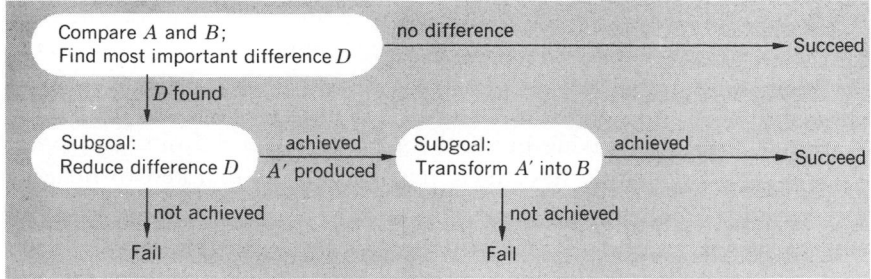

Goal II: Reduce difference D between object A and object B

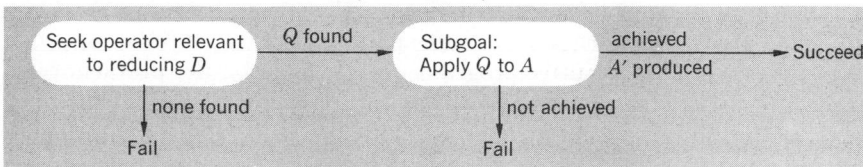

Goal III: Apply operator Q to object A

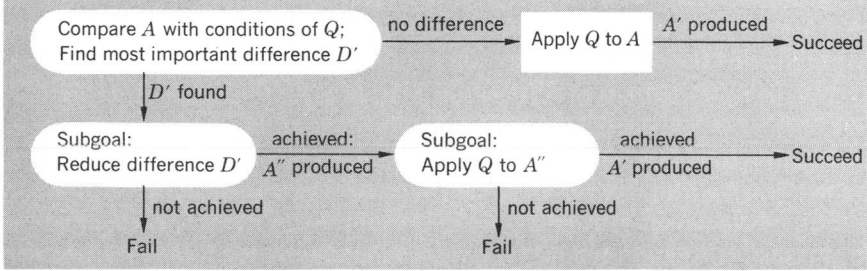

Figure 12-10   **A summary of the major goals and associated methods GPS uses to achieve these goals. The goal of transforming object A into B leads to the subgoal of reducing one or more differences between them. To reduce a given difference, a relevant operator is found. The next subgoal is to apply the operator to A. If that cannot be done, then the next subgoal is to see how A differs from something to which the operator can be applied. At this point the sequence will repeat at this lower level. (From Green, 1963.)**

being done, and will be reported in publications. The authors conclude that the program's point-by point behavior is a fairly accurate simulation of some of the significant features of the subject's verbal output and sequence of rule-selections.

It is clear nevertheless that the General Problem-Solver is still very far from attaining the general capabilities of the human adult. It requires that the goal be described in exactly the same way as the givens of a problem. From this common description, it then tries to transform the givens into the goal. This constitutes a restriction, of course, on the class of problems it can attempt to solve. For example, the Letter Series Completion and the Geometric Analogies tasks have goals not describable in this manner, and it is clear that GPS would have no way of handling these or similar problems. Having in mind the various "special purpose" problem-solving programs we have reviewed, we may be tempted to imagine that a complete model of man would be a supersystem that somehow combines all these various programs into one. Few scientists have even attempted to suggest how this might be done in a really ingenious way. The trivial logical solution, of course, would be to have an executive program that is a pattern recognizer and dispatcher. All special programs would be linked to this dispatcher, either waiting on separate computers or in a call-up library. The executive program would recognize the problem type, and dispatch it to the appropriate special-purpose computer, which would work on it and relay back the answer. This is not an elegant solution to the dream-problem of getting a general-purpose machine. However, except for duplication of processes in the linked computers, it is difficult to say exactly how and where the dispatcher system differs very much from what humans do.

LANGUAGE PROCESSING PROGRAMS

It is hardly possible to doubt that the unique capability of men is their competence in using language—listening to it, understanding it, reading it, and producing more of it in speech and writing. Modeling of these capabilities is currently the most formidable project confronting those at work in the simulation and artificial intelligence fields. The magnitude of this problem has resulted in its break up into many splinter disciplines, each attacking a different aspect of the general problem. There are good general reviews of the chief issues and lines of research by Simmons (1962), Hays (1962), and Green (1963). We shall touch briefly on three of the splinter areas.

Mechanical Translation

After giving the computer text in one language (e.g., Russian), the machine is to output an acceptable translation of it in another language (English). Because of the multiple meanings and usages of a given word in both languages, a simple dictionary-look-up program produces nothing but gibberish. Some syntactic and semantic (meaning) analysis is required, and this is exceedingly difficult to supply.

Information Retrieval

A person places a request for all available documents on some particular topic (e.g., "simulation of learning by machines"). The ideal machine, having a large file of documents and their indexed listing, determines what the request is about and which documents are relevant to it, retrieves them from the files, and delivers them, or a list of their references, to the man making the request. Besides that of understanding the request, the problem here is to design a suitable classification and indexing system, since titles of papers are seldom informative of the range of topics discussed in the article.

Question Answering

These programs take various forms. In one by Green *et al.* (1961), basic factual data are put into the computer in well-organized, tabular form, and then questions are asked of the machine, requiring it to recombine or process the data in sometimes novel ways to compute the answer. Scores of baseball games played by the Yankees in July might be given as the basic data. A question asked might be "In what percentage of their contests did the Yankees beat the Red Sox?" The main job, of course, is getting the machine to understand what is being asked for, and then proceed to find the data relevant to the answer. A program by Lindsay (1963) takes as input Basic English statements about kinship relations, constructs a meaningful model of the family tree, and then answers questions by inference from this kinship model. Given the data that Jane is Jim's sister and Mary's daughter, then the computer when asked will infer that Mary is Jim's mother. If given many relational statements, the family tree may get complex and inferences become difficult to draw out. Lindsay's aim was not to resolve kinship claims but rather to document his belief that realistic models of language must attribute to the subject (program) some ability to construct a usable representation of his (its) environment. The sentences processed by a person refer to things in the world and help him to construct by induction an internal "picture" of that world. Accordingly, questions are answered by referring to his "world-view" rather than by scanning through a file of sentences he has stored away in his memory.

Another language-processing program by Bobrow (1964) solves word problems in algebra. Its main task is to perform a syntactic and semantic analysis of statements in English so as to effect a translation of them into a system of mathematical equations. Methods are employed to identify the mathematical variables and to translate relational statements ("Jim is twice as old as Jane") into equational form, and to interpret just what information is being requested. As most school boys know, once the translation has been successfully achieved, the solution of the system of linear equations is easy (as it is, too, for Bobrow's program).

The problems of language processors arise in large part because of the versatility and multiplicity of forms used. Word strings differing in multiple ways can, in some sense, say exactly the same thing. The two strings "How many times did the Yankees beat the Red Sox in July?" and "What is the figure obtained by counting the occasions on which the Boston team's score was below their opponents' at the termination of the games played with New York between June 31 and August 1?" differ in multiple ways, yet they seem to request the same information. On the other hand, altering a single critical word may alter radically the meaning of a question, and the sequence of information processes needed to answer it. Language problems are difficult and it must be accepted that progress in building a sufficient model for the natural language user will be slow.

LEARNING PROGRAMS

Relevant to the subject of this volume are the information processing models aimed at understanding learning. In the preceding discussion of intelligent automata, we touched briefly on programs incorporating learning subroutines, which are used in modifying other parts of the program with the aim of effecting a better match between the program's response and the correct one reinforced by the trainer. Such subroutines indeed produce adaptive, responsive, optimizing machines. However, in most cases, simulation of how the actual subject might learn and improve his performance is usually not pursued in detail. The information processing models to be considered in this section were devised as first steps toward this aim. Accordingly, the theorists considered below have been more often concerned with describing and modeling experimental results than with actually producing an artificially intelligent machine.

Verbal Learning

A model of general interest to psychologists is the Elementary Perceiver and Memorizer (EPAM) of Feigenbaum and Simon. Their aim was to develop a model that simulates human behavior in a diversity of experimental tasks involving associative learning. Included among these tasks would be paired-associates learning, rote serial learning, recognition learning, immediate or short-term memory tasks, learning to read text, to name objects or pictures, to form concepts, and the like. In principle, the stimuli could be given directly to the machine in any form—visual or auditory. In fact, however, the present version of EPAM has no perceptual processor, so the programmer has to analyze the stimuli into distinctive features, punch this information onto IBM cards, and only then will EPAM be able to deal with the "stimuli."

Because of the comprehensive goals of the model, it is complicated and lengthy. The basic model (Feigenbaum, 1959) has undergone extensive testing and modifications. The version to be discussed below is that described in a paper by Simon and Feigenbaum (1964). We consider its application to paired-associates learning. Specifically, suppose the model is learning a list of nonsense syllable pairs (REH-GIJ, RUZ-FOT, etc.). One part of the program simulates the experimental task; that is, it imitates a paced memory drum which exposes first a stimulus member, then the stimulus and response members together, repetitively cycling through all pairs in the list. The model's task is to anticipate (print out) the correct response when the stimulus is shown.

EPAM learns by building up a sorting tree or discrimination net that makes possible differentiation among the stimuli and responses. The sorting tree is a serial processing system much like that displayed previously in Figure 12-2. Stored at terminal nodes of this sorting tree are compound "images," which are more or less complete representations of the S–R pairs. In general, neither the features used for sorting nor the information stored in the image is complete; that is, no more information is stored than is minimally needed to get by on the task at hand.

Two learning processes, image-building (familiarization) and discrimination learning (tree growing) are postulated. When a stimulus S in view is sorted to a terminal node, it is compared with the stimulus image, S', residing there (from past experience). If no image is there, then part of S is copied as the image at that node. If an image is already there, a comparison of S and S' is made; if differences in detail only are detected, S' is changed or augmented to match S better. Thus is the S' image of S grown. If a positive difference (not just a lack of detail) between S and S' is detected, then the discrimination learning process takes over and constructs two new branches from the former terminal node, with S and S' separately as the images of the new terminals. To illustrate, suppose that we can arrive at a current terminal node by tests on the first letter R, and the current image at this node is R_H. Later RUZ is sorted to this node. In comparing RUZ to the image R_H, the program notes a difference in detail in the second position (not serious) and a positive difference (Z vs H) in the third position. It would then set up a third-letter test at this node as shown in Figure 12-11b. With this new node added to the tree, the stimuli REH and RUZ are no longer sorted to the same node so that confusion errors between them will be avoided.

Although the sorting (recognizing) is done on the stimulus member of the pair, both the stimulus and response syllables are represented as a compound image S'–R' at the terminal node. The response image, R', is retrieved when S gets sorted to and makes contact with the stimulus image S'. The response image R' contains information enabling the program to locate another terminal node R″ in the net, and R″ will, after learning, contain the images of the three letters of the response syllables (G, I, J) and the information required to produce them (print them out). Eventually, then, presentation of stimulus REH causes the machine to print out GIJ and it has learned.

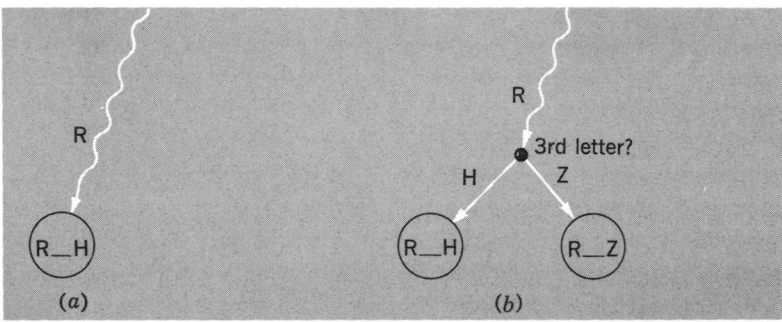

Figure 12-11   An example of how a formerly terminal node in EPAM's discrimination net will be elaborated, to differentiate previously confused stimuli. In (*a*), by first letter tests on R one arrives at a terminal node bearing the image R-H. Later, when RUZ is sorted to this node, causing a confusion error, a new test is added based on the third letter (*b*) and two lower nodes are sprouted from this terminal.

One virtue of this system is that it treats the nominal stimulus and response terms in comparable fashion, namely, as images to be built up in the sorting tree. Also the S–R pair to be associated requires no special representation as it is simply a compound image constructed from two simpler images. In addition to the recognition and learning processes mentioned above, EPAM has a higher-level executive routine that oversees and "runs the show." Part of its job is to keep the central processes in contact with the environment (e.g., "stop processing that last item; respond to the new S that has just appeared in the drum window"), to schedule where and how it shall distribute the processing effort and time at its disposal, since image building and net growing take processing time. It uses feedback about its current performance on an S–R pair to decide, roughly speaking, what is the matter and what part of the knowledge-structure needs more polishing. There are many more details to EPAM, but this sketch is not intended to do more than describe the basic processes it uses.

Simon and Feigenbaum (1964) have put the EPAM model through a variety of simulated learning experiments and compared its trial-by-trial output with that of human subjects. It shows a number of similarities to the data. Like human subjects, EPAM takes longer to learn a list in which the stimulus items are highly similar (many common letters). It displays positive or negative transfer in learning a second list depending upon the stimulus–response relations of the two lists, in much the same way that the human data depend on these relations. It shows the beneficial effect of prior familiarization with the stimulus and response terms before these are used in a paired-associate learning task. The model shows stimulus confusion errors and retroactive interference to a degree depending upon the similarity of stimulus items in the original learned list and the interpolated list. It shows a serial position effect in rote serial learning that corresponds closely to those obtained (cf. Feigenbaum and Simon, 1962). The simulation of the data is sometimes fairly accurate in a relative quantitative sense, i.e., the ratio of trials to learn under condition A to that for condition B is about the same for the model as for the human data. In an early paper, Feigenbaum and Simon (1961) showed that EPAM exhibited an interesting form of mediation (chained associations) seen in the training of reading. In phase 1, EPAM learned to associate acoustically coded properties of the spoken word "kahr" with symbolic pointing to a visually coded picture of a car. In phase 2, it learned to associate the visual word CAR with the acoustic pattern "kahr." When later tested with the visual word CAR and required to point at a picture, it selected the car-picture. This is a simple example of mediated transfer, and is of the elementary sort that most stimulus-response analyses would predict.

EPAM is an important and promising model, primarily because of its promise of comprehensibility rather than because of its accomplishments up to now. Considerably less elaborate alternative models can be written to handle the data presently offered in support of the EPAM model. However, the prospective operations and tasks it is capable of performing may very likely leave the simpler alternative models trailing behind in a cloud of dust. To be sure, there are several well-known phenomena of verbal learning that EPAM presently does not account for (e.g., backward associations and proactive interference). Though these could be handled by *ad hoc* supplements, the theory designers apparently prefer to wait until a more elegant and parsimonious mechanism suggests itself for their explanation.

The Binary Choice Program

Feldman (1961, 1962) has worked on a model to simulate the behavior of subjects in the binary choice experiment known as "probability learning." Such experiments were described earlier in Chapter 11 (cf. p. 348). In them, the subject tries to predict successive members in a sequence of binary events (e.g., C or P) that are shown to him one at a time. The sequences are constructed randomly (e.g., 70% C and 30% P events), although subjects frequently believe the sequence is lawful and orderly and they try to discover its pattern. The standard account of behavior in this situation is given by stochastic learning models (cf. Chapter 11) which suppose that the subject's probability of predicting C increases or decreases trial by trial depending on whether the C or P event occurs.

Feldman's model supposes that in this situation the subject is trying to discover local patterns (or trying out sequential hypotheses) to explain the event sequence and to extrapolate (predict) the next member of the series. To get information relevant to these notions, Feldman has his subjects "think aloud" and state their reasons trial by trial for the prediction they make. A subject's protocol consists then of the sequence of his predictions and the reasons he gave for each. Feldman's model attempts to account for the sequence of reasons, since the subject almost always made a prediction that was consistent with the reason he gave. The model is tailored specifically to simulate a particular subject, and details of the program vary for different subjects.

The program proceeds by the testing out of hypotheses which are attempts to explain the event sequence. The trial-by-trial cycle for the model is as follows: Use the current hypothesis to predict the next event; the next event occurs, and it is explained by an explanation hypothesis; a prediction hypothesis is developed, and is used to predict the next event; the next event occurs and the cycle repeats.

Each hypothesis consists of two components: an event-pattern hypothesis and a guess-opposite component. The event-pattern hypothesis is selected from a list of pattern hypotheses such as "progression of C's," "alternation of 2 C's and 2 P's," and so forth. The patterns are put on this list by the theorist after examining what types the subject said he used. The guess-opposite component may be either "on" or "off": if the pattern hypothesis is a progression of C's and this component is off, the model predicts C; if the guess-opposite component is on, the model predicts P, the opposite of the pattern.

Various rules are employed whereby feedback from the event sequence is used to select, alter, or maintain the current hypothesis. If a hypothesis predicts correctly, it is retained for another trial. If it predicts incorrectly, it is likely to be replaced temporarily. In this case, the events from the last 3 or 4 trials are used to select the plausible candidates from the pattern-hypothesis list. If several candidates are plausible, the program chooses that pattern-hypothesis which has been used most often in the past. The circumstances for modification of the guess-opposite component are more complicated and cannot be easily summarized.

Feldman (1962) has published the outcome of fitting the model to the behavior of one subject. His procedure was to continually revise the model until it gave a good fit. Feldman summarizes the process as follows:

The completion of the model was a lengthy task involving the iterative procedure of proposing a detailed model, testing the model against the data, modifying the model, testing again, and so on. During this procedure, almost every part of the model originally proposed was modified or replaced (Feldman, 1962, p. 342).

A unique feature of Feldman's model assessment was his use of "conditional prediction." If the model's prediction of the subject's hypothesis on trial n proved incorrect, then the model was set back on the correct track by replacing its "predicted" hypothesis with the subject's actual hypothesis. The supposition was that the model is strongly path-dependent, in the sense that if it is "off" on trial n, it will get progressively farther off from the data if it is not set back on the track.

These two methodological points, models tailored for individuals and contingent predictions, are novel to Feldman's work. They will be discussed later in the section on evaluation of simulation models. Suffice it to say, that by using these techniques, Feldman demonstrated that his model was able to predict his subject's protocol with a high degree of accuracy.

Concept Learners

Psychologists have for many years carried out investigations of concept learning, most of the more recent ones falling within the framework of the kind of experimental tasks whose analysis was proposed by Hovland (1952). Stimulus objects or patterns are characterized according to a list of attributes each with a number of values. For example, geometric patterns can differ in the attributes of size, color, shape, orientation, and so on. If there are n attributes with v values each, then there are potentially v^n patterns in all. A concept can be defined by a division of this set into two parts, with the patterns in one part belonging to class A and the remainder belonging to the complement class $\bar{A}$.

To illustrate, the universe of patterns might be four-letter nonsense strings; in each letter position ("attribute") either of 3 letters ("values") can appear. If the attribute-values are (X,Z,T), (P,M,K), (J,W,R), and (B,T,S), then XPJB and ZPRT are elements of the universe while XZTP and XPTW are not. For convenience in the following, we use abbreviations such as 3J to indicate the letter J at position 3. In Hovland's initial scheme, concepts were defined by specifying one attribute-value (e.g., 2K) or several attribute-values with logical connectives between them. In a *conjunctive* problem (e.g., 1X *and* 2P), patterns containing both 1X and 2P go into class A; otherwise, into class $\bar{A}$. In other words, 1X (as is 2P) is separately necessary but not a sufficient condition for class A. Several varieties of logical connectives are available besides these: exclusive disjunction (2M or 4S but not both), implication (4S or not 2M or both), and biconditional (1X and 2P, or not 1X and not 2P).

Hunt (1962) and Hunt, Marin, and Stone (1965), following early notions of Hunt and Hovland (1961), have developed an information processing model which learns or solves such concept problems. Although the model uses several strategies that humans apparently also do (e.g., having a bias for conjunctive solutions), it contains features which humans quite certainly do not show (e.g., perfect memory for many previous patterns, perfect rationality, errorless checking and validation of a hypothesis).

The program proceeds roughly as follows: as successive instances of the A and $\bar{A}$ class are given to the machine, they are stored away on two separate lists in memory. The model learns a concept by growing a sorting tree (serial processor); the sorting tree and the concept labels, A and $\bar{A}$, stored at its terminal nodes are then sufficient to classify all further instances. For example, a tree for the inclusive disjunction (2M or 4S or both) is shown in Figure 12-12a and for exclusive disjunction (2M or 4S but not both) in Figure 12-12b. The nodes of the tree ask a question about an attribute-value; depending upon how an input pattern "answers" this question, it is shunted by the left or right branch to a lower node.

Hunt's concept learner is an algorithm embodying a "wholist strategy," which looks for common features of objects classified similarly. Given the current lists of A and $\bar{A}$ patterns, it looks for one or more characteristics always present in one list but not in the other. If such features are found they are made the first node of the sorting tree and the problem is solved. This alone suffices if the concept is the affirmation or denial of either one element (e.g., "not 2M") or a conjunction of elements. If no such feature is found, then a first node is composed of that feature which occurs most frequently in the positive instances. This node produces two new pairs of sublists, namely, lists of positive and negative instances which do or do not have the first feature. Treating each pair of sublists as a separate problem, the program uses the wholist strategy again (recurses back to the beginning) on each subproblem, and therefrom constructs a second and third node for the sorting tree. The reader may verify that two such recursions will suffice to solve any two-element concept, e.g., the disjunctions in Figure 12-12. The recursion continues, or the decision tree grows, until all patterns in memory have been correctly classified.

In Hunt's program, the tree-growing routines will eventually come to a solution in the sense of correctly sorting all members of its A and A list. The decision tree it grows is not guaranteed to be the simplest in a logical sense, but in fact, it was so in most of the simulated runs of the program. Hunt, Marin, and Stone (1965) report results of conducting several experiments on the model's behavior. The main evidence offered for considering this as an initial candidate for simulation of how people solve

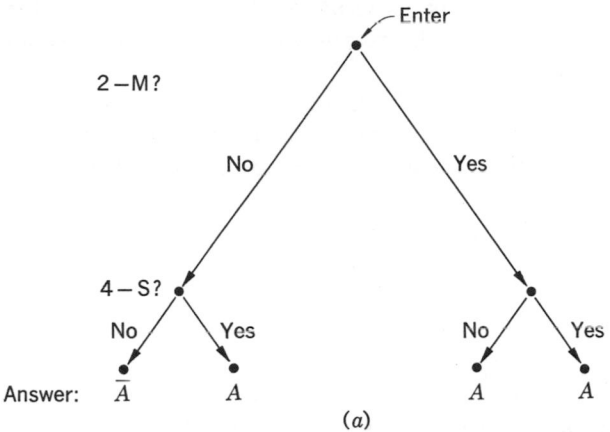

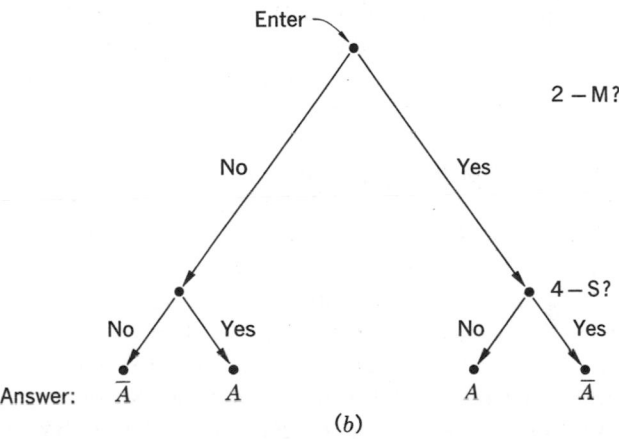

Figure 12-12   Examples of optimally efficient binary sorting trees for classifying stimuli. In (*a*), the A-concept is "2M or 4S or both." The first node asks whether the input pattern has an M in the second position; the second node asks whether it has an S in the fourth position. In (*b*), the A-concept is "2M or 4S but not both."

concept problems is that the rank order of difficulty in solving concepts of different logical types turns out to be about the same for the program as for most people. At best, this is a weak constraint and not a very demanding test for a reasonable model to pass. The difficulty of acquiring a given concept is roughly correlated with the length of the logical statement required to define it. For example, "2M" is easiest, "2M and 4S" is next, "2M or 4S or both" is next, and "2M and 4S, or not 2M and not 4S" is hardest. A somewhat more convincing result is that a subject's trial-by-trial classifications of patterns (while learning) were predicted better by the model than by the responses of another subject going through the same problem.

The deficiencies of the model considered as a simulation are its large memory, its rationality, and its reliance upon a wholist strategy. Humans have error-prone memories, are not always rational, and have flexible search strategies that are easily modified by instructions or by a small amount of practice on problems of one type (e.g., Haygood and Bourne, 1965). A more general limitation of the model stems from its concentration on only the Hovland-type of concepts; that is, its dependence on the format of attribute-value descriptions where the concepts are defined by Boolean operations on attribute-value pairs. Such description spaces are simply not rich enough to represent many of the concepts that people learn and use. For example, relational and metric notions, such as *"x* is *above y," "x* is *longer than y,"* cannot be represented in these terms, nor can so many of our concepts that are defined by relations among their parts. The "concept" of the letter E, for instance, requires a listing of its parts (three horizontal short lines, one vertical long line) in certain relations to each other (horizontal lines above one another and parallel, their left ends making contact with vertical line, etc.).

Another concept learning program has been described in detail by Johnson (1964). Johnson had his subjects think aloud while working on a variety of concept learning problems. He tried to tailor the model so that it would mimic trial by trial the hypotheses particular subjects entertained while working on a problem. At the outset the model is endowed with a long list of hypotheses regarding the form of the solution, and these have probability weights determining their selection. A hypothesis is selected and checked out against the data; if it is valid for the past instances, it is used until disconfirmed. When disconfirmed, its probability weight is lowered, and the selection of a hypothesis starts anew. Other mechanisms are postulated to get the model to try out compound hypotheses and also to display maladaptive behavior (e.g., incomplete checking of a proposed hypothesis, patching up a wrong hypothesis by addition of exceptions, etc.). Johnson published results comparing the model's trial-by-trial output to that of his three subjects. It is difficult to judge exactly how accurate the simulation was, although Johnson concludes that it was adequate.

By way of summary, it may be seen that simulation models of learning have tended to tackle the more "complicated" learning situations and, generally speaking, have developed rather involved models of the subject. No efforts have been directed at modeling the so-called "simple" learning situations such as classical or instrumental conditioning. A significant distinction in strategy may be made between theorists who construct a model of subjects in general (Feigenbaum, Simon, Hunt) and those who tailor a model for a specific subject (Feldman, Johnson). The argument for the latter is that individuals differ, and may do so considerably, and it is wise not to ignore this fact. In constructing a model, one puts in various general processes or assumptions but then leaves it open with respect to a fringe of possible specific processes or their parameters which may be altered to model a particular subject. Hopefully, only these fringe processes will have to be changed to make the model fit other subjects. In a way analogous to factor analysis, the worth of the modeling enterprise depends on the weight of the common factors (general processes) relative to the specific or unique factors which are altered to produce the fits with different subjects. At present, the theorists have to admit that these relative weights are unknown.

DISCUSSION AND EVALUATION

Having briefly described several of the information processing models that have a relevance to behavior theory, it may be helpful to discuss some of the advantages and accomplishments of this approach as well as a few of the problems connected with it. We take up the latter first, since we prefer to end the section in a positive forward-looking vein. The main problems are those of communication and evaluating goodness of fit.

The Communication Problem

The communication problem is a serious one and there can be little hope for its solution in the immediate future. Despite the obvious contributions of the developments in computer simulation, psychologists (who should be among the major beneficiaries) have been very slow to adopt these techniques placed at their disposal. Still, ten years following the appearance of the Logic Theorist and the conceptual revolution it initiated, the major portion of the personnel engaged in simulation are not psychologists by training. Instead they come from such disciplines as the computer sciences, engineering, business administration, mathematics, and linguistics. Probably several inferences can be drawn from this fact: one has to do with historical vested interests of psychologists in analytic problems of ancient vintage; another concerns the cultural lag that interferes with modifying graduate training practices in psychology in order to accommodate the new computer technology. Perhaps the most obvious fact is one emphasized by Reitman (1964); namely, the impoverished communication between experimental psychologists and computer simulators. Simulation programs are comprised of exceedingly long sequences of instructions, with an almost dumbfounding welter of complex details, and all wrapped up and coded in a special programming language adapted to communication to an IBM 7090, not to a psychologist who understands nothing of IPL-V. Acquiring facility with one or more list-processing languages is difficult and time-consuming, especially so for the older scientists who are very pressed for time by their usual research commitments. As Reitman notes:

. . . the description of a recent version of the Newell, Shaw, and Simon General Problem Solving program (GPS) runs to more than 100 pages and even so covers only the main details of the system. Furthermore, the discussion assumes a knowledge of an earlier basic paper on GPS and a knowledge of Information Processing Language V (IPL-V), the computer language in which it is written. Finally, the appendix, which simply *names* the routines and structures employed, takes another 25 pages. Unless one is familiar with similar systems, a thorough grasp of the dynamic properties of so complex a model almost certainly presupposes experience with the running program and its output (Reitman, 1964, p. 4).

In place of a prolonged apprenticeship with a model's program and the computer, the ordinary experimentalist is dependent upon an intermediary to interpret the program for him, provided such an intermediary is available, as usually he is not. Because of the incompleteness of an "outsider's" knowledge of the program, he is unsure what the psychological assumptions in the theory are, or fails to grasp the importance and critical nature of one or another feature in the overall performance, such as the way a particular subroutine is coded. The difficulty is compounded by the fact that the simulation theorist is also constantly modifying his model (intending to improve it, of course), with the consequence that in discussions the uninformed have difficulty keeping track of one version, let alone three or four newer versions.

Perhaps because they are put off by the omnibus appearance of many simulation programs, experimentalists are not inclined to tease out critical hypotheses from the overall model and put these to experimental test. It is a significant though perplexing fact that, after ten years' production of simulation theories, the amount of novel experimental testing that has been instigated by them can only be described as miniscule compared to the effort put into the theoretical enterprise. As a result, the enterprise has turned up few new empirical facts about behavior. The simulation theorist may well agree that this is true, but presumably he would reply: "Facts? We've got plenty of them already. What's needed is a general model sufficient for the facts at hand." This and similar rejoinders encounter a mixed reception depending on the biases of the audience.

Evaluating Goodness of Fit

The other major problem associated with computer *simulation* theories (which purport to be models of the person) lies in evaluating the goodness of fit of the model to the data. First of all, because of the complexity of such models, practically no *general* theorems can be proved regarding specific features of its behavior in particular situations. They differ in this regard from mathematical theories (at least those where explicit solutions can be obtained). Such general theorems are usually explicit equations of the form: "if the data statistics x_1, x_2, have known values, then the data statistics x_3 and x_4 should have the values $x_3 = f_1(x_1, x_2)$ and $x_4 = f_2(x_1, x_2)$." In the case of most information processing theories, the results of a single simulation run are relatively uninformative about the general characteristics of the behavior the program can display. Hence, many simulation runs must be made, usually under slightly varying circumstances or model parameters, in the hope that one can infer some general properties of the behavior it exhibits by examining this sample of results. Newell and Simon note the issue as follows:

. . . we can study the model empirically, exploring its behavior under variations of parameters and so on. But to date there is no body of theorems and general means of inference that allow us to derive general properties of the program given in symbolic form. Almost no interesting theorems, in the accepted mathematical sense of the word, have ever been proved about particular programs (Newell and Simon, 1963, p. 375).

The accumulation of knowledge about a program's specific capabilities by this method is often slow. In consequence of this slow accumulation the theorist often cannot answer specific questions about his model until he has run his program under just those specific conditions. Thus, information-feedback to the questioning experimentalist is often much delayed.

In lieu of general theorems, the favored method for testing the validity of a simulation model is by direct comparison of the trial-by-trial statements of the subject while thinking aloud and the corresponding "reasonings" output by the computer program. Comparison with a single computer trace from the program will obviously not do if the program involves many probabilistic elements and, as a consequence, displays quite variable behavior over different runs. However, in the programs employing this method to date (Feldman's binary choice machine and GPS), few or no probabilistic elements are involved, so the same trace is always obtained, given the same starting state and sequence of experimental events.

Despite its several advantages, the "thinking aloud" technique also has some drawbacks. Often the subject's remarks have to be edited, "content analyzed," and coded in terms comparable to the computer's trace of GPS. In Feldman's binary choice situation, it may be plausibly argued that the format and content of the subject's "thinking aloud" statements are determined in part by incidental, selective reinforcements by the experimenter. For example, in one published protocol (Feldman, 1961), it would appear that during the early trials the subject was learning what kinds of "thinking aloud" statements were acceptable to the experimenter. The effect of casual reinforcement (through facial expression, tone of voice, etc.) upon behavior in such ambiguous situations is well established (cf. Krasner, 1958). If pressed, an S–R theorist might argue that the content of the thinking-aloud statements could be considered as rationalizations of the more primitive effects of reinforcement of prediction responses produced by the event series. The subject might "just feel that it'll be a C event," but learns to add on a rationalization of this ("You'll continue the progression"). Other studies argue for such "primitive" learning without awareness. Even more relevant is Verplanck's experiment (1962) showing that by incidental reinforcement the subject's motor responses and the content of his verbal rationalizing of them could be shaped almost independently of each other, even to the point of putting them entirely out of phase.

Setting aside these cautions, suppose we accept the validity of the thinking-aloud statements and ask about the goodness of fit of the model. Here Newell and Simon have made this succinct comment:

> Thus, in gaining a form of prediction (single trials of protocols) that seems hard to achieve by classical numerical models, we lose most of our standard statistical techniques for treating data and raise many difficult problems about assessing the goodness of our theories (Newell and Simon, 1963, p. 376).

Feldman (1962) lists three possible tests. The first, Turing's test (can an uninformed judge discriminate between a human protocol and the computer's protocol?), Feldman rejects as too weak, as it surely is. The second, simple difference counting (between the model's and subject's trial-by-trial output), he also rejects because of the strong path dependency implicit in certain models. The third method, contingent prediction, sets the model back on the right track each time it makes an error (i.e., replace the model's prediction hypothesis with the subject's stated hypothesis). Feldman argues that only this method gives the model a fair chance. The fit of the model to one subject using this method is impressive, but this is difficult to assess when we recall how the model was repeatedly revised in terms of the data. Also, some of the more accurate predictions test only trivial aspects of the complex model (e.g., on 117 of 120 trials the subject kept his hypothesis for another trial when it was confirmed; in 193 of 195 trials he made his prediction consistent with his stated hypothesis, etc.).

It appears certain that alternative methods of testing goodness of fit must be developed as more simulation models get down to the hard business of exact trial-by-trial predictions, which after all, is advertised as one of their chief merits. Feldman is one of the few in the IP area who has discussed the issue in any depth, probably because his model was the first to arrive at this advanced stage of development and testing. The conditional-prediction proposal will not be generally applicable (see Reitman, 1964). For some models, a given prediction depends upon such a complex network of prior decisions and arrangements of list structures that once the model errs (as it surely must, being only a model), it is not clear how to proceed in setting it back on the track of the subject. The deficiencies of the IP models on this score are well known and widely deplored by the scientists working with simulation models. We may count on vigorous and varied efforts to rectify this specific problem.

Advantages in Simulation

Let us conclude this section by mentioning a few of the accomplishments, benefits, and advantages of the simulation approach. First of all, the simulation approach has been a strong antidote to the predominately analytic trend that has generally characterized experimental psychology. The job of a scientist is only half done when he has carried through a thorough, analytic breakdown of a behavioral phenomenon. An equally important, and often neglected, part of his job is to show how to reconstruct or synthesize the behavior from his analytic units. If the behavior is complex, then there is all the more reason to demand a synthesis (a model) that can be proven sufficient unto the phenomena it purports to explain. The computer is a tool for helping us prove that our theory specifies enough parts, together with sufficient detail concerning their exact rules of operation to make it behave. There can be no hidden or implicit assumptions in the model: if it is not explicitly written in the program, the computer prints back "Garbage!" and throws you off, a sobering lesson in the necessity of being explicit and complete.

A second point that we have learned is that the higher mental processes arc neither so mysterious nor so complicated as to defy exact modeling, as had been formerly believed. Newell and Simon state this conclusion clearly:

The first thing we have learned—and the evidence is by now quite substantial—is that we can explain many of the processes of human thinking without postulating mechanisms at subconscious levels which are different from those that are partly conscious and partly verbalized. The processes of problem solving, it is turning out, are the familiar processes of noticing, searching, modifying the search direction on the basis of clues, and so on. The same symbol-manipulating processes that participate in these functions are also sufficient for such problem-solving techniques as abstracting and using imagery. It looks more and more as if problem solving is accomplished through complex structures of familiar simple elements. The growing proof is that we can simulate problem solving in a number of situations using no more than these simple elements as the building blocks of our programs (Newell and Simon, 1963, p. 402).

The general position that problem-solving involves organized sequences of only elementary processes is not itself a testable proposition. Rather, it is an orientation or strategy for undertaking the theory-constructing enterprise. In one sense, it is true that every complex process is eventually understood in terms of sequences of elementary (familiar) operations. So this position really reflects a confidence that the higher mental processes will eventually be understood by the rational methods of science. The quoted comment of Newell and Simon regarding subconscious processes (to which Freudians and others have imputed much "incubation" of thoughts) is difficult to understand and perhaps unfortunate. One might ask how we would ever discover that different processes go on subconsciously than are revealed to us at least partly in conscious verbalizations. The remark presumably means that in the tasks so far simulated, there rarely occurs any thinking-aloud behavior during problem solving that is of a kind *completely* unanticipated by the model. But this is the same as saying that the model is fairly adequate to its job; if it were not, then the sequences of elementary operations would simply be revised to handle the previously unexpected behavior, provided it were thought important enough to do so.

A third benefit of unusually great importance is that the work on simulation has brought the study and explanation of complex cognitive processes within practicable reach. It has redressed the unbalanced trend of behaviorism towards the finer analysis and study of smaller units of behavior under artificial conditions. The argument has been that more complex behaviors—thinking and problem solving—could be more easily understood once simple behaviors under especially simplified conditions were better understood (e.g., rote learning, rats learning mazes, etc.). After some 30 to 40 years without striking advances in our understanding of the capabilities of the human mind, this argument has begun to have a hollow ring. It is one that certainly causes disillusion and discouragement in many students upon their first contact with a formal course in psychology. But the computer simulation technology has given us a tool for dealing with complexity in our theories, and has provided new impetus to the study of man's capabilities for thought. At the conclusion of a review of papers on simulation theories, Shepard cogently remarks:

. . . the start that is so admirably exemplified by many of the papers assembled by Feigenbaum and Feldman establishes a new direction in which those who aspire to precise, rigorous formulations may still find their way back to the heartland of psychology—to the study of those processes that make man unique among known physical systems. Owing to the great complexities inherent in the problem, progress is bound to be slow—perhaps painfully slow. But, unless the goal itself is relinquished, what other alternative do we have? (Shepard, 1964).

SUPPLEMENTARY READINGS

BLAKE, D. V., and UTTLEY, A. M. (Editors) (1959) *Proceedings of the symposium on mechanization of thought processes* (2 vols.).

BORKO, H. (Editor) (1962) *Computer applications in the behavioral sciences.*

FEIGENBAUM, E. A., and FELDMAN, J. (Editors) (1963) *Computers and thought.*

GREEN, B. F., JR. (1963) *Digital computers in research.*

Proceedings of the Western Joint Computer Conference. (*a*) 1955, March 1-3; (*b*) 1959, March 3-5; (*c*) 1960, May 3-5; (*d*) 1961, May 9-11.

REITMAN, W. R. (1965) *Cognition and thought.*

SAYRE, K. M., and CROSSON, F. J. (Editors) (1963) *The modeling of mind.*

UHR, L. (Editor) (1965). *Pattern recognition.*

YOVITTS, M., and CAMERON, S. (Editors) (1960) *Self-organizing systems.*

CHAPTER 13

Neurophysiology of Learning

Nothing is more certain than that our behavior is a product of our nervous system. The proposition is almost more tautological than factual. This being the case, one may wonder why theories of learned behavior have not been more explicitly neurophysiological in their content, constructs, and referents. There are many historical (and, therefore, accidental rather than rational) reasons for this long-standing divorce between neurophysiology and behavior theory, and we will not attempt to discuss the cleavage here. For one thing, during the period from 1930–1950 when most of the *leitmotifs* in our current approaches to learning were developing, it was felt that neurophysiology had very little that was relevant to offer on the psychological issues of the day. But with the explosion of neuropsychological research in the past two decades, this bias is fading away. Secondly, the major theories were never intended to describe the specific, actual events as they go on in the nervous system of their model learner. The tactics have been, and still are in large measure, those of descriptive behaviorism supplemented by intervening variable theorizing. The description of generic "S–R" relationships lies at one level: if you do such-and-so to your subject, he will usually behave in such-and-so a way. The such-and-so in each instance may be replaced by a rather long listing of what are believed to be the relevant variables. At another level of theorizing, one simply postulates the existence within the organism of certain primitive mechanisms that carry out particular functions or that are governed by a particular set of "rules." The behavioral implications of the postulated mechanisms plus their rules of operation are then derived for varying sets of boundary conditions under which the model organism is to be observed. What is important is the logical system of interacting parts—the model—and not the specific details of the machinery that might actually be functioning in a way that embodies it in the nervous system. As an abstraction the logical system could possibly be realized either as sets of equations, or as a mechanical or electrical system, or as a program running inside a high speed computer; the hardware embodiment is irrelevant to the main scientific question, which is whether the theoretical system gives an adequate explanation, description, or prediction of the primary facts relevant to it. If it does so, then psychologists by and large are satisfied with the theory and are willing to leave it at that.

Neuropsychologists by and large are not satisfied to leave matters at that level. They are in fact dedicated to finding out about the specific hardware that evolution has tucked under our skulls. They wish to discover the actual machinery, and how it works in getting an organism around in its everyday commerce with its environment. This is an exceedingly difficult goal because both the nervous system and its behavior are complicated and neither will be understood with any completeness for a long time. In this chapter we are concerned with learning, and, we may be sure, the ability to store information about its history is about the most remarkable capacity of the nervous system. It is also one of the least understood capabilities of nervous tissue.

An act of learning probably involves many different parts of the nervous system. A performance may fail because the organism does not see the stimulus, or does not attend to or register it via his sensory system; he may fail because he forgets how to interpret its meaning, because he never learned it at all, because he is momentarily unable to execute the motor units involved, or because he is no longer motivated to do so or is just not in the mood. This is a loose way to characterize the complex tangle of variables involved in whether and how often a learned act will be performed. It shows too the problems of delineating a research area called the neurophysiology of learning. For example, should receptor physiology be included, since the retina has to transduce a photic signal before it can become a cue for a learned response? Should the study of muscle action be included, since muscles execute the learned performance? By convention such topics are excluded from the research area because these structures are presumed to function similarly whether or not learning is involved. It is usually assumed that a light flash is coded at the retina in an invariant manner whether the light flash is neutral or produces an expectation of reward or punishment due to past learning. Because of this functional distinction, the physiology of the receptors and effectors is usually not considered relevant to the study of learning; their normal operation is a necessary but not a sufficient condition for information storage.

The main search for learning structures, on the other hand, is directed inward from these peripheral structures, to the central nervous system, to the brain in particular. The main question, of course, is what normally happens in the brain during learning? What processes and encoding are involved in storing information in the brain in a relatively permanent manner? Once stored, how is access to this information or retrieval of it achieved to guide later performance? What anatomical structures are involved and how do they operate? Can other structures substitute for them when the original ones are put out of commission? What gets changed during learning, and what is the nature of the change? How does it persist and what, if anything, destroys it? These and many others are the global questions that instigate brain research. Of course, none of them has yet been answered to anyone's satisfaction. Each poses a very large and complicated puzzle, and at any given moment we have only a few pieces of the puzzle before us to aid us in inferring its nature.

Research into the neurophysiology of learning has been slavishly dependent upon the development of techniques for probing inside the brain. Up to about the time of the Second World War, the technique most commonly used was *ablation,* whereby a part of the brain was destroyed or cut out. Following ablation of a part of the brain, the animal is observed for behavior deficits in one or more learning tasks. Although many hundreds of such investigations have been carried out, all who do them are well aware of the limited amount of evidence obtainable from ablation studies when applied to learning. Often, a brain ablation destroys the retention of a formerly learned response, but just about as often the habit can thereafter be relearned. In some cases, an ablation produces a permanent deficit or inability to learn a particular type of performance. Often these appear to be particular kinds of "sensory" deficits. In other cases, the nature of the behavioral deficit itself is incompletely understood and requires extensive psychological analysis with unending batteries of learning tasks. Frequent complications in all of this are variations in the actual site and amount of brain tissue excised, an incomplete description of the specific lesions, and multiple variations in the behavioral tasks used to assess the effect of the brain damage. Thus, a not infrequent happening is the appearance of conflicting reports of behavioral effects of particular lesions. Despite these distressing limitations of the ablation technique, a fair amount has been learned by it and it still remains an indispensable analytic tool for the brain investigator. In this chapter we do not review ablation studies as a specific topic, but references to such studies will come up in the course of reviewing other topics.

More recently, investigations of the central nervous system have either lagged or spurted ahead coincident with failure or success in the discovery of novel recording or stimulation techniques. And most of the techniques having a high information yield have been introduced within the comparatively recent past, mostly since 1945. On the electrical recording side, advances have come largely from the postwar expansion of the electronics industry with the development of various devices for amplifying and faithfully recording or displaying tiny, rapidly changing electrical signals, since such signals act as the "voices" of neural cells. Such amplifiers have made it possible to record a full range of electrical activity in the nervous system, from the gross electroencephalogram (EEG) obtained from the outer skull case down to the present work on microelectrode recording of activity in single neurons. More recently, high-speed computers have been called in to help the electrophysiologist detect regularities and lawful relations in certain forms of "noisy" EEG records in which the significant electrical events are often obscured by random electrical activity of no importance. On the stimulation side, the main techniques being currently exploited are those permitting direct electrical or chemical stimulation of a localized area of the brain of an intact animal that is awake, moving about, and behaving normally. Small bipolar electrodes may be implanted so that they remain in the animal's brain, with the animal living indefinitely with them in place. To stimulate the indicated brain structure, the wire tips of the electrodes protruding from the skull are connected to a source of electrical energy. Similarly implanted cannulae or tiny hollow cylinders may be used to inject chemical solutions or implant crystalline chemicals into a part of the brain. Along with these stimulus-delivery techniques, the electronics industry has kept pace by developing electrical stimulators with precisely adjustable stimulus parameters—wave form, pulse frequency, and so forth—and the pharmaceutical industry has contributed by discovering and synthesizing a variety of new agents (drugs) which act selectively on neural tissue. Conditions have indeed been exceptionally favorable for an expansion of research in neurophysiology, and we appear to be in the midst of a very productive upswing.

The specific topics we shall review are a selected sample of those cultivated mainly within the past 15 years. The work on attention, reward, and motivation is included because of the central influence of these factors upon learning and performance. In each case, our intention will be to give some idea of the type of findings relevant to each topic, describing these in relatively nontechnical language so that results may be understandable to readers unfamiliar with neurophysiology. The specialist in neurophysiology may have to exercise some restraint when he sees his cherished results discussed in somewhat more general terms. Needless to say, more technical as well as exhaustive treatises are available for those who wish to go deeper into each of the subjects (Field *et al.*, 1960; Morgan, 1965; Wooldridge, 1963).

MOTIVATION, AROUSAL, AND ATTENTION

Motivation and learning are intimately related, no matter what position one takes with respect to the role of drive in habit acquisition and in the performance of learned acts. Hence we turn first to neurophysiological knowledge about drive, reward and punishment, arousal and attention, before turning to the more strictly learning topics of memory and association.

Motivational Mechanisms in the Brain

Physiological research has been fairly successful in investigating the neurological mechanisms involved in the common biological motives. Most work has been done on thirst, hunger, and sex. The story is, of course, far from complete, but at least some headway has been made in understanding the brain centers involved. We will briefly review some of the evidence on the neural mechanisms in the brain subserving these consummatory activities.

The study of hunger is by far the most difficult because of its many complex features. Organisms in addition to being simply hungry for food in general, also regulate their behavior in relation to the specific kinds of food they eat and they do this according to their body's special requirements for carbohydrates, proteins, fats, minerals, and vitamins. A variety of diet-selection studies have shown that animals can detect their specific deficits and regulate their intake of appropriate substances with incredible accuracy. However, practically nothing is known about the neural mechanisms that govern such selective intake of various foods according to the body's need. To say simply that salty water "tastes better" to a salt-deprived animal is no help since this is in effect to restate what has to be explained. Despite our ignorance of the mechanisms of selective sub-hungers, a fair amount is known about the regulation of *how much* food in general is consumed. The primary neural structures involved lie within the hypothalamus, at the base of the brain.

The *ventromedial nucleus* close to the midline of the hypothalamus appears to be primarily a "stop" or "satiation-detecting" center. That is, its normal functioning seems required to produce cessation of eating after the animal has eaten a sufficient amount to remove any deficit. This ventromedial nucleus may be destroyed by a localized electrolytic lesion; it is coagulated by a strong electric current delivered through an implanted electrode. When this is done, the animal for a time does not "know how" to stop eating. He overeats by large amounts (hyperphagia) and soon becomes very obese, perhaps to more than double his normal weight. The overeating really appears to stem from simple absence of an appropriate "stop" mechanism rather than an increased hunger drive. Hyperphagic animals will not work very hard to get their food, and they will not tolerate much adulteration of their food with bitter quinine before they reject it, whereas normally hungry animals will both work hard and tolerate quinine in order to get something to eat.

Presumably the way the ventromedial nucleus normally functions is that signals from the mouth, stomach, and certain nutrients (e.g., glucose) circulating in the bloodstream or cerebrospinal fluid stimulate this structure, and its resulting activity through some unknown means stops the eating. It is known that if this structure is artificially stimulated by an electric current (via an implanted electrode), then the hungry animal in the course of eating will be inhibited from further eating while the current is on (Wyrwicka and Dobrzecka, 1960). Also learned responses rewarded by food are similarly inhibited by electrical stimulation of this structure. Likewise, injection of a minute quantity of a salty solution into this area (via an implanted cannula into which a hypodermic needle is fitted) produces inhibition of eating. On the other hand, a temporary increase in eating is produced when the substance injected is procaine (a local anesthetic commonly used by dentists). Presumably the procaine anesthetic temporarily mimics the effect of destroying the tissue (see above). All these effects are consistent with the view that the ventromedial nucleus serves as a regulator to stop eating.

The "start" mechanism for eating appears to lie in the *lateral* areas of the hypothalamus, one on either side of the midline. Destruction of the lateral hypothalamus on both sides (bilateral ablation) produces an animal that refuses to eat (or drink), and if special measures are not taken it will starve to death in a cage filled with food. Teitelbaum and Epstein (1962) report that such animals go through several stages while being nursed back to recovery. For several days after the bilateral ablation the animals (rats) refuse to eat or drink, and spit out substances placed in their mouths. They are kept alive by tube-feeding a nutrient liquid directly into their stomachs. After several days, they still refuse to drink but will eat highly palatable (sugary) foods. Later, they may eat regular lab food, though they still refuse to drink water. Still later, normal drinking may return in some animals. Whether or not and how much an animal will recover seems to depend on the completeness of the original destruction, which is to say that the larger the lesion, the less the likelihood of significant recovery.

This ablation work seems to implicate the lateral hypothalamus in starting both eating and drinking. The two functions have been manipulated separately by localized electrical and chemical stimulation. Electrical stimulation in this area can cause a satiated animal either to eat or to drink depending upon the precise location of the electrode. Injection of a tiny amount of a salty solution into this area of the brain will cause excessive drinking in a satiated animal; injection of pure water causes a thirsty animal to stop drinking. In the case of each of these kinds of stimulation, it has been shown too that learned habits rewarded by food or water can be regulated (turned on or off) by the stimulation. There is little doubt that thirst or hunger "drives," as psychologists use the term, are being manipulated directly in these experiments. A fair amount is known about the mechanisms involved in naturally occurring thirst and drinking. Water losses cause an increase in the concentration of electrolytes in the blood, with a resulting increase in its osmotic pressure. This in turn draws more water out of the cellular stores of the body. A set of neural cells lying in the vascular bed of the lateral hypothalamus put out "thirst" signals when water is needed. These cells—called osmoreceptors—respond to an increase in osmotic pressure of the blood surrounding them. A minute injection of salt water directly into this area mimics the effect of prolonged dehydration by raising the osmotic pressure in the tissue surrounding these osmoreceptors.

An interesting set of experiments by Grossman (1960) indicates differential chemical specificity of the feeding and drinking centers in the lateral hypothalamus of the rat. He found that injection of certain chemicals (adrenergic drugs) into the lateral hypothalamus greatly increased food consumption but did not increase the drinking of water. Injection of other chemicals (cholinergic drugs) produced the opposite effect—increased drinking with no increased eating. Many other chemical effects of this kind have been reviewed by Miller (1965). Of interest here is the fact that the adrenergic drugs used by Grossman (adrenalin and noradrenalin) have been identified as the neural transmitter substance for the sympathetic nervous system, whereas the transmitter for the rest of the nervous system is acetylcholine, a cholinergic substance. This chemical specificity suggests the final link in the communication chain through which the body "informs" the lateral hypothalamic area whether it needs to eat or drink.

Finally, we take a brief look at the brain centers involved with sexual behavior. The pattern of results here is not unambiguous or clearly interpretable from the work on brain lesions. Ablations in some areas sometimes produce a complete loss of sexual behavior whereas ablations in other areas have produced exaggerated, hypersexual behaviors (cf. Morgan, 1965, for a review). More often than not, the effective lesions are in the hypothalamus again, but the exact structures involved are still in dispute. Direct electrical and chemical stimulation of the hypothalamus have produced somewhat clearer results. Vaughan and Fisher (1962) elicited exaggerated sexual behavior in male rats by electrical stimulation in the anterior dorsolateral region of the hypothalamus. The electrical stimulus elicited persistent mounting of a female and produced an excess number of ejaculations, far beyond the satiating requirement of a normal male. Earlier work by Fisher (1956) in which the male sex hormone, testosterone, was injected into the hypothalamus of the male rat produced similar results. When the hormone was applied in one area (lateral preoptic), exaggerated male sexual behavior was elicited from both male and female rats. When injected in a slightly different area (medial preoptic part of hypothalamus), both male and female rats would engage in "maternal" behaviors such as building a home nest and retrieving baby rats from outside the nest. These behaviors normally appear only in female rats after giving birth to a litter. When the testosterone hormone is delivered to a site between these two areas, mixed behavior may result: a male rat may alternate between nest building and mating with an available female. Similar enhancement of sexual behavior in female cats has been reported by Michael (1962) who implanted small paraffin pellets containing estrogen into the hypothalamus. This caused the female to become sexually receptive ("in heat") for a period of 50 to 60 days, as the drug was absorbed very slowly. Though she was sexually receptive, the female cat's vagina and uterus were not in an estrual condition; she would be described as in heat behaviorally, but not physiologically. From these results obtained by Michael and Fisher, it seems safe to conclude that sex drive and receptivity can be induced by direct hormonal stimulation of the hypothalamus.

In concluding this brief sketch of neural drive centers, it is worth remarking that important structures within each drive system are found in the hypothalamus, a very small but phylogenetically very old part of the brain. In addition to the functions mentioned above, the hypothalamus is known to control other behaviors (e.g., "sham rage") and to regulate various physiological functions (e.g., regulation of body temperature). Also, as we shall see, electrical stimulation in this area often produces either rewarding or punishing effects. The effectiveness of the rewarding brain shock to these sites can be enhanced or diminished by increasing or decreasing, respectively, the levels of hunger, thirst, or sex drive (e.g., Hoebel and Teitelbaum, 1962). Indeed, the hypothalamus might be called the "motivational center" of the brain. It now appears plausible that a remarkable range of psychologically significant variables have their eventual impact upon this small, well-packaged nub of neural tissue. The evolutionary advantages obtained by this anatomical tight-packing of many vital functions are not obvious at present.

Reward and Punishment by Brain Stimulation

The motivational significance of the hypothalamus has been enhanced by another set of studies concerned with the effects of reward and punishment. A significant line of research in the past ten years has been the mapping of the locations of reward and punishment centers in the mammalian brain. The initial observations on the reward effect were made by Olds and Milner (1954) and on the punishment effect by Delgado, Roberts, and Miller (1954). The experimental subject—typically a rat, cat, or monkey—is prepared with a two-pole electrode implanted so that it remains in its brain, with the tiny, stimulating tip of the electrode aimed at a particular structure of the brain. Via this electrode, a small electric current can be delivered to that part of the brain surrounding the electrode tip, thereby artificially firing off a probably large population of neural cells in the neighborhood of the electrode tip. In the typical reward experiment, the subject is permitted to operate a switch that delivers brief electric shocks to his brain. If he learns to do this repeatedly, operating the lever at an appreciable rate, then stimulation at that brain site is said to be rewarding. Conversely, if he refrains from stimulating his brain under optimal conditions of learning, the stimulation could be either neutral or punishing. If it is punishing (aversive), then he will learn some response to turn off (escape) the brain shock once it is presented. By means of tests such as these, brain structures may be classified as rewarding, neutral, or punishing.

Upon investigation, it has been found that reward sites are densely and widely scattered throughout the subcortex of the rat's brain. The schematic drawing in Figure 13-1 shows one of the major positive reward systems (labeled FSR), a large "tube" of fibers on the lower floor extending from the hindbrain through the midbrain (hypothalamus) forward to the forebrain. Sites in which electrical stimulation produces punishing effects are situated above these reward fibers. They are labeled MSE in Figure 13-1. These effects depend, of course, upon the intensity and other characteristics of the electrical stimulation to the brain. The intensity of the stimulation has to exceed some threshold value before its behavioral effect is seen. The function relating the behavioral effect to stimulus intensity seems to vary with the structure being stimulated. Roberts (1958) and Bower and Miller (1958) first reported on electrode placements (in cats and rats, respectively) wherein the onset of brain stimulation appeared to be rewarding, but if the stimulation was left on it became aversive after a few seconds or so. Thus, the animals would learn to perform one response to turn on the stimulus and another response to turn it off. A likely account of these dual effects is that the electrode tip was in positive reward cells though there were negative cells in the vicinity, so that during the few seconds of shock the effective site of stimulation spread out from the electrode tip and activated the negative cells. Some of these ambivalent sites are circled in Figure 13-1.

A number of interesting features regarding the electrical reward effect have been uncovered. First, the self-stimulating behavior does not satiate, whereas most naturally occurring positive reinforcers do, as in eating or drinking. This absence of satiation is inferred from the fact that ani-

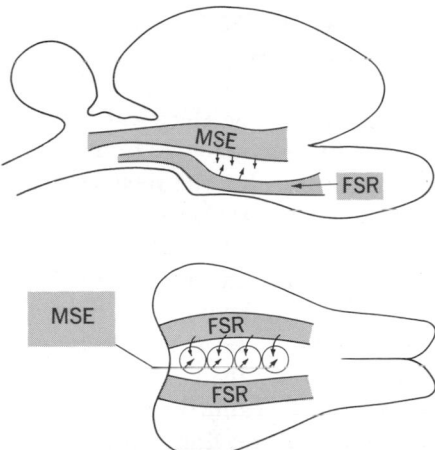

Figure 13-1   Schematic sections of the rat's brain showing locations of major positive and negative reinforcement centers determined by electrical stimulation. The top figure is a sagittal section, slicing fore and aft from the top of brain to the bottom. The bottom figure is a horizontal section, looking down upon the middle interior of the brain. Pure punishing effects were produced by stimulation of the peri-ventricular system of fibers, here labeled MSE (for midbrain substrate of escape); pure positive rewarding effects were produced by stimulation of the lateral hypothalamic tube, here labeled FSR (forebrain substrate of reward). The nuclei (circled in lower figure) into which both these systems project yield ambivalent, that is, positive–negative, reactions. Reproduced from Olds and Olds (1965).

mals will continue to stimulate their brains at a high rate for very many hours, until they drop from fatigue. Secondly, the behavior generally extinguishes very rapidly when the electrical stimulation is shut off, despite the fact that very high response rates had been generated by it. Third, in discrete-trial learning situations (e.g., a runway), performance is generally poor at very long intertrial intervals. At many brain sites, the animal has to be "primed" with one or more free brain shocks before he goes into his act of rapid self-stimulation. Fourth, the reward effect at some locations appears to depend upon the state of one or another motivational (drive) system. Rates of self-stimulation at some sites seem to depend on the animal's hunger drive (i.e., satiation lowers self-stimulation rate), and at other sites it depends on the level of circulating sex hormones (i.e., castration lowers self-stimulation rate). Related to this is Miller's observation that male rats that worked to stimulate hypothalamic sites would frequently show a sexual ejaculation during the brain-shock session. However, the drive-related effects do not appear at all rewarding sites in the brain.

Deutsch and Howarth (1963) have advanced a theory about brain stimulation reward which attempts to handle many of the pertinent facts. We cannot go into details of their theory, but will mention the gist of the main idea, which is that the electrical stimulation in these "reward" experiments is actually serving two functions: reward for the immediate response and motivation for the next response in the series. Each brain shock produces some motivation for the habit which produced the brain shock. The motivation produced by a brain shock decays with the time elapsed since the brain shock, eventually diminishing to zero. The stronger the brain shock, the longer it takes the motivation to decay. The postulated effect of brain-shock reward may be aptly compared with the familiar effect of eating salted peanuts; the behavior is practically self-perpetuating, having a peanut keeps the "desire" for another going, but the urgency of the want declines with the lapse of time since eating the previous peanut.

Deutsch and Howarth present several experimental results consistent with their hypothesis, all essentially showing that the strength of behavior established with a brain-shock reward declines with time since the last brain shock. The hypothesis explains the rapid extinction of self-stimulation habits once the electrical stimulus is removed. They show convincingly that the number of responses left to be emitted in extinction is a function of time elapsed since the last brain shock rather than the prior number of nonreinforced responses. Simply holding the animal away from the lever for a while produces the same effect as letting him respond without reward during that time. The theory predicts too that the brain shock has to be fairly strong (i.e., with long persisting aftereffects) before an animal will perform successfully on a schedule of infrequent reinforcements for barpressing. Since the theory postulates a dual effect of electrical stimulation—excitation of reward and motivational pathways—Deutsch and his associates have investigated means for separating these two effects. A series of experiments are consistent with the assumption that the sensitivity of the two systems differs as stimulation parameters (current intensity, pulse frequency) are varied. Observations in one experiment suggested that the motivational pathway had a lower threshold than the reward pathway. Thus, a brain shock of low intensity could have a motivating but not a rewarding effect. Used as a "reward," such a stimulus was ineffective in promoting lever pressing. However, its motivating effect was seen by injecting it sporadically during the course of extinction of a lever-pressing habit established initially with a strongly rewarding brain shock. Under these circumstances, the animals getting the free delivery of the motivating stimulus persisted in lever pressing longer during extinction than did nonstimulated control animals. In another experiment, frequency (pulses per second) of the brain shock was manipulated along with intensity. Frequency–intensity pairs found to be equally preferred (rewarding) in a T-maze preference test turned out to be unequally motivating in a simple runway test. This suggests that the reward and motivation pathways are maximally sensitive to different frequencies of electrical stimulation. In another set of experiments (Deutsch, 1964), evidence is adduced for the view that the neural "refractory period" of reinforcement pathways is shorter than that of the motivational pathways. The term refractory period refers to a very brief time following the firing of a neuron during which a second stimulus is ineffective and can not fire the neuron again. By purely behavioral tests, Deutsch inferred that the refractory period for the reward pathway was about four-tenths of a millisecond whereas that for the motivational pathway was about six or seven-tenths of a millisecond.

This series of experiments certainly provides rather impressive evidence for Deutsch's hypothesis about brain stimulation reward, although, to be sure, there is some evidence that seems inconsistent with his hypothesis (Pliskoff, Wright, and Hawkins, 1965). In part, actually, the hypothesis looks good because few alternative hypotheses have come forward in competition with it. Recently an alternative interpretation of brain-shock reward effects has been offered by Ball (1965), one of Deutsch's students. Ball noted that stimulation of a rewarding site had the concurrent effect of blocking or severely inhibiting the flow of incoming stimulation over sensory channels. In Ball's preparation, the sensory input consisted of electrical stimulation of the infraorbital nerve. The transmission of this peripheral shock into the brain may be seen by recording the resulting electrical signal passing through the main sensory nucleus of the fifth cranial nerve. The electrical signal is recorded as an *evoked potential* which varies in its amplitude depending on the efficacy of transmission. Ball found that concurrent electrical stimulation in reward sites of the brain would reduce the evoked potential from the peripheral shock by about 90 percent. Thus, the rewarding brain shock was inhibiting or choking off the inflow of sensory stimulation from the periphery. Moreover, in many cases there was a "rebound" effect; which is to say that following the rewarding brain shock, the peripheral shock produced greater than normal evoked potentials for a fairly long period, diminishing with time. From such results, Ball conjectures that self-stimulation in "rewarding" brain sites has the character of a vicious circle in which the animal becomes trapped, and that the behavior is best viewed as escape from the aversive aftereffects of the prior brain stimulus. On this view, the behavior is similar to that of a drug addict who needs the next shot to alleviate the noxious aftereffects of the previous dose. The rebound effect from the preceding brain shock produces an unpleasant barrage of sensory influx ("a booming, buzzing cacophony"), and lever pressing for another brain shock is an efficient way to reduce (inhibit) temporarily this sensory overload. Thus the vicious cycle is maintained once it is started, provided the brain shock is readily available.

The claim that the immediate aftereffect of a brain shock is aversive is supported by a behavioral experiment (Ball and Adams, 1965). This demonstrated that rats would learn to go to the endbox of a T-maze which *avoided* a brain shock if trials were widely spaced (1 every 30 minutes) but would learn to go to the endbox where they received brain shock if trials were massed (1 every 20 seconds). Presumably, at the long intertrial interval, the animal had stopped hurting from his last brain shock (and so did not seek relief from the hurt) but recalled the fact that it hurt.

According to this analysis, self-stimulation behavior is really little different in a functional sense from vicious cycle, escape behavior. An appropriate analog might be the following: a rat is trained to press a lever to escape a painful foot shock. Thereafter the following game is set up: the shock is turned on at a high intensity and then slowly reduced to zero over time; if he responds at any time during this decay, he can bring about an immediate cessation of the shock for 2 seconds, but then the shock reverts to its initial high intensity again. Knowing the program, we can say that in the long run, the optimal thing for the rat is to stop responding, and to withstand some pain for a while so that the shock intensity gets reduced to zero where it will remain so long as he does not respond. But the animal is affected primarily by the short-run contingency, viz., a response terminates shock for two seconds. There is little doubt that he would thus be trapped into this escape behavior that proves maladaptive in the long run.

Many experiments must be done before this interpretation can be accepted. It is clear that if Ball's interpretation is generally supported, then calling self-stimulation sites "reward centers" of the brain is a fundamental misnomer since typical rewarding events (e.g., food to a hungry animal) do not operate at all like this. It is interesting too that Ball's interpretation of self-stimulation reward makes the phenomenon compatible with various "psychological" hypotheses concerning what reinforcing events have in common. Both N. E. Miller and Guthrie have assumed that reinforcement occurs when a response reduces or eliminates strong stimulation. Indeed, Miller (1958) was one of the first to conjecture that "rewarding" brain shocks might achieve their effect by temporarily occluding or reducing other sources of stimulation, although at that time he stressed internal drive stimuli. At the moment, the most convincing evidence against this "escape-circle" hypothesis comes from introspective reports of human patients when stimulated in "pleasure centers" of their brain. Such stimulation is often described as satisfying, or joyful, or relaxing, without unpleasant aftereffects and the patient will willingly take more (Heath and Mickle, 1960). Presumably some resolution of these conflict-

ing interpretations will be achieved in the near future. At present insufficient critical work has been done on Ball's hypothesis to determine
whether it accords adequately with what we now know about self-stimulation behavior.

Arousal and Attention

Within the past 15 years electrophysiological studies have brought
to light many new facts about arousal and attention. The arousal dimension includes variations ranging from excited emotion, to alert attentiveness, to relaxed wakefulness, to drowsiness, to deep sleep, and these are
closely correlated with phenomenal impressions of conscious awareness.
The varying states of arousal are associated with distinctive patterns in the
electroencephalogram (EEG) of the subject. We can gauge the depth of
sleep from the EEG. We can determine too at what times the sleeper is
dreaming; for during dream episodes, the eyes move rapidly, as though
the person were watching a visual scene unfold before him (see Kleitman,
1963).

A host of studies have implicated the reticular activating system (RAS)
of the brain stem as of paramount importance in arousal. This system
seems to be involved in sleeping, wakefulness, and in fine gradations in
attention. Anatomically, this system, which in men is about the size of the
little finger (see Figure 13-2), is located at the core of the brain stem just
above the spinal cord and below the thalamus and hypothalamus.

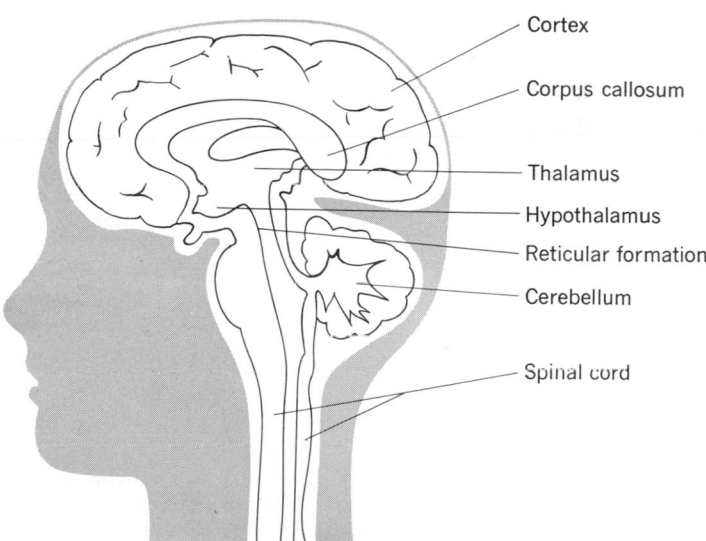

Figure 13-2   Schematic sagittal section of the brain in man. Reproduced from
Kimble (1963).

A number of important facts regarding the RAS are well established. First, selected cells of the RAS are aroused or alerted when signals are being transmitted through sensory input cables from the skin, ear, nose, etc. These sensory input cables send their information to specific "projection" areas in the cerebral cortex, all (except smell) doing so through specific relay nuclei in the thalamus. On the way in, however, these input cables send off collateral branches into the RAS. These collaterals are shown schematically in Figure 13-3. Within the RAS, the collaterals from the various sensory channels are intermingled and lack specificity. Second, the RAS projects its unspecific messages to broad, diffuse areas of the cerebral cortex (see Figure 13-3). Research has indicated that the probable operation of this system is as follows: new sensory information stimulates the RAS which relays the presence of some kind of stimulation to various sensory receiving areas of the cortex. This diffuse stimulation alerts the cortex, essentially telling it that some kind of news is arriving. The alerted cortex is then better able to deal with or process the specific information arriving over the specific sensory input channel to the cortex.

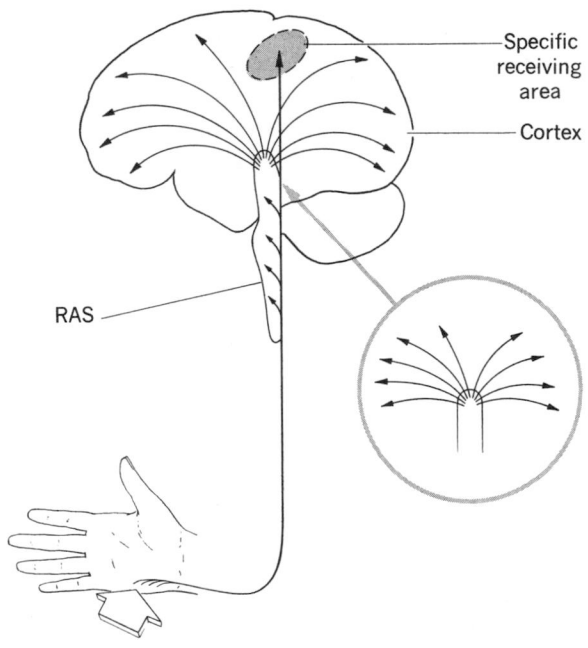

Figure 13-3   Schematic drawing showing how a touch stimulus to the hand is relayed to a specific receiving area in the cerebral cortex. The sensory channel also sends collateral branches into the reticular activating system (RAS), which in turn projects alerting stimulation to many areas of the cerebral cortex. The inset shows the cortical projections arising from the forward end (thalamic section) of the reticular formation. Reproduced from Kimble (1963).

The various parts of this conceptual picture have been pieced together by painstaking research. The alerting function of the RAS has been inferred from various lines of work. Direct electrical stimulation of the RAS at a fast frequency through an implanted electrode will awaken a sleeping cat and produce EEG brain waves characteristic of alertness and excitement. If the RAS is destroyed, a profound and enduring coma results; with the result that for all practical purposes the animal is reduced to a sleeping vegetable. Anesthetic drugs that produce unconsciousness appear to act by depressing the RAS. The coma produced by either the destruction or the anesthetic endures despite the intactness of the sensory projection pathways. Though sounds, touches, lights, etc. still evoke definite electrical responses at the cortex while the animal is comatose, the subject is unaware of these inputs because the RAS switch controlling "consciousness" has been turned down.

It is known too that the cortex itself sends many neural projections back down to the RAS, and these interbrain connections can keep the activity in the RAS at a level sufficient for consciousness. We are all familiar with the fact that we can "think" ourselves into an excited state, or that thinking can keep us awake even when we have successfully shut off most sources of sensory stimulation. Another fact is that the RAS via collaterals from the motor cortex participates with the cerebellum in programing muscle movements produced via the spinal cord, acting like an amplitude control mechanism. For example, the RAS controls the general muscle tone of the body. Lesions in some parts of the RAS can produce extreme muscular contraction, while in other parts their result is relaxation. And in still other parts, the quivering or the shaking palsy characteristic of Parkinson's disease is produced. This variety of functions carried out by the RAS is truly remarkable. Evolution, if we may speak anthropomorphically, seems to have taken great care that all the communication channels going to and from the brain can get together in this reticular formation.

It was said earlier that nonspecific stimulation from the RAS prepares the cortex to process better the incoming sensory information. Some indirect evidence of this perceptual efficiency of an alerted cortex is seen in experiments by Lindsley (1958) and Fuster (1958). The first study examined the cortical resolution of two flashes of light separated by a short period of time. At long interflash intervals, the cortical EEG shows two discrete "evoked potentials," one for each flash; but at very short intervals (around one-twentieth of a second), the cortex responds to the two flashes as though there were one, so that there is only a single evoked response. Lindsley showed that by electrically stimulating the reticular formation just before or during the flashes, the two fast flashes could again be resolved, resulting in two distinct evoked potentials. Thus, a previously undetected fast pair was made detectable by preparing the cortex by means of reticular stimulation. Fuster's experiment showed that concurrent reticular stimulation enabled a monkey to gather more relevant information from a brief tachistoscopic flash illuminating a visual field. The monkey had been trained to get a peanut reward under object A but not under object B. During the test sessions carried out in darkness, the left-right positions of A and B had to be ascertained from a brief flash of light illuminating the field. On half of the trials electrical stimulation of the reticular formation was given during the flash. The results are shown in Figure 13-4. It is apparent that speed and accuracy of the correct response decreased as the duration of the flash decreased. It also shows that performance was facilitated at all intervals by reticular stimulation. From this result we infer that the reticular stimulation alerts the cortex, increasing the speed and efficiency with which it can process and extract information from a brief glimpse of a visual field.

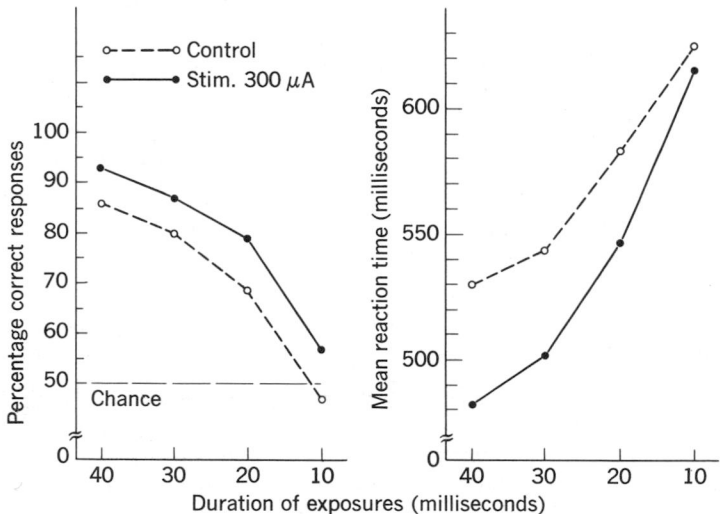

Figure 13-4   Percentage of correct responses (left panel) and mean reaction time (right panel) related to the duration of the flash exposing the visual field. At shorter exposures, the percentage of correct responses is lower and reaction times are longer. During reticular stimulation (solid lines), correct responses increased and reaction times decreased relative to the nonstimulation trials (dashed lines). Reproduced from Fuster (1958).

In recent years many experiments have made it clear that the waking brain exerts considerable control over its sensory input channels. Electrical signals coursing inward from a particular receptor may be subject to modulating influences all along its sensory pathway to the primary receiving area at the cortex. These influences may either enhance or inhibit the inward coursing signal, although inhibition seems to be the predominant mode. These effects may be seen in the changes in the electrically evoked response recorded from various relay stations (synapses) along the sensory input cable. These influences are probably mediated by fibers passing from the cortex and brain stem out alongside the input cable to nearby the peripheral receptors. A fair number of sensory inhibition effects can be produced by electric stimulation in certain parts of the reticular formation.

The main function of these brain-to-periphery neural circuits appears to be that which is ascribed roughly to "attention." By this means the brain can attenuate or "gate out" sensory signals that are of no "interest" to it at the moment, while at the same time amplifying that sensory channel (if any) upon which attention is concentrated. The evidence for this generalization comes from studies of habituation and distraction, and the influence of brain stimulation upon evoked potentials to sensory stimulation.

Consider first the phenomenon of *habituation*. When a novel stimulus of sufficient intensity impinges on a receptor, it evokes a strong and definite electrical response in the relays of that input channel, in the primary sensory cortex for that input channel, and in the reticular formation. This is the electrical accompaniment of the "orienting reflex" discussed by Pavlov and Sokolov (cf. Chapter 3). However, if the stimulus is repeated in a regular, monotonous series, the evoked response diminishes to a low, stable level, often not even detectable. The response has habituated. This habituation can be seen not only at the cortex but also far downstream, at essentially the first sensory relay station beyond the receptor. Such habituatory control is presumably designed to disengage the higher brain centers from dealing with stimuli that have ceased to have any significance for it. The habituation can be temporarily lifted by disturbing the animal (e.g., by electric shock to the feet or an arousing reticular shock). Also, habituation will not occur if the stimulus is converted through conditioning into a signal of biological importance (e.g., by pairing a click with a painful shock or with food). In fact, the evoked electrical response is even larger than normal in this case. Thus, the significance of an input signal is crudely coded almost at once from the receptor inwards.

Consider a second set of observations on distraction. Hernandez-Peon, Scherrer, and Jouvet (1956) recorded in a cat the evoked response to an auditory click at the dorsal cochlear nucleus, a low-level relay station in the auditory pathways. Before habituation occurred, presentation of distracting visual or olfactory stimuli (a mouse or the odor of fresh fish) greatly reduced the evoked auditory response produced at that time by the click. A similar effect was produced by a novel smell or sound upon the evoked response in the optic pathways to a light flash. These observations suggest that the novel stimulus attracted the cat's attention, that stimuli on the attended-to input channel were amplified, whereas stimuli on other input channels not attended to were flattened and blocked out. Moreover, this blockage can go on downstream at sensory relay stations near the receptor. Hernandez-Peon proposed that this blockage was carried out by efferent inhibitory fibers from the reticular formation to sensory relays; meaning that when input on the visual channel captures attention, the reticular formation sends out impulses that temporarily inhibit neuronal activity in other input channels. He reported that direct electrical stimulation of the reticular formation sometimes has such suppressive effects on cochlear potentials. Similar suppression due to reticular stimulation (in other areas) has been reported for the visual pathways (see Livingston, 1959, for a review). However, the reticular formation is but one of several structures whose stimulation or removal affects the incoming sensory information. Spinelli and Pribram (1966) report that stimulation in the "visual association" cortex (infero-temporal lobe) affects the efficiency with which two successive light flashes are resolved at the visual cortex. Similar effects of stimulation in the "auditory association" cortex upon information processing in the auditory pathways have been reported. In addition, Spinelli, Pribram, and Weingarten (1965) found evoked potentials in the optic nerve from the retina when a curarized cat was stimulated with clicks to its ear. These evoked responses could only be efferent messages sent out to the retina from the brain while it was processing clicks in the auditory pathways.

If one accepts the thesis of low-level gating of sensory information via neuronal inhibition from brain-stem efferents, then some of the facts about habituation raise some conceptual puzzles. Habituation turns out to be quite fragile in the face of relatively small stimulus changes. After habituation to a monotonously beeping tone, a change in the frequency of the tone will "release" the habituatory suppression, and the altered tone will now evoke strong electrical responses all along the auditory pathways. A similar phenomenon appears following habituation to a particular temporal pattern of tones—say, the triple "High-Low-Low" repeated indefinitely. Altering the temporal pattern to "High-Low-High" will release the habituation so that evoked responses reappear. The question is, how is this novelty detected if the input along the auditory pathways is being gated or suppressed because of prior habituation? At what level of the brain is this difference-detection carried out? With low-level gating, how does the new stimulus get transported to a high-level comparator?

One way to deal with this difficulty is to assume that the sensory relay stations at the periphery can themselves detect the difference. We could suppose that they can be preset by central efferent commands to act like a selectively tuned attenuator that will not transmit arriving signals having particular properties but will transmit different signals that fall outside the preset band for attenuation.

At first glance, this view appears to attribute considerable "intelligence" to the lowly sensory synapses; and further it might be argued that auditory pattern discriminations require part of the auditory cortex, since its removal disables such learning. But this is not inconsistent with the filter view. An intact auditory cortex would be needed to preset and to maintain a particular setting on the lower filter for it to detect or attenuate particular critical features of the input. Although this idea of a peripheral, differential attenuator preset by the brain handles the conceptual problem, it seems an unlikely mechanism on the basis of what is known of sensory synapses. That is, on the basis of current knowledge few neurophysiologists would be willing to bet that a synapse can respond selectively to such subtle features of an input.

One speculative alternative is to suppose that sensory information, possibly in degraded form, gets transmitted to central analyzers and there weighted for its importance or novelty. During habituation, the reduced signal is fed to a higher-level comparator; if the input matches some stored replica of recent signals, a diminished evoked response occurs and the efferents sustain their inhibitory influence on that input channel. If the input does not match recent signals, then a difference detector releases the efferent inhibition and possibly activates the RAS so that the next stimulus in the series evokes strong electrical activity. Depending upon the complexity of the input stimulus, the comparison of input to stored replica goes on at different levels of the brain. The assumption would be that the neural structures responsible for habituation to a particular stimulus are at the same level as those required for its discrimination. Deutsch and Deutsch (1963) propose a simple mechanism whereby the more important of a group of signals might be selected for attention. Inputs arriving over this selected channel would then be connected to further memorial or motor processes, whereas the remaining signals are not reacted to.

This possibility is speculative and it is difficult to marshal supporting evidence for it. This line of research, seeking to discover at what levels habituation and gating occur, is currently active and vigorous, and it is doubtful whether this interpretation will cover adequately a broad range of the facts once they are all in.

Where are we then? What may we conclude from the studies reviewed? First, it is clear that variations in reticular activation correlate with levels of wakefulness and arousal. Second, the RAS serves a usually facilitatory role in preparing the cortex for processing sensory information. Third, the RAS probably serves as a nonspecific governor or threshold determining the overall level of "importance" any stimulus must have to attract attention. In sleep or drowsiness, only the most important signals will be reacted to (e.g., a baby's cry for its mother). For example, a sleeping cat will not be aroused by a neutral tone but will be awakened by a slightly different tone that was previously paired with shock. Fourth, the RAS and other parts of the brain control and modulate afferent inputs by way of a system of efferent networks. This modulation is usually inhibitory, attenuating channel A when channel B is being listened to. Effects of learning, or associating significance to a stimulus through conditioning, can be seen near the receptor or almost as soon as the signal enters the input channel. These "corticofugal" effects provide some basis for speculation on the perceptual changes that occur during learning, on the attachment of "meaning" to stimuli, and on how stimulation, rather than effecting a passive registration, is selectively edited and distorted for the purposes of the waking organism.

LEARNING AND MEMORY

An organism that could not learn might yet behave differently under various conditions of motivational arousal, might withdraw from noxious stimuli, and might continue to react to favored ones. Such behavior becomes important for learning only when change occurs with experience, that is, when past experiences are somehow stored in memory, so that when stimuli are again encountered reaction to them is altered in the light of what went before. Hence we need to supplement the foregoing account of brain activity with what is known about the changes that take place when learning occurs, and about memory storage and retrieval.

Consolidation of Memory Traces

In broad outline, there are basically two kinds of views about the neural basis for the retention of experience or learning. One view supposes that an experience sets up a continuing electrical activity in appropriate neural circuits and that the persistence of these active circuits is coordinate with the persistence of our memory of the experience coded in this way. When this active trace process stops, we lose that memory. We may call this the "dynamic" view of the engram. Opposed to it is the "structural" view, that learning consists in some enduring physical or structural change in the nervous system, and that this physical change will persist even when the original neuronal circuits responsible for its having been established in the first place have long ago ceased their activity.

It takes very little thought or experiment to reject the "dynamic" view of memory. For example, cooling a hamster down to 5 °C causes it to hibernate, during which time very little, if any, electrical activity can be recorded from its brain. However, when warmed up and tested, it still retains whatever old habits were taught it before the hibernation period. As another example, consider the electrical "brain storms" of *grand mal* epileptic seizures in human patients. Such seizures begin when a local epileptogenic focus (e.g., caused by a brain injury or tumor) starts to re-cruit neighboring clumps of neurons into its abnormal discharge pattern. They fall into lock-step synchrony in firing with the epileptic focus, and then still more areas are recruited. The effective firing area spreads and soon most of the cortex is being driven in synchrony with the epileptic focus and the seizure is in full swing, with practically all the brain par-ticipating in the paroxysmal activity. Upon recovery from such a seizure, the patient is not devoid of memories of his past, as the "dynamic" view would suggest; in fact, it is difficult to detect that the seizure has produced any loss of memory. There are a variety of other lines of evidence that rule out the dynamic view that memory lives in a continual spinning circuit, so this view assumes practically the status of a straw man.

By a process of elimination, we then arrive at the accepted view that memory involves a relatively permanent physical or structural change in the nervous system. Though we cannot prejudge what the nature of this physical change is, it may be innocuous to assume that the change takes place over some span of time following the experience to be learned, pos-sibly even increasing in magnitude with time. If the time span involved is extremely brief, say only a few milliseconds is required to complete the change, then the notion of temporal changes is irrelevant to behavioral experiments. However, the notion does have behavioral implications of interest if the time-span involved is fairly long—say, many seconds, min-utes or hours. It is just this notion that has been pursued under the label of the "consolidation" hypothesis.

One form of such a hypothesis was proposed long ago by Mueller and Pilzecker (1900). They suggested that the neural activity responsible for storing a physical change encoding an experience persists for some time after that experience, and as a consequence of the perseverating neural activity, the physical changes become more firmly fixed or of greater magnitude. This progressive fixation with time is called *consolidation*. If this persisting neural activity is soon interrupted by the intrusion of inter-fering activity, then the physical change is of small magnitude, and reten-tion of the experience should be poor. Hebb (1949) restated this hypothesis and gave a more detailed neurophysiological model for it. The Müller–Pilzecker hypothesis was originally proposed to account for retroactive interference in recall of verbal materials by human subjects (cf. Chapter 14). In that context, it was not very fruitful and has been eclipsed by associative interference theory (cf. Chapter 14) which proved to be more adequate to the factual details in that area. Continuing interest in the con-solidation hypothesis stems partly from clinical observations but primar-ily from experiments with animals, most of them done within the past ten years.

To begin with a clear prototype, we consider a rudimentary form of "posture persistence" that has a clear consolidation period (Gerard, 1963).

If a lesion is made on one side of the cerebellum of a rat, a postural asymmetry of the legs results, due to asymmetrical conduction of motoric impulses down the spinal cord. Cutting the spinal cord below the cerebellar lesion abolishes this asymmetrical discharge down the spinal cord. If done soon enough, this spinal section also abolishes the postural asymmetry of the legs. But if the cord is not cut until the lapse of a critical length of time after the lesion, then the asymmetric posture persists indefinitely despite sectioning of the spinal cord. In this instance, then, we have a relatively permanent change in neuronal circuits of the spinal cord that takes some time to occur. The fixation time turns out to be fairly sharp, namely about 45 minutes from the first appearance of asymmetry following the cerebellar lesion until spinal sectioning. Figure 13-5 shows a graph of the results of one experiment. In most cases of spinal cord sectioning before 45 minutes, the asymmetry was abolished by the section, while for almost all cases of sectioning after 45 minutes, the postural asymmetry persisted after the cord sectioning. Of relevance to our later discussion of neurochemistry, it may be mentioned here that injecting the animals with a drug that retards the rate of synthesis of ribonucleic acid (RNA) prolonged this fixation time to 70 minutes, whereas injecting a drug that

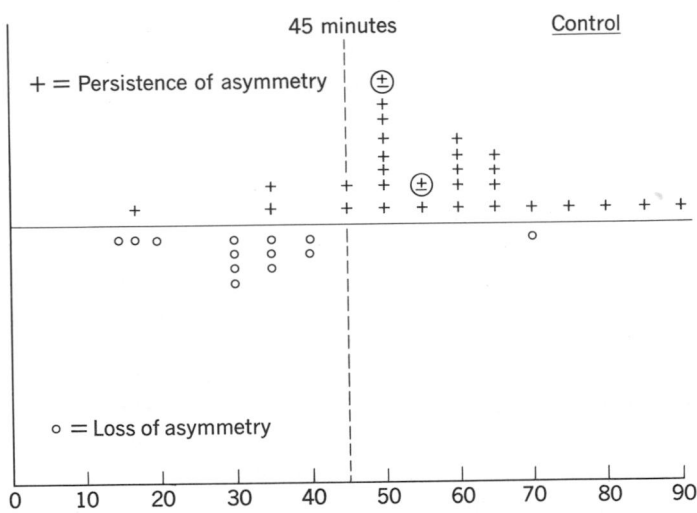

| Figure 13-5 | Each symbol, + or O, represents one animal. + represents animals for whom the postural asymmetry persisted following sectioning of the spinal cord; O represents animals for whom the asymmetry disappeared upon cord sectioning. The time (in minutes) between development of postural asymmetry and sectioning of the spinal cord is indicated on the lower axis of the graph. For all but one animal, asymmetry persisted when the cord section occurred at or after 45 minutes; for 12 of 15 animals sectioned before 45 minutes, the asymmetry was lost. Reproduced from Gerard (1963). |

speeds up the synthesis of RNA shortened the fixation time to 30 minutes.

This experiment is mentioned because it presumably shows a definite time wherein particular neuronal circuits (from the spinal cord to the legs) undergo a kind of permanent change. One might consider the cerebellar preparation as a primitive model of learning from the viewpoint of consolidation theory. It must be admitted, however, that it is only an analogy to learning as we ordinarily conceive of it. Certainly not all consolidation-type analogies are worthwhile. If a man is strangled for about 60 seconds he will die, but little analytic power is gained by viewing death as a process of progressive consolidation.

The main evidence for the consolidation theory of memory comes from studies of disturbing or traumatizing the brain shortly after registration of an experience. In theory, this disruption should prevent consolidation of the neural analogue of the memory, so no learning should be demonstrable at a later test.

In this regard, let us consider the striking clinical phenomenon of retrograde amnesia. After a person receives a hard knock on the head or some traumatic brain injury (such as a combat wound), producing unconsciousness and a coma, when he awakens he is very likely to be unable to recall the events immediately connected with and just prior to the injury. In the more severe and dramatic instances (Russell and Nathan, 1946), the events preceding the trauma by several hours, days, or months may be lost to recall and such a patient is said to have amnesia. In most of these amnestic cases, the person eventually recovers his memories, and the events more remote in time from the injury seem to be recovered first. As recovery continues, events closer in time to the accident can be recalled; yet there usually still remains an unrecoverable portion of those events just immediately prior to the injury. Similar effects in milder degree have been reported in human patients for deep anesthesia, insulin- or metrazol-induced convulsions, and electroconvulsive shock. The consolidation hypothesis would interpret such amnestic phenomena roughly as follows: the injury or trauma prevents the process of consolidation of recent material and additionally raises the threshold for recall of older memories. The older memories, having had more time to consolidate, are stronger. During recovery the threshold for recall declines so that the older, stronger memories return first.

When we turn to the experimental work on amnesia in animals (typically rats), we find that most experimenters have investigated how learning is disrupted when the subject receives an electroconvulsive shock (ECS) shortly after a learning trial. The convulsion, similar in many respects to the synchronized brainstorm in an epileptic seizure, is readily induced by briefly passing a strong electric current between electrodes clipped to the ears of a rat. Starting with work by Duncan (1949), a long series of studies have shown that ECS given to a rat soon after a learning trial interferes with his performance of the appropriate habit when tested the next day after recovery from the short-lived convulsion. Moreover, the closer in time the ECS comes to the end of the learning trial, the greater is the disruption in performance that appears in the subsequent test.

The effect can be illustrated by Duncan's initial experiment. Rats were trained on an active avoidance habit at the rate of one trial a day for 18 days. The trial started by placing the rat on the "danger" side of a two-compartment box. If he did not cross over to the "safe" compartment within 10 seconds, his feet were shocked until he did. Following his crossing over to the safe compartment, the rat received an ECS. The delay between the response and the ECS was varied for different animals, being either 20, 40, 60 seconds, 4 or 15 minutes, 1, 4, or 14 hours. The ECS treatment was given following each of the training trials. Additionally a control group of subjects received no ECS. The effect of the delay between response and ECS is depicted in Figure 13-6 which shows the average number of avoidance responses over the 18 trials for animals given the ECS after each length of delay. The logarithm of the delay before ECS is plotted on the abscissa. Figure 13-6 shows a marked retrograde effect of ECS upon learning. At the shortest interval, 20 seconds, very

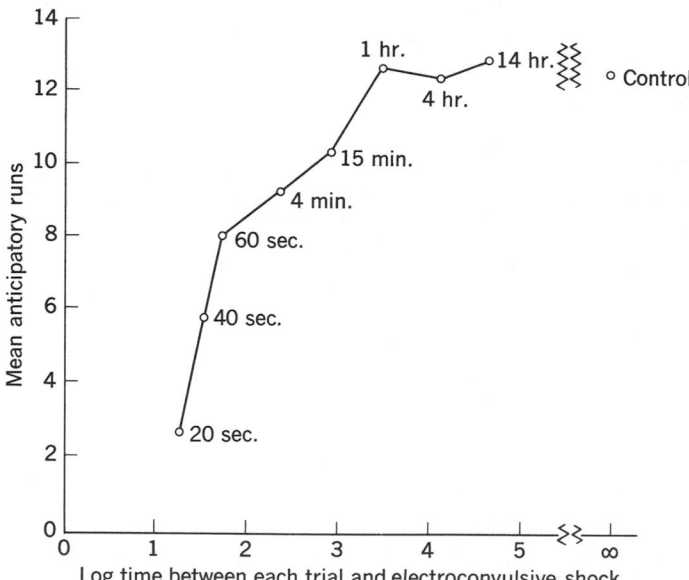

Figure 13-6 The average number of anticipatory runs (avoidance responses) for all 18 trials, related to the logarithm of the delay time between the trial and electroconvulsive shock. Different points on the curve (with delay times indicated) represent different groups of subjects. Reproduced from Duncan (1949), with permission from the American Psychological Association.

little learning occurred. As the time before ECS is lengthened, less decrement occurs. With an ECS delay of one hour or more, the subjects receiving ECS perform as well as the controls receiving no ECS.

These results may be interpreted as reflecting a process of memory consolidation that goes on over about a 60 minute period following each learning trial. The ECS is assumed to interrupt this process, with the amount learned per trial increasing with the time for consolidation before the process is interrupted by ECS.

Unfortunately, an alternative hypothesis would also explain Duncan's finding, namely, the delay-of-punishment gradient. We might assume that the ECS is aversive, so that it punishes and inhibits responses which it shortly follows, doing so according to a typical delay gradient. This would explain Duncan's findings without requiring the consolidation hypothesis. Later experiments have indeed shown that a series of electroconvulsive shocks begin to act like an aversive stimulus which the animal will avoid, although little of this aversion is evident after just one ECS. For this and various other reasons, it is now believed that the best paradigm for showing amnestic effects of ECS is a "one-trial learning" situation into which a single ECS is introduced.

A situation presently in use which meets these requirements is a passive avoidance situation. A rat is placed upon a small raised platform above a grid floor. If this is done with naive rats, they will step down off the small platform within a few seconds. If they are painfully shocked from the grid floor when they step down, a later test will show that they now refuse to leave the platform. They have learned a passive avoidance response in one trial. However, animals given an ECS soon after the foot shock seemingly "forget," so that on the next day's test they still step quickly off the platform (e.g. Chorover and Schiller, 1965). A graded amnesia effect is again obtained, although the time constants seem generally lower than those obtained by Duncan. For example, Chorover and Schiller report practically no ECS-induced amnesia when the ECS is delayed as much as 30 seconds following the learning trial; shorter delays ($\frac{1}{2}$, 2, 5, 10 seconds) had stronger amnestic effects. A partial review of this literature may be found in papers by Chorover (1965) and McGaugh (1965).

The retrograde effect of ECS has by now been repeatedly observed. Similar amnestic effects have been produced by convulsant drugs, heat narcosis, hyperoxia, and certain anesthetic drugs which produce unconsciousness or convulsions. The only serious challenge to the hypothesis of consolidation as an explanation of these results has been put forward by Lewis and Maher (1965 and references cited there). They review a variety of ECS studies showing a diversity of effects beyond those that the consolidation hypothesis presumes to explain. They propose that a useful hypothesis for interpreting many of these effects is that the ECS acts like a Pavlovian unconditioned stimulus producing conditioning of mild inhibition or relaxation to cues in the ECS situation. The retrograde effect is seen to result from poorer conditioning of this relaxation pattern due to a longer "CS-US" interval. They further argue that this conditioned relaxation would often compete with the response being measured as an index of memory, so that ECS would appear to have an "amnestic" effect upon that response. According to this view, then, ECS studies may be understood in terms of the conditioning of competing responses.

Lewis and his co-workers report several experiments supporting his hypothesis of competition which appear inexplicable by the consolidation hypothesis. For example, when ECS is given in a situation quite different from the learning situation, it has less "amnestic" effect than when given in the learning situation; this is predictable on the basis of stimulus generalization decrement of the competing response in the first (dissimilar) case (Yarnell and Adams, 1964). Also a series of convulsions given in the learning situation before training begins is found to retard subsequent learning of an active avoidance response. This is explicable on the basis of proactive interference of the prior-learned relaxation (conditioned by ECS) with the new active response to be learned. If following a prior ECS series animals are merely placed in the situation without ECS for several trials, their subsequent learning of an active avoidance response is improved. This is explained as due to extinction of the ECS-induced responses on the non-ECS trials, so that those responses can no longer effectively compete with the active avoidance to be subsequently learned.

The decision between these two hypotheses is not clear-cut because supporting experiments can be cited for each of them, and various *ad hoc* supplements can be added to each of them to cover the seemingly difficult cases. The human clinical reports on retrograde amnesia, if they can be weighed, seem to support the consolidation hypothesis. Fortunately there is some further evidence for the consolidation view that comes from different experiments by McGaugh. To place these in context, however, we must briefly review Hebb's quasi-neurological view of consolidation.

Hebb (1949) conceived of a short-term and long-term memory store (cf. Chapter 14). The input of stimulation supposedly produces "reverberating" neural activity, representative of that experience, which persists for a while. This dynamic neural trace is coincident with our short-term memory. While this reverberatory activity lasts, the permanent structural change underlying the long-term memory is slowly developing. Once the reverberatory trace dies out, the structural change stops but remains at the level attained. It is plausible, in this theory, to look for variables that influence reverberation rate or the length of time before the short-term trace dies out, since these should affect how much will be consolidated into long-term memory from a learning trial.

McGaugh (1965) has investigated two general classes of variables that may be interpreted by this means, namely, drugs and genetic constitution.

In one line of experiments, he has shown that certain CNS stimulating drugs like strychnine, diazamantan, and picrotoxin given in low doses would speed up maze learning of rats when injected either before *or after* the one trial on each day. Hunt found a similar effect using cardiazol. It is presumed that these stimulants either increase the consolidation rate or prolong the short-term activity trace, resulting in more consolidated learning per trial. In the other line of work, McGaugh has worked with genetic strains of rats that had been selectively inbred by Tryon to be either bright or dull in learning various maze problems. He has tested the implications of the idea that the maze-bright and maze-dull strains differ in their neural reverberation rates or times. For example, one implication that he confirmed is that in the one-trial learning ECS situation, ECS can be delayed longer yet still produce greater memory deficits in the maze-dull rats. Also if maze trials are given widely spaced in time, the maze-dulls can learn as fast as the maze-bright rats, the difference appearing only with massed trials. This is understandable if it is assumed that maze-dulls consolidate more slowly and the consolidation of learning from trial n is cut short when trial $n+1$ starts under the massed condition. Further, it was found that injection of the neural stimulant, picrotoxin, facilitated massed-trial learning of the maze-dulls (in fact, makes them learn as fast as the maze-brights), whereas the maze-bright animals were facilitated at only the higher drug dosages. These observations and several others seem consistent with the view that these two genetic strains differ in rate of memory consolidation.

In closing out our account of the consolidation hypothesis, it is proper to note that Hebb's statement of it employs a "conceptual" nervous system to advantage, without specifying the neural circuitry involved. There is, to be sure, firm evidence of persisting reverberatory neural circuits in the cortex. For example, Burns (1958) reported that a few electrical shocks applied to an isolated slab of quiescent cortex will produce bursts of neural activity that may persist for many minutes (sometimes as long as an hour) after stimulation has stopped. But little is really known of these persisting effects in nonisolated tissue. Nor is much known of the effect on the brain of the drugs like picrotoxin, etc., which facilitate learning, and very little is known of the effect of ECS upon the metabolism and general functioning of the brain. Our point in noting this is that the consolidation hypothesis derives its major, if not its sole, evidential support from "behavioral" studies, not from the observation of events in the central nervous system.

If the consolidation hypothesis is to expand into a viable theory in the future, a variety of further questions will have to be asked and answered by experiments. What causes differences in the time required to consolidate different learning tasks? Is the change gradual, all-or-none, or gradual with a threshold? How do we distinguish poor storage from poor access to a stored engram? What is the generic nature of the sorts of events that disrupt consolidation? How are proactive interference effects on retention to be explained in these terms? How can animals learn to avoid a place where ECS is delivered if that ECS prevents storage of the memory that it was unpleasant? Does consolidation stop when the short-term trace dies out or does it continue if not interfered with? Is there any long-term recovery of a memory disrupted by ECS? These and other questions come to mind. At present the hypothesis is not sufficiently elaborated to know how to answer any of them.

Physiological Changes in Learning

So far we have managed to discuss the neurophysiology of learning by skirting what is surely the central issue, namely, the nature of the physiological change that occurs during learning. The reason for skirting this issue is simple. The nature of this change is far from being understood. A number of speculative hypotheses have been offered over the years, but the evidence for any one of them is very limited and little agreement exists even about what are the more promising leads. The hypotheses, such as there are, vary in their degree of elaboration, from one-line "suggestions" to more elaborate systems of postulates; but for none has it been demonstrated that the hypothesis is sufficient to account for a substantial range of the known facts about learning. This is a sorry state of affairs, but one that seems imposed upon us by the difficulty of the problem. It certainly can not be attributed to any lack of industry or ingenuity by experimenters in the field. In this section, we will touch briefly upon a diverse miscellany of facts and ideas that are relevant to information storage in the nervous system. We can also mention a few of the earlier, more prevalent ideas regarding the physical change in learning, not so much to point to the evidence supporting them but rather to the lack of it.

We begin considerations with the example of a Pavlovian conditioned reflex. This is the simplest context in which to place various notions about the physical change effected by learning. A bell (CS) is paired repeatedly with an electric shock (US) to a forepaw of a dog, eliciting a limb flexion (UR), until with training the bell alone serves to elicit the response (CR). Looking at the process from the anatomical side, at least three classes of structures or cell populations are involved: (a) cells all along the sensory input channel excited by the CS, (b) cells along the sensory input channel excited by the US, and (c) cells along the motor output channel initiating and controlling the response (UR). We will call these multiple structures the CS, US, and UR sites or centers. Because of innate connections, there already exists a strong tendency for activation of the US center to produce activation of the UR center. Most neurophysiological theories of conditioning employ one or another modified version of the *substitution* notion of conditioning. By virtue of many contiguous pairings of activity in the CS center and the US (or UR) center, the former through some means gets "connected" to the latter so that activation of the CS now transmits effective excitation to the US (or UR) center. Thereupon the CS alone mimics or substitutes in some degree for the action of the US. Various hypotheses are then offered regarding the nature of this functional connection and the processes involved in its formation.

One class of hypotheses has to do with a selective increase in the efficiency of existing neural pathways connecting the CS and US centers, which may be assumed to involve many central synapses linked in a chain. Given good conduction between the CS and US centers, it is conceivable that the CS might fire the US center and thus evoke an anticipatory CR. In this case it is supposed that there is some anatomical or biochemical change at the synapses along such critical pathways. Some possibilities are that the presynaptic axon terminals either swell in size, grow in length, or multiply in numbers to make better contact with the postsynaptic neuron, thus aiding future transmission across the synapse.[1] There is slight evidence for the swelling notion and practically none for the growth or the multiplication suppositions. One problem is that normal stimulation across a synapse does not appear to change its efficiency (Brink, 1951). Efficiency can be enhanced, usually for only brief periods (a few minutes), if the synapse is bombarded with a volley of high frequency impulses (e.g., 400 pulses per second), but the relevance of this particular result for normal learning has not been elaborated.

An alternative idea, proposed by Pavlov (cf. Chapter 3) and investigated by the Russians, is cortical irradiation of extraneuronal electrical fields. When activated the cortical sites of the CS and US centers supposedly radiate electrical excitation, spreading out in all directions with diminishing intensity. Because the CS excitation is the weaker of the two, it is supposedly drawn toward the US excitation center by some method unspecified. As a consequence, some kind of cortical pathway (unspecified) would get established between the CS and US center. Beritoff (cited in Konorski, 1948) elaborates on the hypothesis further. However, two immediate problems are encountered by this notion of spreading intracortical electrical fields. First, it is known that animals (dogs) can learn simple conditioned reflexes even after the cortex has been totally removed. Second, an experiment by Sperry and Miner (1955) showed that learning was essentially undisturbed in animals whose cortices had been disturbed by cross-hatching knife cuts, or implantation of wires and mica sheets that serve as electrical conductors or insulators. Such devices must have distorted or destroyed any existing or generated electrical fields in the cortex. Yet they did not interfere at all with the learning of fairly complicated CR's.

[1] The notion of a biochemical change at the synapse is discussed in a later section of this chapter.

As mentioned earlier in our discussion of consolidation, Hebb (1949) and others have proposed that a sequence of stimulus inputs sets up a short-term activity (memory) trace based on reverberatory neuronal circuits involving elements excited by the two (or more) inputs. Neuron A excites neuron B which, through some more or less direct path, excites A again; hence, the loop of A to B to A activity is alleged to perseverate for a time after the inputs. This persisting reverberatory activity is presumed to induce a more enduring structural change (of unknown nature) so that the A-B neural centers will now be aroused as a unit. The fairest statement we can make concerning this notion is that no convincing evidence has been adduced for the existence of reverberatory circuits in the intact brain that (a) are clearly implicated in learning, or (b) that last long enough to have the properties ascribed to them. As mentioned earlier, Burns (1958) reported fairly persistent neural activity following stimulation of the cortex, but that was in an isolated slab of material not subject to dissipating forces from other parts of the brain. In any event, the reverberation idea, even if true, still tells us nothing about the nature of the change effected by learning.

Instead of speculating about the neural changes involved in CR learning, the strategy preferred by many investigators is to search for experimental preparations wherein a few neurons modify their behavior in a way that mimics learning. The hope is that by studying a primitive form of information storage or learning at the level of the single neural cell, we may come up with some fruitful hypotheses about the physical changes in learning. In line with this policy, there have been many efforts to devise preparations that show simple learning in a few neurons. It can be reported that several preparations devised by Morrell (1960, 1961a) appear to be very promising.

The first of such preparations is the "mirror focus" epileptiform phenomenon whereby a cluster of normal brain cells learn to behave in an abnormal way. It has been observed that an abnormally discharging group of brain cells in the cortex of one cerebral hemisphere (the primary focus) will fire off a similar discharge in a corresponding area of the other hemisphere (the secondary focus). The main links connecting the two foci probably pass through the corpus callosum. The primary focus may be produced by local application of various chemicals (ethyl chloride or aluminum hydroxide) to the brain site or by an injury or tumor (as in epilepsy). Initially, discharge of the secondary focus is dependent upon discharge in the primary focus. However, after a time (about 8 weeks in the monkey), the secondary focus begins abnormally discharging on its own, independently of the primary focus. The primary focus can be now ablated, and the secondary focus continues its pattern of paroxysmal discharging. It has "learned" to discharge in an abnormal way. Moreover, if the secondary focus is neuronally isolated by cutting it away from surrounding tissue (but leaving its blood supply intact) and left in a quiescent state for some months, later stimulation of the tissue will still set off the abnormal discharge pattern. Apparently the tissue slab has "retained" this discharge pattern after months of inactivity. Of further interest is the report that abnormally high concentrations of ribonucleic acid (RNA) were found in cells taken from the site of the secondary focus. This observation is placed in better perspective in our next section on neurochemistry. The importance of this preparation is that learning of a primitive sort has been shown to occur in a relatively small group of cortical cells.

The second preparation was devised in the course of pursuing some interesting developments concerning the relation between learning and steady electrical potential shifts in the surface of the cortex. Interest in this latter line of work stems from the fact, observed by Rusinov (1953) and others, that shifts in the steady electrical potential of the brain surface can be recorded during the course of classical conditioning. The supposition is that extraneuronal electrical fields exerting an electrotonic influence on neural cell populations would probably play some important role in the conditioning process. Such shifts in cortical steady potentials have been found to result from direct electrical stimulation of the brain. Indeed, Morrell (1961b) found that a shift of cortical potential elicited by a thalamic electric shock could be conditioned as a "response" to a tone stimulus. Of considerable interest too are studies of the effect of directly modifying the steady potential on the cortical surface. Rusinov modified the steady electrical potential of the brain of rabbits by applying a weak anodal constant direct current to a part of the motor cortex controlling forelimb flexion. Though such a current did not itself produce a motor response, nevertheless while the polarizing current was acting and for up to 30 minutes after it terminated, neutral sensory stimuli such as a light, sound, or touch would produce flexion of the appropriate forelimb. It was as though the brain had been primed in readiness to make this motor response given any sudden sensory signal. Morrell (1961b) replicated these findings and extended them in several ways. In one experiment, it was shown that if a stimulus had been thoroughly habituated, as judged by the eventual absence of an EEG change to its presentation, then that stimulus would not elicit the limb flexion during the heightened excitability period after the polarizing stimulus is switched off. However, novel stimuli that had not been habituated would still trigger the response.

A miniature "learning" preparation was discovered in the course of further study of anodal polarization. In this experiment, a tiny microelectrode was used to record evoked electrical activity in single neurons of the visual cortex (see panels A and B of Figure 13-7). During anodal polarization of the cortex, it was easy to "drive" such cells in synchrony with a flashing light delivered to the eye. "Driving" in this context means that the cell in the visual cortex responds with a short burst of activity for each flash to the eye; for example, if the light flashes three times per second, then the driven cell responds in brief bursts three times per second. Such driving may be seen in panel C of Figure 13-7.

The interesting observation made by Morrell is that such neural cells can learn and retain for a while the particular driving frequency to which they have been exposed. When a cell was driven at 3 per second during anodal polarization, it would later respond to a *single* flash by prolonged 3 per second bursts of activity. The effect is seen in panel D of Figure 13-7. The cell (or its neighbors) apparently learned and retained the specific firing frequency imposed upon it during the "conditioning" phase carried out under anodal polarization.

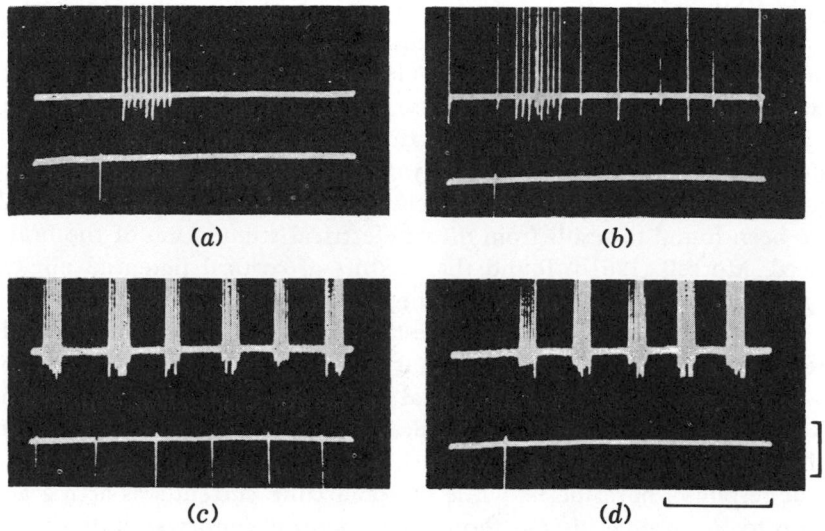

Figure 13-7   Firing of a single neuron in the visual cortex induced by flashes of light. The flash is indicated by the pips on the lower line of each panel; the firing of the neuron is indicated by the pips on the top line of each panel. Time ($\frac{1}{2}$ sec in A and B, 1 sec in C and D) reads from left to right. A single flash elicited a single burst when the cell was quiescent (panel A) or randomly firing (panel B). Flashes occurring at a rate of three per second resulted in unit discharges at a rate of three per second (panel C). A single flash (panel D) delivered 30 seconds after termination of the rhythmic flashes produced repetitive unit discharge at a rate of about three per second. Reproduced from Morrell (1963) in Fields, W. S., and Abbott, W., Information Storage and Neural Control, 1963. Courtesy of Charles C Thomas, Publisher, Springfield, Illinois.

This conditioned rhythmic response was retained over several minutes following the training phase. The three per second response to a single flash became progressively less reliable as time elapsed after the conditioning. The forgetting curve for the neuron is shown in Figure 13-8, depicting the declining percentage of three per second responses to a test flash as time passed. This preparation, then, provides another example of how information about the firing pattern can be retained by the brain, showing up in single neurons an appreciable time after the training phase. The anodal polarization of the cortex enhances the cell's ability to be so modified by input stimulation. Of course, there is no guarantee in this work that learning has occurred in the very cell from which the microelectrode records are taken. Possibly the learning occurs in structures remote from this cell but if this is the case they project their response to the cortical cell from which the record is taken. Thus, one may not have here a cell that learns but rather one that is ganged with others that learn.

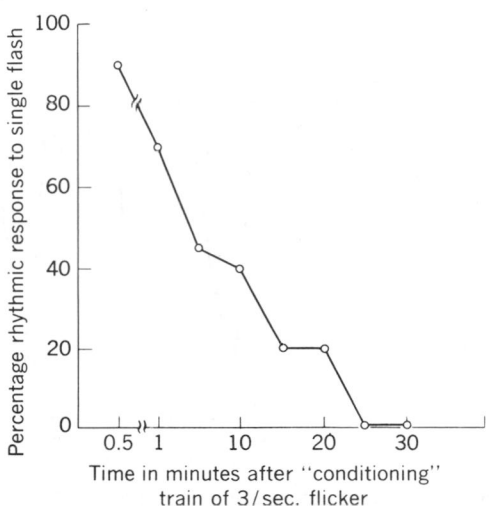

Figure 13-8   **Time course of "forgetting" of conditioned rhythmic response of a single cortical neuron. As time passed following the 3-per-second flashes, a single flash was less likely to elicit the 3-per-second pattern of unit activity. Reproduced from Morrell (1963) in Fields, W. S., and Abbott, W., Information Storage and Neural Control, 1963, Courtesy of Charles C Thomas, Publisher, Springfield, Illinois.**

A further experiment by Morrell and Naitoh (1962) shows the effect upon a conditioned reflex of altering the steady potential of the cortex. Rabbits were trained on a paw flexion CR to avoid shock, the CS being a flashing light. During some training sessions, a weak steady cathodal polarization was applied continuously either to the motor cortex, to the visual cortex, or to the ear lobe (as a control). The effect on a typical animal is shown in Figure 13-9. This figure shows the proportion of CR's over daily training sessions consisting of 20 trials. Several facts are to be noted. First, when a break of one or more days was introduced (on days 17 and 28 in the figure), the animal not being run on those days, performance on the following day was considerably poorer. Though retention decrements of this magnitude are unusual, they appeared to be characteristic of all rabbits in the study. Secondly, cathodal polarization of the visual cortex during an entire session produced considerable loss of CR performance during that session, and for the next several sessions. In fact, the session with visual cathodal polarization mimics the effect of a "rest day" from which the animals show recovery over the following daily sessions. Third, cathodal polarization of the motor cortex or ear had little effect on the CR during that session. In other animals, it was shown that anodal polarization had no effect on the CR when it was applied to the visual cortex.

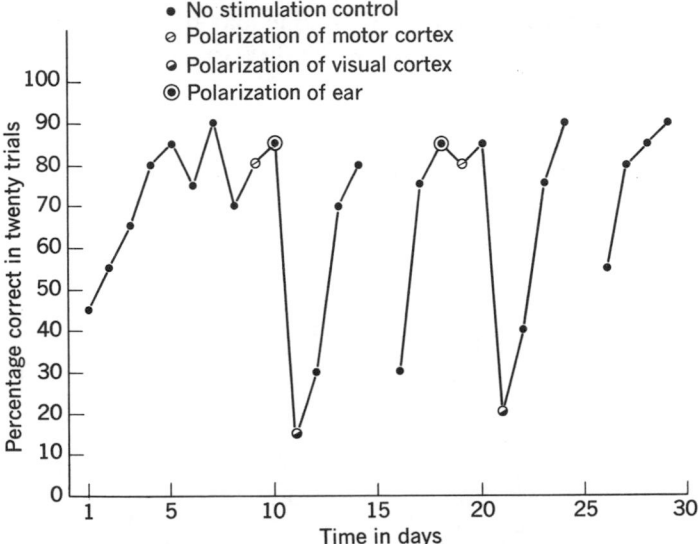

Figure 13-9   **Effect of cathodal polarization upon performance of a conditioned avoidance response in a typical rabbit. Several hundred trials (not shown) preceded the days shown here. The animal was not run on days 15 and 25. Cathodal polarization of visual cortex was continuously applied during the session on days 11 and 21. Controls, consisting of polarization of the motor cortex (days 9 and 19) and of the ear (days 10 and 18), were without effect. Reproduced from Morrell (1963) in Fields, W. S., and Abbott, W., Information Storage and Neural Control, 1963. Courtesy of Charles C Thomas, Publisher, Springfield, Illinois.**

From these results it appears likely that cathodal polarization of the visual cortex acted by preventing the registration of visual events during polarization. Assuming that the visual input is transmitted intact to the visual cortex, the cathodal polarization of that area probably prevents the input signal from being shunted elsewhere, where its "meaning" is interpreted or where it connects to the motor output. It is of interest that the cathodal polarization mimics the spreading depression effect to be reviewed later, both of them producing a functional ablation of a local cortical region, yet one which is temporary and reversible. This technique will very likely be exploited further as one method of studying brain function during learning.

Neurochemistry and Experience

One appealing general hypothesis to explore is that individuals differ in their learning capabilities because of differences in the biochemistry of their brains. This is not an implausible supposition to follow up since developments in neurochemistry have supplied strong evidence that the transmission of neural signals is largely a chemical affair. Perhaps bright and dull individuals differ in the amount or manner of distribution over the brain of particular essential chemicals, or they may differ in the distribution of antagonistic chemicals which must be maintained in delicate balance for good performance. The known effects of powerful hallucinogenic and psychomimetic drugs such as mescaline and LSD offer some support for this thesis. These drugs have powerful and far ranging effects on mental life, producing some of the bizarre mental phenomena characteristic of patients during psychotic episodes. Because some psychomimetic drugs have structural resemblances to chemicals found normally in the brain, much research has been aimed at discovering whether psychotics suffer from some disturbance in the biochemical system that produces these chemicals. Kety (1959) and Rinkel (1958) have given us provocative reviews of the research bearing on this subject.

If we follow up the general idea of seeking to discover how brain chemistry is related to behavior, the first questions to be decided are what chemicals to look for and where in the brain they should be looked for. One approach is to measure the total amount of some chemical in gross areas of the brain, e.g., in the whole cortex of a rat. An alternative measure might be of its amount and how it changes in a few neural cells located in specific brain structures implicated in the behavior we are studying. Another line of research uses brain chemistry alternately as an independent variable and a dependent variable. In the first case, the aim is to find out how behavior varies on some standard task for individuals known to have different distributions of brain chemicals (e.g., because of age or of genetic differences). In the second case, one manipulates the rearing and learning experiences of animals from a common genetic pool, and then determines whether their brain chemistry has been changed as a result of experience. In most instances, both approaches are used by the same investigator. In what follows, we shall review one line of work representative of the relatively "gross" approach to brain chemistry and one representative of the cellular approach.

1. Acetylcholine and Cholinesterase. Nerve cells may be thought of as telephone transmission lines that connect with one another functionally at junctures known as synapses. Line A connects to line B across a synapse, and the synapse is responsible for transmitting to B any nerve impulse (signal) traveling down line A. It is believed that this transmission is largely a matter of biochemistry. An impulse in line A releases, literally squirts out at its end, a small amount of a substance called acetylcholine (ACh); this goes across the tiny gap between A and B, and is absorbed by nerve B, causing an electrical impulse to be generated and propagated down B. ACh is called the *transmitter* substance because of its essential role in this process. Following the firing of B, the enzyme cholinesterase (ChE) comes into play at the synapse. This enzyme works by hydrolizing (neutralizing) the ACh released at the synapse during transmission. In this manner, the ACh is cleared away and the synapse is returned to its prior state, making it ready to conduct further signals. The biochemical reactions here are extremely fast requiring but a few milliseconds, and the interplay of the ACh and ChE systems are in a synchronized and delicate balance at a normal synapse. Small changes in the availability or speed of access to one or the other chemical could result in malfunctioning, or at least reduced efficiency in transmission of finely modulated, temporal patterns of neural impulses across the synapse.

A group of scientists at the University of California—Krech and Rosenzweig the psychologists and Bennett the biochemist—have carried out a research program on ChE concentrations in rat brains. ChE is used because measurements of it are relatively easy to obtain, whereas reliable assays of ACh are difficult. Over a research period of ten years they have shifted their emphasis (due to the incoming data) concerning what brain-chemistry measure should be used to find reliable correlations with behavior. The measure that seems most discriminating is the ratio of total cortical ChE activity to total subcortical ChE activity, called the C/S ratio (for cortical/subcortical). Low values of this C/S ratio are associated with quick learning of maze problems. In one study (Krech, Rosenzweig, and Bennett, 1960), rats reared in an "enriched" sensory environment, one filled with playground toys along with other rats, had lower adult C/S ratios than rats reared under conditions of relative "isolation," where they were in small enclosed cages devoid of other objects and fellow rats. On later tests of maze learning (Krech, Rosenzweig, and Bennett, 1962), the "enriched" subjects also learned more rapidly. Within each rearing condition, individual differences in C/S ratio were correlated with errors in the maze learning problem. The correlation turned out to be .81 for animals reared in the enriched environment and .53 for those reared in isolation. This shows a rather strong correlation between brain chemistry and speed of learning.

In other studies, rats of different genetic strains were examined for differences in C/S ratio. A series of studies has been done with the Tryon maze-bright and maze-dull genetic strains of rats (cf. p. 453). Examination of the brains of these rats showed the C/S ratio was lower for the maze-bright than for the maze-dull subjects. This is consistent with the previous results—that is, lower C/S ratios make for faster learning. In a genetic experiment by Roderick (1960), rats were selectively bred, some for high cortical ChE levels, some for low. After several generations of inbreeding highs with highs and lows with lows, there was little overlap in the distributions of cortical ChE levels in the two populations. Thus, brain chemistry was shown to be manipulable through genetic selection starting from a common genetic stock.

Although these studies have been generally successful in disclosing individual and strain differences in brain chemistry that correlate with learning, the research ran into an interpretative problem. Though the C/S ratio "worked" empirically, no one was able to figure out a very convincing explanation for why it did so. The more recent results, however, provide a new stimulus for fertile hypothesizing. These results have shown, quite simply, that the cerebral cortex of "enriched-reared" (ER) rats is bigger than that of rats kept in the "isolation-reared" (IR) condition! Bennett *et al.* (1964) found that the cortex of the ER rats is both heavier and thicker. Because the increase in cholinesterase activity of the cortex is relatively less than the increase in its weight, the ChE activity per unit of weight decreases in the cortex of the ER rats. The ChE activity of the subcortex remains about the same, whereas the subcortex weight is slightly lower for ER rats, thus making for a higher subcortex ChE activity per unit weight. This explains why the C/S ratio of ChE activity is lower in the ER rats.

This discovery of a change in size of the cortex came as a complete surprise to those familiar with brain research. Before this, few experts would have believed that the effects of a sensorily enriched environment could induce so "obvious" a change in the brain. But the effect has by now been replicated about 8 times, being present each time in the ER-IR comparison. The magnitude of the change varies in different areas over the cortex, being largest (about 10 percent by weight) in the visual cortex. But it will be recalled that complexity of visual input is one of the main factors differentiating the two rearing conditions. In a further study (Rosenzweig *et al.*, 1964), two groups of animals were reared in the same environment, the usual colony room, until they were 105 days of age, making them, roughly, adolescents, and then were separated, some to live in the enriched environment and some in the impoverished environment. After 85 days of such living, the two groups of rats were found to differ significantly in cortical weight and in ChE activity, much as when the differential rearing was done from birth onwards. Thus the brains of rats that have suffered an impoverished early life can be enlarged by placing them at adolescence in an enriched environment. This shows that there is no "critical period" before which the animal has to be exposed to the enriched environment in order to produce an increase in the size of its cortex.

These findings have instigated a number of follow-up studies, investigating individual and strain differences in cortical size and visual learning ability. To date no explanations have been offered for (a) how a stimulating environment leads to a selective increase in cortical size, or (b) why individuals with a slightly larger cortex learn maze problems faster than their slimmer-brained relations. Apparently we may think of neural tissue much as we think of muscles which increase in size with exercise. Such a view would have been considered until very recently incredible nonsense in any respectable neurological discussion.

2. Cellular neurochemistry.   One active line of contemporary research stems from the hypothesis that the physical basis for memory resides in some relatively enduring change in the biochemical constituents of a neuron which selectively control its response. This would suggest that an engram might be built up by certain biochemical changes occurring in many of the cells of a neuronal circuit activated by the learning experience. To push this idea a little further, it might be supposed that if the biochemical constituents of a neuron are of a particular kind, then that neuron will fire readily upon receiving a "familiar" pattern of incoming pulses but will not do so if the incoming pattern is unfamiliar.

For various reasons, ribonucleic acid (RNA) appears to be the logical candidate to assume this role of the memory molecule. It occurs in abundance in neural cells, it contains within its structure a potentially large storehouse for holding encoded information (explained below), and it determines and controls the specific form of proteins that are synthesized within a cell. RNA is a first cousin of DNA (deoxyribonucleic acid) which has been recently established to be the gene-carrying hereditary material in the chromosomes of each cell. DNA contains within its large structure sufficient coded information to specify the phenotypic character of an organism, and it exercises its influence by controlling biochemical reactions in complex ways.

RNA is a very large, single strand molecule (a polymer) consisting of a recurring sequence of a phosphate and sugar pair connected to any one of four "bases," adenine, guanine, uracil, and cytosine. One of the four bases followed by a phosphate and a sugar may be considered as four types of links used to compose a long beaded chain. The RNA molecule is very long (probably several thousand units), so that the number of possible sequential combinations of the four bases is very large. To illustrate, suppose each molecule were 2000 links long and at each position either of the 4 bases could occur. Then the number of different varieties of the molecule would be 4^{2000}, which is indeed a large number. This large number is important because it shows how much information could potentially be encoded in an RNA molecule. This capacity can be appreciated when it is recalled that Morse code translates a letter of the alphabet into a mere string of four or five binary units (a dot or a dash). In metaphorical terms, an RNA strand consisting of 2000 units with 4 alternatives at each unit could encode and store a message about a 1000 letters long. Whether and how biological information is coded in RNA, and what the code is, are at present unanswered questions. However, the point here is that RNA has the potential for filling the role of a biological information storehouse.

If this were all there is to say about RNA, then it would remain merely the subject of idle speculation. But there is a rash of behavioral evidence which, in sum, strongly implicates RNA as the possible memory molecule. For one thing, its concentration in human brain cells first increases with age and then decreases, much as learning ability does. It has been reported that adding RNA supplements to the diet of aged persons improves their immediate memory. Of more direct relevance is the fact that the concentration of RNA in neural cells increases when they are repetitively stimulated.

When the stimulation is to a cell importantly involved in learning some skill, the RNA in that cell not only increases but also changes its character as indexed by the amounts of the four bases (the "base ratio") found in RNA analysis following learning. In one study by Hydén and Egyhâzi (1962), rats were trained to balance upon and walk up an inclined tightrope to get a food reward. Following learning, the RNA in the vestibular nucleus was examined. This is a bundle of fibers that relays signals to the brain from the semicircular canals, which are receptor organs involved in maintaining postural balance. RNA in the nucleus of cells at this site was increased by the learning experience and the dominant species of RNA was of a different kind (different base ratio) than that in control rats subjected to stimulation of their semicircular canals though they had not been given the special training in tightrope balancing and walking. These control rats were instead merely rotated about in a small oscillating cage, movement that stimulates the semicircular canals. Along with this "learning change" in RNA of the vestibular nucleus of the experimental group of rats, there was also a decrease in the amount and a change in the kind of dominant RNA found in the glia cells surrounding the neurons studied.

In a further study (Hydén and Egyhâzi, 1964), right-"handed" rats were trained to use their left "hands" to grab food pellets from the dispenser. Neural cells taken from certain layers of the opposite (right) cerebral cortex showed increases in nuclear RNA concentration and changes in the base ratio of the dominant RNA species. The particular cells were taken from cortical areas involved in use of the left hand; this is inferred from the report that destruction of this cortical area would disable the rat from learning the left-handed grasping skill.

A few difficulties arise in interpreting these results. First is the adequacy of the controls. Since stimulation or exercise *per se* enhances RNA in the neurons involved, the problem is to design the experiment so that the learning subjects and the nonlearning controls receive about the same pattern of input stimulation. It has been argued that the controls run are not adequate in this sense. Second, the changes with learning in the dominant species of RNA are confined only to what is found in the cell's nucleus, not in its cytoplasm. Third, the changes in nuclear RNA are found immediately after the animal has been performing in the learning situation, but are no longer detectable if one waits 24 hours after the learning session before sacrificing the animal and looking at his RNA (see Hydén, 1965); that is, after 24 hours, differences in RNA between the learning subjects and the controls can no longer be detected. Depending on one's attitude, these facts can be interpreted in terms that are either critical of, or sympathetic to, the "RNA memory" hypothesis.

Some other evidence implicating RNA in memory comes from studies on the biological transfer of RNA and memory between two individuals of the same species. One individual is trained until he has learned a habit. Then some of his RNA is extracted and given to a naive subject, and thereafter the naive subject demonstrates that he too can perform the habit to a significant degree. The initial studies along this line were done on flatworms (planaria) by McConnell (1962) and his associates. By pairing a light with a shock evoking body contraction, the planaria may be conditioned to give a contraction or turn the body to the light as a CS. Worms that have been so trained are cut up and fed as food to naive flatworms. Control worms that have been exposed to the same lights and shocks separately, but never paired, are cut up and fed to naive control animals. When later tested for conditioning in the light-shock situation, the worms that have eaten "trained" food outperform control subjects that have eaten "untrained" food. In a related experiment, Ragland and Ragland (1965) reported that a species of planaria that was not conditionable became so after they were fed on trained worms of a different planaria species that was conditionable.

The transfer of learning that is found in these cannibalism studies is evidently due to incorporation by the cannibal of stable chemicals from the trained donor which have been altered in a specific way by learning. Several studies implicate RNA as the transfer substance in these experiments. First, it has been reported that if RNA is specifically extracted from the trained worms and injected into naive worms, the same positive transfer appears in the naive worm, whereas injection of RNA from a naive worm produces no positive transfer (Zelman *et al.*, 1963).

Second, an experiment by Corning and John (1961) is relevant to the theory that the transfer occurs because of RNA. If a trained planarian is cut in half, the head and tail will in the course of several days each regenerate, forming two complete new organisms. Morever, the two regenerated organisms will both show significant retention of the original learning. Corning and John required that this regenerative growth of the two ends occur while the pieces were in a ribonuclease (RNase) solution. Ribonuclease is an enzyme that breaks down free RNA. Without going further into details here, we can say that the effect of RNase upon the regenerating pieces should be to make the brand of RNA present in the regenerated portion different from the brand of RNA present in the old portion of the planaria. The experimenters found that when a new head was regenerated onto an old tail-piece in RNase, no retention of the learned light-shock habit was obtained. However, retention of learning was found when a new tail was regenerated in RNase onto a piece of the old head. And, as expected, retention was also found when either end regenerated in regular pond water. These results suggest that the head-end was dominant in determining test behavior, that the regenerated head-end has its new RNA patterned after that in the trained tail-end if the new head regenerates in pond water, but that the new head contains a different "untrained" species of RNA if it has been regenerated from a tail-end in RNase.

Because of the rather dramatic character of these cannibalism and RNA experiments, many efforts have been made to repeat them, with sometimes marked changes in procedure. At the moment of writing, there is some controversy concerning the repeatability of these planarian results and also concerning the exact experimental conditions under which fairly good learning can be obtained. Because they foresaw that controversy was likely to ensue from reports of their dramatic results, the McConnell group has generally repeated each experiment several times, using double-blind procedures in order to reduce experimenter bias. Still, others have had difficulty replicating the basic results (e.g., Bennett and Calvin, 1964). Presumably debate will subside with further analysis and more exact specification of the small experimental variations that make for good or bad conditioning of planarians.

More recently, the albino rat, the erstwhile and dependable creature of the learning laboratories, has been called upon to supply his testimony. At this writing, the results of three experiments have appeared, all claiming to support memory transfer by RNA in the rat (Fjerdingstad et al., 1965; Babich et al., 1965; Jacobson et al., 1965). The first, however, used too few animals, and the second failed to control for general sensitization of activity; however, the third experiment cited is more convincing. In this experiment by Jacobson et al., two groups of "donor" rats were trained in a Skinner box to approach a food cup and obtain a food pellet when a discriminative stimulus was presented. The discriminative stimulus for approach for one group was an audible click, for the other group a flashing light. After training, RNA was extracted from the brains of these two groups of rats and injected into two groups of naive rats that had been habituated to the same apparatus though they were given no food rewards. Upon testing between 4 and 24 hours after injection (with a double-blind procedure to reduce experimenter bias), the two injected groups showed differential tendencies to approach the food cup upon presentation of the click or the flashing light. Rats injected with RNA from click-trained donors averaged 5.75 approach responses (in 25 click trials) to the click and 1.87 approach responses to the light (again, in 25 light trials). Rats injected with RNA from light-trained donors averaged 3.75 responses to the light and 1.00 response to the click, again each with 25 test trials. Six of the eight click-injected rats gave more responses to click than light; seven of the eight light-injected rats gave more responses to the light than to the click. The group differences in differential reactions to the two stimuli are highly significant by statistical tests, although the amount of transfer is relatively small in an absolute sense.[2]

This sampling of results suffices to explain the current excitement about RNA as a possible carrier of memories. But it is necessary to add that, despite this suggestive evidence, there is still skepticism, or incredulity, in some quarters about the RNA-memory hypothesis. This attitude can be traced in part to the lack of a plausible theory that could throw light on how exactly RNA and memory are, or could be, related.

Several important questions have to be answered by such a theory. The first is, by what means and by what steps is the RNA in a neuron altered (or a particular RNA species selected for a higher rate of synthesis) by experience? The information arriving at a neuron is only electrical impulses, arriving in a particular temporal pattern or frequency. How does this information get translated into biochemical codes within RNA? The second question is, even supposing that information is stored in some fashion in RNA, how is it then retrieved? How does the dominant RNA species in the nucleus of a neural cell selectively control the transmission properties or responsivity of the cell membrane? The information stored in RNA must eventually have its effect at the level of the electrical "language" of the neurons, namely, in modifying the temporal pattern of firing of a neuron to particular inputs.

These are difficult questions, and our ignorance about molecular events at the neural cellular level prevents any satisfactory answer to them at the

[2] The research results are still controversial. Although the original authors report further positive results for RNA-transfer in a light–dark discrimination (Jacobson *et al.*, 1966), failures to find any evidence for RNA-transfer have been reported by Gross and Carey (1965) and Luttges *et al.* (1966).

present time. Various speculative suggestions have appeared (e.g., Hydén, 1965; Roberts, 1965; Landauer, 1964), but these are admittedly sketchy, incomplete, and likely wrong in detail. For example, Roberts tries to show how a given neuronal circuit could be facilitated by the passage of specifically coded RNA from a cell to its adjacent members in the circuit. In effect, he uses the RNA notion to explicate the older idea that learning results from a lowering of synaptic "resistance" along particular neuronal pathways.

To illustrate briefly what a hypothesis about RNA and memory might look like, consider a proposal by Landauer (1964) on how RNA might work, say, in producing learning in a classical conditioning experiment. The theory supposes that neural cells in the brain excited by the CS send out specific frequency modulated signals as electrical waves that spread throughout the surrounding tissue. This specific frequency pattern selects or primes a particular species of RNA from glial cells in such a manner that when the neurons corresponding to the US (or UR) fire, this particular glial RNA in the neighborhood is absorbed into the US (or UR) cells by electrophoresis. This selected-and-absorbed RNA then transforms the membrane protein chemistry of the US (or UR) cells in such a manner as to make them directly sensitive to the frequency modulated signals from the CS cells. Thus, after several contiguous pairings of the CS and US, the changes in the US (or UR) cells may become sufficient to cause them to be fired by excitation of the CS cells alone, thereby giving rise to a conditioned response.

This is the gist of what a hypothesis about storage and retrieval (involving RNA) looks like. Many details are left unspecified for lack of knowledge, and what there are have to be eked out by imaginative guesses. However, there is no denying that such speculative attempts are extremely valuable in guiding and provoking research, and in helping scientists decide what is and what is not a significant finding regarding the process. In preliminary attempts, such hypotheses concentrate upon only a small part of the known facts. For example, the hypotheses proposed by Hydén, Roberts, and Landauer are most relevant only to the Hydén and Egyhâzi studies. The cannibalism and RNA-memory transfer studies would require further assumptions that few theorists have even attempted to formulate.

This concludes our brief tour around the fringes of the neurochemistry of learning. This is a very young field, full of many surprises, perplexities, and promises. There are major technical difficulties in doing research or theorizing at this level, and progress has to be slow. In order to understand the work at all well, one needs a fairly detailed knowledge of biochemistry, and for this reason psychologists are unlikely to rush into this research area in large numbers. It should be clear enough that at this early stage of development, no detailed biochemical account can be given for even the simplest learned act. However, we may look forward to major strides in this area in the next few decades.

TWO HEADS IN ONE SKULL: INTERHEMISPHERIC TRANSFER

One of the more striking features of the vertebrate brain is its bilateral symmetry. Brain structures appear to be duplicated nearly perfectly in homologous positions around the midline of the sagittal plane (i.e., the plane cutting fore and aft from the top of the head to the chin). This bilateral representation of function raises interesting possibilities for research on the localization of the memory trace.

To see some of these possibilities, consider the bilaterality of the visual system in mammals (see Figure 13-10). Visual information is picked up by the retina of each eye and transmitted along separate optic tracts. These tracts meet at a juncture called the optic chiasm. After the juncture the tracts separate again, the left one coursing through various relay stations to project eventually onto the left cerebral hemisphere, the right one coursing similarly to project onto the right cerebral hemisphere. At the chiasm there is appreciable crossing-over of fibers from the two entering tracts, approximately half the fibers of each tract crossing over to the opposite tract as they emerge from the chiasm juncture. The fibers that cross are those that arise mainly from the half of the retina nearest the nose. Because of this cross-over of fibers at the chiasm information from the nose-side of the left retina is projected mainly to the right cortex whereas information from the lateral left-retina is projected to the left cortex. Moving on to the cerebral cortex, the two hemispheres are in direct communication with one another through a series of commissures, the fiber bundles that connect homologous structures on the two sides. The largest of these connecting commissures is the *corpus callosum,* a massive bundle of fibers interconnecting many parts of the two hemispheres.

Interocular Transfer and Its Surgical Abolition

Given this anatomical knowledge, let us now consider the phenomena of interocular transfer of a visual discrimination that an animal (say, cat or monkey) has learned while using only one eye. The animal is forced by some means, such as the use of an occluding contact lens, to learn a visual discrimination using only one eye while the other eye never sees the discriminative stimuli. Following learning with the use of but one eye, the animal is tested with the opposite eye open and the trained eye occluded. Under normal circumstances, the animal will show prac-

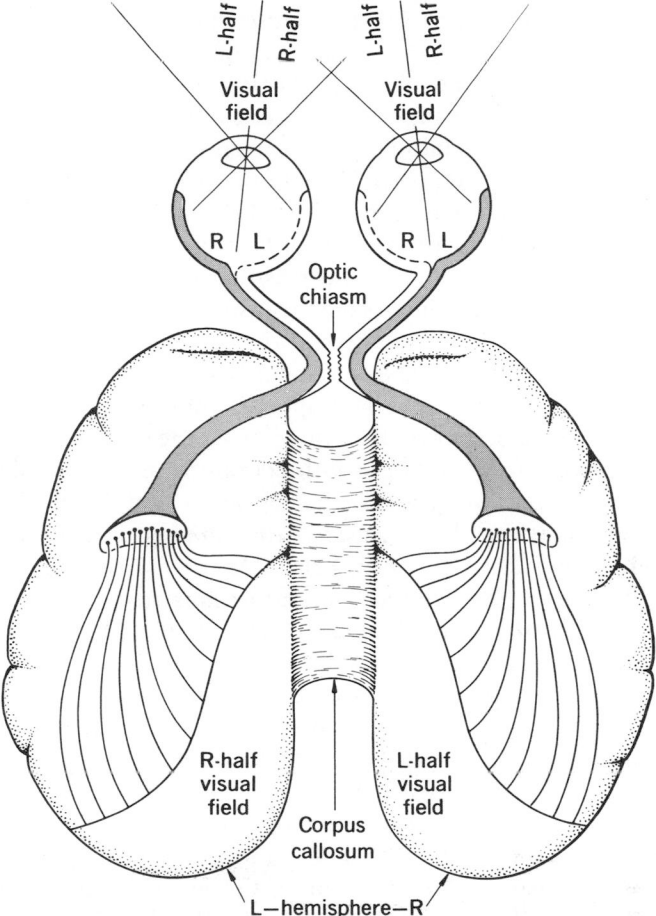

Figure 13-10   Schematic drawing of visual system showing retina, optic chiasm, and projections to visual receiving areas in cerebral cortex. In the figure, the optic chiasm has been sectioned, thus eliminating that half of the visual field normally transmitted by the cross-over fibers from the eye opposite to a cerebral hemisphere. Visual inflow from each eye is restricted to the hemisphere on the same side as the eye. The corpus callosum is shown intact. Reproduced from Sperry (1961).

tically perfect transfer of the habit from the trained to the untrained eye. A series of experiments by Sperry (1961) and his colleagues makes plausible the assumption that in this case the visual knowledge (or engram) mediating the discriminative performance has been laid down in both visual hemispheres during training, and that during testing with the untrained eye its afferent connections with the brain make contact with either one or both of the trained hemispheres, thus retrieving and using the engram to guide correct responses. Let us begin tracking down the systematic evidence for this interpretation.

Consider first the effect of cutting the optic chiasm in the sagittal plane (as shown in Figure 13-10), in such a manner that each eye projects only to its corresponding visual cortex on the same side. This sectioning of the chiasm produces a hemianopia, which means that when only one eye is used, about half of the visual field (the peripheral edge that projects to the nose-side of the retina) is blurred though all aspects can be seen clearly by moving the eye. Surprisingly, cutting the chiasm in this manner does not affect interocular transfer, regardless of whether the cut is made before or after one-eyed training. Although training has restricted visual input to, say, the left hemisphere, later tests with the right eye (projecting to the right hemisphere) show that information along that channel in some way makes contact with the engram.

This contact of right eye with engram is made possible in either of two ways. One possibility is that the engram is laid down only in the left hemisphere that gets direct sensory input during training. The right eye and right hemisphere, however, can make use of this engram during testing by virtue of the callosal communication networks connecting the two hemispheres. The other possibility is that while the primary engram is being established in the left hemisphere during training, the connections through the callosum at the same time permit a duplicate or carbon copy of the engram to be laid down in the right hemisphere. The later test with the right eye would then use this "carbon-copy" engram established in the right hemisphere.

Two experiments indicate that the carbon-copy supposition is more likely the correct one. Suppose that following left-eye training of a chiasm-sectioned cat, we then ablate the visual cortex on the left side. According to the former view, this should disable performance with the right eye because the "informed source" is no longer available to feed information to the naive right hemisphere. But in fact, it is found that animals so treated still show substantial transfer when tested with the right eye. In a second experiment, the callosum is cut following left-eye training of a chiasm-sectioned animal. This should cut the communication lines, so on the basis of the first view we would expect no transfer on tests with the right eye. But such transfer is found. From these experiments, we infer that a duplicate copy of the engram is normally set up via the callosum during one-eyed training of a chiasm-sectioned animal.

With these facts in hand, the reader can readily guess what has to be done to abolish interocular transfer. The effective operation, of course, would be to cut both the chiasm *and* the callosum before the one-eyed visual training begins. And in fact, performing this dual operation before training virtually abolishes interocular transfer; the unseeing eye and hemisphere remain naive about the visual problem learned by the trained eye. This surgical preparation, called the *split brain,* apparently establishes two independent visual systems, one on either side of the brain, and the two sides no longer communicate with one another. For example, by successively occluding one and then the other eye, the animal may easily be trained to conflicting habits to the two eyes—in one case to choose vertical and avoid horizontal stripes when seen by the left eye, and in the other to do the opposite when seen by the right eye. Such conflicting training is extremely difficult for the normal intact animal[3] but is learned with ease by the split-brain cat or monkey. It appears that all of the callosal fibers must be cut to obtain this remarkable independence of visual systems. If even a small portion of callosal fibers are spared, then transfer will still result.

Somewhat similar results have been discovered for transfer of a touch discrimination from one hand to the other, although there are several important differences from the visual system. A touch discrimination (e.g., rough vs smooth surface of objects) learned with the right hand will normally transfer to the left hand. However, if the corpus callosum is cut before the one-hand training, then intermanual transfer is abolished. This is consistent with the anatomical evidence that most, if not all, somesthetic input lines cross over the midline and are projected to the contralateral hemisphere (i.e., touch on left hand projects to right cortex). There is a slight amount of evidence, from evoked potential recordings, that there may be some same-side representation, although it is not normally dominant. An experiment by Glickstein and Sperry (1960) supplied suggestive evidence that this weak ipsilateral route may be used under special circumstances. However, the follow-ups of that work are not sufficiently unambiguous to warrant discussion here.

The split-brain preparation has illuminated many facts about bilaterality of storage in the visual and somesthetic systems, and the important role played by the corpus callosum in providing the connections that permit making a "carbon copy." Additionally, Sperry (1961) points out the many advantages of the split-brain preparation for the investigation of numerous questions regarding brain functions. For one thing, one brain-half can serve as an effective control when lesions and the like partially incapacitate the other brain-half. For another, radical surgical procedures can be carried out on one side only, when doing these bilaterally would seriously disable the animal as a useful experimental subject. Sperry describes a number of novel and ingenious uses that can be made of this split-brain preparation to investigate age-old problems of how the brain functions.

---

[3] Human subjects can probably learn such a problem, with some initial interference, since the eye used becomes a cue for a conditional discrimination. Descriptively, the solution would be "choose vertical stripes when the right eye is occluded; choose horizontal stripes when the left eye is occluded."

Chemical Dissociation of Cerebral Hemispheres

Recently, Bures and Buresovia (1960) have utilized a technique —called *spreading depression*—through which we may *temporarily* knock out the normal functioning of one cerebral hemisphere. This produces a "half-brained" animal for a few hours before recovery from the spreading depression occurs. To induce this effect, a small amount of a potassium chloride solution is applied locally through a small hole in the skull to the surface of the dura membrane surrounding the cortex. Within a short time, the normal electrical activity of the treated hemisphere of the cortex becomes depressed. The depression will persist for roughly as long as the chemical solution is applied. When it is removed, normal electrical activity in the depressed hemisphere is soon restored. In the rat, the depression spreads only over the cortex to which the chemical has been applied. The effect is not that of an anesthetic since even with both hemispheres depressed the animal still moves around normally. Of most interest, however, is the fact that while depressed a hemisphere gives no sign of retaining habits learned when it was intact. Access to the engram has somehow been blocked by the depression. Of further interest is the fact that an animal whose cortex is functioning normally apparently does not remember events that happened when its cortex was depressed; in fact, there is no evidence of learning when both hemispheres are depressed.

The simplest demonstration of this is the absence of interhemispheric transfer of a learned habit. On day 1, a rat is trained to a simple light-shock avoidance habit with, say, its right hemisphere depressed. On day 2, it is tested with either its right or left hemisphere depressed. If the same hemisphere is functioning both days, then the animal shows retention of the habit; if a different hemisphere is functioning on the two days, then it shows no retention. Russell and Ochs (1961) have reported the same results for a barpressing habit taught to rats for food reward. Apparently, the hemisphere functioning during the training session stores the engram, whereas the depressed hemisphere remains naive. On the following test day when the trained hemisphere is depressed, the functioning (but naive) cortex has no access to the engram stored on the depressed side. As with the split-brain monkey, it is also possible, by alternately depressing first one and then the other hemisphere, to train the two hemispheres to conflicting stimulus–response habits, and there is no interference between the two sides and their conflicting habits.

An intriguing question is why the educated hemisphere does not transmit its engram (via callosal connections) to the uneducated hemisphere after its depression has worn off and while the rat is just sitting around its home cage. The lack of interhemispheric transfer shows that this does not happen. However, it turns out that something like this "cross-callosal tutoring" goes on if the rat is replaced in the learning situation and experiences a few trials while both hemispheres are functioning. Russell and Ochs (1961) reported that one trial was sufficient to effect substantial cross-callosal tutoring of the uneducated side; Travis (1964) found less dramatically that 4 or 5 trials were needed to get good transfer of a well-learned habit. These results suggest that stimulation in the learning situation reactivated the engram in the educated cortex, setting up a persisting activity trace, and by way of the callosal links the engram was communicated to and consolidated in the alternate hemisphere.

The interhemispheric transfer for which evidence has been given above has involved, in each case, an active instrumental response, often one controlled by a relatively complicated discriminative stimulus. There is some evidence that conditioned emotional reactions (fear), especially those cued by a simple stimulus (e.g., a change in brightness), can be learned subcortically. Animals learn such CR's despite removal of both cerebral hemispheres. As this suggests, callosal section or spreading depression in one cerebral hemisphere do not prevent the transfer of such classically conditioned "emotions" (cf. McCleary, 1960; Bures et al., 1964). It is known too that simple instrumental brightness discriminations can be learned subcortically—that is, without benefit of cortex. Consequently, it is not too surprising to find that such habits transfer between the eyes despite chiasm and callosal section before one-eyed training (Meikle, 1960; Meikle and Sechzer, 1960). Thus the dramatic absence of transfer from callosal section or spreading depression is seen only for those relatively more complex habits that depend upon a functioning cerebral cortex. This is a small restriction on the generality of the results, but nonetheless a significant one. It tells us that the emotional concomitants of learned instrumental responses are represented subcortically whereas the refined "knowledge" guiding the selective response is likely to be stored cortically.

Drug-induced Dissociation

In preparations with a split-brain or with cortical spreading depression we have managed to dissociate various parts of the brain from one another. Metaphorically speaking, through the dissociation they are forced to lead separate lives, get educated in different schools, and have separate personalities, much like Siamese twins inside one skull case. A related dissociation or split-personality effect has been reported in a fascinating series of drug studies, starting with observations on curare by Girden and Culler (1937). Recent interest in the effect has been aroused by experiments by Overton (1964) using a different drug and testing somewhat more interesting behavior. His work will be reviewed briefly.

Overton finds that the drug, sodium pentobarbital, produces dissociation in rats. This drug, similar to the popularly known "truth serum," is an anesthetic and in sufficient doses puts the rat to sleep. Depending on the strength of the dose, the animal will begin to awake and becomes mobile within 15 to 45 minutes following the injection. At this time the animal can be run through various learning tasks; although somewhat lethargic, it will nevertheless learn simple tasks such as to turn left in a T maze to escape shock delivered to its feet from a grid floor.

The curious fact is that habits learned during this drugged state do not transfer to the nondrugged state, although the habit can be reactivated after putting the animal back into the drugged state. The dissociation works as well in the other direction: a habit learned in the nondrugged state is not available to the subject while he is in the drugged state. The habits are drug-state specific. By giving and withholding the drug on alternate days, it is easy to train the rat to turn left to escape shock when drugged and to turn right when not drugged. The two habits are learned rapidly and independently, with no interfering cross-talk between the two states. Overton showed that complete dissociation is only the extreme pole of a graded continuum. He could obtain more or less dissociation depending on the amount of drug given, with larger dosages yielding a greater degree of dissociation.

It is interesting to speculate on the causes of this dissociation. The notion that immediately comes to mind is that the drugged and nondrugged states are differentiated in terms of differences in (a) how external stimuli are perceived, e.g., vision might be blurred in the drugged state, and (b) the presence or absence of distinctive interoceptive stimuli, as in the different "feelings" we have when we feel drowsy or alert or thirsty or whatever. If these kinds of stimuli were radically different in the drug–nondrug states, then the lack of transfer might be explained. The presence and absence of pentobarbital (and its internal effects) come to be discriminative stimuli to which different responses are attached.

Overton anticipated this "stimulus" interpretation and ran several control conditions to try to assess its plausibility. Discrimination learning of conflicting habits to presence vs absence of pentobarbital was compared to that obtained with presence vs absence of the following "stimuli": the drug Flaxedil (a muscle relaxant), thirst and hunger, an ambient light over the maze, a light and a tone and a stronger shock. Only in the last condition did any significant discrimination learning ("dissociation") occur, and then at a markedly slower rate than under pentobarbital.

To this evidence we can react in either of two ways. The first is to stick to the "stimulus" interpretation and exclaim with wonder at what a strong, effective stimulus a pentobarbital injection is. The other is to reject the stimulus interpretation as *ad hoc* and barren and to seek alternative explanations. One alternative sketchily advanced by Overton is that by modifying the thresholds and firing patterns of neurons, the drug may cause different neural circuits to become active than those that are active in the nondrug state. In this case the differences might consist in different patterns or timing of neural firing so that different circuits or routes of a complex neural network are used. Other speculative hypotheses are available, but research has not yet begun to pin them down with exacting tests. Further theoretical and empirical analysis of this dissociation phenomenon may effect some revolutionary changes in our traditional ways of thinking about the brain and behavior.

CONCLUDING REMARKS

Looking back over our survey, it is apparent that large-scale advances in neuropsychology have been made over the past few decades. Truly, it is impossible to enter upon a thorough discussion today of such topics as consciousness, set, discrimination, attention, arousal, drive, reward, and many others without giving a prominent place to the contributions of neurobehavioral experimentation to what we know about these subjects. This has indeed been a grand accomplishment, for which praise should be bestowed on hundreds of research workers. However, from the point of view of this book, the most refractory problem of them all for neuropsychology has been our prime topic—learning, or information-storage by the nervous system. With a few exceptions,[4] the main lines of neurophysiological research on learning have been touched on here.

Looking at things in neurological terms, as we do in this chapter, the central question remains that of identifying the physiological basis for association. Assuming multiple connections between diverse populations of neurons (structures), we know that temporally proximate activity in two of them causes them to become associated in some primitive or basic manner, so that one is now able to excite the other whereas formerly it did not do so. Several suggestions as to how this might occur have been mentioned. The most likely explanation still is some form of the hypothesis that the "efficiency" of particular neuronal circuits is somehow increased, but specifying what the physical basis for this increased efficiency might be has proved difficult.

Lest the reader think that our discussion of the role of neurons is too far removed from the behavior in which he may be primarily interested, it is apposite to note that appropriate networks of "model neurons" can be easily designed that display rather amazing discrimination and per-

---

[4] The main exceptions include (a) the analysis of brain functions in learning by ablation techniques, on which there is a voluminous literature, and (b) computer analyses of electrical activity in brain structures during learning, on which at the moment there is but a small literature (cf. John, 1961, for an early review).

formance capabilities. This general line of theorizing, modeling performance capabilities by designing nerve networks, began with an early paper
by Pitts and McCulloch (1947) and has been carried further since then.
A book by Culbertson (1962) includes a recent review of some of the results. Roughly speaking, given any transfer function taking various input
information (stimulation) into output information (response), a static
nerve network can be designed to yield that transfer function. The hypothetical neurons in such nets all function by the same simple principles,
which are derived more or less from neurophysiological research. Moreover, if certain premises related to how the efficiency of neural pathways
is changed by feedback from the environment (through reward and punishment) are granted, then the nerve-net models will show adaptive learning in various situations. Rosenblatt (1958, 1962) shows how orderly discriminative performance can be produced (through reinforcement) by a
large neuron network that begins with completely random interconnec-
tions. He also gives us the rationale for this general approach to the construction of models of behavior.

By and large, the people who construct nerve-net automata do not
claim that their design represents exactly the way that the nervous system achieves what it does in a characteristic performance. They remain
content rather with showing that starting with simple neuron elements, networks not obviously contradicted by neurophysiological evidence can be designed to show some of the capabilities of organisms.
As such, the automata are "sufficiency proofs," meaning that they prove
that interesting behavior *can* be produced out of constellations of simple
on–off neural elements. Though the products of such labors are appreciated in some scientific quarters, the fact is that they are not esteemed
in others. From the viewpoint of those working on computer stimulation
of human intelligence (Chapter 12), the nerve-net automata have only
primitive intelligence and their accomplishments are considered to be
rather dull. Then from another side, from the viewpoint of many neurophysiologists, the nerve-net theories are held to ignore too much of what
is known about the neuron and the structure of the nervous system. Be
that as it may, it seems obvious that if neurophysiology is ever to have an
explicit theory capable of making better contact with behavioral data, the
form of it will be little different from the kinds of schemes presently
being designed by those working on nerve-net automata.

Research on the neurophysiology of learning continues at an accelerating pace. Judging from the recent past, its future is likely to be filled
with exciting discoveries, the devising of novel techniques, and profound
alterations in our conceptions of the nervous system and its relation to
behavior. In fact, in few other areas of psychology has there recently been
such a high production rate of significant empirical discoveries as in physiological psychology. Metaphorically speaking, the pearls are easier to

find in a new field than in the older fields that have been intensively cultivated for so many years.

SUPPLEMENTARY READINGS

DELAFRESNAYE, J. F. (Editor) (1961) *Brain mechanisms and learning.*

FIELD, J., MAGOUN, H. W., and HALL, V. E. (Editors) (1960) *Handbook of physiology.* Vol. 3. *Neurophysiology.*

HARLOW, H. F., and WOOLSEY, C. N. (Editors) (1958) *Biological and biochemical bases of behavior.*

KIMBLE, D. P. (Editor) (1965) *Learning, remembering, and forgetting.* Vol. 1. *The anatomy of learning.*

MORGAN, C. T. (1965) *Physiological psychology* (3rd ed.)

WALTER, W. G. (1953) *The living brain.*

WOOLDRIDGE, D. E. (1963) *The machinery of the brain.*

YOUNG, J. Z. (1964) *A model of the brain.*

Recent Developments:
I. The Basic Conditions
of Learning and Retention

Research on the learning process continues at an accelerating pace, and has expanded in a number of directions. Several thousand psychologists and scientists in related fields are doing research that can be roughly classified as investigations of learning. It is next to impossible to characterize the entire field, to cover the full range of phenomena under investigation, and to say where the whole enterprise is leading us. Indeed, it will require two chapters, this and the next, to merely touch upon a selected sample of recent developments. In many respects, research on learning has become more applied, with the development of related behavioral technologies as one consequence. For example, a number of psychologists are engaged in applying learning principles to the acquisition of language, to educational programs for teaching children to read, to modifying the undesirable attitudes and behaviors of psychoneurotic patients, to the efficient training of complex skills for military or industrial personnel, as well as to training retarded children in simple skills. Chapter 16 discusses some of the work on programed instruction, an important area of behavioral technology. Such behavioral engineering has immediate practical goals, and while not irrelevant to theory it can be carried on without becoming distracted by unresolved theoretical issues. The value of learning research lies in its development of techniques of behavioral control, in the general frame of reference it gives us and the concepts to be used in analysis, and finally in the factual knowledge obtained as the product of particular investigations.

The main trend in nonapplied ("pure") research in learning has been away from the large, comprehensive theories of the 1930's and 1940's towards the formulation and testing of smaller hypotheses of local relevance, tailored specifically to fit a limited range of phenomena. Here there is a sacrifice of comprehensiveness in exchange for the definiteness, clarity, and precision of a theoretical explanation. Apparently somewhat disabused by the global theories and by the fact that the grand controversies of the 1930's and 1940's were never resolved, present day psychologists studying learning seem more than willing to submit to this exchange of definiteness for comprehensiveness.

The lines of demarcation between the historical positions have softened, faded, and become all but indistinguishable. The debates have subsided. Increasingly experimentalists talk the same language and listen to one another. It is not uncommon for an experimentalist to work within several different theoretical camps, ranging from Hullian theory to stochastic models to computer simulation. Each empirical subarea has its special phenomena to captivate interest, and we can soon learn the necessary dictionary of concept equivalences to permit moving between subareas.

In this chapter and the next, we shall review a few of the prominent lines of recent research and theorizing in learning. The topics selected are among those in which there have been important developments since the second edition of this text was published (Hilgard, 1956). In that edition, two chapters were also devoted to "recent developments," and they can be read profitably to obtain a background for most of the material in the present chapters. The present chapter reviews recent changes in our conceptions of reinforcement and nonreinforcement, and also theories of short-term memory and forgetting. Chapter 15 which follows discusses new material on discrimination learning, attention, and imitative (observational) learning. Some brief concluding remarks are given at the end of Chapter 15.

CONCEPTIONS OF REINFORCEMENT AND NONREINFORCEMENT

The Relativity of Reinforcement

The law of reinforcement, or law of effect, is the most important principle in all learning theory. It is a rule for shaping behavior by the use of rewards (reinforcers). We train a rat to press a lever by giving it a bit of food when it does so. Because of the central significance of the principle, there have been attempts to state it in a general yet precise way. One commonly accepted formulation is this: a learnable response followed by a reinforcing event (stimulus, state of affairs) will receive an increment in its strength or probability of occurrence. Critics of the law of effect have argued that this formulation is not an empirical law but rather a definition of a reinforcing event. Let us see. If a reinforcer is defined as something that strengthens a response, then by substitution in the statement of the law it becomes: a learnable response followed by something that strengthens a response will receive an increment in its strength! But this is just vacuous circularity. Surely there must be more to the principle than the trivial tautology that "a rose is a rose."

The question whether or not the law has any empirical content was considered by Meehl (1950) in a key paper entitled "On the circularity of the law of effect." Meehl concluded that the law does have empirical content, and that its content concerns the generality of a reinforcer. If I find that scratching a dog behind its ears will reinforce the behavior of lifting a paw to shake hands, then the law of effect makes the prediction that ear scratching can also be used to reinforce other sorts of canine responses—hand licking, tail wagging, ball rolling, stick retrieving, and so forth. The law of effect is used in a "definitional" mode in the initial discovery of ear scratching as a reinforcer; but it is used in an empirical predictive manner when testing ear scratching as a reinforcer for later responses. Meehl's reformulation of the law of effect is: "all reinforcers are transituational." An equivalent, and more understandable version is: "a reinforcer can be used to increase the probability of *any* learnable response."

Meehl's analysis resolved the circulatory charge, and psychologists went on their way satisfied with this formulation of the general law of effect. One implication of Meehl's or Thorndike's statement of the law of effect (see Chapter 2) is what may be called an "absolutist" classification of events as reinforcing or not. That is, given a particular state of the subject (his conditions of deprivation, past training, etc.), we can roughly divide stimulus events into two lists: those that act upon him as reinforcers and those that do not. A list of reinforcers commonly contains biological items like food, water, and sexual contact for appropriately deprived individuals, together with learned (secondary) reinforcers like money, praise, social approval, attention, dominance, the spoken exclamation "good," etc., and a variety of manipulation–curiosity–novelty satisfying types of activities. Given such a partial listing, some psychologists were challenged to try to guess what all these reinforcing things have in common—what is the common essential ingredient that make them all reinforcers. A plausible idea, for example, is Hull's conjecture that all primary reinforcers serve to reduce drives or biological needs, and that secondary reinforcers like praise derive their value from having been associated with many instances of drive reduction, perhaps during the child's early rearing. This conjecture, as well as others like it, has been extensively researched and argued pro and con. Kimble (1961) gives a useful summary of this evidence for the interested student.

Recently, Premack (1959, 1965) has offered a useful reappraisal of reinforcement and the law of effect which promises to increase its generality. As with many useful insights, Premack's argument stems from noting an implicit assumption contained in previous formulations of the law of effect. This implicit assumption is that the response or activities which are to be reinforced are neutral or of no intrinsic value to the subject. But suppose that we take an opposite viewpoint, that the organism engages in a variety of activities (including eating, manipulating, playing, etc., ad infinitum) that vary in their intrinsic value for him. Imagine further that by some means we have ordered these activities in a ranking from most to least preferred, in the order A, B, C, D, ...

Given this ranking of activities (considered in this general sense), what is now an appropriate way to formulate the law of effect? Premack argues that the only sensible formulation ties the reinforcement relation to this preference ordering: a given activity can be used to reinforce those of lesser value but not those of higher value. In our A B C D ranking, we can use B to reinforce C or D, but B will not reinforce A. But acceptance of this point commits us to a "relativity" view of reinforcement. A given event or activity can be used to reinforce some responses but not others. C can reinforce D but not B, even though B is learnable, as we would find when we made A contingent upon B. Thus, not all reinforcers are "transituational," a given reinforcer cannot be used to strengthen any learnable response whatever. Rather, an activity will reinforce only those activities of lesser value, not those of higher value.

An important question is, does this revision of the law of effect now make it completely circular? If Meehl's transituational idea is altered, is there any empirical content left to the law of effect? We can avoid the circularity but it now requires two observations (rather than one) to make an empirical prediction. If we find that activity R reinforces Q and that Q reinforces Z, then the law predicts that R will reinforce Z. That prediction has empirical content and could possibly be false, and so would test the proposed law. Readers familiar with logic will recognize this as a test of the *transitivity* assumption about the reinforcement relation. So the law is testable even if we could find no independent way to assess value or preference.

A central issue is whether we can find an independent way to assess a subject's preference ordering for a set of activities. With human subjects, a verbal estimate of liking or attractiveness would probably serve as a valid index, though a slight hitch arises from the fact that people are occasionally unaware (unconscious) of what kinds of events can reinforce their behavior. But suppose that we wish to have some index of wide application, one that could be used with animals, or nonverbal mental defectives, and so forth. The search for an index of such generality constitutes a real challenge. Premack (1959) proposes that a generally valid index of value would be response rate (or momentary probability) in a "free operant" situation in which the commodity or activity is freely available to the subject. This is a plausible index: the more a person likes an activity, the more often he engages in it when it is freely available with no constraints attached.

To illustrate by a concrete example, suppose the values of four different activities are to be assessed for a kindergarten child: playing a pinball machine (PB), looking at a movie cartoon (M), eating small chocolate candies (C), and hammering on a wooden pegboard (H). The assessment would consist of measuring how frequently (by count or by total time so spent) the child engages in each activity in a standard test room in which opportunity for engaging in each activity is introduced singly and separately. Suppose that the independent rates for a particular child come out in the rank order PB $>$ M $>$ C $>$ H, from highest to lowest. Thus, we would predict that the opportunity to play with the pinball machine can be used to reinforce or increase the rate of either the M, C, or H activities; M can reinforce C or H but not PB; and C can reinforce H but neither M nor PB. The contingent test situation would involve one activity freely available; when it is performed, the other activity becomes available for a brief time and then turns off. For instance, in the M $>$ C test, candy would be freely available at one location. When a candy has been eaten, a movie projector in another part of the room would turn on, showing, say, a 30-second segment of a cartoon. A reinforcing effect would be inferred if the rate of candy-eating increased above its baseline rate when this contingency was introduced. Premack (1959, 1963, 1965) has presented data from children, monkeys, and rats indicating that predictions of this sort are generally accurate.

In some cases, we know that the relative value of two activities or commodities can be altered by altering relevant conditions of deprivation. Thus, I can alter your relative preference for eating versus sleeping by depriving you of food or sleep, respectively. Thus, we should be able to reverse the reinforcement relation between two activities by altering motivation. Premack (1962) demonstrated this effect in rats using water ingestion and running in an activity wheel. The ingestion rate was altered by water deprivation, and the running activity by depriving the rat of access to an activity wheel in an otherwise confining living quarter. When deprived of water but not of activity, water ingestion would reinforce running but not vice versa. When deprived of activity but not water, running would reinforce drinking but not vice versa. Thus, the reinforcement relation was reversible.

Having described Premack's analysis and his experimental methods of checking it, let us go on to evaluate the idea and some of its implications for reinforcement theory. First, on the positive side of the ledger, Premack's approach has the advantage of supplying an apparently valid, operational specification of what contingency arrangements will be reinforcing. The assessment of independent rate and prediction of reinforcement is sensitive to the individual characteristics of a subject and also to his current state (deprivation, past training, etc.). Secondly, Premack's rule appears to accurately characterize many "reinforcers" that are in common use in everyday life, in the school and home environment. Examination of many practical reinforcement procedures shows the operation of a rule like this covering as it does a variety of activities beyond the ingestive or consummatory responses most prototypic of the classical view of reinforcement. A common example is that children are not permitted to watch television until they finish eating their dinner, or they are told they can't have dessert unless they finish their meat and potatoes. Thirdly, acceptance of the rule, or the data reported in support of it, casts a gloomy light upon efforts to identify some essential property of absolute "reinforcing events" considered as isolated elements outside the relational context of the activity that is to be reinforced.

On the negative side of the ledger, several unresolved difficulties still remain for Premack's proposal. One is the problem of generality; another, the validity of response rate as an index of preference. The problem of generality arises when we notice that in almost all human learning studies the reinforcing operation is "information about which is the correct response." Through his motivating instructions, the experimenter or teacher has made being "correct" a reinforcing event for the subject, so that nothing else need be added to promote learning. The effectiveness of this operation probably depends upon a long history of cultural training wherein being "correct" and similar achievements have been associated with parental praise and approval. For instance, in the case of very young preschool children, instructions and information are sometimes not enough, so that material rewards (trinkets, gold stars, candy) must be added if they are to be kept working at difficult learning tasks. In any event, it is unclear how or whether such reinforcement by mere information is or can be covered by what Premack proposes should be done. The same can be said for the topic of vicarious or observational learning which we shall take up in the next chapter.

The other problem is the general validity of the response rate index of preference. Premack admits that it is difficult to get comparable measures on independent rates of different activities; it will not do just to let the calculated rates depend upon arbitrary units imposed upon the behavior by the recording system. Conceived in a general sense, our activities and/or interactions with goal objects vary in multiple ways—in duration of each contact, rate of interaction during contact, time between contacts, and so forth, and it is not at all clear how to combine these features into a single index. Consider, for example, the difficulties of getting comparable measures by which to arrange in rank order the three activities of reading a book, playing a piano, and sleeping. Other problems arise in connection with the rate index (e.g., it can be differentially trained by reinforcement) and this specific proposal seems to be threatened by endless troubles and unavoidable limitations. A less objectionable criterion of relative value would be preferential *choice*, which is the behavioral index most often used in discussions of utility and decision making. If in a free choice between activities A and B, the subject consistently chooses A over B, then we would predict that in a contingent situation we could reinforce activity B by making A contingent on B. This choice index would seem to resolve some of the difficulties encountered by the index of response rate.

Despite these difficulties in the way of carrying out Premack's specific proposal, there seems no escaping the fact that the law of effect must be amended to cover the relativity of the reinforcement relation. Certain kinds of evidence pointing to this necessity have been around for many years in studies on "affective contrast" (see Helson, 1964, for a review). Such studies tend to show that the same stimulus may be judged as pleasant or unpleasant depending on whether the subject has just been seeing other stimuli which are relatively unpleasant or pleasant, respectively, in relation to the one being judged at the moment. Likewise, in studies of learned peformance, a given reward for a response may have either an incremental or a decremental effect upon performance depending on what reward the subject expects or on the range of alternative rewards the subject has been receiving in similar contexts. If a person is expecting a one cent payoff, getting ten cents is going to be positively rewarding; if he is expecting a dollar payoff, then ten cents is frustrating and may have the effect of a punishment. Effects such as these have been observed with animals as well as men (e.g., Bower, 1961b; Bower, 1962c; Bevan and Adamson, 1960). They can all be interpreted in terms of Helson's concept of adaptation level. The rewards obtained over the past trials in a given context determine, by some averaging process, an internal standard or norm called the adaptation level. Each new reward is evaluated in relation to this adaptation level, having a positive influence on behavior if it is above the norm, a negative influence if it is below. A phenomenon closely related to this will be described in the next chapter in the section on behavioral contrast.

Premack's results can be interpreted in terms of adaptation level. In the A, B, C situation, suppose activity B is made freely available. Then, we expect the subject's adaptation level to adjust to a value near B. Since, if we make A contingent on B, the value received is higher than the adaptation level, a positive (reinforcing) effect on the B response will be observed. If we make C contingent on B, the value received is lower than the adaptation level and therefore no reinforcing effect is observed. Thus, the idea of adaptation level implies a relativistic view of reinforcement.

If this line of reasoning is accepted, it becomes apparent that we are moving away from a strict stimulus–response interpretation of the law of effect, and towards a more "cognitive" point of view. The latter, in some ways, seems closer to common sense. It is a conception that makes contact also with the economists' notion of utility and even more obviously with the cognitive theorists' notion of expectancy. The effect on behavior of a given outcome is seen as dependent upon its relation to an internal norm derived via a pooling process from the series of prior outcomes encountered in a given situation. Papers by Bevan (1963) and Bevan and Adamson (1963) provide a tentative reinforcement model based on adaptation-level theory. They use it to explain a number of observed relationships between reinforcement and performance. Whether Bevan's tentative model will stand up under stringent experimental tests is not currently known. But it appears likely that an adaptation-level model of this general sort is going to be needed to handle the range of results on reinforcement. Looking backwards to Meehl's and Thorndike's earlier formulations of the law of effect, we seem to have made some progress in the past fifteen years in formulating the law in a more general and valid way.

Nonreward and Extinction

Along with developments in the contemporary conception of reinforcement and the law of effect, there have also been changes in the interpretation of nonreward and extinction. Almost all of this theory stems from work on nonreward and extinction with animal subjects, although it is presumed that similar ideas apply to at least some types of human learning. Certain earlier interpretations of nonreward of a previously rewarded response had assigned to it an essentially passive role. For example, Tolman supposed that nonreward served simply to disconfirm and weaken an S–R–S_G expectancy. Thorndike gave little systematic consideration to nonreward, and as best we can tell he thought of it as essentially a neutral event. In Hull's theory (Chapter 6), nonrewarded trials are believed to permit inhibitory factors to build up without being offset by a corresponding increase in reaction potential. Hull's ideas about extinction were worked out only in very sketchy fashion and were never really adequate to a very wide range of data on extinction. In the past fifteen years, a number of hypotheses have been proposed regarding nonreward and extinction. Most of these hypotheses have aimed at explaining the increased resistance to extinction of animals trained with a partial reward schedule. That is, a rat rewarded on only, say, 30 percent of its runs down a straight alley will persist longer in going to the goalbox during extinction than will another animal trained with 100 percent rewarded trials. This simple fact, embellished with many ancillary results, has constituted a perennial challenge to theorists. Not that explanations do not abound; it is sorting them out with critical experimental tests that has proved a demanding, though also informative, task. In this section we shall review two conceptions of nonreward and extinction, the frustration interpretation and the dissonance interpretation. These are two of the more prominent hypotheses, and each has a fair amount of evidence in its favor.

Frustrative Nonreward

In contrast to the passive role previously assigned to nonreward, the frustration hypothesis views nonreward of a response as an actively punishing and aversive event. In consequence, many of the effects of nonreward upon responding are now seen as analogous to the effects produced upon that same behavior by punishment.

The psychologist mainly responsible for current acceptance of this point of view is Amsel (1958, 1962) and additional significant contributions to its development have come from Wagner (1963, 1966) and Spence (1960a). We shall first state the hypothesis as directly as we can, and then describe the kinds of experiments that have been adduced in support of it. The hypothesis is roughly outlined in what follows:

The occurrence of nonreward at a moment when the subject is expecting a reward causes the elicitation of a primary frustration reaction (R_F). The feedback stimulation from this reaction is aversive and has short-term, persisting motivational effects upon subsequent instrumental behavior. Fractional parts of this primary frustration reaction become conditioned in the classical manner to stimuli preceding its elicitation. Occurrence of this fractional response in anticipatory form is denoted r_f-s_f. The cues, s_f, from anticipatory frustration are principally connected to avoidance responses, but these connections can be modified through training.

Amsel works within the Hullian framework. Thus, the phrase "is expecting a reward" is translatable into statements about r_g, a mechanism for representing anticipatory reward. This r_g is a learned variable in the Hull–Spence system, varying in its amplitude with trials and with the characteristics of the reward (its amount, sweetness, etc.).

The alleged motivational effect of frustrative nonreward may be seen in the intensifying or speeding up of responses occurring within a short time after the animal experiences nonreinforcement. The standard situation for studying this is a two-link runway. The rat is trained to run to a first goalbox for a reward; after a few seconds there, the entrance is opened to a second runway, which he traverses for a second reward. After training on this two-link sequence, omission of the first reward produces a momentary increase in subsequent speed of running down the second runway on that trial. The difference in running speeds in the second runway following nonreward versus reward in the first goalbox is taken as an index of the size of the frustration effect (FE). As Amsel's theory would predict, the factors that influence the size of the FE tend to be those which would make for stronger arousal of the r_g in the first link of the runway. That is to say, presumably the greater the anticipation of reward, the greater the frustration produced by nonreward. A particularly important finding is that, with 50 percent rewarded and nonrewarded trials at the first goalbox, the FE does not appear during the initial trials but it develops gradually with training, presumably reflecting the further conditioning of anticipatory reward. Additionally, it was claimed that the FE occurs when the amount of reward is merely reduced to a lower (nonzero) level, with the size of the FE graded according to graded reductions in the test reward below the amount customarily expected (Bower, 1961b). However, recent evidence (Barrett *et al.*, 1965) makes it appear that these graded effects are in fact confounded with the temporary depressive effects upon running speed of the rat eating more or less food in the first goalbox.

Wagner (1963) presents data to support the assumption that frustration may be conditioned and that it acts like an aversive drive-stimulus. Rats were run down a runway with half the trials rewarded and half nonrewarded in a haphazard order. A buzzer was presented just a moment before they looked into the empty food cup on nonrewarded trials. This procedure was presumed to associate the buzzer with the frustration reaction elicited when the rat looked into the empty foodcup. Later, this buzzer was shown to enhance the startle reflex to a gunshot, a measure which has proved sensitive to acquired motivational effects of cues. Also the buzzer could be used effectively to train and maintain a response which produced escape from the buzzer. The interpretation is that the escape response is reinforced because it terminates the buzzer, which is associated with aversive frustration.

As applied to extinction of rewarded instrumental responses, frustration is presumed to act like punishment. Since extinction produces repeated frustration at the goal, the animal comes to anticipate frustration (the r_f-s_f mechanism) just as it would anticipate with fear a painful electric shock at the goal. Anticipatory frustration initially produces avoidance of the goal, by evoking responses which interfere with continued approach to the place where frustration occurs. However, it is argued that partial reinforcement effectively trains the animal to tolerate frustration. In particular, the circumstances of such training result in the s_f cues becoming connected to approach rather than avoidance. Thus, extinction is supposed to be slower following partial reinforcement training.

This hypothesis regarding extinction and partial reinforcement has received a fair amount of experimental support. There is little doubt that the conditions under which extinction occurs and their associated stimuli are aversive, and that the animal is reinforced by escaping them. For example, in a Skinner box, animals will learn a new response to remove a stimulus that has been associated with extinction. Azrin (1964) has further shown that during extinction of a food-reinforced response, pigeons will learn a new response for which the payoff is a brief opportunity to aggress against (fight) another pigeon. Under "neutral" control conditions such fighting does not occur. The relevance of this observation to the frustration hypothesis is that such aggressive responses are known to be highly probable mainly when the bird is in pain or otherwise discomforting circumstances. These results are thus explicable if it is assumed that nonreinforced responses produce frustration and that frustration is aversive.

Another related fact is that tranquilizing drugs, which presumably reduce emotional consequences of frustration, will retard extinction and also partially release a response formerly inhibited by frustration. Additionally, Wagner has shown several common elements in training animals to resist the stress of punishment (electric shock) versus frustration for approach to a goal. In particular, if rats have been trained to continue approaching despite punishment at a rewarded goal, then the number of trials required to reach extinction is greater when food and punishment are stopped. Also, animals trained under partial reinforcement will continue responding longer once punishment is introduced at the goal. These results prove that electric shock and nonreward have common properties, so that learning to withstand one of them transfers in some degree to the other. And this supports the interpretation of nonreward as a frustrating, aversive event.

The studies cited plus several others would appear to provide conclusive evidence that nonreward (when reward is expected) has an aversive effect much like a punishment. It is important to realize, however, that this proposition does not commit one to Amsel's interpretation of why partial reinforcement induces great resistance to extinction, since the latter interpretation is not strictly implied by the former. The interpretation of partial reinforcement—that cues from anticipatory frustration are associated with approaching rather than avoiding the goal—does not, at the moment, rest upon much definitive or convincing evidence. Meanwhile, on that question, the jury is still out.

Dissonance Theory

Festinger (1961) and Lawrence and Festinger (1962) have provided an alternative explanation of extinction and how variables influence the rate at which it occurs. Out of a variety of training and testing

variables that influence resistance to extinction these authors have selected for special consideration those variables which might be classified
as producing *deterrents* to performance of an approach response. They
review and present new evidence for the proposition that if a subject can
be induced to respond under conditions of relatively unfavorable reward,
his habit will in consequence exhibit greater persistence during extinction than will that of an animal trained under more favorable conditions
of reward. Festinger's and Lawrence's proposition ties together the following phenomena that have been observed in separate experiments: animals that have been trained to make an effortful response, or those given
mild punishments at the goal, or whose reward has been delayed, or who
have encountered frequent nonreinforcements interspersed among rewarded trials all show greater resistance to extinction than do their fellow animals trained under more favorable conditions, i.e., those trained
to make less effortful responses, or those not given punishment at the
goal, those who have no delay in reward, or those with no nonreinforcement, respectively. An operational criterion for "favorableness" would
consist of a preference choice along the following lines. Take any two
sets of conditions differing as to performance and/or reward variables and
pit them against one another in a preferential choice situation like a T
maze. Suppose in this circumstance, condition A is chosen in preference to
condition B. Then the hypothesis predicts that, in a nonchoice situation
(e.g., a runway), animals trained under condition B will extinguish more
slowly than those trained under condition A. As best we can presently determine, this proposition is valid for a variety of types of A-B differences,
including cases where B (a) has a longer delay of reward, (b) has a smaller
amount of reward, (c) a higher percentage of nonrewards, (d) involves
punishment as well as reward, and (e) involves a more effortful response.

But why is this? Why do organisms "come to love those things for which
they have been made to suffer"? The answer is provided by suitable interpretation of Festinger's (1957) theory of cognitive dissonance. Dissonance
is conceived as tension resulting when the organism is confronted with
two items of information (cognitions) about his behavior which are inconsistent with one another. As an example, dissonance might arise when
(*i*) a hungry rat has just expended much effort to get to a goal, and (*ii*)
there is no food reward there. It is assumed that in a case like this the subject tries to reduce dissonance by modifying either his behavior or his
cognitions about it. In this example, either he can stop responding or he
can develop extra attractions in the goal which will serve to justify continued behavior. Under the training situations of most interest to us (e.g.,
partial reinforcement), the conditions are arranged in such a manner as
to preclude the first alternative, hence he cannot quit entirely. In this
case, the main device available to the subject that will reduce dissonance
is the discovery or elaboration of extra attractions at the goal. In turn, it

is these acquired, extra attractions at the goal, elaborated under conditions of impoverished reward, that will keep the subject responding for a longer time during a subsequent extinction series.

Lawrence and Festinger (1962) report several new experiments consistent with this interpretation. In one study, by interchanging two runways and goalboxes, they showed that the partial reinforcement effect is a goalbox-specific effect and not a runway-specific effect, as though the extra attractions are in the goalbox and not in the runway preceding a partially rewarded goalbox. In another study, they demonstrated that the absolute number of nonrewarded trials during training with partial reinforcement is the main variable controlling resistance to extinction. Holding this number constant, changing the percentage or ratio of nonrewarded to rewarded trials was shown to have no effect upon resistance to extinction following partial training. Another study involved a two-link chain, with a midbox and an endbox. Animals were always rewarded in the endbox. Three groups were run, differing in the percentage of food-reinforced trials in the midbox (100%, 50%, or 0%). After eating on rewarded trials or being delayed for twenty seconds on nonrewarded trials, the rats were permitted to run from the midbox to the endbox to obtain the reward there. The response of running into the midbox was then extinguished (no food there, subject just removed from midbox). The 0% rewarded group persisted in responding the longest, the 50% group next, and the 100% group persisted for the smallest number of trials. In a further study, rats trained to go to the 0% rewarded midbox were extinguished as above but under minimal hunger drive (satiation). In this case, the 0% animals ran more slowly (due to satiation) but showed virtually no extinction, whereas animals trained with 100% reward in the midbox produced regular extinction curves.

These experiments, and others reported in the book by Lawrence and Festinger are easily interpreted in terms of their theory. The extra attractions are relatively specific to the goalbox, they increase with the number of occasions on which dissonance has been aroused and presumably reduced, they are greater for the 0% group in the midbox, and they are more obvious when a strong hunger drive is lacking, thus permitting other motives to intervene. Taken singly, each experiment is usually subject to interpretation in terms of alternative conceptions of partial reinforcement effects (e.g., the discrimination and/or frustration hypotheses). However, considered as an integrated series of experiments, no single alternative hypothesis can deal with all of them as conveniently and parsimoniously as does the dissonance hypothesis. The latter has the additional advantage of giving an integrated and parsimonious account of why resistance to extinction is affected by delayed reward, small magnitudes of reward, punishment mixed with reward, and response effort. Alternative hypotheses about extinction require various *ad hoc* assumptions to bring all these data within their explanatory net.

The most valuable contribution of Lawrence and Festinger has been the generalization that responses trained under relatively poor reinforcement conditions show greater resistance to extinction. Whether and how long their dissonance theory will hold up as an interpretation of these facts remains for future experimentation to decide. Their hypothesis is novel in that it turns upside down some relationships that have been customarily assumed. It goes against the grain of common sense to assume that more value gets attached to stimuli associated with inadequate rewards, that inadequately rewarded responses are, in one sense, stronger than well rewarded responses, and so forth. But it is clear that if this hypothesis continues to receive experimental support, S–R psychologists will have to make room in their conceptual scheme for some peculiar elements, such as accepting rats that compare cognitions, that feel dissonance and that attempt to justify what they do to reduce dissonance. John B. Watson's reaction to such a turn of events in animal psychology, the stronghold of behaviorism, would doubtless be apoplectic. Is it that our heads are now more mature or have they only gone soft?

The Micromolar Approach to Behavior Theory

Along with our changing conception of reinforcement and the law of effect, there has been a corresponding change in our view of what it is that is reinforced, or what is learned when we say that "a response" is reinforced. The micromolar approach, promoted most effectively by Logan (1956, 1960), begins with an argument for expanding the definition of response to include its intensive characteristics (its speed, amplitude, volume, etc.). In the classical view, exemplified by Hull (Chapter 6), response classes are defined in terms of their achievements—running down a runway, pressing a lever, etc. The rule is to aggregate together all instances of behavior which achieve the same end result (e.g., getting the lever down), because they are not differently reinforced by the experimenter. Variations in speed or amplitude of the response during training were taken to be indices of the strength of the response tendency. Hull formalized this idea in his reaction-potential construct, $_sE_r$, which presumably determined the probability, speed, amplitude, and resistance to extinction of the response.

This classical approach runs into difficulties at several points. First, these various response measures frequently fail to be well correlated. During training, a measure like response probability may improve monotonically with practice whereas speed and/or force of the response may at first increase and then decrease over trials. One example is the lengthening latency of the CR in classical conditioning (Pavlov's "inhibition of delay" mentioned in Chapter 3); a second is that forcefulness of lever pressing first increases and then decreases during training, stabilizing at just above that minimal force required to operate the feeder. The second main difficulty of the classical approach results from the fact that one can differentially reinforce intensive characteristics of the response. Skinner (1938) was the first to show this experimentally, demonstrating in the free operant situation differential shaping of slow or fast rates of barpressing, weak or strong forces of barpressing, and long or short durations of barholding. The method is simplicity itself: simply reinforce only responses whose intensive properties fall within a specified criterion range, possibly advancing to stiffer criteria as the animal's performance follows along. It is clear that many skilled performances are differentiated in this way. It is also clear that through such differential reinforcement (e.g., of slow response speeds), the intensive properties of the response (i) may or may not increase monotonically with training, and (ii) may be put in any relation to other intensive properties that we choose to reinforce (e.g., talking slow but loudly, or talking fast but softly).

Logan broadened the notion of "differentiation schedules" to include any variation in some parameter of reinforcement such as its amount, quality, delay, or probability. In conditions of *correlated reinforcement,* one or more dimensions of reinforcement are correlated with some intensive property of the observed behavior, e.g., its speed. The *terms function* specifies what reinforcement the subject receives for particular response speeds; it is similar to the terms of a contract between the subject and a reinforcing agent (the environment or the experimenter). A tremendous variety of terms functions are imaginable, only a few of which have been investigated. Examples in a runway situation might be: the faster the rat runs to the end, the longer his reward may be delayed, or the greater is the amount of reward he receives; or reinforcement is provided only when the speed falls in the interval from x to y, and not otherwise, and so forth. In general, it is found that subjects adjust to such reward conditions, coming eventually to respond at a near optimal level (see Logan, 1960, for some results and a more detailed discussion).

To deal with the behavior of subjects under such conditions, Logan proposed the micromolar approach, or one which identifies different speeds as different responses, selectively influenced by differential reinforcement. Logan proposes essentially a "utility analysis" to deal with this approach, although he specifies the components of utility in terms of the intervening variables of habit, drive, incentive, etc., employed by Hull. The net utility of a particular response speed is given by its positive utility minus its associated negative utility. The main component of positive utility is incentive, which increases with the amount of reward provided for that speed and decreases with the total interval of reinforcement for that speed (total interval = duration of response + delay of reward following that response). The subject is viewed as learning through experience the incentive associated with each speed, adding, however, that it is influenced also by generalization of incentive learned for similar speeds. The main component of negative incentive for a particular speed is its effortfulness, fast responses requiring more effort. The profile of net utility across the speed continuum is then used to calculate the probability distribution of the various speeds. Generally speaking, the expected probability of a particular response speed depends on its net utility relative to that of alternative speeds. Thus, the sole dependent variable of the theory is response probability, but here, response refers to intensive properties of the behavior.

Suffice it to say that such a theory will account qualitatively for the more or less optimal performance subjects achieve under correlated conditions of reinforcement. Because incentive is specific to particular response speeds, the terms function gets mapped into the model's incentive profile, distorted somewhat because of generalization of reinforcement effects among similar responses. Thus does the model take account of and adjust its behavior in relation to the terms function.

Besides accounting for correlated reward conditions, the approach also gives a creditable account of why Hull's conventional approach (called "macromolar") worked when it did and failed when it did. Logan points out that almost all conditions of "constant" reward involve an implicit correlation between response speed and interval of reinforcement: the faster the rat runs to the goalbox, the sooner he gets the reward. The micromolar theory predicts that a particular response dimension will improve monotonically with practice only if some dimension of reinforcement improves with that response dimension. Thus, although speed of level pressing increases with practice because faster responses bring rewards sooner, the forcefulness of the lever press does not increase because more forceful responses require more effort and bring no better reward. Using the same ideas, Logan has shown how the micromolar theory implies the usual effects upon response speed of variations in drive, amount of reward and delay of reward in "constant" reward situations. Many more details might be cited in connection with the theory but we will not elaborate further.

The importance of the micromolar theory has been primarily that of conceptual house cleaning within learning theory. By virtue of Logan's analysis, several conceptual puzzles connected with the problem of how reinforcement shapes behavior have been unraveled and understood. The micromolar approach is general and applies to classical conditioning as well as instrumental conditioning, and it influences the way we talk and think about variables. For example, in cases of classical conditioning the micromolar theory says that the response amplitude learned will be that amplitude elicited by the unconditioned stimulus. This provides a direct interpretation of the fact that amplitude of the conditioned reflex correlates very highly with amplitude of the unconditioned reflex. Thus, the satiated dog that gives a feeble salivary CR has learned his response-amplitude just as well as the hungry dog that gives a large CR amplitude; the first dog is merely learning a smaller-amplitude response. The micromolar approach has been quite useful too in interpreting the influence of various Skinnerian schedules of reinforcement upon rate of responding. At least some schedules may be viewed as more or less inexact terms functions which correlate probability of reinforcement with interresponse time. For example, variable interval schedules generate slow response rates, and this may be explained as due to the differential reinforcement of long interresponse times.

Moreover, the micromolar approach makes somewhat better contact than did the older approach with the learning involved in so many of our everyday performances. Reinforcing consequences typically depend not only upon whether a response is made but also upon whether it is made at the right time, at the right place, at the correct pace or intensity, etc. In fact, it is difficult to imagine human situations in which the payoff does not depend in some way such as in amount, delay, or probability upon the skillfulness with which the response is made. The micromolar theory treats these temporal and intensive aspects of responding as part of what gets learned. In this respect, the treatment of the response is made more comparable to the conventional treatment of the stimulus, where we distinguish quantitative as well as qualitative variations. Just as an 80 db and a 50 db sound are different stimuli, so also a shout and a whisper are different vocal responses. In this manner, the descriptive level of our theory is brought more in line with the realities of many learning situations. The micromolar theory now provides us with the means of analyzing how the learning of differentiated, skillful responses occurs, where previously within the classical tradition no relevant theory had been articulated. All in all, there has been decided progress in this area.

THEORIES OF FORGETTING

Since Ebbinghaus did his inspired work on memory, one of the main occupations of psychologists working on human learning has been to describe and explain the facts of forgetting. Of course, animals forget too, and even forget simple conditioned responses, but animal psychologists have, on the whole, not seemed interested in pursuing the matter in much detail (see recent work by Gleitman and Steinman, 1963, for some exceptions). Thus it comes about that most of the evidence comes from human experiments. With the aim of reducing the cognitive strain involved in understanding, recent experiments have even concentrated on fairly standard, verbal learning situations to yield the main evidence on forgetting.

If one asks the layman why he forgets things, he has a ready answer: he forgets things because he hasn't used them, or "thought of" them for some time. He has forgotten the Spanish he learned in high school because he hasn't used it for the past ten years. But he remembers things he uses right along, like the names of his friends.

The problem with this popular account is that it is vacuous. Lapse of time is not itself a causal variable, although causal events happen in time. If I leave an iron hammer outside, it will progressively rust with time. But it is not the lapse of time that rusts the hammer. Rather it is the reaction of chemical oxidation that occurs in time.

We can give the layman's proposal a more neurological *sound* (if not sense) as follows: each learning experience establishes a neurological trace whose integrity is gradually obliterated by random neuronal noise that occurs at a fixed rate, eroding away the retrievability of the memory trace as the retention interval increases. Does this formulation buy us anything? The answer is "Not really." Unless much more is added, regarding relevant variables and their influence on the hypothetical process (and forgetting), the new proposal is worse than vacuous; it's dangerous because someone is likely to consider it seriously due to its apparent technical jargon.

A variety of substantive proposals concerning the causes of forgetting have appeared, differing considerably in their scope and the range of variables of which forgetting is said to be a function. For example, Freud supposed that some forgetting results from active repression of certain materials in the unconscious. This notion is discussed in Chapter 9. When this idea finally got translated into the laboratory, it had been transformed into the rather limited question of whether one variable—"pleasantness" of the material learned—would influence retention. The research on that issue has been so conflicting and equivocal (see McGeoch and Irion, 1952, for a review) that to build a forgetting theory around such foundations appears to be an admirable act of faith.[1] Another conjecture, contributed mainly by Gestalt psychologists, was that memories were multifaceted systems continually undergoing dynamic changes in their organization, moving towards some better organization (or Gestalt). This notion became translated in laboratory experiments into the question whether a subject's recall of an asymmetric or incomplete figure or line drawing tends to move with retention time towards a good or better Gestalt figure. Riley (1963) in his review of this extensive literature concludes that there is little consistent support for the Gestalt idea. Recall of a figure pattern, more often than not, does tend to move toward cultural

---

[1] For more extensive interpretations of the Freudian theory of repression, see Chapter 9.

stereotypes but such trends as are found turn out more often to be explainable by verbal associations (to the original figure) or proactive interference from prior cultural learning than by Gestalt laws of perceptual organization.

The most serviceable theory of forgetting that has emerged from laboratory experiments is called the *interference* theory. Currently, it has far more adherents, because more evidence in its favor, than any or all alternative theories of forgetting, so it is fair to call it the current dominating theme of experiments on forgetting. This is an association theory; that is, its basic primitive concept is the notion of an associative bond (functional connection) between two or more elements, where the elements may be ideas, words, situational stimuli and responses, or whatnot. In the following exposition, we will use the letters A, B, C, . . . to represent such elements or items, and the notation A-B to represent an associative bond between A and B established by some past training. It is presumed that these associative bonds can vary widely in their strength depending on amount of practice. The experimental situation that best illustrates the theory is paired-associates learning, wherein the subject is taught a set (list) of pairs A-B, C-D, E-F, etc., and then is tested later for retention. The theory applies as well to most other learning tasks, but the paired associates task makes the expositional mechanics easiest to implement.

Interference Theory

The basic ideas of interference theory were first stated explicitly by McGeoch (1932), but through the succeeding years some changes in the theory have occurred. New concepts have been added, unsupported conjectures pruned away, and new experimental methods have been devised to measure more exactly the relevant dependent variables. The changing character of interference theory may be seen by comparing McGeoch's early statements with Postman's (1961b) recent formulation. In what follows, we shall indicate some of the changes and shifts in emphasis.

The first principle of McGeoch's statement seems an absurd one for a theory of forgetting: it says that forgetting does not occur in an absolute sense. The strength of an association between two items, A-B, is established by training, and it is maintained at that level despite disuse of the association. The cause of a measurable retention loss over time is not that the strength of A-B decays, but rather that alternative associations, A-C or A-D, have by some means (to be specified) gained strength in the absence of continued training on A-B. Thus, on a retention test, the subject may give C or D as the associate to A, so we record a retention loss for the A-B association. The A-B association has not been lost or forgotten in any absolute sense; it is still there, but B has been temporarily displaced, losing out in competition with elements C and D at the moment of recall.

On the basis of this theory, then, an association once learned is permanently stored, and forgetting is due to declining accessibility, a lessening probability of retrieval from the storehouse. And this declining accessibility results from competing associations. Such an approach has at least the substrate required to account for the clinically puzzling instances of hypermnesia in which a person demonstrates exceptional recall or believes his recall is genuine, of experiences from long before. Such heightened recall may occur in manic states, in the hours anticipating some emotionally exciting event (e.g., soldiers about to go into combat), in a hypnotic trance, or while following a line of free associations while on the psychoanalyst's couch (see Stratton, 1919; Pascal, 1949; Stalnaker and Riddle, 1932).

According to this theory, the way the A-B association is tested is by presenting one of the elements, say A, whereupon the subject tries to produce the associated B. We may think of A as a stimulus term and B as a response. This suggests an experiment in which we manipulate the degree of similarity of a test stimulus (call it A') to the original training stimulus A. The principle of stimulus generalization predicts that A' is less likely to activate the A-B association so that B is produced in proportion as A' is dissimilar to A. This is empirically true. Moreover, we may expand our conception of A to include any background contextual stimulation that is present when the A-B association is learned. Changes in such contextual stimuli have been found to result in poorer recall (Pan, 1926; Abernethy, 1940). Thus, if the subject is tested for recall in a different room than that in which he learned, or with a different type of stimulus-presenting device, or with the material presented on different backgrounds, or when he adopts a different posture, or whatnot, his recall is poorer than when during testing precisely the original stimulating context present during learning is reproduced. Such results seem consistent with the analytic position of interference theory.

Earlier we mentioned that retention loss on a learned A-B association results from competition of conflicting associations, A-C, at the moment of recall. If we ask where these conflicting associations come from, the logical answer is that they (or ones similar to them, A'-C) come from learning either before or after the A-B learning but before the retention test. This analysis has led to the intensive investigation of situations in which the A-B and A-C learning is explicitly controlled. There are two basic paradigms, called retroaction or proaction, depending on whether the experimenter's interest is in retention of the first-learned or the second-learned material. These paradigms, together with the appropriate control conditions, and some hypothetical recall data are illustrated in Table 14-1. In the retroaction paradigm, the control group first learns the A-B associations, then rests, and later is tested for recall of B when given the A term. The experimental group learns A-B, then learns new pairs A'-C, and then tries to recall B when given A. The retroactive interference index calculated for the hypothetical data is 67%. The proaction conditions may be read similarly.

A variety of task variables can be studied in this context, and on the whole the recall results fall in line with what would be expected from interference theory. For example, recall on the A-B test is better the greater the number of practice trials on A-B and the fewer the practice trials on A'-C. Recall of A-B is better as the difference increases between A and A' measured on some scale of similarity. Also, as one increases the time from the end of learning list 2 until the recall test, the relative magnitude of retroaction decreases and of proaction increases. A paper by Slamecka and Ceraso (1960) systematically reviews much data obtained from both paradigms.

Table 14-1

	Retroaction		Proaction	
	Experimental	Control	Experimental	Control
List 1	A-B	A-B	A'-C	rest
List 2	A'-C	rest	A-B	A-B
Recall Test	A-B	A-B	A-B	A-B
% Correct Recall	20	60	60	80
Effect	$\dfrac{60-20}{60} = 0.67$		$\dfrac{80-60}{80} = 0.25$	

McGeoch's hypotheses predict a perfect correlation between retention loss of A-B and the occurrence on testing of intruding associates, C or D. This correlation is not always found: on the A-B retention test following the A'-C learning, the subject often is unable to respond with any associate. Two hypotheses have been proposed to account for this and both probably have some validity. One notion, due to Thune and Underwood (1943), is that the subject can discriminate the list membership (first or second) of associates that come to mind; to the extent that he does this, he will censor and reject response C when trying to recall the first-list response, B. This is plausible since it is known (Yntema and Trask, 1963) that it is possible to judge with fair accuracy which of two events has occurred more recently in the past. Another idea, first expressed by Melton and Irwin (1940), is that during the A-C interpolated learning, the first pair A-B is unlearned or extinguished. If so, then, when the test occurs soon after the A-C learning, B is temporarily unavailable as an associate. The clearest evidence for unlearning comes from a recall method first used by Barnes and Underwood (1959). Using the A-B, A-C paradigm, the subject was asked on the later test to recall both list responses to stimulus A and to indicate their list membership. This is a noncompetitive recall situation, and failures are ascribed to unavailability of the responses. Barnes and Underwood found that recall of C responses increased with trials of A-C learning but, more importantly, recall of B responses decreased with trials on A-C. Thus, as the A-C training is extended, the first-list associates become increasingly unavailable, presumably due to unlearning. A variety of follow-up experiments have confirmed and extended these results, so that the concept of unlearning is now widely accepted.

But if A-B is unlearned in acquiring A-C, how is proactive interference to be accounted for? One answer to this question that has been offered is based on a critical fact, that proactive effects (poor recall of A-C due to prior learning of A-B) increase with time after A-C learning and before the retention test. It is hypothesized that during this time the unlearned A-B associates spontaneously recover some of their prior strength. The analogy is to Pavlov's observations that conditioned responses recover during a rest period after a series of extinction trials. Clearly, if the A-B associates spontaneously recover, they will cause disruption with A-C recall (proactive interference), increasingly so as recovery increases over time. Briggs (1954) and Adams (1961) have reported evidence that may be interpreted as supporting this idea of recovery in the case of the A-B verbal associations.

One major shift in interference theory that has occurred consists in the powerful role now assigned to proactive sources of interference in forgetting. In a major paper, Underwood (1957) employed the proactive notion to clear up what had been a major source of embarrassment to interference theory. Most of the major studies of retention had shown rather massive forgetting—about 80%–90% over 24 hour intervals. The claim that this was due to interference from casual interpolated learning seemed unconvincing since it was difficult to imagine much everyday learning that would interfere with nonsense materials learned in the laboratory. By collating various reports, Underwood determined that those studies reporting massive forgetting had used the same subjects under many list-learning conditions. The more lists a subject had learned, the more he tended to forget the last one when recall of it was measured the next day. Thus, proactive effects presumably accumulated over the lists learned earlier. Interestingly and in confirmation, if a subject learned only a single list of verbal material, then his recall was fairly high—around 75%–80% after 24 hours.

In a later paper, Underwood and Postman (1960) have attempted to account for the remainder of what is forgotten by appealing to extra-experimental sources of interference. They point out that in learning arbitrary verbal associations or nonsense material in the laboratory, the subject probably has to unlearn the prior verbal habits which he shares with other members of his particular linguistic community. These prior verbal habits may be of several types—letter-sequences associations and unit (word) sequence associations. To give a transparent example, a subject is certain to enter the experiment possessing prior word associations like "table-chair" and "light-dark." Suppose the learning task requires him to form the new associates "table-dark" and "light-chair." During a rest interval, spontaneous recovery of the unlearned prior associates will produce a decrement in the probability of his recalling the associations learned in the laboratory. The experiments by Underwood and Postman plus related follow-up studied show the merits of this analysis. New materials that clash with prior verbal habits are forgotten more readily, usually being distorted in the direction of agreement with the prior habits.

A novel demonstration of this effect is to be found in a study by Coleman (1962). He took a 24-word passage of prose from a book and scrambled the words into random order. This order was given to a subject for brief study, and he then tried to reconstruct verbatim the serial order of the words he had studied. This reconstructed order was then given to a second subject to study, whose reconstructed order was then studied by a third subject and recalled, etc. The passage was successively filtered through 16 subjects. As it went from subject to subject, its recall (reconstructed order) was distorted more and more from the original jumble in the direction of sensible English sentences. One of Coleman's original passages and the sixteenth reconstruction of it is given in Table 14-2. The amount of change is dramatic, especially so considering that each subject was trying to reproduce verbatim the exact order of words he had studied. The change illustrates vividly the powerful effect of prior verbal habits in distorting recall of conflicting associations.

Table 14-2 Illustration of sequential interference due to language habits (Coleman, 1962).

Original Passage studied by first subject:	"about was good-looking way and treating made of that a him the quiet youngster nice he manners a them girls wild go with" . . .
Reproduction of sixteenth subject in the chain:	"he was a youngster nice quiet with manners good-looking and a way of treating them that made the girls go wild about him" . . .

This brief tour through interference theory will have to suffice as an indication of its major features. The main shifts in it that have occurred have been acceptance of the notion of unlearning, a changed emphasis on proactive interference, and identification of a potent source of proactive effects in those prior language habits that conflict with the temporary verbal associations set up in a laboratory experiment. There have also been changes in the experimental techniques employed. For example, Barnes and Underwood's modified recall procedure mentioned earlier is now widely used because of the additional information it yields on what the person remembers. This is an active field of research and no brief discussion can do justice to the range of variables that have been investigated in relation to forgetting. For more comprehensive reviews, see Postman (1961b), McGeoch and Irion (1952), Bower (1966a) or Cofer (1961).

Current studies of human learning and forgetting appear to be in a highly analytical phase, with attention progressively on finer analysis of smaller aspects. As happens during analytical phases in other specialties, synthesis of the knowledge into a broader conception of the phenomena has been shunted aside temporarily. As a result, the possible uses of our scientific knowledge for solving practical problems has been only cursorily explored, and then in an often stumbling fashion. To mention just one major applied problem: educators or anyone engaged in training personnel would surely like to know how best to teach a student something so that he will retain it for a long time. The laboratory work relating retention to the conditions under which training has occurred is clearly relevant; but it is often so far removed from the kind of task, background and other variables that make up the applied situation that some ingenious extrapolation is required before the principles can be applied. Writings by Voeks (1964), Gagné (1964), Bugelski (1964), and a collection of papers edited by Hilgard (1964a) represent a few recent attempts at reasonable extrapolations. It is a hope, possibly forlorn, that more work will be done in the future bridging the gulf between the laboratory on the one hand and the classroom, shop or office on the other.

Short-Term Memory

In studies of "immediate" memory, a subject's recall of information is tested within a few seconds after he has briefly studied it. If only one or two items (words, nonsense syllables) are involved, then he usually shows perfect immediate recall. Moreover, he will show perfect recall over an interval of 30 to 60 seconds, provided he is not distracted. But if he is distracted by some means, say, by having to respond to other material, then his ability to recall the first material drops off precipitously within the space of a few seconds. Such phenomena are familiar to most of us; after looking up a telephone number or street address, we forget it if something distracts us before we have written it down or used it. Figure 14-1 below shows some measurements of this effect in the laboratory. In this particular experiment, by Peterson and Peterson (1959), the subject read off a nonsense trigram (e.g., CHQ), and then engaged in doing mental arithmetic (successively subtracting 3's from a random number). The curve shows the decreased probability that the trigram was correctly recalled after intervals of up to 16 seconds devoted to successive subtracting.

Phenomena of this general type have stimulated much experimental research in recent times. In appearance, the findings seem to imply a *short-*

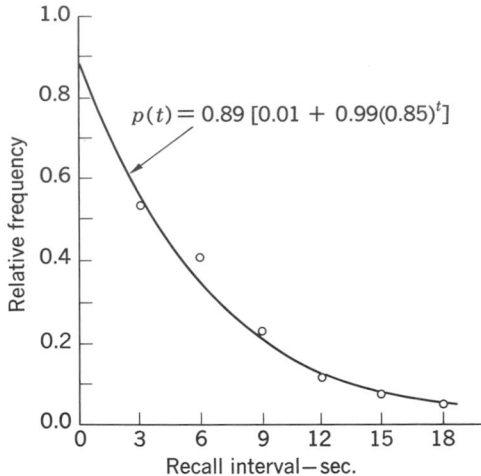

Figure 14-1   **Percentage of correct recalls of a nonsense trigram after varying intervals of distraction by successively subtracting 3's. The equation fit to the data points (open dots) is derived from Estes' stimulus fluctuation theory (see Chapter 11). From Peterson and Peterson (1959), with permission from the American Psychological Association.**

term memory of extreme fragility, lasting only a few seconds when distracting material is presented. But what is the functional use of this short-term memory system in the overall economy of the mind? What relation does this short-term system have to our relatively "long-term" memories? How are we to describe the operation of this short-term system? What are its laws? These and other questions have inspired some interesting theoretical conjectures and a spate of experimentation.

If one asks the functionalist question "What purpose does short-term memory have, or what functions does it carry out?," it takes little thought to enumerate several. One main function of a short-term memory would seem to be as a store for temporarily holding incoming information either while our attention is occupied doing something else or until we collect sufficient information to act upon or reach a judgment about the input. A secretary taking dictation in shorthand provides an example of this first function. She "shadows" the speaker, lagging behind by several words. Each successive word heard is held temporarily until the process of transcribing in shorthand catches up to it. Then she writes it down in its proper code, and this act appears almost to erase it from the short-term store. An example of the second function is illustrated by the way we are able to understand long strings of spoken words as sentences or propositions despite the fact that the major grammatical elements (subject, verb, object) may be far apart in time. Suppose I say "Tom Jones, the kid who's so skinny that he looks like a beanpole, swung the bat, lined the baseball to center field, and slid into second base with a roaring double." The words "slid into second base" come a fairly long time after the words "Tom Jones," but few listeners would fail to recall by the time they reach the sentence's end that it was Tom Jones who slid into second base. The initial elements of the sentence would seem to be held in a temporary store until all the information the sentence supplies has been turned in. After carrying out certain operations on this word string (e.g., rehearsing it, assimilating it, or reacting to it), the store seems to be partly cleared out to process the next sentence arriving in the discourse. Still another possible function for short-term memory is as a temporary "working space," like a scratchpad, to which elements are brought and used now and again during thinking. This is clearly involved, for instance, when a person tries to add three 3-digit numbers "in his head." It is involved too when we actively rehearse some material which we are to retain for a longer time or when we try to construct mnemonic associations to aid later retention. I briefly show you the nonsense trigram VTK to read and remember. You may rehearse "Vee-Tee-Kay" subvocally over and over, but you can retrieve "Vee" after having just thought "Tee-Kay." Alternatively, you may construct the mnemonic V = very, T = thin, K = kitty, and then rehearse "Very Thin Kitty." In either case, a brief information holder is needed so you can shift attention from one to another element, and return to the first one before it gets lost. There are probably still other functions that could be served by such a short-term memory, but the ones mentioned tend to show its functional importance.

Several theorists, notably Hebb (1949) and Broadbent (1957, 1958), have argued for treating short-term memory on a different basis from long-term memory. Some of Hebb's neurophysiological speculations were mentioned in Chapter 13, and the section there on consolidation of memory traces may be read in relation to the material that follows here. In Hebb's view, immediate memory is a reflection of reverberating, neuronal circuits set in motion by sensory input, which may be tapped for immediate recall, but which tend to dissipate with time. On the other hand, long-term memories result from relatively permanent, structural changes in neuronal connections resulting from frequent contiguous firing of two or more units. Thus, if two neural cell populations are frequently stimulated sequentially in a repetitive, reverberating cycle, a structural change in neuronal connections between the two may be induced, producing a long-acting association. Broadbent's account is functional: material is input to a short-term storage system in which it is recirculated (rehearsed) for storage into a long-term memory. If attention is switched to something else (e.g., some other input or mental activity), then the original material decays with time from the short-term store and becomes unavailable. In what amounts to the same assumption, Broadbent assumes that the first few items that enter the short-term store can be displaced (or erased) by subsequent material coming in soon afterwards which overloads the short-term store. The basic idea is to represent the short-term store as a system of limited capacity that can hold only a small amount of information at one time, and to conceive of attention as a selective filter that allows only small amounts of information to be processed (acted upon, thought about) at one time. Much of Broadbent's work (1958) is concerned with discovering the properties of this selective filter system; the main procedure employed is to determine the person's capabilities for handling information when he is being simultaneously stimulated by different signals in several sensory channels (different messages to the two ears, to the eye and the ear, etc.).

In a very lucid paper, Melton (1963) has identified the main issues and questions in research on short-term memory. Of these issues we have space to discuss but one to illustrate the type of research and thinking going on in this area. The issue is whether the distinction between short-term and long-term memory is a truly conceptual dichotomy based on basic differences in principles, or whether it is only a conventional fiction for referring to different parts of a continuum along which interference principles operate all the way. What is needed, then, is evidence to aid in deciding whether the variables affecting short-term memory and their functional laws are different in kind from the variables and laws discovered in dealing with phenomena of long-term memory and forgetting.

According to one version of the dichotomy viewpoint, recall from the short-term store is governed by a trace-decay principle whereas recall from the long-term store is governed by principles of associative interference, response competition, and the like. The alternative view is that interference principles are adequate to deal with the entire range of facts, and that the short-term vs long-term memory distinction is a convenient but not a fundamental one. The question becomes, then, how best to explain the decrements in short-term recall.

The trace theory simply sticks to the autonomous decay principle. Any material put into the short-term store establishes a trace. This trace decays simply as a function of the time since the material was last attended to, and is revealed by the decreased availability of the item for recall as time passes. A trace can be kept active by rehearsal of the material, but doing so requires attending to it. If attention is diverted to some other task (e.g., responding to new inputs), the first trace at once begins to decay. This decay may be thought of as the progressive loss of the information in the trace—by analogy to the gradual smudging and erasure of a word printed in chalk on a blackboard. Progressively more distinctive features are lost, as is our facility for reconstructing the original copy. With complete smudging, the signal-properties of the trace become indistinguishable fom the random "noise" in the nervous system, and thereafter its retrieval (recall) has become impossible.

Let us consider some of the facts offered in support of this view. A first point is that the progress of decay of a trace is assumed to be independent of the means used to switch attention away from it (provided the means is effective). Thus, an interpolated counting backwards task is effective in promoting forgetting of a nonsense syllable unit (see Figure 14-1). This forgetting would seem difficult to explain by any theory of interference since it is not immediately clear how numbers could effectively compete with the recall of a nonsense syllable according to the principle of associative interference. But suppose we make the interpolated material more like the target material originally learned and now to be recalled, while in some way assuring that the load on the short-term store is not changed as we do this. For this case, the trace theory makes an interesting prediction. The target trace should decay at the same rate no matter whether similar or different material is interpolated. However, the relative discriminability of the target trace at any given time does depend on what other traces are present. The retrieval mechanism scans these and picks the most likely candidate for recall. If the trace selected is similar in gross properties to the correct one (e.g., is a syllable rather than a number), it may be given in recall and then an intrusion error will be recorded; if it is different from the correct one, no recall occurs and an omission error is recorded. Brown (1958) reported data which he interpreted as supporting this view. His percentage of correct recalls did not vary appreciably in relation to the similarity of the interpolated material to the target item; however, the errors tended to be mainly overt intrusions when the materials were similar and omissions when they were dissimilar. Wickelgren (1965) disputed this finding. He found that absolute level of recall was lower when similar material was interpolated between the target items and the recall. This is a result that has been obtained by several other investigators, including experiments by Bruning and Schappe (1965). The explanation of Brown's discrepant finding is at present lacking, though it will probably turn out to be due to crucial differences in the materials used.

A later experiment by Conrad (1964) demonstrated the partial information that remains in a trace during its decay. Subjects were shown a visual display of 6 alphabetic letters which they then tried immediately to recall. Analysis of such errors as intruded in recall then revealed rather stable clusters of easily confused letters (e.g., B, D, P, Z). The same confusion clusters occur also in auditory recognition tasks when a subject is asked to identify what letter is spoken against a noisy background. From the similarity of the confusion in the two cases, Conrad concluded (1) that subjects encode letters presented visually by sounding them subvocally, thus setting up an "auditory" trace, and (2) as this trace decays, the first information lost consists of the details needed to discriminate one item from other members of its confusion class (i.e., B is recalled in place of D). A further process of decay would presumably spread the replacements over a broader range, extending beyond the immediate confusion class. Hintzman (1965) obtained similar results and suggested that the confusions between letters that he obtained in recall were explicable by overlap in the patterns of movements of the vocal musculature as particular letters were sounded subvocally. Letters having the same place of articulation (front, middle, or back of the tongue) are especially prone to be confused as also are letters with the same voicing (either voiced or unvoiced).

We turn now to review a few experiments that appear favorable to the alternative view. A first question concerns the effect of repetitions of a verbal unit upon its later recall from short-term memory. The interference hypothesis sees each repetition as one that strengthens further the association between the contextual cues and the verbal response, so recall should be better following more repetitions. Figure 14-2 below supplies evidence that this beneficial effect is indeed obtained. There it is shown that the more times the target item is presented and rehearsed before the backwards-subtracting activity is begun, the better is the recall of the target item at every retention test interval. However, it is doubtful whether this effect really clashes with the theory of trace-decay. It is possible to make several assumptions about repetitions of the target unit. To list a few of these: repetitions may (a) establish multiple copies (traces) of the target item, (b) change the rate of decay of a single copy, (c) increase the probability that the item gets put into the long-term store, from which decay will be very slow, or (d) simply delay the onset of the normal decay

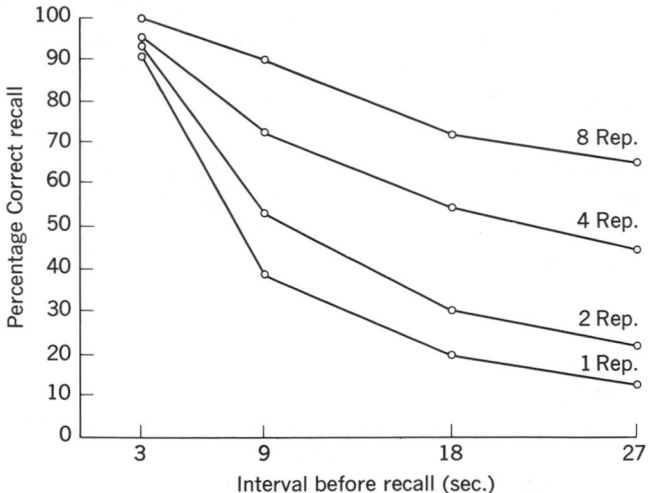

Figure 14-2   Percentage of correct recalls as a function of the duration of retention interval filled with counting backwards. The curves differ according to the number of consecutive presentations of the target item before the retention interval begins. From Hellyer (1962), with permission from the American Psychological Association.

process. Of these possibilities, only the latter (as Brown conjectured, 1958) predicts no benefit of repetition upon later recall.

Consider another type of experiment. We present a list of verbal items at a fast or slow rate, and by some means determine the immediate recall of a particular target item in this list. Then two important facts will emerge. First, proactive and retroactive interference effects operate within the list; that is, probability of recall of the target item decreases the greater the number of prior and/or following items around the target. Second, it often turns out that the recall of the target varies primarily with the number of intervening items between it and the test but is independent of the time that elapses between its initial presentation and its recall test (e.g., Murdock, 1961; Waugh and Norman, 1965). The rate of presentation of the intervening items determines the retention time interval for the target; yet in the studies cited, the presentation rate (and hence, time *per se*) was not significantly related to recall of the target. The trace-decay theory can handle the first set of facts; Broadbent (1957) gives a plausible account of such serial-position effects from his trace theory, an account emphasizing differential attention and rehearsal of items throughout the serial list. The second point, on the potency of interfering items versus the comparative ineffectiveness of elapsed time *per se*, becomes more critical if one is attempting to uphold the time-decay idea. But there are still several possible ways of defending the latter. First of all, this kind of result is not always obtained; some experiments find that recall is poorer when it is delayed than when it is not, even though the same number of intervening events occur in either case. For example, Conrad and Hille (1958) presented short series of verbal items to their subjects and then forced them to recall the series either at a fast or slow rate (in pace with a rapidly or slowly ticking metronone). They found recall to be consistently poorer when it was forced to occur slowly—a result in line with the time-decay idea. Consider another defense of the trace theorist in reacting to the Murdock (1961) and Waugh and Norman (1965) findings mentioned above. It could be argued that when the items to be memorized are presented slowly, the subject has a greater opportunity to rehearse, i.e., go over, each item as well as those prior to it. The beneficial effects of such extra rehearsals could suffice to offset the longer time interval (from target presentation till test) associated with the slower presentation rate. Thus, the Murdock (1961) and Waugh and Norman (1965) experiments appear not to be definitive, although their interpretation in terms of interference surely seems more natural.

An important question that must be answered by the interference theory is how interpolated tasks involving materials differing from the target can interfere with recall of the target. How can the numbers spoken in subtracting successively by 3's compete with recall of a nonsense syllable? The answer that has been advanced is that the source of the interference is not the numbers but rather the nonsense syllables that were encountered previously in the experiment. Thus, proactive interference is proposed as an explanation. The hypothesis is that during the backward counting, the contextual associations to previous syllables spontaneously recover, and these compete with recall of the target item. Some data are consistent with this idea. First, many of the overt errors in short-term recall are indeed intrusions from among the prior syllables encountered in the experiment. In fact, there is a recency gradient to this: the target syllable on trial $n + 1$ is most likely to be replaced, if at all, by the one from trial n, and next most likely by the one from trial $n - 1$, and so on. Second, the subject's immediate recall of the very first target item he encounters in the experiment is very good, showing less of a temporal decay gradient than do the target items encountered following the first few items (Keppel and Underwood, 1962; Loess, 1964). The argument is that proaction by definition can not operate to reduce recall of the first item in the session, but that it builds up very quickly over the session. Wickens, Born, and Allen (1963) showed too that this proactive effect could be "released" by shifting to a new type of target item (e.g., trigrams made up of a new and different set of letters) midway through the experiment. The first item after the switch is recalled better than later ones.

To continue the dialog just a step farther, let us see how a trace-decay theorist might handle these factors. First, the gradient of intrusion errors from past target items fits neatly into the decay notion. If the subject forgets target $n + 1$, then he comes out with whatever syllable-trace is available, and this is likely to be one that comes from the recent past. The trace theorist is quick to point out, in addition, that overt intrusion errors are relatively infrequent in comparison to the high proportion of omission errors (inability to supply any association). And the trace-theorist has a simpler explanation of such omissions than does the interference theorist. Turning to the other finding, i.e., to the within-session effects found by Keppel and Underwood and by Wickens *et al.*, the trace theorist might begin his defense by noting that recall in this task normally involves discriminating among memory traces according to their recency or time of arrival, and memory for this arrival time decays with time elapsed (Yntema and Trask, 1963). As the Peterson-type experiment proceeds, it is really only this tag of recency that discriminates the trace of the item to be recalled from traces of previous items. On this view, the first item encountered in the experiment has a special status simply because it is the only "nonsense syllable trace" active in the short-term store at the moment of recall, there being nothing else in the store with which to confuse it. Hence, the first item of the experimental series is recalled very well. To handle what was found in the experiment of Wickens *et al.*, it is supposed that the shift in the type of material to be recalled adds an extra cue for retrieval of this new trace as distinct from the traces of the different types of items that came before. To illustrate, suppose the target items are changed from the nonsense syllables used previously to three-digit numbers. On the initial test after the shift, the subject would know that he is to recall a number, not a syllable; so this cue along with the usual recency tag would aid retrieval of the recent "number trace" from a short-term store filled with "syllable traces." As the series of consecutive number items continues, the retrieval process should revert to one directed solely by recency judgments. This analysis leads to several testable predictions. One, for example, is that the optimal block size for alternating number and syllable items is one of each (single alternation). This should produce better average recall than larger blocks of similar items.

We suspend the dialog at this point. Our sketch has been intended to give the flavor of the thinking and some of the ideas and experiments that have developed around just one of the several issues which Melton (1963) considers as central to theories of memory. As is the case with many such scientific debates, there is no completely clear resolution of this one. Conceivably, the issue is beyond resolving and may be destined to become one of those hardy perennials that continue to send up new sprouts every so often in the field of learning theory. One problem in such a debate is that the theories propounded are not molded in concrete but rather become progressively altered and elaborated to handle new findings as they come in. Each approach has its inelegancies. A trace-decay principle really has little more to recommend it as a causal account of forgetting than does the "law of disuse" which we mentioned and criticized earlier. But by the same token, the interference theorist's postulate of the spontaneous recovery of proactive associations is little more than the "law of disuse" in reverse. The contacts between the theories and the data are loose enough so that explanations are rather easily generated *ad hoc* in an attempt to account for certain results. It appears that the next useful step in research strategy would be to develop explicit mathematical models designed to predict quantitative details of the data. Such models tend to curtail debate because standard goodness-of-fit tests are available for their assessment. And because of their explicit nature, proposals for modifying the model can be investigated to see whether the proposed new wrinkle does in fact account quantitatively for the data discrepant from the original formulation. At this writing, only a few mathematical models have been formulated for experiments on immediate memory (Atkinson and Shriffrin, 1965; Bernbach, 1965; Bower, 1966b). However, this kind of theoretical activity will probably increase in this area in the near future.

SUPPLEMENTARY READINGS

The readings appropriate to this chapter appear with those following Chapter 15.

Recent Developments: II. Discrimination Learning and Attention

While discrimination learning has long been a familiar area of investigation within laboratory studies of learning, the usual assumption has been that the stimuli presented were well above the organism's capacity for discrimination, so that the investigator of learning was little interested in the perceptual problems involved, leaving them to the investigator of sensory phenomena or psychophysics. Although any such generalization has its conspicuous exceptions, it is true, as we shall see, that the traditional problems of attention, of perceptual selectivity, of learning through observation, were rather neglected but have more recently commanded new interest. This chapter is devoted to some of these newer developments within discrimination learning, along with some fresh light on the standard problems set by a discriminative task.

DISCRIMINATION LEARNING

Discrimination learning is the name we give to the process by which stimuli come to acquire selective control over behavior. Discrimination is the term used to describe the control so achieved. The basic evidence required to infer that an organism can discriminate between two stimuli is that he can be induced, under suitable circumstances, to respond differently in the presence of the two stimuli, and to do this reliably. In brief, we require a correlation between changes in the stimulus and changes in behavior.

The range of variables operating during discrimination learning may be classified roughly into those referring to the stimuli and their reception at the organism's sense organs, and those referring to the subject's conditions of motivation and his reinforcements for responding in various ways to the several stimuli. We may call these the stimulus conditions and the performance conditions, respectively. Discriminative behavior may fail to appear because of a deficiency in either set of conditions. The subject may not show differential responding either because his sensory equipment is incapable of detecting the desired difference (e.g., variations in ultraviolet light to the human eye), or because he will gain nothing he wants by so differentiating in this instance. Of course, psychologists interested in learning have been most concerned with investigating the performance variables as they arise in the context of discrimination learning, whereas they have tended to use rather straightforward stimulus arrangements. Thus, they are only rarely asking the question, "Can this subject discriminate this difference?" since it probably is already widely known that subjects of this particular species can so discriminate. The questions instead are usually asking, e.g., how a particular learning history or particular combination of learning variables influences how fast and by what means the subject comes to perform a particular discrimination, and how we can best describe what the subject has learned when he has completed training.

Many different paradigms of discrimination learning can be set up and investigated. A thorough classification of many different types has been made by Bush, Galanter, and Luce (1963). However, their classification scheme is more extensive than will be required in our discussion below. To begin with some labeling conventions, we will let S_1 and S_2 denote two classes of stimulus patterns that are to be discriminated by the subject. The two classes of patterns may share many common stimulus elements, but in our cases there will always be some elements unique to S_1 (not shared with S_2) and some elements unique to S_2 (possibly only the "absence" of the unique elements of S_1). In the *simultaneous* paradigm, instances from both classes S_1 and S_2 are simultaneously presented on each trial and the subject preferentially chooses one of them. In the *successive* paradigm, instances from the two classes are presented singly, one per trial, and the subject's response to each instance is recorded. This paradigm can be further subdivided depending upon the type of differential response required of the subject. In one subparadigm, the response required is a preferential choice between, say, two available responses, and the discriminative performance would be described by the rule "Choose response 1 if an instance of S_1 occurs; choose response 2 if an instance of

S_2 occurs." In the other subparadigm, the differential behavior is of the "go – no go" type in regard to a single reference response (e.g., salivating, barpressing). Here the discriminative performance would be described by the rule "Respond at a high rate if S_1 occurs; respond at a lower rate (or not at all) if an instance of S_2 occurs." Traditionally, studies of discrimination involving classical conditioning have almost always used this latter paradigm, although it is not strictly necessary to the Pavlovian situation.

The simplest situation of this "go – no go" type is one in which the subject, usually an animal, is positively reinforced for responding in the presence of one stimulus (called the positive stimulus, denoted conventionally as S^+), and not reinforced for responding in the presence of another stimulus (the negative stimulus, denoted S^-), With training, the subject comes eventually to respond promptly to S^+ but not to S^-. The classical view of this situation, as first elaborated by Spence (1936) and later by Hull (1952a), was that analysis of such discrimination learning should require no new concepts beyond the notions of simple conditioning, extinction, and stimulus generalization. It was assumed that cumulative effects from reinforced responding to the positive stimulus would build up a strong habit tendency at S^+. Similarly, it was assumed that conditioned inhibition would accumulate at S^- from the frustration consequent upon nonreinforced responses made in the presence of S^-. These habit and inhibition tendencies established at S^+ and S^- are assumed to generalize to similar stimuli, with the amount of generalization decreasing with decreasing similarity. The net tendency to respond to any stimulus is then given by the generalized habit minus generalized inhibition to that particular stimulus (cf. Figure 15-2, page 524).

This simple theory has proved extremely serviceable and has provided good accounts of much that we know about discrimination learning (cf. Kimble, 1961, for a summary). As a result, the significance of work on discrimination learning is often assessed using this classical theory as a foil. Any exceptional behavioral phenomenon is pursued just because it appears to be consistently at variance with the classical theory, or because it reveals some incompleteness in the classical theory. The facts to be reviewed below fall within this category.

Behavioral Contrast

One implication of the assumption of stimulus generalization in the classical theory is that responding in the presence of one stimulus, S_1, should be positively related to responding in the presence of the other, S_2. Suppose we were to fix the reinforcement conditions in S_1, and manipulate the reinforcement conditions in S_2. As we make the reinforcement in S_2 relatively more favorable or unfavorable, responding to S_2 will increase or decrease, accordingly. The expectation is that responding to the fixed stimulus, S_1, should also increase or decrease, respectively, to an extent dependent upon the generalization of response tendency between the two stimuli. This expected pattern of positive correlation between the two response rates has been called *positive induction*. This phenomenon has been observed in several instances and the general principle plays a central role in many S–R analyses.

It has, therefore, been of interest to discover a class of discrimination situations which yield just the opposite result, *negative induction*. In this case, response rates are negatively correlated. This is to say that a reduction in the reinforcement for responding in S_2 reduces response rate to that stimulus but *increases* response rate to S_1, even though S_1 has been maintained on the same condition of reinforcement. Reynolds (1961a) has labeled this phenomenon *behavioral contrast* since the response rate in S_1 (denoted by r_1) changes in a direction (up or down) opposite to the direction of change of response rate in S_2 (denoted r_2).

Reynolds first called attention to the importance of this phenomenon, to its consistency and reliability, and initiated a concerted series of experiments to discover the variables that control it. We will briefly review some of his experimental findings. All of his experiments and those by his co-workers have been carried out in the free operant Skinner box using pigeons as subjects and key pecking as the response. It may be added, however, the effect has been observed in other situations and using different species of animals.

In the typical experiment by Reynolds the discriminative stimuli (e.g., red or green colors) are projected onto the pecking key. They occur in repeated cycles of, say, six minutes duration: first red key (S_1) for three minutes, then green key (S_2) for three minutes, the cycle repeating indefinitely over, say, a two-hour experimental session. In the presence of S_1, one schedule of reinforcement for keypecking is adopted; in S_2, a possibly different reinforcement schedule for keypecking prevails. During an initial phase, the reinforcement schedule is the same in S_1 and S_2, so that this establishes a baseline with which to compare subsequent changes. Following this period, the reinforcement conditions are changed in S_2 only, and we observe the subsequent changes in r_1 and r_2 response rates over the next several experimental sessions. Over an entire experiment, which may last several months, a number of changes may be examined for their effects, with frequent returns to the baseline to recover the performance.

In this experimental context, it has been found that an S_2-schedule change which reduces r_2 (below its value on the prior schedule) will increase the r_1 rate, and an S_2 change that increases r_2 will decrease the r_1 rate. These changes in r_1 rate are contrast effects. They occur despite the fact that the S_1 schedule remains fixed and is of such a nature that the number of reinforcements in S_1 remains relatively fixed. For example, if fixed or variable interval schedules are used, rate of reinforcement is relatively unaffected by rate of responding.

Reynolds (1961a, 1961b) has shown that the amount of change in the r_1 rate due to contrast increases with the amount of change in the relative rate of reinforcement in S_1. Table 15-1 gives some hypothetical data which illustrate this effect. In this case, in stimulus S_1 keypecking is always reinforced on a two-minute variable interval schedule. The table shows the effect of changing from the baseline condition to one of four conditions, in two of which r_1 increases and in two of which r_1 decreases. The relative rate of reinforcement is calculated as a percentage of the total reinforcements in a session that occurs during the presence of each stimulus. The table illustrates (with hypothetical data) the kinds of effects found: the rate of responding increases 10, then 20, responses per minute when the relative reinforcement rate in S_1 increases $+25\%$, then $+50\%$; similarly, r_1 decreases 8, then 20 responses per minute when the relative reinforcement rate in S_1 decreases -16.7%, then -38.9%. This general result has been observed with a variety of reinforcement schedules in S_1 and S_2. Moreover, preliminary evidence (Reynolds, 1961c) suggests that the size of the contrast effect is greater the more similar (up to a limit) stimulus S_2 is to S_1; this outcome is precisely the opposite of what would be expected from the classical theory, which requires that positive induction should increase with stimulus similarity.

A theoretical account of contrast effects is currently lacking, although it is a clear focus of activity. In what he has published concerning his work, Reynolds leaves the matter at the level of description: the relative goodness of a stimulus condition depends on what are the reinforcement conditions when alternative stimuli successively control the behavior. All the obviously simple explanations have been ruled out by various experiments: it appears that contrast is not a drive-satiation phenomenon for it does not occur if differential stimuli are absent, and it is not a response-fatigue phenomenon because it still occurs if the S_1 and S_2 components occur singly on alternate days. Also, it does not occur if keypecking is extinguished in S_2 but the same rate of reinforcement—for other behavior—is maintained in S_2. Two likely candidates for its explanation are being pursued. The first is Amsel's frustration-drive notion: lowering the reinforcement rate in S_2 produces frustration reactions, these become conditioned to apparatus cues, and their motivational consequences feed into increasing responding to S_1. The Terrace results to be discussed below bear on this interpretation. An alternative hypothesis, proposed by Wertheim (1964), treats contrast as an example of a general class of "adaptation-level" effects previously observed in affective and perceptual judgments. This general idea was mentioned in the discussion in Chapter 14 of interpretations of reinforcement. Helson (1964) gives a thorough re-

Table 15-1 Hypothetical data used to illustrate behavioral contrast.

Condition	Stimulus	Schedule	Reinforcements per hour	Response rate (R/min)	Relative rate (%) of reinforcement	Change from baseline in % of rf in S_1	Change from baseline in Response rate in S_1
BASELINE	S_1	2 min. VI	30	60	50	...	...
	S_2	2 min. VI	30	60	50	...	...
CONTRAST INCREASES RESPONSE RATE IN S_1	S_1	2 min. VI	30	70	75	+25	+10
	S_2	6 min. VI	10	22	25	...	...
	S_1	2 min. VI	30	80	100	+50	+20
	S_2	Extinction	0	3	0	...	...
CONTRAST DECREASES RESPONSE RATE IN S_1	S_1	2 min. VI	30	52	33.3	−16.7	−8
	S_2	1 min. VI	60	80	66.7	...	...
	S_1	2 min. VI	30	40	11.1	−38.9	−20
	S_2	Const. Rf.	240	90	88.9	...	...

Key to abbreviations: VI means variable interval reinforcement schedule; rf means reinforcements.

view and explication of adaptation-level theory. According to this notion, the subject is viewed as making a "judgment" about his current rate of reinforcement in a particular stimulus, and that judgment is made in comparison with an adaptation level which is affected in turn by the reinforcement rates prevailing in the alternative stimuli. By reducing the reinforcement rate in S_2, the overall adaptation-level is lowered; consequently, the same reinforcement rate in S_1 is now judged as higher in relation to this new adaptation level. It is further assumed that the rate of responding in a stimulus is correlated with this judgment of its apparent rate of reinforcement. From these assumptions, the results on behavioral contrast may be derived.

It is important that Wertheim applied these ideas to explain his data on contrast effects obtained with shock *avoidance* performance. He used rats in a Skinner box in which each barpress postponed the next shock for some number of seconds, called the response-shock interval. In this situation, response rate falls off proportionately to the length of time that the next shock is postponed by a response. Wertheim's animals were trained with two successive stimuli, each with its corresponding response-shock interval (or shock rate). Much as in the case of the analogous results with positive reinforcement, changes in the shock rate to one stimulus produced contrasting changes in the response rate to the other stimulus. And the amount of contrast shown in response rates was highly correlated with the amount of change in the relative shock rate. The occurrence of contrast effects in such shock-avoidance situations establishes the generality of the phenomenon. This is important because the adaptation-level hypothesis may be applied to both positive and negative reinforcement, whereas the alternative frustration hypothesis probably makes sense only when applied in the case of positive reinforcement. Thus, the adaptation-level hypothesis regarding contrast effects has the advantage of greater generality. It has the advantage too of integrating the behavioral contrast effect with a large body of other results concerning the way in which contextual stimulation biases affective and psychophysical judgments (see Helson, 1964, for a review). It is conceptual links such as this between learning theory and constructs that have proved their worth in other fields of research that serve to give some unity to our science.

Errorless Discrimination Learning

The classical view is that discrimination is achieved by extinguishing generalized responses in S^-. The repeated frustration by nonreinforcement of responding to S^- is presumed to cause the development of inhibition, conditioned to S^-.

Terrace (1963a) has devised a procedure for teaching a pigeon a perfect discrimination in such a manner that it never responds to S^- throughout the entire experiment; in other words, without ever making an "error." The initial studies have been done with different colored lights on the pecking key serving as S^+ and S^-. The procedure involves (*i*) introducing S^- very early before the response to S^+ is well conditioned, and (*ii*) introducing S^- gradually, initially for very brief durations and at very dim intensities. Over successive trials, the intensity and duration of S^- are gradually increased to their full values. The method hinges in part upon certain peculiarities of pigeons such as the fact that they are unlikely to peck a darkened key, so how far the method may be applicable to other species is not known.

By using this simple procedure Terrace proved that it is possible to get perfect discrimination without the occurrence of a nonreinforced response to S^-. In contrast, suppose that S^- is introduced, as it usually is, for the full duration and at full brightness after the pigeon has had several sessions to exposure to S^+ and has become well conditioned. Under these conditions, the pigeon may emit several thousand responses to S^- before learning acceptable differential behavior. Thus, the difference produced by Terrace's simple procedure is truly enormous whether one thinks in terms of ease of training a discrimination or also, by inference, of the amount of emotional frustration that the subject has been spared.

In a related experiment, Terrace (1963b) was able to show that an errorless discrimination learned to, say, red vs green key colors could be transferred to two new stimuli (a white vertical bar as positive and horizontal bar as negative) by a special method. The special method consisted in (*i*) first superimposing the vertical bar on the positive red key, and the horizontal bar on the negative green key, and (*ii*) after several sessions of such superimposed conditions, gradually fading out (dimming) the red and green colors on the key, eventually ending up with only the vertical or horizontal bar on a dark key. By this procedure, stimulus control is transferred from red vs green to vertical vs horizontal bars, and here, again, no errors occur in the course of the gradual transfer. It is of significance that Terrace was unable to train a vertical vs horizontal discrimination from scratch without errors (by manipulating brightness of S^-). This suggests that if a difficult discrimination is to be trained, an optimal method is to train without errors another discrimination that is inherently easy for the subject (as colors surely are for pigeons), and then superimpose and fade into the more difficult stimuli. It is of interest too that if following the superimposition phase the colors were abruptly removed, the animals did make a number of errors on the vertical vs horizontal discrimination. Moreover, when later retested on the red vs green discrimination, the animals that had the abrupt change started to make errors (responses to S^-) despite their initial errorless training on red vs green. Terrace points out the relevance of all his results to Skinner's claim that the optimal arrangement of programed instruction sequences (in teaching machines) is the one in which the student never makes an error in answering questions during learning.

There are several intriguing auxiliary features of errorless discrimination performance as compared to what is obtained under the customary, error-spotted procedure. First of all, the discriminative performance itself is far superior. Animals trained by the errorless method never respond to S⁻ whereas birds whose training routine is spotted with errors continue indefinitely to put out sporadic bursts of responses to S⁻. Secondly, observation reveals that the error-prone birds display a large amount of emotional behavior in S⁻, suggesting that it is probably an aversive stimulus for them, apparently because of the frustration generated by nonreinforced responding. In comparison, an errorless-trained bird displays little or no emotional behavior in S⁻. Third, giving the animal an injection of the tranquilizing drug, chlorpromazine, "releases" large quantities of responses to S⁻ in the error-prone trained birds but not in the errorless-trained birds. Presumably, the tranquilizer dispels some of the frustration which had been inhibiting responses to S⁻ for the animals trained with errors. Fourth, the errorless-trained birds do not show the behavioral contrast effect discussed in the prior section, whereas the error-prone birds do; however, if an errorless-trained bird is induced to start making errors in S⁻ (say, by the abrupt transfer mentioned above), then it begins to show contrast by speeding up its response to S⁺. Fifth, a generalization gradient taken following discrimination training shows a "peak shift" for the error-prone birds but not for the errorless birds. Peak shift refers to the fact that the peak (maximum) rate of responding is produced not at S⁺ but at a value displaced from S⁺ in a direction away from S⁻. Figure 15-1 below shows this effect in Terrace's experiment (1964). The stimulus continuum is wavelength of light (corresponding to color changes to the human eye) measured in millimicrons. The S⁺ was at 580 and S⁻ at 540 millimicrons. The peak rate of responding during generalization testing is at 580 (the S⁺) for the errorless-trained birds, but is at 590 for the error-prone-trained birds.

What does all this mean? How is it best interpreted? A possible account might go somewhat as follows. Errorless discrimination is possible because of conditioning by sheer contiguity of the last response made before a stimulus terminates. Because the pigeon does not peck a dark key and because the S⁻ color is presented initially dim and for short durations, the likely response to these initial S⁻ presentations is either withdrawal or just "sitting still," and this behavior is what gets conditioned to S⁻. This is roughly the account Guthrie or Spence would give for the phenomenon, since both are contiguity theorists. Behavioral contrast and peak shift are effects that depend upon S⁻ having been converted into an aversive stimulus, and this is ordinarily achieved by the frustration generated by nonreinforced responding to S⁻. Since the errorless procedure produces no

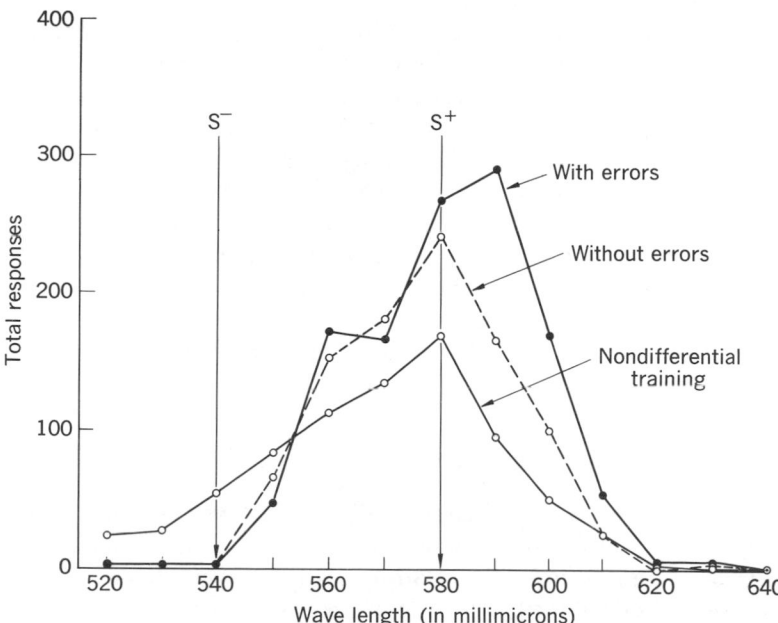

Figure 15-1   Generalization gradients obtained under three different conditions, relating response output to variations in the wavelength (color) of a light projected on the pecking key. The lower gradient was obtained following simple conditioning at 580 mμ without a discrimination procedure. The other two gradients followed discrimination training on 580 mμ as S$^+$ and 540 as S$^-$, one procedure involving errors to S$^-$, the other not. A peak shift appears in the former gradient since responding to 590 mμ was greater than to 580, the S$^+$ of training. From Terrace (1964).

frustrated responses, no aversion is conditioned to S$^-$, and so contrast and peak shift do not occur in this case. In line with this reasoning, Grusec (1965) found that errorless-trained birds did show peak shift if they were shocked in association with S$^-$, thus converting it into an aversive stimulus. Though plausible, this account leaves several facts unexplained. Why was Terrace unable to train from scratch a vertical-horizontal discrimination without errors? Why does abrupt removal of colors following superimposition of vertical vs horizontal lines produce errors? Why, thereafter, do errors begin occurring on the retest with red vs green? A hypothesis to tie together all these unexplained facts is conspicuously lacking at the moment.

Despite the absence of a hypothesis to explain all the facts, the significance of the errorless result still stands. It shows that the conventional extinction procedure can be sidestepped in establishing a discrimination and that the performance obtained is better than the ones usually obtained. Terrace's procedure brings out strikingly a point of view on learning research that has often been lacking in the past. The viewpoint is one concerned with optimality, and asks questions regarding the best arrangement of training conditions, one that permits the subject to achieve some criterion of good performance. The strategy here would be to devise training sequences to optimize or minimize some such variable as the goodness of the eventual performance achieved, the speed of effecting a given change in performance, or producing a desired change with a minimum of errors, or a minimum of frustration, or of difficulty, and so forth. Such a research strategy will assuredly yield results of practical relevance to educators, psychotherapists, and others whose concern is with practical behavioral engineering.

Transfer of Relational Responding

All theoretical approaches to discrimination learning begin by trying to specify, either formally or intuitively, what it is that a subject has learned in his discrimination training. How are we to characterize the subject's knowledge gained by this educational procedure? For behaviorists, this question gets translated into one about stimulus control of responses: what is the *effective stimulus* controlling the subject's discriminative performance? At one level of analysis, practically all theories answer this general question in a similar manner: the effective stimulus variable that comes eventually to control discriminative performance is that feature (cue, attribute, etc.) or set of features present in S^+ and absent (or different) in S^-. Such features are called relevant cues because their variations correlate with presence or absence of reinforcement for responding. Cues not so correlated are termed irrelevant.

But let us consider a problem where the relevant cues consist of different values along some ordered stimulus continuum (such as size, brightness or heaviness, etc.). For example, suppose a monkey is trained to use size as a cue for securing a food reward. The setup may consist of simultaneously presenting two boxes between which the monkey is to choose; the one containing the reward has a top with an area of 160 square centimeters, whereas the other box, containing no reward, has a smaller top 100 square centimeters in area. The *relational* theory supposes that in this situation, the subject would learn the relation "the *larger* area is correct." The *absolute* theory supposes that the subject has learned specific stimulus–response connections; in particular, that the reaching response is conditioned positively to the specific value of the rewarded stimulus (160) whereas the response is inhibited to the value of the non-rewarded stimulus (100).

Which mode of description of "what is learned" is better is more than a matter of taste, because transfer tests with new stimuli provide us with data for inferring what the subject has learned in the 160 vs 100 situation. If the subject learned a relation ("choose the larger one of the stimuli"), then he should in some degree be able to transfer his response to this relation to new stimulus pairs differing from those used in training. That is, the relation he has learned is one that transcends the specific stimulus pair used to exemplify the relation. Thus, if we test the animal with the new pair 256 vs 160, he should still choose the larger stimulus in this pair, namely, 256, in preference to 160, despite the fact that 160 was rewarded in the prior training series. The usual experimental result is that animals do choose the 256 stimulus in preference to the 160 stimulus. That is, they *transpose* the relation "larger" along the size continuum. Such studies are thus called transposition experiments.

This kind of transposition has been found with fair regularity in experiments, and it has been offered as evidence for the relational view of what the animal learns (e.g., Köhler, 1918). It was formerly thought that such a transposition was inconsistent with the absolute theory since, on that basis, how could one ever predict that a new stimulus (256) would be chosen in preference to the one (160) that had been so often rewarded in prior training?

It was in this context that Spence published a classic paper in 1937 demonstrating that transposition and several related phenomena are perfectly predictable from an absolute stimulus theory of what is learned. All that is required, according to Spence, is the assumption that the generalization gradients of habit strength and inhibition around the specific S^+ and S^- values of training have a certain reasonable form. This view is best illustrated in Figure 15-2 which depicts a theoretical view of the situation established by the 160 vs 100 size discrimination training. Figure 15-2 shows a habit gradient set up around the reinforced stimulus of training (160), and an inhibition gradient set up around the nonreinforced stimulus (100). The net tendency to respond to any size stimulus is given by the difference between the generalized habit and inhibition at that point. These difference scores are indicated in Figure 15-2. In a choice test between two stimuli, that stimulus having the larger net response tendency will be chosen. For example, for the training pair of 160 vs 100, the net tendency to respond to 160 is 51.7 and to 100 is 29.7; so in this pair, the 160 stimulus would be chosen.

A number of implications follow from this "absolute" stimulus theory. It does predict transposition over a short range of stimulus pairs close to the training pair, e.g., from the difference scores shown in Figure 15-2, the animal would be expected to choose the 256 stimulus (which has a difference score of 72.1) in preference to the 160 stimulus (difference score of 51.7). It is on this same basis that the theory predicts the "peak shift" phenomenon in net generalization gradients following discrimination training; this phenomenon was mentioned in the prior section and was

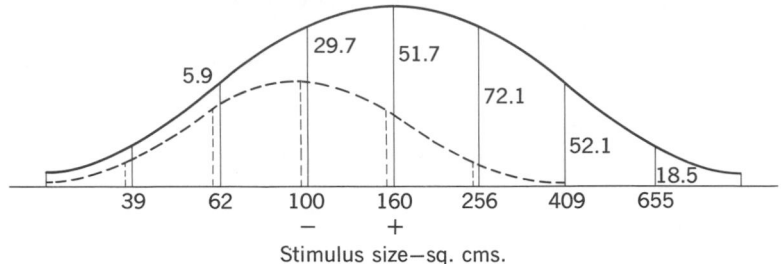

Stimulus size—sq. cms.

Figure 15-2 Hypothetical generalization gradient for habit (solid curve) around 160 (+) and inhibition (dashed curve) around 100 (−). The difference, habit minus inhibition, is indicated numerically at various points. The stimulus values are equally spaced on a logarithmic scale. From Spence (1942), with permission from the American Psychological Association.

illustrated in Figure 15-1. Examination of Figure 15-2 shows too that prediction of how the animal will choose on a given test pair of stimuli depends critically on how far the pair is from the training pair. As the test pair is moved above and away from the training pair, the theory first predicts transposition for near test pairs, then reversal of transposition (choosing the smaller) for pairs of intermediate distance (e.g., as in 409 vs 256), and then random choices for test pairs very far removed from the training pair (as in, say, 900 vs 1300). This decline in transposition with distance has indeed been found many times and it provides a difficulty for the relational view. Furthermore, according to Spence's theory, S^+ and S^- need not be simultaneously present for comparison in order to establish the conditions required by the theory to predict transposition in later pairwise tests. Single stimulus presentation of S^+ and S^- with reinforcement and nonreinforcement of responding should serve suitably to produce later transposition choices on paired tests. Transposition is found following such single stimulus training, although various procedural changes generally cause it to be somewhat less than that following simultaneous-presentation discrimination training. Several other predictions are derivable from Spence's theory; for example, the test stimulus range over which transposition is observed should be less when S^- is even farther below the S^+ of training. In general, the effects predicted by Spence's theory have been confirmed by experiments. A study by Honig (1962) is particularly clear in showing several of these effects within a single experiment. Because of confirmation of its determinate predictions, Spence's absolute-stimulus theory won the day because no similarly developed relational theory was then advanced to explain the facts.

Carrying matters a step further, Spence (1942) extended his theory to cover cases involving three training stimuli. In the *intermediate size* problem, the animal would be trained to choose the 160 stimulus from the triple consisting of 100, 160, and 256. Figure 15-3 depicts Spence's analysis of the situation in terms of his specific stimulus theory. An inhibition gradient is set up around both nonreinforced stimuli, with the two gradients being summated (see Hull's "behavioral addition") at points where they overlap. From this diagram, several implications are evident. First, the intermediate size problem should be much more difficult to learn than a two-choice problem. This may be seen by comparing Figure 15-3 with 15-2, noting that the net differential reaction tendency to S^+ is much less for the intermediate size task. Second, learning to choose the intermediate stimulus should prove more difficult than learning to choose either of the end stimuli of the three (largest or smallest). This is true and is easily derived, although it is not shown in Figure 15-3. Third, there should be no transposition following training on the middle-size problem but there should be transposition after training on one of the end stimuli of the triad. In Figure 15-3, for example, following training on the middle-sized stimulus, a test with the triad 160, 256, and 409 should lead to choice of 160, the positive stimulus of training. In fact, for any test triad, the preferred stimulus should be that one closer in size to 160. Spence (1942) reported data showing indeed that his subjects (chimpanzees) did not transpose the middle-size relation to the test triad (160, 256, 409) following training on 100, 160, 256.

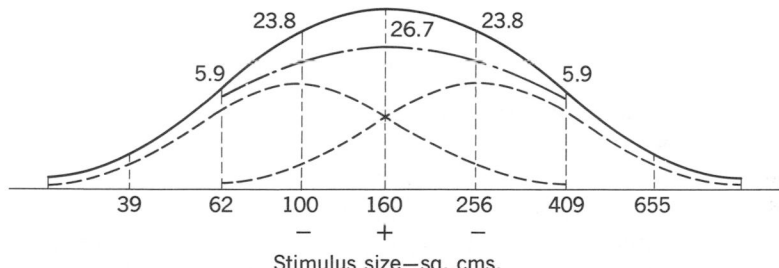

Stimulus size—sq. cms.

Figure 15-3   Hypothetical gradients following learning of the middle-size problem, where 160 was rewarded and 100 and 256 were non-rewarded. The inhibition gradients (dashed curves) around 100 and 256 are summated to yield a single net inhibition curve with a peak at 160. The difference, habit minus net inhibition, is indicated numerically at various points. From Spence (1942), with permission from the American Psychological Association.

Despite the attractive parsimony of Spence's theory and the evidence that can be marshaled for it, reports of other results that have continued to appear suggest that it is either incomplete or inadequate in some other way. Some of these studies, such as those by Smith (1956) and Riley (1958), have emphasized, at least for the brightness continuum, the importance of the background contextual stimulation surrounding the focal stimulus patches to which the subject responds. Thus, a test patch of a particular brightness may be seen as lighter or darker depending upon whether its surrounding background is darker or lighter, respectively, than the test patch. Riley, for example, showed that the decline in transposition on the "far tests" did not occur if the test patch-to-surround brightness ratio was kept the same in training and testing (although absolute intensity levels were changed for the tests). In other work, Lawrence and DeRivera (1954) demonstrated that rats apparently learned relational cues when the training situation promoted the effectiveness of cues involving brightness-contrast. Moreover, in various follow-up experiments on the middle-size problem, transposition has often been found (contrary to Spence's result), although not in every instance.

It is upon this scene of increasingly confusing results that Zeiler (1963) has come out with a theory that appears to account beautifully for most of the results, including those cited for and against Spence's theory. Zeiler develops his theory for the middle-sized problem, although judging from the prior work by James (1953) the theory can easily be extended to cover the two-choice problems as well. Zeiler's is a ratio theory involving the adaptation-level concept. His basic proposition is that the subject's perception of a stimulus depends upon its ratio to an internal norm or standard, the adaptation level (AL). Earlier in Chapter 14 and in this chapter, the AL notion was used to interpret reinforcement and behavioral contrast. Zeiler's use of the AL concept is actually closer to the psychophysical judgmental situations for which Helson originally developed the AL theory. The AL is assumed to be an average value (actually geometric mean) obtained by pooling the focal and background stimulation currently present and the stimulation that has been effective in the recent past. Without going into details here, Zeiler's theory assumes that the three training stimuli establish a particular AL, and that the subject learns to choose that stimulus (the middle-sized one) bearing a particular ratio (call it r^+) to the prevailing AL. When later tested with a new set of three stimuli, a new test adaptation level (call it AL*) has to be computed from the theory: it is a weighted average of the training AL and the different AL that would be appropriate were only the three test stimuli acting. In the test, the subject is assumed to choose that stimulus whose ratio to the test AL* is closest to r^+, the stimulus ratio reinforced during training. If neither test stimulus ratio is close to r^+, in a special sense defined by Zeiler, then random responding on the test is predicted.

This theory can predict transposition, transposition reversal, or random responding in the middle-size problem depending upon the precise set of training and test stimuli involved. In general, the theory does a remarkably good job of accounting for most of the previous data on the middle-size problem. In addition, it predicts fairly well the results of an extensive series of experiments which Zeiler carried out with 4- and 5-year-old children. Part of the beauty of the theory is the manner in which it nicely integrates parts of the "relational" and "specific stimulus" theories. According to the specific stimulus theory, the response tendency to any stimulus is established in a definite way by the training conditions and it is assumed to be aroused independently of the alternative test stimuli that are present; according to the relational approach, the specific stimuli of the test set are irrelevant, since the relation that the subject has learned supposedly transcends particular elements. But in Zeiler's account, the attractiveness of a stimulus depends upon the context in which it is embedded. It is the composition of the test set that partly determines the new norm, AL*, in relation to which the stimuli are judged. Just as the relational theory would have it, Zeiler supposes that the subject has indeed learned to respond to a particular ratio. However, contrary to the strict relational viewpoint, the test stimulus ratio most similar to that reinforced in training depends on both the current (test) stimulation and the previous (training) stimulation which influence the current adaptation level. Zeiler's theory is moderately complex, but this would be true of any adequate theory since the patterns of the experimental results that have to be accounted for are also complex.

As is often the case in the evolution of scientific explanations, the initial alternative hypotheses (relational vs absolute) are both eventually proved to be inadequate or insufficiently comprehensive. The new explanation emerging involves some novel concepts but also retains certain of the features of the previously competing theories. The transposition phenomenon engendered a controversy only in regard to the behavior of animals and possibly preverbal children. Spence himself restricted his theory's application to nonverbal organisms, believing that the human's use of symbolic language introduces novel factors not covered by his theory. It is indeed true that humans learn and use relational concepts in abundance and our language is replete with relational terms which we use properly hundreds of times each day ("greater, above, farther, to the west of," etc.). Several investigators have been concerned with how transposition responding varies as the human child develops and becomes more proficient in the use of language. The general trend of the findings is that transposition improves with the mental age and/or linguistic proficiency of the child, although there have been a few discrepant reports (see Hebert and Krantz, 1965, for a review).

Attention and Its Role in Discrimination Learning

If a subject has been trained with several redundant relevant cues serving for differential behavior, later tests may show that his behavior is primarily under the control of only one component of the entire stimulus complex. Of many instances of this selectivity we shall describe just one example. In an experiment by Trabasso and Bower (1966) college students were trained to give response A to red circles and response B to blue triangles, with several irrelevant or misleading cues added to the learning situation to slow down the learning rate. Following learning, subjects were given special tests on the single color and form components. In this way it was discovered that some subjects had learned the significance of the color cue but knew nothing about the shape cue, other subjects had learned about shape but not about color, and other subjects had learned perfectly well about both the color and shape cues.

The control of behavior by only selected aspects of a complex stimulus has been classed as an *attention* phenomenon. The historical tradition of radical behaviorism was to reject mentalistic constructs, including that of attention. In accordance with Occam's razor, demanding parsimony of explanations, the traditional strategy has been to see how much data could be explained without postulating central selector mechanisms. Surprising as it may seem at first glance, theories that introduce no such construct as attention have been fairly successful in accounting for a variety of discrimination results from animal experiments. The classical theory of Spence's outlined at the beginning of this section is one example of such a theory.

The explanatory power of such an approach is considerably enhanced when it is supplemented by the construct of "peripheral orienting acts." An example would be turning the head and adjusting the eyes so that the visual image of some object is projected onto the retina under maximally favorable conditions. Such acts of orientation and receptor adjustment involve the peripheral musculature, so their introduction into the system seemed not to violate the spirit of the behavioristic Zeitgeist. Because such orienting acts are responses, they are presumably learned by the usual laws of reinforcement. Holland and Skinner (1961) give the customary account when they point out that such observing responses are secondarily reinforced because they produce or clarify a discriminative stimulus, which itself controls some instrumental, goal-directed response. Experiments by Holland (1958), Wyckoff (1952), and Atkinson (1961) give nice illustrations of the use of this approach for studying the learning of explicit observing responses.

The question remains whether such peripheral receptor acts are sufficient to carry the entire explanatory burden or whether some of the facts demand more central selector mechanisms or filters. The problem here is to decide what qualifies as "peripheral" and what as "central" filters. The neurophysiological work of Hernandez-Peon *et al.* (1956) and many others (briefly reviewed in Chapter 13) attests to the existence of low-level filters or blocking mechanisms at the receptor and/or the first major synapse of the sensory tract. But is it a peripheral or a central act when a person modifies the tension on his tympanic membrane to attenuate extraneous sounds while he is attending to visual input? When a person is looking at an open circle outlined in red pencil, does his eye move differently when he is attending to its redness rather than to its circularity? When a person is judging the pitch of a tone, is his entire hearing apparatus set differently from when he is judging its loudness? The factual questions involved here are difficult to answer and are largely neurophysiological in nature. In turn, the issue of peripheral vs central selectors is not one likely to be decided on psychological grounds. It is probably the wrong type of question for psychologists to be trying to answer.

A more relevant question is to ask what are some of the variables influencing stimulus selection of any sort during learning (see Berlyne, 1960, and Treisman, 1964, 1966, for a review of some of this literature). Another relevant question is to ask how fertile are theories which adopt attention constructs—what explanatory power do they achieve in doing so? A topic that comes up for immediate discussion is: What does an attention theory look like? How might one employ the construct of attention in a theory? The best worked out theories of this variety are those of Sutherland (1959, 1964), Broadbent (1957), Zeaman and House (1963), and Lawrence (1963). These theories involve a common network of concepts and assumptions and though the verbal labels for these concepts may differ, their substance is more or less the same. Zeaman and House (1963) have worked out a stochastic model based on their theory, similar in many respects to an earlier model by Atkinson (1961). Lovejoy (1966) has also developed a stochastic model for Sutherland's theory. Lawrence and Broadbent have not worked through any formalization of their ideas. In the following discussion, we shall adopt primarily the terminology that Lawrence introduces.

The basic construct is that of a "coding operation" or a "coding response." A coding operation is a procedure for labeling or representing objects in one domain by objects or symbols in another domain. It can be used as a means for describing a complex stimulus by one or more of its properties (attributes). Because most stimuli can be described or classified in a multitude of ways, each way represents the output from a particular coding operation available to the subject. The carrying out of a coding operation upon an input yields one of a range of values, the stimulus-as-coded (sac). If the coding response is to ask of the stimulus complex "What color is it?," the stimulus-as-coded might be the implicit description "Blue."

To illustrate all this with a discrimination learning problem, suppose that the stimulus patterns vary in a number of independent attributes such as their shape, size, color, orientation, position, etc., and that the relevant attribute (with which reward is correlated) is color. We suppose that for each attribute there is a corresponding coding response. These coding responses may be of different strengths (or alternatively, are more or less likely to occur). During the course of learning, the subject tries out first one, then another coding response until by a trial-and-error procedure he settles upon the coding response for the relevant cue (color here). Once he settles upon a relevant coding response and has learned what instrumental responses to make to the sac's from this coding response, the problem is solved. Thus, the subject would learn to encode the complex stimulus pattern according to its color; and he learns to give response A if it's red and response B if it's blue. The sac is the functional stimulus in the sense that (i) it controls the instrumental response made on any trial, and (ii) the reinforcement or outcome on a trial influences the associative connection of only the sac employed on that trial. Features of the stimulus that are not encoded on a particular trial neither influence the response selected nor have their associative connections to the instrumental responses changed as the result of reinforcing events. The coding response is presumably conditioned to those stable background or situational cues which prevail despite changes in the proximal stimulus from trial to trial.

This general scheme, although plausible, is practically useless until more details are specified about variables affecting strengths of the coding responses, and the actual mechanics of the trial and error procedure for eventual discovery and learning of the relevant coding response. To deal with the mechanics first: the common rule is one or another version of the "win-stay; lose-shift" strategy. Following a correct (rewarded) response, the encoding response used on that trial receives an increment in its probability and the sac-correct response connection used on that trial is also incremented. Following an incorrect (nonreinforced) response, the encoding response employed on that trial receives a decrement as does the sac-error response connection involved on that trial. The processes of associating the relevant sacs to the correct responses and of selecting the relevant coding response are strictly interactive and govern or regulate one another. The change in a sac-correct response association on a trial depends upon whether that coding response is selected. The change in the probability that a coding response is selected depends on whether it is followed by a correct response, which depends in turn on the strength of the sac-correct response association. It has long been known that mathematical analysis of such interactive systems leads to intractable mathematics. It is noteworthy that Lovejoy and Zeaman and House obtained predicted results by using Monte Carlo methods to run through their model with a high-speed computer, since explicit prediction equations could not be derived. A tractable mathematical system is possible if one of the learning processes is assumed to be degenerate; for example, Bower and Trabasso (1964) used a model which assumed that the selection of a relevant coding response was an all-or-none process, and that the sac-correct response association was completely established on the first occasion that a sac was used. Although these simplifications seemed warranted by their data on human concept identification, the assumptions are probably of limited generality.

Many quantitative and qualitative predictions about discrimination learning follow from such schemes. Unfortunately, some of the qualitative predictions differ depending upon the relative learning rates of the two processes in the model. For example, if the attention-learning rate is slow but the association-learning fast, then the model predicts a learning curve characterized by a long plateau of chance responding for many trials, followed by a rapid increase in correct responding at the end. The initial probability of selecting the relevant coding response determines the length of this plateau and the difficulty of the problem (cf. Zeaman and House, 1963, for illustrations and data). If, on the contrary, the attention-learning is fast and the association-learning slow, then a progressive, slow climb in correct responding is predicted. Such theories have many implications for discrimination learning. For example, Sutherland uses the theory to explain why overtraining on a difficult discrimination facilitates rate of subsequent learning to reverse responses to the two values of the relevant attribute, but retards subsequent learning to use a different, newly relevant attribute when the first-learned attribute is made irrelevant. The theory also explains why a habit differential trained to the values of an attribute can be preserved more or less intact over an interpolated series of random reinforcement, when the subject presumably begins to use other coding responses. The papers by Atkinson (1961), Lovejoy (1966), or Zeaman and House (1963) may be consulted for many other details and predictions.

It was stated earlier that the coding responses are initially arranged in a hierarchy according to how they vary in strength or in their probability of being employed. The position of a coding response in this hierarchy will determine the difficulty for the subject of a problem which requires use of the corresponding cue for solution. Therefore, one is interested in the factors which influence the initial hierarchy at the beginning of work on a problem. These factors may be classified in three groups: innate, stimulus-bound, and those involved with past learning. The "innate" label merely refers to the common knowledge that there are interspecies differences in the saliency or importance of particular properties of stimuli. Spatial location and smell are salient cues for rats; colors and visual stimuli generally, for pigeons; smells and sounds, for dogs; and so on. Since knowledge of this kind is limited, the "innate" label attached simply covers our ignorance. The stimulus-bound factors affecting the saliency of an attribute have also been little investigated, although it is of great interest to psychologists working in the advertising business. We know various tricks for *emphasizing* a particular cue, essentially by marking it with a distinctive tag that itself is not a discriminative cue. For example, the critical part of a picture may be colored differently or more brightly than the rest, or an arrow may point at it, etc. The emphasizer is essentially telling the subject, "Look here." Trabasso (1963) reports a neat study of emphasizing effects. Other stimulus factors affecting the likelihood that an attribute is selected are the intensity, vividness, and discriminability of the different values of that attribute which run throughout a series of patterns. For example, it takes a subject longer to notice that, say, the sizes of the figures vary if there is only a small range of differences in their sizes. If a small-size discrimination is to be trained, then a net saving can be achieved by starting with a large size difference. Once the subject is attending to the size attribute, then its discriminability can be reduced without any ill effect on the subject's performance.

Past learning also influences the initial hierarchy of coding responses, and these are the influences that have been most studied. Past learning is broadly defined to include instructions to human subjects prior to their judging a stimulus series. Thus, they can react appropriately when they are instructed to judge the tones of a series by pitch, and later are instructed to judge them by loudness. The past learning experiences of animals can often be interpreted as having much the same effect as verbal instructions with human subjects. We can train animals over a series of problems to "look for" variations in a particular attribute simply because it has usually been relevant in the past. Experiments by Lawrence (1950) illustrate this clearly with rats. A trained bias towards using a particular type of cue (call it cue A) can be made to show itself by comparison with control ("unbiased") subjects during the learning of a new problem, and by one of three methods: (1) facilitation of learning when the relevant cue is still of type A, (2) interference with learning when a different cue is relevant whereas cue A, though present, is now irrelevant to the correct solution, and (3) a preference for learning mainly about cue A when cue A and a different cue, B, are made redundant and equally relevant in the new problem. It is not yet known whether the salience of a cue can be demoted in an absolute sense by making it irrelevant over a series of problems (i.e., if in the test problem it is paired with novel cues), although this seems likely.

The preceding discussion has focused upon the situation where stimuli are analyzable by the subject into various dimensions or attributes (color, shape, size, etc.). A relevant question not touched upon is how the person learns in the first place what a stimulus dimension or attribute is, and how to isolate it perceptually. No firm answers are known, although several interesting conjectures are available (e.g., Solley and Murphy, 1960; Gibson and Gibson, 1955). Another question is how a person later learns to compound several attributes into what appears to be a single coding operation (as when we immediately judge a wine as dry or a woman as beautiful). The best guess as to how this combining occurs is that several stimulus attributes are processed in parallel or simultaneously (cf. Figure 12-5) by their specific analyzers (coding operations), yielding a set of patterned joint outputs. Through feedback (reinforcement) from the environment, a basic set of analyzers required for a given discrimination is selected, and the patterns of joint outputs from this set of analyzers get associated with appropriate overt responses.

A problem related to the first one is how the coding-response theories are to account for learning with unitary stimuli for which subjects have few, if any, relevant coding operations. Shepard (1963) has observed that discriminating certain color patches is an instance of this sort. Since the layman does not know the scientific classification system, he often has no ready means of analysis of slight color variations. Then he may resort to the use of stereotypes: "This color is a rose red, that a tomato-soup red," etc. In such an instance, the errors subjects make while learning to divide a set of color patches into two classes (chosen arbitrarily by the experimenter) are quite predictable from perceptual confusions between the stimuli involved (Shepard and Chang, 1963).

The presumption would be that with more experience, the subject would invent or discover coding operations (not necessarily in verbal awareness) to help order these stimuli. This is probably what happens in the training of expert wine or coffee tasters, or when a South Sea island native acquires a capability of discriminating several degrees of ripeness in coconuts. Gibson and Gibson (1955) have stressed this discovery of new features that comes from increased familiarity with stimulus variations for which the person initially had few relevant coding operations.

Despite the intriguing nature of such *de novo* discrimination-learning phenomena, very few investigators have tried to teach subjects discriminations that they could not make initially with suitable instructions. In the human laboratory, we tend to use stimulus variations that the culture has trained our subjects to notice and to label. But it is not too difficult to invent novel stimulus variations that subjects can not initially discriminate. For example, W. P. Tanner (personal communication, 1964) utilized very brief tones of 50 milliseconds (1/20 sec) duration with different rise and fall characteristics produced by accurate electronic equipment. Such small tonal variations are not noticed in everyday life, and Tanner's college students as subjects were at first totally unable to discriminate among them any better than chance even after many hundreds of trials. But when daily listening to and responding to the tones was continued over many weeks, all the subjects improved to a very high level of discriminative performance. It is significant, however, that despite their high level of discrimination, the subjects were still unable to describe how the tones differed or how, phenomenologically, they were able to discriminate between them. Tanner obtained similar long-term improvement in discrimination of pitch (frequency) by Punjabi Indian students who were "tone deaf" at the beginning of the experiment, i.e., very poor at identifying large differences in pitch.

There are no really relevant hypotheses in the field to account for such long-term gains in discriminative performance, nor any neural model of the sensory channels that helps us explain why improvement comes so very slowly. But it appears likely that a similar slow development of relevant "attribute" discriminations normally occurs during early infancy. It appears too that the successes in extending discriminative capabilities argue for caution in setting "absolute limits" to men's sensory capabilities. Just as exceptional and hitherto "impossible" performances are now occurring annually in track and field events, so too exceptional sensory feats could perhaps be produced if our environmental reinforcements were sufficiently stepped up.

OBSERVATIONAL LEARNING

If someone were to ask how we acquire new response patterns, current stimulus–response theory has a reasonably pat answer: by reinforcement of variations in behavior that successively approximate the final form desired. In shaping a behavior sequence by successive approximations, we wait for and then reinforce some response that is at least grossly similar to the first element of the final pattern desired. Thereafter, reinforcement is provided only for variations of this first element that correspond more closely to the one desired. After the first element of a series is learned, we go on to teach the second response element in a similar manner and this is chained to the first element. After the two are learned, they are chained to the third element, and so on. Skinner was one of the first to describe the shaping method as a means for increasing an organism's repertoire. The procedure is often illustrated by training animals to perform tricks or complex behavioral sequences that make an interesting spectacle. Thus, pigeons can be trained to play competitive ping-pong, a raccoon to put a basketball through a hoop, a mynah bird to say strings of English words, and so forth. Shaping an animal to perform such a chain has by now become a standard laboratory exercise in most college courses in learning.

Shaping through differential reinforcement is indeed an important method for establishing new responses, but is it the only method? Examination of everyday learning by human beings suggests another method and in almost all cases it is more efficient than the shaping method. This other method is simply to have the learner *observe* someone else performing the response that the learner is to acquire. By this means, the learner can often perform the novel responses sometime later without ever having performed them before or having been reinforced for them (since they have never occurred before). It seems obvious that a large portion of human learning is observational and, in one sense, imitative. It is obvious too that many skills (e.g., driving a car, pronouncing foreign words) are learned more readily by this method than they would be were the successive approximation method (without verbal instructions) used exclusively.

In several papers, Bandura (1962, 1965) has pointed out the ubiquity and efficiency of such observational learning in humans and has emphasized its unique features not found in the standard paradigms of shaping and instrumental conditioning. He has also carried out an admirable series of studies with young children that throw light upon the variables influencing such observational learning.

In the typical experiment, a kindergarten child (the subject) sits and watches some person (the model) perform a particular behavioral sequence. Later the subject is tested under specified conditions to determine to what extent his behavior now mimics that displayed by the model. What he does is compared to what control subjects do who are tested without having observed the model. A variety of factors can be varied in this situation, and many can be shown to affect the extent of imitative behavior performed by the subject. We list a few of those studied by Bandura:

A. Stimulus properties of the model
  1. The model's age, sex, and status relative to that of the subject. High status models are more imitated.
  2. Model's similarity to the subject: the model is another child in the same room, a child in a movie, an animal character in a movie cartoon, etc. Imitation induced in the subject decreases as the model is made more dissimilar to a real person.
B. Type of behavior exemplified by the model
  1. Novel skills vs novel sequences of known responses. Presumably, the more complex the skills, the poorer the degree of imitation after one observation trial.
  2. Hostile or aggressive responses. These are imitated to a high degree.
  3. Standards of self-reward for good vs bad performances. The subject will adopt self-reward standards similar to those of model. Also the subject will imitate the type of moral standards exhibited by an adult model.
C. Consequences of model's behavior
  1. Whether model's behavior is rewarded, punished, or "ignored" (neither reinforced nor punished) by other agents in the drama. Rewarded behaviors of the model are more likely to be imitated.
D. Motivational set given to subject
  1. Instructions given the subject before he observes the model provide him with high or low motivation to pay attention to and learn the model's behavior. High motivation might be produced by telling the subject that he will be paid commensurate with how much of the model's behavior he can reproduce on a later

test. Under minimal instructions, learning is classified mainly as "incidental."

2. Motivating instructions after the subject views the model and before he is tested. This aids in distinguishing learning from performance of imitative responses.

This listing of variables in the observational learning situation is not exhaustive; it is intended to show the range of possibilities. A wide range of behaviors can be transmitted under these conditions by the model and with the effect that the fidelity of the subject's mimicry (even under incidental learning conditions) is often remarkable.

It was mentioned above that the model's behavior is more often imitated when the model has been rewarded rather than punished for his behaviors. Bandura was able to show that this reward-punishment variable affected the subject's performance of imitative responses but not his learning of them. After the observation trial, attractive rewards were offered to the subjects if they would reproduce the model's responses. This increased the display of imitative responses and totally wiped out the differential effect of having seen a rewarded vs a punished model. Thus it was noted that the observer had learned the "bad guy's" responses even though he did not perform them until the incentive to do so was offered.

The mechanisms required for such observational learning have been insufficiently analyzed. Bandura (1965) mentions two processes. One process is the learning by contiguity of stimulus sequences (see also Sheffield, 1961). During the exposure to modeling stimuli, sequences of sensory experiences ("images") occur and become associated or integrated. Later, the recall of the integrated sensory experiences will guide the observer's behavior in imitation. Following some early dispute about the phenomenon, there now seems abundant evidence from many sources that direct sensory-sensory conditioning of this sort occurs (cf. Seidel, 1959). The most cogent evidence comes from EEG recordings of brain activity; for example, if a soft tone precedes a flickering light, after a few pairings the characteristic EEG response produced by the light begins to occur to the tone alone (cf. Morrell, 1961b).

The other process utilizes verbal descriptions by the human subject. Once verbal labels are available for the subject, he can describe to himself the model's behavior as it unfolds and can learn these verbal descriptions. Their later recall can serve as cues for directing or guiding the subject through the imitative responses. In an attempt to manipulate this factor, Bandura, Grusec and Menlove (reported in Bandura, 1965) had children view the model (shown in a film) under three different conditions. In one, the subject verbalized aloud the sequence of novel responses performed by the model. In another, the subject was instructed merely to observe carefully. In the third, the subject was required to count rapidly while watching the film, and this presumably interfered with implicitly verbalizing and learning the model's behavior. A later performance test, under either high or low incentive for imitation, showed the three groups ranked in the order in which we listed them in their ability to imitate the model's behavior. That is to say, the subjects who described in words the model's behaviors learned best, and those who had to engage in the interfering counting task during observation learned the least.

The student may rightly be puzzled as to why such studies of observational learning can be considered something of an innovation as recently as 1965. The main subject investigated is not a new notion, by any means; since the late nineteenth century, psychologists have recognized observation followed by imitation as a principal mode of learning. However, the idea has had its ups and downs in popularity. It was muddied by some rather bad speculation, and it generally fell into disrepute during the behavioristic revolution, perhaps because evidence for it was lacking in a few animal experiments. The notion of sensory-sensory conditioning boggled the biases of the S–R behaviorist, and the animal orientation of S–R learning theory was clearly what triumphed during the 1930's and 1940's. Except for a few rare flings at it by such psychologists as Miller and Dollard (1941), the topic of imitation was pushed aside and not really dealt with while the S–R reinforcement theorists went about cultivating their own traditionally preferred problems. Bandura's contribution has been to call attention to this long neglected mode of learning, and to sharpen the unique features that differentiate it from the operant conditioning paradigm of learning-by-doing plus reinforcement. And then, in addition, he instigated an admirable series of detailed studies that aimed at analysis of the variables influencing observational learning.

In one sense, the facts so far uncovered about observational learning are not particularly surprising. As adults, we already have a considerable store of common-sense knowledge about observational learning, owing to the fact that so much of our learning has been of this type. Also, as he himself notices, Bandura's experimental situation is really not much different from the typical laboratory experiment in verbal learning where a subject observes nonsense syllables exposed by a memory drum and later recites them back. Presumably, the same type of verbal associative learning is going on when a subject observes the stimuli produced by the behavior of a model. It would appear that to a large extent, variables similar to those found to influence verbal learning will apply to learning by observation (e.g., proactive and retroactive interference, complexity of material to be learned, etc.). Additionally, motivating and rewarding variables seem importantly involved in whether imitative responses will be performed once they have been learned.

As a final word on the topic, it is important in a practical sense to point out that an optimal training program for transmitting many behaviors to human beings would use the observational method in conjunction with differential reinforcement. By having the person observe a model, we increase the initial probability that a response pattern resembling the one desired will occur. After it occurs, the response can be further refined or differentiated and its rate stepped up by reinforcement. For some finely skilled performances, once started on it, more benefit derives from actual practice in the skill than from further observing of the model. The division and order of allotment of time for observing a model vs practicing with reinforcing feedback will surely have different optimal arrangements depending on the nature of the particular task performance to be shaped. Such questions concerning what is optimal would seem, at present, to have no general answers and each must be worked out under appropriate field conditions.

CONCLUDING REMARKS

It is out of the question to attempt an integrative summary that will neatly wrap up in one package all the topics discussed in the past two chapters, along with accompanying prognostications of the future. We do not know how to do this, and we doubt whether it can be done in an intellectually honest, and yet satisfactory, manner. The analytical trend of modern experimental psychology has succeeded almost too well in breaking up the study of learning into many subfields and specialties. These specialties pursue their particular problems eagerly and penetratingly, but almost independently of one another. The behavioral modifications produced by experience (learning) constitute a vast subject matter. Specialization within it is to be expected, even required, if investigators are to uncover the myriad facts out of which a complex science is built. Regretfully, the day of the complete generalist in psychology has for quite some time gone into eclipse.

Examination of the section headings of the past two chapters—reinforcement, extinction, forgetting, discrimination, attention—may at first glance suggest that the same old problems are being currently worked upon which have occupied psychologists almost since their profession was first recognized. A critic could interpret this in a depreciative manner to mean that no progress has been made in the solution of these problems, since they are still with us. The observation may be correct but the interpretation is not. Each of the terms we use has considerable scope and is merely a convenient chapter-heading label that is helpful in classifying and pigeonholing the volume of research knowledge, laws, theories, and small-scale hypotheses that have collected around a particular class of behavioral phenomena which presumably reveal fundamental processes or capabilities of some organism. As our techniques for manipulating and controlling behavior develop, we acquire the means for generating genuinely novel behavioral patterns, some of a type never before encountered in just this form. As this is done, the range of an older term is simply extended to cover the new phenomena.

In a fundamental sense, the global problems of a particular science rarely change and the notion that they can be solved turns out to be inapplicable and naive. To cite an example, "understanding the nature of matter" was a problem set for physics by Aristotle, and it still remains today as a major problem for modern physics. But thousands upon thousands of small subgoals have been set and passed, advances have been made, and these in turn have generated and will continue to generate without limit further subgoals, questions, and searches for answers. Science is an enterprise that continues without end, because each good answer is sure to raise even more probing questions. What is true in the physical sciences applies also to the study of memory, or discrimination, or any of the classical global problems in psychology.

The science-game is infinitely more complicated than chess though it shares the same elements of skill, strategic planning, and fun. A general problem generates many subproblems, each in turn generating further subproblems, expanding quickly into an enormous tree of small issues, none of which ever really terminates. There are few criteria for evaluating the worth or importance of getting a partial answer to a given subproblem because the goal of the entire enterprise is never sharply defined. At best, the goal is envisioned in terms of "understanding" the problem or satisfying our curiosity. Many branches of the search tree are explored vigorously for a while and then abandoned for lack of satisfaction to the investigator, either because the results are understood too little or too well (until new doubts are raised).

How does one evaluate progress in such an ever-shifting search tree? The only relevant criterion that comes to mind is the logical depth of the search—the number of subproblems that have been more clearly defined and investigated, or perhaps supplanted or bypassed in order to investigate more "fundamental" problems, and so forth. By such criteria, there has been a fair degree of progress in the research on learning. We are loaded with problems that we do not know how to solve and their numbers seem to multiply daily.

SUPPLEMENTARY READING

BROADBENT, D. E. (1958) *Perception and communication.*

DEUTSCH, J. A. (1960) *The structural basis of behavior.*

GOLDSTEIN, H., KRANTZ, D. L., and RAINS, J. D. (Editors) (1965) *Controversial issues in learning.*

HONIG, W. K. (Editor) (1966) *Operant behavior: areas of research and application.*

KIMBLE, G. A. (1961) *Hilgard and Marquis' Conditioning and Learning.*

KOCH, S. (Editor) Vol. 2 (1959) and Vol. 5 (1963) *Psychology: A study of a science.*

LAWRENCE, D. H., and FESTINGER, L. (1962) *Deterrents and reinforcement.*

LOGAN, F. A. (1960) *Incentive.*

MELTON, A. W. (Editor) (1964) *Categories of human learning.*

MOSTOFSKY, D. I. (1965) *Stimulus generalization.*

MOWRER, O. H. (1960) *Learning theory and behavior.*

PROKASY, W. F. (Editor) (1965a) *Classical conditioning.*

SIDMAN, M. (1960) *Tactics of scientific research.*

SPENCE, K. W. (1960b) *Behavior theory and learning.*

Learning and the
Technology of Instruction

Any isolation of basic science from applied science, when it persists, is unfortunate. Over the years the advances in science have occurred
in intimate relation with advances in technology. Thus the instrument-
makers (producing microscopes, telescopes, vacuum tubes, computers)
have opened new fields of basic research; invention has all along gone
hand in hand with scientific discovery. If we were to apply the historical
lessons from astronomy, physics, biology (and their related technologies)
to the psychology of learning, we would expect an equal intimacy between
theory and research in the basic processes of learning and the applied
aspects of instruction and training in the schools.

Educational institutions are under a large measure of social control,
whether they are public or private; hence they are open to improved methods of teaching if it can be demonstrated that these methods are an outcome of scientific research. Because of this, it might be assumed that the
psychologist interested in the study of learning would be very eager to
have his theories embodied in the arts of instruction, and validated by
the greater efficiency and effectiveness of teaching techniques that result
from his findings.

While many students of learning are indeed interested in instruction,
this is not universally true. The uneven interest in applications comes
about in part through division of labor and specialization of knowledge:
there are "pure science" aspects to the study of learning, just as in other
fields of inquiry, and the scientist delving into basic problems may not

be concerned with applying what he knows. Thus one does not expect every geneticist to be interested in the breeding of farm animals, even though what he learns may ultimately be useful to the animal breeder. While many investigators of learning are interested in "pure" science, apart from applications, some investigators are very much interested in the technology of instruction. In this chapter we wish to examine some of the problems that are involved in bridging the gap from the laboratory to the classroom, in the conviction that a sound theory of learning must eventually be validated by its influence upon the arts of practice. If educational practices cannot be improved as a result of research investigations of learning, something is wrong with that research. Whether or not what we know is now being used raises some other questions.

EDUCATION AND TRAINING

Although educational psychology developed rapidly under Thorndike's influence early in this century, the greatest mass efforts to apply psychological research methods to practical problems of training have not been in the schools but in the armed services. Because a good deal has been written about training research, we will examine its results to see whether or not it provides lessons for schooling generally.

Two differences between *education* and *training* have been delineated by Glaser (1962). First, training tends to be toward specific objectives, such as repairing a radio or piloting an airplane, while education tends to be toward broader objectives, such as becoming a responsible citizen or a creative scientist. Second, training seeks a certain uniformity, a competency that can be counted upon (e.g., the typing skill that leads to typing 60 words per minute with a minimum number of errors), while education seeks to maximize individual differences by discovering and releasing individual potential. Competent research on ways to improve learning toward specific objectives is doubtless easier than research on ways to improve education toward vaguer and broader objectives. The lesson to be learned from research on training may be stated in this way: *It has been found enormously difficult to apply laboratory-derived principles of learning to the improvement of efficiency in tasks with clear and relatively simple objectives. We may infer that it will be even more difficult to apply laboratory-derived principles of learning to the improvement of efficient learning in tasks with more complex objectives.*

This inference is not necessarily true, for it is possible that one might control the teaching of highly generalized skills, such as those of observation, concept formation, and problem-solving through the application of laboratory-derived principles, even though individual tasks might have to be mastered through sheer exposure to them because the highly specific aspects of task structure do not permit much use of principles. There is little evidence at present to support this view that we are more competent in teaching higher order skills than lower order ones. In any case, it behooves us to learn all that we can from training research to gain perspective on the problems that we face in educational research more broadly conceived.

The Problem of Objectives

Objectives take on different roles in basic and applied research. In basic research, the objective is to get evidence bearing on a problem, often within quite arbitrary limits set by the investigator at his convenience. Thus he may study the learning of white rats of a given stock raised with a given diet, tested within a standard maze, imposing some parameters (e.g., number of trials per day) at his own discretion. The objective is to find whether there is some difference, say, between one trial per day and two trials per day, often in relation to some hypothesis respecting the outcome. In training research, however, the constraints are those of some socially defined task, such as correctly reading the instruments that control a particular operation, or building a safe bridge over a river. The standards of a "good enough" performance are not those set arbitrarily by the investigator. All of the manuals that have come from training research units consistently stress the need to begin with clearly specified objectives defined by what the trained person is expected to do. How well these are met is evaluated by practical tests that he must pass within a given time and within stated margins of error. This emphasis is well illustrated in a small book on objectives for planned instruction by Mager (1961a). He stresses eliminating vagueness from objectives by clear communication to all concerned of just what is expected. For example, some words commonly used in stating objectives are vague and open to many interpretations; others are precise and tell you what to expect. His lists of words to illustrate this point is given in Table 16-1. If objectives are to be communicated clearly it is necessary to specify the kind of behavior that will be accepted as evidence that the learner has reached the objective, to state the conditions under which this behavior is expected to occur, and to specify the criteria of an acceptable performance. This is not so different from the objectives of a formal laboratory experiment, except that a practical psychologist may have no freedom in choosing objectives, but must discover the actual demands upon the learner in terms of a task or job analysis. He has to train toward objectives that are not really his own to assign. Instead of discovering what kind of results a given situation yields, he must discover a situation that yields given results.

The problem of teaching toward objectives becomes different not in kind but in complexity when the whole field of education is concerned

(Bloom, 1956; Krathwohl, Bloom, and Bertram, 1964). In general, anything worth spending time to teach is worth analyzing for its goals of instruction.

Importance of Appropriate Appraisal of Outcomes

Those who work on applied problems of training are necessarily interested in a precise outcome that can be measured, such as proficiency in a skill meeting standards of time and errors, an outcome which also remains available as needed after a lapse of time (e.g., Frederiksen, 1962; Wilson, 1962).

Table 16-1 Words commonly used in stating objectives of training or education (Mager, 1961a, page 11).

Words Open to Many Interpretations	*Words Open to Fewer Interpretations*
to know	to write
to understand	to recite
to *really* understand	to identify
to appreciate	to differentiate
to *fully* appreciate	to solve
to grasp the significance of	to construct
to enjoy	to list
to believe	to compare
to have faith in	to contrast

Any measure of a training outcome embodies the objectives in some kind of an evaluation instrument. Ideally, an instructor should have prepared his final examination before he begins to teach his course: if his objectives are attainable, he ought to be directing his training toward them. This is equally true if he is seeking widely generalizable kinds of learning: then his outcome criteria must include a wide range of applications to test whether or not what has been learned is indeed generalizable. It is not surprising that Bloom, who has been most concerned with objectives, is in charge of the examinations at the University of Chicago.

The dependence of college teachers upon written final examinations may or may not be a good thing, depending upon how fully such examinations reflect the purposes of the training. Most of these instruments are highly verbal, and for many purposes ought to be supplemented with performance measures. Many other questions arise in respect to adequate examinations, but the point here is that a good examination should reflect clearly what it is that a course attempts to do.

Some Results of Training Research in the Armed Forces

The experience of elaborate studies of training carried on within the armed services during and since World War II is somewhat sobering.

Doubtless much good has come of it, but the testimony of those who have taken leadership in these studies is that there is no easy transition from principles of learning to the improvement of practice. Glaser (1964) has assembled some of this testimony. He quotes Webb (1957) as reporting "a tough time getting research and the market place together." Webb finds on the one hand that generalizations from the laboratory are usually unjustifiably broad considering the highly specific circumstances of experimentation; on the other hand, results from field experimentation are obtained under circumstances so complex that generalizations are difficult to establish. Gagné (1962) finds the best-known psychological principles of learning (practicing a response, reinforcement, distribution of practice, meaningfulness) "strikingly inadequate to handle the job of designing effective training situations" (page 85). He notes that in several specific tasks (gunnery, procedures of switch-pressing, trouble-shooting complex equipment) practice, even under presumably favorable conditions (according to established "principles"), was not very effective; the learner instead had to learn what to look for, what was to be done, and the classes of situation likely to be met. After reviewing the comments of several others (Melton, 1959; Travers, 1962; Lumsdaine, 1961), Glaser concludes that what we need is an integration of a *task analysis* and the pertinent *learning variables*. Without a task analysis we will never know how to apply what we have discovered about learning.

Although a number of summary volumes have been published, it is not easy to assess the implications of the vast research on training for the problems of education generally, or indeed to state with any confidence the proper relationship between laboratory learning studies and applied investigations. One way to approach this is to take a look at the research outcomes in some representative fields. For this purpose we may examine some of the results on skill training (because perceptual-motor skills have long been favorites in the laboratory), and on trouble-shooting (because this involves problem-solving, another basic area). While we shall be concerned first of all with the upshot of the empirical research in these areas, the background question is of course the relationship between learning theory and what has been discovered about these performances.

1. Skill training. A useful summary of some of the results of studies of skill training has been given by Fitts (1962). In common with most of those who have faced actual training problems, he begins with the problem of *task taxonomy*, that is, a description of the structure of what has to be learned. He notes that in perceptual-motor skills one is concerned with at least the following, differing from task to task: (1) stimulus and response sequences, their coherence, continuity, frequency, and complexity; (2) stimulus–response coding and code transformations; (3) nature and amount of input and external feedback information; (4) nature of internal (proprioceptive) feedback; (5) dynamics of physical systems (lags, oscillations, etc.); and (6) overall task complexity. Fitts is impressed by the amount of *cognitive* activity that is involved in skill learning. He believes that the learning of a complex skill progresses through a cognition phase, then through a fixation phase, and finally to a stage of automation. The importance of intellectualization in the early stages of skill training was demonstrated in some studies of airplane pilot training (Williams and Flexman, 1949; Flexman, Matheny, and Brown, 1950). They tried to make use of "principles" that had come from the psychology of learning, and appeared to be quite successful in this effort, in part because they included some cognitive principles. The principles identified were (a) motivation, (b) knowledge of results, (c) anticipatory set, (d) judicious use of both part and whole learning, (e) performance of the task while receiving verbal instructions, (f) overlearning, (g) judicious use of spaced practice, and (h) intellectual knowledge of maneuvers. Fitts was particularly impressed by their promoting an understanding of flight problems: knowledge of results, appropriate expectancies, "talking through" the maneuvers, and "intellectualization." Their results were rather dramatic, with the mean time to solo for 42 students turning out to be 3.82 hours, as against 5.28 hours for a prior group of 48 students trained without the special procedures.

The implications of the many studies in which Fitts took a central role, and of others with which he was familiar, led him to single out three important suggestions. The first of these concerns *overpractice*. It is important to continue practice beyond the point at which some arbitrary criterion is met. This is particularly true if the task is one requiring habit-patterns that are not much practiced in ordinary experience. Extensive overtraining is needed to counteract the possibility of disintegration of such habits in periods of stress, likely, of course, to be met in combat. The second concerns *training in subroutines*. If parts of a task are clearly separable, it is desirable to have practice in these subroutines. If they can become automatized, then it is easier to add new aspects of a complex task. The illustration he uses is that of the pilot thoroughly familiar with his aircraft, who can then add a new task (such as a gunnery one) without losing control of his plane.

The third suggestion concerns *elimination of artificial limits to performance*. Studies of skilled performances carried on for long periods of time show that slight increases in speed tend to continue after errors have been virtually eliminated. Hence artificial barriers (such as instruments with fixed limits) are to be avoided, and encouragement should be given for continued improvement. The general improvement in competitive skills, such as running a mile race once a record has been broken, shows the importance of the motivational factor.

This all seems very plausible, but it is not very impressive as an outcome of such a tremendous amount of research effort, for essentially the same advice could have been given in 1910 on the basis of evidence then available. The main advance seems to have come in task description, not in psychological principles.

In another summary chapter, Fleishman (1962) reviews a slightly different approach to perceptual-motor skill learning. His taxonomy is based on a factor analysis of the abilities involved in different skills, at different stages of practice. Presumably the results of such a research enterprise ought to provide leads for skill teaching in the schools (reading and writing, computation, typing, etc.). His conclusions from the various studies for which he was responsible are (1) that the pattern of abilities contributing to the performance changes with practice, and (2) each task gives rise, at its later stages, to a factor specific to that stage of practice. Again we are confronted with the necessity of a prior task analysis, before suggestions for training can be given. *When there has been such an analysis,* it is possible to make use of some of the analytical information. Thus one factor analysis of a complex tracking task had shown the importance of spatial orientation early in training and multilimb coordination late in training. This knowledge was used later in giving special instructions first about spatial aspects of the task, and later about coordination requirements. When the results for the specially instructed groups were compared with two other groups, the instructed group was found to do better (Figure 16-1).

While this result is encouraging, it is not a very dramatic finding, and is, indeed, subject to some reservations. For one thing, no generalization from one task to another was involved, because the factor analysis had been done on exactly this task; it would ordinarily be clumsy to have to do a factor analysis for every specially arranged task to be taught. Second, the motivational control is somewhat inadequate, for there were no alternate instructions given with the same hope that they would lead to more effective performance.

If there is a lesson from both the Fitts and Fleishman summaries of motor-skill learning, it is that even what appear to be simple tasks are indeed quite complex, the psychological processes involved run the whole gamut from simple associative learning to higher forms of information processing, and, while research efforts are likely .o lead to some improvement in the efficiency of training, the results will seldom be very dramatic.

2. Trouble-shooting. The mushrooming of electronics equipment calls for the training of a great many technicians to keep the equipment in order. One of the things that has to be taught is how to find out what is the matter with a bit of equipment that doesn't work. This diagnostic

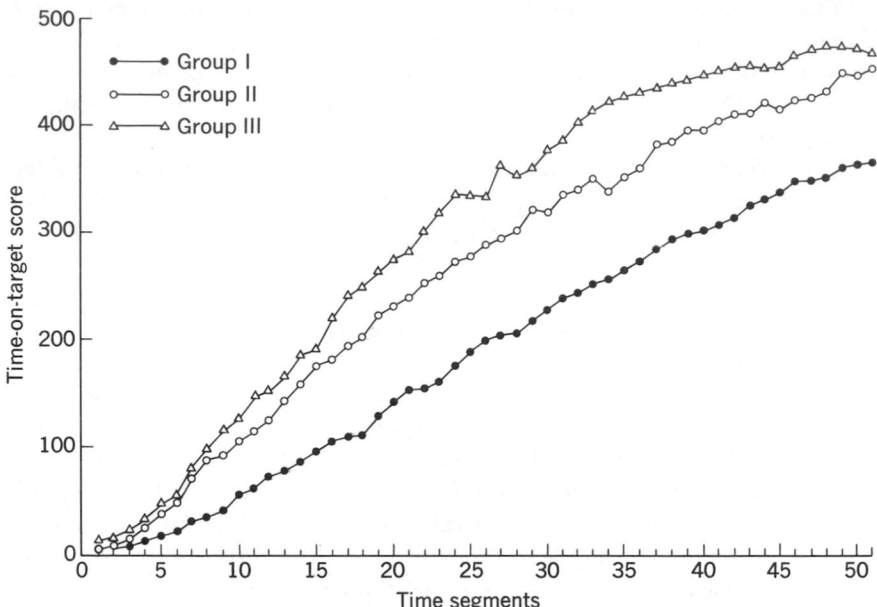

Figure 16-1   Training in a tracking task based on prior factorial analysis of component abilities. A time-on-target score is plotted for three groups, Group I with minimum instructions, Group II with "common sense" training, and Group III with training based on prior factor analysis. From Fleishman (1962, page 171), based on data from Parker and Fleishman.

task is known as "trouble-shooting" and is obviously a form of problem-solving. Bryan (1962) has discussed how this was taught to electronics technicians in the armed services. In one study, Bryan and Schuster (1959) divided a group of 162 students in a Navy Electronics Training School into a number of subgroups, trained by different methods to trouble-shoot a fairly complicated navigational aid (DAS-3 Loran). While sheer practice, without guidance, led to measurable improvement, various guidance techniques were better. One of the best made use of an instrument known as the Optimal Sequence Trainer. The trainee had to examine the symptom material given to him, and then decide what to check. If his choice did not agree with that of an expert (whose choices were coded into the machine) he had to try something else, until a green light came on. When the green light finally came on, he got the result of his check, and went on to the next. In this manner, he soon "learned to think like an expert," without having any formal pronouncements about trouble-shooting principles. In view of various theories of trouble-shooting (such as the advantage of the half-split technique, Miller, Folley, and Smith, 1953), it is a bit disconcerting to have the rather blind "apprentice" method work so well, though of course the optimal sequence may have had all the necessary "theory" built into it.[1]

3. Comments on training research. These few specimens of training research do not by any means exhaust what has been done, particularly in the use of various simulators, audio-visual aids, programs, and the preparation of countless manuals and training aids for specific devices or routines. The small sample of investigations was given for the purpose of raising the question of what happens in the interchange between theory and practice. With respect to motor skills, it was pointed out that principles derived from learning experiments did indeed guide those preparing an instructional plan for pilots, but the thing that impressed Fitts was the use of "intellectualization," a feature commonly missing from traditional laboratory studies of skill learning. The other impressive matter is the insistence on taxonomy, whether through a logical analysis of the requirements of the task, or one derived from factor analysis. The discussions of trouble-shooting went on with little reference to conventional learning principles. It appears that when the trainer is up against actual requirements then the nature of the tasks set, the abilities that are required, become of primary importance, and "principles of learning," however valid, fade into the background.

TECHNOLOGICAL AIDS IN TRAINING AND INSTRUCTION

Teachers have always used such aids to instruction as were available to them: slates, blackboards, libraries, textbooks, workbooks, laboratories, studios, stages, playgrounds. There have been educational innovations over the years, and educational technology, as such, is not new. What is new is the pace at which new devices have been developed, and a better opportunity to ask what research tells us about their effectiveness.

This is a book about learning theory, not about teaching. However, a review of some of the instructional aids will help highlight the interplay between theory and practice, and help us to find an acceptable position on the role of research. To this end four aids will be examined: simulators, films (including television), the language laboratory, and programed learning.

Simulators

Gagné (1962) has reviewed the successful use of simulators in military training, not only aircraft simulators for training pilots, but trainers

[1] The account may give the impression that trouble-shooting is easily taught. Actually the field is a large and difficult one, with many research reports. Standlee, Popham, and Fattu (1956) listed 110 studies in their annotated bibliography.

for aircraft controllers and control tower operators, missile guidance operators, and technicians of various kinds. He points out that it is not necessarily the *device* that is simulated, but the *operations* or *tasks* related to it: procedures, skills, identifications, trouble shooting, team skills, such as communication of information.

He believes that the educational use of simulators should be at fairly advanced stages of instruction, as in the training of civilian technicians, and perhaps in some kinds of performance assessment (e.g., assessment of automobile driving skill).

The generalizations, so far as theory of learning is concerned, again bear more upon task analysis than upon learning processes involved, though of course problems of degree of similarity between simulated and real situation have to be considered. This is essentially a practical matter, however, and not helped too much by theories of generalization and transfer.

Films and Television

Films and television are similar in that both use animated pictures with sound. Films may of course be presented over closed-circuit television sets, with some advantage in that room darkening is less necessary, and remote projectors or video tape recorders can present the films. Television may also be "live," again either from a remote source, or over closed-circuit from near sources, including the lecturer's own desk, if he wishes to permit a room full of students to look over his shoulder as he dissects or performs some other demonstration. We are not here interested in how the equipment can be made more convenient, although that of course has something to do with its use. Instead our concern is with the kind of teaching that takes place with such audio-visual aids.

In a very incisive review of the research on learning from films, Hoban (1960) classified the results of some 400 investigations of teaching films into three zones of certainty with respect to the findings: low certainty, intermediate certainty, and high certainty. To achieve high certainty results had to satisfy four criteria: (1) they should be intuitively reasonable, (2) they should have been reported by a competent and constructively imaginative investigator, (3) they should be related to some systematic formulation, and (4) the investigation should have been replicated. Other degrees of certainty were attached to those findings which did not satisfy these four criteria. Skipping over the findings of low and intermediate certainty (areas in which more research is urgently needed) we may examine the results that Hoban felt met his high-certainty criteria. These can be stated fairly concisely:

1. People learn from films.

2. Learning from films varies in amount with audience characteristics, such as age and formal education.
3. The amount of learning from films can be increased by the use of one or more of the following tested mechanisms and methods:
   a. *Redundancy.* Film-makers (and English teachers) make the use of redundancy an uphill fight, according to Hoban, yet repetition of information, even repetition of whole films, can be demonstrated to provide increments in learning.
   b. *Participation.* If student activity can be encouraged, such as answering questions inserted in a film, learning is enhanced, particularly if there is some feedback so that the student knows whether or not he answered correctly. Experimentation has shown that this is not merely a motivational device (to be sure that the student notices what is going on) but that there is a genuine practice effect from making relevant responses.
   c. *Attention-directing devices and methods.* A motion picture can use arrows that appear on a chart (or picture) to call attention to some feature, or in other ways can help the student search out the desired critical information. Such devices and teaching methods appropriate to them produce gains in learning from films.

Again, using this summary to ask about the background of learning theory, we find that the basic principles are familiar and not, as principles, very incisive: individual differences, repetition of presented materials and ideas, practice in making responses that are desired, paying attention to what is relevant. What is more important, as the actual research is studied, is how these principles are embodied in detail, taking into consideration again the structure of what is being taught.

The importance of task analysis is brought into focus again by some experiments on teaching by film conducted by Sheffield and Maccoby (1961), and their associates. They found, for example, that in teaching an assembly task, if the sequential task was broken down into distinctive subunits the total sequence was easily learned as a sequence of these subsequences. In line with Fitts' emphasis upon cognitive elements in skill-learning, they found a genuine gain from using what they called an "implosion" device in their filmed demonstrations of a sequential assembly (Sheffield, Margolius, and Hoehn, 1961). In this visual demonstration, parts of a subassembly are spread out before the viewer, and then each one "jumps" into its proper place in the proper sequence. The results, by several measures, showed the advantage of the implosion form of presentation (performance rate is plotted in Figure 16-2). The gains with the implosion device are all the more striking because without implosion these were already excellent instructional films, constructed on the basis of considerable prior research. The authors speak of implosion furthering a kind of *perceptual blueprinting* of the task, a statement reminiscent of Tolman's discussion of cognitive structures as maplike. We shall return later to some of the theory proposed by Sheffield and Maccoby.

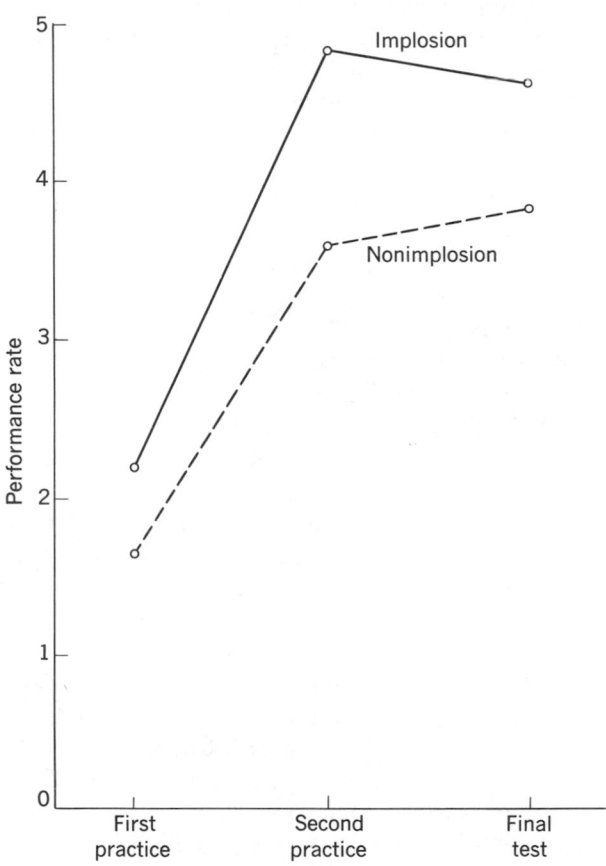

Figure 16-2   Performance rate in assembling a waste-gate motor following demonstration film with and without implosion (Sheffield, Margolius, and Hoehn, 1961, page 114).

The Language Laboratory

While in World War I we tended to show our distaste for the enemy by burning books and eliminating the teaching of the enemy's language, in World War II the importance of language learning was emphasized, and considerable effort was expended on ways to facilitate such learning. Here, if anywhere, we should expect a payoff for education, because language teaching has always been one of the standard school tasks, although there has been some vacillation between teaching the language as something to be spoken or as something to be read. The military training emphasized the spoken language, and the emphasis has shifted within schools and colleges back to the spoken language and away from reading knowledge. This has come about in part because better devices are available for bringing acceptably pronounced utterances to students in smaller schools who might lack teachers fully proficient in the language being taught.

A language laboratory is simply a class of devices which allows speech recorded on phonograph records, or now more commonly on electromagnetic tape, to be used in instruction. The more elaborate contemporary devices permit the student to imitate what is heard, and then to listen to his own production, or to have the teacher monitor what he has said. The "console" at which the teacher sits may have two-way communication with a number of students at once.

Sometimes the public impression is that the methods developed during the war were so revolutionary that language learning was easy. This is by no means the case. In the Army Language School at Monterey, California, a student typically spends nearly all of his time for 8 months working on a language if it is not one of the more difficult, and 12 months for the more difficult languages. Even so, many are unsuccessful. In one of the earlier studies of language learning in the armed services, Williams and Leavitt (1947) reported that 80 percent of those who undertook to learn Japanese dropped out before they completed their mastery of the language. There are no easy roads to the mastery of any difficult learning task.

Carroll (1963), reviewing research on foreign language teaching, gives the impression that we know next to nothing about the effectiveness of the procedures that have been adopted in language laboratories, such as the student hearing his own speech, practice on particular patterns of speech, and so on. Very little help has come from conventional laboratory learning experiments. For example, it might be supposed that the work on paired-associates learning is directly relevant to vocabulary learning, but as Carroll points out, vocabulary is not actually learned this way (particularly when the "natural method" is used in which only the language to be learned is the vehicle of communication). Furthermore, it assumes a one-to-one correspondence of words, which is inappropriate; a good bilingual speaker does not translate word for word.

There have been some reasonably satisfactory comparisons of the language laboratory type of teaching with conventional methods. Thus a study done by faculty members at Antioch College compared conventional teaching of 20 students in a class taught six times a week by a regular instructor with a language laboratory in which 60 students met twice a week with a regular instructor and four times a week with student laboratory assistants (Antioch College, 1960). The experimental procedures saved about 12 hours per week of the time of the regular instructors. The laboratory periods of one and one-half hours each were divided into the presentation of audio-visual materials (slides and accompanying tape-recorded sound), individual work in language laboratory booths, and drill and practice in face-to-face contact with the student assistants. In two separate years, achievement tests at the end of the year showed no significant differences to be attributed to the two forms of instruction; because the laboratory method was better liked by the students and saved the time of regular instructors, it still had something to recommend it. Pickrel, Neidt, and Gibson (1958) showed that teachers untrained in Spanish could teach conversational Spanish to seventh-grade students effectively if they based their teaching on tapes prepared by a specialist in Spanish; the children did not differ in oral fluency from those taught by the Spanish teacher. Thus the new methods offer promise, but no great revolution in teaching effectiveness. In the study just cited, the groups taught by the Spanish teacher were superior on written tests of Spanish to those taught by tapes.

In his analysis of what is involved in foreign language learning, Carroll (1962) identified the following aspects of foreign language aptitude: phonetic coding, grammatical sensitivity, rote memory for foreign language materials, and inductive language learning ability. It may be noted that the ordinary verbal factor or verbal knowledge factor (tested often by vocabulary in the familiar language) is not a good predictor of ability to learn a foreign language, in part because in the first stages of learning a foreign language it is not necessary to master a large vocabulary. In his model of the learning process as it applies to foreign language learning, he (Carroll, 1962, 1963) believes that success is a function of the following five elements, the first three of which reside in the learner, the final two in the instructional process:

1. The learner's language aptitude.
2. The learner's general intelligence.
3. The learner's perseverance.
4. The quality of the instruction.
5. The opportunity for learning afforded the student.

Again we note the importance of analyzing the nature of the performance both in order to specify the requisite component abilities and to design an appropriate instructional program.

Programed Learning

Attention to programed learning began with the introduction of the *teaching machine* as a technological aid, although, as we shall see, the essence of programing does not reside in the particular kind of equipment used. The first of these machines was developed by Sidney L. Pressey at Ohio State University many years ago (Pressey, 1926, 1927). While originally developed as a self-scoring machine to facilitate the taking and scoring of objective examinations, the machine soon demonstrated its ability to actually teach. The student reads the question presented in the aperture of the machine, selects an answer from among several alternatives, and then presses the button corresponding to this chosen answer. If he is correct, the next question appears in the slot; if he has made a mistake, the original question remains. The machine counts his errors but the tape does not move on to the next question until the right button has been pressed. Because the student knows that he is correct when the question moves, he has immediate information (reinforcement, feedback) and thus he learns while testing himself. Because the machine has counted his errors, his score can be read off as soon as he has finished taking the test. This machine of Pressey's did not become popular, although a number of studies by him and his students showed it to be effective as a teaching device.

A new forward push was given to the idea of automatic self-instruction by the publication of a paper by Skinner (1954), whose operant conditioning work had already given him authority in the field of learning. The time was now right, and work on teaching machines and programed learning flourished shortly thereafter. Now it is a very large-scale international scientific, educational, and commercial enterprise. Skinner's machine differed from Pressey's chiefly in that the student was not given alternatives to choose from, but instead was asked to write his own response in the spaces provided, and then, as a printed tape advanced, the correct answer appeared for comparison with what he had written. He thus "emitted" his own response to be "reinforced" by the comparison response. A further difference is involved, in that the material is so planned that it is not essentially a review of partially learned material, but rather a "program" in which the responses of the learner are "shaped" as he learns. We shall return to the problems of programming after considering another set of technological aids.

Far more complex instructional devices have been developed beyond those of Pressey and Skinner. Quite different sets of devices were developed somewhat earlier in the U.S. Air Force. Lumsdaine, who had a prominent role in their development, has given a description of some of them (Lumsdaine, 1959). For example, in one arrangement a step-by-step film projection is used to teach a technician how to operate a piece of electronic equipment. A single demonstrational segment appears on the screen until the learner has mastered it. He then presses the button to bring on the next illustration, and so on, until he has learned the complete operation. Modern electronic computers have been brought into the picture, occasionally to combine slide projection, motion picture projection, and other materials within the program for a single learner, occasionally to make possible the management of learning for a group of learners. The flexibility provided makes possible almost any arrangement that the investigator desires, as long as the costs can be met.

The essence of learning by means of a teaching machine lies not in the machinery but in the material to be presented, and it has been found that properly designed programed books can serve about the same purpose as the simpler forms of teaching machines. The simple machines are sometimes derogated as "mechanical page turners" because they do little more than the student can as well do for himself. Obviously the more complex machines do much more than this, but the teasing of the simple machine is intended to point to the importance of the program over the technology. The programed book is not to be confused with the earlier "workbook" in common educational use; the "workbook" was primarily a place to practice on examples of what had been taught by the teacher or a textbook, but the program is designed to do the teaching itself. Hence the program necessarily must begin with what the learner already knows, and it then adds to this by supplying answers that are at first *hinted at* or *prompted* in order to make the correct answers highly probable. These answers, once "reinforced," are then overlearned through their repeated use as new material is grafted on that already learned. It is evident that the person who constructs a program must be aware of the *organization of knowledge,* both its logical organization and its psychological organization, in order to build knowledge and understanding in this way. The programer does his best to anticipate what will happen, but in practice he corrects the programs through tryout until the program can be mastered by its intended learners with a minimum of errors, usually in one run through the program. The result of the learning is then tested by a conventional-type examination to see if the material has indeed been mastered and can be applied appropriately in new contexts.

In order to correct misapprehensions about programing being just another form of mass education, Skinner (1958) made the case for a similarity between programed instruction and individual tutoring. He pointed out several resemblances to a tutor:

1. A good tutor begins where the pupil is, and does not insist on moving beyond what the pupil can comprehend.
2. A good tutor moves at the rate that is consistent with the ability of the pupil to learn.
3. A good tutor does not permit false answers to remain uncorrected.
4. A good tutor does not lecture; instead by his hints and questioning he helps the pupil to find and state answers for himself.

According to Skinner, these qualities are all found in a good program.

Varieties of programing. The type of program advocated by Skinner, that which moves step by step through a single set of materials, has come to be called *linear programing.* Another type, commonly associated with the name of Norman Crowder, is called a *branching program.*[2] In the programed books which use this method (e.g., Crowder and Martin, 1961), multiple-choice answers are provided, and the answer the student selects directs him to a different page in the book. The book is thus a "scrambled one" which is read most irregularly. The correct answer leads to a page on which the next bit of instruction is given, with new alternatives. An incorrect answer is pointed out, with some comments as to why this might have been selected, and then the learner is sent back to make another choice. Crowder believes that students who are ill-prepared should always have a way to go back to simpler materials, and if well-prepared should be able to bypass some of the material; hence his later developments provide for these alternative paths through the material. Linear programs of more modern sort also provide for some kind of review for those who wish to go back to earlier parts of the program, and some kind of skipping for those ready to go ahead (Markle, 1963). Computer-based programs provide the maximum amount of flexibility in these respects, including alternative paths and different examples for those who may need them. Thus programing is no more a single line of development than the teaching machine is a single type of equipment.

Some problems within programed learning. The literature on programed learning has been building up at an accelerated rate, so that a review at this time would soon be outmoded (Figure 16-3). Still a few of

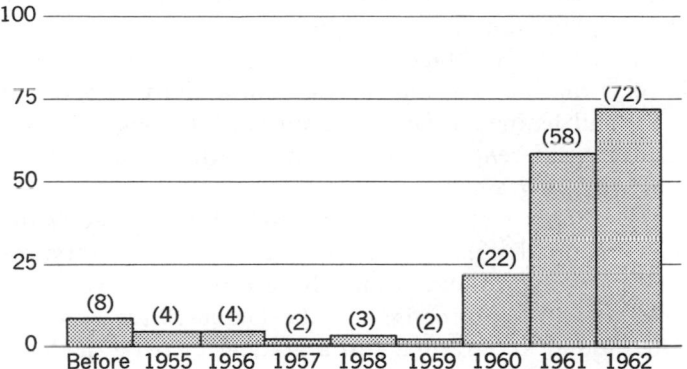

| Figure 16-3 | Research papers on programed learning (after Schramm, 1964d, page 465). |

---

[2] Another name is *intrinsic* programing. Although this is Crowder's own name for his program (e.g., Crowder, 1959), it is less descriptive than *branching.*

the pressing problems can be highlighted, with some illustrations of the results of investigation.

Schramm (1964a), having reviewed some 165 papers on programed learning, was able to summarize some of the generalizations that could be made from the research reports at that time. Because his summaries, and a number of others, are readily available,[3] what he reports will be digested without references to the original sources. He begins by asking the general question, do students learn from programed instruction? The answer is clearly in the affirmative, but we need more information to know whether or not programed instruction is a more efficient form of instruction than other forms that we now use. Of 36 reports comparing programs with conventional classroom instruction (at all levels from primary school to college and adult education) the general summary is that 17 showed superiority for programed over conventional instruction, 18 showed no significant difference, and but 1 showed a f.nal superiority for the conventional classroom method. While such a summary has its defects, there is little doubt that programing is an educational method to be taken seriously.

With respect to more analytical problems of the program, Schramm considers a number of questions which have troubled programers:

1. *Is the ordered sequence essential?* The assumption in most programs is that the substance in the form of "frames" is arranged in an optimum order for learning, the later knowledge being built upon the earlier. Even something as plausible as this can be questioned on the basis of research findings. Of five studies comparing the immediate and delayed post-test results of an ordered sequence with a random ordering, three showed no difference, one showed an immediate advantage for the ordered sequence, but none on a delayed test, and only one showed clear advantage for the ordered sequence! In a different kind of experiment, but not unrelated, Mager (1961b) permitted some electronics students to do their own sequencing by asking questions. They were highly motivated, and learned what was required, but their orders of presentation were very different from the orders in which the topics would typically have been programed.

2. *Are short steps to be preferred?* The typical Skinnerian program moves in small steps, leading the students along very gradually. While, with a few exceptions, studies have come out favorable to small steps, some kind of compromise may be better. Thus Maccoby and Sheffield (1961) found an advantage in a gradual increase in the size of step in a demonstrational film sequence before interrupting for practice.

[3] For example, Coulson (1961), Galanter (1959), Hanson (1963), Lumsdaine (1961, 1962, 1963, 1964), Lumsdaine and Glaser (1960), Schramm (1964b), Smith and Moore (1962).

3. *What form of response is to be preferred?* Skinner favored a response constructed by the learner, hence "emitted" by him, rather than some other form of response, such as selecting from a group of multiple-choice possibilities. The research results are confusing, usually with no significant difference between constructed and multiple-choice responses, and often no difference between overt and covert (thinking) responses. In some cases, presenting the word normally sought as a reply, underlined for emphasis, works as well as having the student actually write the response himself, and this, of course, saves the student a great deal of time (when it works). The research is beginning to sharpen those circumstances under which one form of response is better than another, and the differential effects on long-term retention. In any case, dogmatic assertions are inappropriate in view of the varied findings.

4. *Is immediate knowledge of results helpful?* In the theory of programed learning no principle taken over from the laboratory has had more prominence than "reinforcement" or "feedback," in the form of immediate knowledge of results. While the results are generally favorable to knowledge of results, they are not universally so; delay may not matter, and confirmatory knowledge on but a fraction of the trials (corresponding to "intermittent reinforcement") may be just as effective as every-trial feedback. It may be that in well-cued programs there are so few errors that the learner knows he is correct when he catches the cue, without any external verification.

As in laboratory types of reinforcement, some cue other than a fully informative one may be used. Such cues have been compared with the informative type of feedback in which the correct answer is given as reinforcement. Apparently trinkets, small monetary rewards, or flashing lights can be used to reinforce correct responses in programed learning, with results not significantly different from the more usual informative feedback.

It should be pointed out that what is learned is not limited to the response that eventually appears in the space provided for responses, for this response, like other cues used for reinforcement, is designed to reinforce the behavior that leads to the response. This behavior presumably depends upon the comprehension of a line of thought. To make this clear, consider a program designed in true-false style, so that all blanks can be filled in by either "yes" or "no." Such a program could teach, but it would be teaching something besides how to emit "yes" and "no." This means that a program should not be judged by examining the tape to see what answers occur on it; such an appraisal could be very misleading. It would be something like judging an arithmetic test by seeing a set of numerical answers to its questions, without inquiring what the operations were that these answers served to check.

5. *Should the learner set his own pace?* One of the intuitively appealing features of programed instruction is that it recognizes individual differences in the learner, and each learner is free to move through the program at his own pace. The results are, however, not unequivocably in favor of self-pacing. Schramm found two studies in which self-pacing was indeed better than external pacing, but he located eight others in which no significant differences were found. These included presentations by teaching machines, programed texts, television and films. An interesting conjecture by Frye (1963) was that self-pacing would prove more advantageous for heterogenous groups of students than for more homogeneous ones, a result which he found to be the case. He reasoned that for students of equal background and ability, self-pacing would not be necessary to meet individual differences in rate of learning.

While many other comparisons have been made (linear vs branching programs, sex differences, the use of explanations supplementing informative feedback, programs as supplementary to textbook material vs teaching by program alone, having more than one student use the same program and discuss their answers) the foregoing questions, with their tentative answers, help orient us to the place of programing in relation to learning theory.

It is often supposed that programs are appropriate chiefly for materials that can be learned by "drill," that is, materials subject to rote learning, such as number combinations, vocabulary, geographical locations. This is a mistake; in fact, the programed method is cumbersome for teaching such materials and is better adapted to more complexly structured bodies of materials in which what is learned later depends upon what has been learned before. A quite satisfactory programed book exists on teaching the appreciation of poetry (Reid, Ciardi, and Perrine, 1963), and programing has been used to train for creativity and problem-solving (Crutchfield, 1965). It is evident that the programing method is not limited to any one kind of subject-matter.

There remain the questions about the extent to which programing has been adopted in school systems, and what its success has been when used in a wholesale fashion. The most informative report to date is another one edited by Schramm (1964b), which reports on experiences in four widely separated geographical locations: Manhasset, New York; Denver, Colorado; Chicago, Illinois; and Provo, Utah. The Manhasset experience (Herbert and Foshay, 1964) is that of a junior high school that pioneered in introducing programs, but after three years of sympathetic encouragement by the principal, only one program, having to do with English grammar, remained in regular use. The Denver schools spent three years in which they made their own programs in grammar, Spanish, French, and one on the constitution (Schramm, 1964c). While they interpret this experience as valuable, they believe that in the future they will use more commercial programs. In one of the studies on the advantages of individualization of instruction, a comparison was made of which students, according to ability level, profited most from the program on English usage. The hope of programing is that individual differences will be reduced, but this was not found to be the case: the students who profited most were the superior ones, although they complained most about the programs. The least able students (in the so-called modified classes) learned more from regular class instruction than from the programs. The report on experiences in the Chicago area (Thelen and Ginther, 1964) draws some generalizations from a number of different tryouts of programed learning. The authors conclude that programed materials used by themselves are likely to satisfy neither pupils nor teachers; the programs will have to be more fully appropriate to a pupil's individual needs, and some kinds of reward beyond the program's self-contained feedback will have to be provided for the pupil working alone with a program. Individualized instruction—each pupil moving at his own rate—conflicts with the notion of "teaching a class," and makes it difficult to use the other enriching experiences open to the teacher and pupil. Thus far the programs have failed "to turn education into a meaningful inquiry by the students." The experiences in the Brigham Young University Laboratory School (Edling, 1964) are among the more encouraging. The school has operated since 1959 on what is called a Continuous Progress Plan, whereby the student moves through the school at his own rate, and is thus unusually well prepared for the use of programed instruction. Even in this favorable setting it is clear that programed materials will be used to supplement rather than supplant present teaching methods and materials. The need for better and more widely ranging programs is evident. Programs use teacher time as well as save it; teachers will probably have to be given more clerical help than is usually provided them if many programs are adopted.

Comments on Technological Aids

The brief characterizations of the research on simulators, teaching by films and television, the language laboratory, and programed learning, help to create a context in which to discuss the role of learning research and learning theory in relation to practical problems. It is abundantly clear that each new device requires research to find its most appropriate use; in no case is a derivation from learning theory sufficient to specify just what arrangement will be most feasible. This does not imply, however, that learning theory is either invalid or impractical. We shall turn now to a consideration of its role in relation to the kinds of learning tasks that have just been reviewed.

APPLICABILITY OF LEARNING "PRINCIPLES" AND OF LEARNING THEORIES

It is a purpose of basic research to question assumptions and to attempt to make our knowledge more precise and more systematic. Basic research is necessarily patient, working on such problems as are manageable at present. Applied research, however, must move ahead and solve as best it can the pressing problems. Hence basic research looks for weaknesses in present conceptions that need re-examination; applied research looks to what we now know well enough to provide hints upon which we can make decisions affecting the present. It turns out that many of the quarrels of the theorists are over matters of uncertainty, important to them in establishing a firmer foundation for their theories, but not very important in relation to problems of training. There are, in fact, a great many experimental relationships of practical importance upon which the theorists are in substantial agreement. We shall examine these first, and then turn to some attempts to use more unified theory in relation to practice.

Some "Principles" Potentially Useful in Practice

The reason for writing "principles" in quotation marks is that the generalizations to be listed are mere summarizations of empirical relationships that hold rather widely, although many of them are not stated with sufficient precision to consider them to be "laws" of learning. Students of learning who have not devoted themselves primarily to problems of instruction can still give some very useful advice. Some of this advice comes from those whose orientation is toward S–R theories, some from those who are oriented toward cognitive theories, some from those whose concern is with motivation and personality. The following suggestions for practice are in large part acceptable to all parties (with reservations with respect to detailed applicability that the foregoing account of training research makes necessary); the assignment to one or another source is a matter of emphasis (and vocabulary) rather than an indication that the statement is controversial.[4]

A. *Principles emphasized within S–R theory*
   1. The learner should be *active,* rather than a passive listener or viewer. The S–R theory emphasizes the significance of the learner's *responses,* and "learning by doing" is still an acceptable slogan.
   2. *Frequency of repetition* is still important in acquiring skill, and in bringing enough overlearning to guarantee retention. One does not learn

[4] The suggestions have been adapted from Hilgard, 1960, with some changes.

to type, or to play the piano, or to speak a foreign language, without some repetitive practice.

3. *Reinforcement* is important; that is, repetition should be under arrangements in which desirable or correct responses are rewarded. While there are some lingering questions over details, it is generally found that positive reinforcements (rewards, successes) are to be preferred to negative reinforcements (punishments, failures).

4. *Generalization* and *discrimination* suggest the importance of practice in varied contexts, so that learning will become (or remain) appropriate to a wider (or more restricted) range of stimuli.

5. *Novelty* in behavior can be enhanced through imitation of models, through cueing, through "shaping," and is not inconsistent with a liberalized S–R approach to learning.

6. *Drive conditions* are important in learning, but all personal–social motives do not conform to the drive-reduction principles based on food-deprivation experiments. Issues concerning drives exist within S–R theory; at a practical level it may be taken for granted that motivational conditions are important.

7. *Conflicts* and *frustrations* arise inevitably in the process of learning difficult discriminations and in social situations in which irrelevant motives may be aroused. Hence these have to be recognized and their resolution or accommodation provided for.

B. *Principles emphasized within cognitive theory.*

1. The *perceptual features* according to which the problem is displayed to the learner are important conditions of learning (figure-ground relations, directional signs, "what-leads-to-what," organic interrelatedness). Hence a learning problem should be so structured and presented that the essential features are open to the inspection of the learner.

2. The *organization of knowledge* should be an essential concern of the teacher or educational planner. Thus the direction from simple to complex is *not* from arbitrary, meaningless parts to meaningful wholes, but instead from *simplified wholes* to *more complex wholes*. The part–whole problem is therefore an organizational problem, and cannot be dealt with apart from a theory of how complexity is patterned.

3. *Learning with understanding* is more permanent and more transferable than rote learning or learning by formula. Expressed in this form the statement belongs in cognitive theory, but S–R theories make a related emphasis upon the importance of meaningfulness in learning and retention.

4. *Cognitive feedback* confirms correct knowledge and corrects faulty learning. The notion is that the learner tries something provisionally and then accepts or rejects what he does on the basis of its consequences. This is of course the cognitive equivalent of reinforcement in S–R theory but

cognitive theory tends to place more emphasis upon a kind of hypothesis-testing through feedback.

5. *Goal-setting* by the learner is important as motivation for learning and his successes and failures are determiners of how he sets future goals.

6. *Divergent thinking,* which leads to inventive solutions of problems or to the creation of novel and valued products, is to be nurtured along with *convergent* thinking, which leads to logically correct answers. Such divergent thinking requires the subject to perceive himself as potentially creative through appropriate support (feedback) for his tentative efforts at originality.

C. *Principles from motivation and personality theory.*

1. The learner's *abilities* are important, and provisions have to be made for slower and more rapid learners, as well as for those with specialized abilities.

2. *Postnatal development* may be as important as hereditary and congenital determiners of ability and interest. Hence the learner must be understood in terms of the influences that have shaped his development.

3. Learning is *culturally relative,* and both the wider culture and the subculture to which the learner belongs may affect his learning.

4. *Anxiety level* of the individual learner may determine the beneficial or detrimental effects of certain kind of encouragements to learn. The generalization appears justified that with some kinds of tasks high-anxiety learners perform better if *not* reminded of how well (or poorly) they are doing, while low-anxiety learners do better if they *are* interrupted with comments on their progress.

5. The same objective situation may tap *appropriate motives* for one learner and not for another, as for example, in the contrast between those motivated by affiliation and those motivated by achievement.

6. The *organization of motives* and values within the individual is relevant. Some long-range goals affect short-range activities. Thus college students of equal ability may do better in courses perceived as relevant to their majors than in those perceived as irrelevant.

7. The *group atmosphere* of learning (competition vs cooperation, authoritarianism vs democracy, individual isolation vs group identification) will affect satisfaction in learning as well as the products of learning.

If one reviews such a list of suggestions as the foregoing, it becomes apparent that laboratory knowledge does not lead automatically to its own applications. Any teacher reading the list will say: "How can I do these desirable things, with the many pupils in my classes, and with the many demands upon me?" Or even: "How would I do it if I had only a single student to tutor?" As in the development of any technology, further steps are needed between the pure science stage and the ready application of what has been found out.

It is still worthwhile to attempt to assemble suggestions such as these from the general knowledge of learning, for then the steps of application will presumably be taken more economically.

Approaches to Practical Problems Via Unified Theories

The effort to arrive at unified conceptions of learning is commendable. The scientific enterprise tends in general to favor elegant and simple theories; parsimony and esthetic appeal help guide the search for comprehensive theories. Within applied science, however, the constraints are somewhat different. For one thing, applied science cannot wait for the answers of pure science to come in: crops have to be planted and gathered, the sick have to be treated, and children have to be taught with whatever tools and knowledge are now available. It is natural that in the early development of the relevant sciences the applied users, the technologists, will tend to be eclectic, picking up a plausible idea here and there, and using it somewhat inventively in the practical situation. Thus skilled teachers contribute to educational advance, with students of the psychology of learning sometimes bringing up the rear. Only when science is further advanced can pure science take the lead in developing practice, as it does in the aiming of shots to the moon.

The option is still open of attempting to guide practical developments by way of one or the other of the prevailing theories, or by developing some new model which has more unity than a set of eclectic "principles." Some psychologists have chosen this approach, and a number of their positions may be examined briefly in turn. The classical position in this respect was of course that of Thorndike, for his position on learning was developed as an educational psychology, with its emphasis upon elements, transfer, measurement, and the law of effect. The functionalism of John Dewey, although a related viewpoint, had a very different influence upon the schools; while his position was called "experimentalism" it was not synonymous with the "experimentation" of Thorndike, and, while victorious over Thorndike in some respects (McDonald, 1964), it did not lead to much research within educational psychology. The exciting newcomer on the field in the 1930's was gestalt psychology, which became the accepted educational psychology for a time, but its excesses in the hands of some of its educational enthusiasts, who were not experimentally oriented, led to its declining influence (Hilgard, 1964c). We may, for illustrative purposes, consider four of the views represented in earlier chapters (Guthrie, Skinner, Hull, and gestalt) in terms of some contemporaries who have attempted to use these theories in relation to practical problems, and then turn to one newer viewpoint, that of Gagné, which uses a hierarchical set of principles, possibly less unified than the major theories, but more unified than a sheer empiricism.

1. Applications of Guthrie's contiguous conditioning. In giving a rationale for their applied psychological research, Lumsdaine, Sheffield, and Maccoby, all at one time students of Guthrie, defer repeatedly to his theoretical position.

Lumsdaine (1964), for example, believes that much that is done in programed learning can be accounted for better according to Guthrie's views than according to Skinner's. The chief issue is over *prompting* vs *shaping*.[5] According to Guthrie, one learns by assimilating cues to responses, so that the *cueing* of responses follows directly from his theory. The programer frequently does just that: he tries to give enough cues to guarantee a high order of successful responses. Maintaining the responses with fewer stimulus supports ("fading") is also coherent with Guthrie's theory. This emphasis upon the *responses* of the learner, reflected in the title of one of the books that Lumsdaine edited, *Student responses in programed instruction* (Lumsdaine, 1961), follows from Guthrie's position that we learn what we do. Skinner's emphasis upon the role of reinforcement, by contrast, emphasizes the rewarding of approximate responses, and then, through differential reinforcement, strengthening those responses that better meet the specifications of what is wanted. While this works pretty well in free operant behavior, the programed type of learning is more constricted, and, according to Lumsdaine, the practice accords more to cueing and prompting than to shaping.

Sheffield (1961) outlined the theory that guided the work that he and Maccoby and their collaborators did on learning complex sequential tasks from combinations of filmed demonstrations and practice. Sheffield's theory is pure Guthrie[6] (association by contiguity, referred to as conditioning), except for an important amendment: perceptual responses are said to follow the same principles as motor responses. It must be noted that this does *not* mean that perceptual responses *are* motor responses (e.g., discriminatory reactions, subvocal speech, etc.), but rather that one can take them for what they are phenomenally, and then apply the associative rules to them.

The position taken here is that what is usually called "perception" refers to cases in which the immediate sensory stimulation is not only eliciting its innate sensory responses, but is also eliciting other sensory responses which have been conditioned to the immediate stimulation in past experience (Sheffield, 1961, page 15).

[5] The notions of *prompting, shaping,* and *fading* are all from within Skinner's conceptions of programing. We are here concerned with the theory of their operation.
[6] See earlier discussion in Chapter 4.

The word "response" has here lost its original behaviorist meaning of a muscular movement or a glandular secretion; a new category of innate response, *sensory response*, has been added, which, through conditioning, becomes a perceptual response. This gives Sheffield great freedom in introducing cognitive processes into an essentially S–R type of system. For example:

In the same vein, a wristwatch is completely "transparent" to a skilled watch repairman. From the outside he can note the distinctive brand and model; this is sufficient for him to "fill in" all of the internal parts—their sizes, shapes, arrangements, and so forth. When he takes the watch apart he is completely prepared for everything he sees because his anticipatory conditioned sensory responses correspond with his immediate unconditioned sensory responses when he opens it and makes the inner works visible (Sheffield, 1961, page 16).

Without questioning either the validity or the usefulness of the ideas embodied in this quotation, it is the kind of statement, which had it been expressed in terms of sensations and their revival as images, would have been most repugnant to an early behaviorist. It is clear enough that a functionalist would accept such a statement, but even a contemporary S–R theorist must have some trouble with this kind of response. Having ignored this hurdle, Sheffield is able to do some very cogent theorizing about what goes on in sequence learning, and in response organization. Many of the conceptions have overtones of gestalt or cognitive theory, such as the distinction between *imposed* and *inherent* organization, "natural units" of a sequential task, perceptual "blueprinting." The concept of natural structure was much emphasized by Wertheimer, and the notion of mapping, as mentioned earlier, by Tolman. Although in Sheffield's opinion he has gone beyond gestalt or cognitive psychology in deriving their truths from conditioning theory, the major leap is to interpreting organization in perception as the conditioning of innate sensory responses. Whether or not one sees these additions as natural extensions or consequences of Guthrie's theory, from a practical standpoint one can only celebrate the trend toward consensus on some of the implications for instruction.

2. Applications of Skinner's operant conditioning. Part of Skinner's success in gaining adoption for programed learning (originally for the teaching machine) came because of his insistence that he was basing this instructional device strictly on what had been found out from his experiments on rats and pigeons. The major concepts of emitted response and its strengthening through carefully timed reinforcement, of the importance of reward over punishment, of shaping through small-step gains, of the subject's control of his own pace, all came from the experimental background of operant conditioning. In his original announcement of programed learning, Skinner (1954) was very clear that he was deriving the principles of programed learning from his laboratory work; the child was simply a new organism to be studied:

There are certain questions which have to be answered in turning to the study of any new organism. What behavior is to be set up? What reinforcers are at hand? What responses are available in embarking upon a program of progressive approximation which will lead to the final form of the behavior? How can reinforcements be most efficiently scheduled to maintain the behavior in strength? These questions are all relevant in considering the problem of the child in the lower grades (Skinner, 1954, page 93).

The notion of shaping through reinforcement is clearly implied. One of his associates enunciated the laboratory principles as they applied to programed learning as suggested by the following six topics (Holland, 1960):
1. Immediate reinforcement.
2. Emitted behavior.
3. Gradual progression to complex repertoires.
4. Fading; gradual withdrawal of stimulus support.
5. Controlling observing (attentive) behavior.
6. Discrimination training (abstractions; concepts).

There can be little doubt that the background of laboratory experience contributed strongly to what was done in Skinner's laboratory as programing was introduced.

Several comments are in order. In the first place, the direct application of these principles has not proved to be universally the only efficient way in which to proceed. Reservations apply to immediate reinforcement, the necessity to emit behavior (in the form of constructed responses), even to some aspects of gradual progression. Others have also noted that Skinner has not moved as directly from his free operant model as his writings sometimes have suggested; for example, Zeaman (1959) showed that it would be possible to consider programed learning as an illustration not of a free operant but of a controlled operant, and in some respects like classical conditioning. Finally, specific inventiveness, ingenuity, and empiricism (revising programs through tryout) have played a role equal to that of any generalizations from the animal laboratory. Hence all credit is due to Skinner, but not necessarily on the basis of the authority of any principles learned from the rat or the pigeon.

3. Drive-reinforcement theory applied in the Miller-Dollard version. Miller and Dollard (1941) introduced a simplified version of a theory very near to that of Hull in which they stressed the sequence drive-cue-response-reward, a theory since developed more fully by Miller (1959). Miller has shown that his less mathematical version of a theory similar in type to Hull's can be used to derive practical consequences. This is best illustrated by way of a small book on graphical methods in education that Miller edited, and much of which he wrote (Miller, 1957).

In applying his theory to propose the conditions for maximum learning from motion pictures, Miller fell back upon the four-stage analysis he and Dollard had originally proposed:

1. Drive: The student must want something.
2. Cue: The student must notice something.
3. Response: The student must do something.
4. Reward: The student must get something he wants.

This manner of talking about what Hull would have talked about in terms of stimuli, reaction potential, habit strength, and drive, permits Miller to summarize the findings from experiments in a very sensible manner. The outline proved not quite sufficient, however, and he added another chapter after one on each of these four stages. The added chapter discussed such issues as the specificity versus generality of the influence of watching a teaching film, the superiority of logical over rote learning, meaningfulness and organization of material, forgetting and review, the value of demonstrating errors (as well as correct responses) in the visual material, dramatic versus expository presentation, types of audience, and the need to train students to profit from films.

While the theory thus provides a structure around which to give an exposition of research, a reader cannot but note how few of the principles from research of other kinds give any very direct guidance for motion picture learning, and how other principles, besides the more formal ones, seem necessary when a practical instructional situation is to be faced.

4. The applicability of Gagné's hierarchical model. The only new model being introduced here is that of Gagné (1965). He accepts eight types or categories of learning, each with its own rules, but arranges them in a hierarchy from simple to complex, on the assumption that each higher order learning depends upon the mastery of the one below it. Hence the theory is not strictly an eclectic theory (which chooses good principles from here and there without any order among them), but is the beginning of a unified theory on the assumption that appropriate transformation equations could be found for moving from one level to the next. The proposal of eight kinds of learning is sufficiently elaborated to be deserving of review.

His own summary of the eight types is as follows (Gagné, 1965, pages 58-59).

Type 1. Signal learning. The individual learns to make a general diffuse response to a signal. This is the classical conditioned response of Pavlov (1927).

Type 2. Stimulus–response learning. The learner acquires a precise response to a discriminated stimulus. What is learned is a connection

(Thorndike, 1898) or a discriminated operant (Skinner, 1938), sometimes called an instrumental response (Kimble, 1961).

Type 3. Chaining. What is acquired is a chain of two or more stimulus–response connections. The conditions for such learning have been described by Skinner (1938) and others, notably by Gilbert (1962b).

Type 4. Verbal association. Verbal association is the learning of chains that are verbal. Basically the conditions resemble those for other (motor) chains. However, the presence of language in the human being makes this a special type because internal links may be selected from the individual's previously learned repertoire of language (cf. Underwood, 1964).

Type 5. Multiple discrimination. The individual learns to make n different identifying responses to as many different stimuli, which may resemble each other in physical appearance to a greater or lesser degree. Although the learning of each stimulus–response connection is a simple Type 2 occurrence, the connections tend to interfere with each other's retention (cf. Postman, 1961b).

Type 6. Concept learning. The learner acquires a capability of making a common response to a class of stimuli that may differ from each other widely in physical appearance. He is able to make a response that identifies an entire class of objects or events (cf. Kendler, 1964).

Type 7. Principle learning. In simplest terms, a principle is a chain of two or more concepts. It functions to control behavior in the manner suggested by a verbalized rule of the form "If A, then B," where A and B are concepts. However, it must be carefully distinguished from the mere verbal sequence "If A, then B," which, of course, may be learned as Type 4.

Type 8. Problem solving. Problem solving is a kind of learning that requires the internal events usually called thinking. Two or more previously acquired principles are somehow combined to produce a new capability that can be shown to depend on a "higher-order" principle.

The notion that each of the higher stages requires the next lower as a prerequisite is limited for Gagné only by some uncertainty with respect to Types 1 and 2; he is not convinced with Mowrer (1960) that Type 2 has Type 1 as its essential background.

Gagné rejects the interpretation that learning is basically the same for all types; their differences are said to be more important than their similarities. Despite the position of conditioning at the base of the hierarchy, the sufficiency of conditioning is pointedly rejected:

> There can be little doubt that Watson's idea that most forms of human learning can be accounted for as chains of conditioned responses is wildly incorrect; and this has been pretty generally conceded for many years (Gagné, 1965, page 13).

It is intuitively clear that Gagné, having proposed so many different kinds of learning, will find it relatively easy to describe many kinds of school learning according to one or another of his types. It is not so clear, however, how he will work in the concept of hierarchy.

Two conceptions of hierarchy have to be distinguished. One of these is the hierarchy of learning types (from Type 1 through Type 8); another is the organization of knowledge according to hierarchies of principles, all of which may be, for example, at the learning level of Type 7. How Gagné deals with these matters can best be illustrated by examples.

Gagné has illustrated the hierarchical organization of school instruction, according to his types, for mathematics, science, foreign languages, and English (1965, pages 175-203). The structure for reading is reproduced in Figure 16-4.

While there is a certain plausibility to such an outline as that of Figure 16-4, it is by no means clear that a sequence of instruction can be designed upon it, or that the basic notion is sound that the lower steps of the hierarchy have to be mastered before the higher steps can be learned. There may well be a kind of cyclical development in learning, in which the various stages repeatedly assert themselves.

When actual empirical studies are done, they tend to deal with the second concept of hierarchy, that is, of hierarchies of principles at a single stage of learning (e.g., Gagné and others, 1962; Gagné and Bassler, 1963). Gagné has used some principles implied in the understanding of the vector resolution of forces (all at the level of Type 7 in the hierarchy of learning types) to show what he means (Figure 16-5). In order to understand the principle at the top of the hierarchy (to identify horizontal and vertical components of forces as vectors) it is necessary to act in accordance with all of the principles lower in the hierarchy.

A strong emphasis within Gagné's analysis is upon *the structure of knowledge,* an important supplement to principles of learning whenever a practical instructional task is under consideration.[7]

Some Comments on Theory and Practice

The review of "principles" and of the effort to make use of unified theories tends to substantiate the conclusions arrived at in the review of training and technology. When the practical conditions of learning

[7] Emphasis upon the structure of knowledge appears also in the writings of Bruner (1960, 1964), whose position is well summarized in the often-quoted hypothesis that "any subject can be taught effectively in some intellectually honest form to any child at any stage of development" (1960, page 33). This position reflects to some extent an influence from Piaget (e.g., Piaget, 1952). The meaning of Piaget for learning theory has not been well enough worked out for exposition here, but attention may be called again to the work of Aebli (1951), and to the discussion of education and learning in Flavell (1963, pages 365-379).

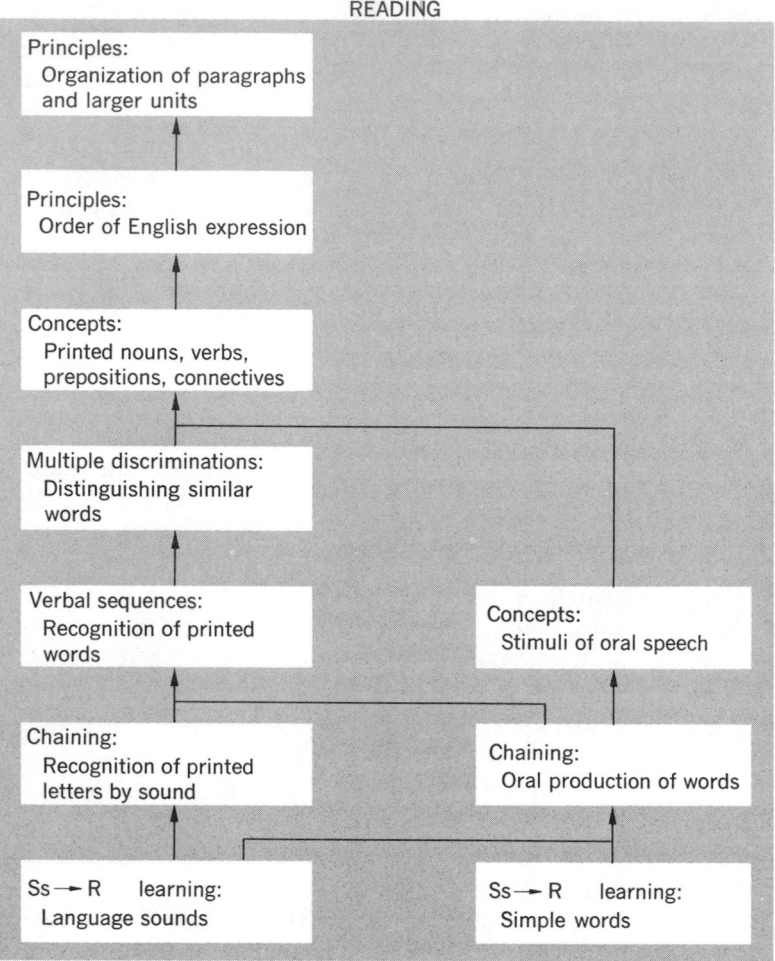

Figure 16-4   A learning structure for the basic skills of reading (Gagné, 1965, page 201).

have to be arranged for particular learners, there is general agreement that attention has to be paid to the nature of the learners, to careful analysis of the tasks that confront them; beyond that, there is rather general agreement on some broad generalizations from learning experiments and theory, but these are not uniquely bound to particular theoretical viewpoints, and are not very instructive in respect to specific problems of improving efficiency of learning. A large element of empirical testing has to enter in. This leads us somewhat away, then, from the basic science of learning, important as we may believe this to be, toward some considerations having to do with research and development, as these terms have been used in other technological fields.

VECTOR RESOLUTION OF FORCES

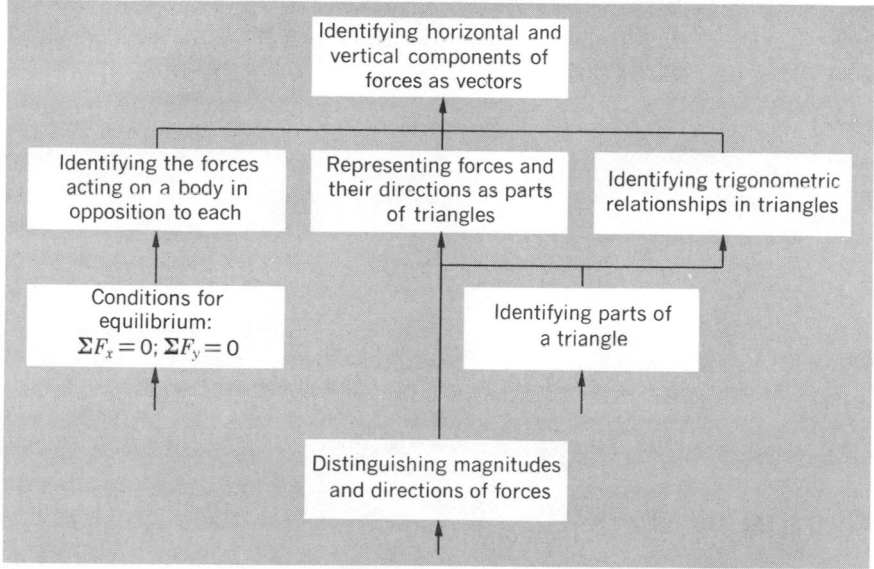

Figure 16-5   A hierarchy of principles comprising the topic "Vector Resolution of Forces" (Gagné, 1965, page 155).

THE RESEARCH AND DEVELOPMENT PROBLEM IN RELATING LEARNING TO EDUCATION

It is by now commonly recognized that it is not possible to move from basic science directly to applied science without a number of intervening steps, some of which require all the ingenuity and scientific acumen of basic research itself. We may approach this problem by considering some of the stages in the continuum between basic science research in learning and the widespread modification of educational practices based on research.

Stages from Basic Research to Widespread Adoption

The stages from the "purest" of research on learning to the most "applied" research (concerned with the adoption of a recommended educational practice) may conveniently be broken up into six steps according to their relevance to the educational enterprise.[8] Three of these may be placed within the "basic research" end of the continuum, three within the "technological research and development" end, as shown in Figure 16-6.

[8] This section leans heavily on an earlier discussion (Hilgard, 1964b).

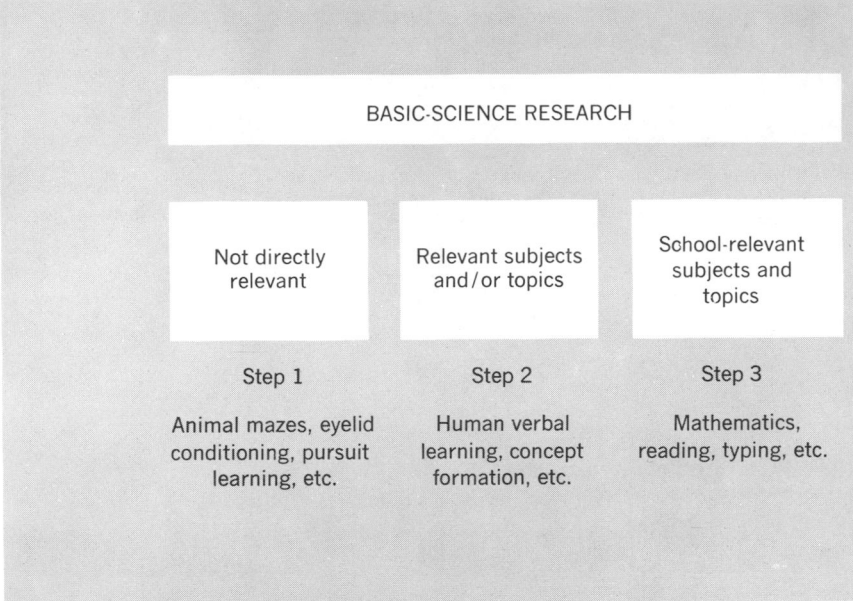

Figure 16-6   Steps from basic research on learning to technological development (modified slightly from Hilgard, 1964b, page 406).

Basic-science research on learning. By basic-science research is meant that which is guided by the problems which the investigator sets himself, without regard for the immediate applicability of the results to practical situations. This does not mean that the investigator has no practical interests, or that he does not want his results used; it is only that he is patient and uses the methods and procedures appropriate to the topic on which he works. Within learning research we may divide the stages of relevance to learning into the following three, expanding somewhat the left three boxes of Figure 16-6.

Basic-Science Research in Learning

Step 1. Research on learning with no regard for its educational relevance, e.g., animal studies, physiological, biochemical investigations. Learning in the flatworm and learning in the rat with transected spinal cord classify here.

Step 2. Research on learning which is not concerned with educational practices but which is more relevant than that of Step 1 because it deals with human subjects and with content that is nearer to that taught in school, e.g., nonsense syllable memorization and retention. The principles being tested are likely to be theoretical ones, such as the relative importance of proactive and retroactive inhibition.

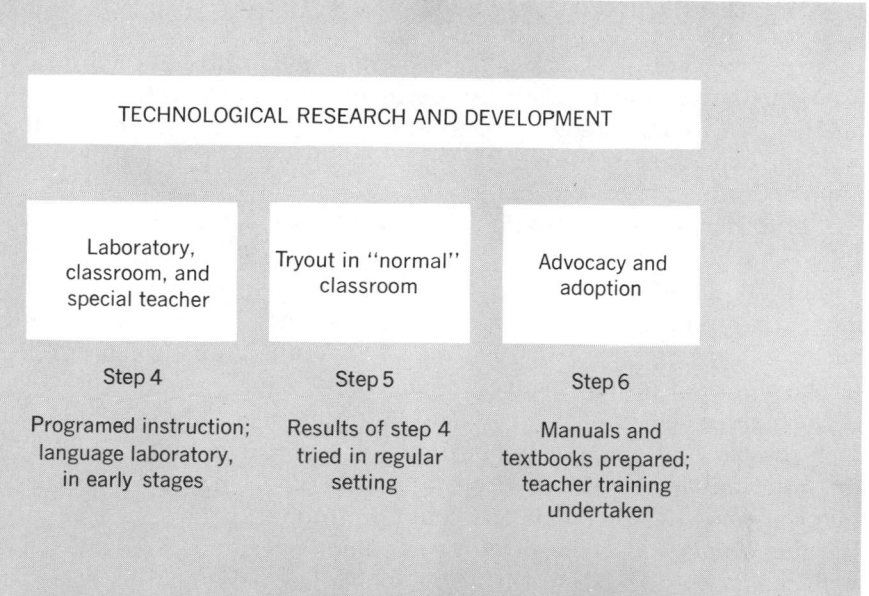

TECHNOLOGICAL RESEARCH AND DEVELOPMENT

Laboratory, classroom, and special teacher	Tryout in "normal" classroom	Advocacy and adoption
Step 4	Step 5	Step 6
Programed instruction; language laboratory, in early stages	Results of step 4 tried in regular setting	Manuals and textbooks prepared; teacher training undertaken

Step 3. Research on learning that is relevant because the subjects are school-age children and the material learned is school subject matter or skill, though no attention is paid to the problem of adapting the learning to school practices, e.g., foreign language vocabulary learned by paired-associate method with various lengths of list and with various spacing of trials.

These three steps of relevance all classify as basic-science research because the problems are set by the investigators in relation to some theoretical issues and do not arise out of the practical needs of instruction. Of course there may be bridges from any basic-science project to a practical one: perhaps drugs discovered in brain studies of rats may aid remedial reading, studies of interference may suggest intervals between classes or what should be studied concomitantly, and language-vocabulary results in a pure context may guide language acquisition in schools. The main point is that the scientist has not committed himself to relevance. He may even disavow it, in line with a cult of pure science that seems to have been developing. According to this view, something is valuable precisely because it is remote from application; so long as it is precise, it does not matter how trivial it is. This is a faulty conception of basic science, and for the investigator to escape responsibility for the relevance of his work by falling back upon this "pure science" conception is as likely to be a sign of weakness as of strength.

A further word on Step 3 is in order. The best work will be done at this stage by combining the skills of the subject-matter specialist with those of the experimenter upon learning. For example, it is fruitful to combine the work of linguist and psychologist, as in the use of Hockett's linguistic analysis by Gibson, Gibson, Danielson, and Osser (1962), and in the joint work of experts in mathematical learning theory and in linguistics in Suppes, Crothers, Weir, and Trager (1962).

A brief characterization of the report by Suppes and others will be useful in showing some of the characteristics of Step 3 investigations. The authors consist of a logician sophisticated with respect to mathematical models, a psychologist whose work lies particularly in the field of mathematical learning, and two linguists. The studies, which concern the teaching of the Russian language, used actual language students, working in the familiar setting of the language laboratory in one of the local junior high schools. The material to be studied was prepared with the aid of a linguist familiar with the structure of the Russian language, so that certain conjectures about linguistics could be studied at the same time that learning theory was being investigated. The discriminations called for were real ones—Russian words being spoken into the tape by someone fluent in Russian. Contrast this with the usual preparation of a list to be memorized in the laboratory! Without going into detail, consider kinds of things that come from such a study:

1. Linguists have offered some conjectures about which combinations of phonemes can be most easily identified and how easily allophones can be recognized. (An allophone is a phoneme that is acoustically a variant: the phoneme that is represented by the letter *p* in English is not equally explosive in s*p*eech, *p*each, and to*p*most. Hence these three *p*'s are allophones.) The investigation gave evidence that most of the conjectures of the linguist were indeed correct. A native speaker has no trouble in hearing two allophones as the "same" phoneme, but the student hearing a foreign language has a great deal of trouble, and in constructing a good program these details are important.

2. The effort to work up by small steps from the easier combinations to the more difficult ones, which seemed plausible enough from the theory of programing, turned out not to be advantageous. The students who received random presentations from the start did somewhat better than those who had the orderly progression from easy to difficult.

3. The mathematical model that proved to fit these data best was a two-stage model, as though learning took place in two jumps from no learning through an intermediate stage to mastery. What this means in terms of the underlying process is not yet clear; it may mean that first comes a stage of discriminating the stimuli and responses, and then a stage of connecting them. (See Chapter 11.)

This investigation belongs at Stage 3 because it is essentially a basic-science project, concerned with phoneme-allophone discrimination, on the one hand, and mathematical models of learning, on the other. Its relevance to classroom learning comes about because of its choice of subjects, laboratory conditions, and subject-matter. It is close to the technology of instruction but is not yet designed to indicate just how Russian should be taught. The order of presentation (increasing difficulty versus random difficulty) is the most technologically relevant of the suggestions coming from the study, but this has to do with only a small aspect of learning Russian and requires more substantiation before it can be generalized. At the same time, it is fairly obvious that experimentation closely related to the instructional task is likely to bear educational fruit more quickly than experiments classifiable within Steps 1 and 2.

Applied or technological research and development. We are ready to consider what happens on the right-hand side of Figure 16-6, in the steps having to do with applied- rather than basic-science research. The steps may be described as follows:

Technological Research and Development

Step 4. Research conducted in special laboratory classrooms, with selected teachers, e.g., bringing a few students into a room to see whether or not instruction in set theory or symbolic logic is feasible, granted a highly skilled teacher.

Step 5. A tryout of the results of prior research in a "normal" classroom with a typical teacher. Whatever is found feasible in Step 4 has to be tried out in the more typical classroom, which has limited time for the new method, and may lack the special motivation on the part of either teacher or pupil.

Step 6. Developmental steps related to advocacy and adoption. Anything found to work in Steps 4 and 5 has to be "packaged" for wider use, and then go through the processes by which new methods or procedures are adopted by those not party to the experimentation.

It is evident that the mood has changed in the transition from basic-science research to technological research, although the distinction between Steps 3 and 4 may be slight under some circumstances, as indeed in the experiment by Suppes and others used in illustration of Step 3.

If one were to review the relationship between experimentation on learning by psychologists in its relation to education over the past several decades, it would be fair to say that too much of the research has rested at Steps 1 and 2 to be educationally relevant; educational psychologists, too, have tended to work at this end of the spectrum and then to jump, by inference, to Step 6, without being sufficiently patient about Steps 4 and 5. In this respect the introduction of programed learning has been helpful, because of the serious concern both with the structure of subject matter and with the individual learner for whom the program is designed.

The Problem of Educational Innovation

In something as complex as a school system, we need at a high level a special research strategy which may be called the *strategy of innovation*. The best of equipment may lie idle, the best of resources remain unused, the best of techniques sabotaged, unless there is care in introducing the new methods or new materials to all concerned. Once the basic-science principles have been established and the applications validated in practice schoolrooms, the more widespread adoption is by no means guaranteed or, if the adoption is forced, there is no assurance that the desired results will be forthcoming. Abstractly, the steps of innovation are clear enough: Provide (a) a sound research-based program, validated in tryout, (b) the program packaged in such a way as to be available, as in good textbooks, supplementary readings in the form of pamphlets, films, programs for teaching machines, and guides for the teacher, (c) testing materials by which it can be ascertained if the objectives of the program have indeed been realized, with appropriate normative data on these evaluative instruments, (d) in-service training of the teacher to overcome the teacher's resistance to something new and to gain his enthusiastic acceptance of the program as something valuable as well as to train him in its use,[9] and (e) support for the program from the community, school boards, parents, and others concerned with the schools.

We have not done very well in appraising carefully our strategies of innovation. We have sometimes gone overboard for the novel and untried, just to keep up with the Joneses ("we have teaching machines, too"); at other times we have been very resistant. Commercialism and vested interests enter in unpleasant ways, sometimes supported, unfortunately, by factions of the educational profession itself. Here, then, is a task calling for wisdom and sensitivity. The psychological contributions may come more from social psychology than from the psychology of learning, because the processes are those of social control and attitude change; but unless there is serious concern about the appropriate ways in which to bring innovation about, schools are likely to be the victims of whims, rather than the heirs of the best tradition we can establish through cooperative effort.

---

[9] A puzzling problem with respect to innovations arises, on the one hand, from resistance by both teachers and students to something untraditional, and, on the other hand, by a "placebo" or "Hawthorne effect" from the hope and enthusiasm developed by something new and promising. Care must be taken to avoid either distortion. For a relevant discussion, see Miles (1964).

There are some specific suggestions that might be given consideration. It would be desirable, for example, for every school system, of whatever size, to have somewhere within it a school building, or at least a set of schoolrooms, devoted to in-service training of teachers and to innovation; these are on-going matters important at the community level and cannot be left to teacher-training colleges or universities. Both children and teachers could be rotated through these rooms in order to try out innovations before there is firm commitment to them. Thus, a few teaching machines or closed-circuit television projectors could be tried out without investing in them for a whole school system; teachers could have a voice in saying whether or not they wanted the new devices, or in selecting among various possibilities. Usually no harm would be done in waiting for a while if teachers were not ready, for methods imposed on teachers are unlikely to prove successful. Some of the innovations to be tried out might be those of successful local teachers themselves, here given the opportunity to show their colleagues how they do it in their own classrooms. Members of the school board and representatives of the parents could be brought in also to see things being tried out. The principles of tryout before acceptance, of choice by those who are to use the method, seem to be sound ones. If the new methods are indeed good, they will find acceptance.

In order to build a sound bridge from the experimental studies of learning to the classroom, we need a series of steps, for applied science consists of more than applying principles to practice. The main points are that in the research and development phases a collaboration is called for between psychologist, subject-matter specialist, and teacher; beyond this, careful consideration has to be given to techniques of innovation. If we achieve success in integrating these phases, we will move toward that improvement of education which will be satisfying to us all.

The Role of Major Research and Development Centers

The history of research on the technology of education suggests that the approach through multitudinous small research projects does not have satisfactory consequences. For example, the thousands of small studies that have been done on the teaching of reading have yielded remarkably little in the way of sound knowledge (Russell and Fea, 1963; Carroll, 1964a). What is apparently needed is large-scale programs which will do for teaching and learning what large-scale testing enterprises, such as the Educational Testing Service, have done for evaluation. Educational measurements have been improved through basic studies in statistics, theory of scaling, factor analysis, and so on; at the same time the arranging of materials and the determination of norms have proceeded only because the applied aspects were taken as seriously as the basic-science aspects.

Little of this kind of effort, until recently, went into the problems of providing better teaching materials and tested instructional methods. We now have a number of experiences of large-scale cooperative efforts in producing better teaching materials through the collaboration of subject-matter experts, learning specialists, and teachers. The U. S. Office of Education has seen fit to establish large regional research centers, substantially financed. The experience in the military establishments shows that results do not come either quickly or cheaply, but there appears to be no alternative to carefully conceived massive attacks on the learning problems involved in instruction. A plea for such centers has been made in various forms by Travers (1962), Gilbert (1962a), Glaser (1964). Now that some of them are coming into being, it will be of interest to study their output.

FINAL COMMENTS ON WHERE WE NOW STAND AND WHERE WE ARE GOING

The most difficult kind of history to write is contemporary history, for we do not know what threads from the present will later, in retrospect, be the ones that have led to the most significant development. Still, it is important to try as best one can to get some distance from the present, to keep things in perspective, and to attempt a kind of general stock-taking. In this we are thinking of the status of learning theory generally, as well as its relationship to practical concerns.

Some Consequences of the Lessened Interest in Major Disputes

It is fair to say that the era of the great debates in learning theory has faded into the background, so that the theories associated with the names of specific men are not as important as they once were. Why then have we kept alive the chapters which call attention to these somewhat outmoded theories? The answer is that in these debates many important issues were exposed to view, and residues from these theories are still found in the different vocabularies and preferences of those who are no longer partisans to one or another view. The reasons for studying Thorndike, Pavlov, Guthrie, Hull, and the rest are similar to the reasons for studying the classical philosophers; a contemporary philosopher does not have to consider becoming a Platonist or an Aristotelian to justify a knowledge of their views.

There is a kind of tonic influence in being part of a "movement," and something is lost when the sense of discipleship disappears. Among contemporary workers, for example, the loyalty and enthusiasm of the followers of Skinner, who feel that they have a corner on the experimental analysis of behavior, is doubtless motivating for them, and leads to a good deal of productive work along with some narrowness in relation to other views. The lack of such rallying in-group support for the other positions, which are now less confident, must have its toll in attracting younger workers. The center of group identification may, of course, shift to method or content: to mathematical models, to programed learning, to computer simulation, to short-term memory. Men, as Harry Stack Sullivan was fond of saying, are more simply human than otherwise, and they will always find some source of mutual support and encouragement to maintain their convictions that what they are doing is important.

The positive gain in the backing away from the global theory is the patient effort to find out what is so, to find the circumstances under which a generalization holds and does not hold, instead of trying to win a point in a controversy. The debate goes on, but often as between two models which the experimenter may himself propose, so that his ultimate victory, as in a game of solitaire, is only against himself. Thus the abandonment of the global theory does not mean the abandonment of the method of hypothesis-testing, where that method is appropriate.

The Concern for Task Analysis and Categories of Learning

Now that it is somewhat more respectable than it was for a time to pay attention to the applied aspects of learning, people of theoretical bent are finding their theories inadequate. Repeatedly in this chapter we have noted an emphasis upon task analysis, and correlative with that is a raising anew of the questions of how many kinds of learning there are. It will be recalled that Hilgard and Marquis (1940) had expressed some dissatisfaction with attempting to encompass all learning within the two categories of classical and instrumental conditioning, and Tolman (1949) had posited six kinds. Grant (1964), in re-examining classical and instrumental conditioning, concluded that the common principles of associative learning represented only a small part of what went into understanding what actually happened under the great variety of arrangements for learning. The multi-author book edited by Melton (1964) was devoted to the question of taxonomy of learning, that is, the categories needed to encompass the many behaviors involved.

Concern for task analysis and for subcategories of learning leads to attention to detail, and this we find characterizing many of the current research emphases. For example, a project designed to coordinate research efforts concerned with understanding the acquisition of reading skills, known as Project Literacy and directed by Dr. Harry Levin of Cornell University, brings together psycholinguists, anthropological linguists, mathematical model builders, and others interested in physiology, perception, motivation, child development—all focusing on the familiar problem of how a child learns to read and how we can best aid him in this learning.[10] This is a far cry from saying that reading is merely paired-associate learning in which symbols and sounds are connected through differential reinforcement.

Major research programs are under way in other instructional areas, such as mathematics, foreign languages, natural and social sciences, bringing back what was formerly known as "the psychology of special school subjects." That is, when one is genuinely interested in the teaching process, it becomes necessary to pay attention to the organization of knowledge in specific fields, to problems of special ability, of motivation, of aspects that learners find troublesome. While there must of course be some common principles applicable, the specific problems are many also, and the new emphases demand that serious consideration be given to them.

Are Gains in Knowledge Cumulative?

One of the most perplexing problems within psychological research is how to make the gains cumulative, that is, to build a firm foundation from past research on which to plan towards the future. It sounds self-evident that the more we know the more we should be able to find out, but the history of our science does not bear this out. Many questions are never really answered before they are abandoned, and we turn to something else. This does not necessarily mean that they were foolish or unanswerable questions. For example, we have not resolved the many issues within latent learning, continuity versus discontinuity, peripheral versus central mediation, yet such issues get de-emphasized as we turn to something else. The same failure to reach a final conclusion is true at the applied level. We do not have clear answers, for example, on the relationship between handedness and reading or speech defects, on the indications for teaching reading by phonetics or by words, on the advantages and disadvantages of coeducation, and many other topics that have been the occasion for numerous investigations.

It is hard to use the history of other sciences to justify our troubles or to correct them. Other sciences are not simply cumulative either, as the analysis by Kuhn (1962) has shown. He says that science moves by rejecting old paradigms and substituting new ones, and hence shows a kind of discontinuity in its history. Psychology's failure to be more cumulative might perhaps be understood as a search for the more enduring paradigm. However, discontinuity in other sciences is not total; the units of measurement developed within Newtonian physics, for example, are still useful in modern relativity physics. We would wish for psychology that it might be at least as continuous in its accumulation of knowledge as chemistry, physics, and biology.

[10] Project Literacy coordinates the research through a series of research planning conferences, reports of which began to appear in 1964.

Accumulation of knowledge means neither mere fact-gathering nor isolated hypothesis-testing, but thoughtful systematic approaches to meaningful questions leading to *conclusive thinking*. That is, the principles that are asserted to hold true must be such as hold demonstrably under broad but specified conditions. They must be such as can be counted on while new relationships are being studied. The many disagreements in the literature must not be permitted to stand, but must be resolved. We need to move from plausibility to proof in such a convincing manner that principles gain the status of verified laws.

This desirable state of psychological science will not come about by wishing it or by frenetic efforts to investigate everything that is investigatable. Some good high-level thinking is needed, keeping in mind *criteria of relevancy*, so that significant controversies are resolved on the basis of firmer knowledge. Perhaps less stress should be placed upon novelty and more on building more solidly in important areas. The psychology of learning has suffered in the past from a failure to insist upon relevancy, so that materials to be learned, the subjects employed in experiments, and the experimental procedures, have been governed by familiarity and ease of access rather than by cogency. While accuracy and delimited contexts have their place in experimental science, some voices need to be raised to insist that the important problems be solved. Setting problems by what is convenient and manageable still plagues some of our most precise and competent work in the study of learning, as, for example, in the study of mathematical models. We need, along with contemporary *model-building*, some general *psychologizing*, that is, repeated reflection upon the larger questions of psychology, to determine whether or not our approaches are indeed leading to their answer.

The Climate is Favorable

Despite a certain dissatisfaction with progress in firming up our theories of learning in relation to practical needs for training and education, there are many favorable signs at the present.

Psychologists are particularly ingenious in devising research methods applicable to a variety of problems, and here we can indeed point to some cumulative gains. In a chapter on recent development in training problems by Smode (1962), there is a fairly optimistic account of the many innovations available for use. Even he has to recognize the enemy of accumulative knowledge—lack of replication and validation—but the methods exist, many of them are improvements on earlier ones, and they are at hand for use.

The interest of scholars in the substantive fields of knowledge in the educational process, spotty in the past, is now much more widespread, and collaborative efforts between those with substantive training and those with the methodological training of the behavioral scientist are now much more common. These collaborative efforts cover the whole spectrum from basic science through research and development processes. The basic science of learning will be strengthened through these collaborative efforts, as well as the technology of learning and problem solving.

Resources are increasingly available to make possible the large-scale research and development enterprises which many have perceived as essential. Such resources attract talent, and, hopefully with wisdom and effort, problems will eventually reach solution.

SUPPLEMENTARY READINGS

The following books are helpful for appraising the status of learning technology:

GAGE, N. L. (Editor) (1963) *Handbook of research on teaching.*

GLASER, R. (Editor) (1962) *Training research and education.*

HILGARD, E. R. (Editor) (1964a) *Theories of learning and instruction.*

LUMSDAINE, A. A. (Editor) (1961) *Student response in programmed instruction.*

LUMSDAINE, A. A., and GLASER, R. (Editors) (1960) *Teaching machines and programmed learning: A source book.*

While not as directly concerned with applied problems, the following book bears upon the problems of applying learning theory:

MELTON, A. W. (Editor) (1964) *Categories of human learning.*

For the developments in programed instruction, see, in addition to the above:

SCHRAMM, W. (1964a) *The research on programed instruction: An annotated bibliography.*

SCHRAMM, W. (Editor) (1964b) *Four case studies in programed instruction.*

Secretariat, Pädagogischen Zentrum (1964) *Programmierter Unterricht und Lehrmaschinen.* (A report of the International Conference on Programmed Instruction and Teaching Machines, Berlin, 1963, in both German and English.)

REFERENCES AND AUTHOR INDEX

The numbers in italics following each reference give the text pages on which the paper is cited. Citations in the text are made by author and date of publication.

ABERNETHY, E. M. (1940) The effect of changed environmental conditions upon the results of college examinations. *J. Psychol.,* 10, 293–301.—*499*

ABORN, M. (1953) The influence of experimentally induced failure on the retention of material acquired through set and incidental learning. *J. exp. Psychol.,* 45, 225–231.—*289, 290*

ADAMS, H. E. *See* Yarnell and Adams (1964).

ADAMS, P. A. *See* Postman and Adams (1954, 1955).

ADAMSON, R. *See* Bevan and Adamson (1960, 1963).

ADAMS, SUSANNE. (1961) Temporal changes in the strength of competing verbal associates. Unpublished Ph.D. dissertation, Univ. of California; Berkeley, Calif.—*501*

AEBLI, H. (1951) *Didactique psychologique: application à la didactique de la psychologie de Jean Piaget.* Neuchâtel: Delachaux et Niestlé.—*283, 571*

AESCHLIMAN, B. *See* Ritchie, Aeschliman, and Peirce (1950).

ALLEN, C. K. *See* Wickens, Born, and Allen (1963).

ALLPORT, G. W. (1930) Change and decay in the visual memory image. *Brit. J. Psychol.,* 21, 134–148.—*248*

ALLPORT, G. W. (1937) *Personality: a psychological interpretation.* New York: Holt, Rinehart and Winston.—*122, 306*

ALLPORT, G. W., and POSTMAN, L. (1947) *The psychology of rumor.* New York: Holt, Rinehart and Winston.—*251*

AMMONS, R. B. (1947) Acquisition of motor skill: 1. Quantitative analysis and theoretical formulation. *Psychol. Rev.,* 54, 263–281.—*322*

AMMONS, R. B. (1962) Psychology of the scientist: II: Clark L. Hull and his "Idea Books." *Percept. Motor Skills,* 15, 800–802.—*190*

AMSEL, A. (1958) The role of frustrative nonreward in noncontinuous reward situations. *Psychol. Bull.,* 55, 102–119.—*488*

AMSEL, A. (1962) Frustrative nonreward in partial reinforcement and discrimination learning. *Psychol. Rev.,* 69, 306–328.—*488*

AMSEL, A. (1965) On inductive versus deductive approaches and neo-Hullian behaviorism. In B. B. Wolman (Editor) *Scientific psychology.* New York: Basic Books, 187–206.—*169*

ANDERSON, N. H. (1964) An evaluation of stimulus sampling theory: Comments on Professor Estes' paper. In A. W. Melton (Editor), *Categories of human learning.* New York: Academic.—*353*

ANGELL, J. R. (1906) Review of *Studies in philosophy and psychology* (Garman Commemorative Volume), *J. Phil. Psychol. sci. Meth.,* **3**, 637–643.—*307*

ANGELL, J. R. (1907) The province of functional psychology. *Psychol. Rev.,* **14**, 61–91.—*300*

ANGELL, J. R., and MOORE, A. W. (1896) Reaction-time: a study in attention and habit. *Psychol. Rev.,* **3**, 245–258.—*298*

Antioch College (1960) *Experiment in French language instruction:* Second report, 1959–1960. Yellow Springs, Ohio: Antioch Press.—*554*

ANTONITIS, J. J. *See* Schoenfeld, Antonitis, and Bersh (1950).

ARNOLD, W. J. (1947) Simple reaction chains and their integration. I. Homogeneous chaining with terminal reinforcement. *J. comp. physiol. Psychol.,* **40**, 349–363.—*170, 171*

ASHBY, W. R. (1952) *Design for a brain.* New York: Wiley.—*382*

ASRATYAN, E. A. (1961) The initiation and localization of cortical inhibition in the conditioned reflex arc. In N. S. Kline (Editor) Pavlovian conference on higher nervous activity. *Annals of the New York Academy of Science,* 1141–1159.—*63*

ATKINSON, J. W. *See* McClelland and Atkinson (1948); McClelland, Atkinson, Clark, and Lowell (1953).

ATKINSON, R. C. (1961) The observing response in discrimination learning. *J. exp. Psychol.,* **62**, 253–262.—*528, 529, 531*

ATKINSON, R. C. (Editor) (1964) *Studies in mathematical psychology.* Stanford, Calif.: Stanford Univ. Press.—*379*

ATKINSON, R. C. *See also* Dear and Atkinson (1962); Myers and Atkinson (1964); Suppes and Atkinson (1960).

ATKINSON, R. C., BOWER, G. H., and CROTHERS, E. J. (1965) *Introduction to mathematical learning theory.* New York: Wiley.—*352, 369, 379*

ATKINSON, R. C., and CROTHERS, E. J. (1964) A comparison of paired-associate learning models having different acquisition and retention axioms. *J. math. Psychol.,* **1**, 285–315.—*373*

ATKINSON, R. C., and SHIFFRIN, R. M. (1965) *Mathematical models for memory and learning.* Technical report #79, Psychology Series, Institute for Mathematical Studies in the Social Sciences. Stanford: Stanford Univ. Press.—*511*

AUSTIN, G. *See* Bruner, Goodnow, and Austin (1956).

AZRIN, N. (1964) Aggression. A speech to American Psychological Association, Sept. 6, 1964, Los Angeles. Title listed in *Amer. Psychol.,* **17**, 501.—*490*

BABICH, F. R., JACOBSON, A. L., BUBASH, S., and JACOBSON, A. (1965) Transfer of learning to naive rats by injection of ribonucleic acid extracted from trained rats. *Science,* **149**, 656–657.—*467*

BABICH, F. R. *See* Jacobson, Babich, Bubash, and Jacobson (1965); Jacobson, Babich, Bubash, and Goren (1966).

BABKIN, B. P. (1949) *Pavlov, a biography.* Chicago: Univ. of Chicago Press.—*49, 73*

BAHRICK, H. P. *See* Fitts, Bahrick, Noble, and Briggs (1965).

BALL, G. G. (1965) Personal communication. Paper in preparation.—*437*

BALL, G. G., and ADAMS, D. W. (1965) Intracranial stimulation as an avoidance or escape response. *Psychonomic Sci., 3,* 39–40.—*438*

BALL, J. *See* Lashley and Ball (1929).

BANDURA, A. (1962) Social learning through imitation. In M. R. Jones (Editor), *Nebraska Symposium on motivation: 1962.* Lincoln: Univ. of Nebraska Press, 211–269.—*534*

BANDURA, A. (1965) Vicarious processes: a case of no-trial learning. In L. Berkowitz (Editor) *Advances in experimental social psychology,* Vol. II. New York: Academic.—*534–536*

BANDURA, A., and WALTERS, R. H. (1963) *Social learning and personality development.* New York: Holt, Rinehart and Winston.—*295, 309*

BARKER, R. G., DEMBO, T., and LEWIN, K. (1941) Frustration and regression: a study of young children. *Univ. Ia. Stud. Child Welf.,* 18, No. I.—*277*

BARNES, J. M., and UNDERWOOD, B. J. (1959) Fate of first-list associations in transfer theory. *J. exp. Psychol., 58,* 97–105.—*500*

BARRETT, R. J., PEYSER, C. S., and McHOSE, J. H. (1965) Effects of complete and incomplete reward reduction on a subsequent response. *Psychonomic Sci., 3,* 277–278.—*489*

BARTEL, H. (1937) Über die Abhängigkeit spontaner Reproduktionen von Feldbedingungen. *Psychol. Forsch., 22,* 1–25.—*251, 253*

BARTLETT, F. C. (1932) *Remembering.* Cambridge: Cambridge Univ. Press.—*249, 250*

BASSLER, O. C. *See* Gagné and Bassler (1963).

BATESON, G. (1941) The frustration-aggression hypothesis and culture. *Psychol. Rev.,* 48, 350–355.—*277*

BAUER, F. J., and LAWRENCE, D. H. (1953) Influence of similarity of choice-point and goal cues on discrimination learning. *J. comp. physiol. Psychol., 46,* 241–248.—*224*

BAVELAS, A. *See* Seashore and Bavelas (1941).

BEACH, F, A. (1955) The descent of instinct. *Psychol. Rev., 62,* 401–410.—*3*

BEACH, F. A., and JAYNES, J. (1954) Effects of early experience upon the behavior of animals. *Psychol. Bull., 51,* 239–263.—*281*

BENNETT, E. L., and CALVIN, M. (1964) Failure to train planarians reliably. *Neurosciences Research Program Bulletin,* 2, July–August issue.—*467*

BENNETT, E. L., KRECH, D., and ROSENZWEIG, M. R. (1964) Reliability and regional specificity of cerebral effects of environmental complexity and training. *J. comp. physiol. Psychol., 57,* 440–441.—*463*

BENNETT, E. L. *See* Krech, Rosenzweig, and Bennett (1960, 1962); Rosenzweig, Bennett, and Krech (1964).

BENTLEY, A. F. *See* Dewey and Bentley (1949).

BERLYNE, D. E. (1960) *Conflict, arousal, and curiosity.* New York: McGraw-Hill.—*68, 529*

BERNBACH, H. A. (1965) Stimulus learning and recognition in paired-associate learning. Ph.D. dissertation, University of Michigan. Also Technical report #05823–7–T under Contract No. AF 49(638)–1235.—*371, 373, 511*

BERSH, P. J. (1951) The influence of two variables upon the establishment of a secondary reinforcer for operant responses. *J. exp. Psychol.*, **41**, 62–73. *—121*

BERSH, P. J. *See* Schoenfeld, Antonitis, and Bersh (1950a); Schoenfeld and Bersh (1952).

BERTRAM, B. M. *See* Krathwohl, Bloom, and Bertram (1964).

BEVAN, W. (1963) The pooling mechanism and the phenomena of reinforcement. In O. J. Harvey (Editor), *Motivation and social interaction: cognitive determinants.* New York: Ronald, 18–44, 453–472.*—487*

BEVAN, W., and ADAMSON, R. (1960) Reinforcers and reinforcement: Their relation to maze performance. *J. exp. Psychol.*, **59**, 226–232.*—486*

BEVAN, W., and ADAMSON, R. (1963) Internal referents and the concept of reinforcement. In N. F. Washburne (Editor) *Decisions, values, and groups,* Vol. 2. New York: Pergamon.*—487*

BINDER, A., and FELDMAN, S. E. (1960) The effects of experimentally controlled experience upon recognition responses. *Psychol. Monogr.*, **74** (No. 496).*—350*

BIRCH, H. G. (1945) The relation of previous experience to insightful problem-solving. *J. comp. Psychol.*, **38**, 367–383.*—240*

BIRENBAUM, J. (1930) Das Vergessen einer Vornahme. *Psychol. Forsch.*, **13**, 218–284.*—258*

BLAKE, D. V., and UTTLEY, A. M. (Editors) (1959) *Proceedings of the symposium on mechanization of thought processes.* National Physical Laboratories, Teddington, England. London: H. M. Stationary Office. (2 vols.)*—425*

BLODGETT, H. C. (1929) The effect of the introduction of reward upon the maze performance of rats. *Univ. Calif. Publ. Psychol.*, **4**, 113–134.*—200*

BLODGETT, H. C., and McCUTCHAN, K. (1947) Place versus response-learning in the simple T-maze. *J. exp. Psychol.*, **37**, 412–422.*—197*

BLODGETT, H. C., and McCUTCHAN, K. (1948) The relative strength of place and response learning in the T-maze. *J. comp. physiol. Psychol.*, **41**, 17–24. *—197*

BLOOM, B. S. (Editor) (1956) *Taxonomy of educational objectives. Handbook I: Cognitive domain.* New York: Longmans.*—544*

BLOOM, B. S. *See also* Krathwohl, Bloom, and Bertram (1964).

BLOUGH, D. S. (1961) Experiments in animal psychophysics. *Sci. Amer.* **205**, July, 113–122.*—131*

BLUM, G. S. (1953) *Psychoanalytic theories of personality.* New York: McGraw-Hill.*—282*

BOBROW, D. G. (1964) Natural language input for a computer problem-solving system. Project MAC—Technical report no. 1, Mass. Inst. of Tech., Sept. Cambridge. Unpublished Ph.D. thesis from MIT in 1964.*—409*

BODE, B. H. (1940) *How we learn.* Boston: Heath.*—299*

BORING, E. G. (1933) *The physical dimensions of consciousness.* New York: Appleton-Century-Crofts.*—303*

BORING, E. G. (1941) Communality in relation to proaction and retroaction. *Amer. J. Psychol.*, **54**, 280–283.*—314*

BORING, E. G. (1950) *A history of experimental psychology,* Second edition. New York: Appleton-Century-Crofts.*—261, 264, 297*

Borko, H. (Editor) (1962) *Computer applications in the behavioral sciences.* Englewood Cliffs: Prentice-Hall.—*389, 425*

Born, D. G. *See* Wickens, Born, and Allen (1963).

Bourne, L. E. *See* Haygood and Bourne (1965).

Bower, G. H. (1959a) Choice-point behavior. In R. R. Bush and W. K. Estes (Editors), *Studies in mathematical learning theory.* Stanford: Stanford Univ. Press, 109–124.—*360*

Bower, G. H. (1959b) A theory of serial discrimination learning. In R. R. Bush and W. K. Estes (Editors) *Studies in mathematical learning theory.* Stanford: Stanford Univ. Press, 76–93.—*173.*

Bower, G. H. (1961a) Application of a model to paired-associate learning. *Psychometrika,* **26**, 255–280.—*369, 370*

Bower, G. H. (1961b) A contrast effect in differential conditioning. *J. exp. Psychol.,* **62**, 196–199.—*486, 489*

Bower, G. H. (1962a) Response strengths and choice probability: a consideration of two combination rules. In E. Nagel, P. Suppes, and A. Tarski (Editors) *Logic, methodology, and philosophy of science: Proceedings of the 1960 International Congress.* Stanford: Stanford Univ. Press, 1962, 400–412.—*360*

Bower, G. H. (1962b) An association model for response and training variables in paired-associate learning. *Psychol. Rev.,* **69**, 34–53.—*221, 370*

Bower, G. H. (1962c) The influence of graded reductions in reward and prior frustrating events upon the magnitude of the frustration effect. *J. comp. physiol. Psychol.,* **55**, 582–587.—*486*

Bower, G. H. (1966a) Verbal learning. In H. H. Helson and W. Bevan (Editors), *Theories and data in psychology.* Princeton: Van Nostrand.—*356, 503*

Bower, G. H. (1966b) A descriptive theory of human memory. In O. P. Kimble (Editor), *Learning, remembering and forgetting,* Vol. 2. New York: New York Academy of Science.—*511*

Bower, G. H. *See also* Atkinson, Bower, and Crothers (1965); Trabasso and Bower (1964, 1966).

Bower, G. H., and Miller, N. E. (1958) Rewarding and punishing effects from stimulating the same place in the rat's brain. *J. comp. physiol. Psychol.,* **51**, 669–674.—*434*

Bower, G. H., and Theios, J. (1964) A learning model for discrete performance levels. In R. C. Atkinson (Editor), *Studies in mathematical psychology.* Stanford: Stanford Univ. Press.—*367, 373*

Bower, G. H., and Trabasso, T. R. (1964) Concept identification. In R. C. Atkinson (Editor), *Studies in mathematical psychology.* Stanford: Stanford Univ. Press, 32–94.—*370, 530*

Bowlby, J. (1958) The nature of the child's tie to his mother. *Int. J. Psychoanal.,* **39**, 350–373.—*291*

Braly, K. W. (1933) The influence of past experience in visual perception. *J. exp. Psychol.,* **16**, 613–643.—*237*

Breland, K., and Breland, M. (1951) A field of applied animal psychology. *Amer. Psychologist,* **6**, 202–204.—*126*

Breland, M. *See* Breland and Breland (1951).

Brelsford, J. W., Jr. (1965) Experimental manipulation of state occupancy in a

Markov model for avoidance conditioning. Ph.D. dissertation, Univ. of Texas, May. Also Tech. report no. 7 of Conditioning Research Laboratory, Dept. of Psychol., Univ. of Texas, Austin, Texas.—*374*

BRELSFORD, J. W., Jr. *See* also Theios and Brelsford (1966).

BRETNALL, E. P. *See* Tolman, Hall, and Bretnall (1932).

BRIGGS, G. E. (1954) Acquisition, extinction and recovery functions in retroactive inhibition. *J. exp. Psychol.*, 47, 285–293.—*501*

BRIGGS, G. E. *See* Fitts, Bahrick, Noble, and Briggs (1965).

BRINK, F., Jr. (1951) Synaptic mechanisms. In S. S. Stevens (Editor), *Handbook of experimental psychology.* New York: Wiley, 94–120.—*455*

BROADBENT, D. E. (1957) A mechanical model for human attention and immediate memory. *Psychol. Rev.*, 64, 205–215.—*505, 509*

BROADBENT, D. E. (1958) *Perception and communication.* New York: Pergamon. —*505, 506, 539*

BROGDEN, W. J. (1939) Sensory pre-conditioning. *J. exp. Psychol.*, 25, 323–332.— *65*

BROWN, E. L. *See* Flexman, Matheny, and Brown (1950).

BROWN, F. D. *See* Pechstein and Brown (1939).

BROWN, J. F., and FEDER, D. D. (1934) Thorndike's theory of learning as gestalt psychology. *Psychol. Bull.*, 31, 426–437.—*28*

BROWN, J. (1958) Some tests of the decay theory of immediate memory. *Quart. J. exp. Psychol.*, 10, 12–21.—*507, 509*

BROWN, J. S. (1942) The generalization of approach responses as a function of stimulus intensity and strength of motivation. *J. comp. Psychol.*, 33, 209–226.—*176*

BROWN, J. S. (1948) Gradients of approach and avoidance responses and their relation to levels of motivation. *J. comp. physiol. Psychol.*, 41, 450–465.— *176*

BROWN, J. S. *See also* Miller, Brown, and Lipofsky (1943).

BROWN, T. (1820) *Lectures on the philosophy of the human mind.* 16th edition, 4 vols. Edinburgh: William Tait, 1846.—*50, 310*

BROWN, W. (1935) Growth of "memory images." *Amer. J. Psychol.*, 47, 90–102.— *249*

BROWN, W. L. *See* Gentry, Brown, and Kaplan (1947).

BROWN, W. O. *See* Muenzinger, Brown, Crow, and Powloski (1952).

BRUNER, J. S. (1960) *The process of education.* Cambridge, Mass.: Harvard Univ. Press.—*571*

BRUNER, J. S. (1964) Some theorems on instruction illustrated with reference to mathematics. In E. R. Hilgard (Editor), *Theories of learning and instruction.* Chicago: Univ. of Chicago Press, 306–335.—*571*

BRUNER, J. S., GOODNOW, J., and AUSTIN, G. (1956) *A study of thinking.* New York: Wiley.—*389*

BRUNING, J. L., and SCHAPPE, R. H. (1965) Type of interpolated activity and short-term memory: a note. *Psychol. Rep.*, 17, 256.—*507*.

BRUNSWIK, E. (1939) Probability as a determiner of rat behavior. *J. exp. Psychol.*, 25, 175–197.—*203, 204, 268*

BRUNSWIK, E. (1955) Representative design and probabilistic theory in a functional psychology. *Psychol. Rev.*, 62, 193–217.—*332*

BRUNSWIK, E. *See also* Tolman and Brunswik (1935).

BRYAN, G. L. (1962) The training of electronics maintenance technicians. In R. Glaser (Editor), *Training research and education*. Pittsburgh: Univ. of Pittsburgh Press, 295–321.—*548*

BRYAN, G. L., and SCHUSTER, D. H. (1959) *An experimental comparison of trouble shooting training techniques*. Los Angeles: Univ. of Southern Calif., Electronics Personnel Research Group Technical Report No. 3, p. 10.—*548*

BRYAN, W. L., and HARTER, N. (1897) Studies in the physiology and psychology of the telegraphic language. *Psychol. Rev.*, 4, 27–53.—*1*

BRYAN, W. L., and HARTER, N. (1899) Studies on the telegraphic language. The acquisition of a hierarchy of habits. *Psychol. Rev.*, 6, 345–375.—*1*

BUBASH, S. *See* Babich, Jacobson, Bubash, and Jacobson (1965); Jacobson, Babich, Bubash, and Jacobson (1965); Jacobson, Babich, Bubash, and Goren (1966).

BUCK, C. *See* Luttges, Johnson, Buck, Holland, and McGaugh (1966).

BUGELSKI, B. R. (1956) *The psychology of learning*. New York: Holt, Rinehart, and Winston.—*14*

BUGELSKI, B. R. (1964) *The psychology of learning applied to teaching*. Indianapolis: Bobbs-Merrill.—*503*

BUGELSKI, B. R., and CADWALLADER, T. (1956) A reappraisal of the transfer and retroactive surface. *J. exp. Psychol.*, 52, 360–366.—*316*

BUREŠ, J., and BUREŠOVÁ, O. (1960) The use of Teão's spreading depression in the study of interhemispheric transfer of memory traces. *J. comp. physiol. Psychol.*, 53, 558–563.—*474*

BUREŠ, J., BUREŠOVÁ, O., and FIFKOVÁ, E. (1964) Interhemispheric transfer of a passive-avoidance reaction. *J. comp. physiol. Psychol.*, 57, 326–330.—*475*

BUREŠOVÁ, O. *See* Bureš and Burešová (1960); Bureš, Burešová, and Fifková (1964).

BURKE, C. J., ESTES, W. K., and HELLYER, S. (1954) Rate of verbal conditioning in relation to stimulus variability. *J. exp. Psychol.*, 48, 153–161.—*344*

BURKE, C. J. *See* Friedman, Burke, Cole, Keller, Millword, and Estes (1964); Keller, Cole, Burke, and Estes (1965).

BURNS, B. D. (1958) *The mammalian cerebral cortex*. London: Edward Arnold and Co.—*153, 156*

BUSH, R. R. (1960) A survey of mathematical learning theory. In R. D. Luce (Editor) *Developments in mathematical psychology*. Glencoe: The Free Press.—*380*

BUSH, R. R. *See also* Luce, Bush, and Galanter (1963a, 1963b, 1965a, 1965b).

BUSH, R. R., and ESTES, W. K. (Editors) (1959) *Studies in mathematical learning theory*. Stanford: Stanford Univ. Press.—*380*

BUSH, R. R., GALANTER, E., and LUCE, R. D. (1963) Characterization and classification of choice experiments. In R. D. Luce, R. R. Bush, and E. Galanter, *Handbook of mathematical psychology*. Vol. 1. New York: Wiley, 77–102.—*513*

BUSH, R. R., and MOSTELLER, F. (1951) A mathematical model for simple learning. *Psychol. Rev.*, 58, 313–323.—*335*

BUSH, R. R., and MOSTELLER, F. (1955) *Stochastic models for learning*. New York: Wiley.—*335, 360, 364, 380*

BUXTON, C. E. (1943) The status of research on reminiscence. *Psychol. Bull.*, 40, 313–340.—*327*

Bykov, K. M. (1957) *The cerebral cortex and the internal organs.* (Translated by W. H. Gantt.) New York: Chemical Publishing.—*65, 73*

Cadwallader, T. *See* Bugelski and Cadwallader (1956).

Cain, L. F., and Willey, R. de V. (1939) The effect of spaced learning on the curve of retention. *J. exp. Psychol.,* 25, 209–214.—*324*

Caldwell, W. E., and Jones, H. B. (1954) Some positive results on a modified Tolman and Honzik insight maze. *J. comp. physiol. Psychol.,* 47, 416–418.—*198*

Calvin, M. *See* Bennett and Calvin (1964).

Cameron, N. (1938a) Reasoning, regression, and communication in schizophrenics. *Psychol. Monogr.,* 50, No. 1.—*277*

Cameron, N. (1938b) A study of thinking in senile deterioration and schizophrenic disorganization. *Amer. J. Psychol.,* 51, 650–664.—*277*

Cameron, S. *See* Yovitts and Cameron (1960).

Campbell, A. A. *See* Hilgard and Campbell (1936).

Campbell, R. K. *See* Hilgard, Campbell, and Sears (1938).

Canaday, R. H. (1962) The description of overlapping figures. Unpublished Masters thesis in electrical engineering, Mass. Inst. of Tech.—*405*

Cannicott, R. G., and Umberger, J. P. (1950) An investigation of the psychoanalytic "mechanism" of repression: the retention of verbal material associated with noxious stimulation. *Proc. Okla. Acad. Sci.,* 31, 176–178.—*289*

Cantor, N. (1946) *Dynamics of learning.* Buffalo, N.Y.: Foster and Stewart.—*283, 296*

Carey, F. M. *See* Gross and Carey (1965).

Carmichael, L., Hogan, H. P., and Walter, A. A. (1932) An experimental study of the effect of language on the reproduction of visually perceived form. *J. exp. Psychol.,* 15, 73–86.—*249*

Carr, H. A. (1925) *Psychology, a study of mental activity.* New York: Longmans.—*299, 302, 308*

Carr, H. A. (1930) Teaching and learning. *J. genet. Psychol.,* 37, 189–219.—*309*

Carr, H. A. (1931) The laws of association. *Psychol. Rev.,* 38, 212–228.—*304, 310*

Carr, H. A. (1933) The quest for constants. *Psychol. Rev.,* 40, 514–532.—*303*

Carr, H. A. (1935) *An introduction to space perception.* New York: Longmans. —*304*

Carr, H. A. (1938) The law of effect. *Psychol. Rev.,* 45, 191–199.—*308*

Carroll, J. B. (1962) The prediction of success in intensive foreign language training. In R. Glaser (Editor), *Training research and education.* Pittsburgh: Univ. of Pittsburgh Press, 87–136.—*554*

Carroll, J. B. (1963) Research on teaching foreign languages. In N. L. Gage (Editor), *Handbook of research on teaching.* Chicago: Rand, McNally, 1060–1100.—*579*

Carroll, J. B. (1964a) The analysis of reading instruction: Perspectives from psychology and linguistics. In E. R. Hilgard (Editor), *Theories of learning and instruction.* Chicago: Univ. of Chicago Press, 336–353.—*579*

CARROLL, J. B. (1964b) *Language and thought.* Englewood Cliffs: Prentice-Hall. —*133*

CARTWRIGHT, D. (1959) Lewinian theory as a contemporary systematic framework. In S. Koch (Editor), *Psychology: A study of a science,* Vol. 2. New York: McGraw-Hill, 7–91.—*262*

CASON, H. *See* also Trowbridge and Cason (1932).

CERASO, J. *See* Slamecka and Ceraso (1960).

CHANG, J. J. *See* Shepard and Chang (1963).

CHILD, I. L. *See* Whiting and Child (1953).

CHILDS, J. L. (1931) *Education and the philosophy of experimentalism.* New York: Appleton-Century-Crofts.—*299*

CHOMSKY, C. *See* Green, Wolf, Chomsky, and Laughery (1961).

CHOMSKY, N. (1959) Review of Skinner's *Verbal behavior. Language,* 35, 26–58.—*133*

CHOROVER, S. L. (1965) Rapid memory consolidation: Effect of electroconvulsive shock upon retention in the rat. In D. P. Kimble (Editor), *Learning, remembering and forgetting,* Vol. 1. *The anatomy of memory.* Palo Alto: Science and Behavior Books.—*451*

CHOROVER, S. L., and SCHILLER, P. H. (1965) Short-term retrograde amnesia in rats. *J. comp. physiol. Psychol.,* 59, 73–78.—*451*

CHOW, K. L. *See* Lashley, Chow, and Semmes (1951).

CIARDI, J. *See* Reid, Ciardi, and Perrine (1963).

CLAPARÈDE, E. (1934) La genèse de l'hypothèse. *Arch. de Psychol.,* 24, 1–154.— *72*

CLARKSON, J. K. *See* Deutsch and Clarkson (1959).

CLAYTON, K. N. (1964) T-maze choice learning as a joint function of the reward magnitudes for the alternatives. *J. comp. physiol. Psychol.,* 58, 333–338.— *345*

CLEMES, S. R. (1964) Repression and hypnotic amnesia. *J. abnorm. soc. Psychol.,* 69, 62–69.—*287*

COAN, R. W., and ZAGONA, S. V. (1962) Contemporary ratings of psychological theorists. *Psychol. Record,* 12, 315–322.—*72*

COFER, C. N. (Editor) (1961) *Verbal learning and verbal behavior.* New York: McGraw-Hill.—*333, 503*

COHEN, L. H., HILGARD, E. R., and WENDT, G. R. (1933) Sensitivity to light in a case of hysterical blindness studied by reinforcement-inhibition and conditioning methods. *Yale J. Biol. Med.,* 6, 61–67.—*96*

COLE, M. *See* Friedman, Burke, Cole, Keller, Millword, and Estes (1964); Keller, Cole, Burke, and Estes (1965).

COLEMAN, E. B. (1962) Sequential interference demonstrated by serial reconstruction. *J. exp. Psychol.,* 64, 46–51.—*502*

CONRAD, R. (1964) Acoustic confusions in immediate memory. *Brit. J. Psychol.,* 55, 75–84.—*507*

CONRAD, R., and HILLE, B. A. (1958) The decay theory of immediate memory and paced recall. *Canad. J. Psychol.,* 12, 1–6.—*509*

COOK, S. W., and SKINNER, B. F. (1939) Some factors influencing the distribution of associated words. *Psychol. Rec.,* 3, 178–184.—*132*

COOK, T. W. (1934) Massed and distributed practice in puzzle solving. *Psychol. Rev.,* **41**, 330–355.—*324*

CORNING, W. C., and JOHN, E. R. (1961) Effect of ribonuclease on retention of conditioned response in regenerated planarians. *Science,* **134**, 1363–1365.—*467*

COTTRELL, L. S., Jr., and GALLAGHER, R. (1941) Important developments in American social psychology during the past decade. *Sociometry,* **4**, 107–139.—*299*

COULSON, J. E. (Editor) (1961) *Programmed learning and computer-based instruction.* New York: Wiley.—*558*

COWLES, J. T., and NISSEN, H. W. (1937) Reward expectancy in delayed responses of chimpanzees. *J. comp. Psychol.,* **24**, 345–358.—*196*

CRISLER, G. *See* Kleitman and Crisler (1927).

CROSSON, F. J. *See* Sayre and Crosson (1963).

CROTHERS, E. J. (1965) Learning model solution to a problem in constrained optimization. *J. math. Psychol.,* **2**, 19–25.—*377*

CROTHERS, E. J. *See* Atkinson, Bower, and Crothers (1965); Atkinson and Crothers (1964); Suppes, Crothers, Weir, and Trager (1962).

CROW, W. J. *See* Muenzinger, Brown, Crow, and Powloski (1952).

CROWDER, N. A. (1959) Automatic tutoring by means of intrinsic programming. In E. H. Galanter (Editor), *Automatic teaching: The state of the art.* New York: Wiley, 109–116.—*557*

CROWDER, N., and MARTIN, G. (1961) *Trigonometry.* Garden City: Doubleday.—*557*

CRUTCHFIELD, R. S. (1965) Instructing the individual in creative thinking. In *New approaches to individualizing instruction.* Princeton: Educational Testing Service, 13–25.—*560*

CRUTCHFIELD, R. S. *See also* Krech and Crutchfield (1948).

CULBERTSON, J. T. (1962) *The Minds of Robots.* Urbana: Univ. of Illinois Press.—*478*

CULLER, E. A. *See* Girden and Culler (1937).

CUNNINGHAM, L. M. *See* Jenkins and Cunningham (1949).

DANIELSON, A. *See* Gibson, Bigson, Danielson, and Osser (1962).

DASHIELL, J. F. (1949) *Fundamentals of general psychology,* Third edition. Boston: Houghton Mifflin.—*305*

DEAR, R. E. *See* Karush and Dear (1964).

DEAR, R. E., and ATKINSON, R. C. (1962) Optimal allocation of items in a single two-concept automated teaching model. In J. Coulson (Editor), *Programmed learning and computer-based instruction.* New York: Wiley, 25–45.—*377*

DEESE, J. (1958) *The psychology of learning,* Revised. New York: McGraw-Hill.—*14*

DEGROOT, A. (1946) *Het Denken van den Schaker.* Amsterdam: Noord-Hollandsche Uitgevers Maatschappij.—*389*

DELAFRESNAYE, J. F. (Editor) (1961) *Brain mechanisms and learning.* Oxford: Blackwell.—*479*

DELGADO, J. M. R., ROBERTS, W. W., and MILLER, N. E. (1954) Learning motivated by electrical stimulation of the brain. *Amer. J. Physiol.*, 179, 587–593.—*434*

DEMBO, T. *See* Barker, Dembo, and Lewin (1941).

DERIVERA, J. *See* Lawrence and DeRivera (1954).

DEUTSCH, D. *See* Deutsch and Deutsch (1963).

DEUTSCH, J. A. (1954) A machine with insight. *Quart. J. Exp. Psychol.*, 6, 6–11. Also reprinted as Chap. X in J. A. Deutsch, *The structural basis of behavior.* Chicago: Univ. of Chicago Press, 1960.—*225, 382*

DEUTSCH, J. A. (1960) *The structural basis of behavior.* Chicago: Univ. of Chicago Press.—*218, 225, 539*

DEUTSCH, J. A. (1964) Behavioral measurement of the neural refractory period and its application to intracranial self-stimulation. *J. comp. physiol. Psychol.*, 58, 1–9.—*437*

DEUTSCH, J. A., and CLARKSON, J. K. (1959) Reasoning in the hooded rat. *Quart. J. exper. Psychol.*, 11, 150–154.—*198, 225*

DEUTSCH, J. A., and DEUTSCH, D. (1963) Attention: Some theoretical considerations. *Psychol. Rev.*, 70, 80–90.—*445*

DEUTSCH, J. A., and HOWARTH, C. I. (1963) Some tests of a theory of intracranial self-stimulation. *Psychol. Rev.*, 70, 444–460.—*436*

DEWEY, J. (1896) The reflex arc concept in psychology. *Psychol. Rev.*, 3, 357–370.—*298*

DEWEY, J. (1910) *How we think.* Boston: Heath.—*298*

DEWEY, J. (1920) *Influence of Darwin on philosophy.* New York: Holt, Rinehart, and Winston.—*298*

DEWEY, J. (1929) *The quest for certainty.* New York: Minton, Balch.—*332*

DEWEY, J. (1938) *Logic: the theory of inquiry.* New York: Holt, Rinehart, and Winston.—*300*

DEWEY, J., and BENTLEY, A. F. (1949) *Knowing and the known.* Boston: Beacon.—*300*

DILL, J. B. *See* Seward, Dill and Holland (1944).

DIVEN, K. (1937) Certain determinants in the conditioning of anxiety reactions. *J. Psychol.*, 3, 291–308.—*288*

DOBRZECKA, C. *See* Wyrwicka and Dobrzecka (1960).

DODGE, R. (1931) *Conditions and consequences of human variability.* New Haven: Yale Univ. Press.—*242*

DOLLARD, J., and MILLER, N. E. (1950) *Personality and psychotherapy.* New York: McGraw-Hill.—*266, 267, 269, 273*

DOLLARD, J., DOOB, L. W., MILLER, N. E., MOWRER, O. H., SEARS, R. R., FORD, C. S., HOVLAND, C. I., and SOLLENBERGER, R. T. (1939) *Frustration and aggression.* New Haven: Yale Univ. Press.—*188, 277*

DOLLARD, J. *See also* Miller and Dollard (1941).

DOOB, L. W. *See* Dollard, Doob, Miller, Mowrer, Sears, Ford, Hovland, and Sollenberger (1939).

DORÉ, L. R., and HILGARD, E. R. (1937) Spaced practice and the maturation hypothesis. *J. Psychol.*, 4, 245–259.—*321*

DOYLE, W. (1960) Recognition of sloppy hand-printed characters. *Proc. 1960 Western Joint Computer Conference.* New York: IRE, 133–142.—*395*

DuBois, P. H., and Forbes, T. W. (1934)   Studies of catatonia: III. Bodily postures assumed while sleeping. *Psychiat. Quart.*, **8**, 546–552.—*277*

Dudycha, G. J., and Dudycha, M. M. (1941)   Childhood memories: a review of the literature. *Psychol. Bull.*, **38**, 668–682.—*282*

Dudycha, M.   *See* Dudycha and Dudycha (1941).

Duncan, C. P. (1949)   The retroactive effect of electroshock on learning. *J. comp. physiol. Psychol.*, **42**, 32–44.—*449, 450*

Duncan, C. P. (1951)   Stimulus-generalization and spread of effect. *Amer. J. Psychol.*, **64**, 585–590.—*38*

Duncker, K. (1945)   On problem-solving. Trans. by L. S. Lees from the 1935 original. *Psychol. Monogr.*, **58**, No. 270.—*248, 389, 402*

Dykman, R. A.   *See* Reese, Dykman, and Peters (1964).

Ebbinghaus, H. (1885)   *Memory*. Translated by H. A. Ruger and C. E. Bussenius. New York: Teachers College, 1913. Reissued as paperback, New York: Dover, 1964.—*1, 151, 310, 354*

Edgren, R. D.   *See* Hilgard, Edgren, and Irvine (1954).

Edling, J. V. (1964)   Programmed instruction in a "continuous progress" school —Provo, Utah. In W. Schramm (Editor), *Four case studies of programmed instruction*. New York: Fund for the Advancement of Education, 65–94.—*561*

Edwards, A. C.   *See* Mayhew and Edwards (1936).

Edwards, A. L. (1941)   Political frames of reference as a factor influencing recognition. *J. abnorm. soc. Psychol.*, **36**, 34–61.—*288*

Edwards, A. L. (1942)   The retention of affective experiences—a criticism and restatement of the problem. *Psychol. Rev.*, **49**, 43–53.—*288*

Edwards, A. L.   *See also* Guthrie and Edwards (1949).

Edwards, W. (1954)   The theory of decision making. *Psychol. Bull.*, **51**, 380–417.—*225*

Edwards, W. (1962)   Utility, subjective probability, their interaction, and variance preference. *J. Conflict Resolution,* **6**, 42–51.—*225*

Egyházi, E.   *See* Hydén and Egyházi (1962, 1964).

Elliott, M. H. (1928)   The effect of change of reward on the maze performance of rats. *Univ. Calif. Publ. Psychol.,* **4**, 19–30.—*196*

Epstein, A. N.   *See* Teitelbaum and Epstein (1962).

Ericksen, S. C. (1942)   Variability in attack in massed and distributed practice. *J. exp. Psychol.*, **31**, 339–345.—*324*

Erickson, M. H.   *See also* Huston, Shakow, and Erickson (1934).

Estes, W. K. (1944)   An experimental study of punishment. *Psychol. Monogr.*, **57**, No. 263.—*124, 135, 136, 137*

Estes, W. K. (1950)   Toward a statistical theory of learning. *Psychol. Rev.*, **57**, 94–107.—*92, 97, 335*

Estes, W. K. (1954)   Kurt Lewin. In Estes, Koch, MacCorquodale, Meehl, Mueller, Schoenfeld, and Verplanck, *Modern learning theory*. New York: Appleton-Century-Crofts, 317–344.—*262*

Estes, W. K. (1955a)   Statistical theory of spontaneous recovery and regression. *Psychol. Rev.*, **62**, 145–154.—*354–356*

Estes, W. K. (1955b) Statistical theory of distributional phenomena in learning. *Psychol. Rev.*, 62, 369–377.—*356*

Estes, W. K. (1958) Stimulus-response theory of drive. In M. R. Jones (Editor), *Nebraska symposium on motivation*. Vol. 6. Lincoln: Univ. of Nebraska Press.—*80, 361, 362*

Estes, W. K. (1959a) The statistical approach to learning theory. In S. Koch (Editor), *Psychology: A study of a science*. Vol. 2. New York: McGraw-Hill.—*335, 349, 356, 359, 380*

Estes, W. K. (1959b) Component and pattern models with Markovian interpretations. In R. R. Bush and W. K. Estes (Editors) *Studies in mathematical learning theory*. Stanford: Stanford Univ. Press.—*365*

Estes, W. K. (1962) Theoretical treatments of differential reward in multiple-choice learning and two-person interactions. In Joan Criswell, H. Solomon, and P. Suppes (Editors), *Mathematical methods in small group processes*. Stanford: Stanford Univ. Press.—*349*

Estes, W. K. (1964) Probability learning. In A. W. Melton (Editor), *Categories of human learning*. New York: Academic.—*349, 353*

Estes, W. K. *See also* Burke, Estes, and Hellyer (1954); Bush and Estes (1959); Friedman, Burke, Cole, Keller, Millword, and Estes (1964); Keller, Cole, Burke, and Estes (1965).

Estes, W. K., Koch, S., MacCorquodale, K., Meehl, P. E., Mueller, C. G., Jr., Schoenfeld, W. N., and Verplanck, W. S., (1954). *Modern learning theory*. New York: Appleton-Century-Crofts.—*14*

Evans, S. (1936) Flexibility of established habit. *J. gen. Psychol.*, 14, 177-200. —*198*

Evans, T. C. (1963) A heuristic program for solving geometric analogy problems. Unpublished Ph.D. dissertation, Mass. Inst. Tech., Cambridge.—*402, 403*

Eysenck, H. J. (1952) The effects of psychotherapy: An evaluation. *J. consult. Psychol.*, 16, 319–324.—*294*

Fagan, C. A., and North, A. J. (1951) A verification of the guessing sequence hypothesis about spread of effect. *J. exp. Psychol.*, 41, 349–531.—*35*

Farber, I. E. (1954) Anxiety as a drive state. *Current theory and research on motivation*. In M. R. Jones (Editor), *Nebraska symposium on motivation*. Lincoln: Univ. of Nebraska Press, 1-46.—*273*

Fattu, N. A. *See* Standlee, Popham, and Fattu (1956).

Fea, II. R. *See* Russell and Fea (1963).

Fechner, G. T. (1873) Einige Ideen zur Schöpfungs—und Entwicklungsgeschichte der Organismen. Leipzig.—*266*

Feigenbaum, E. A. (1959) An information processing theory of verbal learning. A RAND Corp. Paper, P–1817, October.—*411*

Feigenbaum, E. A., and Feldman, J. (1963) *Computers and thought*. New York: McGraw-Hill.—*389, 401, 425*

Feigenbaum, E. A., and Simon, H. A. (1961) Performance of a reading task by an elementary perceiving and memorizing program. *A RAND Corp. Paper*, P–2358, July.—*413*

FEIGENBAUM, E. and SIMON, H. A. (1962) A theory of the serial position effect. *Brit. J. Psychol.,* 53, 307–320.—*413*

FEIGENBAUM, E. A. *See* Simon and Feigenbaum (1964).

FELDMAN, J. (1961) Simulation of behavior in the binary choice experiment. *Proc. 1961 Western Joint Computer Conference,* New York: IRE, 133–144.—*413, 421*

FELDMAN, J. (1962) Computer simulation of cognitive processes. In H. Borko (Editor), *Computer applications in the behavioral sciences.* Englewood Cliffs: Prentice-Hall.—*413–415, 422*

FELDMAN, J. *See* Feigenbaum and Feldman (1963).

FELDMAN, S. E. *See* Binder and Feldman (1960).

FELSINGER, J. M., GLADSTONE, A. I., YAMAGUCHI, H. G., and HULL, C. L. (1947) Reaction latency (stR) as a function of the number of reinforcements (N). *J. exp. Psychol.,* 37, 214–228.—*161*

FELSINGER, J. M. *See* Gladstone, Yamaguchi, Hull, and Felsinger (1947); Hull, Felsinger, Gladstone, and Yamaguchi (1947); Yamaguchi, Hull, Felsinger, and Gladstone (1948).

FENICHEL, O. (1945) *The psychoanalytic theory of neurosis.* New York: Norton. —*269, 270, 275*

FERSTER, C. S., and SKINNER, B. F. (1957) *Schedules of reinforcement.* New York: Appleton-Century-Crofts.—*117, 118, 120, 143, 145*

FESTINGER, L. (1942) Wish, expectation, and group standards as affecting level of aspiration. *J. abnorm. soc. Psychol.,* 37, 184–200.—*227*

FESTINGER, L. (1957) *A theory of cognitive dissonance.* New York: Harper & Row.—*227, 491*

FESTINGER, L. (1961) The psychological effects of insufficient rewards. *Amer. Psychologist,* 16, 1–11.—*490*

FESTINGER, L. *See* Lawrence and Festinger (1962).

FIELD, J., MAGOUN, H. W., and HALL, V. E. (Editors) (1960) *Handbook of physiology,* Vol. 3. Washington, D. C.: American Physiological Society.—*429, 479*

FIFKOVA, E. *See* Bures, Beuesova, and Fifkova (1964).

FISHER, A. E. (1956) Maternal and sexual behavior induced by intracranial chemical stimulation. *Science,* 124, 228–229.—*433*

FISHER, A. E. *See* Vaughan and Fisher (1962).

FISKE, D. W., and MADDI, S. R. (Editors) (1961) *Functions of varied experience.* Homewood, Ill.: Dorsey Press.—*281*

FITCH, F. B. *See* Hull and others (1940).

FITTS, P. M. (1962) Factors in complex skill training. In R. Glaser (Editor) *Training research and education.* Pittsburgh: Univ. of Pittsburgh Press, 177–197.—*545*

FJERDINGSTAD, E. J., NISSEN, Th., and RØIGAARD-PETERSEN, H. H. (1965) Effect of ribonucleic acid (RNA) extracted from the brain of trained animals on learning in rats. *Scand. J. Psychol.,* 6, 1–6.—*467*

FLAVELL, J. H. (1963) *The developmental psychology of Jean Piaget.* Princeton: Van Nostrand.—*571*

FLEISHMAN, E. A. (1962) The description and prediction of perceptual-motor skill learning. In R. Glaser (Editor) *Training research and education.* Pittsburgh: Univ. of Pittsburgh Press, 137–175.—*547, 548*

FLEISHMAN, E. A. *See also* Parker and Fleishman (1959).

FLEXMAN, R. E. *See* Williams and Flexman (1949).

FLEXMAN, R. E., MATHENY, W. G., and BROWN, E. L. (1950) Evaluation of the school link and special methods of instruction. *Univ. of Illinois Bull.,* 47, No. 80.—*546*

FOLLEY, J. D., JR. *See* Miller, Folley and Smith (1953).

FOORD, E. N. *See* Hebb and Foord (1945).

FORBES, T. W. *See* DuBois and Forbes (1934).

FORD, C. S. *See* Dollard, Doob, Miller, Mowrer, Sears, Ford, Hovland, and Sollenberger (1939).

FORGIE, J. W., and FORGIE, C. D. (1959) Results obtained from a vowel recognition computer program. *J. Acoust. Soc. Am.,* 11, 1480–1489.—*397*

FORGIE, C. D. *See* Forgie and Forgie (1959).

FOSHAY, A. W. *See* Herbert and Foshay (1964).

FRANKMANN, R. W. *See* Suppes, Rouanet, Levine, and Frankmann (1964).

FREDERIKSEN, N. (1962) Proficiency tests for training evaluation. In R. Glaser (Editor), *Training research and education.* Pittsburgh: Univ. of Pittsburgh Press, 323–346.—*544*

FREUD, A. (1935) *Psychoanalysis for teachers and parents.* New York: Emerson. —*282, 296*

FREUD, S. (1911) Formulations regarding the two principles in mental functioning. In *Collected papers.* London: Hogarth, 1925, IV, 13–21.—*267*

FREUD, S. (1915a) Repression. In *Collected papers.* London: Hogarth, 1925, IV, 84–97.—*274*

FREUD, S. (1915b) The unconscious. In *Collected Papers.* London: Hogarth, 1925, IV, 98–136.—*277, 293*

FREUD, S. (1920a) *A general introduction to psychoanalysis.* New York: Liveright.—*271*

FREUD, S. (1920b) *Beyond the pleasure principle.* Translation, 1950. New York: Liveright.—*265, 266, 269, 285, 295*

FREUD, S. (1921) *Group psychology and the analysis of the ego.* Translation, 1922. New York: Liveright.—*277*

FREUD, S. (1923) *The ego and the id.* Translation, 1927. London: Hogarth.—*295*

FREUD, S. (1926) *The problem of anxiety.* Translation, 1936. New York: Norton. —*271, 272, 273, 296*

FREUD, S. (1940) *An outline of psychoanalysis.* Translation, 1949. New York: Norton.—*296*

FRIEDMAN, M. P., BURKE, C. J., COLE, M., KELLER, L., MILLWORD, R. B., and ESTES, W. K. (1964) Two-choice behavior under extended training with shifting probabilities of reinforcement. In R. C. Atkinson (Editor), *Studies in mathematical psychology.* Stanford: Stanford Univ. Press.—*353*

FRIEDMAN, S. M. (1952) An empirical study of the castration and oedipus complexes. *Genet. Psychol. Monogr.,* 46, 61–130.—*282*

FROLOV, Y. P. (1937) *Pavlov and his school.* New York: Oxford Univ. Press.— *49, 73*

FRYE, C. H. (1963) *Group vs individual pacing in programmed instruction.* Portland, Ore.: Oregon State System of Higher Education.—*560*

FUSTER, J. M. (1958) Effects of stimulation of brain stem on tachistoscopic perception. *Science,* 127, 150.—*441, 442*

GAGE, N. L. (Editor) (1963) *Handbook of research on teaching.* Chicago: Rand McNally.—*584*

GAGNÉ, R. M. (1962) Simulators. In R. Glaser (Editor), *Training research and education.* Pittsburgh: Univ. of Pittsburgh Press, 223–246.—*545, 549*

GAGNÉ, R. M. (1964) The analysis of instructional objectives for the design of instructions. In R. Glaser (Editor), *Teaching machines and programmed learning: II. Data and directions.* Washington: Nat'l Educ. Assoc.—*503*

GAGNÉ, R. M. (1965) *The conditions of learning.* New York: Holt, Rinehart, and Winston.—*569–573*

GAGNÉ, R. M., and BASSLER, O. C. (1963) Study of retention of some topics of elementary non-metric geometry. *J. educ. Psychol.,* 54, 123–131.—*571*

GAGNÉ, R. M., MAYOR, J. R., GARSTENS, H. L., and PARADISE, N. E. (1962) Factors in acquiring knowledge of a mathematical task. *Psychol. Monogr.,* 76, No. 526.—*571*

GALANTER, E. H. (Editor) (1959) *Automatic teaching: The state of the art.* New York: Wiley.—*558*

GALANTER, E. (1966) Comments on "A descriptive theory of memory." In D. P. Kimble, (Editor), *Learning, Remembering, and Forgetting. The organization of memory.* Vol. 2, Palo Alto: Science and Behavior Books.—*376*

GALANTER, E. *See* Bush, Galanter, and Luce, (1963); Luce, Bush, and Galanter (1963a, 1963b, 1965a, 1965b); Miller, Galanter, and Pribram (1960).

GALLAGHER, R. *See* Cottrell and Gallagher (1941).

GANTT, W. H. (1965) Pavlov's system. In B. B. Wolman and E. Nagel (Editors), *Scientific psychology.* New York: Basic Books, 127–149.—*61, 73*

GARSTENS, H. L. *See* Gagné, Mayor, Garstens, and Paradise (1962).

GEIER, F. M., LEVIN, M., and TOLMAN, E. C. (1941) Individual differences in emotionality, hypothesis formation, vicarious trial and error, and visual discrimination learning in rats. *Comp. Psychol. Monogr.,* 17, Serial No. 87.—*202*

GEIS, G. L., STEBBINS, W. C., and LUNDIN, R. W. (1965a) *Reflexes and conditioned reflexes: A basic system program.* New York: Appleton-Century-Crofts.—*73*

GEIS, G. L., STEBBINS, W. C., and LUNDIN, R. W. (1965b) *Reflexes and operant conditioning: A basic systems program.* New York: Appleton-Century-Crofts.—*145*

GELB, A., and GOLDSTEIN, K. (1918) Zur Psychologie des optischen Wahrnehmungs—und Erkennungsvorganges. *Z. ges. Neurol. Psychiat.,* 41, 1–143.—*259*

GELERNTER, H. (1959) Realization of a geometry-theorem proving machine. *Proc. of the international conference on information processing.* New York UNESCO, 273–282.—*398*

GENGERELLI, J. A. (1928) Preliminary experiments on the causal factors in animal learning. *J. comp. Psychol.,* 8, 435–457.—*75*

GENTRY, G., BROWN, W. L., and KAPLAN, S. J. (1947) An experimental analysis of the spatial location hypothesis in learning. *J. comp. physiol. Psychol.,* 40, 309–322.—*197*

GERARD, R. W. (1963) The material basis of memory. *J. verb. Learn. verb. Behav.,* 2, 22–33.—*447, 448*

GIBSON, E. J. (1940) A systematic application of the concepts of generalization and differentiation to verbal learning. *Psychol. Rev.,* 47, 196–229.—*318*

GIBSON, E. J. (1942) Intralist generalization as a factor in verbal learning. *J. exp. Psychol.,* 30, 185–200.—*318*

GIBSON, E. J. *See also* Gibson and Gibson (1955).

GIBSON, E. J., GIBSON, J. J., DANIELSON, A., and OSSER, H. (1962) A developmental study of the discrimination of letter-like forms. *J. comp. physiol. Psychol.,* 55, 897–906.—*576*

GIBSON, J. J. (1929) The reproduction of visually perceived forms. *J. exp. Psychol.,* 12, 1–39.—*248*

GIBSON, J. J. *See also* Gibson, Gibson, Danielson, and Osser (1962).

GIBSON, J. J., and GIBSON, Eleanor J. (1955) Perceptual learning: Differentiation or enrichment. *Psychol. Rev.,* 62, 32–41.—*532, 533*

GIBSON, R. *See* Pickrel, Neidt, and Gibson (1958).

GILBERT, T. F. (1962a) A structure for a coordinated research and development laboratory. In R. Glaser (Editor) *Training research and education.* Pittsburgh: Univ. of Pittsburgh Press, 559–578.—*580*

GILBERT, T. F. (1926b) Mathetics: the technology of education. *J. Mathetics,* 1, 7–73.—*570*

GILHOUSEN, H. C. (1931) An investigation of "insight" in rats. *Science,* 73, 711–712.—*269*

GINSBERG, A. (1954) Hypothetical constructs and intervening variables. *Psychol. Rev.,* 61, 119–131.—*218*

GINSBERG, R. *See* Suppes and Ginsberg (1962, 1963).

GINTHER, J. R. *See* Thelen and Ginther (1964).

GIRDEN, E., and CULLER, E. A. (1937) Conditioned responses in curarized striate muscle in dogs. *J. comp. Psychol.,* 23, 261–274.—*475*

GLADSTONE, A. I., YAMAGUCHI, H. G., HULL, C. L., and FELSINGER, J. M. (1947) Some functional relationships of reaction potential (sER) and related phenomena. *J. exper. Psychol.,* 37, 510–526.—*161*

GLADSTONE, A. I. *See also* Felsinger, Gladstone, Yamaguchi, and Hull (1947); Hull, Felsinger, Gladstone, and Yamaguchi (1947); Yamaguchi, Hull, Felsinger, and Gladstone (1948).

GLASER, R. (Editor) (1962) *Training research and education.* Pittsburgh: Univ. of Pittsburgh Press.—*542, 545, 584*

GLASER, R. (1964) Implications of training research for education. In E. R. Hilgard. (Editor), *Theories of learning and instruction.* Chicago: Univ. of Chicago Press, 153–181.—*580*

GLASER, R. *See* Lumsdaine and Glaser (1960).

GLASER, N. M. *See* Maier, Glaser, and Klee (1940).

GLEITMAN, H., *See also* Tolman and Gleitman (1949).

GLEITMAN, H., and STEINMAN, F. (1963) The retention of runway performance as a function of proactive interference. *J. comp. physiol. Psychol.,* 56, 834–838.—*496*

GLICKMAN, S. E. (1961) Perseverative neural processes and consolidation of the memory trace. *Psychol. Bull.,* 58, 218–233.—*324*

GLICKSTEIN, M., and SPERRY, R. W. (1960) Intermanual somesthetic transfer in split-brain rhesus monkeys. *J. comp. physiol. Psychol.,* 53, 322–327.—*473*

GOAD, D. *See* Underwood and Goad (1951).

GOLD, B. (1959)   Machine recognition of hand-sent Morse code. *IRE Trans. on Inform. Theory*, IT–5, 17–24.—*395*

GOLDSTEIN, H., KRANTZ, D. L., and RAINS, J. D. (1965)   *Controversial issues in learning*. New York: Appleton-Century-Crofts.—*14, 539*

GOLDSTEIN, K. (1939)   *The organism: A holistic approach to biology derived from pathological data in man*. New York: American Book.—*259*

GOLDSTEIN, K. (1940)   *Human nature*. Cambridge: Harvard Univ. Press.—*259*

GOLDSTEIN, K. (1948)   *Language and language disturbances*. New York: Greene and Stratton.—*259*

GOLDSTEIN, K.   *See* Gelb and Goldstein (1918).

GOODNOW, J.   *See* Bruner, Goodnow, and Austin (1956).

GOODSON, F. E.   *See* Marx and Goodson (1956).

GORDON, K. (1905)   Über das Gedächtnis für affektiv bestimmte Eindrücke. *Arch. ges. Psychol.*, 4, 437–458.—*275*

GORDON, K. (1925)   The recollection of pleasant and unpleasant odors. *J. exp. Psychol.*, 8, 225–239.—*275*

GOREN, C.   *See* Jacobson, Babich, Bubash, and Goren (1966).

GOTTSCHALDT, K. (1926)   Über den Einfluss der Erfahrung auf die Wahrnehmung von Figuren, I. *Psychol. Forsch.*, 8, 261–317. Translated and condensed as "Gestalt factors and repetition" in W. D. Ellis (1938) *A source book of gestalt psychology*. New York: Harcourt, Brace and World, 109–122.—*236*

GRANT, D. A. (1962)   Testing the null hypothesis and the strategy and tactics of investigating theoretical models. *Psychol. Rev.*, 69, 54–61.—*375*

GRANT, D. A. (1964)   Classical and operant conditioning. In A. W. Melton, (Editor), *Categories of human learning*. New York: Academic, 1–31.—*64–66, 581*

GRANT, D. A., HAKE, H. W., and HORNSETH, J. P. (1951)   Acquisition and extinction of a verbal conditioned response with differing percentages of reinforcement. *J. exp. Psychol.*, 42, 1–5.—*206*

GRAY, J. A. (Editor) (1964)   *Pavlov's typology: Recent theoretical and experimental developments from the laboratory of B. M. Teplov*. New York: Macmillan.—*73*

GREEN, B. F., JR. (1963)   *Digital computers in research*. New York: McGraw-Hill. —*385, 389, 408, 425*

GREEN, B. F., WOLF, A., CHOMSKY, C., and LAUGHERY, K. (1961)   Baseball: an automatic question-answerer. *Proc. 1961 Western Joint Computer Conference*. New York: IRE, 219–224.—*409*

GREEN, E. J. (1956)   Stimulus variability and operant discrimination in human subjects. *Amer. J. Psychol.*, 69, 269–273.—*344*

GREENO, J. G., and STEINER, T. E. (1965)   Markovian processes with identifiable states: general considerations and application to all-or-none learning. *Psychometrika*, 29, 309–333.—*371*

GREENO, J. G.   *See also* Polson and Greeno (1965).

GREENSPOON, J. (1955)   The reinforcing effect of two spoken sounds on the frequency of two responses. *Amer. J. Psychol.*, 68, 409–416.—*134*

GREENSPOON, J. (1962)   Verbal conditioning in clinical psychology. In A. J. Bachrach, *Experimental foundations of clinical psychology*. New York: Basic Books.—*134*

GRINKER, R. R., and SPIEGEL, J. P. (1945a) *Men under stress.* New York: Blakiston.—*290*

GRINKER, R. R., and SPIEGEL, J. P. (1945b) *War neuroses.* New York: Blakiston. —*290*

GROSS, C. H., and CAREY, F. M. (1965) Transfer of a learned response by RNA injection: failure of attempts to replicate. *Science, 150,* 1749.—*468*

GROSSMAN, S. P. (1960) Eating or drinking elicited by direct adrenergic or cholinergic stimulation of the hypothalamus. *Science, 132,* 301–302.—*432*

Group for the Advancement of Psychiatry (1964) *Pavlovian conditioning and American psychiatry.* Symposium No. 9. New York: Group for the Advancement of Psychiatry.—*61*

GRUSEC, T. (1965) Aversive conditioning and peak shift in stimulus generalization. Ph. D. dissertation, Stanford Univ.—*521*

GUTHRIE, E. R. (1930) Conditioning as a principle of learning. *Psychol. Rev., 37,* 412–428.—*97, 106*

GUTHRIE, E. R. (1934) Pavlov's theory of conditioning. *Psychol. Rev., 41,* 199–206.—*76*

GUTHRIE, E. R. (1935) *The psychology of learning.* New York: Harper & Row. —*77, 79, 80, 82–86, 97, 101, 104, 106, 243*

GUTHRIE, E. R. (1936a) Psychological principles and scientific truth. *Proc. 25th Anniv. Celebr. Inaug. Grad. Stud.,* Univ. Southern California.—*86*

GUTHRIE, E. R. (1936b) Thorndike's concept of "belonging." *Psyhol. Bull., 33,* 621.—*28*

GUTHRIE, E. R. (1938) *The psychology of human conflict.* New York: Harper & Row.—*80, 106*

GUTHRIE, E. R. (1940) Association and the law of effect. *Psychol. Rev., 47,* 127–148.—*81*

GUTHRIE, E. R. (1942) Conditioning: A theory of learning in terms of stimulus, response, and assoiation. Chapter 1 in *The psychology of learning. Natl. Soc. Stud. Educ.,* 41st Yearbook, Part II, 17–60.—*77, 81, 87, 104, 106*

GUTHRIE, E. R. (1952) *The psychology of learning,* Revised. New York: Harper & Row.—*80, 90, 104, 106, 206, 224*

GUTHRIE, E. R. (1959) Association by contiguity. In S. Koch, (Editor), *Psychology: A study of a science,* Vol. 2. New York: McGraw-Hill, 158–195.— *91, 92, 106*

GUTHRIE, E. R. *See also* Smith and Guthrie (1921).

GUTHRIE, E. R., and EDWARDS, A. L. (1949) *Psychology: A first course in human behavior.* New York: Harper & Row.—*80*

GUTHRIE, E. R., and HORTON, G. P. (1946) *Cats in a puzzle box.* New York: Holt, Rinehart, and Winston.—*80, 81, 87, 89, 90, 243, 245*

GUTHRIE, E. R., and POWERS, F. F. (1950) *Educational psychology.* New York: Ronald.—*80*

GWINN, G. T. (1949) The effects of punishment on cats motivated by fear. *J. exp. Psychol., 39,* 260–269.—*83*

HAKE, H. W. *See* Grant, Hake, and Hornseth (1951).

HALL, C. S. (1954) *A primer of Freudian psychology.* Cleveland: World Publishing.—*272*

HALL, C. S. *See also* Tolman, Hall, and Bretnall (1932).

HALL, M. *See* Hull and others (1940).

HALL, V. E. *See* Field, Magoun, and Hall (1960).

HAMILTON, J. A., and KRECHEVSKY, I. (1933) Studies in the effect of shock upon behavior plasticity in the rat. *J. comp. Psychol.,* 16, 237–253.—*276*

HANAWALT, N. G. (1937) Memory traces for figures in recall and recognition. *Arch. Psychol.,* New York, No. 216.—*249*

HANAWALT, N. G. (1952) The method of comparison applied to the problem of memory change. *J. exp. Psychol.,* 43, 37–42.—*249*

HANSON, L. F. (Editor) (1963) *Programs.* Washington, D. C.: U. S. Office of Education.—*558*

HARLOW, H. F. (1949) The formation of learning sets. *Psychol. Rev.,* 56, 51–65. —*241*

HARLOW, H. F., and WOOLSEY, C. N. (Editors) (1958) *Biological and biochemical bases of behavior.* Madison: Univ. of Wisconsin Press.—*479*

HARSH, C. M. (1937) Disturbance and "insight" in rats. *Univ. Calif. Publ. Psychol.,* 6, 163–168.—*198*

HARTER, N. *See* Bryan and Harter (1897, 1899).

HARTMANN, G. W. (1941) Frustration phenomena in the social and political sphere. *Psychol. Rev.,* 48, 362–363.—*277*

HARTMANN, H. (1958) *Ego psychology and the problem of adaptation.* New York: Intern. Univ. Press.—*268*

HARTMANN, H., and KRIS, E. (1945) The genetic approach in psychoanalysis. *Psychoanal. Stud. Child,* 1, 11–30.—*280*

HAWKINS, T. D. *See* Pliskoff, Wright, and Hawkins (1965).

HAYGOOD, R., and BOURNE, L. E. (1965) Attribute and rule learning aspects of conceptual behavior. *Psychol. Rev.,* 72, 175–195.—*418*

HAYS, D. G. (1962) Automatic language-data processing. In H. Borko (Editor), *Computer applications in the behavioral sciences.* Englewood Cliffs: Prentice-Hall.—*408*

HAYS, Ruth (1962) Psychology of the scientist: III. Introduction to "Passages from the 'Idea Books' of Clark L. Hull." *Percept. Motor Skills,* 15, 803–806.—*190*

HEATH, R. G., and MICKLE, W. A. (1960) Evaluation of seven years' experience with depth electrode studies in human patients. In Ramey and O'Doherty (Editors), *Electrical studies on the unanesthetized brain.* New York: Harper & Row, 214–247.—*438*

HEATHERS, L. B., and SEARS, R. R. (1943) Experiments on repression. II. The Sharp technique. (Unpublished: see Sears, 1943.)—*286*

HEBB, D. O. (1949) *The organization of behavior.* New York: Wiley.—*220, 447, 452, 456, 505*

HEBB, D. O., and FOORD, E. N. (1945) Errors of visual recognition and the nature of the trace. *J. exp. Psychol.,* 35, 335–348.—*249*

HEBERT, J. A., and KRANTZ, D. L. (1965) Transposition: A re-evaluation. *Psychol. Bull.* 63, 244–257.—*527*

HEIDBREDER, E. (1933) *Seven psychologies.* New York: Appleton-Century-Crofts. —*298*

HEINEMAN, C. *See* Schlosberg and Heineman (1950).

HEINZE, S. J. *See* Stein and Heinze.

HELD, R. *See* Köhler and Held (1949); Köhler, Held, and O'Connell (1952).

HELLYER, S. (1962) Supplementary report: Frequency of stimulus presentation and short-term decrement in recall. *J. exp. Psychol.,* 64, 650.—*508*

HELLYER, S. *See* Burke, Estes, and Hellyer (1954).

HELSON, H. (1964) *Adaptation-level theory.* New York: Harper & Row.—*486, 516, 518*

HENLE, M. (1942) An experimental investigation of past experience as a determinant of visual form perception. *J. exp. Psychol.,* 30, 1–22.—*237*

HENLE, M. (1961) *Documents of Gestalt psychology.* Berkeley and Los Angeles: Univ. of California Press.—*263*

HENLE, M. *See also* Wallach and Henle (1941) (1942).

HERBERT, J., and FOSHAY, A. W. (1964) Programed instruction in the Manhasset Junior High School. In W. Schramm (Editor) *Four case studies of programed instruction.* New York: Fund for the Advancement of Education.—*560*

HERNANDEZ-PEON, R., SCHERRER, H., and JOUVET, M. (1956) Modification of electric activity in cochlear nucleus during "attention" in unanesthetized cats. *Science,* 123, 331–332.—*443, 528*

HESS, E. H. (1958) "Imprinting" in animals. *Sci. American,* 198, March, 81–90.—*3*

HESS, W. R. (1929) The mechanism of sleep. *Amer. J. Physiol.,* 90, 386–387.—*59*

HILGARD, E. R. (1931) Conditioned eyelid reactions to a light stimulus based on the reflex wink to sound. *Psychol. Monogr.,* 41, No. 184.—*96*

HILGARD, E. R. (1940) Review of *Mathematico-deductive theory of rote learning: The psychological system. Psychol. Bull.,* 37, 808–815.—*151, 152*

HILGARD, E. R. (1948) *Theories of learning,* First edition. New York: Appleton-Century-Crofts.—*232*

HILGARD, E. R. (1956) *Theories of learning,* Second edition. New York: Appleton-Century-Crofts.—*161, 202, 481*

HILGARD, E. R. (1958) Intervening variables, hypothetical constructs, parameters, and constants. *Amer. J. Psychol.,* 71, 238–246.—*12, 218*

HILGARD, E. R. (1960) Learning theory and its applications. In W. Schramm (Editor), *New teaching aids for the American classroom.* Stanford: Institute for Communication Research, 19–26.—*562*

HILGARD, E. R. (1962) Impulsive versus realistic thinking: an examination of the distinction between primary and secondary processes in thought. *Psychol. Bull.,* 59, 477–488.—*283*

HILGARD, E. R. (Editor) (1964a) *Theories of learning and instruction.* 63rd Yearbook, National Soc. for Study of Educ., Part I. Chicago: Univ. of Chicago Press.—*14, 503, 584*

HILGARD, E. R. (1964b) A perspective on the relationship between learning theory and educational practices. In E. R. Hilgard (Editor), *Theories of learning and instruction.* Chicago: Univ. of Chicago Press, 402–415.—*573, 575*

HILGARD, E. R. (1964c) The place of gestalt theory and field theories in contemporary learning theory. In *Theories of learning and instruction.* Chicago, Ill.: 63rd Yearbook, Part I. Nat'l Soc. for the Study of Education, 54–77. —*261, 565*

HILGARD, E. R. *See also* Cohen, Hilgard, and Wendt (1933); Umemoto and Hilgard (1961); Doré and Hilgard (1937).

HILGARD, E. R., and CAMPBELL, A. A. (1936) The course of acquisition and retention of conditioned eyelid responses in man. *J. exp. Psychol.,* **19,** 227–247.—*79*

HILGARD, E. R., CAMPBELL, R. K., and SEARS, W. N. (1938) Conditioned discrimination: the effect of knowledge of stimulus-relationships. *Amer. J. Psychol.,* **51,** 498–506.—*204*

HILGARD, E. R., EDGREN, R. D., and IRVINE, R. P. (1954) Errors in transfer following learning with understanding: further studies with Katona's card-trick experiments. *J. exp. Psychol.,* **47,** 457–464.—*257*

HILGARD, E. R., IRVINE, R. P., and WHIPPLE, J. E. (1953) Rote memorization, understanding, and transfer: an extension of Katona's card-trick experiments. *J. exp. Psychol.,* **46,** 288–292.—*257*

HILGARD, E. R., and MARQUIS, D. G. (1940) *Conditioning and learning.* New York: Appleton-Century-Crofts.—*49, 53, 64, 65, 110, 114–116, 166, 581*

HILGARD, E. R., and SMITH, M. B. (1942) Distributed practice in motor learning: score changes within and between daily sessions. *J. exp. Psychol.,* **30,** 136–146.—*323*

HILGARD, J. R. (1953) Anniversary reactions in parents precipitated by children. *Psychiatry,* **16,** 73–80.—*270*

HILL, W. F. (1963) *Learning: A survey of psychological interpretations.* San Francisco: Chandler.—*14*

HILL, L. M. *See* Keller and Hill (1936).

HILL, W. F. (1964) Contemporary developments within stimulus-response learning theory. Chap. 2 in *Theories of learning and instruction.* Natl. Soc. Stud. Educ., 63rd Yearbook, Part I, 27–53, esp. 40–46.—*106*

HILLE, B. A. *See* Conrad and Hille (1958).

HINDE, R. A., and TINBERGEN, N. (1958) The comparative study of species-specific behavior. In A. Roe, and G. G. Simpson (Editors), *Behavior and evolution.* New Haven: Yale Univ. Press, 251–268.—*3*

HINTZMAN, D. L. (1965) Classification and aural coding in short-term memory. *Psychonomic Science,* **3,** 161–162.—*508*

HOBAN, C. F. (1960) The usable residue of educational film research. In W. Schramm (Editor), *New teaching aids for the American classroom.* Stanford: Institute for Communication Research, 95–115.—*550*

HOEBEL, B. G., and TEITELBAUM, P. (1962) Hypothalamic control of feeding and self-stimulation. *Science,* **135,** 375–376.—*433*

HOEHN, A. J. *See* Sheffield, Margolius, and Hoehn (1961).

HOFFMAN, H. S. (1962) The analogue lab: a new kind of teaching device. *Amer. Psychologist,* **17,** 684–694.—*382*

HOGAN, H. P. *See* Carmichael, Hogan, and Walter (1932).

HOLLAND, J., *see* Luttges, Johnson, Buck, Holland, and McGaugh (1966).

HOLLAND, J. G. (1958) Human vigilance. *Science,* **128,** 61–67.—*528*

HOLLAND, J. G. (1960) Teaching machines: An application of principles from the laboratory. In A. A. Lumsdaine and R. Glaser (Editors), *Teaching machines and programmed learning: A source book.* Washington, D.C.: National Education Association, 215–228.—*568*

HOLLAND, J. G., and SKINNER, B. F. (1961) *The analysis of behavior: A program for self-instruction.* New York: McGraw-Hill.—*107, 132, 145, 528*

HOLLAND, M. A. *See* Seward, Dill, and Holland (1944).

HOLLINGWORTH, H. L. (1928) General laws and redintegration. *J. gen. Psychol.,* 1, 79–90.—*100*

HOLLINGWORTH, H. L. (1931) Effect and affect in learning. *Psychol. Rev.,* 38, 153–159.—*27*

HOLMBERG, A. R. (1950) Nomads of the Long Bow: the Siriono of Eastern Bolivia. *The Smithsonian Institute of Social Anthropology.* Washington, D.C.: Publication No. 10.—*266*

HOLT, E. B. (1915) *The Freudian wish and its place in ethics.* New York: Holt, Rinehart, and Winston.—*292*

HONIG, W. K. (1962) Prediction of preference, transposition, and transposition reversal from the generalization gradient. *J. exp. Psychol.,* 64, 239–248.—*524*

HONIG, W. K. (Editor) (1966) *Operant behavior: Areas of research and application.* New York: Appleton-Century-Crofts.—*131, 145, 539*

HONZIK, C. H. (1936) The sensory basis of maze learning in rats. *Comp. Psychol. Monogr.,* 13, No. 64.—*78*

HONZIK, C. H. *See also* Krechevsky and Honzik (1932); Tolman and Honzik (1930a, 1930b).

HORENSTEIN, B. R. *See* Kimble and Horenstein (1948).

HORNSETH, J. P. *See* Grant, Hake, and Hornseth (1951).

HORTON, G. P. *See* Guthrie and Horton (1946).

HOUSE, B. J. *See* Zeaman and House (1963).

HOVLAND, C. I. (1938) Experimental studies in rote-learning theory. III. Distribution of practice with varying speeds of syllable presentation. *J. exp. Psychol.,* 23, 172–190.—*322*

HOVLAND, C. I. (1939) Experimental studies in rote-learning theory. IV. Comparison of reminiscence in serial and paired associate learning. *J. exp. Psychol.,* 24, 466–484.—*322*

HOVLAND, C. I. (1952) A "communication analysis" of concept learning. *Psychol. Rev.,* 59, 461–472.—*415*

HOVLAND, C. I. *See* Dollard, Doob, Miller, Mowrer, Sears, Ford, Hovland, and Sollenberger (1939); Hull, Hovland, Ross, Hall, Perkins, and Fitch (1940); Hunt and Hovland (1961).

HOVLAND, C. I., and KURTZ, K. H. (1951) Experimental studies in rote-learning theory. IV. Influence of work-decrement factors on verbal learning. *J. exp. Psychol.,* 42, 265–272.—*322*

HOWORTH, C. I. *See* Deutsch and Howorth (1963).

HULL, C. L. (1917) The formation and retention of associations of concepts; an experimental study. *Amer. J. Psychol.,* 28, 419–435.—*152*

HULL, C. L. (1920) Quantitative aspects of the evolution of concepts; an experimental study. *Psychol. Monogr.,* 28, No. 123.—*150*

HULL, C. L. (1928) *Aptitude testing.* Yonkers-on-Hudson: World Book.—*150, 210*

HULL, C. L. (1929) A functional interpretation of the conditioned reflex. *Psychol. Rev.,* 36, 498–511.—*150*

HULL, C. L. (1932) The goal gradient hypothesis and maze learning. *Psychol. Rev.*, **39**, 25–43.—*168*

HULL, C. L. (1933) Differential habituation to internal stimuli in the albino rat. *J. comp. Psychol.*, **16**, 255–273.—*213*

HULL, C. L. (1934a) The concept of the habit-family hierarchy and maze learning. *Psychol. Rev.*, **41**, 33–54; 134–152.—*169*

HULL, C. L. (1934b) Learning: II. The factor of the conditioned reflex. In C. Murchison (Editor), *A handbook of general experimental psychology.* Worchester, Mass.: Clark Univ. Press, 382–455.—*51*

HULL, C. L. (1935a) The conflicting psychologies of learning—a way out. *Psychol. Rev.*, **42**, 491–516.—*147, 150, 187*

HULL, C. L. (1935b) Special review of Thorndike's *The fundamentals of learning. Psychol. Rev.*, **32**, 807–823.—*30*

HULL, C. L. (1937) Mind, mechanism, and adaptive behavior. *Psychol. Rev.*, **44**, 1–32.—*147, 151, 169*

HULL, C. L. (1938) The goal-gradient hypothesis applied to some "field-force" problems in the behavior of young children. *Psychol. Rev.*, **45**, 271–299. —*168, 169*

HULL, C. L. (1939) Modern behaviorism and psychoanalysis. *Trans. N. Y. Acad. Sci.*, Ser. II, **1**, 78–82.—*188*

HULL, C. L. (1943) *Principles of behavior.* New York: Appleton-Century-Crofts. —*151, 153–161, 163, 183, 189*

HULL, C. L. (1945) The place of innate individual and species differences in a natural-science theory of behavior. *Psychol. Rev.*, **52**, 55–60.—*182, 210*

HULL, C. L. (1950) Behavior postulates and corollaries—1949. *Psychol. Rev.*, **57**, 173–180.—*161*

HULL, C. L. (1951) *Essentials of behavior.* New Haven: Yale Univ. Press.—*150, 151, 161, 189*

HULL, C. L. (1952a) *A behavior system: An introduction to behavior theory concerning the individual organism.* New Haven: Yale Univ. Press.—*149, 151, 161–163, 168, 171–173, 175, 177, 178, 181, 184, 189, 514*

HULL, C. L. (1952b) Autobiography. In *A history of psychology in autobiography*, IV. Worcester, Mass.: Clark Univ. Press.—*190*

HULL, C. L. (1962) Psychology of the scientist: IV. Passages from the "Idea books" of Clark L. Hull. *Percept. Motor Skills*, **15**, 807–882.—*150, 190*

HULL, C. L. *See* Felsinger, Gladstone, Yamaguchi, and Hull (1947); Gladstone, Yamaguchi, Hull, and Felsinger (1947); Yamaguchi, Hull, Felsinger, and Gladstone (1948).

HULL, C. L., FELSINGER, J. M., GLADSTONE, A. I., and YAMAGUCHI, H. G. (1947) A proposed quantification of habit strength. *Psychol. Rev.*, **54**, 237–254.—*161*

HULL, C. L., HOVLAND, C. I., ROSS, R. T., HALL, M., PERKINS, D. T., and FITCH, F. G. (1940) *Mathematico-deductive theory of rote learning.* New Haven: Yale Univ. Press.—*150, 151, 153, 189, 322*

HULL, C. L., and LUGOFF, L. S. (1921). Complex signs in diagnostic free association. *J. exp. Psychol.*, **4**, 111-136.—*273*

HUMPHREY, G. (1933) *The nature of learning in its relation to the living system.* New York: Harcourt Brace & World.—*5*

HUMPHREYS, L. G. (1939a) The effect of random alternation of reinforcement on the acquisition and extinction of conditioned eyelid reactions. *J. exp. Psychol.,* **25**, 141–158.—*204*

HUMPHREYS, L. G. (1939b) Acquisition and extinction of verbal expectations in a situation analogous to conditioning. *J. exp. Psychol.,* **25**, 294–301. —*204, 205, 222*

HUNT, E. B. (1962) *Concept learning.* New York: Wiley.—*416*

HUNT, E. B., and HOVLAND, C. I. (1961) Programming a model of human concept formulation. *Proc. 1961 Western Joint Computer Conference.* New York: IRE, 145–156.—*416*

HUNT, E. B., MARIN, J., and STONE, P. (1966) *Experiments in induction.* New York: Academic.—*416*

HUNT, J. McV. (1941) The effects of infant feeding-frustration upon adult hoarding in the albino rat. *J. abnorm. soc. Psychol.,* **36**, 338–360.—*281*

HUSTON, P. E., SHAKOW, D., and ERICKSON, M. H. (1934) A study of hypnotically induced complexes by means of the Luria technique. *J. gen. Psychol.,* **11**, 65–97.—*288*

HYDÉN, H. (1965) Activation of nuclear RNA in neurons and glia in learning. In D. P. Kimble (Editor), *Learning, remembering, and forgetting.* Vol. 1. *The anatomy of memory.* Palo Alto: Science and Behavior Books, 170–239.—*466, 469*

HYDÉN, H., and EGYHÁZI, E. (1962) Nuclear RNA changes of nerve cells during a learning experiment in rats. *Proc. Nat. Acad. Sci. U. S.,* **48**, 1366–1373.—*465*

HYDÉN, H., and EGYHÁZI, E. (1964) Changes in RNA content and base composition in cortical neurons of rats in a learning experiment involving transfer of handedness. *Proc. Nat'l Acad. Sci. U. S.,* **52**, 1030–1035.—*465*

IREY, E. *See* Muenzinger, Koerner, and Irey (1929).

IRION, A. L. (1949) Reminiscence in pursuit-rotor learning as a function of length of rest and of amount of pre-rest practice. *J. exp. Psychol.,* **39**, 492–499.—*322*

IRION, A. L. *See also* McGeoch and Irion (1952).

IRVINE, R. P. *See* Hilgard, Edgren, and Irvine (1954); Hilgard, Irvine, and Whipple (1953).

IRWIN, J. McQ. *See* Melton and Irwin (1940).

IVANOV-SMOLENSKY, A. G. (1927) On the methods of examining the conditioned food reflexes in children and in mental disorders. *Brain,* **50**, 138–141.— *65, 66*

JACKSON, L. L. (1943) VTE on an elevated maze. *J. comp. Psychol.,* **36**, 99–107. —*202*

JACKSON, T. A. (1942) Use of the stick as a tool by young chimpanzees. *J. comp. Psychol.,* **34**, 223–235.—*241*

JACOBSON, A. *See* Babich, Jacobson, Bubash, and Jacobson (1965); Jacobson, Babich, Bubash, and Jacobson (1965).

JACOBSON, A. L., BABICH, F. R., BUBASH, S., and JACOBSON, A. (1965) Differential approach tendencies produced by injection of ribonucleic acid from trained rats. *Science,* 150, 636–637.—*467*

JACOBSON, A. L., BABICH, F. R., BUBASH, S., and GOREN, C. (1966) Maze preferences in naive rats produced by injection of ribonucleic acid from trained rats. *Psychon. Sci.,* 4, 3–4.—*468*

JACOBSON, A. L. *See also* Babich, Jacobson, Bubash, and Jacobson (1965).

JACOBSON, R. *See* Zelman, Kabot, Jacobson, and McConnell (1963).

JAMES, H. (1953) An application of Helson's theory of adaptation level to the problem of transposition. *Psychol. Rev.,* 46, 345–351.—*526*

JAMES, W. (1890) *The principles of psychology.* New York: Holt, Reinhart, and Winston.—*50*

JANET, P. (1935) *Les debuts de l'intelligence.* Paris: E. Flammarion.—*72*

JAYNES, J. *See* Beach and Jaynes (1954).

JENKINS, W. O. (1943) Studies in the spread of effect. *J. comp. Psychol.,* 35, 41–72.—*43*

JENKINS, W. O. *See also* Sheffield and Jenkins (1952).

JENKINS, W. O., and CUNNINGHAM, L. M. (1949) The guessing-sequence hypothesis, the "spread of effect," and number-guessing habits. *J. exp. Psychol.,* 39, 158–168.—*35*

JENKINS, W. O., and POSTMAN, L. (1948) Isolation and "spread of effect" in serial learning. *Amer. J. Psychol.,* 61, 214–221.—*38*

JENKINS, W. O., and SHEFFIELD, F. D. (1946) Rehearsal and guessing habits as sources of the "spread of effect." *J. exp. Psychol.,* 36, 316–330.—*35, 43*

JENKINS, W. O., and STANLEY, J. C., JR. (1950) Partial reinforcement; a review and critique. *Psychol. Bull.,* 47, 193–234.—*144, 206*

JENSEN, D. D. *See* DeBold, Miller, and Jensen (1965).

JOHN, E. R. (1961) Higher nervous functions (brain function and learning). *Ann. Rev. Physiol.,* 23, 451–484.—*477*

JOHN, E. R. *See* Corning and John (1961).

JOHNSON, E. S. (1964) An information-processing model of one kind of problem solving. *Psychol. Monog.,* 78, No. 581.—*418*

JOHNSON, T., see Luttges, Johnson, Buck, Holland, and McGaugh (1966).

JONES, H. B. *See* Caldwell and Jones (1954).

JOUVET, M. *See* Hernandez-Peon, Scherrer, and Jouvet (1956).

JUDD, C. H. (1908) The relation of special training to general intelligence. *Educ. Rev.,* 36, 28–42.—*258*

KABOT, L. *See* Zelman, Kabot, Jacobson, and McConnell (1963).

KALISH, D. *See* Tolman, Ritchie, and Kalish (1946, 1947).

KATONA, G. (1940) *Organizing and memorizing.* New York: Columbia Univ. Press.—*237, 254, 255, 256*

KATONA, G. (1942) Organizing and memorizing: a reply to Dr. Melton. *Amer. J. Psychol.,* 55, 273–275.—*257*

KEET, C. D. (1948) Two verbal techniques in a miniature counseling situation. *Psychol. Monogr.,* 62, No. 204.—*286*

KELLER, F. S., and HILL, L. M. (1936) Another "insight" experiment. *J. genet. Psychol.,* 48, 484–489.—*198*

KELLER, F. S., and SCHOENFELD, W. N. (1950) *Principles of psychology.* New York: Appleton-Century-Crofts.—*121, 122, 129, 130, 140, 142*

KELLER, L., COLE, M., BURKE, C. J., and ESTES, W. K. (1965) *Paired associate learning with differential reward.* Tech. report no. 66, Psychology Series, Institute for Mathematical Studies in the Social Sciences, Stanford Univer., Stanford, Calif., Sept. 3.—*370*

KELLER, L. *See also* Friedman, Burke, Cole, Keller, Millword, and Estes (1964).

KELLEY, E. C. (1947) *Education for what is real.* New York: Harper & Row.—*300*

KENDALL, J. W., Jr. *See* Kimble and Kendall (1953).

KENDLER, H. H. (1946) The influence of simultaneous hunger and thirst drives upon the learning of two opposed spatial responses of the white rat. *J. exp. Psychol.,* **36**, 212–220.—*224*

KENDLER, H. H. (1952) Some comments on Thistlethwaite's perception of latent learning. *Psychol. Bull.,* **49**, 47–51.—*202*

KENDLER, H. H. (1959) Learning. *Annual Rev. Psychol.,* **10**, 43–88.—*261*

KENDLER, H. H. (1964) The concept of the concept. In A. W. Melton (Editor) *Categories of human learning.* New York: Academic, 212–236.—*570*

KEPPEL, G., and UNDERWOOD, B. J. (1962) Proactive inhibition in short-term retention of single items. *J. verb. Learn. verb Behav.,* **1**, 153–161.—*510*

KETY, S. S. (1959) Biochemical theories of schizophrenia. *Science,* **129**, 1528–1532.—*461*

KILPATRICK, W. L. (1925) *Foundations of method.* New York: Macmillan.—*299*

KIMBLE, D. P. (1963) *Physiological psychology: A unit for introductory psychology.* Reading, Mass.: Addison-Wesley.—*439, 440*

KIMBLE, D. P. (Editor) (1965) *Learning, remembering, and forgetting,* Vol. 1. *The anatomy of memory.* Palo Alto: Science and Behavior Books.—*479*

KIMBLE, G. A. (1961) *Hilgard and Marquis' Conditioning and learning,* Second edition. New York: Appleton-Century-Crofts.—*14, 49, 54, 64, 65, 70, 73, 77, 110, 483, 514, 539, 570*

KIMBLE, G. A., and HORENSTEIN, B. R. (1948) Reminiscence in motor learning as a function of length of interpolated rest. *J. exp. Psychol.,* **38**, 239–244.—*322*

KIMBLE, G. A., and KENDALL, J. W., Jr. (1953) A comparison of two methods of producing experimental extinction. *J. exp. Psychol.,* **45**, 87–90.—*99*

KINTSCH, W. (1964) Habituation of the GSR component of the orienting reflex during paired associate learning before and after learning has taken place. *J. math. Psychol.,* **2**, 330–341.—*370*

KINTSCH, W., and MORRIS, C. J. (1964) Application of a Markov model to free recall and recognition. *J. exp. Psychol.,* **69**, 200–206.—*371*

KLEE, J. B. *See* Maier, Glaser, and Klee (1940).

KLEITMAN, N. (1963) *Sleep and wakefulness,* Revised edition. Chicago: Univ. of Chicago Press.—*439*

KLEITMAN, N., and CRISLER, G. (1927) A quantitative study of a salivary conditioned reflex. *Amer. J. Physiol.,* **79**, 571–614.—*51*

KLINE, N. S. (Ed.) (1961) Pavlovian conference on higher nervous activity. *Annals of the New York Academy of Science,* **92**, 813–1198.—*62*

KOCH, S. (1954) Clark L. Hull. In Estes, Koch, MacCorquodale, Meehl, Mueller, Schoenfeld and Verplanck, *Modern learning theory.* New York: Appleton-Century-Crofts, 1–176.—*174, 190*

KOCH, S. (Editor) (1959) *Psychology: a study of a science.* Vol. 2. New York: McGraw-Hill.—*539*

KOCH, S. (Editor) (1963) *Psychology: a study of a science.* Vol. 5. New York: McGraw-Hill.—*539*

KOERNER, L. *See* Muenzinger, Koerner, and Irey (1929).

KOESTLER, A. (1964) *The act of creation.* New York: Macmillan.—*284*

KOFFKA, K. (1924) *The growth of the mind.* Translated by R. M. Ogden. London: Kegan Paul, Trench, Trubner and Co., Ltd.—*229, 231, 235, 263*

KOFFKA, K. (1933) Review of Tolman's *Purposive behavior in animals and men. Psychol. Bull.,* 30, 440–451.—*217*

KOFFKA, K. (1935) *Principles of gestalt psychology.* New York: Harcourt, Brace & World.—*232, 234–239, 258, 263*

KOHLER, I. (1963) The formation and transformation of the perceptual world. *Psychol. Issues, 3,* Monogr. 12.—*304*

KÖHLER, W. (1917) *Intelligenz-prufungen an Menschenaffen.* See Köhler, 1925. —*230*

KÖHLER, W. (1918) Nachweis einfacher Strukturfunktionen beim Schimpansen und beim Haushuhn. *Abb. d. königl Preuss. Ak. d. Wissen,* Phys. Math. Klasse, Nr. 2, 1–101. Translated and condensed as "Simple structural functions in the chimpanzee and in the chicken" in Ellis, W. D. (1938) *A source book of gestalt psychology.* New York: Harcourt, Brace, & World, 217–227.—*523*

KÖHLER, W. (1920) Die physische Gestalten in Ruhe und in stationären Zustand, Ein naturphilosophische Untersuchung. Braunschweig Verlag. (Portions condensed and translated in Ellis, W. D. (1938) *A source book of gestalt psychology.* New York: Harcourt, Brace, and World, 17–54.— *259*

KÖHLER, W. (1925) *The mentality of apes.* Translated by E. Winter. New York: Harcourt, Brace & World.—*229, 263*

KÖHLER, W. (1929) *Gestalt psychology.* New York: Liveright.—*263*

KÖHLER, W. (1938) *The place of value in a world of facts.* New York: Liveright. —*237, 251, 260*

KÖHLER, W. (1940) *Dynamics in psychology.* New York: Liveright.—*251, 254, 263*

KÖHLER, W. (1941) On the nature of associations. *Proc. Amer. phil. Soc.,* 84, 489–502.—*234, 235*

KÖHLER, W. (1943) Review of McGeoch's *The psychology of human learning. Amer. J. Psychol.,* 56, 455–460.

KÖHLER, W. (1947) *Gestalt psychology.* New York: Liveright.—*246, 259, 262, 263*

KÖHLER, W. (1958) Gestalt psychology today. *Amer. Psychologist,* 14, 727–734. —*263*

KÖHLER, W., and HELD, R. (1949) The cortical correlate of pattern vision. *Science, 110,* 414–419.—*259*

KÖHLER, W., HELD, R., and O'CONNELL, D. L. (1952) An investigation of cortical currents. *Proc. Amer. phil. Soc.,* 96, 290–330.—*259*

KÖHLER, W., and RESTORFF, H. VON (1935) Analyse von Vorgangen im Spurenfeld. *Psychol. Forsch.,* 21, 56–112.—*251–253*

KONORSKI, J. (1948) *Conditioned reflexes and neuron organization.* Cambridge: Cambridge Univ. Press.—*73, 455*

KONORSKI, J. (1964) On the mechanism of instrumental conditioning. *Proc. XVII International Congress of Psychology.* Amsterdam: North-Holland Publishing Co., 45–59.—*64*

KONORSKI, J., and MILLER, S. (1937a) On two types of conditioned reflex. *J. gen. Psychol.,* 16, 264–272.—*65*

KONORSKI, J., and MILLER, S. (1937b) Further remarks on two types of conditioned reflex. *J. gen. Psychol.,* 17, 405–407.—*65*

KONORSKI, J. *See also* Miller and Konorski (1928).

KOTOVSKY, K. *See* Simon and Kotovsky (1963).

KRAELING, D. *See* Miller and Kraeling (1952).

KRANTZ, D. L. *See* Goldstein, Krantz, and Rains (1965); Hebert and Krantz (1965).

KRASNER, L. (1958) Studies of the conditioning of verbal behavior. *Psychol. Bull.,* 55, 148–170.—*134, 422*

KRASNER, L. (1965) Verbal conditioning in psychotherapy. In L. Krasner and L. P. Ullman (Editors) *Research in behavior modification.* New York: Holt, Rinehart and Winston, 211–228.—*66, 134, 295*

KRATHWOHL, D. R., BLOOM, B. S., BERTRAM, B. M. (1964) *Taxonomy of educational objectives: Handbook II: Affective domain.* New York: David McKay.—*544*

KRECH, D. *See also* Bennett, Krech, and Rosenzweig (1964); Rosenzweig, Bennett, and Krech (1964).

KRECH, D., and CRUTCHFIELD, R. S. (1948) *Theory and problems of social psychology.* New York: McGraw-Hill.—*251*

KRECH, D., ROSENZWEIG, M., and BENNETT, E. L. (1960) Effects of environmental complexity and training on brain chemistry. *J. comp. physiol Psychol.,* 53, 509–519.—*462*

KRECH, D., ROSENZWEIG, M., and BENNETT, E. L. (1962) Relations between brain chemistry and problem-solving among rats raised in enriched and impoverished environments. *J. comp. physiol. Psychol.,* 55, 801–807.—*462*

KRECHEVSKY, I. (1932a) "Hypotheses" in rats. *Psychol. Rev.,* 39, 516–532.—*202, 206*

KRECHEVSKY, I. (1932b) "Hypotheses" versus "chance" in the presolution period in sensory discrimination-learning. *Univ. Calif. Publ. Psychol.,* 6, 27–44.—*206*

KRECHEVSKY, I. (1933a) Hereditary nature of "hypotheses." *J. comp. Psychol.,* 16, 99–116.—*206*

KRECHEVSKY, I. (1933b) The docile nature of "hypotheses." *J. comp. Psychol.,* 15, 429–443.—*206*

KRECHEVSKY, I. *See* Hamilton and Krechevsky (1933).

KRECHEVSKY, I., and HONZIK, C. H. (1932) Fixation in the rat. *Univ. Calif. Publ. Psychol.*, **6**, 13–26.—*216*

KRETSCHMER, E. (1925) *Physique and character.* (Translated from second edition.) New York: Harcourt, Brace & World.—*60*

KRIS, E. (1947) The nature of psychoanalytic propositions and their validation. In S. Hook and M. R. Konvitz (Editors), *Freedom and experience.* Ithaca, N. Y.: Cornell Univ. Press, 239–259. Also in Marx (1951), pp. 332–351.—*280*

KRIS, E. (1952) *Psychoanalytic explorations in art.* New York: Intern. Univ. Press.—*283*

KRIS, E. *See* Hartmann and Kris (1945).

KUBIE, L. S. (1952) Problems and techniques of psychoanalytic validation and progress. In E. R. Hilgard, L. S. Kubie, and E. Pumpian-Mindlin, *Psychoanalysis as science.* Stanford: Stanford Univ. Press, 46–124.—*280, 295*

KUBIE, L. S. (1953) Some unsolved problems of the scientific career. I. *Amer. Scientist*, **41**, 596–613.—*284*

KUBIE, L. S. (1954) Some unsolved problems of the scientific career. II. *Amer. Scientist*, **42**, 104–112.—*284*

KUHN, T. S. (1962) *The structure of scientific revolutions.* Chicago: Univ. of Chicago Press.—*228, 582*

KUO, Z. Y. (1937) Forced movement or insight? *Univ. Calif. Publ. Psychol.*, **6**, 169–188.—*198*

KURTZ, K. H. *See* Hovland and Kurtz (1951)

LaBERGE, D. L. (1959) A model with neutral elements. In R. R. Bush and W. K. Estes (Editors), *Studies in mathematical learning theory.* Stanford: Stanford Univ. Press.—*347*

LANDAUER, T. K. (1964) Two hypotheses concerning the biochemical basis of memory. *Psychol. Rev.,* **71**, 167–179.—*469*

LASHLEY, K. S. (1929) Learning: I. Nervous mechanisms in learning. In C. Murchison (Editor), *The foundations of experimental psychology.* Worcester, Mass.: Clark Univ. Press, 524–563.—*208*

LASHLEY, K. S., and BALL, J. (1929) Spinal conduction and kinesthetic sensitivity in the maze habit. *J. comp. Psychol.*, **9**, 71–105.—*196*

LASHLEY, K. S., CHOW, K. L., and SEMMES, J. (1951) An examination of the electrical field theory of cerebral integration. *Psychol. Rev.,* **58**, 123–136.—*259*

LAUER, L. W. *See* Moore and Lauer (1963).

LAUGHERY, K. *See* Green, Wolf, Chomsky, and Laughery (1961).

LAWRENCE, D. H. (1950) Acquired distinctiveness of cues: II. Selective association in a constant stimulus situation. *J. exp. Psychol.*, **40**, 175–188.—*532*

LAWRENCE, D. H. (1963) The nature of a stimulus. In S. Koch (Editor), *Psychology: a study of a science.* Study II, Vol. 5. *Process Areas.* New York: McGraw-Hill.—*529*

LAWRENCE, D. H. *See also* Bauer and Lawrence (1953).

LAWRENCE, D. H., and DeRIVERA, J. (1954) Evidence for relational discrimination. *J. comp. physiol. Psychol.*, **47**, 465–471.—*526*

LAWRENCE, D. H., and FESTINGER, L. (1962) *Deterrents and reinforcement: The psychology of insufficient reward.* Stanford: Stanford Univ. Press.—*227, 490, 492, 540*

LEAVITT, H. J. *See* Williams and Leavitt (1947).

LEEPER, R. (1935a) The role of motivation in learning: a study of the phenomenon of differential motivational control of the utilization of habits. *J. genet. Psychol., 46,* 3–40.—*213*

LEEPER, R. (1935b) A study of a neglected portion of the field of learning—the development of sensory organization. *J. genet. Psychol., 46,* 41–75.—*233*

LEEPER, R. (1943) *Lewin's topological and vector psychology, a digest and a critique.* Eugene: Univ. Oregon Press.—*262*

LEEPER, R. *See also* Waters and Leeper (1936).

LEVIN, M. *See* Geier, Levin, and Tolman (1941).

LEVINE, M. *See* Suppes, Rouanet, Levine, and Frankmann (1964).

LEVY, D. M. (1941) The hostile act. *Psychol. Rev., 48,* 356–361.—*277*

LEWIN, K. (1933) Vectors, cognitive processes, and Mr. Tolman's criticism. *J. gen. Psychol., 8,* 318–345.—*217*

LEWIN, K. (1935) *A dynamic theory of personality.* Translated by D. K. Adams and K. E. Zener. New York: McGraw-Hill.—*263*

LEWIN, K. (1942) Field theory and learning. Chapter 4 in *The psychology of learning.* Natl. Soc. Stud. Educ., 41st Yearbook, Part II, 215–242.—*262, 263*

LEWIN, K. *See* Barker, Dembo, and Lewin (1941).

LEWIS, D. J., and MAHER, B. A. (1965) Neural consolidation and electroconvulsive shock. *Psychol. Rev., 72,* 225–239.—*451*

LIDDELL, H. S. (1936) Pavlov, the psychiatrist of the future. *J. Mt. Sinai Hosp., 3,* 101–104.—*61*

LIDDELL, H. S. (1961) Pavlov, the psychiatrist of the future. In N. S. Kline (Editor), Pavlovian Conference on Higher Nervous Activity. *Ann. New York Acad. Sci., 92,* 981–983.—*61*

LINDSAY, K. J. (1959) Transfer and retroaction as a function of response similarity, materials, and experimental design. Unpublished Ph.D. Dissertation, Stanford Univ. (*Diss. Abstr.,* 1960, *20,* 3400–3401.)—*316*

LINDSAY, R. K. (1963) Inferential memory as the basis of machines which understand natural language. In E. A. Feigenbaum and J. Feldman (Editors), *Computers and thought.* New York: McGraw-Hill.—*409*

LINDSLEY, D. B. (1958) The reticular system and perceptual discrimination. In H. H. Jasper *et al.* (Editors), *Reticular formation of the brain.* Boston: Little, Brown, Chap. 25.—*441*

LINDSLEY, O. R. (1960) Characteristics of the behavior of chronic psychotics as revealed by free-operant conditioning methods. *Dis. nerv. System, Monogr. Supp., 21,* 66–78.—*134*

LINDSLEY, O. R. (1963) Free-operant conditioning and psychotherapy. *Current psychiatric therapies,* Vol. 3. New York: Grune and Stratton, 47–56.—*295*

LIPOFSKY, H. *See* Miller, Brown, and Lipofsky (1943).

LIVINGSTON, R. B. (1959) Central control of receptors and sensory transmission systems. In *Handbook Physiol., Sect. I, Neurophysiol.,* Vol. 1, pp. 741–760. Washington, D. C.: Am. Physiol. Soc.—*444*

LOESS, H. (1964) Proactive inhibition in short-term memory. *J. verb. Learn. verb. Behav.,* **3,** 362–368.—*510*

LOGAN, F. A. (1956) A micromolar approach to behavior theory. *Psychol. Rev.,* **63,** 63–73.—*493*

LOGAN, F. A. (1959) The Hull-Spence approach. In S. Koch (Editor), *Psychology: A study of a science,* Vol. 2. New York: McGraw-Hill, 293–358.—*189*

LOGAN, F. A. (1960) *Incentive.* New Haven: Yale Univ. Press.—*493, 494, 540*

LORENZ, K. Z. (1952) *King Solomon's ring.* New York: Crowell.—*3*

LOUCKS, R. B. (1933) An appraisal of Pavlov's systematization of behavior from the experimental standpoint. *J. comp. Psychol.,* **15,** 1–47.—*58*

LOVEJOY, E. P. (1966) Analysis of the overlearning reversal effect. *Psychol. Rev.,* **73,** 87–103.—*529, 531*

LUCE, R. D. (1959) *Individual choice behavior.* New York: Wiley.—*380*

LUCE, R. D. *See also* Bush, Galanter, and Luce (1963).

LUCE, R. D., BUSH, R. R., and GALANTER, E. (Editors) (1963a) *Handbook of mathematical psychology.* Vols. I and II. New York: Wiley.—*380*

LUCE, R. D., BUSH, R. R., and GALANTER, E. (Editors) (1963b) *Readings in mathematical psychology.* Vol. I. New York: Wiley.—*380*

LUCE, R. D., BUSH, R. R., and GALANTER, E. (Editors) (1965a) *Handbook of mathematical psychology.* Vol. III. New York: Wiley.—*380*

LUCE, R. D., BUSH, R. R., and GALANTER, E. (Editors) (1965b) *Readings in mathematical psychology.* Vol. II. New York: Wiley.—*380*

LUCHINS, A. S. (1942) Mechanization in problem solving. The effect of Einstellung. *Psychol. Monogr.,* **54,** No. 248.—*239, 262*

LUCHINS, A. S. (1951) An evaluation of some current criticisms of gestalt psychological work on perception. *Psychol. Rev.,* **58,** 69–95.—*235*

LUCHINS, A. S. (1961) Implications of gestalt psychology for AV learning. *Audiovisual Communication Review,* Supplement IV, 7–31.—*262*

LUCHINS, A. S., and LUCHINS, EDITH H. (1959) *Rigidity of behavior.* Eugene: Univ. of Oregon Books.—*262*

LUCHINS, EDITH H. *See* Luchins and Luchins (1959).

LUGOFF, L. S. *See* Hull and Lugoff (1921).

LUMSDAINE, A. A. (1959) Teaching machines and self-instructional materials. *Audiovisual Communica. Rev.,* **7,** 163–172.—*555*

LUMSDAINE, A. A. (Editor) (1961) *Student response in programmed instruction: A symposium.* Washington, D. C.: National Academy of Sciences—National Research Council.—*545, 558, 566, 584*

LUMSDAINE, A. A. (1962) Experimental research on instructional devices and materials. In R. Glaser (Editor), *Training research and education.* Pittsburgh: Univ. of Pittsburgh Press, 247–294.—*558*

LUMSDAINE, A. A. (1963) Instruments and media of instruction. In N. L. Gage (Editor), *Handbook of research on teaching.* Chicago: Rand McNally, 583–682.—*558*

LUMSDAINE, A. A. (1964) Educational technology, programmed learning, and instructional sciences. In E. R. Hilgard (Editor), *Theories of learning and instruction.* Chicago: Univ. of Chicago Press, 371–401.—*558, 566*

LUMSDAINE, A. A. *See* May and Lumsdaine (1958).

LUMSDAINE, A. A., and GLASER, R. (1960) *Teaching machines and programmed learning: A source book.* Washington, D. C.: National Education Assn.— *558, 584*

LUNDIN, R. W. *See* Geis, Stebbins, and Lundin (1965a, 1965b).

LURIA, A. R. (1961) *The role of speech in the regulation of normal and abnormal behavior.* New York: Lippincott.—*66, 67*

LURIA, A. R. (1965) *The higher cerebral activity in man.* New York: Basic Books.—*73*

LUTTGES, M., JOHNSON, T., BUCK, C., HOLLAND, J., and McGAUGH, J. (1966) An examination of "transfer of learning" by nucleic acids. *Science,* 151, 834–837.—*468*

MACCORQUODALE, K., and MEEHL, P. E. (1948) On a distinction between hypothetical constructs and intervening variables. *Psychol. Rev.,* 55, 95–107.—*12, 218*

MACCORQUODALE, K., and MEEHL, P. E. (1953) Preliminary suggestions as to a formalization of expectancy theory. *Psychol. Rev.,* 60, 55–63.—*221, 224*

MACCORQUODALE, K., and MEEHL, P. E. (1954) Edward C. Tolman. In Estes, Koch, MacCorquodale, Meehl, Mueller, Schoenfeld, and Verplanck, *Modern learning theory.* New York: Appleton-Century-Crofts, 177–266. —*202, 221, 228*

MACCORQUODALE, K. *See also* Meehl and MacCorquodale (1948); Estes, Koch, MacCorquodale, Meehl, Mueller, Schoenfeld, and Verplanck (1954).

MACLEOD, R. B. (1962) Retrospect and prospect. In H. E. Gruber, G. Terrell, and M. Wertheimer (Editors), *Contemporary approaches to creative thinking.* New York: Atherton Press, 175–212.—*262*

McCLELLAND, D. C., and ATKINSON, J. W. (1948) The projective expression of needs: I. The effects of different intensities of the hunger drive on perception. *J. Psychol.,* 25, 205–223.—*266*

McCLELLAND, D. C., ATKINSON, J. W., CLARK, R. A., and LOWELL, E. L. (1953) *The achievement motive.* New York: Appleton-Century-Crofts.—*266*

McCONNELL, J. V. (1962) Memory transfer through cannibalism in planarians. *J. Neuropsychiat.,* 3 (Suppl. 1), 542.—*466*

McCONNELL, J. V. *See also* Zelman, Kabot, Jacobson, and McConnell (1963).

McCULLOCH, W. S. *See* Pitts and McCulloch (1947).

McCUTCHAN, K. *See* Blodgett and McCutchan (1947) (1948).

McDONALD, F. J. (1964) The influence of learning theories on education. In E. R. Hilgard (Editor), *Theories of learning and instruction.* 63rd Yearbook of the Natl. Soc. Study Educ. Chicago: Univ. of Chicago Press, 1–26.—*300, 565*

McGAUGH, J. C. (1965) Facilitation and impairment of memory storage processes. In D. P. Kimble (Editor), *Learning, remembering, and forgetting.* Vol. 1, *The anatomy of memory.* Palo Alto: Science and Behavior Books, 240–291.—*451, 452*

McGAUGH, J. *See* Luttges, Johnson, Buck, Holland, and McGaugh (1966).

McGEOCH, J. A. (1932) Forgetting and the law of disuse. *Psychol. Rev.,* 39, 352–370.—*312, 498*

McGEOCH, J. A. (1936) The vertical dimensions of mind. *Psychol. Rev.*, 43, 107–129.—*303*

McGEOCH, J. A. (1942) *The psychology of human learning.* New York: Longmans.—*309, 318*

McGEOCH, J. A., and IRION, A. L. (1952) *The psychology of human learning.* Revised. New York: Longmans.—*14, 210, 312, 329, 332, 333, 497, 503*

McGILL, W. J. (1963) Stochastic latency mechanisms. In R. D. Luce, R. R. Bush, and E. Galanter (Editors), *Handbook of mathematical psychology.* Vol. I. New York: Wiley.—*360*

McHOSE, J. H. *See* Barrett, Peyser, and McHose (1965).

McLEARY, R. A. (1960) Type of response as a function of interocular transfer in the fish. *J. comp. physiol. Psychol.*, 53, 311–321.—*475*

MACCOBY, N., and SHEFFIELD, F. D. (1961) Combining practice with demonstration in teaching complex sequences: Summary and interpretations. In A. A. Lumsdaine (Editor), *Student response in programmed learning: A symposium.* Washington, D. C.: Natl. Acad. of Sci., 77–85.—*558*

MACCOBY, N. *See also* Sheffield and Maccoby (1961).

MACFARLANE, D. A. (1930) The role of kinesthesis in maze learning. *Univ. Calif. Publ. Psychol.*, 4, 277–305.—*196*

MADDI, S. R. *See* Fiske and Maddi (1961).

MAGER, R. F. (1961a) *Preparing instructional objectives.* Palo Alto: Fearon Publishers.—*543, 544*

MAGER, R. F. (1961b) On the sequencing of instructional content. *Psychol. Reports,* 9, 405–413.—*558*

MAGOUN, H. W. *See* Field, Magoun, and Hall (1960).

MAHER, B. A. *See* Lewis and Maher (1965).

MAHLER-SCHOENBERGER, M. (1942) Pseudoimbecility: a magic cap of invisibility. *Psychoanalyt. Quart.*, 11, 149–164.—*283*

MAIER, N. R. F. (1930) Reasoning in humans. I. On direction. *J. comp. Psychol.*, 10, 115–143.—*241, 243*

MAIER, N. R. F. (1931) Reasoning and learning. *Psychol. Rev.*, 38, 332–346.—*6*

MAIER, N. R. F. (1949) *Frustration, the study of behavior without a goal.* New York: McGraw-Hill.—*270*

MALTZMAN, I. (1952) The Blodgett and Haney types of latent learning experiment: Reply to Thistlethwaite. *Psychol. Bull.*, 49, 52–60.—*202*

MARGOLIUS, G. J. *See* Sheffield, Margolius, and Hoehn (1961).

MARIN, J. *See* Hunt, Marin, and Stone (1966).

MARKLE, S. M. (1963) Programming '63: The straight line bends. In *Programmierter unterricht und Lehrmaschinen.* Report of International Conference on Programmed Instruction and Teaching Machines. Berlin: Pädagogische Arbeitstelle, Secretariat Pädagogisches Zentrum, 368–386.—*557*

MARQUIS, D. G. *See* Hilgard and Marquis (1940).

MARTENS, D. (1946) Spread of effect in verbal serial learning. (Abstract) *Amer. Psychologist*, I, 448–449.—*31, 33*

MARTIN, G. *See* Crowder and Martin (1961).

MARX, M. H. (1951) Intervening variable or hypothetical construct? *Psychol. Rev.*, 58, 235–247.—*218*

MARX, M. H. (1956) Spread of effect: A critical review. *Genet. Psychol. Monogr.*, 53, 119–186.—*35, 41, 47*

MARX, M. H. (1957a) Gradients of error-reinforcements in a serial perceptual-motor task. *Psychol. Monogr.*, **71**, No. 437.—*40*

MARX, M. H. (1957b) Spread of effect: Animal studies. *J. genet Psychol.*, **90**, 219–226.—*43*

MARX, M. H. (Editor) (1963) *Theories in contemporary psychology.* New York: Macmillan.—*14*

MARX, M. H., and GOODSON, F. E. (1956) Further gradients of error reinforcement following repeated reinforced responses. *J. exp. Psychol.*, **51**, 421–428.—*40, 41*

MASLOW, A. H. (1941) Deprivation, threat, and frustration. *Psychol. Rev.*, **48**, 364–366.—*277*

MATHENY, W. G. *See* Flexman, Matheny, and Brown (1950).

MAY, R. (1950) *The meaning of anxiety.* New York: Ronald.—*271*

MAYHEW, K. C., and EDWARDS, A. C. (1936). *The Dewey school: the laboratory school at the University of Chicago, 1896–1903.* New York: Appleton-Century-Crofts.—*299*

MAYOR, J. R. *See* Gagné, Mayor, Garstens, and Paradise (1962).

MAZE, J. R. (1954) Do intervening variables intervene? *Psychol. Rev.*, **61**, 226–234.—*218*

MEEHL, P. E. (1950) On the circularity of the law of effect. *Psychol. Bull.*, **47** 52–75.—*47, 482*

MEEHL, P. E. *See also* MacCorquodale and Meehl (1948, 1953, 1954); Estes, Koch, MacCorquodale, Meehl, Mueller, Schoenfeld, and Verplanck, (1954).

MEEHL, P. E., and MACCORQUODALE, K. (1948) A further study of latent learning in the T-maze. *J. comp. physiol. Psychol.*, **41**, 372–396.—*224*

MEER, B. *See* Stein and Meer (1954).

MEIKLE, T. H. (1960) Role of corpus callosum in transfer of visual discrimination in the cat. *Science*, **132**, 1496.—*475*

MEIKLE, T. H., and SECHZER, J. A. (1960) Interocular transfer of brightness discrimination in "split-brain" cats. *Science*, **132**, 734–735.—*475*

MELTON, A. W. (1941a) Learning. In W. S. Monroe (Editor), *Encyclopedia of educational research.* New York: Macmillan.—*303*

MELTON, A. W. (1941b) Review of Katona's *Organizing and memorizing. Amer. J. Psychol.*, **54**, 455–457.—*256*

MELTON, A. W. (1950) Learning. In W. S. Monroe (Editor), *Encyclopedia of educational research* (Revised). New York: Macmillan, 668–690.—*303, 305, 309*

MELTON, A. W. (1959) The science of learning and the technology of educational methods. *Harvard educ. Rev.*, **29**, 96–106.—*545*

MELTON, A. W. (1963) Implications of short-term memory for a general theory of memory. *J. verb. Learn. and verb. Behav.*, **2**, 1–21.—*506, 511*

MELTON, A. W. (Editor) (1964) *Categories of human learning.* New York: Academic.—*12, 14, 304, 333, 540, 581, 584*

MELTON, A. W., and IRWIN, J. McQ. (1940) The influence of degree of interpolated learning on retroactive inhibition and the overt transfer of specific responses. *Amer. J. Psychol.*, **53**, 173–203.—*500*

MELTZER, H. (1930) Individual differences in forgetting pleasant and unpleasant experiences. *J. educ. Psychol.*, **21**, 399–409.—*287*

MICHAEL, R. P. (1962) Estrogen-sensitive neurons and sexual behavior in female cats. *Science,* **136**, 322–323.—*433*

MICKLE, W. A. *See* Heath and Mickle (1960).

MILES, M. B. (Editor) (1964) *Innovation in education.* New York: Teachers College, Columbia University.—*578*

MILES, W. R. *See* Miller and Miles (1935).

MILLER, G. A., GALANTER, E., and PRIBRAM, K. H. (1960) *Plans and the structure of behavior.* New York: Holt, Rinehart and Winston.—*262*

MILLER, N. E. (1935) A reply to "Sign-Gestalt or conditioned reflex?" *Psychol. Rev.,* **42**, 280–292.—*186*

MILLER, N. E. (1941) The frustration-aggression hypothesis. *Psychol. Rev.,* **48**, 337–342.—*277*

MILLER, N. E. (1944) Experimental studies in conflict. In J. McV. Hunt (Editor), *Personality and the behavior disorders.* New York: Ronald, 431–465.—*176, 177*

MILLER, N. E. (1948a) Studies of fear as an acquired drive. I. Fear as motivation and fear-reduction as reinforcement in the learning of new responses. *J. exp. Psychol.,* **38**, 89–101.—*272*

MILLER, N. E. (1948b) Theory and experiment relating psychoanalytic displacement to stimulus-response generalization. *J. abnorm. soc. Psychol.,* **43**, 155–178.—*278, 279*

MILLER, N. E. (1957) *Graphic communication and the crisis in education.* Washington, D. C.: National Educational Association.—*569*

MILLER, N. E. (1958) Central stimulation and other new approaches to motivation and reward. *Amer. Psychol.,* **13**, 100–108.—*438*

MILLER, N. E. (1959) Liberalization of basic S-R concepts: Extensions to conflict behavior, motivation and social learning. In S. Koch (Editor), *Psychology: A study of a science,* Vol. 2. New York: McGraw-Hill, 196–292.—*189, 568*

MILLER, N. E. (1965) Chemical coding of behavior in the brain. *Science,* **148**, 328–338.—*432*

MILLER, N. E. *See* Bower and Miller (1958); DeBold, Miller, and Jensen (1965); Delgado, Roberts, and Miller (1954); Dollard and Miller (1950); Dollard, Doob, Miller, Mowrer, Sears, Ford, Hovland, and Sollenberger (1939); Murray and Miller (1952).

MILLER, N. E., BROWN, J. S., and LIPOFSKY, H. (1943) A theoretical and experimental analysis of conflict behavior: III. Approach-avoidance conflict as a function of strength of drive and strength of shock. (Unpublished: see Miller, 1944).—*176*

MILLER, N. E., and DOLLARD, J. (1941) *Social learning and imitation.* New Haven: Yale Univ. Press.—*148, 537, 568*

MILLER, N. E., and KRAELING, D. (1952) Displacement: Greater generalization of approach than avoidance in a generalized approach-avoidance conflict. *J. exp. Psychol.,* **43**, 217–221.—*278*

MILLER, N. E., and MILES, W. R. (1935) Effect of caffeine on the running speed of hungry, satiated, and frustrated rats. *J. comp. Psychol.,* **20**, 397–412.—*168*

MILLER, N. E., and MURRAY, E. J. (1952) Displacement and conflict: Learnable drive as a basis for the steeper gradient of avoidance than of approach. *J. exp. Psychol.,* 43, 227–231.—*278*

MILLER, R. B., FOLLEY, J. D., Jr., and SMITH, P. R. (1953) Systematic trouble shooting and the half-split technique. *USAF Human Resources Cent.,* Tech. Report No. 53–21.—*548*

MILLER, S., and KONORSKI, J. (1928) Sur une forme particulère des réflexes conditionnels. *C. R. Soc. Biol. Paris,* 99, 1155–1157.—*64, 65, 71*

MILLER, S. *See also* Konorski and Miller (1937a, 1937b).

MILLWORD, R. B. *See* Friedman, Burke, Cole, Keller, Millword, and Estes (1964).

MILNER, P. *See* Olds and Milner (1954).

MINER, N. *See* Sperry and Miner (1955).

MINSKY, M. (1961a) Steps toward artificial intelligence. *Proc. of Inst. of Radio Engineers,* 49, 8–30. Also reprinted in E. Feigenbaum and J. Feldman (Editors) (1963) *Computers and thought.*—*389*

MINSKY, M. (1961b) A selected descriptor-indexed bibliography of the literature on artificial intelligence. *IRE Transactions on Human Factors in Electronics,* 2, 39–55. Reprinted in E. Feigenbaum and J. Feldman (Eds.) (1963) *Computers and thought.*—*389*

MOORE, A. W. *See* Angell and Moore (1896).

MOORE, J. W. *See* Smith and Moore (1962).

MOORE, M. G. (1930) Gestalt vs. experience. *Amer. J. Psychol.,* 42, 453–455.—*237*

MOORE, R. K., and LAUER, L. W. (1963) Hypnotic susceptibility in middle childhood. *Int. J. clin. exp. Hyp.,* 11, 167–174.—*282*

MOORE, J. W. *See* Smith and Moore (1962).

MORGAN, C. T. (1965) *Physiological psychology,* Third Edition. New York: McGraw-Hill.—*429, 432, 479*

MORGENSTERN, O. *See* Von Neumann and Morgenstern (1944).

MORRELL, F. (1960) Secondary epileptogenic lesions. *Epilepsia,* 1, 538–560.—*456*

MORRELL, F. (1961a) Effect of anodal polarization on the firing pattern of single cortical cells. *Ann. N. Y. Acad. Sci.,* 92, 860–876.—*456*

MORRELL, F. (1961b) Electrophysiological contributions to the neural basis of learning. *Physiol. Rev.,* 41, 443–494.—*457, 536*

MORRELL, F. (1963) Information storage in nerve cells. In W. S. Fields and W. Abbott (Editors), *Information storage and neural control.* Springfield, Illinois: Charles C Thomas.—*458, 459, 460*

MORRELL, F., and NAITOH, P. (1962) Effect of cortical polarization on a conditioned avoidance response. *Exp. Neurol.,* 6, 507–523.—*459*

MORRIS, C. J. *See also* Kintsch and Morris (1965).

MOSTELLER, F. *See* Bush and Mosteller (1951, 1955).

MOSTOFSKY, D. I. (Editor) (1965) *Stimulus generalization.* Stanford, Calif.: Stanford Univ. Press.—*540*

MOWRER, O. H. (1938) Preparatory set (expectancy): A determinant in motivation and learning. *Psychol. Rev.,* 45, 62–91.—*266*

MOWRER, O. H. (1939) A stimulus-response analysis of anxiety and its role as a reinforcing agent. *Psychol. Rev.,* 46, 553–565.—*272*

MOWRER, O. H. (1940a) An experimental analogue of "regression" with incidental observations on "reaction-formation." *J. abnorm. soc. Psychol.*, **35**, 56–87.—*276*

Mowrer, O. H. (1940b)   Anxiety reduction and learning. *J. exp. Psychol.*, **27**, 497–516.—*272*

Mowrer, O. H. (1947)   On the dual nature of learning—A re-interpretation of "conditioning" and "problem-solving." *Harv. educ. Rev.*, **17**, 102–148.—*65*

Mowrer, O. H. (1950)   *Learning theory and personality dynamics.* New York: Ronald.—*269, 273*

Mowrer, O. H. (1960)   *Learning theory and behavior.* New York: Wiley.—*189, 540, 570*

Mowrer, O. H.   *See* Dollard, Doob, Miller, Mowrer, Sears, Ford, Hovland, and Sollenberger (1939).

Mowrer, O. H., and Ullman, A. D. (1945)   Time as a determinant in integrative learning. *Psychol. Rev.*, **52**, 61–90.—*272*

Mueller, C. G., Jr., and Schoenfeld, W. N. (1954)   Edwin R. Guthrie. In Estes, Koch, MacCorquodale, Meehl, Mueller, Schoenfeld, and Verplanck, *Modern learning theory.* New York: Appleton-Century-Crofts, 345–379.—*90, 105, 106*

Muenzinger, K. F. (1935)   Motivation in learning. I. Electric shock for correct response in the visual discrimination habit. *J. comp. Psychol.*, **17**, 267–277.—*207*

Muenzinger, K. F. (1938)   Vicarious trial and error at a point of choice. I. A general survey of its relation to learning efficiency. *J. genet. Psychol.*, **53**, 75–86.—*202*

Muenzinger, K. F. (1942)   *Psychology: The science of behavior.* New York: Harper & Row.—*299*

Muenzinger, K. F., Brown, W. O., Crow, W. J., and Powloski, R. F. (1952)   Motivation in learning. XI. An analysis of electric shock for correct responses into its avoidance and accelerating components. *J. exp. Psychol.*, **43**, 115–119.—*207*

Muenzinger, K. F., Koerner, L., and Irey, E. (1929)   Variability of an habitual movement in guinea pigs. *J. comp. Psychol.*, **9**, 425–436.—*90*

Müller, G. E., and Pilzecker, A. (1900)   Experimentelle Beiträge zur Lehre vom Gedächtnis. *Z. Psychol.*, Ergbd. I.—*312, 322, 447*

Müller, I. (1937)   Zur Analyse der Retentionsstörung durch Häufung. *Psychol. Forsch.*, **22**, 180–210.—*251, 253*

Murdock, B. B., Jr. (1961)   The retention of individual items. *J. exp. Psychol.*, **62**, 618–625.—*509*

Murphy, G. (1947)   *Personality.* New York: Harper & Row.—*270*

Murphy, G.   *See also* Solley and Murphy (1960).

Murray, E. J., and Miller, N. E. (1952)   Displacement: Steeper gradient of generalization of avoidance than of approach with age of habit controlled. *J. exp. Psychol.*, **43**, 222–226.—*278*

Murray, E. J.   *See* Miller and Murray (1952).

Myers, J. L., and Atkinson, R. C. (1964)   Choice behavior and reward structure. *J. math. Psychol.*, **1**, 170–203.—*349*

NAITOH, P. *See* Morrell and Naitoh (1962).

NATHAN, P. W. *See* Russell and Nathan (1946).

NEIDT, C. *See* Pickrel, Neidt, and Gibson (1958).

NEISSER, U. *See* Selfridge and Neisser (1960).

NEWCOMB, T. M. (1950) *Social psychology.* New York: Dryden.—*299*

NEWELL, A. (Editor) (1961) *Information processing language V manual.* Englewood Cliffs: Prentice-Hall.—*386*

NEWELL, A., SHAW, J. C., and SIMON, H. (1958) Elements of a theory of human problem solving. *Psychol. Rev.,* **65,** 151–166.—*387, 389*

NEWELL, A., SHAW, J. C., and SIMON, H. A. (1959) A report on a general problem-solving program. *Proc. of the International Conference on Information Processing,* New York: UNESCO, 256–265.—*406*

NEWELL, A., and SIMON, H. A. (1956) The logic theory machine. *IRE Transactions on Information Theory.* IT–2, 61–69.—*387*

NEWELL, A., and SIMON, H. A. (1961) Computer simulation of human thinking. *Science,* **134,** 2011–2017.—*406*

NEWELL, A., and SIMON, H. A. (1963) Computers in psychology. In R. D. Luce, R. R. Bush, and E. Galanter, (Editors), *Handbook of mathematical psychology,* Vol. I. New York: Wiley.—*421–423*

NISSEN, H. W. *See* Cowles and Nissen (1937).

NISSEN, Th. *See* Fjerdingstad, Nissen, and Røigaard-Petersen (1965).

NOBLE, M. E. *See* Fitts, Bahrick, Noble, and Briggs (1965).

NOLAN, C. Y. *See* Webb and Nolan (1953).

NORMAN, D. A. *See* Waugh and Norman (1965).

NORMAN, M. F. (1964) *A probabilistic model for free-responding.* Technical report #67, Psychology Series: Institute of mathematical studies in the social sciences; Stanford Univ., Stanford, Calif., Dec. 14.—*360*

NORTH, A. J. *See* Fagan and North (1951).

NUTTIN, J. (1949) "Spread" in recalling failure and success. *J. exp. Psychol.,* **39,** 60–699.—*39*

NUTTIN, J. (1953) *Tâche, réussite et échec.* Louvain, Belgium: Publications Univ. de Louvain.—*39, 47*

NYSWANDER, D. B. *See* Stone and Nyswander (1927).

OCHS, S. *See* Russell and Ochs (1961).

O'CONNELL, D. L. *See* Köhler, Held, and O'Connell (1952).

O'KELLY, L. I. (1940a) An experimental study of regression. I. Behavioral characteristics of the regressive response. *J. comp. Psychol.,* **30,** 41–53.—*276*

O'KELLY, L. I. (1940b) An experimental study of regression. II. Some motivational determinants of regression and perseveration. *J. comp. Psychol.,* **30,** 55–95.—*276*

OLDS, J. (1953) The influence of practice on the strength of secondary approach drives. *J. exp. Psychol.,* **46,** 232–236.—*220*

OLDS, J. (1954) A neural model for sign-gestalt theory. *Psychol. Rev.,* **61,** 59–72. —*220*

OLDS, J., and MILNER, P. (1954) Positive reinforcement produced by electrical stimulation of septal area and other regions of rat brain. *J. comp. physiol. Psychol.*, 47, 419–427.—*434*

OLDS, J., and OLDS, MARIANNE. (1965) Drives, rewards, and the brain. In *New directions in psychology, II*. New York: Holt, Rinehart, and Winston.—*435*

OLDS, M. *See* Olds and Olds (1965).

OSGOOD, C. E. (1949) The similarity paradox in human learning: A resolution. *Psychol. Rev.*, 56, 132–143.—*314, 315*

OSGOOD, C. E. (1950) Can Tolman's theory of learning handle avoidance training? *Psychol. Rev.*, 57, 133–137.—*220*

OSGOOD, C. E. (1953) *Method and theory in experimental psychology*. New York: Oxford Univ. Press.—*14, 251, 312, 332, 333*

OSGOOD, C. E., SUCI, G. J., and TANNENBAUM, P. H. (1957) *The measurement of meaning*. Urbana: Univ. of Ill. Press.—*330*

OSSER, H. *See* Gibson, Gibson, Danielson, and Osser (1962).

OVERTON, D. A. (1964) State-dependent or "dissociated" learning produced by pentobarbital. *J. comp. physiol. Psychol.*, 57, 3–12.—*475*

PAN, S. (1926) The influence of context upon learning and recall. *J. exp. Psychol.*, 9, 468–491.—*499*

PARADISE, H. E. *See* Gagné, Mayor, Garstens, and Paradise (1962).

PASCAL, G. R. (1949) The effect of relaxation upon recall. *Amer. J. Psychol.*, 62, 32–47.—*499*

PAVLOV, I. P. (1902) *The work of the digestive glands*. London: Griffin.—*49*

PAVLOV, I. P. (1903) Experimental psychology and psychopathology in animals. In Pavlov (1928), pp. 47–60; also in Pavlov (1955), pp. 151–168.—*73*

PAVLOV, I. P. (1927) *Conditioned reflexes*. London: Oxford Univ. Press.—*49, 52, 53, 58, 71, 73, 146*

PAVLOV, I. P. (1928) *Lectures on conditioned reflexes*. Translated by W. H. Gantt. New York: International.—*49, 51, 73*

PAVLOV, I. P. (1932) The reply of a physiologist to psychologists. *Psychol. Rev.*, 39, 91–127.—*76*

PAVLOV, I. P. (1941) *Conditioned reflexes and psychiatry*. New York: International Publishers.—*49, 62, 73*

PAVLOV, I. P. (1955) *Selected works*. Moscow: Foreign Languages Publishing House.—*49, 56, 59, 60, 61, 69, 72, 73*

PAVLOV, I. P. (1957) *Experimental psychology and other essays*. New York: Philosophical Library.—*49, 73*

PEAK, H. (1933) Reflex and voluntary reactions of the eyelid. *J. gen. Psychol.*, 8, 130–156.—*108*

PEARSON, G. H. J. (1952) A survey of learning difficulties in children. *Psychoanal. Stud. Child.*, 7, 322–386.—*283*

PEARSON, G. H. J. (1954) *Psychoanalysis and the education of the child*. New York: Norton.—*283, 296*

PECHSTEIN, L. A., and BROWN, F. D. (1939) An experimental analysis of the alleged criteria of insight learning. *J. educ. Psychol.*, 30, 38–52.—*244*

PEIRCE, P. See Ritchie, Aeschliman, and Peirce (1950).

PERKINS, F. T. (1932) Symmetry in visual recall. *Amer. J. Psychol.*, 44, 473–490. —*248*

PERKINS, D. T. See Hull, Hovland, Ross, Hall, Perkins and Fitch (1940).

PERKINS, F. T. See also Wheeler and Perkins (1932).

PERRINE, L. See Reid, Ciardi, and Perrine (1963).

PERRY, R. B. (1918) Docility and purposiveness. *Psychol. Rev.*, 25, 1–20.—*193*

PETERS, J. E. See Reese, Dykman, and Peters (1964).

PETERSON, J. (1922) Learning when frequency and recency factors are negative. *J. exp. Psychol.*, 5, 270–300.—*75*

PETERSON, L. R., and PETERSON, M. J. (1959) Short-term retention of individual verbal items. *J. exp. Psychol.*, 58, 193–198.—*503, 504*

PETERSON, M. J. See Peterson and Peterson (1959).

PEYSER, C. S. See Barrett, Peyser, and McHose (1965).

PIAGET, J. (1952) *The child's conception of number.* New York: Humanities Press.—*571*

PICKREL, G., NEIDT, C., and GIBSON, R. (1958) Tape recordings are used to teach seventh grade students in Westside Junior-Senior High School, Omaha, Nebraska. *Nat. Ass. Sec. Sch. Principals Bull.*, 42, 81–93.—*554*

PIERS, G., and SINGER, M. B. (1953) *Shame and guilt.* Springfield, Ill.: Charles C Thomas.—*272*

PILZECKER, A. See Müller and Pilzecker (1900).

PITTS, W., and McCULLOCH, W. S. (1947) How we know universals, the perception of auditory and visual form. *Bull. Math. Biophysics,* 9 (No. 3), 127–147.—*478*

PLATONOV, K. I. (1959) *The word as a physiological and therapeutic factor,* Second edition. Moscow: Foreign Languages Publishing House (original in Russian, 1955).—*59*

PLATT, C. E. See Wickens and Platt (1954).

PLISKOFF, S. S., WRIGHT, J. E., and HAWKINS, T. D. (1965) Brain stimulation as a reinforcer: Intermittent schedules. *J. exp. anal. Behav.,* 8, 75–88.—*437*

POLSON, M. C., RESTLE, F., and POLSON, P. G. (1965) Association and discrimination in paired-associates learning. *J. exp. Psychol.,* 69, 47–55.—*374*

POLSON, P. G. See Polson, Restle, and Polson (1965).

POLSON, P. G., and GREENO, J. G. (1965) Nonstationary performance before all-or-none learning. Paper read at Midwestern Psychol. Assoc. Meetings, Chicago, May 1. (Reprints available from J. G. Greeno.)—*371*

POPHAM, W. J. See Standlee, Popham, and Fattu (1956).

POSTMAN, L. (1947) The history and present status of the Law of Effect. *Psychol. Bull.,* 44, 489–563.—*47*

POSTMAN, L. (1961a) Spread of effect as a function of time and intraserial similarity. *Amer. J. Psychol.,* 74, 493–505.—*41*

POSTMAN, L. (1961b) The present status of interference theory. In C. N. Cofer (Editor), *Verbal learning and verbal behavior.* New York: McGraw-Hill, 152–179.—*498, 503, 570*

POSTMAN, L. (1962) Rewards and punishments in human learning. In L. Postman (Editor), *Psychology in the making.* New York: Knopf, 331–401.—*16, 29, 33, 35, 47*

Postman, L.   *See* Allport and Postman (1947); Jenkins and Postman (1948); Underwood and Postman (1960).

Postman, L., and Adams, P. A.   (1954)   Performance variables in the experimental analysis of the law of effect. *Amer. J. Psychol.,* **67**, 612–631.—*33, 42*

Postman, L., and Adams, P. A.   (1955)   "Isolation" and the law of effect. *Amer. J. Psychol.,* **68**, 96–105.—*42*

Powers, F. F.   *See* Guthrie and Powers (1950).

Powloski, R. F.,   *See* Muenzinger, Brown, Crow, and Powloski (1952).

Premack, D.   (1959)   Toward empirical behavior laws. I. Positive reinforcement. *Psychol. Rev.,* **66**, 219–233.—*483, 484*

Premack, D.   (1962)   Reversibility of the reinforcement relation. *Science,* **136**, 255–257.—*484*

Premack, D.   (1963)   Rate differential reinforcement in monkey manipulation. *J. exp. Anal. Behav.,* **6**, 81–89.—*484*

Premack, D.   (1965)   Reinforcement theory. In M. R. Jones (Editor), *Nebraska Symposium on motivation: 1965.* Lincoln: Univ. of Nebraska Press.—*483, 484*

Prentice, W. C. H.   (1959)   The systematic psychology of Wolfgang Köhler. In S. Koch (Editor), *Psychology: A study of a science,* Vol. I. New York: McGraw-Hill, 427–455.—*263*

Pressey, S. L.   (1926)   A simple apparatus which gives tests and scores—and teaches. *Sch. and Soc.,* **23**, 373–376.—*555*

Pressey, S. L.   (1927)   A machine for automatic teaching of drill material. *Sch. and Soc.,* **25**, 549–552.—*555*

Pribram, K. H.   *See* Miller, Galanter, and Pribram (1960); Spinelli and Pribram (1965); Spinelli, Pribram, and Weingarten (1965).

Proceedings of the Western Joint Computer Conference. March 1–3, 1955; March 3–5, 1959; May 3–5, 1960; May 9–11, 1961. New York: The Institute of Radio Engineers, 1 E. 79th St.—*425*

Prokasy, W. F. (Editor) (1965a) *Classical conditioning: A symposium.* New York: Appleton-Century-Crofts.—*73, 540*

Prokasy, W. F.   (1965b) An application of a three-state all-or-none model to human eyelid conditioning data. *Psychonomic Sci.* **3**, 349–350.—*373*

Radner, L.   *See* Zeaman and Radner (1953).

Ragland, J. B.   *See* Ragland and Ragland (1965).

Ragland, Rae S., and Ragland, J. B.   (1965)   Planaria: Interspecific transfer of a conditionability factor through cannibalism. *Psychonomic Sci.,* **3**, 117–118.—*466*

Rahn, C. L.   (1914)   The relation of sensation to other categories in contemporary psychology. *Psychol. Monogr.,* **16**, No. 67.—*302*

Rains, J. D.   *See* Goldstein, Krantz, and Rains (1965).

Rapaport, D.   (1951)   *Organization and pathology of thought.* New York: Columbia Univ. Press.—*283*

Rapaport, D.   (1959)   The structure of psychoanalytic theory: A systematizing attempt. In S. Koch (Editor), *Psychology: A study of a science,* Vol. 3. New York: McGraw-Hill, 55–183. Also in *Psychol. Issues,* 1960, **2**, Monogr. 6.—*268*

RAPAPORT, D. *See* Shakow and Rapaport (1964).

RATLIFF, M. M. (1938) The varying function of affectively toned olfactory, visual, and auditory cues in recall. *Amer. J. Psychol.*, **51**, 695–699.—*286*

RATNER, J. (1939) *Intelligence in the modern world: John Dewey's philosophy.* New York: Modern Library.—*300*

RAZRAN, G. (1939) A quantitative study of meaning by conditioned salivary technique (semantic conditioning). *Science*, **90**, 89–91.—*66*

RAZRAN, G. (1957) Recent Russian psychology: 1950–1956. *Contemp. Psychol.*, **2**, 93–101.—*62*

RAZRAN, G. (1961a) The observable unconscious and the inferable conscious in current Soviet psychophysiology. *Psychol. Rev.*, **68**, 81–147.—*66*

RAZRAN, G. (1961b) Raphael's "idealess" behavior. *J. comp. physiol. Psychol.*, **54**, 366–367.—*70*

RAZRAN, G. (1961c) Recent Soviet phyletic comparisons of classical and of operant conditioning: Experimental designs. *J. comp. physiol. Psychol.*, **54**, 357–365.—*64*

RAZRAN, G. (1965) Russian physiologists' psychology and American experimental psychology. *Psychol. Bull.*, **63**, 42–64.—*70*

REESE, W. G., DYKMAN, R. A., and PETERS, J. E. (1964) A gap in GAP Symposium No. 9: "Pavlovian conditioning and American psychiatry." *Amer. J. Psychiat.*, **121**, 555–561.—*61*

REID, J. M., CIARDI, J., and PERRINE, L. (1963) *Poetry: A closer look.* New York: Harcourt, Brace & World.—*560*

REITMAN, W. R. (1964) Information-processing models in psychology. *Science*, **144**, 1192–1198.—*419, 420, 423*

REITMAN, W. R. (1965) *Cognition and thought.* New York: Wiley.

RESTLE, F. (1961) *The psychology of judgment and choice.* New York: Wiley. —*380*

RESTLE, F. (1962) The selection of strategies in cue learning. *Psychol. Rev.*, **69**, 329–343.—*370*

RESTLE, F. (1964a) Sources of difficulty in learning paired associates. In R. C. Atkinson (Editor), *Studies in mathematical psychology.* Stanford: Stanford Univ. Press.—*374*

RESTLE, F. (1964b) The relevance of mathematical models for education. In E. R. Hilgard (Editor), *Theories of learning and instruction: The sixty-third yearbook of the national society for the study of education.* Chicago: Univ. of Chicago Press.—*377*

RESTLE, F. *See* Polson, Restle, and Polson (1965).

RESTORFF, H. VON (1933) Analyse von Vorgangen in Spurenfeld. I. Über die Wirkung von Bereichsbildungen im Spurenfeld. *Psychol. Forsch.*, **18**, 299–342.—*251*

RESTORFF, H. VON *See also* Köhler and Restorff (1935).

REYNOLDS, G. S. (1961a) Behavioral contrast. *J. exp. Anal. Behav.*, **4**, 57–71.—*515, 516*

REYNOLDS, G. S. (1961b) Relativity of response rate and reinforcement in a multiple schedule. *J. exp. Anal. Behav.*, **4**, 179-184.—*516*

REYNOLDS, G. S. (1961c) Contrast, generalization, and the process of discrimination. *J. exp. Anal. Behav.*, **4**, 289–294.—*516*

RICHARDS, I. A. (1943) *Basic English and its uses.* New York: Norton.—*46*

RICHARDSON, H. M. (1932) The growth of adaptive behavior in infants: an experimental study at seven age levels. *Genet. Psychol. Monogr.,* **12,** 195–359.*—240*

RIDDLE, E. E. *See* Stalnaker and Riddle (1932).

RILEY, D. A. (1952) Rote learning as a function of distribution of practice and the complexity of the situation. *J. exp. Psychol.,* **43,** 88–95.*—325*

RILEY, D. A. (1958) The nature of the effective stimulus in animal discrimination learning: Transposition reconsidered. *Psychol. Rev.,* **65,** 1–7.*—525*

RILEY, D. A. (1963) Memory for form. In L. Postman (Editor), *Psychology in the making.* New York: Knopf, 402–465.*—497*

RINKEL, M. (Editor) (1958) *Chemical concepts of psychosis.* New York: McDowell, Obolensky.*—461*

RITCHIE, B. F. (1948) Studies in spatial learning. VI. Place orientation and direction orientation. *J. exp. Psychol.,* **38,** 659–669.*—199*

RITCHIE, B. F., *See* Tolman, Ritchie, and Kalish (1946, 1947).

RITCHIE, B. F., AESCHLIMAN, B., and PEIRCE, P. (1950) Studies in spatial learning. VIII. Place performance and the acquisition of place dispositions. *J. comp. physiol. Psychol.,* **43,** 73–85.*—197*

ROBERTS, E. (1965) Summary and commentary on Professor Hydén's paper. In D. P. Kimble (Editor), *Learning, remembering, and forgetting,* Vol. 1. *The anatomy of memory.* Palo Alto: Science and Behavior Books.*—469*

ROBERTS, W. W. (1958) Both rewarding and punishing effects from stimulation of posterior hypothalamus of cat with same electrode at same intensity. *J. comp. physiol. Psychol.,* **51,** 400–407.*—434*

ROBERTS, W. W. *See* Delgado, Roberts, and Miller (1954).

ROBINSON, E. S. (1927) The "similarity" factor in retroaction. *Amer. J. Psychol.,* **39,** 297–312.*—313, 314*

ROBINSON, E. S. (1932a) *Association theory today.* New York: Appleton-Century-Crofts.*—304, 310, 311, 333*

ROBINSON, E. S. (1932b) *Man as psychology sees him.* New York: Macmillan. *—330*

ROBINSON, E. S. (1935) *Law and the lawyers.* New York: Macmillan.*—331*

ROBY, T. B. *See* Sheffield and Roby (1950).

ROCK, I. (1957) The role of repetition in associative learning. *Amer. J. Psychol.,* **70,** 186–193.*—365*

RODERICK, T. H. (1960) Selection for cholinesterase activity in the cerebral cortex of the rat. *Genetics,* **45,** 1123.*—463*

ROGERS, C. R., and SKINNER, B. F. (1956) Some issues concerning the control of human behavior. *Science,* **124,** 1057–1066.*—145*

RØIGAARD-PETERSEN, H. H. *See* Fjerfdingstad, Nissen, and Røigaard-Petersen (1965).

ROSENBLATT, F. (1958) The perceptron: A probabilistic model for information storage and organization in the brain. *Psychol. Rev.,* **65,** 386–407.*—478*

ROSENBLATT, F. (1962) *Principles of neurodynamics.* Washington, D. C.: Cornell Aeronautical Laboratory, Report 1196–G–8.*—478*

ROSENZWEIG, M. R. (1962) The mechanisms of hunger and thirst. In L. Postman (Editor), *Psychology in the making.* New York: Knopf, 73–143. *—50*

ROSENZWEIG, M. R. *See* Bennett, Krech, and Rosenzweig (1964); Krech, Rosenzweig, and Bennett (1960, 1962).

ROSENZWEIG, M. R., BENNETT, E. L., and KRECH, D. (1964) Cerebral effects of environmental complexity and training among adult rats. *J. comp physiol. Psychol.,* **57,** 438–439.*—463*

ROSENZWEIG, S. (1941) Need-persistive and ego-defensive reactions to frustration as demonstrated by an experiment on repression. *Psychol. Rev.,* **48,** 347–349.*—277*

ROSS, R. T. *See* Hull, Hovland, Ross, Hall, Perkins, and Fitch (1940).

ROTTER, J. B. (1954) *Social learning and clinical psychology.* Englewood-Cliffs: Prentice-Hall.*—221*

ROUANET, H. *See* Suppes, Rouanet, Levine, and Frankmann (1964).

RUJA, H. (1956) Productive psychologists. *Amer. Psychologist,* **11,** 148–149.*—189*

RUSINOV, V. S. (1953) An electro-physiological analysis of the connecting function in the cerebral cortex in the presence of a dominant area. Communications at the XIX International Physiological Congress, Montreal.*—457*

RUSSELL, B. *See* Whitehead and Russell (1925).

RUSSELL, D. H., and FEA, H. R. (1963) Research on teaching reading. In N. L. Gage (Editor), *Handbook of research on teaching.* Chicago: Rand McNally, 865–928.*--579*

RUSSELL, I. S., and OCHS, S. (1961) One-trial hemispheric transfer of a learning engram. *Science,* **133,** 1077–1078.*—474, 475*

RUSSELL, W. A. (1952) Retention of verbal material as a function of motivating instructions and experimentally-induced failure. *J. exp. Psychol.,* **40,** 411–422.*—289, 290*

RUSSELL, W. R., and NATHAN, P. W. (1946) Traumatic amnesia. *Brain,* **69,** 280–300.*—449*

SALZINGER, K. (1959) Experimental manipulation of verbal behavior: A review. *J. genet. Psychol.,* **61,** 65–95.*—134*

SAMUEL, A. (1959) Some studies in machine learning using the game of checkers. IBM J. Research and Development, 3, 210–229. Also reprinted in E. A. Feigenbaum and J. Feldman (Editors), *Computers and thought.* New York: McGraw-Hill.*—400*

SARASON, I. (Editor) (1965a) *Psychoanalysis and the study of behavior.* Princeton: Van Nostrand.*—296*

SARASON, I. (Editor) (1965b) *Science and theory in psychoanalysis.* Princeton: Van Nostrand.*—296*

SAYRE, K. M., and CROSSON, F. J. (Editors) (1963) *The modeling of mind.* Notre Dame, Indiana: Univ. of Notre Dame Press.*—425*

SCHAPPE, R. H. *See* Bruning and Schappe (1965).

SCHERRER, H. *See* Hernandez-Peon, Scherrer, and Jouvet (1956).

SCHEERER, M. (1954) Cognitive theory. In G. Lindzey (Editor), *Handbook of social psychology.* Reading, Mass.: Addison-Wesley, 91–137.*—263*

SCHILLER, P. H. *See* Chorover and Schiller (1965).

SCHLOSBERG, H. (1937) The relationship between success and the laws of conditioning. *Psychol. Rev.*, 44, 379–394.—*65*

SCHLOSBERG, H., and HEINEMAN, C. (1950) The relationship between two measures of response strength. *J. exp. Psychol.*, 40, 235–247.—*273*

SCHLOSBERG, H. *See* Woodworth and Schlosberg (1954).

SCHOEFFLER, M. (1954) Probability of response to compounds of discriminated stimuli. *J. exp. Psychol.*, 48, 323–329.—*346, 347*

SCHOENFELD, W. N., ANTONITIS, J. J., and BERSH, P. J. (1950) A preliminary study of training conditions necessary for secondary reinforcement. *J. exp. Psychol.*, 40, 40–45.—*121*

SCHOENFELD, W. N. *See also* Estes, Koch, MacCorquodale, Meehl, Mueller, Schoenfeld, and Verplanck (1954); Keller and Schoenfeld (1950); Mueller and Schoenfeld (1954).

SCHRAMM, W. (1964a) *The research on programmed instruction: An annotated bibliography*. Washington, D. C.: U. S. Office of Education (OE–34034).—*558, 584*

SCHRAMM, W. (Editor) (1964b) *Four case studies of programmed instruction*. New York: Fund for the Advancement of Education.—*558, 560, 584*

SCHRAMM, W. (1964c) Programmed instruction in Denver. In W. Schramm (Editor), *Four case studies of programmed instruction*. New York: Fund for the Advancement of Education, 29–40.—*560*

SCHRAMM, W. (1964d) The research on programmed instruction. In *Programmierter Unterricht und Lehrmaschinen*. Berlin: Pädagogische Zentrum, 462–483.—*557*

SCHULZ, R. W. *See* Underwood and Schulz (1960).

SCHUSTER, D. H. *See* Bryan and Schuster (1959).

SEARS, P. S. (1951) Doll play aggression in normal young children: Influence of sex, age, sibling status, father's absence. *Psychol. Monogr.*, 65, No. 6.—*279*

SEARS, R. R. (1936) Functional abnormalities of memory with special reference to amnesia. *Psychol. Bull.*, 33, 229–274.—*274, 288*

SEARS, R. R. (1937) Initiation of the repression sequence by experienced failure. *J. exp. Psychol.*, 20, 570–580.—*288*

SEARS, R. R. (1941) Non-aggressive reactions to frustration. *Psychol. Rev.*, 48, 343–346.—*277*

SEARS, R. R. (1943) *Survey of objective studies of psychoanalytic concepts*. New York: Social Science Research Council.—*275, 276, 286*

SEARS, R. R. (1944) Experimental analysis of psychoanalytic phenomena. In J. McV. Hunt (Editor), *Personality and the behavior disorders*. New York: Ronald, 306–332.—*277, 280*

SEARS, R. R. (1951) Effects of frustration and anxiety on fantasy aggression. *Amer. J. Orthopsychiat.*, 21, 498–505.—*279*

SEARS, R. R. *See* Dollard, Doob, Miller, Mowrer, Sears, Ford, Hovland, and Sollenberger (1939); Heathers and Sears (1943).

SEARS, R. R., WHITING, J. W. M., NOWLIS, V., and SEARS, P. S. (1953) Some child-rearing antecedents of aggression and dependency in young children. *Genet. Psychol. Monogr.*, 47, 135–236.—*279*

SEARS, W. N. *See* Hilgard, Campbell, and Sears (1938).

SEASHORE, H., and BAVELAS, A. (1941) The functioning of knowledge of results in Thorndike's line-drawing experiment. *Psychol. Rev.,* **48,** 155–164.—*25*

SECHENOV, I. (1935) *Selected works.* Moscow: State Publishing House.—*50*

SECHZER, J. A. *See* Meikle and Sechzer (1960).

Secretariat, Pädagogisches Zentrum (1964) *Programmierter Unterricht und Lehrmaschinen.* A report of the International Conf. on Programmed Instruction and Teaching Machines. Berlin: Pädagogische Zentrum.—*584*

SEIDEL, R. J. (1959) A review of sensory preconditioning. *Psychol. Bull.,* **56,** 58–73.—*536*

SELFRIDGE, O. G. (1955) Pattern recognition and modern computers. *Proceedings of the 1955 Western Joint Computer Conference,* pp. 85–111.—*387*

SELFRIDGE, O. G., (1959) Pandemonium: a paradigm for learning. In D. V. Blake, and A. M. Uttley (Editors), *Proceedings of the symposium on mechanization of thought processes.* London: H. M. Stationary Office. —*387*

SELFRIDGE, O., and NEISSER, U. (1960) Pattern recognition by machine. *Sci. Amer.,* August, **203,** 60–80.—*392–394*

SELLS, S. B. *See* Woodworth and Sells (1935).

SEMMES, J. *See* Lashley, Chow, and Semmes (1951).

SEWARD, J. P. (1942) An experimental study of Guthrie's theory of reinforcement. *J. exp. Psychol.,* **30,** 247–256.—*99*

SEWARD, J. P. (1955) The constancy of the I-V: A critique of intervening variables. *Psychol. Rev.,* **62,** 155–168.—*218*

SEWARD, J. P., DILL, J. B., and HOLLAND, M. A. (1944) Guthrie's theory of learning: A second experiment. *J. exp. Psychol.,* **34,** 227–238.—*99*

SHAKOW, D. (1960) The recorded psychoanalytic interview as an objective approach to research in psychoanalysis. *Psychoanal. Quart.,* **29,** 82–97.—*285*

SHAKOW, D., and RAPAPORT, D. (1964) The influence of Freud on American psychology. *Psychol. Issues,* **4,** Monogr. 13.—*296*

SHAKOW, D. *See* Huston, Shakow, and Erickson (1934).

SHARP, A. A. (1938) An experimental test of Freud's doctrine of the relation of hedonic tone to memory revival. *J. exp. Psychol.,* **22,** 395–418.—*286*

SHAW, J. C. *See* Newell, Shaw, and Simon (1958, 1959).

SHEEHAN, MARY R. *See* Woodworth and Sheehan (1964).

SHEFFIELD, F. D. (1949a) Hilgard's critique of Guthrie. *Psychol. Rev.,* **56,** 284–291.—*83*

SHEFFIELD, F. D. (1949b) "Spread of effect" without reward or learning. *J. exp. Psychol.,* **39,** 575–579.—*35, 38, 84*

SHEFFIELD, F. D. (1961) Theoretical considerations in the learning of complex sequential tasks from demonstration and practice. In A. A. Lumsdaine (Editor), *Student response in programmed instruction.* Washington, D. C.: National Academy of Sciences–National Research Council, Publication 943, 13–32.—*98, 100, 101, 536, 566, 567*

SHEFFIELD, F. D. (1966a) A drive-induction theory of reinforcement. In R. N.

Haber (Editor) *Current research in motivation.* New York: Holt, Rinehart and Winston, 98–110.—*106*

SHEFFIELD, F. D. (1966b) New evidence on the drive-reduction theory of reinforcement. In R. N. Haber (Editor) *Current research in motivation.* New York: Holt, Rinehart and Winston, 111–121.—*106*

SHEFFIELD, F. D. *See* Jenkins and Sheffield (1946); Maccoby and Sheffield (1961).

SHEFFIELD, F. D., and JENKINS, W. O. (1952) Level of repetition in the "spread of effect." *J. exp. Psychol.,* 44, 101–107.—*35, 38, 39, 42*

SHEFFIELD, F. D., and MACCOBY, N. (1961) Summary and interpretation of organization principles in constructing filmed demonstrations. In A. A. Lumsdaine (Editor), *Student response in programmed instruction.* Washington, D. C.: National Academy of Sciences–National Research Council, 117–131.—*262, 551*

SHEFFIELD, F. D., MARGOLIUS, G. J., and HOEHN, A. J. (1961) Experiments on perceptual mediation in the learning of organizable sequences. In A. A. Lumsdaine (Editor), *Student response in programmed instruction.* Washington, D. C.: National Academy of Sciences–National Research Council, 107–116.—*551, 552*

SHEFFIELD, F. D., and ROBY, T. B. (1950) Reward value of a non-nutritive sweet taste. *J. comp. physiol. Psychol.,* 43, 471–481.—*82*

SHEFFIELD, V. F. (1949) Extinction ~~ a function of partial reinforcement and distribution of practice. *J. exp. Psychol.,* 39, 511–526.—*99*

SHEPARD, R. N. (1963) Comments on Professor Underwood's paper. In C. N. Cofer and B. S. Musgrave (Editors), *Verbal behavior and learning.* New York: McGraw-Hill, pp. 48–69.—*532*

SHEPARD, R. N. (1964) Review of *Computers and Thought. Behavioral Sci.,* 9, 57–65.—*424*

SHEPARD, R. N., and CHANG, J. J. (1963) Stimulus generalization in the learning of classifications. *J. exp. Psychol.,* 65, 94–102.—*533*

SHERRINGTON, C. S. (1906) *The integrative action of the nervous system.* New Haven: Yale Univ. Press.—*85, 306*

SHIFFRIN, R. M. *See* Atkinson and Shiffrin (1965).

SIDMAN, M. (1960) *Tactics of scientific research: evaluating experimental data in psychology.* New York: Basic Books.—*145, 540*

SIDMAN, M. (1962) Operant techniques. In A. J. Bachrach (Editor) *Experimental foundations of clinical psychology.* New York: Basic Books, 170–210. —*134*

SIMMONS, R. F. (1962) Synthex: Toward computer synthesis of human language behavior. In H. Borko (Editor), *Computer applications in the behavioral sciences.* Englewood Cliffs: Prentice-Hall.—*408*

SIMON, H. A., and FEIGENBAUM, E. A. (1964) An information-processing theory of some effects of similarity, familiarization, and meaningfulness in verbal learning. *J. verb. Learn. and verb. Behav.,* 3, 385–396.—*411, 412*

SIMON, H. A., and KOTOVSKY, K. (1963) Human acquisition of concepts for sequential patterns. *Psychol. Rev.,* 70, 534–546.—*402*

SIMON, H. A. *See* Feigenbaum and Simon (1961, 1962); Newell, Shaw, and Simon (1958, 1959); Newell and Simon (1956, 1961, 1963).

SINGER, E. A. (1911) Mind as an observable object. *J. Phil. Psychol. sci. Meth.*, 8, 180–186.—*75*

SINGER, M. B. *See* Piers and Singer (1953).

SKAGGS, E. B. (1925) Further studies in retroactive inhibition. *Psychol. Monogr.*, 34, No. 161.—*313*

SKINNER, B. F. (1931) The concept of the reflex in the description of behavior. *J. gen. Psychol.*, 5, 427–458.—*141*

SKINNER, B. F. (1933) "Resistance to extinction" in the process of conditioning. *J. gen. Psychol.*, 9, 420–429.—*112*

SKINNER, B. F. (1935) Two types of conditioned reflex and a pseudo type. *J. gen. Psychol.*, 12, 66–77.—*71, 141*

SKINNER, B. F. (1936) The verbal summator and a method for the study of latent speech. *J. Psychol.*, 2, 71–107.—*132*

SKINNER, B. F. (1937a) Two types of conditioned reflex: a reply to Konorski and Miller. *J. gen. Psychol.*, 16, 272–279.—*65*

SKINNER, B. F. (1937b) The distribution of associated words. *Psychol. Rec.*, 1, 71–76.—*132*

SKINNER, B. F. (1938) *The behavior of organisms: an experimental analysis.* New York: Appleton-Century-Crofts.—*64, 107, 109–112, 115, 116, 120, 124–126, 128, 130, 144, 494, 570*

SKINNER, B. F. (1939) The alliteration in Shakespeare's sonnets: A study in literary behavior. *Psychol. Rec.*, 3, 186–192.—*132*

SKINNER, B. F. (1941) A quantitative estimate of certain types of sound-patterning in poetry. *Amer. J. Psychol.*, 54, 64–79.—*132*

SKINNER, B. F. (1948) *Walden two.* New York: Macmillan.—*145*

SKINNER, B. F. (1950) Are theories of learning neessary? *Psychol. Rev.*, 57, 193–216.—*79, 107, 111, 116, 123, 142, 143*

SKINNER, B. F. (1951) How to teach animals. *Sci. Amer.*, 185, December, 26–29. *126*

SKINNER, B. F. (1953a) *Science and human behavior.* New York: Macmillan.—*107, 112–114, 117, 122, 123, 128, 130, 133, 134, 139, 140, 142, 144, 145, 332*

SKINNER, B. F. (1953b) Some contributions of an experimental analysis of behavior to psychology as a whole. *Amer. Psychologist*, 8, 69–78.—*121*

SKINNER, B. F. (1954) The science of learning and the art of teaching. *Harvard educ. Rev.*, 24, 86–97.—*555, 568*

SKINNER, B. F. (1957) *Verbal behavior.* New York: Appleton-Century-Crofts.—*132, 133, 145*

SKINNER, B. F. (1958) Teaching machines. *Science*, 128, 969–977.—*556*

SKINNER, B. F. (1961) *Cumulative record*, Revised edition. New York: Appleton-Century-Crofts.—*145*

SKINNER, B. F. *See also* Cook and Skinner (1939); Ferster and Skinner (1957); Holland and Skinner (1961); Rogers and Skinner (1956).

SLAGLE, J. R. (1963) A heuristic program that solves symbolic integration problems in freshman calculus. In E. A. Feigenbaum and J. Feldman (Editors), *Computers and thought.* New York: McGraw-Hill.—*399*

SLAMECKA, N. J., and CERASO, J. (1960) Retroactive and proactive inhibition of verbal learning. *Psychol. Bull.*, 57, 449–475.—*500*

SMITH, C. B. (1964) Background effects on learning and transposition of lightness discriminations. Ph.D. dissertation, University of Texas.—*525*

SMITH, M. B. *See* Hilgard and Smith (1942).

SMITH, M. H., JR. (1949) Spread of effect is the spurious result of nonrandom response tendencies. *J. exp. Psychol.*, **39**, 355–368.—*35, 36, 43*

SMITH, P. R. *See* Miller, Folley and Smith (1953).

SMITH, S., and GUTHRIE, E. R. (1921) *General psychology in terms of behavior.* New York: Appleton-Century-Crofts.—*76, 80, 85*

SMITH, W. I., and MOORE, J. W. (Editors) (1962) *Programmed learning.* Princeton: Van Nostrand.—*558*

SMODE, A. F. (1962) Recent developments in training problems, and training research methodology. In R. Glaser (Editor), *Training research and education*. Pittsburgh: Univ. of Pittsburgh Press, 429–495.—*583*

SNODDY, G. S. (1935) *Evidence for two opposed processes in mental growth.* Lancaster: Science Press.—*322*

SOKOLOV, E. M. (1963) Higher nervous functions: The orienting reflex. *Ann. Rev. Physiology*, **25**, 545-580.—*5, 68*

SOLLENBERGER, R. T. *See* Dollard, Doob, Miller, Mowrer, Sears, Ford, Hovland, and Sollenberger (1939).

SOLLEY, C. M., and MURPHY, G. (1960) *Development of the perceptual world.* New York: Basic Books.—*532*

SPENCE, K. W. (1936) The nature of discrimination learning in animals. *Psychol. Rev.*, **43**, 427–449.—*514*

SPENCE, K. W. (1937) The differential response in animals to stimuli varying within a single dimension. *Psychol. Rev.*, **44**, 430–444.—*223, 523*

SPENCE, K. W. (1942) The basis of solution by chimpanzees of the intermediate size problem. *J. exp. Psychol.*, **31**, 257–271.—*524, 525*

SPENCE, K. W. (1947) The role of secondary reinforcement in delayed reward learning. *Psychol. Rev.*, **54**, 1–8.—*163, 167*

SPENCE, K. W. (1952) Clark Leonard Hull: 1884–1952. *Amer. J. Psychol.*, **65**, 639–646.—*147, 189*

SPENCE, K. W. (1956) *Behavior theory and conditioning.* New Haven: Yale Univ. Press.—*189, 223*

SPENCE, K. W. (1960a) The roles of reinforcement and nonreinforcement in simple learning. Chap. 6 in *Behavior theory and learning: Selected papers of K. W. Spence*. Englewood Cliffs: Prentice-Hall.—*488*

SPENCE, K. W. (1960b) *Behavior theory and learning: Selected papers.* Englewood Cliffs: Prentice-Hall.—*189, 540*

SPERRY, R. W. (1961) Cerebral organization and behavior. *Science*, **133**, 1749–1757.—*471, 473*

SPERRY, R. W. *See also* Glickstein and Sperry (1960).

SPERRY, R. W., and MINER, N. (1955) Pattern perception following insertion of mica plates into visual cortex. *J. comp. physiol. Psychol.*, **48**, 463–469.—*455*

SPIEGEL, J. P. *See* Grinker and Spiegel (1945a, 1945b).

SPINELLI, D. N., and PRIBRAM, K. H. (1966) Changes in visual recovery functions produced by temporal lobe stimulation in monkeys. *Electroencephalog. and Clin. Neurophysiol.*, **20**, 44–49.—*444* nerve responses evoked by auditory and somatic stimulation. *Exper. Neurol.*, 12, 309–319.—*444*

STALNAKER, J. M., and RIDDLE, E. E. (1932) The effect of hypnosis on long-delayed recall. *J. gen. Psychol.*, 6, 429–439.—*499*

STANDLEE, L. S., POPHAM, W. J., and FATTU, N. A. (1956) *A review of trouble shooting research.* Bloomington, Ind.: Indiana Univ. Inst. Educ. Res. Research Report No. 3.—*549*

STANLEY, J. C., JR. *See* Jenkins and Stanley (1950).

STEBBINS, W. C. *See* Geis, Stebbins and Lundin (1965a).

STEIN, M. I., and HEINZE, S. J. (1960) *Creativity and the individual.* Glencoe: The Free Press.—*284*

STEIN, M. I., and MEER, B. (1954) Perceptual organization in a study of creativity. *J. Psychol.*, 37, 39–43.—*284*

STEINER, T. E. *See* Greeno and Steiner (1964).

STEINMAN, F. *See* Gleitman and Steinman (1963).

STEPHENS, J. M. (1934) A change in the interpretation of the law of effect. *Brit. J. Psychol.*, 24, 266–275.—*30*

STEPHENS, J. M. (1941) The influence of symbolic punishment and reward upon strong and upon weak associations. *J. gen. Psychol.*, 25, 177–185.—*32*

STEVENS, S. S. (1939) Psychology and the science of science. *Psychol. Bull.*, 36, 221–263.—*332*

STEVENS, S. S. (Editor) (1951) *Handbook of experimental psychology.* New York: Wiley.—*14*

STONE, C. P., and NYSWANDER, D. B. (1927) Reliability of rat learning scores from the multiple T-maze as determined by four different methods. *J. genet. Psychol.*, 34, 497–524.—*201*

STONE, G. R. (1950) The effect of negative incentives in serial learning. II. Incentive intensity and response variability. *J. gen. Psychol.*, 42, 179–224.—*33*

STONE, G. R. (1953) The effect of negative incentives in serial learning. VIII. Theory of punishment. *J. gen. Psychol.*, 48, 133–161.—*33, 34*

STONE, P. *See* Hunt, Marin, and Stone (1966).

STRASSBURGER, R. C. (1950) Resistance to extinction of a conditioned operant as related to drive level at reinforcement. *J. exp. Psychol.*, 40, 473–487.—*123*

STRATTON, G. M. (1896) Some preliminary experiments on vision without the inversion of the retinal image. *Psychol. Rev.*, 3, 611–617.—*304*

STRATTON, G. M. (1919) Retroactive hypermnesia and other emotional effects on memory. *Psychol. Rev.*, 26, 474–486.—*499*

SUCI, G. J. *See* Osgood, Suci, and Tannenbaum (1957).

SUPPES, P., and ATKINSON, R. C. (1960) *Markov learning models for multiperson interactions.* Stanford: Stanford Univ. Press.—*350–352, 365*

SUPPES, P., and GINSBERG, R. (1962) Application of a stimulus sampling model to children's concept formation with and without an overt correction response. *J. exp. Psychol.*, 63, 330–336.—*370*

SUPPES, P., and GINSBERG, R. (1963) A fundamental property of all-or-none models. *Psychol. Rev.*, 70, 139–161.—*367*

SUPPES, P., CROTHERS, E., WEIR, R., and TRAGER, E. (1962) *Some quantitative studies of Russian consonant phoneme discrimination.* Stanford, Calif.:

Stanford Univ., Inst. for Math. Studies in the Social Sciences, Technical Report 49, Sept. 14.—*576*

SUPPES, P., ROUANET, H., LEVINE, M., and FRANKMANN, R. W. (1964) Empirical comparison of models for a continuum of responses with noncontingent bimodal reinforcement. In R. C. Atkinson (Editor), *Studies in mathematical psychology.* Stanford: Stanford Univ. Press.—*351*

SUTHERLAND, N. S. (1959) Stimulus analyzing mechanisms. In *Proceedings of a symposium on the mechanization of thought processes,* Vol. 2. London: H.M. Stationary Office, 575–609.—*529*

SUTHERLAND, N. S. (1964) The learning of discrimination by animals. *Endeavour,* **23**, 140–152.—*529*

TAIT, W. D. (1913) The effect of psycho-physical attitudes on memory. *J. abnorm. Psychol.,* **8**, 10–37.—*275*

TANNENBAUM, P. H. *See* Osgood, Suci, and Tannenbaum (1957).

TAYLOR, J. A. (1951) The relationship of anxiety to the conditioned eyelid response. *J. exp. Psychol.,* **41**, 81–92.—*273*

TAYLOR, J. A. (1953) A personality scale of manifest anxiety. *J. abnorm. soc. Psychol.,* **48**, 285–290.—*273*

TEITELBAUM, P., and EPSTEIN, A. N. (1962) The lateral hypothalamic syndrome. *Psychol. Rev.,* **69**, 74–90.—*431*

TEITELBAUM, P. *See* Hockel and Teitlebaum (1962).

TEMMER, H. W. *See* Sheffield and Temmer (1950).

TERRACE, H. S. (1963a) Discrimination learning with and without errors. *J. exp. Anal. Behav.,* **6**, 1–27.—*518*

TERRACE, H. S. (1963b) Errorless transfer of a discrimination across two continua. *J. exp. Anal. Behav.,* **6**, 223–232.—*519*

TERRACE, H. S. (1964) Wavelength generalization after discrimination learning with and without errors. *Science,* **144**, 78–80.—*520, 521*

THEIOS, J. and BRELSFORD, J., JR. (1965) A Markov model for classical conditioning: Application to eye-blink conditioning in rabbits. Tech. report no. 9, Conditioning Research Laboratory, Dept. of Psychol., Univ. of Texas, Austin, Texas.—*373*

THEIOS, J., and BRELSFORD, J., Jr. (1966) Theoretical interpretations of a Markov model for avoidance conditioning. *J. math. Psychol.,* **3**, 140–162. Also Tech. report no. 6—Conditioning Research Laboratory, Dept. of Psychol., Univ. of Texas, Austin, Texas, 1965.—*374*

THEIOS, J. *See* Bower and Theios (1964)

THELEN, H., and GINTHER, J. R. (1964) Experiences with programmed materials in the Chicago area. In W. Schramm (Editor) (1964b) *Four case studies of programmed instruction.* New York: Fund for the Advancement of Education, 41–62.—*561*

THISTLETHWAITE, D. L. (1951a) A critical review of latent learning and related experiments. *Psychol. Bull.,* **48**, 97–129.—*202*

THISTLETHWAITE, D. L. (1952) Reply to Kendler and Maltzman. *Psychol. Bull.,* **49**, 61–71.—*202*

THORNDIKE, E. L. (1898) Animal intelligence: An experimental study of the associative processes in animals. *Psychol. Rev., Monogr. Suppl.,* **2**, No. 8.—*1, 16, 71, 570*

THORNDIKE, E. L. (1903) *Educational psychology.* New York: Lemcke and Buechner.—*24*

THORNDIKE, E. L. (1911) *Animal intelligence.* New York: Macmillan.—*16, 47, 65*

THORNDIKE, E. L. (1913a) *The original nature of man* (Educational psychology, I.). New York: Teachers College.—*18*

THORNDIKE, E. L. (1913b) *The psychology of learning.* (Educational psychology, II.) New York: Teachers College.—*17–23, 46, 47, 209*

THORNDIKE, E. L. (1922) *The psychology of arithmetic.* New York: Macmillan.—*47*

THORNDIKE, E. L. (1932a) *The fundamentals of learning.* New York: Teachers College.—*25–28, 47*

THORNDIKE, E. L. (1932b) Reward and punishment in animal learning. *Comp. Psychol. Monogr.,* 8, No. 39.—*26*

THORNDIKE, E. L. (1933a) A proof of the law of effect. *Science,* 77, 173–175.—*28*

THORNDIKE, E. L. (1933b) An experimental study of rewards. *Teach. Coll. Contr. Educ.,* No. 580.—*29, 38*

THORNDIKE, E. L. (1933c) A theory of the action of the after-effects of a connection upon it. *Psychol. Rev.,* 40, 434–439.—*27*

THORNDIKE, E. L. (1935) *The psychology of wants, interests and attitudes.* New York: Appleton-Century-Crofts.—*22, 25, 27, 28, 47*

THORNDIKE, E. L. (1940) *Human nature and the social order.* New York: Macmillan.—*26*

THORNDIKE, E. L. (1949) *Selected writings from a connectionist's psychology.* New York: Appleton-Century-Crofts.—*42, 47*

THORNDIKE, E. L., and others (1927) *The measurement of intelligence.* New York: Teachers College.—*44*

THORNDIKE, E. L., and others (1928) *Adult learning.* New York: Macmillan.—*47*

THORNDIKE, E. L., and WOODWORTH, R. S. (1901) The influence of improvement in one mental function upon the efficiency of other functions. *Psychol. Rev.,* 8, 247–261, 384–395, 553–564.—*24*

THORPE, W. H. (1956) *Learning and instinct in animals.* London: Methuen.—*3, 5*

THUNE, L. E., and UNDERWOOD, B. J. (1943) Retroactive inhibition as a function of degree of interpolated learning. *J. exp. Psychol.,* 32, 185–200.—*500*

THURSTONE, L. L. (1923) The stimulus-response fallacy in psychology. *Psychol. Rev.,* 30, 354–369.—*298*

TILTON, J. W. (1939) The effect of "right"and "wrong" upon the learning of nonsense syllables in multiple choice arrangement. *J. educ. Psychol.,* 30, 95–115.—*30*

TILTON, J. W. (1945) Gradients of effect. *J. genet. Psychol.,* 66, 3–19.—*30, 31*

TINBERGEN, N. (1951) *The study of instinct.* London: Oxford Univ. Press.—*3*

TINBERGEN, N. *See* Hinde and Tinbergen (1958).

TINKLEPAUGH, O. L. (1928) An experimental study of representative factors in monkeys. *J. comp. Psychol.,* 8, 197–236.—*195*

TITCHENER, E. B. (1898) Postulates of a structural psychology. *Philos. Rev.,* 7, 449–465.—*298*

TOLMAN, E. C. (1917) Retroactive inhibition as affected by conditions of learning. *Psychol. Monogr.,* 25, No. 107.—*216, 275*

TOLMAN, E. C. (1922) A new formula for behaviorism. *Psychol. Rev.,* **29,** 44–53. *—219*

TOLMAN, E. C. (1932a) Lewin's concept of vectors. *J. gen. Psychol.,* **7,** 3–15.*—217*

TOLMAN, E. C. (1932b) *Purposive behavior in animals and men.* New York: Appleton-Century-Crofts. (Reprinted, Univ. of California Press, 1949).*— 191, 209–211, 228*

TOLMAN, E. C. (1936) Connectionism; wants, interests, and attitudes. *Character & Pers.,* **4,** 245–253.*—43*

TOLMAN, E. C. (1938) The determiners of behavior at a choice point. *Psychol. Rev.,* **45,** 1, 1–41.*—15, 126, 193*

TOLMAN, E. C. (1939) Prediction of vicarious trial and error by means of the schematic sowbug. *Psychol. Rev.,* **46,** 318–336.*—195, 202, 223*

TOLMAN, E. C. (1941) Discrimination vs. learning and the schematic sowbug. *Psychol. Rev.,* **48,** 367–382.*—195*

TOLMAN, E. C. (1942) *Drives toward war.* New York: Appleton-Century-Crofts.*— 191, 216, 228*

TOLMAN, E. C. (1943) Identification and the postwar world. *J. abnorm. soc. Psychol.,* **38,** 141–148.*—191*

TOLMAN, E. C. (1945) A stimulus-expectancy need-cathexis psychology. *Science,* **101,** 160–166.*—215*

TOLMAN, E. C. (1948a) Kurt Lewin, 1890–1947. *Psychol. Rev.,* **55,** 1–4.*—217*

TOLMAN, E. C. (1948b) Cognitive maps in rats and men. *Psychol. Rev.,* **55,** 189–208.*—101, 202*

TOLMAN, E. C. (1949) There is more than one kind of learning. *Psychol. Rev.,* **56,** 144–155.*—211–213, 581*

TOLMAN, E. C. (1951a) *Collected papers in psychology.* Berkeley: Univ. of Calif. Press. Reprinted as *Behavior and psychological man,* 1961.*—228*

TOLMAN, E. C. (1951b) A psychological model. In T. Parsons and E. A. Shils (Editors), *Toward a general theory of action.* Cambridge, Mass.: Harvard Univ. Press, 279–361.*—218*

TOLMAN, E. C. (1952) A cognition motivation model. *Psychol. Rev.,* **59,** 389–400. *—208*

TOLMAN, E. C. (1955) Principles of performance. *Psychol. Rev.,* **62,** 315–326.*— 214*

TOLMAN, E. C. (1959) Principles of purposive behavior. In S. Koch (Editor), *Psychology: A study of a science,* Vol. 2. New York: McGraw-Hill, 92–157.*—213, 215*

TOLMAN, E. C., and BRUNSWIK, E. (1935) The organism and the causal texture of the environment. *Psychol. Rev.,* **42,** 43–77.*—191, 203, 225*

TOLMAN, E. C., and GLEITMAN, H. (1949) Studies in learning and motivation: I. Equal reinforcements in both end-boxes, followed by shock in one end-box. *J. exp. Psychol.,* **39,** 810–819.*—224*

TOLMAN, E. C., HALL, C. S., and BRETNALL, E. P. (1932) A disproof of the law of effect and a substitution of the laws of emphasis, motivation and disruption. *J. exp. Psychol.,* **15,** 601–614.*—207*

TOLMAN, E. C., and HONZIK, C. H. (1930a) "Insight" in rats. *Univ. Calif. Publ. Psychol.,* **4,** 215–232.*—197, 198, 225*

TOLMAN, E. C., and HONZIK, C. H. (1930b) Introduction and removal of reward, and maze performance in rats. *Univ. Calif. Publ. Psychol.*, **4**, 257–275.— *174, 200*

Tolman, E. C., Ritchie, B. F., and Kalish, D. (1946) Studies in spatial learning. II. Place learning versus response learning. *J. exp. Psychol.*, **36**, 221–229. —*196, 197*

Tolman, E. C., Ritchie, B. F., and Kalish, D. (1947) Studies in spatial learning. V. Response learning vs. place learning by the non-correction method. *J. exp. Psychol.*, **37**, 285–292.—*196*

Tolman, E. C. *See also* Geier, Levin, and Tolman (1941).

Trabasso, T. R. (1963) Stimulus emphasis and all-or-none learning in concept identification. *J. exp. Psychol.*, **65**, 398–406.—*531*

Trabasso, T. R. *See also* Bower and Trabasso (1964).

Trabasso, T. R., and Bower, G. H. (1964) Component learning in the four-category concept problem. *J. math. Psychol.*, **1**, 143–169.—*374*

Trabasso, T. R., and Bower, G. H. (1966) Stimulus selection and additivity of cues in discrimination learning. *Psychol. Monogr.*, in press.—*528*

Trager, E. *See* Suppes, Crothers, Weir, and Trager (1962).

Trask, F. P. *See* Yntema and Trask (1963).

Travers, R. M. W. (1962) A study of the relationship of psychological research to educational practice. In R. Glaser (Editor), *Training research and education*. Pittsburgh: Univ. of Pittsburgh Press, 525–558.—*545, 580*

Travis, R. P. (1964) The role of spreading cortical depression in relating the amount of avoidance training to interhemisepheric transfer. *J. comp. physiol. Psychol.*, **57**, 42–46.—*475*

Treisman, A. M. (1964) Selective attention in man. *Brit. Med. Bull.*, **20**, No. 1 (Experimental Psychology), 12–16.—*529*

Treisman, A. M. (1966) Our limited attention. *Advancement of Science*, February, 600–611.—*529*

Trowbridge, M. H., and Cason, H. (1932) An experimental study of Thorndike's theory of learning. *J. gen. Psychol.*, **7**, 245–258.—*25*

Uhr, L., and Vossler, C. (1963) A pattern-recognition program that generates, evaluates, and adjusts its own operators. In E. A. Feigenbaum and J. Feldman (Editors), *Computers and thought*. New York: McGraw-Hill,— *396*

Ullman, A. D. *See* Mowrer and Ullman (1945).

Umberger, J. P. *See* Cannicott and Umberger (1950).

Umemoto, T. (1962) Paired-associate learning as a function of similarity: Semantic similarity between stimulus- and response-items. *Amer. J. Psychol.*, **74**, 85–93.—*319*

Umemoto, T., and Hilgard, E. R. (1961) Paired-associate learning as a function of similarity: Common stimulus and response items within the list. *J. exp. Psychol.*, **62**, 97–104.—*319*

Underwood, B. J. (1949) *Experimental psychology: An introduction*. New York: Appleton-Century-Crofts.—*312, 323*

Underwood, B. J. (1951a) Studies of distributed practice: II. Learning and retention of paired-adjective lists with two levels of intralist similarity. *J. exp. Psychol.*, **42**, 153–161.—*319*

UNDERWOOD, B. J. (1951b) Studies of distributed practice: III. The influence of stage of practice in serial learning. *J. exp. Psychol.*, 42, 291–295.—*319*

UNDERWOOD, B. J. (1952a) Studies of distributed practice: VI. The influence of rest-interval activity in serial learning. *J. exp. Psychol.*, 43, 329–340.—*325*

UNDERWOOD, B. J. (1952b) Studies of distributed practice: VII. Learning and retention of serial nonsense lists as a function of intralist similarity. *J. exp. Psychol.*, 44, 80–87.—*319*

UNDERWOOD, B. J. (1953a) Studies of distributed practice: VIII. Learning and retention of paired nonsense syllables as a function of intralist similarity. *J. exp. Psychol.*, 45, 133–142.—*319*

UNDERWOOD, B. J. (1953b) Studies of distributed practice: IX. Learning and retention of paired adjectives as a function of intralist similarity. *J. exp. Psychol.*, 45, 143–149.—*319*

UNDERWOOD, B. J. (1953c) Studies of distributed practice: X. The influence of intralist similarity on learning and retention of serial adjective lists. *J. exp. Psychol.*, 45, 253–259.—*319, 321*

UNDERWOOD, B. J. (1953d) Learning. *Ann. Rev. Psychol.*, 4, 31–58.—*327*

UNDERWOOD, B. J. (1954a) Studies of distributed practice: XII. Retention following varying degrees of original learning. *J. exp. Psychol.*, 47, 294–300.—*325*

UNDERWOOD, B. J. (1954b) Intralist similarity in verbal learning and retention. *Psychol. Rev.*, 61, 160–166.—*319, 320*

UNDERWOOD, B. J. (1957) Interference and forgetting. *Psychol. Rev.*, 64, 49–60.—*312, 501*

UNDERWOOD, B. J. (1959) Verbal learning in the educative processes. *Harvard educ. Rev.*, 29, 107–117.—*329*

UNDERWOOD, B. J. (1961) Ten years of massed practice on distributed practice. *Psychol. Rev.*, 68, 229–247.—*318, 328*

UNDERWOOD, B. J. (1964) Laboratory studies of verbal learning. In E. R. Hilgard (Editor), *Theories of learning and instruction.* Chicago: Univ. of Chicago Press, 133–152.—*570*

UNDERWOOD, B. J. (1966) *Experimental psychology,* Second edition. New York: Appleton-Century-Crofts.—*333*

UNDERWOOD, B. J. *See* Barnes and Underwood (1959); Keppel and Underwood (1962); Thune and Underwood (1943).

UNDERWOOD, B. J., and GOAD, D. (1951) Studies of distributed practice: I. The influence of intralist similarity in serial learning. *J. exp. Psychol.*, 42, 125–134.—*318, 319*

UNDERWOOD, B. J., and POSTMAN, L. (1960) Extra-experimental sources of interference in forgetting. *Psychol. Rev.*, 67, 73–95.—*501*

UNDERWOOD, B. J., and SCHULZ, R. W. (1960) *Meaningfulness and verbal learning.* New York: Lippincott.—*329, 330*

UTTLEY, A. M. *See* Blake and Uttley (1959).

VAUGHN, E., and FISCHER, A. E. (1962) Male sexual behavior induced by intracranial electrical stimulation. *Science,* 137, 758–760.—*432*

VERHAVE, T. (Editor) (1966) *The experimental analysis of behavior: Selected readings.* New York: Appleton-Century-Crofts.—*145*

VERPLANCK, W. S. (1954) Burrhus F. Skinner. In Estes, Koch, MacCorquodale, Meehl, Mueller, Schoenfeld, and Verplanck. *Modern learning theory.* New York: Appleton-Century-Crofts.—*142, 143*

VERPLANCK, W. S. (1962) Unaware of where's awareness: Some verbal operants —notates, monents, and notants. In C. W. Eriksen (Editor), *Behavior and awareness.* Duham: Duke Univ. Press.—*422*

VINOGRADOVA, O. S. *See* Luria and Vinogradova (1959).

VOEKS, V. W. (1948) Postremity, recency, and frequency as bases for prediction in the maze situation. *J. exp. Psychol.,* **38,** 495–510.—*77, 94, 95*

VOEKS, V. W. (1950) Formalization and clarification of a theory of learning. *J. Psychol.,* **30,** 341–363.—*77, 93*

VOEKS, V. W. (1954) Acquisition of S–R connections: A test of Hull's and Guthrie's theories. *J. exp. Psychol.,* **47,** 137–147.—*95*

VOEKS, V. (1964) *On becoming an educated person.* Philadelphia: Saunders. —*503*

VON NEUMANN, J., and MORGENSTERN, O. (1944) *Theory of games and economic behavior.* Princeton: Princeton Univ. Press.—*225*

VOSSLER, C. *See* Uhr and Vossler (1963).

WAGNER, A. R. (1963) Conditioned frustration as a learned drive. *J. exp. Psychol.,* **66,** 142–148.—*488, 489*

WAGNER, A. R. (1966) Frustration and punishment. In R. N. Haber (Editor), *Research on motivation.* New York: Holt, Rinehart and Winston.—*488*

WALLACH, H., and HENLE, M. (1941) An experimental analysis of the law of effect. *J. exp. Psychol.,* **28,** 340–349.—*33, 36, 42*

WALLACH, H., and HENLE, M. (1942) A further study of the function of reward. *J. exp. Psychol.,* **30,** 147–160.—*36*

WALTER, A. A. *See* Carmichael, Hogan, and Walter (1932).

WALTER, W. G. (1953) *The living brain.* New York: Norton.—*382, 479*

WALTERS, R. H. *See* Bandura and Walters (1963).

WARD, L. B. (1937) Reminiscence and rote learning. *Psychol. Monogr.,* **49,** No. 220.—*322*

WARREN, H. C. (1934) *Dictionary of psychology.* Boston: Houghton and Mifflin. —*72*

WATERS, R. H., and LEEPER, R. (1936) The relation of affective tone to the retention of experiences in everyday life. *J. exp. Psychol.,* **19,** 203–215.—*288*

WATSON, J. B. (1907) Kinesthetic and organic sensations: Their role in the reactions of the white rat to the maze. *Psychol. Monogr.,* **8,** No. 33.—*75, 78*

WATSON, J. B. (1914) *Behavior, An Introduction to comparative psychology.* New York: Holt, Rinehart and Winston.—*75*

WATSON, J. B. (1916) The place of the conditioned reflex in psychology. *Psychol Rev.,* **23,** 89–116.—*76*

WATSON, J. B. (1924) The unverbalized in human behavior. *Psychol Rev.,* **31,** 273–280.—*293*

WAUGH, N. C., and NORMAN, D. A. (1965) Primary memory. *Psychol. Rev.,* **72,** 89–104.—*509*

WEBB, W. B. (1957) Applied research: Variations on a theme. *Amer. Psychologist*, **12**, 225–226.—*545*

WEBB, W. B., and NOLAN, C. Y. (1953) Cues for discrimination as secondary reinforcing agents: A confirmation. *J. comp. physiol. Psychol.*, **46**, 180–181. —*121*

WEINGARTEN, M. *See* Spinelli, Pribram, and Weingarten (1965).

WEIR, R. *See* Suppes, Crothers, Weir, and Trager (1962).

WEITZENHOFFER, A. M. (1953) *Hypnotism.* New York: Wiley.—*276*

WENDT, G. R. (1937) Two and one-half year retention of a conditioned response. *J. gen. Psychol.*, **17**, 178–180.—*79*

WENDT, G. R. *See* Cohen, Hilgard, and Wendt (1933).

WERNER, H. (1947) The effect of boundary strength on interference and retention. *Amer. J. Psychol.*, **60**, 598–607.—*253, 320*

WERNER, H. (1948) *Comparative psychology of mental development*, Second edition. Chicago: Follett.—*259*

WERTHEIM, G. A. (1964) Performance interactions in multiple avoidance schedules. Unpublished Ph.D. dissertation, Stanford University.—*516*

WERTHEIMER, M. (1923) Untersuchungen zur Lehre von der Gestalt, II. *Psychol. Forsch.*, **4**, 301–350. Translated and condensed as "Laws of organization in perceptual forms" in Ellis, W. D. (1938), *A source book of gestalt psychology.* New York: Harcourt, Brace, & World, 71–88.—*234*

WERTHEIMER, M. (1945) *Productive thinking.* New York: Harper & Row.—*246–248, 263*

WERTHEIMER, M. (1959) *Productive thinking*, Enlarged edition. New York: Harper & Row.—*246, 263*

WHEELER, R. H. (1929) *The science of psychology.* New York: Crowell.—*232*

WHEELER, R. H. (1932) *The laws of human nature.* New York: Appleton-Century-Crofts.—*232, 237*

WHEELER, R. H. (1940) *The science of psychology.* New York: Crowell.—*232*

WHEELER, R. H., and PERKINS, F. T. (1932) *Principles of mental development.* New York: Crowell.—*232, 322*

WHIPPLE, J. E. *See* Hilgard, Irvine, and Whipple (1953).

WHITE, R. K. (1943) The case for the Tolman–Lewin interpretation of learning. *Psychol. Rev.*, **50**, 157–186.—*217*

WHITE, R. W. (1963) Ego and reality in psychoanalytic theory. *Psychol. Issues*, **3**, Monogr. 11.—*268*

WHITEHEAD, A. N., and RUSSELL, B. (1925) *Principia Mathematica*, Second edition. Vol. I. Cambridge: Cambridge Univ. Press.—*388*

WHITING, J. W. M., and CHILD, I. L. (1953) *Child training and personality.* New Haven: Yale Univ. Press.—*281*

WHYTT, R. (1763) *An essay on the vital and other involuntary motions of animals*, Second edition. Edinburgh: J. Balfour.—*50*

WICKELGREN, W. A. (1965) Acoustic similarity and retroactive interference in short-term memory. *J. verb. Learn. verb. Behav.*, 4, 53–61.—*507*

WICKENS, D. D., *Born*, D. G., and ALLEN, C. K. (1963) Proactive inhibition and item similarity in short-term memory. *J. verb. Learn. verb. Behav.*, **2**, 440–445.—*510*

WICKENS, D. D., and PLATT, C. E. (1954) Response termination of the cue stimulus in classical and instrumental conditioning. *J. exp. Psychol.*, 47, 183–186.—*99*

WILCOXON, H. C. (1952) "Abnormal fixation" and learning. *J. exp. Psychol.*, 44, 324–333.—*270*

WILLEY, R. DEV. *See* Cain and Willey (1939).

WILLIAMS, A. C., and FLEXMAN, R. E. (1949) Evaluation of the school link as an aid in primary flight instruction. *Univ. Ill. Bull.*, 46, No. 71.—*546*

WILLIAMS, S. B., and LEAVITT, H. J. (1947) Prediction of success in learning Japanese. *J. appl. Psychol.*, 31, 164–168.—*553*

WILSON, C. L. (1962) On-the-job and operational criteria. In R. Glaser (Editor), *Training research and education.* Pittsburgh: Univ. of Pittsburgh Press, 347–377.—*544*

WILSON, J. T. (1949) The formation and retention of remote associations in rote learning. *J. exp. Psychol.*, 39, 830–838.—*318, 327*

WOLF, A. (1943) The dynamics of the selective inhibition of specific functions in neurosis. *Psychosom. Med.*, 5, 27–38.—*281*

WOLF, A. *See* Green, Wolf, Chomsky, and Laughery (1961).

WOLFE, J. B. (1934) The effect of delayed reward upon learning in the white rat. *J. comp. Psychol.*, 17, 1–21.—*167*

WOLFF, P. H. (1960) The developmental psychologies of Jean Piaget and psychoanalysis. *Psychol. Issues, 2*, Monogr. 5.—*283*

WOLFLE, D. L. (1936) The relative efficiency of constant and varied stimulation during learning. III. The objective extent of stimulus variation. *J. comp. Psychol.*, 22, 375–381.—*344*

WOLPE, J. (1958) *Psychotherapy by reciprocal inhibition.* Stanford: Stanford Univ. Press.—*294*

WOODWORTH, R. S. (1906) Imageless thought. *J. Phil. Psychol. sci. Meth.*, 3, 701–708.—*307*

WOODWORTH, R. S. (1918) *Dynamic psychology.* New York: Columbia Univ. Press.—*85, 302, 305*

WOODWORTH, R. S. (1929) *Psychology,* Revised edition. New York: Holt, Rinehart, and Winston.—*147*

WOODWORTH, R. S. (1931) *Contemporary schools of psychology.* New York: Ronald.—*72*

WOODWORTH, R. S. (1937) Situation- and goal-set. *Amer. J. Psychol.*, 50, 130–140. —*307*

WOODWORTH, R. S. (1938) *Experimental psychology.* New York: Holt, Rinehart, and Winston.—*330*

WOODWORTH, R. S. (1948) *Contemporary schools of psychology,* Revised edition. New York: Ronald.—*297*

WOODWORTH, R. S. (1958) *Dynamics of behavior.* New York: Holt, Rinehart, and Winston.—*306, 307, 333*

WOODWORTH, R. S. *See also* Thorndike and Woodworth (1901).

WOODWORTH, R. S., and SCHLOSBERG, H. (1954) *Experimental psychology,* Revised edition. New York: Holt, Rinehart, and Winston.—*14, 312, 332, 333*

WOODWORTH, R. S., and SHEEHAN, MARY R. (1964) *Contemporary schools of psychology,* Third edition. New York: Ronald.—*333*

WOOLDRIDGE, D. E. (1963)   *The machinery of the brain.* New York: McGraw-Hill. *—429, 479*

WOOLSEY, C. N.   *See* Harlow and Woolsey (1958).

WRIGHT, J. E.   *See* Pliskoff, Wright, and Hawkins.

WULF, F. (1922)   Über die Veränderung von Vorstellungen (Gedächtnis und Gestalt). *Psychol. Forsch.,* I, 333–373. Translated and condensed as "Tendencies in figural variation" in Ellis, W. D. (1938) *A source book of gestalt psychology.* New York: Harcourt, Brace & World, 136–148.*— 237, 248*

WYCKOFF, L. B. (1952)   The role of observing responses in discrimination learning: Part I. *Psychol. Rev.,* 59, 431–442.*—528*

WYRWICKA, W., and DOBRZECKA, C. (1960)   Relationship between feeding and satiation centers of the hypothalamus. *Science,* 123, 805–806.*—431*

YAMAGUCHI, H. G., HULL, C. L., FELSINGER, J. M., and GLADSTONE, A. I. (1948)   Characteristics of dispersions based on the pooled momentary reaction potentials. $(_s\bar{E}_R)$ of a group. *Psychol. Rev.,* 55, 216–238.*—161*

YAMAGUCHI, H. G.   *See also* Felsinger, Gladstone, Yamaguchi, and Hull (1947); Gladstone, Yamaguchi, Hull, and Felsinger (1947); Hull, Felsinger, Gladstone, and Yamaguchi (1947).

YARNELL, T. D., and ADAMS, H. E. (1964)   Electroconvulsive shock and competing responses: Stimulus generalization. *J. comp. physiol. Psychol.,* 58, 470–471.*—452*

YERKES, R. M. (1916)   The mental life of monkeys and apes: A study of ideational behavior. *Behav. Monogr.,* 3, No. 12.*—231*

YERKES, R. M. (1927)   The mind of a gorilla: I. *Genet. Psychol. Monogr.,* 2.*—243*

YERKES, R. M. (1943)   *Chimpanzees: A laboratory colony.* New Haven: Yale Univ. Press.*—242*

YNTEMA, D. B., and TRASK, F. P. (1963)   Recall as a search process. *J. verb. Learn. verb. Behav.,* 2, 65–74.*—500, 510*

YOUNG, J. Z. (1964)   *A model of the brain.* Oxford: Clarendon Press.*—479*

YOUNG, P. T. (1952)   The role of hedonic processes in the organization of behavior. *Psychol. Rev.,* 59, 249–262.*—266*

YOVITTS, M., and CAMERON, S. (Editors) (1960)   *Self-organizing systems.* New York: Pergamon.*—425*

ZAGONA, S. V.   *See* Coan, and Zagona (1962).

ZEAMAN, D. (1959)   Skinner's theory of teaching machines. In E. H. Galanter (Editor) *Automatic teaching: The state of the art.* New York: Wiley, 167–176.*—568*

ZEAMAN, D., and HOUSE, B. J. (1963)   The role of attention in retardate discrimination learning. In N. R. Ellis (Editor), *Handbook of mental deficiency.* New York: McGraw-Hill, 159–223.*—529, 531*

ZEAMAN, D., and RADNER, L. (1953)   A test of the mechanisms of learning proposed by Hull and Guthrie. *J. exp. Psychol.,* 45, 239–244.*—99*

ZEIGARNIK, B. (1927)   Das Behalten erledigter und unerledigter Handlungen,

Psychol. Forsch., **9**, 1–85. Translated and condensed as "On finished and unfinished tasks" in Ellis (1938), *A source book of gestalt psychology.* New York: Harcourt, Brace, & World, 300–314.—*288*

ZEILER, M. D. (1963) The ratio theory of intermediate size discrimination. *Psychol. Rev.,* **70**, 516–533.—*526*

ZELLER, A. F. (1950a) An experimental analogue of repression: I. Historical summary. *Psychol. Bull.,* **47**, 39–51.—*286, 288*

ZELLER, A. F. (1950b) An experimental analogue of repression: II. The effect of individual failure and success on memory measured by relearning. *J. exp. Psychol.,* **40**, 411–422.—*289*

ZELLER, A. F. (1951) An experimental analogue of repression: III. The effect of induced failure and success on memory measured by recall. *J. exp. Psychol.,* **42**, 32–38.—*289*

ZELMAN, A., KABOT, L., JACOBSON, R., and McCONNELL, J. V. (1963) Transfer of training through injection of "'conditioned" RNA into untrained worms. *Worm Runners Digest,* **5**, 14–21.—*466*

ZIRKLE, G. A. (1946a) Success and failure in serial learning. I. The Thorndike effect. *J. exp. Psychol.,* **36**, 230–236.—*34*

ZIRKLE, G. A. (1946b) Success in failure in serial learning. II. Isolation and the Thorndike effect. *J. exp. Psychol.,* **36**, 302–315.—*36, 37, 40, 42*

SUBJECT INDEX

Abient–adient conflict (Hull), 175–181, 183
Ablations, 428, 431, 432
Aborn's theories, 289–290
Absolute theory, 522
Acetylcholine (ACh), 461–464
Action tendency (Thorndike), 18
Activation (MacCorquodale and Meehl), 224
Adaptation level (AL) in Wertheim's theory, 516, 518, 527–528
Adient-abient conflict (Hull), 175–181, 183
Adjusting reinforcement (Ferster–Skinner), 119
Affective contrast, 486
Age-regression (Freud), 276
Aggression, 133, 277–279
AL (adaptation level) in Wertheim's theory, 516, 518, 527–528
Algorithms, 387–388
Alternative reinforcement (Ferster–Skinner), 118
Amnesia, 281–282
  retrograde, 449–452
Amplitude, response, 155, 156, 164, 359–360
  micromolar approach to, 495–496
Amsel's frustrative nonreward hypothesis, 488–489, 490, 516
Analogy, response by, 22
Angell's theories, 297, 298, 300–301, 302
Animal experiments, 131, 206
  Brunswik's, 203
  in classical conditioning, 48, 51, 56, 64, 70
  on consequences of punishment, 136–37
  in contiguous conditioning, 80–83, 85, 87–91
  on discrimination learning, 515–516, 518–522, 525–526, 532
  on displaced aggression, 278–279
  on dissonance, 492
  early, 280–281
  Festinger's, 227
  on frustrative nonreward, 488–490

on insight, 241, 242–245
  Köhler's, 230–231, 233
  on latent learning, 199–202
  limiting nature of, 216, 217
  mathematical data from, 335–336, 345, 359
  in neurochemistry, 461–464, 465–468, 474–475
  neurophysiological, 431–439, 442, 443–444, 446, 448–451, 453, 455, 457, 459–460, 475–476
  neurophysiological, surgical, 472–473
  on place learning, 196–199
  Premack's, 484
  on reward expectancy, 195–196
  Skinner's, 107, 110–111, 113, 117, 119–120, 123–124, 125–126, 129, 144
  on structural model, 225–227
  on systematic behavior, 167, 170, 174, 176–178, 186
  Thorndike's, 16–18, 26
Animal learning:
  in birds, 3–4
  of interocular transfer, 470–472
  latent, 174
  overlearning, 269–270
  reality principle in, 268
  of trained animals, 144, 534
  Watson's theory of, 75
Annoyers (Thorndike), 21, 26, 27
Anodal polarization, 457–459, 460
Anokhin's theories, 62–63
Antedating defense reactions (Hull), 184
Anticipatory response (Hull), 148–149
  See also Fractional antedating goal response
Anti-theory argument, 142–143
Anxiety, 281, 564
  as drive, 271–273, 292
Aperiodic reinforcement (Ferster–Skinner), 115
Armed forces training, research on, 544–549
Arousal, 439–446

Guthrie's final reflections on his theory, 91–93
Hull's theories and, 148–149
lasting contributions of, 105–106
mathematical theory and, 340–341
one law of association, 76–80
puzzle-box experiments on, 87–91
Sheffield's extension of, 98–101
sign learning and, 201, 206, 213, 217
steps toward formalizing, 93–98

Habit-family hierarchy (Hull), 149, 168–169
Habits:
breaking of, 79–80, 84
expectancy vs., 203–206
fixed, 275–276
formation of, 17, 147–148
guessing, 35
strength of (Hull), 25, 154, 156, 157–59, 162, 164, 268–271
Habituation, 443–445
learning vs., 4–5
Hanawalt's experiments, 249
Hardware, robot, 382–383
Harlow's theories, 241
Harter's theories, 1, 17
Hebb's experiments, 249, 452, 453, 456, 505
Hernandez-Peon's animal experiment, 443–444
Heuristics, 387, 388
Hilgard's theories, 64–65, 283
Hoffman's machine, 382
Horton's puzzle-box experiments, 87–91
House's theories, 529, 530–531
Howarth's brain stimulation theory, 436–437
Hull's theories, 104, 146–190, 514
applied to education, 568–569
basic orientation of, 147–150
connectionist theories and, 30
derived intermediate mechanisms, 165–169
estimate of, 182–189
experimental testing of, 169–182
formation of, 150–165
functionalism and, 308, 309
mathematical theory influenced by, 334–335, 338, 360
operant conditioning and, 109, 125
recent developments influenced by, 487, 488, 493, 494–495
sign learning and, 201, 208, 209–210, 217, 218, 224
Human subject experiments, 234
on anxiety, 273, 281
brain-stimulation, 438
on discrimination learning, 526–527, 528, 532–533

on distributed practice, 324
EEG, 439, 441
Gottschaldt's, 236–237
Humphreys', 204–206
on interference theory, 499–500, 501–502
on language laboratories, 553–554
on memory, 248–257
on repression, 285–290
on sexual latency, 282
on SST, 352–353
testing law of effect, 26
Humphreys' experiments, 204–206
Hunger, neural control over, 430–431
Hunt's concept learner, 416–418
Hyperphagia, 430–431
Hypnosis, Pavlov's position on, 59
Hypothalamus, 430–433
Hypothetical constructs, defined, 12–13
Hypothetico-deduction theory:
criticism of, 142–143
Hull's system as, 146

Identical-elements theory, 24–25, 44–45
Image-building, computer, 411
Imitation:
learning by, 534–538, 563
Melton's concept of, 309
Imprinting, defined, 3
Improvement, 2
through repetition, 25, 78–79
Incentives, 7, 174
perceived, 175
Incompatible response, 155
Individual differences, 325
in programed learning, 560, 561
Induction:
in behavioral contrast, 515
reciprocal (Pavlov), 56–59
Skinner's use of term, 125, 140
Inference:
of learning, 4–5, 9
in sign learning, 223
Information processing (computers), 381–425
concepts and models of, 384–397
educational, 556, 557
evaluation of, 419–424
language processing programs of, 408–410
learning programs of, 410–419
problem-solving programs of, 397–408
Information-retrieval computer programs, 409
Information system (Luria), 67
Inhibition:
associative (Guthrie), 79–80
in classical conditioning, 55, 57, 59, 61, 63, 67